The Routledge Physical Education Reader

Physical Education teaching and research is fundamental to the physical and social health of our communities. *The Routledge Physical Education Reader* presents an authoritative and representative selection of the very best international scholarship in PE, drawn from across the full topical range of the discipline.

Containing a rich blend of contemporary, 'classic' and hard-to-find articles, this book helps students gain a full understanding of the historical context in which current issues and debates within PE have emerged. Leading international scholars Richard Bailey and David Kirk weave a thoughtful editorial commentary throughout the book that illuminates each key theme, making insightful and important connections between articles and approaches. The book is divided into eight thematic sections, each of which includes an extensive guide to further reading:

- Nature and values of physical education;
- Physical education and sport;
- Physical education and health;
- Learners and learning;
- Teachers and teaching;
- Curriculum and content;
- Social construction of bodies;
- Researching physical education.

Addressing the most important topics in contemporary physical education, and representing a comprehensive 'one-stop' resource, *The Routledge Physical Education Reader* is essential reading for all serious students of physical education, sport, coaching, exercise and health.

Richard Bailey holds the Chair in Education and Sport at the University of Birmingham, UK, and is a member of the Executive Board of the International Council of Sport Science and Physical Education.

David Kirk is Professor of Physical Education and Youth Sport at Leeds Metropolitan University, UK, where he has been Dean of the Carnegie Faculty of Sport and Education since 2004. He is editor of the journal *Physical Education and Sport Pedagogy*.

The Routledge Physical Education Reader

Edited by

Richard Bailey and David Kirk

Routledge
Taylor & Francis Group

LONDON AND NEW YORK

First published 2009
by Routledge
2 Park Square, Milton Park, Abingdon, Oxon OX14 4RN

Simultaneously published in the USA and Canada
by Routledge
270 Madison Ave, New York, NY 10016

Routledge is an imprint of the Taylor & Francis Group, an informa business

Typeset in Perpetua and Bell Gothic by
RefineCatch Ltd, Bungay, Suffolk
Printed and bound in Great Britain by
The Cromwell Press, Trowbridge, Wiltshire

British Library Cataloguing in Publication Data
A catalogue record for this book is available from the British Library

Library of Congress Cataloging in Publication Data
The Routledge physical education reader / edited by Richard Bailey and David Kirk.
        p. cm.
    1. Physical education and training.   2. Physical education and training—Study and teaching.   3. Physical
education and training—Curricula.   I. Bailey, Richard, 1957–.   II. Kirk, David, 1958–.
GV341.R69 2009
613.7—dc22

                                                                                            2008012570

ISBN10: 0–415–44600–7 (hbk)
ISBN10: 0–415–44601–5 (pbk)

ISBN13: 978–0–415–44600–6 (hbk)
ISBN13: 978–0–415–44601–3 (pbk)

Contents

Acknowledgements

The publishers would like to thank the following for permission to reprint their material:

Armour, K.M. and Duncombe, R. (2004). Teachers' continuing professional development in primary physical education: Lessons from present and past to inform the future. *Physical Education and Sport Pedagogy*, 9(1), Taylor & Francis, pp. 3–21.

Bailey, R.P. (2006) Physical education and sport in schools: A review of benefits and outcomes. *Journal of School Health*, 76(8), Blackwell Publishing, pp. 397–401.

Bain, L.L. (1985). The hidden curriculum re-examined. *Quest*, 37, Human Kinetics, pp. 145–153.

Dyson, B., Griffin, L. and Hastie, P. (2004) Sport education, tactical games, and cooperative learning: Theoretical and pedagogical considerations. *Quest*, 56(2), Human Kinetics, pp. 225–239.

Evans, J. (2004) Making a difference? Education and 'ability' in physical education. *European Physical Education Review*, 10, Sage, pp. 95–108.

Fitzgerald, H. (2005) Still feeling like a spare piece of luggage? Embodied experiences of (dis)ability in physical education and school sport. *Physical Education and Sport Pedagogy*, 10(1), Taylor & Francis, pp. 41–59.

Gard, M. (2003) Being someone else: using dance in anti-oppressive teaching. *Educational Review*, 55(2), Taylor & Francis, pp. 211–223.

Gard, M. and Wright, J. (2001) Managing uncertainty: Obesity discourses and physical education in a risk society. *Studies in Philosophy and Education*, 20(6), Springer, pp. 535–549. With kind permission from Springer Science and Business Media.

Green, K. (2000) Exploring the everyday 'philosophies' of physical education teachers from a sociological perspective. *Sport, Education and Society*, 5(1), Taylor & Francis, pp. 109–129.

Hastie, P. and Siedentop, D. (1999) An ecological perspective on physical education. *European Physical Education Review*, 5(1), Sage, pp. 9–29.

Harris, J. (2005) Health-related exercise and physical education, in K. Green and K. Hardman (eds), *Physical Education: Essential Issues*, Sage, pp. 78–97.

Houlihan, B. (2002) Sporting excellence, school and sports development: The politics of crowded policy spaces. *European Physical Education Review*, 6(2), Sage, pp. 171–194.

Kirk, D. (1986) A critical pedagogy for teacher education: Towards an inquiry-oriented approach. *Journal of Teaching in Physical Education*, 5(4), Human Kinetics, pp. 230–246.

Kirk, D. and Macdonald, D. (1998) Situated learning in physical education. *Journal of Teaching in Physical Education*, 17(3), Human Kinetics, pp. 376–387.

Kirk, D. and MacPhail, A. (2002) Teaching games for understanding and situated learning: Rethinking the Bunker-Thorpe model. *Journal of Teaching in Physical Education*, 21, Human Kinetics, pp. 177–192.

Lee, A.M. (1997) Contributions of research on student thinking in physical education, *Journal of Teaching in Physical Education*, 16, Human Kinetics, pp. 262–277.

Macdonald, D., Kirk, D., Metzler, M., Nilges, L.M., Schempp, P. and Wright, J. (2002) It's all very well in theory: A review of theoretical perspectives and their applications in contemporary pedagogical research. *Quest*, 54(2), Human Kinetics, pp. 133–156.

McNamee, M. (2005) The nature and values of physical education, in K. Green and K. Hardman (eds), *Physical Education: Essential Issues*, Sage, pp. 1–20.

Oliver, K.L. and Lalik, R. (2001) The body as curriculum: Learning with adolescent girls. *Journal of Curriculum Studies*, 33(3), Taylor & Francis, pp. 303–333.

Rink, J. E. (2001) Investigating the assumptions of pedagogy. *Journal of Teaching in Physical Education*, 20, Human Kinetics, pp. 112–128.

Siedentop, D. (2002) Content knowledge for physical education. *Journal of Teaching in Physical Education*, 21(4), Human Kinetics, pp. 409–418.

Siedentop, D. (2002) Junior sport and the evolution of sport cultures. *Journal of Teaching in Physical Education*, 21(4), Human Kinetics, pp. 392–401.

Wright, J., Macdonald, D. and Groom, L. (2003) Physical activity and young people: Beyond participation. *Sport, Education and Society*, 8(1), Taylor & Francis, pp. 17–34.

Foreword

Routledge outline that their Readers provide students with a comprehensive and accessible one-stop resource of essential reading in a subject area. This *Routledge Reader in Physical Education* certainly does this and more. Yet, at a time when ready access to journals and texts is unprecedented, one may question the purpose of a Reader as a one-stop resource comprising previously published materials. I would argue that it is this very proliferation of physical education scholarship that makes this Reader's sophisticated synthesis of scholarship so valuable.

While acknowledging their essential partiality, editors Richard Bailey and David Kirk present 22 papers emanating from North America, the UK, Australia and New Zealand that span 21 years of physical education research. The editors' Introduction, section headings and notes explain how they have 'made sense' of the scholarship conducted over the last 20-odd years in the field. To bypass these parts of the Reader is to miss the intellectual work that has been undertaken in analysing physical education research for key questions, themes, debates, theoretical frameworks and outcomes.

The selected papers have been generated in a socio-political context, characteristic of many Western democracies, described as neoliberalism. Neoliberal practices and discourses aim to reconfigure people as productive economic entrepreneurs who are responsible for making sound choices in their education, work, health and lifestyle. The contribution of physical education to the production of healthy, self-managing citizens, consistent with governments' expectations and educational policies, has generated arguable practices and tensions in the field. The place and value of particular pedagogies (e.g., critical pedagogy), content (e.g., sport, health, dance) or bodies (e.g., overweight), that are subtly proscribed in the neoliberal world, are captured in this Reader.

So too, underpinning many of the papers, are the complex theoretical frameworks of mainstream scholars (alive and dead) such as Basil Bernstein, Michel Foucault, Anthony Giddens, Henry Giroux and Maxine Greene to name a few. Indeed, this collection of papers reveals how scholars in the physical education field have been keen adopters of sophisticated educational and social theories. This has afforded both insightful analyses of research questions, as will be seen in the papers collected in this Reader, as well as physical education scholars making strong contributions to general education research and issues.

A regret shared by Bailey, Kirk and me is that much of the excellent research in physical education does not reach policy-makers and teachers. Elsewhere I have called for more evidence-based decision-making and practices in physical education while being cognisant of the potential misuse of the concept. Evidence-based practice encourages professionals to locate, retrieve, analyse and apply appropriate evidence in their everyday work such that physical education curricula and pedagogies optimise students' learning. This Reader makes a substantial contribution towards realising the goal of evidence-based practice given its accessible and comprehensive material. If physical education is to have a vibrant future it behoves all those within the field to be scholars of the field, and here is a good place to begin.

Doune Macdonald
The University of Queensland

Introduction

■ Richard Bailey and David Kirk

T HE COMPILATION of a Reader is an explicitly selective process and one which is as revealing of the editors' values and perspectives on a field as it is a statement about the field itself. It is appropriate for us to begin with the frank admission that there is nothing objective about the process of compiling this volume. At the same time, this admission does not mean that the selection is necessarily 'biased', 'unreliable' or 'invalid'. If the configuration of a field of knowledge – its form or shape and its content – at any particular time in history is a social construct rather than a naturally occurring phenomenon, this means that the form and content of the field are the result of human endeavour. Often, as curriculum historian Ivor Goodson (1985) has pointed out, human endeavour has been manifest as struggle and contestation between vying individuals and groups over the discursive and material resources that will enable them to have their own perspectives favoured over others. Such struggles are not always or even necessarily noble and they can sometimes be less than pleasant, but there is no reason why they should not be underpinned by an informed and considered view of the field and the contexts in which it is practised.

In this introduction we will seek to outline some of our considered, and hopefully reasonably well-informed, views of scholarship in the field of physical education since the mid-1980s, but mostly over the past decade. We will acknowledge that our choice of what to include and what to leave out is driven by a particular understanding of the field of physical education scholarship in terms of its form and content and where it might be headed in the near future. We will suggest in these opening paragraphs and throughout that this Reader is an intentional and explicit intervention offering a particular definition of physical education scholarship. Our task in this introduction and then through our section commentaries, through the papers we have selected and through our conclusion is to convince you, the reader of this Reader, that our selection of papers and so our favoured definition of the field are not merely reasonable and well-grounded but, more ambitiously, compelling and irresistible.

It is important, first of all, to place the development of physical education scholarship within the broader context of the physical activity field within higher education. Trends towards the academicisation, scientisation, specialisation and fragmentation of the physical activity field in higher education (Lawson, 1991) have been similar in many countries around the world, though developments have followed different timelines country by country. In Britain, the physical activity field in higher education remained focused on teacher education from its inception around the end of the nineteenth century until the late 1940s (Kirk, 1992). Qualifications were typically at sub-degree (diploma) level and with the exception of the USA higher degree study was unusual. The first bachelors degree in Britain was offered by the University of Birmingham in 1949, but it took another 25 to 30 years for degree level qualifications to begin to become commonplace.

With the proliferation of bachelors and then masters degrees during the 1970s and 1980s came an expansion of the field beyond physical education teacher education to include sports science, leisure studies and recreation management. In the process of this expansion, and as the field became increasingly academic, scientific, specialised and fragmented, physical education teaching slipped from the centre to the margins of the field in terms of academic status. Teacher education courses remained popular with young people but, nevertheless, the serious scholarship was widely considered to be found in the biophysical sciences of sport and exercise (Macdonald et al., 1999).

While physical education teaching may have been the main focus of higher education until the 1970s, research into a wide range of topics in sport and exercise had been underway from the early 1900s. Much of this scholarship was focused on the psychology, physiology and biomechanics of the moving body, though there was also a fair amount of philosophical and historical research and writing (McCloy, 1940; McIntosh, 1952). During the 'degree decades' of the 1970s and 1980s, scholarship within college and university departments of physical education came under particular scrutiny as the physical activity field sought to be taken seriously within the academic community. Many institutions built on already well-developed programmes of research in the biophysical sciences as a means of laying claims to high quality scholarship that could underpin proposals for new degree programmes.

In the early stage, educational research in physical education, sport and exercise looked as if it might be left behind as the rush towards academic respectability began. Many individuals who had trained to be physical education teachers undertook higher degree study in biophysical science and effectively re-invented themselves. However, in the English-speaking world scholars did begin to appear, first in the USA during the late 1960s and into the 1970s, then a little later in the 1980s in Britain, Australia and New Zealand, who were interested in researching the educational aspects of physical education such as teaching, learning and teacher education.

In the first decade of the new millennium, any fears about the marginality of physical education scholarship have been dispelled as this 'sub-discipline' of the physical activity field, sometimes described as 'sport pedagogy', has grown rapidly in stature and maturity. In the English-speaking world the field is now served by journals such as the *Journal of Teaching in Physical Education* (in 2008 in its 27th volume), the *European Physical Education Review* (in 2008 in its 14th volume), *Sport, Education and Society* (in 2008 in its 13th volume), *Physical Education and Sport Pedagogy* (in 2008 in its 13th volume) and the *International Journal of Physical Education* (in 2008 in its 66th volume), while there are further specialist journals in other languages. Publication in 2006 of the Sage *Hand-book of Physical Education* (Kirk, Macdonald & O'Sullivan, 2006), containing 45 chapters written by 62 scholars, arguably represented a coming of age for physical education scholarship and presented the 'State of the Art' in considerable detail and quality.

This Reader is then a selection from the field of study that has grown rapidly since the 1970s to establish a secure place in the physical activity field. The core sections of the Reader are Part 4, Learners and learning; Part 5, Teachers and teaching; and Part 6, Curriculum and content. Together, these are the three interdependent dimensions of pedagogy. The papers selected in each section represent a range of theoretical perspectives and topics. For example, the papers in the 'Learners and learning' section draw on cognitive and constructivist approaches to learning, highlight the need to include a perspective on learning in any discussion of pedagogy, and wrestle with issues of equity and social justice in relation to our most basic assumptions about learning in physical education. The papers in the 'Teachers and teaching' section revisit these concerns for equity and social justice and also demonstrate the importance of studies of teacher knowledge, teachers' perspectives and their continuing professional development. Two of the three papers in the 'Curriculum and content' section illustrate the major impact models-based practice has had on physical education scholarship particularly through the 1990s to the present, while the inclusion of dance reveals the breadth of content often embraced by physical education.

The first section of the Reader contains papers on the nature and values of physical education, and in so doing reminds us of the long-term interest of physical education scholars in the critical scrutiny of concepts, assumptions and epistemology. One of the recurring themes of academic writing on physical education has been the exploration (and largely defence) of its educational status. Many writers have offered responses to the claim by some influential philosophers that physical education was a clear example of a non-educational subject because of its apparent lack of cognitive and theoretical foundations. The 1970s were, perhaps, the period during which such debates were fought most vigorously, through the works of David Best, Peter Arnold and David Aspin, but we can still follow the argument today in the writings of Andrew Reid, Bill Morgan and Sheryle Bergmann Drewe. Many have attempted to demonstrate that physical education really is a cognitively orientated subject, and develops students' knowledge (albeit, perhaps, of a different type) as do the more prestigious disciplines. Fewer have questioned the terms of the debate.

In the mid-1980s, Anne Williams (1985) noted the importance of sport and health as two 'legitimating publics' for the existence of physical education in schools. In Part 2, we include two papers that have studied the problematic place of sport in physical education, effectively dispelling a prevailing idea among some physical educators that physical education and sport should be treated as separate practices. In contrast, the papers show that sport has been and remains an integral aspect of physical education but that the ways in which we think about this relationship is mediated by powerful and multiple political and other influences. Health has been a perennial interest of physical educators, but as the papers in Part 3 show, the public's expectations for physical education to resolve various crises such as the so-called 'obesity epidemic' have never been more demanding or potentially unforgiving.

For a field of practice and scholarship that is so centrally concerned with the moving human body, the one-dimensional concern for the animal and machine-like aspects of the body in nature and the neglect of the body in culture has been remarkable. This omission has relatively recently been addressed in physical education scholarship and as these papers show has begun to be better understood in relation to disability, gender and broader social issues such as 'risk society'. While this corpus of scholarship on the social construction of bodies is growing, physical educators still do little explicit teaching about this phenomenon and its very many important social and personal consequences.

Since the nature and quality of scholarship has been so central to the rise of physical education in the physical activity field and in the academic community more broadly, we conclude the Reader with a section on research. The two papers selected here illustrate the wide-ranging theoretical developments that have taken place since the 1970s and the increasing sophistication of research methods as we have deepened and broadened our understanding of physical education.

Taken together, the papers make a statement about the field of physical education scholarship since the mid-1980s, with the emphasis on more recent works from the 1990s and the first decade of the twenty-first century. We think these papers suggest that scholarly work in physical education has reached a relatively sophisticated state in so far as it utilises a range of theoretical and methodological perspectives that are up to date and in regular use in other fields of educational research. Even so, the citation impact factors for the leading journals in the field suggest that much work remains to be done to develop practices of citation that show generations of scholars building on previous work in a systematic fashion. Citation practices in fields such as the physical and biological sciences lead to impact factors that far exceed those in educational research generally and in physical education specifically.

Further challenges exist. For example, there is too little synergy between the scholarship on show in this Reader and policy and curriculum development in physical education in schools and communities. It is not only policy-makers who do not read the research literature. Teachers too seem to have little time for the regular study of research and few take a scholarly approach to their work. The problem here would appear to have its sources in teacher education programmes and in the sedimented and obdurate culture of schools, though there is little evidence to suggest physical educators are any less well read than their colleagues in other subject areas. Nevertheless, there is much to be done including thinking beyond conventional forms of communication in order to improve these synergies.

We trust that the papers contained in this Reader will convince you of the need for the continuing production of high quality scholarly books and papers in physical education and of the salience of the topics they cover. We suggest they provide a window on a field of scholarship that is growing in confidence and sophistication and that is increasingly in touch with the pressing issues of policy and practice. Of course, any collection of papers will be necessarily incomplete. In particular, as is unavoidable, it represents the articles that we have encountered and which seem to us to be important or useful. We are sure that many readers will find glaring omissions. But we hope that they view our selection as indications of a rich past and an exciting future.

References

Goodson, I.F. (1985) Towards curriculum history, in: I.F. Goodson (ed.), *Social Histories of the Secondary Curriculum: Subjects for Study*. London: The Falmer Press.

Kirk, D., Macdonald, D. and O'Sullivan, M. (eds) (2006) *Handbook of Physical Education*. London: Sage.

Kirk, D. (1992) *Defining Physical Education: The Social Construction of a School Subject in Postwar Britain*. London: Falmer.

Lawson, H. (1991). Specialization and fragmentation among faculty as endemic features of academic life. *Quest*, 43, 280–295.

Macdonald, D., Kirk, D. and Braiuka, S. (1999) The social construction of the physical activity field at the school/university interface. *European Physical Education Review*, 5(1), 31–51.

McCloy, C.H. (1940) *Philosophical Bases for Physical Education*. New York: Appleton.

McIntosh, P.C. (1952) *Physical Education in England Since 1800*. London: Bell.

Williams, A.E. (1985) Understanding constraints on innovation in physical education. *Journal of Curriculum Studies*, 17(4), 407–413.

PART 1

Nature and values of physical education

INTRODUCTION

PHYSICAL EDUCATION, like any curriculum subject, can take many forms. As our introduction to this Reader makes clear, the subject has manifested itself in many different ways during its reasonably short history. One might suppose that, as time moves on, the profession would move towards some sort of consensus about its nature and purpose, but the opposite seems to have happened. This is no doubt partly due to the tendency of physical educators to enthusiastically embrace policy agendas of the day, and so fighting the 'obesity epidemic', combating youth crime and laying the foundations for elite sporting success all appear in contemporary advocacy statements. However, disputes about the nature and values of physical education look likely to continue because education is what philosophers call an 'essentially contested concept'. While there is a degree of agreement at a rather abstract level among teachers and writers about the importance of physical education, there is substantial disagreement about the character of that importance. Moreover, no amount of empirical evidence or reasoning is going to settle these disputes once and for all, because they are expressions of competing values.

The papers in this first section approach the question of the nature and values of physical education from quite different directions. **McNamee** reviews attempts to discuss the nature of the subject. In doing so, he highlights a recurring theme within the philosophical literature, namely the different attempts to justify the educational status of physical education. These attempts, he argues, have so far been generally unsuccessful. Nevertheless, he leaves little doubt of the relevance of philosophical tools and techniques for physical educators. **Bailey's** focus is on the empirical basis for the claims made on behalf of physical education. As already stated, there has been a tendency for defenders of physical education to jump on passing policy bandwagons in recent years. One response to such actions is to ask, as McNamee might, whether or not they *ought* to do so; another is to assess the evidence for the claims. Finally, **Bain** draws our attention to the vitally important, but still frequently overlooked, issue of the 'hidden curriculum', which consists of the values and practices that are not written down nor explicitly promoted, but which underlie many of the experiences of learners in lessons.

FURTHER READING

Aspin, D. (1976) 'Knowing How' and 'Knowing That' and physical education. *Journal of Philosophy of Sport*, 3, 97–117.

Best, D. (1978) *Philosophy and Human Movement*. London: George Allen & Unwin.

Kirk, D. (1992) *Defining Physical Education: The Social Construction of a School Subject in Postwar Britain*. London: Falmer.

Morgan, W. (2006) Philosophy and physical education, in: D. Kirk, D. Macdonald and M. O'Sullivan (eds), *Handbook of Physical Education*. London: Sage.

Mike McNamee

THE NATURE AND VALUES OF PHYSICAL EDUCATION

THERE HAS ALWAYS BEEN an air of suspicion about those who think philosophically about the nature and values of physical education. On the one hand, physical education teachers are apt to claim that theirs is essentially a practical vocation; a calling to the teaching of physical activities that can help students to live better lives. What need have they of a philosophy? On the other hand, philosophers of education, notably in the liberal-analytical tradition, have often sought to cast a dim light on physical education, thinking it valuable (on good days at least) – but not educationally so. I shall try in this chapter to say something about the nature and values of physical education; the knowledge and the values that are inherent within its activities and those external ones which can be gained from them. The chapter revolves around a critique of some recent theoretically sophisticated attempts to discuss the nature and educational status of physical education by three philosophers David Carr (1997), Jim Parry (1998) and Andrew Reid (1996a, 1996b, 1997). I try to show where their arguments are both helpful but ultimately inadequate for the task of illuminating what physical education ought properly to consist of and how it might better prove its educational status and value. In particular, I try to show how it is absolutely necessary to think philosophically about the nature and values of activities that are thought to constitute physical education.[1]

On analytical philosophy of education and physical education

Before embarking on an account of the nature of physical education, and its knowledge and values claims, it is necessary to first take a short detour and second, offer an apology. First, it is necessary – if we are to have a reflective view of the philosophical terrain in which sense can be made of the concept of physical education – to understand a little of the nature of philosophical thinking. Second, the account here is itself situated within a particular tradition of thought. I do not speak of continental philosophy where there might be rich seams indeed for philosophers of physical education to plough. In particular, the work of phenomenologists[2] and hermeneuticists[3] have tremendous potential to offer understandings of our experiences in the activities that comprise physical education (whether in sport, games, play or even dance).

The manner in which this 'new' philosophy took a foothold in the UK and the USA — what came to be known as analytical philosophy of education — was nothing short of remarkable. The classic UK texts of the 1960s and 1970s bear testimony to it: Dearden's (1968) *Philosophy of Primary Education*, Hirst and Peters' (1970) *The Logic of Education* and Peters' (1966) *Ethics and Education* are paradigmatic. A cursory glance at their contents pages indicates their subject matter. Each philosopher bore down on their subject matter with microscopic linguistic scrutiny; precisely what was meant by concepts so central to education as 'authority', 'democracy', 'discipline', 'initiation', 'knowledge', 'learning', and so on. No educational concepts escaped their analytical scrutiny. A very similar movement was carrying the day in the USA where philosophers of education centrally saw themselves engaged in the same enterprise — and with surprisingly similar results given the cultural and geographical distance that set them apart. Despite the time that has elapsed since this highly original work, it is genuinely worthwhile to revisit their positions in order to better understand how (and perhaps how not) to think philosophically about physical education as an educational enterprise.

In the UK, Richard Peters developed the most powerful statement about the nature of education. In his inaugural lecture in 1965, he put forward a thesis that was to reach literally across the world through the old British Empire — many of whose educational lecturers were still taught in British universities — that education must be viewed, by all those who seriously investigate its nature, to comprise a certain logical geography. Briefly, his thesis was that education, properly conceived, referred to the initiation of the unlearned into those intrinsically worthwhile forms of knowledge that were constitutive of rational mind. Its shorthand was that education referred essentially to the development of rationality. Despite the hugely influential educational effects of muscular Christianity, physical education enjoyed little more than a Cinderella existence, even in British education, throughout the twentieth century. And now, it was surely not to be invited to the ball. The hegemony of that great thesis cast physical education well and truly into the educational hinterland. I shall now consider that thesis in a little detail.[4]

The particular picture of education favoured by analytical philosophers of education, then, is that of the British philosopher of education Richard Peters and, to a lesser extent, his close colleague Paul Hirst. I shall refer to their theses collectively as the Petersian conception of education. It is familiar enough to anyone who read any English language philosophy of education from 1965 to 1985. For Peters, the many uses of the word 'education' might be reduced to the central case and the philosophical task was to tease out criteria implicit in that case. This led Peters to develop his sophisticated account of education as the transmission of what was intrinsically worthwhile in order to open the eyes of initiates to a vaster and more variegated existence. That same worthwhile knowledge was continuous with the various forms of knowledge that Hirst had delineated by his own set of epistemological criteria. The Petersian thesis was summarised thus:

- 'education' implies the transmission of what is worth-while to those who become committed to it;
- 'education' must involve knowledge and understanding and some kind of cognitive perspective, which are not inert; and
- 'education' at least rules out some procedures of transmission, on the grounds that they lack wittingness and voluntariness on the part of the learner.

(Peters, 1966: 45)

The first two conditions have been referred to as the axiological and epistemological conditions by two other philosophers, Andrew Reid (1996a, 1996b, 1997) and David Carr (1997), both of whom have sought to conceptualise physical education in similar ways, but who have come to rather different conclusions about its educational potential. The third criterion refers to the processes by which such transmission was ethically acceptable. I will comment on the analytical and epistemological dimension of Carr's and Reid's articles and then examine the axiological dimension of Reid's work which is the bedrock of his justification for the educational status of physical education.

What is of significance in Reid (1996a, 1996b, 1997) is the idea that education, as conceived in the Petersian mould, is narrow and restrictive. Despite a lack of argumentation, he signifies a broader conception of education than is found in the accounts of philosophers such as Peters, Hirst, Barrow or, for that matter, anyone housed within the liberal tradition. These philosophers of education conceive of education as the development of individual, rationally autonomous, learners. In their writings they sharply distinguish education from other learning-related concepts such as 'socialisation', 'training' and 'vocation' in terms of their content, scope, value and application. Reid's conceptualisation of a broader account rests on the position of John White (1990) in his book *Education and the Good Life* where educators aim toward the development of personal well-being grounded in rationally informed desires of both a theoretical and practical kind. Education is thus subservient to, and continuous with, the kinds of development that enable an individual to choose activities, experiences and relationships that are affirmations of those informed choices.

By contrast, Carr is more traditional (in the liberal sense) in his account of education and therefore physical education. Like Barrow and Peters before him, he marks the education-training distinction by a thesis about mind. For the earlier writers in liberal philosophy of education, all educational activities were broader and richer in scope than mere training which was a form of instruction with limited, focused ends. Education properly conceived, they argued, aimed at something much richer and more variegated. The educated mind did not focus on things limited in scope, such as training for the world of work, but rather helped learners to better understand their world, and their place within it. As it was often said, education had no specific destination or goal as such; it was rather to travel with a new, enlarged view. Necessarily, this educated view was informed by an initiation into the forms of knowledge or rationality; aesthetic, mathematical, philosophical, scientific, religious, and so on. These were simply what being educated consisted in. Despite the fact that Carr recognises the value of practical as well as theoretical rationality, he undermines Reid's thesis about the importance of physical education conceived of as practical knowledge, and is driven back to the old liberal ground:

> The key idea here is the traditionalist one that certain forms of knowledge and understanding enter into the ecology of human development and formation –

not as theories of a scientist or the skills of a golfer, but as the horizon of significance against which we are able to form some coherent picture of how the world is, our place in it and how it is appropriate for us to relate to others. Strictly speaking, it matters not a hoot on the traditionalist picture whether such received wisdom is theoretical or practical or located at some point in between; what matters is that there should be – in the name of education – some substantial initiation into this realm (or these realms) of human significance *alongside any training in vocational or domestic or merely recreational skills.* This is not to deny any proper normative conception of the latter, or that any pursuit of such skills may involve considerable rational judgement and discrimination; it is rather to insist that the sort of rationality they do exhibit may not and need not have anything much to do with education. Very roughly, one might put the point of the liberal-traditionalist distinction between educational and non-educational knowledge by observing that the former is knowledge which informs rather than merely uses the mind.

(Carr, 1997: 201; emphasis added)

Thus, Carr's account is little more than a brave leap back to the Petersian position. Now, as with all philosophical argument, one can dispute a position on its own terms, one can deny the presuppositions of those terms or one can either assert or argue for a counter position. The middle option can be seen in any of a legion of writers[5] who attacked the liberal position for its normative presuppositions. Under the banner of ideological neutrality, it seemed to smuggle in an awful lot of values. Moreover, nearly every self-respecting sociologist of education (and physical education) cried that it entailed little more than a crystallisation of the kind of curriculum favoured by British grammar and public schools in the UK over the last 100 years or so. I shall not discuss the normative presuppositions in the liberal account of education. Instead, I will merely indicate here that I am persuaded by a less restricted account of the contents of education based on the notion of a worthwhile life which is not exhausted by those activities that, so to speak, inform the mind. I lay out the contours of such an account in the final section below.

There is a point of considerable agreement between Carr and Reid that is typical of the liberal theory of education, and it is one that is typically used against the educational advocates of physical education. Both writers are keen to hold on to the liberal ideal that education has its own ends. This of course cuts across the grain of 'common sense' thinking that it is the job of education to effect socialisation, or produce a more efficient workforce, and so on. Reid says that a broader view of what education entails – the introduction to cultural resources – must not simply be thought of as the development of qualities of mind:

The idea of *introduction to cultural resources* is to be taken here as an abbreviated way of referring to the complex and lengthy processes associated with the knowledge condition of education, with the teaching and learning which are required for effective appreciation and use of those resources. The sports and games which figure in physical education, then, are to be distinguished from work, the arts, intellectual illumination and so on in terms of their fundamentally hedonic orientation, but not in terms of their role as major cultural institutions, and thus (on the view which sees personal well-being and its component values in terms of socialisation and acculturation) in terms of their educational importance.

(Reid, 1997: 15–16; original emphasis)

It seems, therefore, that Reid is not unhappy with the general model of education as initiation into sports and games as major cultural institutions.[6] As we have seen, Carr parts company with Reid on epistemological issues to do with the development of rational mind, though not only there. Despite recognising the value of such initiation, Carr pejoratively refers to sports and games (following Barrow, 1981) as merely a valuable part of one's schooling – but, note, not education. Carr's logical geography is restricted to the Petersian-liberal continent. Like many others before him, Reid wants to shift the ground of education away from the development of intellect as the sole basis and look also to a kind of 'pleasure principle'. Reid suggests that the nature and value of physical education is best characterised by a 'fundamentally hedonic orientation'. I shall consider these points in that order.

Epistemological aspects

One major strand in physical education teachers' collective insecurity complex is to be found in epistemological aspects of their subject which, in the UK at least, has undergone significant professional changes. Central among those changes is the emergence of a graduate profession armed (supposedly) with a greater breadth and depth of theoretical knowledge. For my part, I harbour three suspicions about such claims. First, I am simply not sure if it is true that the development of an all-graduate profession has produced a teacher base that is characterised as having a broader and deeper knowledge base and I know of no empirical study to dis/prove the claim. Second, even if this were true, it does not follow necessarily that this would bring about better learning and teaching in physical education lessons. Third, over the last 20 years or so we have seen witnessed the introduction of significant elements of propositional knowledge into the school subject (taught in a fashion more typical of the classroom than the gymnasium) which has been incorporated systematically into syllabi, culminating in examinations.[7] Yet, it is not the mere snobbery of the physics or maths teacher that is problematic here. Carr, as we have seen above, gives it its most pithy statement: education comprises those forms of knowledge that do not merely use but, rather, inform rational mind. The distinction is both clear and elegantly put. But what follows from it? The answer is 'nothing necessarily'. Further exploration is required.

Reid claims that the family of activities of physical education are best conceived of as expressions of 'knowing how', to use Gilbert Ryle's famous phrase. That is to say, the activities and their knowledge contents are not merely the handmaiden of theoretical knowledge, but a species of knowledge in their own right. They are better captured under the title 'practical knowledge'. Similarly, Parry (1988) claims that it is the practical knowledge required for successful participation in physical education activities that satisfies the epistemological criterion of education. On a technical point, it could be argued that the phrase 'epistemological criterion' requires correction. Peters' remarks on the epistemological criteria of education are better subdivided thus: (a) the development of knowledge and understanding which are not inert; and that (b) such knowledge and understanding must be framed in some 'cognitive perspective'. This distinction is important since, among other objections, one could argue that the knowledge and understanding of the activities of physical education may well come to characterise part of one's way of viewing the world. The phrase 'having a healthy and active lifestyle' (of late, barbarously misused) might well capture the idea of a person considered physically educated; one whose knowledge was tied to action in important respects. It could be said that most adults 'know' what a healthier and more active lifestyle looks like but they are unable to incorporate it into their lives. On the stronger epistemological account, one could not be said *properly* to know this whilst acting in a contrary way. But it is really the second epistemological aspect – the cognitive perspective – that offends both Peters' and Carr's rationalism. Lest it be said that I am erecting a strawman, consider Peters' construction of the value of theoretical knowledge. Note that it is in contrast to theoretical knowledge that he dismisses, among other things, sports and games:

> To get attached to pets, people or possessions is a bad bet *sub specie aeternitatis;* for there is one thing we know about them – they will die or become worn out with use or age. No such fate awaits the objects of theoretical activities; for as long as there is an order of the world there will always be further things to find out about it.
>
> (Peters, 1966: 157)

> In so far as knowledge is involved in games and pastimes, this is limited to the hived off end of the activity which may be morally indifferent. A man (sic) may know a great deal about cricket if he is a devotee of the game; but it would be fanciful to pretend that his concern to find out things is linked with any serious purpose, unless the game is viewed under an aesthetic or moral purpose. Cricket is classed as a game because its end is morally unimportant. Indeed an end has almost to be invented to make possible the various manifestations of skill.
>
> (Peters, 1966: 158)

In a passage that should be etched on the hearts and minds of all physical education student teachers, he continues:

> Curriculum activities, on the other hand, such as science or history, literary appreciation, and poetry are 'serious' in that they illuminate other areas of life and contribute much to the quality of living. They have, secondly, a wide ranging cognitive content which distinguishes them from games. Skills, for instance, do not have a wide ranging cognitive content. There is very little to know about riding bicycles, swimming, or golf. It is largely a matter of knowing how rather than of 'knowing that', of knack rather than of understanding. Furthermore, what there is to know throws little light on much else.
>
> (Peters, 1966: 159)

While Reid, therefore, presents a sophisticated account of practical knowledge and reasoning (ironically enough, following Carr and others), he fails to attack the proper target and to give an account for the specific epistemological aspects of the activities of physical education. It would seem to me that a more fruitful place to start would be to interrogate Peters' account of 'seriousness' which is used to demarcate knowledge considered educational from that which is not. Two brief sets of points can be made here. In what sense is the illumination of things other than themselves a necessary condition for what is said to be 'serious'? Why, furthermore, should wide-ranging cognitive content similarly be viewed as a logically necessary condition of educational activities? The criterion does indeed distinguish practices such as science from sport but, again, what follows from this? Second, note how the notion that certain ranges of knowledge contribute to the quality of living, gets sidelined thereafter. Surely this is one of the palpable claims that all physical educators would make as a hypothetical justification of the subject? As a matter of fact, one could survey the millions of people for whom sports and related practices are central to their quality of living. As a justification, of course, this form of argument is hypothetical since its success is contingent upon the satisfactions enjoyed by those persons. We should not need reminding that many children simply detest sports and games just as others come to love and care for them (both in spite of, and because of, the manner of a child's initiation into them).[8] If we agree the philosophical point that to be physically educated, what one knows must characterise the way one acts in the world, then as physical educators, it is our duty to both habitualise children into patterns of activity and engagement with social practices such as hockey and basketball, and to open up to our students the significant sporting inheritance of our cultures so that they too may come to savour its joys and frustrations *and* to know a little about that aspect of the cultures which sporting practices instantiate (for no one would seriously deny their enormous significance in modern societies).[9]

Thus Reid's exploration of the underlying logic of practical knowledge is, despite Parry's assertion, a worthwhile task. But Reid fails significantly to take that analysis further. This omission is manifest in his observation that there are profoundly complex kinds of practical knowledge required, for example, in playing Tchaikovsky or flying a plane. Howsoever these examples are used to illustrate the potential complexity of forms of practical knowledge, they are not representative of the kinds of knowledge definitive of physical education. Nor can they be used helpfully as analogues in such an argument. There is a further complication, moreover, in the contrast between the serious forms of knowledge and sports and games which relates to the ease with which children are initiated into cultural practices. Like physical education, the 'serious' educational subjects too have easy skills and techniques at their onset, yet these are the first steps in practices of immense rational sophistication in range and depth. Sports do not possess this range of cognitive complexity and it would be folly to argue that they do. Yet there is more to them than *mere* knack: a forward roll is a skill and so is a double twisting back somersault but compare the range of complexity. The capacity to generate immensely technical skills aligned to perceptive judgement and anticipation in a time-compressed manner is typical of any invasion game (though they too have their basic techniques). Sports skills are not comparable in density or range to classical music or philosophy. This is why Tchaikovsky's concertos or landing aeroplanes are inappropriate analogues. It might, however, be profitable to explore other areas of the curriculum that embody overt performative knowledge as opposed to intellectual ones with respect to the embodiment of that knowledge.

What has to be acknowledged in this debate is the exceptional difficulty in talking about sporting experiences especially where they refer significantly to the emotional dimension that accompanies success and failure. It is not so much that one can give a full account of action if only sports people were linguistically sophisticated (a point lamentably true of most media, post-performance, interviews); the point is that these descriptions occupy different worlds. A phenomenological account simply does not try to do the same thing as, say, a physiological or biomechanical one.[10] But that is a discussion for another day. This entire area has been largely neglected in the philosophy of physical education since David Best's (1978) and David Carr's work (1979) in the 1970s. Reid has done the profession a service by reminding us of their importance.

Characteristic of early analytical philosophers of education, however, Reid proceeds as if the logic of his philosophical analysis carries itself forward to a conclusion in the minds of any reasonable person (including policy makers, headteachers, and other curriculum tutors competing for scarce resources). Like so much earlier work in analytical philosophy of education Reid fails to accord sufficient weight to contextual particulars and specifically the power-related discourses of the school-as-institution (rather than mere concept) and the dominance of the academic therein. Reid merely gestures towards this problematic. Despite the clarity of his arguments regarding physical education, it is the widespread experiences of physical education teachers who have been demeaned by the hierarchical dominance, or positioning, of propositional over performative knowledge. I am certain that this is the core root of the professional insecurity that has always characterised the physical education profession, and which has culminated in the apparent 'academicisation' of our profession.

Finally, the greatest weakness in the epistemological aspect of Reid's account of physical education as education is his failure to offer a value argument for the kinds of knowledge representative of physical education. It is a point that Peters flagged up 30 years ago: 'It is one thing to point to characteristics of activities that are usually thought to be worth while; it is quite another to show why these sorts of characteristics make them worth while' (1966: 152).

Like any philosophical thesis, one may challenge the Petersian position by rejecting the manner in which it is presented rather than looking for inconsistencies or incoherence within it. One could, so to speak, reject the paradigm completely; that is to say, reject the very terms in which it is presented and the bases it presupposes. In doing so we could reconceptualise some or all of the notions of 'rationality', 'knowledge' or 'education' to find an account more conducive to physical education and its claims to proper educational status. Despite making a case for the necessary existence of practical rationality in edu-cational matters, on Reid's case, physical educationists would still be left to argue whether the activities of physical education were *productive* of practical rationality and *why* the particular practical rationality employed or exemplified in the activities were of particular value. Equally unfortunate, we have seen how Carr's position appears little more than a retrenchment into a broadly Petersian education. Reid's best hopes appear to be based on the pluralism of value conferred by the range of activities, but particularly in reference to their essentially hedonic character. While I think that it is clear that the range of activities represent a family (with some close relations and some more distant ones) I think the policies of both Carr and Reid are misguided. It is, therefore, to issues of axiology and physical education that I will now turn.

Axiology and physical education

What Reid attempts, more generously than other liberal philosophers of education, is to connect the ways in which different kinds of knowledge in physical education activities embody different kinds of value. He sets out a fuller list of the sources of value and attempts to relate physical education to them. In addition to arguments about the value of theoretical knowledge, he articulates the following range: intellectual, ethical, aesthetic, economic, hedonic and health. As we have seen, anyone attempting to argue for the educational value of physical education on the grounds that the playing of games conferred a wide-ranging cognitive perspective on the world would be barking up the wrong tree. A more circumscribed claim regarding theoretical knowledge in physical education is plausible. Understanding sports and other forms of 'physical activities' from the appropriate field of theoretical standpoints (anatomy, biology, history, sociology, and so forth) illuminates the ways in which those activities can contribute to a worthwhile life. For example, I can benefit from knowing that steady state, medium intensity, exercise over 20 minutes' duration draws significantly upon aerobic rather than anaerobic metabolism and is therefore more appropriate to my maintaining lower levels of fat. Conversely, I may come to appreciate that circuit training is more conducive to anaerobic fitness and that by altering my body positions while performing sit-ups I may more specifically target my abdominal muscles and reduce the contribution of my hip flexors. Moreover, I may begin critically to appreciate the highly gendered atmosphere of the locker room or the deep offensiveness engendered by racist or anti-Semitic attitudes in some sports crowds. The point remains, however, that despite these benefits, the value-arguments for physical education ought not to be erected on *exactly* the same grounds as other curriculum subjects that are palpably different in nature. This inspires Reid's search for a broader range of values.

There is a sense in which Reid has brought this problem upon himself *because* of the way in which he conceives physical education. He recognises that no satisfactory account of the subject will flow simply from an examination of the ways in which the words 'physical' and 'education' are used. Rather, such an account must begin from an analysis of the historical practices and traditions that have been prominent in giving shape and form to physical education. Rather, Reid thinks the task is to elucidate

> the conceptual features of a set of well-founded educational practices and traditions. What is 'given', from this standpoint, is not some set of axioms or intuitions about the nature of 'physicality' and 'education', but what might rather be called physical education as a form of life, that is the practices and traditions of physical education as they have evolved historically and continue to evolve, in concrete social, cultural and institutional contexts.
>
> (Reid, 1997: 10)

This is absolutely the right way to go about things. Not only should we look historically at those practices and traditions but also at their contemporary instantiations. But it is problematic to argue merely that physical education is the sum of its practices and traditions without also offering an account that articulates and brings together the disparate nature of those practices and traditions.[11] For which practices are we to opt? Into whose traditions ought we to initiate our young? Compare what values Rugby Union stood for only ten years ago with its new professional metamorphosis. To what extent does it represent the same kind of practice into which we once thought it worthwhile for our children to be initiated?[12] Is the ethos of girls' hockey or cricket really full of camaraderie as is stereotypically thought? What is entirely unhelpful, is to argue that what holds the different activities, their practices and traditions together, is the notion of hedonic pleasure.

In terms of ethical value, Reid points out the inherent normativity of physical education activities. Here, it must be pointed out, the diversity of what goes under the heading physical education renders generalisations problematic. In sporting games, the moral educational features are written into their very nature (that is to say, the regulative rules). Where games are taught properly, ethical notions such as equality, fairness, honesty and rule-abiding action necessarily arise. The extent to which these notions are merely caught rather than taught is another matter. Precisely, how these values infuse dance, health-related exercise, or orienteering is quite another matter and Reid's recognition of eclectic argumentation is helpful. Yet in his final paper (see Reid, 1997) there is a tendency to use only sporting games as the vehicle for his own justificatory argument. Reid makes two points that are designed to defuse the arguments of those who deny sports' ethical dimension. While I am in agreement with the point of arguing for the ethical dimension of sports I will dispute his specific argumentation below. Reid writes:

> The first relates to the discussion earlier on the relations between the constituents of our axiology, which concluded in favour of the priority of ethical values (when competing values are entertained). In the context of games teaching, this reflects the traditional principle that fair play, sportsmanship and respect for one's opponent take precedence over the competitive objectives of winning and avoiding defeat. The second point, likewise, concerns questions of priority. The position adopted in this paper . . . is that games and sports are forms of play, aimed essentially at promoting pleasure enjoyment, excitement, recreation, and the like; their primary value, in short, is hedonic. Winning, from this point of view, is not, as is sometimes supposed, the ultimate goal of competitive games: enjoyment is, and competitive action, structured in highly specific ways by the operation of the norms, rules, codes, conventions and so on of the various particular sports and games, is the way in which the conditions of enjoyment are fulfilled, its possibilities realized.
>
> (Reid, 1997: 12)

He continues: 'games themselves are, as essentially hedonic activities, fundamentally self-contained and in some sense non-serious . . . and this observation gives some weight to the scepticism sometimes expressed about the prospects for extending those ethical principles beyond the boundaries of the game'.

Here Reid answers Peters' question regarding the source of value. But is it a satisfactory one? I will make a few general points about Reid's general argument here, and then move specifically to the adequacy of his hedonic direction. First, Reid has failed to apply his own reasoning to his analysis of the logic of competitive games viz. their ethical dimension. He posits that where there is conflict between the competitive urge to win and other, ethical, principles such as fairness and honesty the latter should prevail. Yet he has already informed the reader that to play games logically entails the observance of such principles. This being the case there can be no such conflict, for where players are dishonest, or unfair or not rule-abiding (assuming they are breaking the rules, in being dishonest, or violent or disrespectful) they are *ipso facto* not playing the game. This point is commonly referred to as the 'logical incompatibility thesis'. Adherents of the thesis argue that to play a game one must play by the rules and to do otherwise is to be engaged in behaviours that are, by definition, not part of the game.[13]

Second, on an historical note, Reid's move can be compared with Robert Carlisle's (1969) doomed essentialistic argument.[14] Where Carlisle attempted to locate the educational status of physical education in terms of their essentially aesthetic character Reid opts for the hedonic. This sort of essentialism appears in marked contrast to his earlier recognition of the disparate nature of the constituent activities of physical education. Similarly, despite his earlier eclecticism, Reid appears to have turned physical education into competitive games. It is not a new sleight of hand; the National Curriculum for PE in the UK underwent such a reduction in the highly politicised policy formulation stages. And there are some clear benefits to such a strategy though there are burdens too. The dietary narrowness of competitive games has been the object of much rancorous debate and the breadth of modern physical education curricula is something welcomed not only by egalitarians of the left.[15] Nevertheless, from a philosophical point of view, it seems clear that if one were to conceptualise or justify physical education solely in terms of sports and games then this would beg questions as to the educational place of the other members of the family of activities that traditionally fall under the heading of physical education, in the UK at least. Furthermore, if one were to alter the conception of physical education it seems clear that one's arguments concerning the types of knowledge entailed therein, the aims, value and educational justification of the subject ought correspondingly to alter too. Reid's failure to acknowledge this is problematic since he later discusses at length the benefit of health values wrought by a physical education curriculum.[16] The precise picture of physical education Reid wants to defend is not specified though the contours are visible; a distaste for theoretical engagement; a predominance of sporting games; a reductionism to hedonic values. What Reid argues later is for a kind of eclecticism that blurs the emphasis on competitive sporting games. He urges that the full value of physical education is to be found in its manifold contributions to different sorts of value but that as a matter of logic, on his analysis, their value is essentially hedonic.

I have argued at length elsewhere (see McNamee, 1994) of the weakness of reducing sports and related practices to the value of felt pleasures and I will merely rehearse those arguments briefly here.[17] The central reason why the hedonic thesis should not be considered adequate is that it offers no criteria (and hence no logical basis over and above mere preference) against which to evaluate such practices or make subsequent policy decisions. If, for instance, we are concerned with the questions 'what practices are worth pursuing/providing/committing ourselves to?' we find ourselves without logical assistance since the first and last words of the hedonist's thesis are 'it gives me pleasure' or 'I enjoy it'. This response is sometimes referred to as a 'stopper'. It fails to provide any sort of logical answer to a sceptical questioner but stops them from further exploration. Of course, many children and adults who are committed to sports find the exercise of skilful acts deeply satisfying, fulfilling or pleasurable and attribute their value to nothing other than the experience or engagement in the activity. The language in which their accounts of the value of their experiences are often couched is hedonic in the sense that they refer exclusively to the subjective value of pleasurable feelings. Reid fails to instantiate in detail what the hedonic thesis amounts to.

By way of criticism, consider first those activities that are ill-characterised by felt pleasure. For instance, there may be many qualities, goods or values associated with, for instance, outdoor and adventurous activities in the winter time. It may be assumed, however, that fun or pleasure may not commonly be among them. These activities may come to be enjoyable but only after some considerable time and effort and this may only be afforded to a limited number of people who are genetically predisposed to them or who, through training, have come to be committed to them. Second, as Parry noted, the pursuit of pleasure itself does not demarcate any special class of activities except those logically thus defined. The corollary of the hedonic view would entail the justification of whatsoever people found pleasurable simply because they found it pleasurable. And the contents list of such an account could render some fairly unthinkable items for education. Third, pleasures differ in quality. The pleasures derived by a six-year-old child from engaging in simple motor actions are considered inappropriate for sixteen-year-olds who demand something more complex. To the best of my knowledge no one has explored this idea in the context of sport from a philosophical point of view yet the classification of games by Celia Brackenridge and John Alderson presupposes it.[18] It has been called the 'Aristotelian Principle' by John Rawls who writes:

> other things equal, human beings enjoy the exercise of their realized capacities (their innate or trained abilities), and this enjoyment increases the more the capacity is realized, or the greater its complexity. The intuitive idea here is that human beings take more pleasure in doing something the more they become proficient at it, and of two activities they do equally well, they prefer the one calling on a larger and more intricate and subtle discrimination.
>
> (Rawls, 1972: 435)

Indeed the value of sports and games may themselves be considered time-related goods.[19] No one would want to deny that the satisfactions afforded by the successful grasping of timing a boast in squash or spotting a somersault are tremendously rewarding but are they always so, and is pleasure the right concept to denote the attendant satisfactions?

Every account of the value presupposes a particular *weltanschauung* and, moreover, a particular philosophical anthropology. Any particular and substantive account of the value of sports and related practices will therefore be related conceptually to an account of a person that is thought desirable for one to become. Sports and related practices thus become seen as one of a family of engineering processes (less deterministically, practices and traditions) that are constitutive of a person's becoming just that: a person. Each culture, indeed each epoch, has more or less tightly defined horizons that inform and are informed symbiotically by each other.

How are such horizons informed by the hedonic thesis? Let me start with a logical point. One cannot pursue pleasure in isolation. Pleasure is derived *through* actions and activities. A similar point is made by Nozick in one of his thought experiments, the 'experience machine'.[20] A thought experiment is a typical tool used by philosophers to get people to imagine a hypothetical scenario and then to show how this sheds light on a real case by analogy. So Nozick asks his readers, 'What else matters to us other than how life feels on the inside?' He asks us to consider whether we would hook ourselves up to a machine which simulates the feelings experienced when having any and all the wonderful experiences we desired. I have tried the experiment out with students over 20 years of lecturing. The vast majority, on the first run through of the argument opt to plug in. After considerable discussion many change their mind. The reasons for this are illuminating for our consideration of the value of physical education. In the experience machine one remains essentially passive. But *as* persons,[21] we want to *do* certain things; to achieve the attendant satisfactions of being a successful teacher or pupil, cricketer, or athlete. To *be* such things is to be committed to various activities, roles and relationships which define the sort of persons we are. Plugging into the machine is a form of suicide. In a sense, we cease to be the same person since the relationship between our experiences and our acts no longer holds. Many of my students have used the language of merit: 'you don't deserve those experiences because you have not got the ability, or trained for years, or sacrificed your life to the goals of sport' they say. In the machine, all these pleasurable experiences would not be related to us in the strong way that flows from our being attached to particular plans and projects. On the contrary the status of those experiences would be contingent to, rather than definitive of, our identity. The experience machine effectively lives our lives for us. This is not the life of a person.

It should be noted that I have not denigrated the value of pleasure as an action guiding reason *per se*. It is in need of some focus if it is to be used in offering a sound account of the value of the activities, practices and traditions of physical education. Moreover, a value argument ought not to be built in terms of the pursuit of pleasure alone. Pleasure, as was noted above, can only be pursued through particular acts and activities.

All these arguments about the inadequacy of educational justification being based upon hedonic lines leaves untouched the philosophical questions concerning the nature of value itself and classes of value used to account for physical education. Parry discerned the blurring of the intrinsic/instrumental distinction by Linda Bain (in the USA) and Keith Thompson (in the UK).[22] Carr correctly offers a similar critique of Reid, and Peters before him, who employ the terms 'intrinsic', 'extrinsic', 'inherent' and 'instrumental' to refer to both the value of an activity and the motivational states of a person. It is helpful here to stipulate linguistic usage in the interests of conceptual clarity. Let the terms 'intrinsic' and 'extrinsic' refer to my motivations or valuing of an activity but preserve the terms 'inherent' and 'instrumental' to refer to the (potential) value of a given thing or activity. For one can be intrinsically motivated to bang one's head against a wall (i.e., where one did it for its own sake and sought no further end) whereas no one would want to maintain that it was an inherently valuable act. On the other hand, it could be argued that while sport was inherently valuable, any particular athlete only valued it instrumentally and therefore that their motivations were entirely extrinsic. Much confused debate in physical education has occurred precisely for the want of drawing these distinctions with care.

Though I have captured the heart of Carr's point here I have expressed it somewhat differently. Moreover, I want to say that the highest goods, after Plato,[23] should be called mixed goods; those which are inherently valuable *and* valuable as means to further valuable ends. Furthermore, we could extend the debate to consider not only the relationality between means and ends, but also between particular persons who have particular capacities, abilities, dispositions and potentialities, and those means and ends. The very same activity might be inherently valuable but, as a matter of fact, be valued intrinsically by one person, extrinsically by another, both by the same and or not at all by a third person.

Having set out the inadequacies of Reid's hedonic argument in terms of its inherent weaknesses, the essentialism his position embodies and, finally, the classification of value it rests upon, it is now incumbent upon me to offer the beginnings of an alternative picture of the nature and educational value of physical education.

Persons, practices and physical education

Parry (1988) captured the bigger picture with respect to the nature and values of physical education when he urged upon the profession a fundamental re-examination of the central concepts education, culture and personhood.[24] He observed that any educational ideology could be challenged at a variety of levels: first, at the level of actual practices as legitimate expressions of the educational theory, or as efficient means to its goals; second, at the level of educational theory as a legitimate expression of the ideology; and, finally, at the level of ideology. The radical kind of conceptualisation was never fully taken up. But neither analytical philosophy of education nor the physical education profession at large is sympathetic to this dense continental philosophy that employs a language all of its own and seems antithetical to the common-sense strand of English-speaking analytical philosophy.[25] Parry urged a less cognitivist conceptualisation of education and personhood.

I have elsewhere attempted to answer that call by suggesting a conception of personhood based strongly around Charles Taylor's account which emphasised the human capacity not merely for weak, instrumental, evaluation (means–ends reasoning) but also for strong, qualitative, evaluation (ends–ends reasoning) and which also contains at its core the centrality of the emotions in the life of persons. I think that the move of situating a less rationalistic view of persons necessarily opens up a proper consideration of the role of the emotions in our lives and especially in sports where they are channelled, frustrated, exposed, and potentially explored in self-critical ways. But this has rarely been addressed either theoretically or in the professional education of physical educators where spaces for non-applied, or immediately relevant, professional matters are rarely created. Elsewhere I have attempted to situate that argument in a broader philosophical account about the nature of education, analytical philosophy of education, and an alternative account of value and the broader nature of practices that can inform one's identity and constitute an important component of one's evaluative picture of a worthwhile life.[26] I can only set out the skeleton of that argument here.

I would urge a less than radical evaluation of Petersian thinking; one that loosens the shackles tying education to the development of theoretical rationality embodied by the distinct forms of knowledge. I would not argue for a wholesale rejection of the thesis since, so it seems to me, education is concerned precisely with initiation into significant cultural practices. Neither would I set great store by those radical or revolutionary philosophers of education who are antithetical to the nature of authority as encapsulated by education and its constituent practices. This very thin conceptualisation is preferable at two levels to the position made famous by Peters and retained by Carr. In the first instance, it is preferable on normative grounds in that it recognises a plurality of conceptions of education that emerge from some shared understanding of the need for societies to seek the grounds of their own continuance. How is this to be done other than by capturing the hearts and minds (and lungs!) of its young? On analytical grounds, so open a position does not prescribe in precise terms how this is to be done though one would want, as Peters did, to proscribe certain procedures on ethical grounds. To set out the traditional liberal distinctions as Carr does, and as Peters did before him, renders him open to the simple charge of ideology; no matter how internally coherent the thesis, he is always open to counter-ideological critique. It seems that Parry, Reid and I point in a different direction but none of us have travelled down it any distance here. We have all signposted a less restricted account of education as the initiation into a range of cultural practices that have the capacity to open up the possibilities of living a full and worthwhile life. Reid has given us no clues as to a broader *weltanshauung* that informs the shared position against cognitive imperialism: he is merely at pains to stress the primacy of the hedonic. Parry has suggested some liberalised-Olympic thesis while I am inclined towards a communitarian position central to which would be a stronger recognition for the dominant role that social practices like sport play in the formation of our identities and values. I have suggested elsewhere a developed account of how sport can be characterised, within a broad communitarian framework, as a social practice broadly under MacIntyre's description of that term. I have also suggested how that thesis cannot unproblematically be translated into the context of sport as writers such as Peter Arnold have done. Furthermore, it will be clear from the position developed there that I see such practices as one of the foundational bedrocks of character and identity formation which is one of the crucial tasks that fall predominantly, though not exclusively to formal education.[27]

At an analytical level, then, rather than arguing that X is education or not-education on the grounds of a pre-eminent criterion: cognitive depth and breadth (or the capacity to inform rather than merely use the mind, as Carr pithily puts it) recognition must be made for the fact that there are competing conceptions of education. I would not wish to consort with the radical revision of education as an 'essentially contested concept'. If an essence at so basic a level as I have asserted is contestable, I see no grounds for calling it a concept, let alone a concept of education. Instead, as a matter of conceptual necessity, it seems to me that despite the fact that these conceptions embody particular evaluative commitments regarding the nature of persons and society, they all share the formal notion that education is the development of persons towards the living of full and valuable lives. The next step of the argument is to develop an account of persons and the kinds of things that make their lives worthwhile over and above Peters' intellectual pursuits. Persons, on the kind of account I am disposed to, are beings who have the capacity to develop, evaluate, and live out life-plans based on a combination of projects, relationships and commitments. Among this combination of activities are a variety of practices which are valuable by virtue of their internal goods and their capacity to secure external goods in particular and unique ways. The activities of physical education are exemplified by a certain range of sporting practices, which are taken as paradigmatic which can be characterised as mixed goods because they have the capacity to be valued not only for their internal goods but also for the particular manner in which they secure external goods. Physical education can, therefore, contribute to the living of full valuable lives for persons and is thus of educational value. I think this is precisely the kind of rationale that can either be read *into* the work of the American physical educator, Daryl Siedentop (1986), with his enormously influential model of sport education or simply might be explored as a philosophical justification for at least some portions of that model.[28]

This kind of argument, it might be said, holds true only for those practices we recognise as sporting games or athletic activities (and I would add, *pace* Siedentop, dance too). While the argument is long on initiation into those practices that are partly definitive of a culture and its identity(ies) it is short on the kinds of individualised, health-related activities. Historically, there have been two strands in what is called physical education:

sports and health (or in older times hygiene, posture, and so forth). It seems clear to me that a different type of justificatory argument is required to support each. Maybe Carr is right here to classify the latter activities (along with life saving and other 'anomalies' that fall to the task of physical educators) as valuable but not educationally valuable because of their lacking in what can be referred to as cultural significance or cultural capital. Time and space do not allow me to comment in any way here upon these other strands except to note the following. Those who look for *conceptual* unity are simply wasting their time. There is no meaningful essence to the concept in that way. As Reid remarks, one must look rather to culture-specific, historical and political factors that have shaped the professions. Dance is a cultural practice that employs large motor-skilled activity like tennis or football. Some forms of gymnastics require interpretative movements and proceed with music like dance. Sculpting bodies, like training for rugby or netball, often requires the kinds of regimes and exercises that are common. But these similarities are nothing more than that. If all that one can do is to point out commonalities then there is little that is philosophically interesting here for anyone attempting a conceptual analysis by necessary and sufficient conditions of linguistic usage. Reid's peroration towards value pluralism should extend so far as to recognise the inherent openness of the concept of physical education: pluralism in activities; pluralism in values. No universal criterion of demarcation can be raised that will help physical educators to select activities is available, and so we should simply stop looking. Instead we should enquire as to the types and natures of rituals that sports instantiate in our modern world. And if, as Wollheim argues,[29] traditions pass on what they possess, then we should see to it, as guardians of these great cultural rituals, that the values physical education has and gives are kept in good health.[30]

Notes

1   This chapter is a revised version of a paper first published as 'Education, philosophy and physical education: analysis, epistemology and axiology' (McNamee, 1998b). In particular, I have omitted or diluted some of the more technical philosophical points that were made in the original article as well as connecting thoughts there with other material that I have published elsewhere in the ethics of sport, and more generally to other recent contributions to the field.

2   See, for example Whitehead (1990).

3   See, for example, Hogenova (2002).

4   Though the reader is invited to scan at least the veritable legion of writers that have written more and less charitably about it. See for examples of these, respectively, Cooper (1986) and Kleinig (1983).

5   Again, for just one example among many, see Kleinig (1983).

6   Most writers, oddly enough, in the philosophy of physical education, are in agreement with this view. This may well have something to do with the fact that sports typically have conservative forces – notably in the idea of rule-following, and the transmission of dominant norms, via physical activity to the socialisation of the players/athletes/dancers involved. I shall comment later, though only briefly, on this value-conserving function. For much more specific insights, one might look to sociologists of physical education (notably Evans and Penney, 2002) to highlight these latent political functions.

7   This is itself part of that wider trend which might be called 'certificationism' – if I may be excused for introducing a word that looks dangerously postmodern.

8   In a celebrated remark, Peters once observed that 'education cannot be forced upon unwilling minds'. Without recourse to dualism one should also remark that it cannot likewise be forced upon unwilling bodies (or persons with both physical and mental aspects, if you prefer to avoid dualistic, specifically Strawsonian language). See Strawson (1959).

9   Although my point here is somewhat abstractly stated, it seems to me that this is precisely the kind of philosophical orientation that guides the work of Daryl Siedentop in his model of Sport Education and which Kirk (2002) has recently elaborated.

10   On which see Whitehead (1990).

11   The term practice is used in a special way in recent philosophy. It is derived from the work of Alisdair MacIntyre (1985). I note that this way of talking of sports activities is gaining ground in mainstream physical education discourse (Almond, 1996; Kirk, 2002; Siedentop, 2002). Their account, like some philosophers of sport, rarely seeks to acknowledge the problems of considering sports as social practices as opposed to, say, architecture or farming. For an account of some of these subtleties see McNamee (1994, 1995).

12   I am not implying that the 'professionalisation' of that sport has necessarily wrought a morally poorer game. It strikes me that, in the particular case of rugby, we may well witness less violence and more legal but exceptionally harmful aggression. Is that progress? Moreover, I am not at all clear that the phrase 'professionalisation' best characterises the kinds of development we have witnessed in elite, finance-driven, sports.

13   A fuller discussion of this debate can be found in Lehman (1982) and Morgan (1987).

14   See Carlisle (1969).

15   An excellent collection housing a variety of egalitarian criticisms of traditional curricula and pedagogy is Evans and Davies (1993). See especially the editor's introduction, of the same title, pp. 11–27.

16   I have made some critical philosophical remarks about the tenuous relationship involved here while the movement was at its height in McNamee (1988) though I no longer hold to the justificatory argument that I set out there.

17   See McNamee (1994).

18   Brackenridge and Alderson (1982) unpublished. I have benefited from several long discussions with Rod Thorpe on this point in the context of sports.

19   For a discussion of this concept see Slote (1989).

20   Nozick (1974) see especially pp. 42–5.

21   The terms 'person' and 'personhood' are rather special ones in moral philosophy. See McNamee (1992) and Meakin (1982, 1990) for competing analyses and applications of them in physical education contexts.

22   See Bain (1976) and Thompson (1983).

23   See Plato (1974).

24   A footnote is required here as a matter of intellectual honesty. When Parry published the article that is reprinted with additions in this journal I was a doctoral student of his. The subsequent thesis 'The Educational Justification of Physical Education' owes a very significant debt to his intellectual guidance. A portion of one of the chapters sought to satisfy one of his perorations: McNamee (1992).

25   A more recent attempt to offer a phenomenological account of the sports experience (particularly what is often referred to as 'peak experience') from a Heideggerian perspective can be found in Standish (1998).

26   See the unpublished doctoral dissertation cited above, University of Leeds, 1992.

27   See McNamee (1995). With respect to conceptualising social relations more generally
      see, McNamee (1998a).
28   See his classic Siedentop (1986) and most recently Kirk (2002) and Siedentop (2002). In
      saying this I am in no way committing myself to what can sometimes be read into
      Siedentop's earlier work regarding the uncritical socialisation into dominant forms of
      sometimes ethically corrupt (viz. homophobia, racism, sexism, and so forth) values. See
      also McNamee (1995).
29   See Wollheim (1993).
30   I am extremely grateful to Graham McFee for his incisive and generous observations and
      criticisms on an earlier version of this essay.

References

Almond, L. (1996) *The Place of Physical Education in Schools*. 2nd edn. London: Kogan Page.

Bain, L. (1976) 'Play and intrinsic values in physical education', *Quest*, 26: 75–80.

Barrow, R. (1981) *The Philosophy of Schooling*. London: Harvester.

Best, D. (1978) *Philosophy and Human Movement*. London: George Allen and Unwin.

Brackenridge, C. and Alderson, J. (1982) 'A classification of sports', British Association of
      Sports Science Conference.

Carlisle, R. (1969) 'The concept of physical education', *Proceedings of the Philosophy of Education
      Society of Great Britain*, 3: 1–11.

Carr, D. (1979) 'Aims of physical education', *Physical Education Review*, 2 (2): 91–100.

Carr, D. (1997) 'Physical education and value diversity: a response to Andrew Reid', *European
      Physical Education Review*, 3 (2): 195–205.

Cooper, D. (ed.) (1986) *Education, Values and Mind*. London: Routledge and Kegan Paul.

Dearden, R.F. (1968) *The Philosophy of Primary Education*. London: Routledge and Kegan Paul.

Evans, J. and Davies, B. (1993) 'Equality, equity and physical education', in J. Evans (ed.),
      Equality, Education and Physical Education. London: Falmer Press. pp. 11–27.

Evans, J. and Penney, D. (2002) 'Introduction', in D. Penney (ed.) *Physical Education.
      Contemporary Issues and Future Directions*. London: Routledge. pp. 3–13.

Kirk, D. (2002) 'Junior sport as a moral practice, *Journal of Teaching in Physical Education*, 21:
      402–8.

Hirst, P.H. and Peters, R.S. (1970) *The Logic of Education*. London: Routledge and Kegan
      Paul.

Hogenova, M. (2002) 'Legality and legitimacy in sport', *European Journal of Sport Science*, 2 (1):
      1–6.   *http://www.humankinetics.com/EJSS/viewarticle.cfm?aid=120*   *http://www.human
      kinetics.com/EJSS/viewarticle.cfm?aid = 120*

Kleinig, J. (1983) *Philosophical Issues in Education*. Sydney: Croom Helm.

Lehman, C. (1982) 'Can cheaters play the game?', *Journal of Philosophy of Sport*, 8: 41–6.

McIntyre, A. (1985) *After Virtue. A Study in Moral Theory*. London: Duckworth.

McNamee, M.J. (1988) 'Health-related fitness and physical education', *British Journal of
      Physical Education*, 19 (2): 83–4.

McNamee, M.J. (1992) 'Physical education and the development of personhood', *Physical
      Education Review*, 15 (1): 13–28.

McNamee, M.J. (1994) 'Valuing leisure practices: towards a theoretical framework', *Leisure
      Studies*, 13 (1): 288–309.

McNamee, M.J. (1995) 'Sporting practices, institutions, and virtues: a critique and a restate-
      ment', *Journal of Philosophy of Sport*, XXII: 61–82.

McNamee, M.J. (1998a) 'Contractualism and methodological individualism and communitarianism: situating understandings of moral trust', *Sport, Education and Society*, 3 (3): 161–79.

McNamee, M.J. (1998b) 'Education, philosophy and physical education: analysis, epistemology and axiology', *European Physical Education Review*, 4 (1): 75–91.

Meakin, D.C. (1982) 'Moral values and physical education', *Physical Education Review*, 5 (1): 62–82.

Meakin, D.C. (1990) 'How physical education can contribute to personal and social education', *Physical Education Review*, 13 (2): 108–19.

Morgan, W.P. (1987) 'Formalism and the logical incompatibility thesis', *Journal of Philosophy of Sport*, 14: 1–20.

Nozick, R. (1974) *Anarchy, State and Utopia*. Oxford: Blackwell.

Parry, S.J. (1988) 'Physical education, justification and the national curriculum', 11 (2): 106–18.

Parry, S.J. (1998) 'Physical education as Olympic education', *European Physical Education Review*, 4 (2): 153–67.

Peters, R.S. (1966) *Ethics and Education*. London: Allen and Unwin.

Plato (1974) *The Republic*, 2nd edn. (trans.) D. Lee. London; Penguin, pp. 102–4.

Rawls, J. (1972) *A Theory of Justice*. Oxford: Oxford University Press.

Reid, A. (1996a) 'The concept of physical education in current curriculum and assessment policy in Scotland', *European Physical Education Review*, 2 (1): 7–18.

Reid, A. (1996b) 'Knowledge, practice and theory in physical education', *European Physical Education Review*, 2 (2): 94–104.

Reid, A. (1997) 'Value pluralism and physical education', *European Physical Education Review*, 3 (1): 6–20.

Siedentop, D. (1986) *Sport Education*. Champaign, IL: Human Kinetics.

Siedentop, D. (2002) 'Content knowledge for Physical Education', *Journal of Teaching in Physical Education*, 21 (4): 409–18.

Slote, M. (1989) *Goods and Virtues*. Oxford: Clarendon Press.

Standish, P. (1998) 'In the zone: Heidegger and sport', in M.J. McNamee and S.J. Parry (eds) *Ethics and Sport*. London: Routledge. pp. 256–69.

Strawson, P.F. (1959) *Individuals*. London: Methuen.

Thompson, K. (1983) 'The justification of physical education', *Momentum*, 2 (2): 19–23.

White, J.P. (1990) *Education and the Good Life*. London: Kogan Page.

Whitehead, M. (1990) 'Meaningful existence, embodiment and physical education', *Journal of Philosophy of Education*, 24(1): 3–13.

Wollheim, R. (1993) *The Mind and its Depths*. London: Harvard University Press.

Richard Bailey

PHYSICAL EDUCATION AND SPORT IN SCHOOLS
A review of benefits and outcomes

ADVOCATES OF physical education and sport (PES) have listed numerous benefits associated with participation in these activities. For example, Talbot claims that physical education helps children to develop respect for the body—their own and others', contributes toward the integrated development of mind and body, develops an understanding of the role of aerobic and anaerobic physical activity in health, positively enhances self-confidence and self-esteem, and enhances social and cognitive development and academic achievement.[1] Writing specifically about sport, a Council of Europe report suggests that it provides opportunities to meet and communicate with other people, to take different social roles, to learn particular social skills (such as tolerance and respect for others), and to adjust to team/collective objectives (such as cooperation and cohesion), and that it provides experience of emotions that are not available in the rest of life. This report goes on to stress the important contribution of sport to processes of personality development and psychological well-being, stating that there is, "strong evidence . . . on the positive effects of physical activities on self-concept, self-esteem, anxiety, depression, tension and stress, self-confidence, energy, mood, efficiency and well-being."[2]

Such claims have often been criticized for lacking empirical foundations and for confusing policy rhetoric with scientific evidence.[3] This paper seeks to explore some of the scientific evidence that has been gathered on the contributions and benefits of PES for both children and for educational systems. In doing so, it will be using a framework and some of the data derived from a recent international research project,[4] which drew evidence from over 50 countries, including a meta-analysis of statements of aims and standards, and national curricula.[5] Findings suggest that the outcomes of PES can be understood in terms of children's development in 5 domains:

- Physical
- Lifestyle
- Affective
- Social
- Cognitive

As its title suggests, this article is concerned with "physical education and sport." Since the relationship between the concepts "physical education" and "sport" continues to be a cause of debate,[6] it is worthwhile clarifying the use of the terms in this review. In many, predominantly Anglophone, countries, the term "physical education" is used to refer to that area of the school curriculum concerned with developing students' physical competence and confidence, and their ability to use these to perform in a range of activities.[7] "Sport" is a collective noun and usually refers to a range of activities, processes, social relationships, and presumed physical, psychological, and sociological outcomes.[8] In this presentation, there appears to be a relatively clear conceptual distinction between these 2 terms. However, cross-cultural studies have revealed significant differences in the use of terminology in this area, and many educational systems use the terms synonymously, or simply use "sport" as a generic descriptor.[9] For this reason, and in line with international agencies like the United Nations Educational, Scientific and Cultural Organization (UNESCO),[10] the inclusive term "physical education and sport" will be used to refer to those structured, supervised physical activities that take place at school and during the school day.

Physical development

PES in school is the main societal institution for the development of physical skills and the provision of physical activity in children and young people.[11] For many children, school is the main environment for being physically active, through either PES programs or after-school activities.[12] There is evidence that for a growing number of children, school provides the main opportunity for regular, structured physical activity as a combination of economic pressures[13] and parental concerns for safety[14] means that fewer children are able to play games in nonschool settings. Moreover, school-based PES offers a regulated opportunity for usually qualified, accountable teachers to introduce physical activities and lifestyle skills and knowledge in a structured way to all children, within a safe and supportive environment.[15]

The physical health benefits of regular physical activity are well established.[16] Regular participation in such activities is associated with a longer and better quality of life, reduced risk of a variety of diseases, and many psychological and emotional benefits.[17] There is also a large body of literature showing that inactivity is one of the most significant causes of death, disability, and reduced quality of life across the developed world.[18] Evidence is starting to appear suggesting a favorable relationship between physical activity and a host of factors affecting children's physical health, including diabetes, blood pressure,[19] bone health,[20] and obesity.[21]

Basic movement skills, like those developed in PES, form the foundation of almost all later sporting and physical activities.[22] There is evidence that those who have developed a strong foundation in fundamental movement skills are more likely to be active, both during childhood and later in life.[23] There is also a frequently cited, but underresearched, hypothesis that the development of a broad range of these basic movement skills through PES programs is a necessary condition for excellence in sport.[24] Conversely, children who have *not* been able to acquire an adequate base of movement competences are more likely to be excluded from participation in organized sports and play experiences with their friends because of a lack of basic physical skills.[25] So, as one of the most highly valued aspects of many children's and young people's lives, such omission from the activities that make up PES is likely to have far-reaching and harmful consequences to the development and education of many children.[26]

Lifestyle development

Physical inactivity has been identified as a major risk factor for coronary heart disease,[27] as well as being associated with premature mortality[28] and obesity.[29] It is not surprising, then, that PES programs — some of the few opportunities to promote physical activities amongst all children[30] — have been proposed as a cost-effective way to influence the next generation of adults to lead physically active lives.[31]

The mechanisms by which active young people become active adults are unclear. However, research suggests that a number of factors contribute to the establishment of physical activity as part of a healthy lifestyle. There is some evidence that health-related behaviors learned in childhood are often maintained into adulthood.[32] The extent to which physical activity patterns are maintained over time is less clear.[33] The Amsterdam Growth Study did not find evidence of tracking of physical activity from 13 and 27 years.[34] Other studies, however, *have* found that youth activity carries on into later life.[12] A review of retrospective and longitudinal studies reported that physical activity and sports participation in childhood and youth represents a significant predictor of later activity. Interestingly, studies also show how strongly *inactivity* in youth tracks to adulthood,[35] so exclusion from PES can be associated with a legacy of inactivity and associated ill-health in the years to come.

There have been frequent claims that school PES create important contexts in which physical activity levels are influenced.[36] Studies have found that school-based programs can contribute to physical activity levels, both during youth and later in life.[37] The potency of PES' influence on physical activity seems to be greatest when programs combine classroom study with activity,[38] when they allow students' experiences of self-determination and feelings of competence in their own abilities,[39] and when they emphasized enjoyment and positive experiences.[40]

Affective development

There is now fairly consistent evidence that regular activity can have a positive effect upon the psychological well-being of children and young people, although the underlying mechanisms for explaining these effects are still unclear.[41] The evidence is particularly strong with regards to children's self-esteem.[42,43] Other associations with regular activity that have been reported include reduced stress, anxiety, and depression.[44] All of these lend support to the claim that well-planned and presented PES can contribute to the improvement of psychological health in young people.

One especially relevant set of findings, in this regard, relates to the development of perceived physical competence. It has been suggested that self-esteem is influenced by an individual's perceptions of competence or adequacy to achieve,[45] and that it is also worth considering the growing interest in the relationship between PES and students' general attitudes toward school.[46,47] The evidence supporting such claims is limited and is mostly based on small-scale studies or anecdotal evidence.[48] However, some studies report generally positive outcomes in terms of pupil attendance following the introduction of PES schemes, and there is evidence from studies of pupils at risk of exclusion from school that an increase in the availability of PES programs would make the school experience more attractive.[49]

On the theme of the relationship between PES and attitudes to school, it ought to be acknowledged that not all pupils enjoy such activities, at least when presented in certain ways. For example, many girls acquire a progressive disillusionment with certain aspects of PES and totally disengage from participation as they move through secondary schooling.[50] So it would be misleading to suggest that PES will *necessarily* contribute toward positive attitudes to school in all pupils as inappropriate provision might actually increase disaffection and truancy.[51] More positively, though, there is a great deal of research showing that when PES activities are presented in attractive and relevant ways to girls, they can enjoy participation as much as boys.[52]

Social development

The idea that PES positively affect young people's social development and prosocial behavior goes back many years.[53] PES settings are considered an appealing context because both naturally occurring and contrived social interactions frequently emerge[54] and because the public nature of participation usually makes both socially appropriate and inappropriate behaviors evident.[55]

The research literature on the relationship between PES and social development is equivocal.[56] It does not seem to be the case that prosocial behavior necessarily improves as a result of engagement,[57] and there is evidence that in some circumstances behavior actually worsens.[58] However, numerous studies have demonstrated that appropriately structured and presented activities *can* make a contribution to the development of prosocial behavior,[2] and can even combat antisocial and criminal behaviors in youth.[59]

The most encouraging findings come from school-based studies, especially those focusing on PES curriculum programs.[60] While a wide range of physical activities seem able to offer valuable environments for social development, school-based programs have a number of advantages, such as access to nearly all children,[61] fewer external pressures to emphasize outcome and competition, and the ability to integrate social education with the similar teaching across the school curriculum.[62] Intervention studies have produced generally positive results, including improvements in moral reasoning,[63] fair play and sportspersonship,[64] and personal responsibility.[65] It also seems that the most promising contexts for developing social skills and values are those mediated by suitably trained teachers and coaches who focus on situations that arise naturally through activities, by asking questions of students and by modeling appropriate responses through their own behavior.[66]

Of related concern is the issue of social inclusion and exclusion. Combating social exclusion, or the factors resulting in people being excluded from the normal exchanges, practices and rights of modern society,[67] has become a focus of attention for governments and nongovernment organizations in recent years.[68] Some writers have argued that PES not only reflects but can also contribute to some groups' social exclusion.[69] However, positive experiences do seem to have the potential to, at least, contribute to the process of inclusion by bringing individuals from a variety of social and economic background together in a shared interest, offering a sense of belonging to a team or a club, providing opportunities for the development of valued capabilities and competencies, and developing social networks, community cohesion, and civic pride.[3]

Cognitive development

There is a long tradition claiming that a "healthy body leads to a healthy mind," and that physical activity can support intellectual development in children.[70] However, there is also an increasing concern by some parents that, while PES has its place, it should not interfere with the real business of schooling, which many believe to be academic achievement and examination results.[71]

Researchers have suggested that PES can enhance academic performance by increasing the flow of blood to the brain, enhancing mood, increasing mental alertness, and improving self-esteem.[72] The evidence base of such claims is varied and more research is still required. However, existing studies do suggest a positive relationship between intellectual functioning and regular physical activity, both for adults and children.

The classic study of the relationship between PES and general school performance was carried out in France in the early 1950s.[73] Researchers reduced "academic" curriculum time by 26%, replacing it with PES; yet, academic results did not worsen, and there were fewer discipline problems, greater attentiveness, and less absenteeism. More recent studies have found improvements for many children in academic performance when time for PES is increased in their school day.[74] A review of 3 large-scale studies found that academic performance is maintained or even enhanced by an increase in a student's levels of PES, despite a reduction in the time for the study of academic material.[75]

Overall, the available research evidence suggests that increased levels of physical activity in school—such as through increasing the amount of time dedicated to PES —does not interfere with pupils' achievement in other subjects (although the time available for these subjects in consequently reduced) and in many instances is associated with improved academic performance.

Concluding comments

Clearly, PES have the potential to make significant contributions to the education and development of children and young people in many ways, although further research and evaluation will help us better understand the nature of these contributions. Nevertheless, in each of the domains discussed—physical, lifestyle, affective, social, and cognitive— there is evidence that PES can have a positive and profound effect. In some respects, such an effect is unique, owing to the distinctive contexts in which PES take place. Consequently, there is a duty for those who teach and acknowledge the value of PES to act as advocates for its place as a necessary feature of the general education of all children. They need to argue not just for the inclusion of PES within the curriculum, and for the provision of sufficient time, but also to stress the importance of the *quality* of the program and share information on the benefits of PES among administrators, parents, and policy makers.

A note of caution should be sounded, too. The scientific evidence does *not* support the claim that these effects will occur automatically. There is no reason to believe that simply supporting participation in PES will necessarily bring about positive changes to children or to their communities. The actions and interactions of teachers and coaches largely determine whether or not children and young people experience these positive aspects of PES and whether or not they realize its great potential. Contexts that emphasize positive PES experiences, characterized by enjoyment, diversity, and the engagement of all, and that are managed by committed and trained teachers and coaches, and supportive and informed parents, are fundamental.

References

1. Talbot M. The case for physical education. In: Doll-Tepper G, Scoretz D, eds. *World Summit on Physical Education*. Berlin, Germany: ICSSPE; 2001:39–50.
2. Svoboda B. *Sport and Physical Activity as a Socialisation Environment: Scientific Review Part 1*. Strasbourg, France: Council of Europe; 1994.
3. Bailey R. Evaluating the relationship between physical education, sport and social inclusion. *Educ Rev*. 2004;56(3):71–90.
4. Bailey R, Dismore H. Sport in Education (SpinEd)—the role of physical education and sport in education. Project Report to the 4th International Conference of Ministers and Senior Officials Responsible for Physical Education and Sport (MINSEPS IV), December 2004; Athens, Greece.
5. NASPE. *Physical Activity for Children: A Statement of Guidelines for Children Ages 5–12*. 2nd ed. Reston, Va: NASPE; 2004.
6. Bergmann Drewe S. *Why Sport? An Introduction to the Philosophy of Sport*. Toronto, Ontario: Thompson; 2003.
7. Department for Education and Employment. *Physical Education: The National Curriculum for England and Wales*. London, UK: Department for Education and Employment; 2000.
8. Council of Europe. *Recommendation No. R. (92) 13 REV of the Committee of Ministers of Members States on the Revised European Sports Charter*. Strasbourg, France: Council of Europe; 2001.
9. Bailey R, Dismore H. *Sport in Education (SpinEd)—The Role of Physical Education and Sport in Education. Final Report*. Berlin, Germany: International Council for Physical Education and Sport Science; 2004.
10. UNESCO. Declaration of Athens: Fourth International Conference of Ministers and Senior Officials Responsible for Physical Education and Sport, MINEPS IV, December 6–8, 2004; Athens, Greece. Paris, France: UNESCO; 2004.
11. Sallis J, McKenzie T, Alcaraz J, Kolody B, Faucette N, Hovell M. The effects of a 2-year physical education (SPARK) program on physical activity and fitness of elementary school children. *Am J Public Health*. 1997;87:1328–1334.
12. Telama R, Yang X, Laakso L, Viikari J. Physical activity in childhood and adolescence as predictor of physical activity in adulthood. *Am J Prev Med*. 1997;13:317–323.
13. Kirk D, Carlson T, O'Connor T, Burke P, Davis K, Glover S. The economic impact on families of children's participation in junior sport. *Aust J Sci Med Sport*. 1997;29:27–33.

14. Ollendick T, King N, Frary R. Fears in children and adolescents: reliability and generalizability across gender, age and nationality. *Behav Res Ther*. 1989;27:19–26.

15. National Association for Sport and Physical Education. Is it physical education or physical activity? NASPE position statement. *Strategies*. 2005;19(2):33–34.

16. World Health Organisation/Fédération Internationale de Médecine du Sport—Committee on Physical Activity for Health. Exercise for health. *Bull World Health Organ*. 1995;73:135–136.

17. Sallis J, Owen N. *Physical Activity and Behavioral Medicine*. Thousand Oaks, Calif: Sage; 1999.

18. US Department of Health and Human Services. *Physical Activity and Health: A Report of the Surgeon General*. Atlanta, Ga: Centers for Disease Control; 1996.

19. Malina R, Bouchard C. *Growth, Maturation and Physical Activity*. Champaign, Ill: Human Kinetics; 1991.

20. Bailey D, Martin A. Physical activity and skeletal health in adolescents. *Pediatr Exerc Sci*. 1994;6:348–360.

21. Gutin B, Barbeau P, Yin Z. Exercise interventions for prevention of obesity and related disorders in youth. *Quest*. 2004;56:120–141.

22. Gallahue DL, Ozmun JC. *Understanding Motor Development: Infants, Children, Adolescents, Adult*. 5th ed. Boston, Mass: McGraw-Hill; 1998.

23. Okely A, Booth M, Patterson JW. Relationship of physical activity to fundamental movement skills among adolescents. *Med Sci Sports Exerc*. 2001;33:1899–1904.

24. Abbott A, Collins D, Martindale R, Sowerby K. *Talent Identification and Development: An Academic Review*. Edinburgh, UK: Sport Scotland; 2002.

25. Ignico A. The influence of gender-role perception on activity preferences of children. *Play Culture*. 1990;3:302–310.

26. President's Council on Physical Fitness and Sport. *Physical Activity and Sport in the Lives of Girls: Physical and Mental Health Dimensions from an Interdisciplinary Approach*. Washington, DC: President's Council on Physical Fitness and Sport; 1997.

27. Freedman D, Kettel Khan L, Dietz W, Srinivasan S, Berenson G. Relationship of childhood obesity to coronary heart disease risk factors in adulthood: the Bogalusa Heart Study. *Pediatrics*. 2001;108:712–718.

28. Paffenberger R, Hyde R, Wing AL, Hsieh C. Physical activity, all-cause mortality and longevity of college alumni. *N Engl J Med*. 1986;314:605–613.

29. Sallis J, Patrick K. Physical activity guidelines for adolescents: a consensus statement. *Pediatr Exerc Sci*. 1994;6:307–330.

30. Fox K. Physical activity promotion and the active school. In: Armstrong N, ed. *New Directions in Physical Education*. London, UK: Cassell; 1996:94–109.

31. Shephard R, Trudeau F. The legacy of physical education: influences on adult lifestyle. *Pediatr Exerc Sci*. 2000;12:34–50.

32. Kelder S, Perry C, Klepp K, Lytle L. Longitudinal tracking of adolescent smoking, physical activity and food choices behavior. *Am J Public Health*. 1994;84:1121–1126.

33. Pangrazi R, Corbin C. Health foundations: toward a focus on physical activity promotion. *Int J Phys Educ*. 2000;37:40–49.

34. Van Mechelen W, Kemper H. Habitual physical activity in longitudinal perspective. In: Kemper H, ed. *The Amsterdam Growth Study: A Longitudinal Analysis of Health, Fitness and Lifestyle*. Champaign, Ill: Human Kinetics; 1995:135–158.

35. Raitakari O, Porkka K, Taimela R, Telama R, Räsänen L, Viikari J. Effects of persistent physical activity and inactivity on coronary risk factors in children and young adults. *Am J Epidemiol*. 1994;140:195–205.

36.   Sallis J, McKenzie T. Physical education's role in public health. *Res Q Exerc Sport*. 1991;62:124–137.

37.   Trudeau F, Laurencelle L, Tremblay J, Rajic M, Shephard RJ. Daily primary school physical education: effects on physical activity during adult life. *Med Sci Sports Exerc*. 1999;31:111–117.

38.   Dale D, Corbin C, Cuddihy T. Can conceptual physical education promote physically active lifestyles? *Pediatr Exerc Sci*. 1998;10:97–109.

39.   Ferrer-Caja E, Weiss M. Predictors of intrinsic motivation among adolescent students in physical education. *Res Q Exerc Sport*. 2002;71:267–279.

40.   McKenzie T, Sallis J, Kolody B, Faucett F. Long-term effects of a physical education curriculum and staff development work: SPARK. *Res Q Exerc Sport*. 1997;53:326–334.

41.   Dishman R. Physical activity and public health: mental health. *Quest*. 1995;47:362–385.

42.   Fox K. The self-esteem complex and youth fitness. *Quest*. 1988;40:230–246.

43.   Fox K. The effects of exercise on self-perceptions and self-esteem. In: Biddle S, Fox K, Boutcher S, eds. *Physical Activity and Psychological Well-being*. London, UK: Routledge; 2000:88–117.

44.   Hassmen P, Koivula N, Uutela A. Physical exercise and psychological well-being: a population study in Finland. *Prev Med*. 2000;30:17–25.

45.   Harter S. The determinants and mediational role of global self-worth in children. In: Eisenberg N, ed. *Contemporary Topic in Developmental Psychology*. New York, NY: Wiley; 1987:219–242.

46.   Sabo D, Melnick M, Vanfossen B. *The Women's Sports Foundation Report: Minorities in Sports*. East Meadow, NY: Women's Sports Foundation; 1989.

47.   Marsh H, Kleitman S. School athletic participation: mostly gain with little pain. *J Sport Exerc Psychol*. 2003;25:205–228.

48.   Berger B. Psychological benefits of an active lifestyle: what we know and what we need to know. *Quest*. 1996;48:330–353.

49.   Fejgin N. Participation in high school competitive sports: a subversion of school mission or contribution to academic goals? *Sociol Sport J*. 1994;11:211–230.

50.   Fuchs R, Powell K, Semmer N, Dwyer J, Lippert P, Hoffmoester H. Patterns of physical activity among German adolescents: the Berlin Bremen study. *Prev Med*. 1988;17:746–763.

51.   Kirk D, Fitzgerald H, Wang J, Biddle S. *Towards Girl-Friendly Physical Education: The Nike/YST Girls in Sport Partnership Project—Final Report*. Loughborough, UK: Institute for Youth Sport; 2000.

52.   Sabo D, Miller K, Melnick M, Heywood L. *Her Life Depends on It: Sport, Physical Activity and the Health and Well-Being of American Girls*. East Meadow, NY: Women's Sports Foundation; 2004.

53.   Weiss M, Bredemeier B. Moral development in sport. In: Pandolf K, Hollowszy J, eds. *Exercise and Sport Sciences Reviews—Volume 18*. Baltimore, Md: Williams and Wilkins; 1990:331–374.

54.   Bailey RP. The value and values of sport. In: Bailey R, ed. *Teaching Values and Citizenship Across the Curriculum*. London, UK: Kogan Page; 2000:105–115.

55.   Miller S, Bredemeier B, Shields D. Sociomoral education through physical education with at-risk children. *Quest*. 1997;49:114–129.

56.   Kleiber D, Roberts C. The effects of sport experience in the development of social character: an exploratory investigation. *J Sport Psychol*. 1981;3:114–122.

57.   Reddiford G. Morality and the games player. *Phys Educ Rev*. 1981;4:8–16.

58. Beller J, Stoll S. Moral reasoning of high school student athletes and general students: an empirical study versus personal testimony. *Pediatr Exerc Sci*. 1995;7:352–363.

59. Morris L, Sallybanks J, Willis K, Makkai T. *Sport, Physical Activity and Antisocial Behaviour in Youth. Trends and Issues in Crime and Criminal Justice—No. 249*. Canberra, Australia: Australian Institute of Criminology; 2003.

60. Wandzilak T, Carroll T, Ansorge C. Values development through physical activity: promoting sportsmanlike behaviors, perceptions, and moral reasoning. *J Teach Phys Educ*. 1988;8:13–22.

61. Caine D, Krebs E. The moral development objective in physical education: a renewed quest? *Contemp Educ*. 1986;57:197–201.

62. Shields D, Bredemeier B. *Character Development and Physical Activity*. Champaign, Ill: Human Kinetics; 1995.

63. Romance T, Weiss M, Bockoven J. A program to promote moral development through elementary school physical education. *J Teach Phys Educ*. 1986;5:126–136.

64. Gibbons S, Ebbeck V, Weiss M. Fair play for kids: effects on the moral development of children in physical education. *Res Q Exerc Sport*. 1995;66:247–255.

65. Hellison D. Teaching responsibility in school physical education. In: Feingold R, Rees C, Barrette G, Fiorentino L, Virgilio S, Kowalski E, eds. *Education for Life: Proceedings of the 1998 AIESEP Conference*. New York, NY: Adelphi University; 1998.

66. Ewing M, Gano-Overway L, Branta C, Seefeldt V. The role of sports in youth development. In: Gatz M, Messner M, Ball-Rokeach SJ, eds. *Paradoxes of Youth and Sport*. New York, NY: State University of New York; 2002:31–47.

67. *Commission of the European Communities Background Report: Social Exclusion—Poverty and Other Social Problems in the European Community*. Luxembourg, Luxembourg: Office for Official Publications of the European Communities; 1993.

68. Micklewright J. *Social Exclusion and Children: A European View for a US Debate*. Florence, Italy: UNICEF Innocenti Research Centre; 2002. Innocenti Working Papers No. 9.

69. Collins M, Kay T. *Sport and Social Exclusion*. London, UK: Routledge; 2003.

70. Snyder E, Spreitzer E. Sport education and schools. In: Lueschen G, Sage G, eds. *Handbook of Social Science of Sport*. Champaign, Ill: Stipes; 1977:119–146.

71. Lau P, Yu C, Lee A, So R, Sung R. The relationship among physical fitness, physical education, conduct and academic performance of Chinese primary school children. *Int J Phys Educ*. 2004;12:17–26.

72. Hills A. Scholastic and intellectual development and sport. In: Chan K-M, Micheli L, eds. *Sports and Children*. Champaign, Ill: Human Kinetics; 1998:76–90.

73. Hervet R. Vanves, son Experience, ses Perspectives. *Rev Institut Sports*. 1952;24:4–6.

74. Sallis J, McKenzie J, Kolody B, Lewis M, Marshall S, Rosengard P. Effects of health-related physical education on academic achievement: project SPARK. *Res Q Exerc Sport*. 1999;70:127–134.

75. Shephard R. Curricular physical activity and academic performance. *Pediatr Exerc Sci*. 1997;9:113–126.

Linda L. Bain

THE HIDDEN CURRICULUM RE-EXAMINED

THE TERM "hidden curriculum" has been used extensively in educational literature since the early 1970s to refer to "what is taught to students by the institutional regularities, by the routines and rituals of teacher/student lives" (Weis, 1982, p. 3). Some time ago I discussed the hidden curriculum in physical education in *Quest* 24 (Bain, 1975). Now, a decade later, it seems appropriate to re-examine the topic in light of the research completed since that time.

Interest in the hidden curriculum provided much of the early impetus for examining the lived culture in schools and for use of qualitative research methodologies in educational research, A review of the theoretical bases for this research may shed light not only on the hidden curriculum but also on theoretical issues related to qualitative research. Although the hidden curriculum in physical education has received only limited attention, the research completed has extended our knowledge of the implicit values communicated by physical education programs.

Approaches to the study of the hidden curriculum

Four approaches to the study of the hidden curriculum can be identified in general education literature. This review will rely primarily upon American authors, but it is important to note that they were influenced by European social theory in general and British sociology of education in particular. Although many researchers can be identified within each of the four approaches. Table 1 identifies one representative work that exemplifies each of the approaches being described.

Phillip Jackson (1966, 1968) conducted some of the earliest research on the topic and popularized the term "hidden curriculum." Jackson conducted intensive observations of

Table 1 Approaches to the study of the hidden curriculum

Theoretical perspective	Mode of analysis	Representative work
I. Atheoretical	Observation and description	Jackson, *Life in Classrooms,* 1968
II. Functionalist theory	Theoretical analysis	Dreeben, *On What is Learned in Schools,* 1968
III. Correspondence theory	Theoretical analysis	Bowles & Gintis, *Schooling in Capitalist America,* 1976
IV. Critical theory of reproduction and transformation	Ethnographic and phenomenological studies and theoretical analysis	Apple & Weis, *Ideology and Practice in Schooling,* 1983

elementary school classrooms and noted that the day-to-day conduct of schooling seemed to be a powerful mechanism for transmitting values and beliefs to children. He describes those classrooms as characterized by crowds (the homogenous grouping of students), power (the authority of the teacher and the powerlessness of students), and praise (a teacher-controlled system of evaluation). He suggests that students learn patience, acceptance of impersonal prescriptive authority, and distinctions between work and play. Students also learn to conform to institutional expectations but to maneuver in this setting by seeking privilege through "apple polishing" and by hiding behaviors that might displease those in authority, Jackson's work could best be described as atheoretical in that he described the events in classrooms without attempting to relate those descriptions to a theory about schooling and society. While such work clearly has limitations, it served an important role in raising the issue of the impact of the hidden curriculum. Debate ensued about whether these routines and rituals of schooling were functional or dysfunctional, harmful or harmless.

Some early examinations of the effects of the hidden curriculum were based upon a functionalist perspective which examined how the school prepares students for effective participation in adult society. Robert Dreeben's (1968) analysis of what is learned in schools suggests that the hidden curriculum is an effective mechanism for teaching students essential norms. Specifically he suggests that students learn the norms of independence, achievement, universalism, and specificity. That is, students learn to work independently and to accept responsibility for competing against a standard of excellence. Children also learn to accept that in public life, in contrast to family life, one is treated by others as a member of a category (universalism) and that the scope of one person's interest in another is confined to a narrow range specific to the purpose of the interaction (specificity). This permits students to distinguish between persons and their social positions, a capacity Dreeben describes as crucially important in occupational and political life. He suggests that schooling, occupation, and politics are reasonably well integrated and that schools contribute to the creation of capacities required by the political economic system.

Not everyone who examines the hidden curriculum sees it as beneficial to students. Critics claim that the schools contribute to the maintenance of political and economic systems of domination, exploitation, and inequality and that the hidden curriculum is a central aspect of this process. Although several writers have proposed such a correspondence between school and society, the most complete analysis was proposed by Bowles and

Gintis (1976) in *Schooling in Capitalist America*. They posit that through the day-to-day regularities of schools, students learn social class definitions, the discipline of the work-place, the legitimacy of hierarchical arrangements and loss of control over their own work. The correspondence theory suggests that "the hierarchically structured patterns of values, norms, and skills that characterize the work force and the dynamics of class interaction under capitalism are mirrored in the social dynamics of the daily classroom" (Giroux, 1981a, p. 6).

It should be noted that both the functionalist and the correspondence analyses of the relationship between schooling and society assume that certain meanings and values are taught by schools without examining directly the meanings held by teachers and students. Both also view the school as functioning to maintain society but they differ in their judgment as to whether such a society is fundamentally just or unjust.

The most recent work on the hidden curriculum builds upon the neo-Marxist analyses of the correspondence theorists, but rejects both their determinism and their treatment of the school as a "black box" (Apple, 1979, 1982; Giroux, 1981a, 1981b). Apple (1982, p. 14) argues that "schools are not 'merely' institutions of reproduction, institutions where the overt and covert knowledge that is taught inexorably molds students into passive beings who are able and eager to fit into an unequal society." He suggests that "student reinterpretation, at best only partial acceptance, and often outright rejection of the planned and unplanned meanings of schools, are more likely." For this reason, schools contain the potential for both reproduction and transformation of society. To understand the hidden curriculum one must study the lived culture of the school and analyze its relationship to the structure of the larger society. Such research assumes that knowledge is socially constructed (Berger & Luckmann, 1966) and begins with an analysis of meaning that utilizes ethnographic and phenomenological studies. However, this analysis of mean-ing is combined with an analysis of ideology and reproduction (Apple, 1978). The recent work edited by Apple and Weis (1983) contains several examples of research employing this analysis of both meaning and ideology. Other important examples are Paul Willis's *Learning to Labour* (1977), a study of working-class boys in a comprehensive secondary school in England, and Robert Everhart's (1983) *Reading, Writing and Resistance,* a study of an American junior high school.

The steps involved in conducting research on schooling following this critical theory model are outlined below. In contrast to the positivist approach which assumes research to be value-free, this perspective sees all knowledge including research as socially con-structed and therefore begins with a clarification of the standpoint of the researcher. Steps 2 and 3 take the researcher inside the "black box" of the school to observe behavior and to discover its meaning to teachers and students. This microanalysis is followed by a macro-analysis of the relationship of the lived culture to the reproduction or transformation of class, race, and gender relations. Because the researcher is not assumed to be value-free but instead a politically committed person, the final step in the process is the identification of actions which might assist in the transformation of schools and society, an approach sometimes called emancipatory or radical pedagogy (Giroux, 1981a, 1981b). The five steps in the implementation of a critical theory approach are these:

1   Identification of the standpoint of the researcher;
2   Description of patterns of behavior;
3   Analysis of the participants' social construction of meanings;

4   Analysis of ideology and social relations;
5   Identification of action to assist transformation.

Research on the hidden curriculum in physical education

While little if any of the research on the hidden curriculum in physical education has employed the approach just described, the steps outlined in that model serve as a useful way to organize the review of the research. Almost all studies of the hidden curriculum in physical education have assumed the positivist stance of value-free research and therefore have not made the researcher's standpoint explicit. Most of this work seems to be either atheoretical or based upon a liberal functionalist perspective which endorses the basic justice of a meritocratic society but calls for reforms to guarantee equal opportunity for all. A few scholars have made explicitly critical analyses of sport in society (Boutilier & San Giovanni, 1983; Gruneau, 1975; Hargreaves, 1982) but they have not included analysis of pedagogical process in sport and physical education.

Some of the work on the hidden curriculum in physical education can best be characterized as descriptions of patterns of behavior fitting step 2 of the model. My studies of secondary physical education classes in Chicago (Bain, 1975, 1976) and of physical education classes and athletic team practices in Houston (Bain, 1978) used systematic observation to describe regularities of teacher behavior and class organization which communicated values and norms to students. Male and female classes were compared but no attempt was made to examine the meanings that teachers and students attached to these routines nor to examine their relationship to social theory. The research indicated there are patterns of behavior in physical education classes that can be interpreted as emphasizing orderliness, achievement, universalism, specificity, autonomy, and privacy, and that differences exist between the experiences of male and female students, urban and suburban students, and athletes and physical education students.

Recent work which examines the causes and effects of teacher expectations in teaching and coaching performs a similar function of describing patterns of behavior (Martinek, Crowe, & Rejeski, 1982). Although this work does not specifically address the hidden curriculum, it has considerable relevance. In general the research on teacher expectations in physical education indicates that teachers' perceptions of students are influenced by gender, appearance, and perceived effort, and that these expectations influence the interactions between teacher and student in a way that is consistent with the teacher's expectations (Martinek, 1983).

The second set of research studies on the hidden curriculum in physical education are those which have attempted not only to describe behavior but to examine the meanings that participants attach to those experiences. These studies have employed ethnographic and phenomenological research methodologies. Tindall (1975) conducted a participant observation study of physical education classes and a community basketball program. His analysis indicated that the game of basketball was experienced as a lesson in proper personal behavior. The premise underlying the game, that individuals ought to and do control other individuals, was accepted by most students hut rejected by those for whom it conflicted with their native American culture.

Wang (1977) conducted a participant observation study of a fifth grade physical education class. She discovered a teacher-sponsored curriculum and a separate, contradictory student-imposed curriculum. The teacher-sponsored curriculum promoted an ideal of integrated, democratic living in which rules of individual worth were tempered with emphasis upon cooperation, equality, and social responsibility. The student-imposed curriculum revealed patterns of discrimination based on gender, race, social class, personality, and skills. Skillful sport performance had a property-like nature in the student society. Wang suggests that a more active instruction in skills might be the most effective way to counter discrimination.

Kollen (1981, 1983) conducted a phenomenological inquiry into the perceptions of 20 high school seniors regarding their physical education classes. Based on her interviews, she concluded that the physical education environment is perceived as sterile (stressing conformity) and unsafe (characterized by embarrassment and humiliation). Students respond to the environment by "withholding something of themselves through minimal compliance, lack of involvement, manipulation of the teacher, false enthusiasm, rebellion, leaving, failing class, isolation or giving up" (Kollen, 1983, p. 87). Kollen suggests that the movement standard in physical education is masculine-athletic-competitive and that it creates a fragmented rather than an integrated movement experience.

Griffin (1983) observed sixth and seventh grade gymnastics classes and found that students' behavior revealed patterns of differentiation based on sex. Serious participation in specific gymnastics events was governed by perceived sex appropriateness of the event. Boys participated in "girl appropriate" events either frivolously or reluctantly; girls' participation in "boy appropriate" events was exploratory or reluctant. Boys limited the girls' opportunity to learn by hassling them, and limited their own opportunity to learn by clowning. Girls did not limit boys' opportunity to learn but spent most of their time trying to ignore boys or separate themselves from them. Students segregated themselves by sex and reinforced that segregation by sex differentiated participation and interactions.

These ethnographic studies which address the social construction of meanings in the physical education setting reflect an important step forward in the research. They have extended our understanding of the hidden curriculum in those settings and have suggested aspects of social relations such as gender which may have relevance for examining that hidden curriculum. However, they have not attempted a systematic analysis of the relationships of the lived culture of sport and physical education to social structure and ideologies. Apple (1978, p. 500) suggests that such omission may in fact lend support to the existing social order: "Without the overt recognition of the subtle connections between ideology and meaning, research that is limited to a description of meaning could itself be considered an aspect of reproduction." For this reason, physical educators interested in the hidden curriculum need to proceed to the final steps of the model, analysis of ideology and determination of action. The final section of this paper will address this possibility.

Feminist analysis of the hidden curriculum in physical education

The fundamental goal of research on the hidden curriculum is not only to understand the experience of schooling but also to comprehend the relationship between schooling and society. We live in a patriarchal society in which the maintenance of gender roles supplies society with the most basic form of hierarchical social organization and order (Eisenstein, 1981). Patriarchal power results in sexual division of labor and a division between the public (male) and private (female) domains of life. The critical component of patriarchal ideology is the transformation of the biological role of woman as childbearer into the political role of woman as childrearer. The assignment of motherhood as the primary occupation of women in society has functioned to maintain and to legitimate the political and economic inequities in patriarchal societies (Firestone, 1970).

Patriarchy interacts with the economic mode of society, but is a relatively autonomous system operating alongside the economic system not derived from it. Patriarchy has thrived in feudalist, capitalist, and socialist societies. Nevertheless, to understand the operation of patriarchy in a particular society one must examine it in relation to the structure of that society. This analysis will focus upon patriarchy and sexism in the United States. It should be noted that while this analysis focuses upon sexism, it is recognized that the efforts of sexism interact with those of racism and class. The concentration upon sexism is not intended to diminish the importance of either race or class.

American society can be characterized as a capitalist society based on an ideology that has been identified as liberal because of its emphasis upon the values of independence, individualism, and equality of opportunity. Jaggar and Struhl (1978) have identified four approaches to feminism in America. Most widespread is a liberal feminism which endorses the basic principles of the existing society and seeks to ensure that the doctrine of equal opportunity is extended to include women. The assumption is that if women are allowed equal access to education, employment, and political office, the present inequities of status will disappear. The other three forms of feminism that Jaggar and Struhl identify (Marxist feminism, radical feminism, and socialist feminism) assume that basic structural changes in society are needed in order to eliminate patriarchy and the oppression of women, although they differ on the kind of changes needed.

Most feminists, regardless of category, would concur that the system of patriarchy and sexism is maintained both by force (laws and practices that discriminate against women) and by ideology (beliefs about gender that are accepted by men and women). The hidden curriculum in schools may incorporate discriminatory practices and transmit a gender-based belief system.

This gender-based ideology may be accepted or resisted by students and teachers, Anyon (1982) suggests that gender development "involves not so much passive imprinting as active response to social contradictions." Girls have to cope with and resolve contradictory social messages about appropriate behavior for females on the one hand and appropriate behavior for achievers in the competitive world of school and work on the other. Anyon suggests that their responses often involve both accommodation and resistance to these contradictions.

Examining the hidden curriculum from a feminist perspective is particularly important in physical education because of the strong association between sport and masculinity (Boutilier & SanGiovanni, 1983) and because of the extreme "feminine" concern about the appearance of the female body (Brownmiller, 1984; Chernin, 1981; Orbach, 1978). The liberal feminist emphasis in such research tends to focus upon equal opportunity: girls' access to instruction, practice, and playing time. A critical analysis must go beyond this to an examination of the culture in physical education as it relates to and maintains patriarchy.

Several aspects of the lived culture in physical education seem worthy of study. The way in which the individualistic, competitive performance environment affects males and females is of particular importance. Willis (1982, p. 120) suggests that critical theory "accepts differences in sport performance between men and women, accepts that cultural factors may well enlarge this gap, but is most interested in the manner in which this gap is understood and taken up in the popular consciousness of our society." He asks why some differences but not others are viewed as important. Why for example are differences in strength important while differences in flexibility are not? Willis argues that sports performance serves to reinforce ideology about male supremacy. He and others (Boutilier & SanGiovanni, 1983; Felshin, 1974; Heide, 1978) have suggested that feminists may need to redefine sport and its standards of performance if sexism is to be eliminated.

A second area to be investigated is the social construction of body image for males and females. Heinemann (1980) proposes that the body is a social fact, that the handling of the body, the regulation and control of its functions, and our attitudes toward it are not "natural" but socially created, Willis (1982) indicates that the media treatment of women in sport often has a sexual innuendo in which the sexual identity often takes precedence over the sport identity of female athletes. Chernin (1981) suggests that women's obsession with diet and exercise reflects a dislike for the female body. Kollen (1981) found that students in physical education classes experience self-consciousness and embarrassment as a result of being continually on display. Each of these threads suggest that physical education's role in the development of body image needs to be examined.

The final aspect of the hidden curriculum in physical education that requires examination from a feminist perspective is the dualism which reflects and reinforces the separation of the private and public domains of life. Such a division which sees the public domain of work and politics as the man's world and the private realm of the family and emotion as the woman's sphere is at the heart of the patriarchal system (Eisenstein, 1981), This separation is ideologically represented by the dualisms of mind and body, instrumental and expressive activity, and work and play. To the extent that physical education programs reflect such dualisms, they may reinforce the sexual division of labor in society.

Conclusion

This paper has attempted to examine the theoretical bases for research on the hidden curriculum, summarize related research in physical education, and propose a model for feminist analysis of the hidden curriculum in sport and physical education. To some extent, it reflects my own journey from a naive, atheoretical description of the hidden curriculum to a radical feminist analysis of how patriarchal society is reproduced and transformed in the process of schooling, particularly within sport and physical education.

This analysis has focused upon sexism, but pervasive effects of class and especially race in sport and physical education should also be noted. Future examinations of the hidden curriculum need to investigate each of these (gender, class, and race) not only separately but in interaction with each other.

The final step in the critical theory model for research is the identification of action which leads to transformation of society. One role of the research is to identify "gaps and tensions" in the process of social reproduction which provide possibilities for political action (Giroux, 1981a). Giroux (1981c, p, 218) states, "While it would be naive and misleading to claim that schools alone can create the conditions for social change, it would be equally naive to argue that working in schools does not matter."

References

Anyon, J, (1982). Intersections of gender and class: Accommodations and resistance by working class and affluent females to contradictory sex-role ideologies. *Issues in education: Schooling and the reproduction of class and gender inequalities* (pp. 46–79). Occasional Paper #10, SUNY at Buffalo.

Apple, M.W. (1978). The new sociology of education: Analyzing cultural and economic reproduction. *Harvard Educational Review*, **48**, 495–503.

Apple, M.W. (1979). *Ideology and curriculum.* London: Routledge & Kegan Paul.

Apple, M.W. (1982). *Education and power.* Boston: Routledge & Kegan Paul.

Apple, M.W., & Weis, L. (Eds.). (1983). *Ideology and practice in schooling.* Philadelphia: Temple Press.

Bain, L.L. (1975). The hidden curriculum in physical education. *Quest*, **24**, 92–101.

Bain, L.L. (1976). Description of the hidden curriculum in secondary physical education. *Research Quarterly*, **47**, 154–160.

Bain, L.L. (1978). Differences in values implicit in teaching and coaching behaviors. *Research Quarterly*, **49**, 5–11.

Berger, P., & Luckmann, T. (1966). *The social construction of reality.* New York: Doubleday.

Boutilier, M.A., & SanGiovanni, L. (1983). *The sporting woman.* Champaign, IL: Human Kinetics.

Bowles, S., & Gintis, H. (1976). *Schooling in capitalist America.* New York: Basic Books.

Brownmiller, S. (1984). *Femininity.* New York: Linden Press/Simon & Schuster.

Chernin, K. (1981). *The obsession: Reflections on the tyranny of slenderness.* New York: Harper & Row.

Dreeben, R. (1968). *On what is learned in schools.* Reading, MA: Addison-Wesley.

Eisenstein, Z. (1981). *The radical future of liberal feminism.* New York: Longman, Inc.

Everhart, R. (1983). *Reading, writing and resistance.* Boston: Routledge & Kegan Paul.

Felshin, J. (1974). The triple option . . . for women in sport. *Quest*, **21**, 36–40.

Firestone, S. (1970). *The dialectic of sex.* New York: Bantam Books.

Giroux, H. (1981a). Hegemony, resistance, and the paradox of educational reform. *Interchange*, **12**(2–3), 3–26.

Giroux, H. (1981b). *Ideology, culture and the process of schooling.* London: Falmer Press.

Giroux, H. (1981c). Pedagogy, pessimism and the politics of conformity: A reply to Linda McNeil. *Curriculum Inquiry*, **11**(3), 211–222.

Griffin, P.S. (1983). "Gymnastics is a girl's thing": Student participation and interaction patterns in a middle school gymnastics unit. In T.J. Templin & J.K. Olson (Eds.), *Teaching in physical education* (pp. 71–85). Champaign, IL: Human Kinetics.

Gruneau, R.S. (1975). Sport, social differentiation and social inequality. In D. Bell & J.W. Long (Eds.), *Sport and social order* (pp. 117–184). Reading, MA: Addison-Wesley.

Hargreaves, J. (Ed.). (1982). *Sport, culture and ideology.* London: Routledge & Kegan Paul.

Heide, W.S. (1978). Feminism for a sporting future. In C.A. Oglesby (Ed.), *Women and sport: From myth to reality.* Philadelphia: Lea & Febiger.

Heinemann, K. (1980). Sport and the sociology of the body. *International Review of Sport Sociology*, **3**, 41–54.

Jackson, P.W. (1966). The student's world. *Elementary School Journal*, **66**, 345–357.

Jackson, P.W. (1968). *Life in classrooms.* New York: Holt, Rinehart, & Winston.

Jaggar, A.M., & Struhl, P.R. (Eds.). (1978). *Feminist frameworks: Alternative and theoretical accounts of the relations between women and men.* New York: McGraw-Hill.

Kollen, P. (1981). *The experience of movement in physical education: A phenomenology.* Unpublished doctoral dissertation, University of Michigan.

Kollen, P. (1983). Fragmentation and integration in movement. In T.J. Templin & J.K. Olson (Eds.), *Teaching in physical education* (pp. 86–93). Champaign, IL: Human Kinetics.

Martinek, T.J. (1983). Creating Golem and Galatea effects during physical education instruction: A social psychological perspective. In T.J. Templin & J.K. Olson (Eds.), *Teaching in physical education* (pp. 59–70). Champaign, IL: Human Kinetics.

Martinek, T.J., Crowe, P.B., & Rejeski, W.J. (1982). *Pygmalion in the gym*. West Point, NY: Leisure Press.

Orbach, S. (1978). *Fat is a feminist issue*. New York: Berkley Books.

Tindall, B.A. (1975). Ethnography and the hidden curriculum in sport. *Behavioral and Social Science Teacher*, **2**(2), 5–28.

Wang, B.M. (1977). *An ethnography of a physical education class: An experiment in integrated living*. Unpublished doctoral dissertation. University of North Carolina at Greensboro.

Weis, L. (1982). Schooling and the reproduction of aspects of structure. *Issues in education: Schooling and the reproduction of class and gender inequalities* (pp. 1–16). Occasional Paper #10, SUNY at Buffalo.

Willis, P. (1977). *Learning to labour*. Sussex, England: Teakfield Ltd.

Willis, P. (1982). Women in sport in ideology. In J. Hargreaves (Ed.), *Sport, culture and ideology* (pp. 117–135). London: Routledge & Kegan Paul.

PART 2

Physical education and sport

INTRODUCTION

GIVEN THE CENTRAL ROLE of gymnastics in defining physical education historically, the association of sport with physical education is a relatively recent phenomenon, dating from the 1950s and the emergence in Britain of physical education in secondary schools. Even though there has been an increasing amount of sport-related activity in physical education programmes since this time, the place of sport in physical education has remained problematic for some sections of the physical education community, at least in theory. The common response from these physical educators to the politician or lay-person who makes the mistake of using 'sport' in place of 'physical education' is that physical education is more than sport and indeed has different purposes that are more educationally focused than the purposes of sport. In practice, physical educators have since the 1950s increasingly replaced gymnastics and other aspects of physical education with sport-related activities.

The two papers in this section explore this tension between physical education and sport. Siedentop is clear that sport is properly a central aspect of physical education and that the purposes of physical education and sport coincide. He is, however, highly critical of the ways in which sport is commonly presented in physical education and he argues for an alternative means of doing this which he labels 'Sport Education'. Houlihan explores the politics around this tension and shows that there are competing perspectives on the relationship between sport and physical education. He points out that in the crowded policy spaces around sport, physical educators' views are often marginal and sometimes drowned-out by more powerful groups.

FURTHER READING

Bailey, R.P. (2005) Evaluating the relationship between physical education, sport and social inclusion. *Educational Review*, 57(1), 71–90.

Bailey, R.P. and Morley, D. (2005) Towards a model of talent development in physical education. *Sport, Education and Society*, 11(3), 211–230.

Kirk, D. (2002) Junior sport as a moral practice. *Journal of Teaching in Physical Education*, 21, 402–408.

Murdoch, E.B. (1990) Physical education and sport: the interface, in N. Armstrong (ed.), *New Directions in Physical Education*, London: Cassell.

Penney, D. (2000) Physical education, sporting excellence and educational excellence. *European Physical Education Review*, 6, 135–150.

Daryl Siedentop

JUNIOR SPORT AND THE EVOLUTION OF SPORT CULTURES

I AM GRATEFUL TO BE ASKED to share some thoughts with you on the topic of junior sport. I have enormous respect for the sport culture of New Zealand, and I have been impressed with the serious efforts taken in recent years in New Zealand to strengthen and make more educative the junior sport aspects of your larger sport culture. Sport has been the central, defining focus of my life and I owe much to it, but as a famous coach at my university once said, "You can't pay back, you can only pay forward." I take it that many here assembled have been similarly influenced by their sport experiences and have come together to see how you might collectively pay forward to improve the junior sport experiences for Kiwi juniors of the future.

It has become increasingly difficult over the past quarter-century for intellectuals to poke fun at adults who take sport seriously, not just during competition, but who also take it seriously as a cultural form, a major thread woven into and holding together the fabric of society. A generation ago, if you took sport seriously as an adult, many thought that you had spent too much time in the toy department! Over the past 20 years, sport has commanded the attention of scholars such as A. Bartlett Giamatti (1989) and Michael Novak (1976), each of whom argued that sport played a central, civilizing role in culture. Sport has also attracted the attention of neo-Marxist scholars who see it as a central mechanism for continued hegemonic patriarchal control in the developed democracies of the world. Either way, it's better to be taken seriously than to be ignored.

I assume that sport is central to your culture, as it has become to the cultures of most developed nations, and that New Zealand sport embodies certain cultural values you wish to transmit to future generations. I also assume, using a biological analogy, that sport practices evolve. They are always changing, albeit often so slowly that we don't immediately recognize the changes. That doesn't mean that sport cultures necessarily get better —there is no teleological force ensuring good sport and a healthy and sane sport culture.

Sport practices can devolve also, and in so doing contribute to the demise of a culture through the spread of values that are antithetical to a free, progressive society.

You are assembled here to try to ensure the continued progress of the New Zealand sport culture, and you rightly assume that junior sport policies and practices are crucial to that progress. Graham Dalton, in the *Sunday Auckland Star-Times*, suggested that this forum would be the most important event in New Zealand sport for many years to come.

The first suggestion I have is to urge you to examine junior sport with the seriousness it deserves given its crucial role in the future of your sport culture. Junior sport policies and practices need serious examination, serious debate, and continual dialogue. They don't need competing mythologies and unexamined creeds.

Let me give an example of what I mean. In my country there has been a prevailing mythology that boys will turn into men only if they experience the magic elixer of football competition. This is particularly true for troubled boys who, as the creed goes, if brought under the influence of some tough coaches and experience competition that is character-ized primarily by physical confrontation between opponents, will emerge with newly attained qualities of character such as persistence, courage, and the willingness to over-come physical discomfort, all of which are ascribed as nearly automatic benefits of these experiences.

This mythology is a vulgarization of Arnoldism, the mid-19th-century philosophy of fair play that took the name of the headmaster at the Rugby School in England. Arnodlism in its pure form was a philosophy that not only taught how one ought to behave in sport, but used sport as a metaphor for how life should be lived. Needless to say, there is nothing inherently positive about the influence of sport on developing children and youths. I have always been a bit leery of the "learning to play the game of life" speeches that I too often had to endure in sports banquets when I was an athlete and later when I coached. It is a creed that doesn't fairly represent the reality.

I do believe that sport, properly conceived and conducted, can teach important qualities of character, but these qualities do not come automatically, and there are many negative qualities that poorly conducted sport also teaches.

For example, we might note that a form of what the American sport psychologist Mary Duquin (1988) has called sado-aesceticism has crept gradually into sport in recent years, an obsessive asceticism imposed on athletes, sometimes inadvertently, by overzeal-ous coaches and parents, and eventually by athletes on themselves and those around them. While "no pain, no gain" has been a slogan around sport for generations, it has taken on a new, more sinister meaning. Pain is redefined as discomfort and "real athletes" are taught to work through it; indeed, some eventually come to embrace it. This is seen not only in con-tact sports but also in gymnastics, distance running, rowing, and in the many sports that rely on extensive strength training as necessary preparation for competition, and in sports where weight control and reduced body fat are associated with competitive advantage.

As Duquin pointed out, however, the wisdom of the body is to deny pain. Children, when left to themselves, often quit when they experience pain. Their slogan would be "no pain is sane!" Generally, all of us try to avoid pain, injury, and unpleasant physical situations unless they are necessary for achieving some immediate goal that represents a sufficiently higher good to make the risk of pain and injury justifiable. While it may be understandable that adults choose sometimes to sacrifice their bodies for their perceptions of truth, it is unacceptable when in junior sport, "the truths are those of adults, the sacrificial bodies those of children" (Duquin, 1988, p. 35).

Where is the mythology and where is the truth? How do we steer a middle course, protecting children and respecting their developing sensibilities, yet at the same time attempting to put them in situations where qualities such as perseverance, courage, and the willingness to subordinate their own goals and gratification to those of the group can be learned? When you take abstract notions about junior sport and test them with concrete situations, you can provoke a dialogue, serious study, and eventually, perhaps, approved policies and practices that guide a collective response to such issues. Too often, however, such issues provoke only conditioned responses, both from those who want to defend questionable junior sport practices no matter what and those who want to condemn them no matter what, with a lot of heat generated from both sides, but very little light.

One of the ongoing problems for those whose task it is to develop and implement junior sport policies and practices is to sort out which goals the junior sports programs should serve from the multiple goals that might reasonably be put forward. Goals for sport programs, of course, don't have to be mutually exclusive, and one is tempted to argue that all goals can be met equally through one system; but that smacks of theology rather than theory, and the evidence doesn't support that particular theology.

There are three primary goals that can be put forward to define junior sport programs: the educative goal, the public health goal, and the elite-development goal. There is a fourth goal that is less apparent but nonetheless important, that of preserving, protecting, and enhancing sport practices. Those who have invested themselves for years in the practice of cricket or the practice of tennis are rightly concerned that their sport practices thrive and grow so that more persons can experience the satisfaction they have taken from their own involvement. This is a goal for national associations and sport clubs, who are the main bearers of sport practices in this culture. I will refer to this goal throughout this paper.

The most frequently cited goal for junior sport is what I will call the educative goal; that is, junior sport is supported primarily for the developmental and educational benefits it provides participants. This is also often referred to as a youth development goal. The evidence does support the assertion that a number of benefits accrue from well-conducted junior sport programs. The most commonly attributed benefits would be learning useful skills, cooperation, leadership skills, submerging individual interests to collective goal, and perseverance. If the educative goal were to dominate a sport program, it would be as inclusive as possible, attractive to diverse children and youth, modified physically and emotionally to fit developing bodies, talents, and spirits, and administered and coached with the educative benefits clearly reflected.

A second goal is to contribute to the public health goals of a nation. It is now clear that physical inactivity is related to all-cause morbidity, with particular emphasis on the marked differences between adults who are inactive and those do get moderate to vigorous, regular activity. Physical inactivity has been linked to a number of degenerative diseases, and it is becoming increasingly clear that regular activity has both prophylactic and remedial benefits. Nations that can induce their citizens to become and remain physically active can reduce their health costs dramatically.

Data in America show an alarming trend toward obesity and inactivity among adolescents, and although the evidence is quite thin, no pun intended, most of us believe that the best predictor of an active adult lifestyle is being active and gaining skills as a young person. An article in the *Wellington Post* just this Wednesday reported similarly alarming data for New Zealand youth and expressed concerns that are now being heard throughout the developed world, as health costs consume an increasingly large proportion of national wealth. If junior sport were organized primarily around a public health goal, it would emphasize playful activity above all and would specifically target for inclusion those children and youths who are most at risk on indices of cardiovascular performance and body composition, exactly those children and youth who typically do not participate in most junior sports programs.

A third goal, what I call the elite-development goal, is for junior sport to allow the most talented and interested young athletes to pursue excellence, to realize their full potential. A fair portion of the attention in sport cultures is devoted to sport heroes—and increasingly, I'm happy to report, to sport heroines. Does it matter whether New Zealand athletes do well in Atlanta next August? Did the America's Cup victory stir the national pride? Did the successes of Mark Todd and Charisma find their way into your cultural history? Did anyone care that the All-Blacks lost to France yesterday?

A junior sport program organized around the development of elite athletes would, of course, be markedly different from one devoted to educative or public health goals. We know that the development of sport expertise takes years and years of what psychologists most often refer to as "deliberate practice" (Ericcson, Krampe, & Tesch-Romer, 1993). We also know that sustaining children and youths through the 10 to 15 years of deliberate practice necessary to develop an elite sportsperson requires a network of supportive adults. The question, then, is how to balance these goals when formulating policies and practices for junior sport, and which goals the bearers of sports practices—the national sport associations, clubs, and schools—choose to emphasize.

In the United States, the school-sport portion of our junior sport system has chosen an exclusionary, varsity model in which fewer athletes participate as they grow through their teen years, and more resources are differentially devoted to those fewer, more talented athletes. Teens who have been excluded from participation in varsity programs have very limited access to other quality sport experiences.

At a recent Board of Education meeting in a suburb of Columbus, Ohio, the high school athletic director made an emotional plea to sustain resources for the boys' varsity football team so that they could continue to employ 12 coaches for the 60 boys on that team, with the main thrust of the argument being that any fewer coaches would put them at a competitive disadvantage. No one questioned whether those resources might be better used to extend participation opportunities to more boys and girls.

In a typical American high school of 2,000 students, 12 boys and 12 girls will make the varsity basketball teams this winter, and there is relatively little opportunity for continued development and competition for the 100 or 200 other girls and boys who would gladly participate if there were reasonable opportunity. The varsity model serves the elite-development goal quite effectively. Teens now regularly specialize in a single sport, spending their off-season training and developing strength and endurance specific to their sport and position. The day of the multiple-sport high school athlete in my country is rapidly waning. The high school system weeds out the less talented, and the intercollegiate system then picks up the most talented and repeats the training/development cycle for another 4 or 5 years.

There is increasing evidence that the educative and public health goals of sport are lost in the varsity system, particularly as the most talented athletes move up the system into Division I NCAA sport at the university level. A study of Division I athletes has shown that they tend to experience low quality of life compared to their noncompeting peers at the university (Wrisberg, 1996). These athletes spend most of their time doing, witnessing, or talking about their sports. Many are chronically fatigued and frequently injured. The pressure to use banned substances is great. Many feel isolated from and misunderstood by other students. So much for the luxurious life of the scholarship athlete! And, so much for the educative and public health goals of sport programs.

Please do not infer that I am against programs that allow for talented children and youths to pursue their interests in sports to the fullest extent. Quite to the contrary, I understand that expertise and heroism in sport are crucial to a culture's values and its collective sense of itself.

The central organizing ethic of ancient Greek culture was heroism, what the Greeks called "arete," a concept that does not translate well into English, but which typically meant heroic striving for excellence (Siedentop, 1972). The British philospher Alasdair MacIntrye (1981) has put forward a highly regarded moral philosophy—a modern version of this ancient Greek ethic—in which culture is seen to advance as members of what he calls practices strive for excellence in order to win the admiration of their peers within the practice, a social good that is available only to those who submit themselves to the rigor of the particular practice, be it chemistry, architecture, or football. MacIntrye argued that it is through the striving for excellence within practices that cultures progress.

Every culture needs heroes and heroines who stretch the limits, who through their own heroic performances show us new possibilities, who provide models to be emulated, not just as performers but as persons who embody the qualities we value and wish to transmit to our children and youths. It is impossible to achieve that standard of excellence today without years of toil and sacrifice, whether in sport, music, or medicine. It also seems clear that in the long road toward excellence in sport, the support system of coaches, parents, and governments that sustain the journey become necessary components of elite development programs.

What this does suggest, however, is that one can legitimately question the degree to which the elite-development goals of a junior sport system can be served as part of a comprehensive system and still direct sufficient resources to achieve the educative and public health goals that are more fundamental to the system as a whole. It also suggests that policies are needed within the elite-development portion of the system that protect the developing athlete from abuses that are far too common in elite junior sport throughout the world.

What should be the characteristics of junior sport, particularly from the educative and public health perspectives? There is little doubt what children and youth want from their junior sport experiences—the evidence throughout the world is remarkably reliable.

- Youth want to participate. They would rather play on a losing team than sit and watch on a winning team.
- Youth want to get better at their sports. A growing sense of competence in a valued activity is a central developmental task of adolescence.
- They want to be among friends. Voluntary participation in leisure sport as an adult has a strong social component. Social outcomes are prominent at every level of amateur sport. Why should we expect less in junior sport?
- They want to have fun. Teens often report "no fun" as the biggest reason for dropping out of sport.

Yet, I must caution you that the concept of fun is among the most badly understood in the sport field. We all too often use the concept and interpret the use of the term more restrictively than we should. When having fun in sport is discussed, it is too often done so framed by a view of children having fun—gaiety, frivolity, and the like. For adults, however, fun often means becoming totally absorbed in an activity in which they are trying to improve, a kind of fun that is found in training, a taste for rules, and a taste for imposed difficulty, exactly the characteristics that define adult forms of play (Caillois, 1961).

Children and youth also want to compete and win, yet this is not a priority for them to the extent that it overwhelms these other reasons they have for participating. When children and youths allow winning to overwhelm the other reasons for participating, it is because this value has been imposed on them prematurely by adults.

There are two other characteristics I would add from an adult perspective, that is, outcomes from junior sport experiences that adults would like to see occur more frequently. The first is a growing independence through decision-making. The second is the moral sensibility engendered through a shared community devoted to a common purpose. Children and youth react positively to programs that have these characteristics, but these aren't such that boys and girls would mention them when asked what they like about their sport experiences.

I am convinced that junior sport must increasingly allow for decision-making and foster independence as youth grow through their teens. The research and evaluation of Sport Education in New Zealand and Australia provide evidence for the degree to which youths respond positively to such opportunities (Alexander & Taggart, 1994; Aussie Sport Action, 1995; Carlson, 1995; Grant, 1992). If we are to have adults who choose to participate in sport, we must take more seriously the goal of helping youngsters become more independent and make good choices in sport. Unfortunately, models of coaching throughout the world tend to emphasize coach control over athletes that limits their independence and decision-making.

I also believe junior sport must foster moral sensibilities and caring among young athletes, and must inspire a sense of community and belonging. This is important if we expect junior sport to provoke a lifelong commitment not only to sport participation but to the health and vitality of sport practices which can provide positive experiences for sportsmen and sportswomen throughout life.

This suggests that junior sport should strive to do more to develop what in Sport Education (Siedentop, 1994) I have defined as the literate and enthusiastic sportsperson. Literate sportspersons understand and are committed to the rules, traditions, rituals, and values of a sport, and they have learned to distinguish between good and bad actions and procedures within a sport. Enthusiastic sportspersons participate and behave in ways that preserve, protect, and enhance the practice of their sport. They are activists for their sport and are involved in ensuring its continued health and growth.

One of the weaknesses of junior sport programs throughout the world is that they teach little more than the performer role. Boys and girls learn to be forwards, outside hitters, midfielders, or goalies. For sport systems to develop and be sustained, however, we must have women and men who willingly serve in the central roles of coaches, managers, trainers, referees, umpires, and also persons serving in a host of supportive roles, often on a volunteer basis. We have assumed that boys and girls who learn and play sport when they are children and youths will, as adults, become competent volunteers in these central and supportive roles, when in fact they have had no preparation to fulfill those roles competently and may not understand how crucial those roles are to good sport systems. Subsequently, they may not feel any obligation to fulfill a central or supportive role for the future development of their sport practice.

The skills to fill these roles well can be learned in a more complete sport education. The predisposition to become obligated to sustaining the future development of a sport practice by becoming involved in central and supportive roles can also be nurtured in junior sport programs. Indeed, sport programs should lay claims on their members that produce exactly these obligations.

If one thinks of junior sport as an infrastructure of opportunity, there are good lessons to be learned from the more general fields of activity programming, fields as seemingly disparate as early childhood education, youth development, worksite fitness, and elder care. First, it is clear that access is fundamental to program success. A compelling analysis of urban youth programs describes the most successful programs as tangibly local. Friends of mine in the senior retirement housing business tell me that beyond a certain distance, measured in feet, not miles, senior residents simply don't use available programs and facilities. The worksite fitness and exercise adherence literatures reach similar conclusions; for programs to be effective for voluntary participation, they have to be accessible, safe, and attractive, which are some of the most compelling reasons for developing and sustaining a comprehensive, inclusive school sport program.

A second characteristic of successful programs is membership in an inclusive, persisting group. We have thoroughly underestimated the power of persisting groups, and how the informal social contingencies within groups keep members engaged. A significant factor in persisting groups for children and youth is the continuing presence of competent, caring adult leadership. There is no evidence anywhere to suggest that children and youths in sport programs don't want adult leadership. To the contrary, the evidence supports the opposite view; however, they want leadership to be caring, supportive, and instructive, rather than authoritarian.

The third characteristic of successful activity programs is the provision of challenging activities that offer active participation which results in real accomplishments, as defined by the participants themselves as well as by significant others in their lives. It is here, of course, that sport has such an extraordinary advantage and perhaps the main reason why it captures the enthusiasm of so many young persons. This is also why many of us believe that sport is such an appropriate vehicle through which to influence young lives in a positive way.

The persisting group, and the competent, caring adult leadership associated with it, form the basis for community and provide the opportunity for the development of what the American sociologist James Coleman (1987) called social capital. Social capital refers to the values, norms, predispositions, and sense of self that children and youth develop through regular contact with significant adults across time. Notice here that I said regular contact with significant adults, and across time. It is the diminution of social capital among children and youth that is alarming adults throughout the developed world, where discussions about at-risk youth have become commonplace.

When this persisting group and adult leadership forms around a particular sport, then it also provides the opportunity for what the British philosopher Alasdair MacIntyre (1981) called a "practice." A practice, to quote MacIntyre, is a "socially established cooperative human activity through which goods internal to that form of activity are realized in the course of trying to achieve the standards of excellence which are appropriate to, and partially definitive of, that form of activity, with the result that human powers to achieve excellence, and human conceptions of the ends and goods involved, are systematically extended" (p. 175). Architecture, law, and medicine are practices in this sense, but so too is farming, and so too are football and equestrian disciplines.

The persisting group with competent, caring adult leadership, when formed around a sport, provides an initiation into the practice of that sport and allows for the development of social capital among girls and boys. It is within this community of caring that many good things can happen. Without it, without the community of caring and expectations, without the moral overtones of a practice, few good things result except performance, and even great performances are not sufficient to sustain practices. If performance and entertainment become the main focus, the practices eventually devolve.

When initiated into and sustained in a sport practice, children and youth can learn to care about that sport and care about its future in a sport culture. This happens because to become a member of a sport practice, one must learn about and accept the standards of excellence in that sport, accept the authority of those standards, and subject oneself to the rules and traditions that define the practice as one attempts to achieve the goods that are defined by participation in that sport and the respect and admiration of those with whom one is engaged in that sport practice.

Put simply, if you want to be a cricket player and earn the admiration and respect of other cricket players, there is only one way to achieve that social good; to wit, you must enter the practice of cricket and subordinate yourself to the standards of excellence within cricket and seek to pursue excellence within the traditions and rules of cricket. You can't buy that respect and admiration. You can earn it only by becoming a cricket player. Being a cricket player, however, has traditionally meant something different, something more than being a cricket performer. To the extent that performance as entertainment is what we care about and reward most, then sport loses its educative and moral power.

The persisting sport group, and the particular practice of that sport in which the group is embedded, can provoke the development of rich qualities of character and spirit among children and youth—honesty, caring for your fellow sportspersons, humility in achievement, empathy in victory, resilience in defeat, perseverance, appreciation for the aesthetics of quality sport performance, courage, and a sense of fairness and justice— exactly the social capital that ensures the continued development of a free, progressive society.

A sport practice can do so by communicating these standards and qualities to young persons in ways they understand, engaging them in activities and experiences which reflect these standards and qualities, and developing relationships with boys and girls that communicate these qualities and virtues. Helping to initiate youngsters into sport practices can help them form a belief in and dedication to something larger than themselves, building a sense of purpose and identity that is surely an antidote to youthful demoralization. There is no automaticity here, however. This sense of purpose is communicated and reinforced by the community of older youths and adults who are members of the practice, both by what they say and in how that is congruent with the way they live their lives.

Children in sport who are encouraged to take real responsibilities as members of a persisting sport group, who perform services to others and for their sport, have the best chance of developing life commitments to the practice of that sport. If these youngsters experience honest, fair, and caring relationships with older youth and adults, and come to understand the moral meanings of the choices they make within their sport, they will not only sustain the practice of that sport but will help it grow and thrive within a sport culture.

The sociologist Amitai Etzioni (1993) has written, "Communities speak to us in moral values. They lay claims on their members" (p. 41). It is clear that in many societies it is becoming less popular to "lay moral claims" on members of any communities sporting practices included. Educator William Damon (1995) has argued that this disinclination to lay moral claims lies at the heart of our failure to maintain communities that provide protection and guidance for young persons.

A junior sport charter that is not built on the firm conviction that its guiding principles will provide programs for children and youths that lead them in appropriate directions will be impotent. The policies that such a charter suggests must lead to procedures and programs that faithfully reflect the developmental and moral sense of those policies. In the end, it will be the procedures and programs that determine how junior sport impacts the lives of children and youths. It is one thing to suggest a policy that asserts that all young persons in junior sport programs should have a fair-go at participation. It is quite another thing to develop and enforce procedures that ensure equal playing time and equal opportunity to learn different positional play.

I envy the opportunity you have. You are a small nation with an extraordinary sporting tradition. You have the very real opportunity to help junior sport develop in ways which extend that sporting tradition into a brilliant future, while at the same time contributing to the development of honest, caring citizens who value fairness and understand the meaning of commitment to a common goal and the purposefulness necessary to realize the commitment and achieve the goal. I wish you well.

References

Alexander, K., & Taggart, A. (1994). Sport education in physical education, *Aussie Sport Action*, **5**, 5–9.

Aussie Sport Action (1995). Sport education: A proven alternative. *Aussie Sport Action*, **6**(4), 5–8.

Caillois, R. (1961). *Man, play and games*. New York: The Free Press.

Carlson, T. (1995). "Now I think I can": The reaction of Year eight low-skilled students to sport education. *ACHPER Healthy Lifestyles Journal*, **42**(4), 6–8.

Coleman, J. (1987). Families and schools. *Educational Researcher*, **16**(6), 32–38.

Damon, W. (1995). *Greater expectations: Overcoming the culture of indulgence in America's homes and schools*. New York: The Free Press.

Duquin, M. (1988). Gender and youth sport: Reflections on old and new fictions. In F. Smoll. R. Magill, & M. Ash (Eds.). *Children in sport* (pp. 31–42). Champaign, IL: Human Kinetics.

Ericcson, K., Krampe, R., & Tesch-Romer, C. (1993). The role of deliberate practice in the acquisition of expert performance. *Psychological Review*, **100**, 363–406.

Etzioni, A. (1993). *The spirit of community*. New York: Crown.

Giamatti, A.B. (1989). *Take time for paradise*. New York: Summit Books.

Grant, B. (1992). Integrating sport into the physical education curriculum in New Zealand secondary schools. *Quest*, **44**, 304–316.

MacIntyre, A. (1981). *After virtue*. Notre Dame, IN: University of Notre Dame Press.

Novak, M. (1976). *The joy of sports*. New York: Basic Books.

Siedentop, D. (1972, January). Differences between Greek and Hebrew views of man. *Canadian Journal of Sports History*.

Siedentop, D. (1994). *Sport education: Quality PE through positive sport experiences*. Champaign, IL: Human Kinetics.

Wrisberg, C. (1996). Quality of life for male and female athletes. *Quest*, **48**, 392–408.

Barrie Houlihan

SPORTING EXCELLENCE, SCHOOLS AND SPORTS DEVELOPMENT
The politics of crowded policy spaces

Introduction

THE INCREASED EMPHASIS on the pursuit of elite international sporting achievement has inevitably meant that the role of the education system in England and Wales, and schools in particular, in contributing to elite success has been the subject of considerable debate and a focus for government intervention. While highly political debates over the content of the Physical Education (PE) curriculum dominated the late 1980s and early 1990s, they were only a relatively minor element in a series of broader and more politically divisive debates about the future role and organization of schools. The funding of schools, the role of the LEA, the balance of power between teachers, governors and parents, and the content of the curriculum were only the most prominent in a series of issues that were focused on the school. The school was an arena in which a complex range of interests attempted to assert control over policy. Some interests, such as teacher's unions and subject specialist bodies, were largely internal to the education policy community, while others, including the major political parties and employer's associations, were powerful but external. As a consequence of the heightened salience of education as a policy issue and schools as an arena for the exercise of policy influence, new policy initiatives are the focus of intense political activity during all phases of the policy process and especially during the later stages of implementation. The focus of this paper is on one policy initiative, specialist sports colleges (SSCs) and the intention is to explore the degree to which the formulation of the SSC initiative represented a compromise between competing interests and also to examine the early experience of four SSCs in order to identify indications of the extent to which the competing interests are affecting the policy during implementation.

School sport since the 1980s

The last 20 years or so have been a turbulent period for education in Britain. Of particular note is the extent to which education policy has been affected by the broader reorientation of British politics away from a model of welfare, in which the state, operating through a series of central and local government level bureaucracies, was secure in its role as the provider of a broad range of services and in which relatively autonomous professions played a central role in defining need and controlling access. During the 1980s the attack on public expenditure, the challenge to the professional model of service control and autonomy, and the rejection of the role of the state as the automatic primary service provider left few parts of the public sector untouched. Particularly in the late 1980s, housing, personal social services and education were frequently in the forefront of the Thatcherite assault on comfortable assumptions of public service provision.

Apart from the Thatcherite challenge to the post-war welfare consensus, the Conservative government had a specific agenda in relation to education. In essence the Conservatives sought to assert the priority of the needs of the economy over other conceptualizations of the purpose of education. The commitment to reshape the curriculum to support more effectively the perceived needs of the economy was complemented by a determination to weaken the influence of both the local education authority and the teaching profession. Nested within the broad agenda for educational reform was a specific agenda for physical education and sport, reflected most sharply in the design of the National Curriculum for Physical Education (DES, 1991) and in the policy statement *Sport: Raising the Game* (DNH, 1995).

The politics of the formulation of the NCPE is well documented and needs only brief comment (see Evans and Penney, 1995; Houlihan, 1997; Penney and Evans, 1999; Talbot, 1995). The determination of the content of the NCPE took place within a complex and multilayered context. Part of that context was the long-standing debate about the status of PE relative to other elements of the curriculum and, by implication, the status of PE teachers relative to their peers. A further element of the context, and one particularly relevant to the focus of this paper, is the more recent tension between PE on the one hand and competitive team sports on the other. For the Thatcherite right in the government the perceived dominance of PE over competitive team sport in schools was used as a convenient metaphor 'to signify all else that was wrong with state education' (Evans, 1992: 234). More specifically, PE was seen as being at best well meaning but essentially muddled, while sport was lauded as promoting positive personal and social values and outcomes. Although in large part a manufactured polarization, the political distinction between sport and PE had the effect of legitimizing the marginalization of PE teachers in the curriculum design process and legitimizing a degree of political direction which was exceptional in comparison to most other areas of the curriculum.

The strong political lead from the government resulted, not surprisingly, in a curriculum constructed around conventional disciplines and traditional content. The membership of the PE curriculum working group was notable for the strong representation of interests associated with performance sport and the absence of any practising physical education teachers. Despite its composition, the interim report of the working party was generally welcomed by PE teachers for the extent to which it emphasized cognitive as well as practical elements. However, any satisfaction with the report was short-lived as the strong intervention by the Secretary of State, supported by the sports lobby, forced a

reworking of the NCPE such that the 'final report seemed a substantial "surrender"'
(Penney and Evans, 1999: 57). A key change in emphasis was the clear subordination
of the educational objectives associated with 'planning' and 'evaluating' in favour of
'performing'. The centrality of performance in 'games' was reinforced by the work of
the National Curriculum Council, whose responsibility it was to refine the report in
preparation for presentation of the final version of the curriculum to Parliament. Further
reinforcement came from the Dearing review, which reduced the content of the NCPE
but left the 'games' element largely intact, thus giving it an increased share of the available
curriculum time (DES, 1995). However, it should be borne in mind that, far from
representing a break with the then current practice of PE, the NCPE represented an
endorsement of the long-established practices which prioritized gender-based team games
over a more thematic and integrated physical education curriculum.

The political direction of the content of the NCPE and the explicit emphasis on the
role of competitive team games was indicative of the government's broader orientation
towards sport which received its clearest articulation with the publication, in 1995, of
the policy statement *Sport: Raising the Game* (DNH, 1995). In the introduction John Major
declared that 'My ambition is simply stated. It is to put sport back at the heart of
weekly life in every school' (p. 2). He added that 'I am determined to see that our great
traditional sports – cricket, hockey, swimming, athletics, football, netball, rugby, tennis
and the like – are put firmly at the centre of the stage' (p. 3). A key underlying assumption
was that compliance with these exhortations was unproblematic for teachers and for their
schools. Throughout the statement teachers were identified as the key agents for realizing
successful policy implementation. Moreover, *Sport: Raising the Game* re-emphasized the
priority of competitive team sports within the National Curriculum:

> . . . in the revised National Curriculum the Government has greatly increased
> the importance of competitive sport, including team games played in a
> form appropriate to each age group. The focus of this Policy Statement is
> deliberately on sport rather than physical education.
>
> (DNH, 1995: 7)

A variety of proposals were included in the statement designed to promote sport
in schools. OFSTED was to be asked to inspect the quality and range of games within the
PE curriculum and also to conduct an audit of initial teacher training in PE. The Sportsmark and Gold Star schemes were proposed to be awarded to schools that met specified
criteria for the effective promotion of sport. Although not included in the statement, the
introduction of specialist sports colleges (SSCs) was also part of the government's drive to
reinvigorate school sport. In the review of progress published the following year, the
launch of SSCs was mentioned as 'a further avenue for secondary schools to focus on
physical education and sport' (DNH, 1996: 16).

Although the policy statement was dominated by its proposals regarding schools and
its reinforcement of the thrust of the National Curriculum for PE, it should be borne in
mind that the statement also constituted an outline of the government's broader sports
development policy. From the late 1980s the Great Britain Sports Council had attempted
to retain an integrated sports development strategy centred around the model of the
sports development continuum, which conceptualized sport as comprising four tightly
integrated elements: foundation, participation, performance and excellence. While the

model was not without its tensions, it proved to be durable and to be an effective representation of the interrelatedness of apparently disparate policies and interests. The model provided a degree of conceptual coherence to the broad range of investment required to support mass participation and elite development and also to the range of disparate and potentially antagonistic organizations that sought a share of Sports Council and later National Lottery funding. The model had the virtue of linking (if at times only in theory) the interests of elite performers with those of the general participant. More importantly, the sports continuum provided support for a broader view of PE in schools than the government was prepared to accept. *Sport: Raising the Game* undermined the sports continuum model and hastened the fragmentation of the range of sports interests that it had previously encompassed.

Sport: Raising the Game abandoned any pretence of an integrated and multidimensional approach to sports development. Its twin emphasis on school sport and excellence made little attempt to demonstrate the potential areas of overlap or common interest. It also promoted a narrower definition of the foundation and participation elements of the sports continuum than had the GB Sports Council. Although mass participation and elite development are referred to in parallel in the section dealing with further and higher education, the preoccupation is with the potential contribution of universities to the development of elite talent. More significantly, the absence of any discussion of the role and contribution of local authorities in the area of mass participation is explicable only in terms of the persistent hostility of the Conservatives to local government. It is against this background of a clear prioritization of elite development, and the replacement of the sports development continuum with a linear view of sports development, that the Labour government was elected in 1997.

Despite rhetorical flourishes about reinvigorating the concept of Sport for All, it is the extent of continuity between the in-coming Labour government and its predecessor that has been most striking over the last two years. The Labour Party's preelection policy document *Labour's Sporting Nation* argued strongly that its objectives were to provide 'opportunities for the many not the few' (1996: 6) and to develop 'excellence at all levels' (p. 4). It also reasserted both the central role of local authorities as leisure and sports providers and the 'crucial role played by local authority sports development officers in widening sporting opportunities' (p. 9). However, although the document endorsed the sports continuum and made generalized policy commitments in each area, the central thrust of the document was to reinforce the twin emphasis of the out-going government. In many ways the Labour Party sought to outshine the Conservatives in its commitment to competition and elite achievement. Beginning with ritual statements lamenting the decline in time allocated to PE, the decline of extracurricular school sport and the importance of the curriculum containing a range of sports activities, the document ended by asserting that 'Labour supports the teaching of competitive team games. We believe they should continue to be the mainstay of school sports provision' (p. 8). The party also emphasized its commitment to the establishment of a British academy of sport to meet the needs of elite, especially Olympic, athletes.

In the period since the 1997 election the Labour government has begun to make good its policy commitments in the area of sport, but it is notable that there has been far greater progress in addressing the issues associated with the elite end of the sports continuum. Most notably, the elite sports institute has been announced, albeit after a period of confusion over the precise nature of the body, and elite athletes are now provided with funding through the World Class Performance plan. At the mass participation end of the continuum progress in policy implementation, and even policy formulation, has been far less rapid, indicating a lower degree of certainty about precise direction and purpose. Perhaps the most notable development regarding mass participation concerned the work of the Football Taskforce, which is far more concerned with the good govern-ance of an element of the entertainment industry than with participation in soccer as a sport.

The uncertainty of policy direction was not lessened in the first major debate in the House of Commons. Despite the Secretary of State for Culture, Media and Sport's declaration that 'The concept of sport for all will govern and permeate all that the government do for sport, as well as being the badge for specific policies by which we shall seek to widen opportunity and access' (House of Commons, 1997) there has generally been little of substance to support the claim, beyond the endorsing of a number of existing schemes, such as the TOPs programmes and the Sportsmark and Sportsmark Gold award. However, the recently published Sport England lottery strategy may mark the reinvigoration of a Sport for All policy. Under the new arrangements, at least two-thirds of available funding will be invested in community facilities or activities of which 50 percent will be directed towards areas of greatest need (Sport England, 1999).

In the absence of a clear lead from government, the sports councils were left in the position of having to anticipate government policy. Sport England in particular had had a fairly unhappy relationship with previous governments. A succession of weak minis-ters during the 1980s, rarely in post for a substantial period, and an antipathetic prime minister produced a general policy climate of neglect interrupted by occasional clumsy and often ill-thought-out interventions. The election of John Major as party leader brought to the prime minister's office someone who was passionate about sport, if in a sentimental and highly romantic way. However, while the Conservative Party has little difficulty empathizing with sport as an element of national heritage, it has always found it difficult to acknowledge sport, especially soccer, as an element of popular culture. As a result the sports councils have experienced a prolonged period of organizational uncertainty, and a degree of policy drift. However, in the mid-1990s the GB Sports Council attempted to anticipate the policy thrust of the in-coming Labour government.

Under the slogan of 'More people, more places, more medals', the English Sports Council, as the GB Sports Council was retitled, introduced four linked programmes of which Active Schools was one (the others being Active Communities, Active Sports and World Class).[1] Although not explicitly linked to the sports development continuum, which appears to have fallen out of favour, it was clear that the four new programmes corresponded to stages in the continuum. The aim of the Active Schools programme was to 'provide every young person at school in England with high quality, sustainable opportunities to learn foundation skills and participate in the sport or physical activity of their choice'. The content of the programme was a series of initiatives, many of which already featured in the National Junior Sport Programme, and included well established schemes such as Sportsmark, TOP Play and TOP Sport as well as new schemes such as the creation of School Sport Co-ordinators. The DfEE Specialist Sports Colleges initiative was mentioned in passing, with the comment that the 50 or so colleges expected to be in place by 2003 would provide a network of regional centres of excellence.

Conceptualizing school sport policy: Talent identification, physical education and sports development

It was suggested earlier that public services are affected by a series of layered policy influences, ranging from the broad ideological orientation of the government through policies targeted specifically at general service sectors to policies targeted at specific aspects of individual services (see figure 1). The present government's broad ideological orientation is best reflected in the promotion of social inclusion and best value. The clear expectation that these ideological priorities should permeate all public services is mediated by the existence of policy targeted at specific policy sectors. Thus the pursuit of Olympic medals may take priority over (or at least moderate) the goal of social inclusion to the extent that a disproportionate representation of social classes A and B will be accepted if it brings Olympic or other international sporting success.[2] At the more specific level of individual sports, the goal of international prestige might result in a particular sports event, such as the 2000 World Flyfishing Championships, being refused support by the UK Sports Council, despite the fact that the UK boasts a number of current world champions in the sport. The UK Sports Council stated that 'The event is not regarded as a priority on the grounds of public profile, performance development and economic impact' (House of Commons, 1999: 22). Similarly, Tony Banks's preference for providing lottery funding for chess, despite the fact that the Sports Council had declared it ineligible,

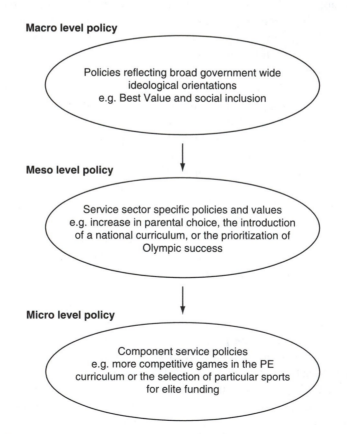

Figure 1 Policy layers.

is a further example of a highly specific policy intervention. In addition to the layered quality of policymaking there is also a sectoral dimension where policies primarily focused on one service area spill over into others or where a number of different policy areas share a common focus on a particular constituency or client group.

School sport is a good illustration of the latter form of sectoral complexity (see figure 2). The boundaries of school sport policy are especially difficult to determine. It might be possible to define the policy boundaries in relation to the pattern of activities and resource allocation within the physical boundaries of the school, the temporal divisions of the school day, term or academic year, the pattern of legal and moral duties imposed upon or assumed by teachers, or the network of intra and inter-professional relationships of which PE teachers are a part. Yet it is clear that the process of policy-making for school sport is not confined by any of these boundaries, thus making it difficult for core interests, such as PE teachers, to assert policy leadership. As was made clear above, the debates around school sport and especially the NCPE show just how permeable the organizational and professional boundaries have been. Most significantly the elite development policy community has greatly strengthened its voice and influence over government policy in the last 10 years even if this has been the result of a fortuitous coincidence of circumstance (sympathetic ministers and prime ministers and an upsurge

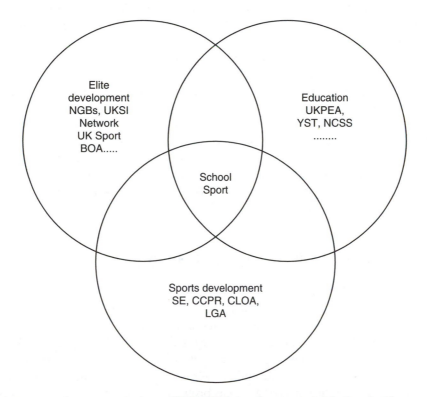

Key: NGB (national governing bodies); UKSI (UK Sports Institute); BOA (British Olympic Associ-ation); UKPEA (UK Physical Education Association); YST (Youth Sport Trust); NCSS (National Council for Schools' Sports); SE (Sport England); CCPR (Central Council of Physical Recreation); CLOA (Chief Leisure Officers Association); LGA (Local Government Association)

Figure 2 Major policy sectors at micro (service component) level.

in popular sentiment) rather than the product of successful lobbying.[3] In contrast to the context for policy debate provided by education interests, those within the elite development community perceive young people as the seed-corn for future elite squads. They are to be identified, trained, protected from poaching by other sports and gradually assimilated into the competitive culture and routine of the particular sport. For many of the national governing bodies of sport, school is as much a threat as an ally.

An additional external interest is that of the local authorities, whose dominant perception of young people is as citizens and customers. For local authorities young people are increasingly the primary focus for sports development strategies whether the motive be health, achieving social inclusion or simply an increase in participation. Finally, there is the commercial sector which views young people as an important source of profit through the provision of water-based facilities, adventure centres (such as Quasar) and ski-centres.

The constituent interests or client groups in less clearly defined or less effectively defended policy areas, of which school sport is a prime example, are correspondingly more vulnerable to imposition of policy over which they have exercised little influence. Frequently their role is reactive rather than proactive, buffeted by policy currents rather than steering a course through them. Sports-related policies which take as their focus either schools or young people enter a policy arena which is already congested and targeted by different policy communities that have very different and often conflicting policy objectives. On the one hand the school, and young people as a group, are sharply contested policy targets, being of interest to a series of policy communities, most significantly the advocates of sports development (as defined by the sports continuum and reflected in the priorities of the series of linked programmes of which Active Schools is one), the advocates of PE (as reflected in the TOPs schemes and the work of UKPEA) and finally the promoters of elite development and talent identification policy (as reflected in the strategic plans of most sports governing bodies and the UK Sports Institute network). On the other hand the variety of sports policy priorities focused on schools and young people have to operate within a broader policy context of educational reform (literacy hours and an increased emphasis on vocationalism) and general government priorities associated with social inclusion. It is within this sectorally competitive and multilayered environment that new policy initiatives have to operate.

Policy at the margin: The school sport policy process

Much of the case-study literature on policy analysis focuses on major political issues which can be defined reasonably clearly and where policy actors and interests are readily identifiable. A preference for exploring such issues is understandable, but this focus often obscures the extent to which policy in one area is the result of the spillover from other adjacent or overlapping policy areas. Indeed, it is valuable to conceptualize issues as being located on a spectrum. At one end of the spectrum are those major issues that may be accurately portrayed as possessing a clear profile in relation to the public and policymakers, are the focus of attention of specialized and influential interest groups and agencies, where policy debate takes place within clearly designated arenas or forums, and where the history and antecedents of a policy can be identified. At the other end of the spectrum are those issues which generally possess a far less distinct profile (both in the eyes of those operating within the policy area and those in its immediate environment), are rarely the subject of specialist or influential interest groups or agencies, which lack a stable forum for policy debate, and where policy direction and momentum is frequently determined (incidentally and inadvertently) by the deliberations and decisions of contiguous policy agendas.

The preference for examining major issues is not simply that they tend to be more amenable to empirical investigation, but also that they tend to be the more politically salient issues within society. However, such a focus fails to reflect the large number of public policy issues where images of proaction, power, self-confident advocacy and policy*making* are seriously misleading. Just as 'policy space' is occupied by an institutional infrastructure, so too is it occupied by existing policy and competing claims for influence over future issues (Hogwood and Gunn, 1984; Wildavsky, 1980). As was pointed out by the OECD, 'Public policy has become a crowded field, with complex, overlapping and even competing programmes addressing increasingly closely specified or targeted categories of client' (1987: 26). One important implication of the increasingly densely packed policy space is that 'as the population of policies grows relative to the size of the policy space, individual policies necessarily become more interdependent. The consequences produced by one policy are increasingly likely to interfere with the working of other policies' (Majone, 1989: 159). I have suggested elsewhere that some issues are better conceptualized as travelling in the slipstream of more politically salient issues and that 'debates on sport and PE were frequently merged with, and occasionally submerged by, other issues, including curriculum reform, parental control of schools, budget cuts and teacher (and subject) status' (Houlihan, 1997: 264).

In densely packed policy spaces such as school sport it is likely that, in contrast to the image of robust proactive policymaking resulting in a clarity of policy direction, the actual position will be one of intense policy competition, where a number of interests are forced to adopt a reactive stance in relation to policy initiatives and where policy is determined by the balance of exogenous interests. Dery provides a useful distinction between policymaking and policytaking. Policymaking 'implicitly presumes control over key variables that shape policy in a given area', whereas policytaking:

> . . . denotes the pursuit of a given set of policy objectives, which is primarily or entirely shaped by the pursuit of other objectives . . . the resulting policy . . . [is] . . . the by-product of policies that are made and implemented to pursue objectives other than those of the policy in question.
>
> (Dery, 1999: 165–6)

Thus rather than conceptualizing new policy initiatives, such as SSCs, Sportsmark and the NCPE, as self-contained programmes where there is clarity of both ends and means, it is more realistic to acknowledge the likelihood of reinterpretation and renegotiation of policy during implementation. Each policy sector with an interest in school sport has the capacity to initiate policy and to influence the interpretation of the policy initiatives of others. Thus a description of school sport policy is going to be closer to a simple statement of the sum of existing policies rather than a comprehensive policy reflecting both purpose and coordinated action. New policy is introduced into a context where differing and often competing interests will view young people variously as future or potential workers and citizens, health sector clients, elite athletes, consumers of leisure services, etc. Moreover, new policies are introduced into a policy space which may not only be crowded but which already possesses a pattern of power relations established as a result of the implementation of earlier policy. For example, the process of designing the NCPE not only resulted in the production of a particular policy but also produced a revised set of relationships between the various interests concerned with young people and school sport and which would constitute the environment for future policy initiatives. SSCs are one such example of a policy initiative that entered a crowded policy space.

Sports development, talent identification or education: The case of specialist sports colleges

The SSC was a policy initiative that was of undeniable significance to many sports related interests, but was also an initiative introduced into a policy space that was already crowded if not congested. The significance of the education system in general and secondary schools in particular for competitive and elite sport is easily demonstrated. In a recent English Sports Council survey of the elite squads of 12 sports, it was found that the average age at which athletes began to take part in competitive (performance level) sport was 11 years and 6 months, with the lowest entry age being for swimming (8 years 6 months) and the highest being for women's rugby union (17 years 4 months).[3] For many athletes involvement at elite level also began during the school years. In women's judo, athletes moved to the elite level at an average age of 15 years 11 months and athletes in five other sports (men's judo, swimming, netball, women's hockey and sailing) also moved to the elite level before the age of 18 years.

Not only is the secondary school period when athletes begin to compete and move into or towards the elite ranks, the school is frequently where athletes are introduced to their sport. Introduction to a particular sport was most commonly by a parent, but schools were the second most commonly cited source (29 percent) and were especially significant for black athletes, 53 percent of whom were introduced to their sport at school. The school was the first entry route for over one-third of elite athletes in athletics, hockey, netball and rowing, and for between a fifth and one-third for cricket, rugby league and swimming. For athletes at the participation level the school was almost twice as likely to be the main facility used (40 percent as opposed to 22 percent who cited a facility linked to a sports club), at the performance level the college or school facility was mentioned by 18 percent as the main facility used (in comparison to 26 percent who mentioned a facility linked to a club) and even at the excellence level 11 percent still cited the school or college as the main facility used.

Of elite athletes 39 percent were still in full-time education and one in five had attended or were currently attending private schools, where it was suggested that the level of coaching support was better than that available in the state sector. Interestingly, 39 percent of elite athletes who had attended private schools considered that the support that they had received from their school had contributed to their progress towards the elite level, while only 20 percent of those from state schools felt able to make the same claim. One rugby union coach reported that 'the emphasis put on sport in most of the independent schools means that many really do develop into very good players by the time they reach 18'. In hockey, where 49 percent of the elite squad attended private schools, one player remarked that 'the facilities and coaching are much better than in the state schools – it's taken seriously', while in rowing, where 58 percent and 46 percent of the men's and women's squads respectively attended private schools, a coach commented that 'rowing, at the younger ages, is effectively run by the independent schools' (all three quotes are from English Sports Council, 1998: 27). According to the ESC report, 'The contribution of schools to progress in sport is particularly notable in men's rugby union and hockey and to a lesser extent in women's hockey and men's cricket' (1998: 29). A final indicator of the centrality of schools to the development of elite talent was the fact that, of the 12 sports surveyed, seven national governing bodies (NGBs) mentioned schools as part of their hierarchy of competition squads.

The first SSCs were designated in 1996 and there were, in mid-1999, a total of 34 SSCs in operation, out of a total of over 330 specialist schools of all types.[4] Nearly all SSCs are comprehensive schools and although they are allowed to accept up to 10 percent of pupils on the basis of aptitude in sport there is a clear warning not to misuse this flexibility to select on the basis of more general academic ability. In order to qualify for SSC status, schools should normally already be of Sportsmark standard and those seeking redesignation after their first three years of operation 'will be expected to show that they are of Sportsmark Gold standard' (DfEE, 1998a: 14). Additional requirements include access to a wide range of local sports facilities, an established track record of attainment in sports and that they be in a sound financial position. The application process requires the preparation of a three-year development plan, the capacity to raise £100,000 from sponsors and the willingness to develop a continuing relationship with the sponsors. The development plan should include a set of performance indicators which cover both curriculum developments and output measures of students' attainment in the specialist subjects. Although the performance measures should be tailored to the needs of the particular school, all applications must include targets relating to indicators which measure the increased provision of specialist subjects, the increased take up of such courses and improved attainment in specialist subjects. Not surprisingly, the DfEE is insistent that 'if applicant schools are not already providing a full GCSE or its equivalent in physical education and sport for key stage 4 pupils their Development Plans must include clear targets for doing so' (1998b: 14).

One of the key tangible benefits of SSC status is additional financial support from government. Government will not only match the £100,000 sponsorship with a £100,000 capital grant but will also pay an additional £100 per pupil for at least the first two years following designation. The additional funding may be used to appoint new staff, to purchase in-service training or to acquire specialist equipment. SSCs can also use their sponsorship and capital grant as matching funding to support a bid to the National Lottery. However, the basis of the lottery bid has to be an expansion of community access to school facilities.

In many respects the specialist sports colleges appear to sit uneasily at the intersection of at least three distinct sectoral interests, the first of which is that of the national governing bodies of sport and especially their concerns with talent identification and development. The DfEE stipulates that SSCs should commit themselves to:

> . . . becoming local and regional centres of achievement in their specialist subjects . . . [and] . . . provide enhanced opportunities to fulfil the potential of talented performers and . . . help prepare many young people for careers in professional sport, coaching, teaching and the leisure industry.
>
> (DfEE, 1998a: 1 and 14)

According to the Youth Sport Trust, 'it is hoped that the Sports Colleges will in time serve as feeder institutions to the government's proposed British Academy of Sport' (1996: 3). Elsewhere in the DfEE document, the vocational orientation of the schools and the importance of cultivating a close relationship with business and industry is stressed. To encourage and support the links with external bodies, it is a requirement of the SSC status that schools raise £100,000 in sponsorship from business, charitable or other private sector organizations and it is noted that 'the sponsor can also contribute to the school's curriculum, adding a sharper and more vocational edge to courses' (DfEE, 1998a: 19).

The second sectoral interest is that of educationalists and their concern, inter alia, with the needs of all children, the promotion of lifelong learning and the establishment of beacon schools. To this end the DfEE refers to the objective of 'raising standards of achievement for all their students, of all abilities; developing and sharing their good practice; and being active partners in a learning society' (DfEE, 1998a: 1). Moreover, SSCs should seek to increase diversity of secondary school education, 'enhance self-esteem, interpersonal and problem-solving skills' (1998a: 3), sharpen the identity of the school and 'develop within the school characteristics which signal their changed identity and which are reflected in the school's aims' (1998b: 1). The final sectoral interest is that broader coalition concerned with a set of sports/community development interests. Here the specialist school is seen as a resource for 'their local families of schools and their communities' (DfEE, 1998a: 1). Moreover, SSCs 'will form a focal point for revitalising education in areas of socio-economic disadvantage, particularly in the new Education Action Zones' (1998a: 1).

It is within this context of varied, if not competing, interests that the current 34 SSCs operate. Most are only in the early stage of their development, but the first group designated in 1996 are now approaching the deadline for redesignation. The central question for investigation is how SSCs have interpreted or managed the conflicting expectations set by the DfEE and the extent to which they perceive themselves fulfilling a talent identification and development role on behalf of national governing bodies.

At first sight the majority seem to have been selected on the basis of economic and social indicators rather than current excellence in sport. Although Table 1 relies on district level rather than catchment area data it suggests that there is a close relationship between indicators of socioeconomic deprivation and the location of SSCs. The table has been constructed using Gordon and Forest's analysis (1995) of indicators of poverty and wealth based on data from the 1991 census. The schools were grouped by quintile using 16 economic and social indicators. In general, the districts in which SSCs are located tend to be those which possess the following dominant characteristics: high youth unemployment, high 'poor child' ranking, high number of traditional families (married couples with children), high percentage of 'young families' and a high number of young people not in education. Of the 34 SSCs all but six could be described as being located in areas of relative deprivation.

The impression of relative deprivation is reinforced when educational performance is considered. According to the DfEE guidelines, 'it is unlikely that a school whose examinations results are on a declining trend will be successful in its application unless there are good reasons to explain the trend' (DfEE, 1998b: 5–6). At the level of local or regional comparisons, the majority of the SSCs are average in terms of academic performance, although 12 are relatively poor, but when the comparison is with national data the SSCs appear to be average or better in terms of 'one or more GCSEs' and 'five or more

Table 1 Distribution of schools by indicators of economic and social deprivation

	A	B	C	D	E
Economic variable					
'the poor' (A = the poorest quintile)	9	10	6	3	6
'the wealthy' (A = the least wealthy)	12	3	7	8	4
inequality (A = most unequal)	11	8	6	6	3
mean earnings (A = lowest)	11	6	4	8	5
multi-earners (A = lowest)	11	9	3	7	4
the free (hidden) economy (A = highest %)	11	6	4	9	4
manufacturing/service jobs (A = most manufacturing)	7	6	6	8	7
class (A = highest % working)	9	8	5	4	8
Social variable					
youth unemployment (A = highest)	12	11	5	1	5
young people not in education (A = most)	10	10	5	5	4
young people on YTS (A = most)	7	8	9	5	2
young families (A = highest number)	13	3	8	2	4
'poor child' (A = highest)	14	10	3	4	3
'working parents' (A = highest)	10	8	4	8	4
traditional families (married couple with children) (A = highest)	11	9	3	9	2
health care (A = highest)	9	7	6	9	3
highly educated (A = lowest number)	9	5	4	10	6

Source: Gordon and Forest, 1995

GCSEs'. More importantly, in the year in which they were designated or in the year prior to designation, most SSCs showed an improved academic performance. In the short time since designation the picture has been variable, with there being no clear sign of continued improvement, indeed of the seven schools that offer GCE A level courses, performance in five had declined. However, a longer time period would be required before reliable conclusions about the impact of SSC status on academic performance could be drawn.

For the present study, four SSCs were examined in order to assess where the new sports/educational initiative lay in relation to the series of interests and to assess the potential contribution that the colleges might make to the achievement of elite success.[5] The experience of each school will be discussed in terms of the impact of designation on its pattern of external relationships with the wider community, the impact on the organization of the school and finally the effect on sport within the school.

School W is a large upper school (14–16 age range) and was one of the first SSCs to be designated. It is located in a catchment area that has a stable population and does not score especially high in terms of indicators of socioeconomic deprivation. Its sponsorship was received from a charitable foundation. One of the most notable consequences of designation has been the extent to which the school has sought to develop partnerships with external organizations in three particular areas: with local government, with schools in its 'family' and with NGBs. Although the relationship with the local authority is getting stronger, the lack of a proactive authority was mentioned as a barrier to expanding the broader sports development role of the school in relation to community needs. However, the recent appointment of sports development staff by the authority has substantially eased the relationship. The school clearly accepts its community development role, has sought to expand opportunities for community use of school sports facilities and has also sought to target members of particular underparticipating ethnic groups.

Links with local schools have also been strengthened, best illustrated by access being encouraged both to coaching courses offered at the SSC and to the school's facilities. Relations with the local university are reasonably good and it is hoped within the school that the recent announcement that the university was to be a site of one of the UK Sports Institute regional centres will lead to further opportunities to build closer links, in terms of access to university facilities for school squads.

Designation as a SSC has also prompted the school to formalize its links with the national governing bodies responsible for its priority sports, which include football, basketball, netball, tennis and badminton. To date the school has developed links with local clubs in each of its priority sports. As well as providing exit routes for talented students through links with external clubs, the school has also agreed that one of the 'less resource rich' NGBs, table tennis, would be able to use the school as a base, thus effectively bringing a club into the school and adding a sixth potential priority sport to the range available to students.

The overall impact on the quality and quantity of sport available to students has been significant. There has been a clear increase in the range of sports coaching and competition, which will enable a greater proportion of the students to be involved at performance level. There has also been an increase in the opportunities for involvement at the participation level through the increased allocation of time to physical education within the curriculum (to over three hours per week) and through opportunities for more extensive community use, some of which includes students using facilities outside school hours. As far as the impact within the school is concerned, there were signs initially of a sense of grievance from other departments at the flow of additional resources to PE. As a result there is some pressure for an internal reallocation of resources to placate the dissident staff.

School X was designated a SSC in 1998 and is a comprehensive school in a catchment area that scores highly in terms of both a concentration of the poor and the wealthy. High youth unemployment, a large number of young people not in education, a high number of children in poor families are combined with a high number of multi-income families. Sponsorship was raised from a series of local charities. The school already has a high level of community use and sports club use of its facilities and the SSC grant has been used to extend the range of facilities available. The development plan of the school was similar to that of school W insofar as it reflected the same trio of objectives, namely, to increase the opportunities for sports participation in the curriculum, to develop the position of the school as a resource for 'feeder' schools and to enhance links with local clubs and thereby create pathways into a hierarchy of competition. However, according to the head of PE, the primary benefit of SSC status will be to enhance community links rather than foster curriculum innovation.

As with school W there has been considerable progress in developing new partnerships, for example, with the NCF who have recently granted the school Premier Coaching Centre status, and enhancing existing links, for example, with the Youth Sports Trust and with the local authority sports development section. The most significant impact to date has been within the school where there has, according to the head of PE, been a noticeable rise in the level of self-esteem among students. It was also suggested that the school now had a higher and sharper profile within the local community. Interestingly, designation has apparently had a very positive impact on the recruitment of PE staff, many of whom see working in a SSC as a strong foundation for their career. More surprisingly, a number of existing non-PE staff have also shown an interest in registering for sports-related courses (coaching and TOPS delivery, for example) due to a belief that sports-related qualifications will enhance their career prospects.

School Y is a large 11–18 years comprehensive also in its first year of designation. Although the catchment area is socially mixed, the immediate location is within a socially deprived ward. The school had some problems raising the necessary sponsorship, which eventually came from a variety of sources, mainly from charities but also a small amount from the private sector.

As with the two previous schools School Y's development plan emphasizes the contribution that it will be able to make, as a SSC, to increasing participation, improving community access and developing sporting talent. At first sight the capacity of the school to provide enhanced opportunities for sports participation is limited, due to the restricted range of current facilities. Even with utilization of grant income and sponsorship the facilities will still be modest by comparison to the other three schools. However, the school's commitment to supporting talent development is indicated by the decision to appoint a coordinator with responsibility for performance level sports development and the securing of 'pathways' for talented students through closer links with local clubs.

The head of PE argued that the requirement to produce a development plan was a valuable planning exercise in itself, irrespective of the outcome of the bid. It helped the school to identify its priority sports and has fostered closer links with local clubs. The development plan was constructed around the five sports (soccer, athletics, swimming, cricket and rugby) that were traditionally strong in the area, plus netball and gymnastics. Although the head of PE noted that a much more coherent approach to sports development was emerging, he also stressed that the school had taken the decision to retain its traditional pattern of fixtures rather than seek out fixtures against schools with higher standards of competition. In many ways this decision highlights the tension between what the head referred to as the PE/education perspective and the sports perspective promoted by Sport England. He referred to 'some pressure' from Sport England to adopt particular programmes, but stressed that the school had maintained its discretion to select only those programmes that complemented its development plan.

There is a strong emphasis on developing the school's facilities for greater community use and increasing the participation of girls and women has been identified as the immediate priority. Since the initiation of the bid for SSC status, the school has cultivated successfully a network of partnerships with local clubs and their NGBs, feeder schools and other local schools, and the county sports development unit. Although the network of partnerships is in its infancy, the management of the network is a clearly identifiable additional call on the time of the school's head of PE. However, the recent appointment by the county council of four additional sports development officers with a brief to work with schools has gone some way to alleviate that burden.

As regards the impact of designation on the school, the impact has been similar to that of school X insofar as the school reported a noticeable increase in the quality of applicants for PE posts and no discernible negative impact on applications for posts in other subject areas. Although there was some initial resistance to SSC designation from among staff and from some governors, the attitude seems to be becoming more positive.

Finally, school Z, designated a SSC in 1997, is a large 11–16 comprehensive in an area of a major conurbation characterized by many indicators of deprivation such as high youth unemployment: 41 percent of students are eligible for free school meals. The school is also within an Education Action Zone, a Health Action Zone and a Single Regeneration Budget area. Existing sports facilities are poor: there is no sports hall nor any all-weather pitches.

Given the socioeconomic profile of the school, it is not surprising that there is a tension between the PE staff and the senior managers about the relative priority of participation and performance. For the senior management the priority is 'participation over performance', which contrasts with the view of the PE staff and also that of the Youth Sports Trust who see the school as well placed to develop sporting potential. While on the one hand there is a clear vision for the school in which it establishes itself as part of a hierarchy of opportunity linked to local clubs and their NGBs for talented athletes to progress in a series of sports, there is on the other hand a body of opinion within the school that would prefer to give priority to a community and participation focused strategy.

Progress to date would suggest that the community/participation orientation is dominant. Although five new PE staff have been appointed, priority has been given to social objectives including strengthening the links between improved health, fitness, attendance and academic performance within the school and developing a closer relationship with other schools in the area.

Discussion and conclusion

The template for the introduction of specialist sports colleges was set by the earlier introduction of specialist technology, arts and language colleges. In some respects the objectives and disciplinary focus of SSCs fits comfortably within that broader specialist schools template. In particular the requirements to develop partnerships with their 'family' of local schools and to seek to become a local/regional centre of excellence build upon the traditional inter-school networking that is evident in much extra-curricular sport. Similarly, the expectation that specialist schools should seek to work closely with their local communities complements and reinforces the policy of community use of sports facilities that many schools have already developed.

However, there are also a number of respects in which the attempt to fit SSCs into the existing specialist schools framework looks awkward. First, the objective of vocationalism is far less obvious when applied to SSCs than technology colleges, for example, as it is unclear whether the definition of vocation relates to elite performance or employment in a service or management capacity in the leisure industry. Second, the expectation of sponsor involvement in curriculum matters also fits less comfortably within the specialist sports college model. In the four schools examined, none had received significant sponsorship from industry-related organizations. Furthermore it is unlikely that any NGB would have sufficient funds to fulfil the sponsorship role and if leisure industry sponsors had been found it is likely that their concerns would have been with the management of, rather than the practice of, sports and leisure. However, it should be borne in mind that there is a long-established tradition of NGB involvement in curriculum development in sport and PE. Swimming, athletics and basketball have all promoted their own award schemes and coaching/lesson plans for use in PE classes. More recently the work of the Youth Sport Trust in promoting the TOPs schemes is further evidence of the weakness of curriculum control exercised by the PE profession. A third example of the tension between the broader specialist school model and sport and PE is the requirement, on the one hand, to demonstrate a commitment to the practice of sport by, for example, achieving Sportsmark and Sportsmark Gold standard and, on the other, to pursue an academic vision of sport through the introduction of GCSE courses in sport.

If the design of the SSC policy shows the imprint of, and conflicts with, previous policymaking for specialist schools, implementation has, so far at least, been far less tense. The four schools examined showed little evidence of strain and were generally coping well with the requirement to balance the range of objectives relating to community regeneration, the enhancement of educational standards and the development of sporting achievement. In particular, all four schools were enthusiastic about the benefits of net-working and partnership building, with new or strengthened links between the school and clubs, local authority sports development officers and local schools being seen as of especial value. Such a positive view is not surprising at this relatively early stage of policy implementation and, while all those interviewed were positive about their early experience, there were some signs of emerging problems and conflicts. In particular, the incipient tensions between 'participation' and 'performance', identified explicitly by one school, between the practice of sport and the pursuit of academic achievement in sports-related GCSEs, and between elite sporting success and vocational training for the leisure industry, are all unresolved and potentially divisive.

The resolution of these tensions is not necessarily a substantial problem as it is unlikely that either the DfEE or any of the other external interested bodies possess the capacity to monitor implementation in detail, thus leaving the schools with a substantial degree of discretion to determine implementation at the 'street level'. However, if it is the case that the capacity to shape the precise character of each SSC will rest with interests internal to the school, it is worth noting that there is little evidence that PE teachers will play a determin-ing role. While there is some evidence from the case studies that the designation of a school as a SSC raises the profile of PE specialists within the school, there is less evidence that it is this group of teachers who are shaping the precise character of sport in the school. Rather the discretion of PE teachers appears limited with decisions about priority sports, curric-ulum content and design influenced by external organizations. Thus the selection of priority sports is likely to reinforce Sport England's national priority sports or those of the local authority. Similarly, curriculum content and design is likely to reflect the requirements of Sportsmark standards or the content of TOPs programmes rather than a process of profes-sional innovation internal to the school. Of particular importance are the signs that it will be the school that will determine the balance between the trio of sectoral interests identi-fied above. It is clear from the case studies that many schools will perceive SSC status as primarily a public relations opportunity through which they will be better able to market the school within the local area. This preference is likely to be reinforced if, as seems probable, many SSCs fall within future Education Action Zones.

In summary, specialist sports colleges will be significant in contributing to the achievement of objectives associated with the regeneration of individual schools and the wider regeneration and reinvigoration of local communities, but will be far less significant in affecting elite development policy. The modest contribution of SSCs to elite sports development is partly due to the submersion of sports objectives beneath broader and more influential educational and social agendas, an effect that is likely to be reinforced if the government is successful in pursuing its demand for 'joined up' thinking in policymaking and implementation. However, the limited potential contribution of SSCs is also the result of the decision by an increasing number of NGBs to pursue their own talent identification and elite development strategy at school level. The SSCs were never intended to fulfil the role of the hierarchy of sports schools developed in the former Soviet Union. Thus while NGBs appear willing to support their local clubs who wish to develop closer links with SSCs, they do not see the initiative as making more than a marginal contribution to their development strategies. Indeed the trend among NGBs is for them to withdraw talented children from the school sports system. Some sports, soccer for example, have begun to develop a network of academies focused on their major clubs, while others have sought to relocate the members of their national squad to their national training centre, with the junior members attending a local school but receiving all their sports training at the centre. Both gymnastics and table tennis operate this system, with the latter encouraging its senior and junior squad members to relocate to the national training centre at Holme Pierrepoint with the juniors attending the local Daynford School. A further indication of the growing gap between school sport and the development strategy of the NGBs is the increasing reluctance of some NGBs, most notably soccer and rugby union, to allow their junior elite squad members to play competitive matches for their school. The Football Association, for example, recently announced that it would take over the running of under-15 competition and there is some evidence of pressure being applied to talented children as young as eight years not to participate in inter-school soccer matches.

Despite the potential for specialist sports colleges to reinvigorate the concept of the sports development continuum, it is highly unlikely that the establishment of 50 or so SSCs will reverse the tend towards a greater degree of fragmentation in the organization and conceptualization of sport. Over the last 20 years or so, not only has there been a steady separation of elite sport, especially within the commercially successful sports, from mass performance sport, but that separation has been occurring at an increasingly early stage in the career of athletes. Promising athletes in an increasing range of sports and the NGBs to which they are affiliated are now less likely to see school sport as a significant opportunity to develop, refine and practise skills. The pressure from Sport England that NGBs develop more sophisticated talent identification procedures will make the system of school sport a safety net rather than an essential part of the elite sports development process. Successful talent identification techniques will enable NGBs to concentrate their coaching resources on a smaller group of potential elite athletes. While the network of specialist sports colleges will fulfil a number of valuable educational and social functions, it is likely that they, and indeed much of the system of school sport, will become increasingly marginal to the system of talent identification and development.

Notes

1   When the GB Sports Council was abolished it was replaced by two new organizations, the English Sports Council and the UK Sports Council. The sports councils for Northern Ireland, Scotland and Wales were largely unaffected by these changes.

2   A recent English Sports Council report showed that, out of 12 sports surveyed, the elite squad of all but one were disproportionately drawn from social classes A and B (ESC, 1998).

3   The concept of a policy community is best defined as a relatively stable group of policy actors, often including both the relevant government department or agency and a profession, which regularly interact to resolve routine issues within the policy area. Probably the key defining characteristic of a policy community is the existence of a set of core values that will inform the ways in which problems are identified and defined and in which solutions are selected (see Houlihan, 1997, for a fuller discussion).

4   The 12 sports included in the survey were athletics, cricket, cycling, gymnastics, hockey, judo, netball, rowing, rugby league, rugby union, sailing and swimming.

5   The other types of specialist school are technology, languages and arts. At the end of 1998 there were 227 technology colleges, 58 language colleges and 19 arts colleges.

6   The schools were examined through a combination of interviews, reviews of development plans and the analysis of national statistical data relating to school performance.

References

Department for Education and Employment (1998a) *Specialist Schools: Education Partnerships for the Twenty-First Century*. London: DfEE.

Department for Education and Employment (1998b) *Sports Colleges: A Guide for Schools*. London: DfEE.

Department of Education and Science (1991) *Physical Education in the National Curriculum*. London: DES.

Department of Education and Science (1995) *Physical Education in the National Curriculum*. London: DES.

Department of National Heritage (1995) *Sport: Raising the Game*. London: DNH.

Department of National Heritage (1996) *Sport: Raising the Game: The First Year Report*. London: DNH.

Dery, D. (1999) 'Policy by the Way: When Policy is Incidental to Making Other Policies', *Journal of Public Policy* 18(2): 163–76.

English Sports Council (1998) *Development of Sporting Talent, 1997: Report of Findings*. London: ESC.

Evans, J. (1992) 'A Short Paper about People, Power and Educational Reform', in A. G. Sparkes (ed.) *Research in PE and Sport: Exploring Alternative Visions*. London: Falmer Press.

Evans, J. and Penney, D. (1995) 'Physical Education, Restoration and the Politics of Sport', *Curriculum Studies* 3(2): 183–96.

Gordon, D. and Forrest, R. (1995) *People and Places 2: Social and Economic Distinctions in England*. Bristol: SAUS, University of Bristol.

Hogwood, B.G. and Gunn, L.A. (1984) *Policy Analysis for the Real World*. London: Oxford University Press.

Houlihan, B. (1997) *Sport, Policy and Politics: A Comparative Analysis*. London: Routledge.

House of Commons (1997) *Hansard Report*, Adjournment debate, 27 June, columns 1059–1129. London: HMSO.

House of Commons (1999) *Fourth Report of House of Commons Select Committee for Culture, Media and Sport*, 'Staging International Sports Events', vol. 2, 'Evidence'. London: The Stationery Office.

Majone, G. (1989) *Evidence, Argument and Persuasion in the Policy Process*, New Haven, CT: Yale University Press.

Organisation for Economic Co-operation and Development (1987) *Administration as Service: The Public as Client*. Paris: OECD.

Penney, D. and Evans, J. (1999) *Politics, Policy and Practice in Physical Education*. London: E&FN Spon.

Sport England (1999) *Investing for the Future: Sport England Lottery Fund Strategy, 1999–2009*. London: Sport England.

Talbot, M. (1995) 'Physical Education and the National Curriculum: Some Political Issues', *Leisure Studies Association Newsletter* 41: 20–30.

The Labour Party (1996) *Labour's Sporting Nation*. London: The Labour Party.

Wildavsky, A. (1980) *The Art and Craft of Policy Analysis*. London: Macmillan.

Youth Sports Trust (1996) *Sports Colleges: You can be Part of our Sporting Future*. London: YST.

PART 3

Physical education and health

INTRODUCTION

BY FAR THE most common justifications for the inclusion of physical education in the school timetable in recent years have been framed within discussions of health. This represents the discourse of physical education as compulsory physical activity, and physical activity as a necessary component of well-being, both during childhood and in later life. As the most visible societal institution for the promotion of physical activity among children, this is perhaps not surprising. But many researchers have sought to problematise the discussions, both by examining the empirical foundations of such goals and by questioning the appropriateness of them in the first place.

Harris usefully clarifies some of the terms of recent debates about the role of physical education in the public health agenda. She goes on to review some of the expectations made on behalf of physical education, and suggests some of the ways in which the subject might indeed contribute to the promotion of healthy, active lifestyles. Wright, Macdonald and Groom report on evidence from interviews with young people about the place and importance of physical activities in their lives. What emerges is a complex picture of the different spaces for being active, and the kinds of personal identities that are constructed in relation to physical activity. Their paper is a good example of disappointingly rare research exploring young people's voices, rather than presuming passive consumption of health and well-being messages from adults.

FURTHER READING

Bailey, R.P., McNamee, M. and Bloodworth, A. (2007) Gender, sport and well-being, in
I. Wellard (ed.), *Rethinking Gender and Youth Sport*. London: Routledge.

Gard, M. and Wright, J. (2005) *The Obesity Epidemic: Science, Morality and Ideology*.
London: Routledge.

McKenzie, T. (2007) The preparation of physical educators: a public health perspective. *Quest*,
59, 346–57.

Wallhead, T. and Buckworth, J. (2004) The role of physical education in the promotion of youth
physical activity. *Quest*, **56**(3).

Jo Harris

HEALTH-RELATED EXERCISE AND PHYSICAL EDUCATION

Introduction

THIS CHAPTER WILL REVIEW health-related exercise developments within the school curriculum and identify enduring themes and contemporary issues. At the outset, it is important to clarify the meaning of 'health-related exercise' (HRE) both within and beyond the school setting. In broad terms, HRE is physical activity associated with health enhancement and disease prevention (Health Education Authority, 1998, p. 2). More specifically within an educational context, HRE refers to:

> the teaching of knowledge, understanding, physical competence and behav-
> ioural skills, and the creation of positive attitudes and confidence associated
> with current and lifelong participation in physical activity.
>
> (Harris, 2000, p. 2)

Of course, the close relationship between physical education (PE) and health is hardly a new concept. PE was driven by this objective at the beginning of the twentieth century (Sleap, 1990) although other objectives such as skill development and self-discovery later came to the fore, at the expense of a concern for health. Nevertheless, health once again became an important objective of the PE curriculum in the early 1980s, and since then there has been a well documented and active interest by many physical educators in promoting health-related physical activity in schools in the UK (Almond, 1989; Williams, 1988).

There is little doubt that the school is an appropriate setting for the promotion of health-related learning and behaviours, not least because there is the potential for sustained exposure to an environment which can positively influence the behaviour of virtually all children for about 40–45 per cent of their waking time (Fox & Harris, 2003). It is known that school-based intervention studies have positively influenced young people's health, fitness and physical activity levels, as well as their knowledge, understanding and attitudes towards physical activity (Almond & Harris, 1998; Cale & Harris, 1998; Harris & Cale, 1997; Stone et al., 1998).

Physical education is considered to play a key role in the promotion of health and activity in young people (Armstrong, 2002; Cale, 2000a; Cardon & De Bourdeaudhuij, 2002; McKenzie, 2001; Shephard & Trudeau, 2000). Indeed, McKenzie (2001) views PE as the most suitable vehicle for the promotion of active, healthy lifestyles among young people whilst Green (2002, p. 95) refers to the 'taken-for-granted role of PE in health promotion'. Both Green (2002) and Harris and Penney (2000) have noted how government policy in recent years has identified PE and school sport as important in educating and providing opportunities for young people to become independently active for life (Department of Health (DoH), 1999; Department for Culture, Media and Sport (DCMS), 2001). This is exemplified by the following significant statement:

> The government believes that two hours of physical activity a week, including the National Curriculum for Physical Education and extra-curricular activities, should be an aspiration for all schools.
> (Department for Education and Employment & Qualifications and Curriculum Authority (DfEE & QCA), 1999b, p. 17)

A further example is the government's PE, School Sport and Club Links Strategy which is designed to transform PE and school sport, and carries with it an investment of £459 million over three years (Department for Education and Skills (DfES) & DCMS, 2003). These examples are clearly encouraging in terms of the future provision and quality of health-related learning and activity opportunities for young people.

Although it is accepted that PE represents much less than two per cent of a young person's waking time and therefore cannot in itself satisfy the physical activity needs of young people or address activity shortfalls (Fox & Harris, 2003), there is a strong belief that PE can affect leisure time physical activity through positive activity experiences and exercise education (Vilhjalmsson & Thorlindsson, 1998). It is therefore essential to carefully consider how PE can most effectively contribute to promoting active lifestyles and providing opportunities for all pupils to experience appropriate levels of physical activity (Cardon & De Bourdeaudhuij, 2002). In this respect, the content and delivery of the health-related learning in the PE programme within the context of the National Curriculum, as well as the provision of activity opportunities within and beyond the school, are critical.

Review of HRE within the National Curriculum

The first National Curriculum for Physical Education (NCPE) formally addressed health issues (Department of Education and Science and the Welsh Office (DES & WO), 1992) and identified HRE as a component of the cross-curricular theme of health education (National Curriculum Council, 1990). However, its position and mode of expression in the curriculum were unclear (Harris, 1997a). At the time, some feared that the area would be marginalised or overlooked as it was not afforded the status of a separate programme of study but was instead identified as a theme to be delivered through the activity areas (Cale, 1996; Fox, 1992; Penney & Evans, 1997). These fears were all but confirmed by Harris' (1997a) research which revealed the teaching of HRE in PE in secondary schools to be characterised by much confusion and considerable variation in practice, resulting in limited systematic expression of health. In short, HRE meant different things to different people, and it was evident that health promotion as a key goal of physical education was neither universally accepted nor well understood (Harris, 1995).

In these early days of the NCPE, the absence of an activity area for HRE was interpreted by some to indicate that HRE should be delivered solely through the activity areas (Oxley, 1994). However, Harris and Almond (1994) pointed out that the National Curriculum should permit scope for professional judgment regarding how best to deliver content within the context of different schools. Consequently, a number of different approaches to the delivery of HRE have emerged (i.e. permeation/integration; focused/discrete; combined/multi-method), each with specific strengths and limitations (see Table 1). Cale (2000a) has revealed a combination of approaches to be the most common (i.e. focused units of work in PE, integration through the activity areas, and delivery within other areas of the curriculum) which suggests that HRE is now being addressed in a more explicit and structured manner in schools. However, the critical issue remains the effectiveness of the learning more than the particular approach adopted (Harris, 2000).

Subsequent revisions of the NCPE (Department for Education and the Welsh Office (DfE & WO), 1995; Department for Education and Employment & Qualifications and Curriculum Authority (DfEE & QCA), 1999a) have arguably provided a stronger positioning of health-related issues which implies a more explicit prompt for the area to be addressed in curriculum planning and delivery (Fox & Harris, 2003). For example, 'knowledge and understanding of fitness and health' is now one of four aspects of the NCPE through which learning is developed at each key stage. A more explicit approach to HRE is also evident in Curriculum Wales 2000 which provides a detailed programme of study for HRE at each key stage, and incorporates 'exercise activities' (non-competitive forms of exercise, such as step aerobics, jogging, weight-training, cycling, circuit-training and skipping) as one of four areas of experience at Key Stage 4 (Welsh Assembly, 1999). Similarly, in England, in line with a call from Government for the broadening of provision within the PE curriculum to enhance lifelong learning and healthy lifestyles, the compulsory requirement to study games activities for 14 to 16 year olds was removed (DfEE & QCA, 1999a).

Not before time, these developments have opened the doors to more flexible, creative and relevant provision of PE for older pupils. Indeed, Green (2002) acknowledges the trend identified by Roberts (1996b) of schools beginning to respond to the changing lifestyles and activity interests of young people and supplementing the traditional PE diet with a broader range of activities. This was acknowledged in an Office for Standards in Education (Ofsted) summary of secondary school physical education reports (2000–02) which made a positive reference to the provision of more indoor alternative activities such as aerobics, fitness, badminton, volleyball and access to accredited courses, as well as changes to gender groupings and kit requirements (Ofsted, 2002, p. 2).

Table 1 Approaches to HRE within the National Curriculum

Approach	Strengths	Limitations
Permeation/integration An integrated approach in which HRE is taught through the PE activity areas (i.e. through athletics, dance, games, gymnastics, swimming, and outdoor and adventurous activities).	HRE knowledge, understanding and skills can be seen as part of and integral to all PE experiences. Children learn that all physical activities can contribute towards good health and can become part of an active lifestyle.	HRE knowledge, understanding and skills may become 'lost' or marginalised amongst other information relating to skills and performance; there may be an overload of information for pupils; much liaison is required to ensure that all pupils receive similar information from different teachers; the approach may be somewhat ad hoc and piecemeal.
Focused/discrete An approach involving teaching HRE through specific focused lessons or units of work either within a PE or health education programme. During PE lessons, the main focus is the learning concept rather than the activity itself.	A specific focus can help to ensure that HRE does not become lost or take second place to other information; there is less likelihood of HRE being regarded as an assumed 'by-product' of PE lessons; HRE is perceived as important through having its own time slot and identity; the value and status of the associated knowledge, understanding and skills is raised.	HRE may be seen in isolation and not closely linked to the PE activity areas; the HRE knowledge, understanding and skills may be delivered over a period of time with long gaps in between which is problematic in terms of cohesion and progression (e.g. one short block of work per year); the knowledge base may be delivered in such a way as to reduce lesson activity levels (e.g. through 'sitting down' lessons with too much talk).
Combined/multi-method Any combination of permeation, focused and topic based approaches is possible.	A combination of approaches can build on the strengths of different approaches and, at the same time, minimise their individual limitations; it can ensure that value is placed on HRE and that the area of work is closely linked to all PE experiences and other health behaviours.	Combined approaches may be more time consuming initially to plan, structure, implement and co-ordinate within the curriculum.

Supporting the teaching of HRE in schools

In response to ongoing concerns over the expression of health in PE, and teachers' relatively limited knowledge and understanding of the area (Almond & Harris, 1997; Cale, 1996; Fox, 1992; Harris, 1997a), a HRE working group comprising representatives from schools, higher education, the advisory service, and key sport, health and PE organisations was established in 1997 to produce good practice guidelines on HRE for primary and secondary teachers. The published resource provided an interpretation of the health and fitness requirements of the NCPE in England and Wales expressed in the form of learning outcomes, and incorporated links with aspects of related subjects such as Personal, Social and Health Education (PSHE) and Science (Harris, 2000). The learning outcomes are placed in four categories (safety issues; exercise effects; health benefits; activity promotion) to clarify the range of coverage and the progression of learning within and across the key stages. Table 2 presents examples of these learning outcomes for Key Stage 2 (7–11 years) and Key Stage 3 (11–14 years) pupils.

Reassuringly, a study conducted with 500 secondary schools revealed that the HRE guidance had a positive impact on many PE teachers' knowledge, attitudes and confidence, and on their planning, content, evaluation, organisation and delivery of HRE (Cale *et al.*, 2002). However, it was less successful in changing teachers' philosophies and teaching methods. Clearly, resources by themselves are limited in their ability to bring about 'real' change. To quote Sparkes (1994), what results represents 'innovation without change' in that new ideas are taken on board but only at a superficial level, or they are integrated within already well-established philosophies and paradigms.

During and since the development of the guidelines on HRE, resources have been produced to reflect and exemplify the consensus guidance. Examples include *Fit for TOPs*

Table 2 Examples of HRE learning outcomes for pupils 7–14 years

Category of HRE learning outcomes	HRE learning outcomes at Key Stage 2 (7–11 yrs)	HRE learning outcomes at Key Stage 3 (11–14 yrs)
Safety issues	Know the purpose of a warm up and cool down and recognise and describe parts of a warm up and cool down.	Understand the value of preparing for and recovering from activity and the possible consequences of not doing so, and be able to explain the purpose of and plan and perform each component of a warm up and cool down.
Exercise effects	Experience and understand the short-term effects of exercise (e.g. increase in rate and depth of breathing to provide more oxygen to the working muscles; increase in the heart rate to pump more oxygen to the working muscles; varied feelings and moods).	Understand and monitor a range of short-term effects of exercise on body systems (e.g. cardiovascular system – changes in breathing and heart rate, temperature, appearance, feelings, recovery rate, ability to pace oneself and remain within a target zone).
Health benefits	Know that exercise strengthens bones and muscles (including the heart) and keeps joints flexible.	Know and understand a range of long-term benefits of exercise on physical health (e.g. reduced risk of heart disease, osteoporosis, obesity, back pain).
Activity promotion	Be aware of their current levels of activity; know when, where and how they can be active in school and outside.	Be able to access information about a range of activity opportunities at school, home and in the local community, and know ways of incorporating activity into their lifestyles.

for primary teachers of PE (Youth Sport Trust *et al.*, 1998) and *Fit for Life* for secondary PE teachers (Youth Sport Trust, 2000). Furthermore, the YMCA has produced a series of 'health and fitness' resources to support the teaching of HRE at Key Stage 4 in secondary schools (Elbourn & YMCA Fitness Industry Training, 1998; Elbourn *et al.*, 1998a, 1998b, 1998c; YMCA, 2000, 2002). These resources provide primary and secondary teachers of PE with a much needed and long awaited support structure to assist them in designing and delivering effective HRE programmes in schools. Nevertheless, it cannot be assumed that teachers are aware of these resources and are able to access them, or that the resources and/or associated training will necessarily be successful in bringing about changes in philosophical approaches underpinning the content and delivery of current programmes.

Parallel health-related developments of significance

A parallel health-related development of much significance was the launch of the Health Education Authority's (HEA) (now the Health Development Agency (HDA)) policy framework for the promotion of health-enhancing physical activity for young people 'Young and Active?' (HEA, 1998). This framework identifies the Education Sector as one of the key organisations which has a role to play in promoting health-enhancing physical activity and includes a series of key recommendations for schools, including:

- Schools should recognise the importance of health-related exercise within the National Curriculum and ensure that the requirements are fully implemented in practice.
- Health-related exercise should take the form of an effectively planned, delivered and evaluated programme of study.
- Professional development, training and support services, including FE and HE colleges, should provide appropriate training (including initial teacher and in-service training) that includes the teaching of health-related exercise.

(Health Education Authority, 1998, p. 8)

In addition, the policy framework contained the following recommendations about how active young people (i.e. all people aged 5–18 years) should be (see Table 3).

Table 3 Physical activity recommendations for young people (5–18 years)

Primary recommendations

- All young people should participate in physical activity of at least moderate intensity *for one hour per day*.
- Young people who currently do little activity should participate in physical activity of at least moderate intensity for *at least half an hour per day*.

Secondary recommendation

- *At least twice a week,* some of these activities should help to enhance and maintain muscular strength and flexibility and bone health.

(Health Education Authority, 1998, p. 3)

These recommendations are significant and timely. They represent a concise response to the key question 'How active should young people be?' and they provide a consistent message for young people and for adults involved in caring for and working with young people. Disappointingly though, many PE teachers appear to be unaware of these recommendations as they rarely integrated within schemes and units of work. Teachers of PE and PSHE (Personal, Social and Health Education) clearly need to be informed of these exercise recommendations and their implications for practice, as well as their limitations (Cale & Harris, 1993, 1996).

Further significant developments within the education sector include the expansion of the Specialist Sports Colleges infrastructure and the School Sport Co-ordinator partnerships, and QCA's PE and school sport (PESS) investigation into the impact of high quality PESS on young people and schools. Each of these developments has now become an element of the government's PESSCL Strategy (DfES & DCMS, 2003) and the potential influence of these programmes collectively is promising in terms of sharing good practice amongst schools in relation to innovative HRE programmes and increasing the number of young people who benefit from being active.

Limited and limiting interpretations of HRE within PE

With respect to enduring themes, research has highlighted examples of narrow interpretations of HRE that often equate the area with some or all of the following: vigorous activity such as cross country running; fitness testing; safety and hygiene issues such as warming up and cooling down, lifting and carrying equipment, and taking showers (Harris, 1997b). Such narrow interpretations are worrying as they have the potential to lead to undesirable practices such as: forced fitness regimes; directed activity with minimal learning; inactive PE lessons involving excessive theory or teacher talk; dull, uninspiring drills; or an over-emphasis on issues relating to safety and hygiene (Harris, 2000). Furthermore, the knowledge base associated with HRE is not always fully acknowledged and consequently activity-based units (e.g. blocks of work on aerobics, cross country, circuit-training) may be delivered with minimal learning and limited pupil involvement. Evidence also suggests that physiological issues, such as the physical effects of exercise and fitness testing, tend to dominate HRE courses in schools (Harris, 1995, 2000). Indeed, one could argue that many health-related programmes designed, taught and evaluated in schools are oriented more towards 'fitness for sports performance' than 'fitness for healthy lifestyles'.

This is perhaps not surprising given that Green (2002) and Penney and Evans (1999) have observed that both teachers and Government appear to view sport, and particularly team games, as the primary focus of PE and the primary vehicle for the promotion of on-going involvement in health-promoting, active lifestyles. Certainly, despite successive revisions of the NCPE, and notwithstanding the loosening of the constraint towards games at Key Stage 4 within Curriculum 2000 (DfE & WO, 1995; DfEE & QCA, 1999a), competitive sports and team games with an emphasis on performance still dominate the curriculum (Fairclough et al., 2002; Penney & Evans, 1999; Penney & Harris, 1997). In addition, changes in the terminology towards 'fitness' and 'training', evident within the new requirements (DfEE & QCA, 1999b), further highlight the continued and powerful influence of the focus on sport and performance in PE (Hargreaves, 2000; Penney & Evans, 1997, 1999).

This is despite the fact that the relevance and appeal of competitive sports and team games to many youngsters in the UK has been questioned (Fairclough *et al.*, 2002; Fox & Harris, 2003; Green, 2002; Roberts, 1996a) and concern has been expressed that the continued emphasis and privileging of 'traditional PE' may be turning many young people off physical activity participation (Fox & Harris, 2003; Harris & Cale, 1998; Roberts, 1996a). Green (2002, p. 97) suggests that much official and semi-official government rhetoric concerning school sport and PE fails to acknowledge participatory trends in young people towards lifestyle activities and non-competitive, more recreational sporting forms, and away from competitive performance-oriented sports. He also suggests that this results in a substantial disservice to physical educators committed to promoting lifelong participation by proposing an inappropriate response. Similarly in the US, Douthitt and Harvey (1995) consider that the PE profession has 'been trying to force youth into a PE curriculum mold which does not include sensitivity to individual psycho-emotional needs and preferences' (p. 34).

Indeed, this is partly exemplified by the prevalence of fitness testing in schools (American College of Sports Medicine, 2000; Harris, 1995; Cale & Harris, 2002) despite controversy about its value and place in the curriculum (American College of Sports Medicine, 1988; Armstrong, 1987, 1989; Cale & Harris, 2002; Harris, 2000; Harris & Cale, 1997; Physical Education Association, 1988; Rowland, 1995). A key concern with testing in PE lessons is, of course, the amount of time spent on it without necessarily positively influencing either pupils' activity levels or their attitudes towards physical activity (Cale & Harris, 2002; Harris & Cale, 1997). Indeed, Rowland (1995) considers programmes of field testing children to be anti-ethical to the goal of promoting physical activity in children, demeaning, embarrassing and uncomfortable to those children about which there is most concern, and believes that they serve to reinforce the notion that exercise is competitive and unpleasant. To assist PE teachers in critically evaluating the place of fitness testing in the curriculum, the HRE guidance material (Harris, 2000) identifies the main issues associated with testing and recommends that any testing should: promote activity; develop understanding; be safe and developmentally-appropriate; be individualised; and be enjoyable. The national PESS programmes both in England and in Wales include plans to develop resources on monitoring pupils' health, activity and fitness through developmentally-appropriate procedures linked to criterion referenced standards. These resources should do much to help teachers overcome the limitations of commonly practised fitness testing, and maximise the benefits that pupils can obtain from being involved in informative, individualised and positive monitoring of health, activity and fitness.

Linked to this are concerns over the low level of moderate to vigorous physical activity during PE lessons (Babiarz *et al.*, 1998; Curtner-Smith *et al.*, 1995; Fairclough, 2003; Stratton, 1996, 1997) although it is known that intervention studies have successfully shown that PE can be made more active for pupils, and teachers can make a difference to the amount of activity achieved during lessons (e.g. McKenzie *et al.*, 1996, 1997; Sallis *et al.*, 1997; Simons-Morton *et al.*, 1991). However, Harris and Cale (1998) caution how increasing activity levels within PE prompts a range of potential responses including those that may be misguided and undesirable. For example, some teachers may respond by forcing pupils into 'hard, uncomfortable' exercise, such as arduous cross-country running or fitness testing, at the expense of developing understanding and physical and behavioural skills and enhancing attitudes through positive activity experiences. Likewise, Fairclough (2003) also suggests that by employing interventions and activities aimed to increase pupils' heart rates (e.g. Baquet *et al.*, 2002), other teaching objectives within PE may be compromised. Cale and Harris (1998) believe that such examples serve only to simplify the complex nature of health enhancement and overlook the multi-faceted nature of exercise education and activity promotion.

Strengths and areas for development

An analysis of health-related learning within the PE curriculum reveals that the PE profession addresses some areas of learning well but there are areas which are less well addressed. These areas of strength and areas for development are summarised in Table 4 and are supported by the findings of a critical document analysis of Ofsted inspection reports (1997–2000) of 33 secondary schools in the Midlands, focusing on the 'knowledge and understanding of health and fitness' aspect of the PE curriculum, which revealed variations in both the quantity and quality of the comments and inconsistencies in the range of the statements. In summary, the comments were generally narrow in scope, focusing predominantly on 'safety issues' and 'exercise effects', with minimal attention to 'health benefits' and 'activity promotion'. Typical comments included:

> Pupils know the value of a warm-up activity, such as stretching, to prevent muscles tearing. Some pupils know and locate the muscles in their legs to be stretched, for example, the hamstrings and calf muscles.
>
> (11–14 school; November 1999)

> Fitness knowledge is appropriate, with all students able to conduct their own warm-up and stretching exercises.
>
> (14–18 years; January 1997)

> Most know the names of large muscle groups and can locate them accurately.
>
> (11–18 school; September 2000)

The analysis indicated a limited expression of 'health and fitness' within Ofsted inspection findings, reflecting a narrow interpretation by teachers and/or inspectors of health-related issues within physical education. For example, while some health-related topics and

Table 4 Strengths and limitations of health-related learning in PE

HRE: Strengths What does the PE profession do well?	HRE: Areas for development What does the PE profession do less well?

Addressing safety issues
  e.g. providing a safe learning
  environment; warming up
	Understanding health benefits
	  e.g. explaining the links with energy balance and
	  healthy weight management; emphasising the
	  social and psychological benefits of activity

Explaining exercise effects
  e.g. describing the effects of exercise
  on heart rate and breathing rate
	Promoting activity
	  e.g. routinely informing all pupils where they can
	  do more activity; informing pupils about how
	  active they should be; monitoring involvement in
	  activity

concepts were adequately addressed in inspection reports, if not overdone (e.g. warming up), others were neglected (e.g. cool down; health benefits of exercise; exercise recommendations for young people; the role of physical activity in healthy weight management; personal exercise programming). The comments within Ofsted inspection reports reflected the physiological domination of health-related PE programmes and their limited attention to social and psychological issues. For example, it was rare to find statements relating to pupils' learning about the health benefits of physical activity, how active they should be, and about opportunities to be active in the community. This is disappointing, especially given the increasing profile of 'health' in the public domain and concerns about sedentary lifestyles, low activity levels and increasing obesity levels. It would seem that by focusing on such a narrow range of health-related issues, Ofsted inspectors are doing little to encourage teachers to move the area forward. This clearly has implications for the future expression of health within physical education.

Disparate agendas for PE and public health

It remains evident that physical education has not yet fully acknowledged, addressed or embraced its potential contribution to public health. Furthermore, PE does not appear to be perceived by significant others as a major contributor to public health. For example, 'physical activity' is frequently absent from National Healthy School Standard (NHSS) developments in schools and PE teachers are usually not centrally involved in such initiatives. The NHSS is one component, along with the 'Wired for Health' website and 'Strategies for Safer Travel to School', within the 'Healthy Schools Programme' (DoH, 1999) which is a key part of the Government's drive to improve standards of health and education and to tackle health inequalities. The 'Healthy Schools Programme' aims:

> to make children, teachers, parents and communities more aware of the opportunities that exist in schools for improving health.
>
> (www.wiredforhealth.gov.uk)

Principally, a 'Healthy School' seeks to achieve healthy lifestyles for the entire school population by developing supportive environments conducive to the promotion of health. 'Wired for Health' is a series of websites which provides health information for a range of audiences, including pupils. The following websites:

> www.welltown.gov.uk (for 5–7 year olds)
> www.galaxy-h.gov.uk (for 7–11 year olds)
> www.lifebytes.gov.uk (for 11–14 year olds)
> www.mindbodysoul.gov.uk (for 14–16 year olds)

include messages about physical activity such as:

> A lot of young people are active for a total of 30 minutes a day. This may sound okay but actually it's not enough to keep your heart and body in good health. You should be aiming for at least one hour per day of moderate

intensity physical activity. Activities like brisk walking, cycling and dancing are all excellent examples of moderate activity. Moderate activity makes you feel warmer and slightly out of breath.

(www.lifebytes.gov.uk)

Once you know how much activity you should be aiming for and the types of activity you can do, how are you going to find time and opportunity to do it all? After all, you're at school all day, and have homework and other commitments in the evening. Sound familiar? Check out the excuse busters.

(www.mindbodysoul.gov.uk)

In addition to the above developments, a number of recommendations to guide physical activity promotion within schools have been published in recent years (Harris, 2000; HEA, 1998; National Audit Office, 2001; National Heart Forum, 2002; Centers for Disease Control & Prevention, 1997, 2000; Morrow et al., 1999). These recommendations identify the need for a whole-school approach to physical activity promotion, targeted physical activity interventions, and further research into school-based approaches to promote physical activity. However, it is disappointing that the PE profession is not more centrally involved in whole-school initiatives to promote health, and that many PE teachers remain unaware of the NHSS programme and its component parts as these could be used to reinforce and develop learning in and through PE and school sport. It is also a pity that comparatively limited attention appears to have been paid to the formally recognised concept of an 'Active School' which maximises opportunities for children and adults associated with the school to be active by exploring all opportunities and avenues to promote physical activity (Cale, 1997; Fox, 1996; Fox & Harris, 2003; National Heart Forum, 2002).

With respect to the notion of disparate and possibly conflicting agendas for PE and public health, it would appear that PE tends to reflect and reinforce concepts relating to fitness, sport and performance, whilst health education is more closely associated with health, activity and participation. Consequently, PE teachers tend to be viewed outside the PE profession as sports teachers or coaches, more interested in performance and excellence, than participation and health. Furthermore, and perhaps surprisingly, rather than promoting equity and inclusion, Harris and Penney (2000) found that health-related PE programmes often reflected, expressed and reinforced gendered practices.

Clearly, in order to promote health and activity, the way in which health-related information and activity experiences are presented is critical. PE should involve enjoyable, positive and meaningful exercise experiences, a practical knowledge base and caring teaching strategies (Fox & Harris, 2003). There should also be a clear emphasis on the beneficial short- and long-term effects of exercise, improved functional capacity, weight management, and psychological well-being associated with exercise participation. Fox (1993) reminds us that merely highlighting the risks of inactivity is ineffective as teenagers believe that they are either immortal or immune from such risks. Young people need to be helped to shift from dependence on the teacher to independence, by acquiring the necessary understanding, competence and confidence to be active independently (Harris, 2000). This needs to be taught, not relied upon to be 'caught'. Smith and Biddle (1995) and Harris (1995, 2000) have pointed out that limited attention is paid in schools to socio-cultural, environmental and behavioural factors influencing children's participation in activity. Yet, it is commonly accepted within health promotion that knowledge alone is insufficient to bring about behaviour change (Douthitt & Harvey, 1995) and that simply encouraging children to be more active takes no account of key socio-cultural, environmental and behavioural factors (Smith & Biddle, 1995).

Teachers who do address these factors within the curriculum typically adopt educational or behavioural approaches to the promotion of physical activity, presenting arguments for and relevant information about physical activity, and possibly involving pupils in learning self-management and regulatory skills such as goal setting, programme planning, self-reinforcement and monitoring or time management to encourage participation in physical activity. These skills are considered critical to lifestyle change and activity independence (Corbin, 2002). However, this approach has major limitations as it holds the individual totally responsible for their activity behaviour, and fails to acknowledge other factors in the social environment which influence physical activity. In recognition of such limitations, there has been growing interest and support for environmental or ecological approaches to physical activity promotion in recent years (Sallis et al., 1998). For example, many aspects of the school can either promote or inhibit the adoption of an active lifestyle, and understanding gained through the 'formal' curriculum can be reinforced and supported or completely undermined by the 'hidden' curriculum. Thus, to increase the likelihood of physical activity promotion being successful and leading to sustainable behaviour change, it needs to be more than just a curriculum activity focusing on individual behaviour change strategies (Cale, 1997).

So why is the PE profession not more successful in terms of fostering lifelong activity in young people (Douthitt & Harvey, 1995; Harris & Cale, 1998)? Possible contributory reasons include limited PE time and low subject status. The time allocated to PE in the UK has consistently been among the lowest in Europe (Cale, 2000a; Harris, 1994; Fairclough & Stratton, 1997; Morrow et al., 1999) and the health and PE curricula are generally seen as competing with core subjects (e.g. maths/numeracy; English/literacy) and in times of high academic priority, viewed as more expendable (Fox & Harris, 2003). Hardman and Marshall's (2000) international study of school PE similarly highlighted issues of restricted or decreasing curriculum time for PE, low subject status and negative attitudes of significant others such as headteachers and parents towards PE. More encouragingly, however, the Government's recent 'PE, School Sport and Club Links Strategy' aims to increase the percentage of school children in England who spend a minimum of two hours each week in high quality PE and school sport within and beyond the curriculum from 25 per cent in 2002, to 75 per cent by 2006 (DfES & DCMS, 2003). Yet, even with increased PE time, there can be no guarantee that health and activity promotion will become central features of the curriculum. Fox and Harris (2003) highlight how, despite a stronger positioning of health issues within the curriculum in recent years, the effect may be minimal because many teachers continue to prefer to focus on competitive sport in the curriculum.

Additional reasons for the somewhat narrow approach to HRE may be PE teachers' limited health-related (Cale et al., 2002; Harris, 1995; Office for Standards in Education (Ofsted), 1996) and physical activity promotion knowledge (Cale, 2000b; Cardon & De Bourdeaudhuij, 2002), despite a positive attitude towards physical activity and fitness goals (Cale, 2000b; Kulinna & Silverman, 2000). Cardon and De Bourdeaudhuij (2002), for example, revealed that many PE teachers were not sufficiently aware of the health-promoting role of PE, and Cale (2000b) reported that a number had limited understanding of the concept and how it could be approached in their school. Of course, the above may partly be explained by the fact that few physical educators have been adequately trained to address health-based work and physical activity promotion (Cardon & De Bourdeaudhuij, 2002; Harris, 1997a; Fox & Harris, 2003; Pate *et al.*, 1999). Corbin (2002, p. 132) reminds us that children 'do activity in different ways than adults' and Fox and Harris (2003) describe young children's activity as 'kiss-and-chase' or 'kick-and-run' type bursts of energy and teenagers' activity as more adult-like, involving sustained moderate activity through sports or exercise. It is also evident that young people's activity occurs in a range of settings, in a variety of modes, and at particular times of the day including: active transport to and from school; informal play during school breaks and lunchtimes; informal play after school; formal sports, PE and exercise training; active jobs (Fox & Harris, 2003, p. 187).

Finally, in terms of constraining factors within the PE profession, Fox and Harris (2003) suggest that the structure and funding of initial teacher training courses often serve to limit prospective teachers' experience of health-related exercise within the curriculum. Furthermore, the approach many PE teachers adopt to the area is inevitably influenced by the highly scientised sports science courses (which typically focus on a bio-physical conception of the body and of health) from which PE teachers normally graduate (Colquhoun, 1994).

Contemporary issues

A contemporary issue associated with HRE relates to future plans for the 14–19 curriculum. The Government's Green Paper '14–19: extending opportunities, raising standards' (DfES, 2002) states that there should be an emphasis on physical fitness, health and well-being during the 14–19 stage in PE. The Qualifications and Curriculum Authority (QCA)'s website (www.qca.org.uk/pess) contains guidance on key objectives and signs of success. The key objectives are considered to be:

- To improve pupils' knowledge and understanding of fitness, health and well-being.
- To improve pupils' commitment to healthy, active lifestyles.
- To increase pupils' involvement in healthy, active lifestyles.

Examples of 'signs of success' which teachers might expect to see from their pupils when there has been an increased emphasis on fitness, health and well-being at Key Stage 4 are presented in Table 5.

In response to concerns that the traditional PE programme is neither relevant nor appealing to a large proportion of older pupils, and taking into account psycho-social factors influencing young people's participation, Fox and Harris (2003) identified a number of features which, in their view, might produce more successful programmes. These features included: introducing more individual sports and fitness activities; providing activities acceptable to a range of adolescent subcultures; teaching the 'why' of physical activity in the curriculum; helping youngsters to develop self-management skills that equip them to make lifestyle changes; and, creating a learning environment in which young people can develop a sense of responsibility.

Relatively little systematic research has been undertaken on the effectiveness of

Table 5 Example of 'Signs of Success': fitness, health and well-being at Key Stage 4 (adapted from www.qca.org.uk)

Key objectives of increasing the emphasis on fitness, health and well-being	Examples of signs of success You will see pupils who:
Knowledge and understanding of fitness, health and well-being	• can explain more clearly what H, F & WB are and the relationships between them; • can explain more clearly the value and benefits of being involved in healthy, active lifestyles; • have a greater understanding of the barriers to getting involved and how to overcome them.
Commitment to healthy, active lifestyles	• are clearer about the targets and goals they want to set for themselves; • show an increased interest in joining or setting up clubs and groups; • show a greater interest in how they travel to school and consider alternatives to car travel.
Involvement in healthy, active lifestyles	• have clearer exercise and health plans that they monitor and evaluate regularly; • take part in organised physical activity groups and clubs more often and effectively; • choose healthy travelling and eating options more often.

school-based approaches to the promotion of young people's physical activity, particularly in the UK and mainland Europe (Almond & Harris, 1998; Fox & Harris, 2003; Harris & Cale, 1997). This lack of rigorous evaluation has meant that there has been little opportunity to build an evidence base regarding programme effectiveness and successful mechanisms for change. Consequently, no definitive guidelines are available for schools outlining which types of programmes and strategies are most successful and why. Fox and Harris (2003) suggest that until such an evidence base is constructed, the design and delivery of effective health and activity promotion initiatives are likely to remain uninformed, undirected and sporadic.

It is good news then that current government initiatives (DfES & DCMS, 2003) incorporate monitoring and evaluation procedures to determine their impact on pupils and to ascertain whether high quality PE and school sport has influences which extend beyond the gymnasium and playing field. Hence the government agenda on learning through PE and school sport (as opposed to learning in PE and school sport) and the focus on whole-school improvement and the promotion of healthy, active lifestyles.

Conclusion

Despite an improving picture of health in PE and a number of key health-related developments, it is suggested that many schools are still not maximising their potential in terms of promoting lifelong healthy, active lifestyles. Indeed, some responses by schools to combat sedentary lifestyles and rising obesity figures may be misguided and could consequently dissuade some young people from being more active. However, the Government's major investment of funding through the PESSCL Strategy provides much hope in England of enhanced status and increased time for PE and school sport, additional professional development to help teachers effectively address health-related learning and promote health and activity, and increased confidence to transform PE and school sport programmes so that they are central to whole school improvement, and relevant and appealing to children. It would seem that the time for PE has finally arrived and it us up to the PE profession to make the most of it for the sake of its own future and for the benefit of today's young people.

References

Almond, L. (1989). New wine in a new bottle – implications for a national physical education curriculum. *The British Journal of Physical Education*, 20(3): 123–125.

Almond, L., & Harris, J. (1997). Does health related exercise deserve a hammering or help? *British Journal of Physical Education*, 28(2): 25–27.

Almond, L., & Harris, J. (1998). Interventions to promote health-related physical education. In: Biddle, S., Sallis, J., & Cavill, N. (eds) *Young and Active? Young People and Health-enhancing Physical Activity – Evidence and Implications*, London: Health Education Authority, pp. 133–149.

American College of Sports Medicine (ACSM) (1988). Opinion statement on physical fitness in children and youth. *Medicine and Science in Sport and Exercise*, 20(4): 422–423.

American College of Sports Medicine (ACSM) (2000). Exercise testing and prescription for children, the elderly, and pregnant women. In: *ACSM's Guidelines for Exercise Testing and Prescription*. Sixth edition, Lippincott Williams & Wilkins, pp. 217–234.

Armstrong, N. (1987). A critique of fitness testing. In: Biddle, S. (ed.) *Foundations of Health Related Fitness in Physical Education*, London: Ling Publishing House, pp. 19–27.

Armstrong, N. (1989). Is fitness testing either valid or useful? *British Journal of Physical Education*, 20: 66–67.

Armstrong, N. (2002). Promoting physical activity and health in youth: The active school and physical education. Abstract presented at the 12th Commonwealth International Sport Conference, 19–23 July, 2002. Manchester, Association of Commonwealth Universities, pp. 37–40.

Babiarz, B., Curtner-Smith, M.D., & Lacon, S.A. (1998). Influence of national curriculum physical education on the teaching of health-related exercise: A case study in an urban setting. *Journal of Sport Pedagogy*, 4: 1–18.

Baquet, G., Berthoin, S., & Van Praagh, E. (2002). Are intensified physical education sessions able to elicit heart rate at a sufficient level to promote aerobic fitness in adolescents? *Research Quarterly for Exercise and Sport*, 73(3): 282–288.

Cale, L. (1996). Health related exercise in schools – PE has much to be proud of! *British Journal of Physical Education*, 27(4): 8–13.

Cale, L. (1997). Physical activity promotion in schools – beyond the curriculum. *Pedagogy in Practice*, 3(1): 56–68.

Cale, L. (2000a). Physical activity promotion in secondary schools. *European Physical Education Review*, 6(1): 71–90.

Cale, L. (2000b). Physical activity promotion in schools – PE teachers' views. *European Journal of Physical Education*, 5(2): 158–167.

Cale, L., & Harris, J. (1993). Exercise recommendations for children and young people. *Physical Education Review*, 16(2): 89–98.

Cale, L., & Harris, J. (1996). Understanding and evaluating the value of exercise guidelines for children. In: Lidor, R., Eldar, E. & Harari, I. *Proceedings of the 1995 AIESEP World Congress, Wingate, Israel*, pp. 161–166.

Cale, L., & Harris, J. (1998). The benefits of health-related physical education and recommendations for implementation. *Bulletin of Physical Education*, 34(1): 27–41.

Cale, L., & Harris, J. (2002). National fitness testing for children – issues, concerns and alternatives. *British Journal of Teaching Physical Education*, 33(1): 32–34.

Cale, L., Harris, J., & Leggett, G. (2002). Making a difference? Lessons learned from a health-related exercise resource. *Bulletin of Physical Education*, 38(3): 145–160.

Cardon, G., & De Bourdeaudhuij, I. (2002). Physical education and physical activity in elementary schools in Flanders. *European Journal of Physical Education*, 7(1): 5–18.

Centers for Disease Control & Prevention (1997). Guidelines for school and community programs to promote lifelong physical activity among young people. *Morbidity and Mortality Weekly Report*, 46: RR-6.

Centers for Disease Control & Prevention (2000). Promoting Better Health for Young People through Physical Activity and Sports. A report to the President from the Secretary of Health and Human Services and the Secretary of Education.

Colquhoun, D. (1994). Health and physical education in the health promoting school. *Healthy Lifestyles Journal*, 41(1): 32.

Corbin, C.B. (2002). Physical activity for everyone: what every physical educator should know about promoting lifelong physical activity. *Journal of Teaching in Physical Education*, 21: 128–144.

Curtner-Smith, M.D., Chen, W., & Kerr, I.G. (1995). Health-related fitness in secondary school physical education: a descriptive-analytic study. *Educational Studies*, 21(1): 55–66.

Department for Culture, Media and Sport (DfCMS) (2001). *A Sporting Future for All. The Government's Plan for Sport*. London: Author.

Department for Education and the Welsh Office (DfE and WO) (1995). *Physical Education in the National Curriculum*. London: HMSO.

Department for Education and Employment & Qualifications and Curriculum Authority (DfEE & QCA) (1999a). *Physical Education. The National Curriculum for England*. London: HMSO.

Department for Education and Employment & Qualifications and Curriculum Authority (DfEE & QCA) (1999b). *The National Curriculum. Handbook for Secondary Teachers in England*. London: HMSO.

Department for Education and Skills (DfES) (2002). *14–19: Extending opportunities; raising standards*. London: Author.

Department for Education and Skills (DfES) and Department for Culture, Media and Sport (DCMS) (2003). *Learning Through PE and Sport. A Guide to the Physical Education, School Sport and Club Links Strategy*. London: Author.

Department of Education and Science and the Welsh Office (DES and WO) (1992) *Physical Education in the National Curriculum*. London: HMSO.

Department of Health (DoH) (1999). *Our Healthier Nation*. London: HMSO.

Douthitt, V.L., & Harvey, M.L. (1995). Exercise counseling – how physical educators can help. *Journal of Physical Education, Recreation and Dance*, 66(5): 31–35.

Elbourn, J., & YMCA Fitness Industry Training (1998). Planning a personal exercise programme. London: YMCA Fitness Industry Training.

Elbourn, J., Brennan, M., & YMCA Fitness Industry Training (1998a). Exercise technique resource pack. London: YMCA Fitness Industry Training.

Elbourn, J., Brennan, M., & YMCA Fitness Industry Training (1998b). Assisting a circuit training instructor. London: YMCA Fitness Industry Training.

Elbourn, J., Brennan, M., & YMCA Fitness Industry Training (1998c). Assisting an exercise to music instructor. London: YMCA Fitness Industry Training.

Fairclough, S. (2003). Physical activity lessons during key stage 3 physical education. *British Journal of Teaching Physical Education*, 34(1): 40–45.

Fairclough, S., & Stratton, G. (1997). Physical education curriculum and extra curriculum time: A survey of secondary schools in the North West of England. *British Journal of Physical Education*, 28(3): 21–24.

Fairclough, S., Stratton, G., & Baldwin, G. (2002). The contribution of secondary school physical education to lifetime physical activity. *European Physical Education Review*, 8(1): 69–84.

Fox, K.R (1992). Education for exercise and the national curriculum proposals: A step forwards or backwards? *British Journal of Physical Education*, 23(1): 8–11.

Fox, K. (1993). Exercise and the promotion of public health: More messages for the mission. *British Journal of Physical Education*, 24(3): 36–37.

Fox, K. (1996). Physical activity promotion and the active school. In: Armstrong, N. (ed.) *New Directions in Physical Education*, London: Cassell Education, pp. 94–109.

Fox, K., & Harris, J. (2003). Promoting physical activity through schools. In: McKenna, J., & Riddoch, C. (eds) *Perspectives on Health and Exercise*, Basingstoke: Palgrave Macmillan, pp. 181–201.

Green, K. (2002). Physical education and the 'couch potato society' – part one. *European Journal of Physical Education*, 7(2): 95–107.

Hardman, K., & Marshall, J. (2000). The state and status of physical education in the international context. *European Physical Education Review*, 6(3): 203–229.

Hargreaves, J. (2000). Gender, morality and the national physical education curriculum. In: Hansen, J., & Nielsen, N. (eds) *Sports, Body and Health*, Odense: Odense University Press.

Harris, J. (1994). Physical education in the national curriculum: Is there enough time to be effective? *British Journal of Physical Education*, 25(4): 34–38.

Harris, J. (1995). Physical education: A picture of health? *British Journal of Physical Education*, 26(4): 25–32.

Harris, J. (1997a). Physical Education: A Picture of Health? The Implementation of Health-Related Exercise in the National Curriculum in Secondary Schools in England. Unpublished doctoral thesis, Loughborough University.

Harris, J. (1997b). A health focus in physical education. In: Almond, L. (ed.) *Physical Education in Schools* (2nd edition), London: Kogan Page, pp. 104–120.

Harris, J. (2000). *Health-Related Exercise in the National Curriculum. Key Stages 1 to 4.* Champaign, IL: Human Kinetics.

Harris, J., & Almond, L. (1994). Letter in response to OFSTED inspector's view of HRE in the National Curriculum. *Bulletin of Physical Education*, 30(3): 65–68.

Harris, J., & Cale, L. (1997). How healthy is school PE? A review of the effectiveness of health-related physical education programmes in schools. *Health Education Journal*, 56: 84–104.

Harris, J., & Cale, L. (1998). Activity promotion in physical education. In: Green, K., & Hardman, K. (eds) *Physical Education, A Reader*, Oxford: Meyer & Meyer, pp. 116–131.

Harris, J. & Penney, D. (2000). Gender issues in health-related exercise. *European Physical Education Review*, 6(3): 249–273.

Health Education Authority (1998). *Young and Active? Policy Framework for Young People and Health-enhancing Physical Activity*. London: Author.

Kulinna, P.H., & Silverman, S. (2000). Teachers' attitudes toward teaching physical activity and fitness. *Research Quarterly for Exercise and Sport*, 71(1): 80–84.

McKenzie, G. (2001). Physical activity and health: school interventions. Abtracts of the 6th Annual Congress of the European College of Sports Science, 24th–28th July, p. 17.

McKenzie, T.L., Nader, P.R., Strikmiller, P.K., Yang, M., Stone, E., Perry, C.L., *et al.*, (1996). School physical education: effect of the child and adolescent trial for cardio-vascular health. *Preventive Medicine*, 25: 423–431.

McKenzie, T.L., Sallis, J.F., Kolody, B., & Faucett, F.N. (1997). Long-term effects of a physical education curriculum and staff development work: SPARK. *Research Quarterly in Exercise and Sport*, 68: 280–291.

Morrow, J.R., Jackson, A.W., & Payne, V.G. (1999). Physical activity promotion and school physical education. *President's Council on Physical Fitness and Sports Research Digest*, 3(7): 1–7.

National Audit Office (2001). *Tackling Obesity in England*. London: The Stationery Office.

National Curriculum Council (1990). *Curriculum Guidance 5: Health Education*. London: HMSO.

National Heart Forum (2002). *Young@Heart: A Healthy Start for a New Generation*. London: National Heart Forum.

Office for Standards in Education (Ofsted) (1996). Subjects and Standards. Issues for School Development Arising from OFSTED Inspection Findings. 1994/95. Key Stages 3 and 4 and Post 16. London: HMSO.

Office for Standards in Education (Ofsted) (2002). Secondary Subject Reports 2000/01: Physical Education. HMI 381. London: HMSO.

Oxley, J. (1994). HRE and the national curriculum – an OFSTED inspector's view. *Bulletin of Physical Education*, 30(2): 39.

Pate, R.R., Small, M.L., Ross, J.G., Young, J.C., Flint, K.H., & Warren, C.W. (1999) *School Physical Education*. NASPE Speak II Advocacy Kit, pp. 19–26.

Penney, D., & Evans, J. (1997). Naming the game. Discourse and domination in physical education and sport in England and Wales. *European Physical Education Review*, 3(1): 21–32.

Penney, D., & Evans, J. (1999). *Politics, Policy and Practice in Physical Education*. London: E & FN Spon.

Penney, D., & Harris, J. (1997). Extra-curricular physical education: More of the same for the more able? *Sport, Education and Society*, 2(1), 41–54.

Physical Education Association (PEA) (1988). Health related fitness testing and monitoring in schools. A position statement on behalf of the PEA by its Fitness and Health Advisory Committee. *British Journal of Physical Education*, 19(4/5): 194–195.

Qualifications and Curriculum Authority website: www.qca.org.uk

Roberts, K. (1996a). Young people, schools, sport and government policy. *Sport, Education and Society*, 1(1): 47–57.

Roberts, K. (1996b). Youth cultures and sport: the success of school and community sport provisions in Britain. *European Physical Education Review*, 2(2): 105–115.

Rowland, T.W. (1995). The horse is dead; let's dismount. *Pediatric Exercise Science*, 7: 117–120.

Sallis, J.F., Bauman, A., & Pratt, M. (1998). Environmental and policy interventions to promote physical activity. *American Journal of Preventive Medicine*, 15(4): 379–397.

Sallis, J.F., McKenzie, T.L., Alcaraz, J.E., Kolody, B., Faucette, N., & Hovell, M.F. (1997) The effects of a 2 year physical education programme (SPARK) on physical activity and fitness in elementary school students. Sports, play and active recreation for kids. *American Journal of Public Health*, 87: 1328–1334.

Shephard, R.J., & Trudeau, F. (2000). The legacy of physical education: influences on adult lifestyle. *Pediatric Exercise Science*, 12: 34–50.

Simons-Morton, B.G., Parcel, G.S., Baranowski, T., Forthofer, R., & O'Hara, N.M. (1991) Promoting physical activity and a healthful diet among children: results of a school-based intervention study. *American Journal of Public Health*, 81: 896–991.

Sleap, M. (1990). Promoting health in primary school physical education. In: Armstrong, N. (ed) *New Directions in Physical Education*, Volume 1, Champaign, IL: Human Kinetics, pp. 17–36.

Smith, R.A., & Biddle, S.J.H. (1995). Psychological factors in the promotion of physical activity. In: Biddle, S.J.H. (ed) *European Perspectives on Exercise and Sport Psychology*, Champaign, IL: Human Kinetics, pp. 85–108.

Sparkes, A. (1994). Curriculum change: on gaining a sense of perspective. In: Armstrong, N., & Saprkes, A. (eds) *Issues in Physical Education*, London: Cassell.

Stone, E.J., McKenzie, T.L., Welk, G.J., & Booth, M.L. (1998). Effects of physical activity interventions in youth: review and synthesis. *American Journal of Preventive Medicine*, 15(4): 298–315.

Stratton, G. (1996). Children's heart rates during physical education lessons: a review. *Pediatric Exercise Science*, 8: 215–233.

Stratton, G. (1997) Children's heart rates during British physical education lessons. *Journal of Teaching in Physical Education*, 16: 357–367.

Vilhjalmsson, R., & Thorlindsson, T. (1998). Factors related to physical activity: a study of adolescents. *Social Science and Medicine*, 47: 665–675.

Welsh Assembly (1999). Curriculum 2000. Author: Cardiff.

Williams, A. (1988). The historiography of health and fitness in physical education. *British Journal of Physical Education Research Supplement*, 3: 1–4.

Wired for Health Website (2003). http://www.wiredforhealth.gov.uk.

YMCA Fitness Industry Training (2000). *Teaching about HRE in a fitness room at Key Stage 4*. London: Author.

YMCA Fitness Industry Training (2002). *Teaching about HRE through Exercise to Music/Aerobics at Key Stage 4*. London: Author.

Youth Sport Trust, YMCA Fitness Industry Training & English Sports Council (1998). *Fit for TOPs*. Loughborough: Youth Sport Trust.

Youth Sport Trust (2000). *Fit for Life*. Loughborough: Author.

Jan Wright, Doune Macdonald and Lyndal Groom

PHYSICAL ACTIVITY AND YOUNG PEOPLE

Beyond participation

Introduction

A S WEARING AND WEARING (1990) point out, the theorisation of leisure has moved beyond simplistic assumptions of 'free time' and 'free choice' to an understanding that any study of leisure must take into account structural relations of power. They point to inequities in the allocation of resources which are based on particular dominant social agendas and meanings associated with the 'benefits' of leisure to the state. This has seen resources allocated to support sport as a major site of 'productive' leisure— that is, a site where attributes of individual achievement, striving and so on judged desirable for citizenship in a patriarchal capitalist society are developed. In addition achievement at the elite level is intimately linked to government concerns with national identity (Penney & Evans, 1999). While sport continues to claim a substantial proportion of the state funded 'leisure' resources in countries like Britain and Australia, in the last decade, imperatives around fitness and the so-called 'obesity epidemic' have produced a discursive context in which the health benefits of physically active leisure have also received prominence (Gard & Wright, 2001).

In this context, the health promotion and movement science research literature has been dominated by concerns with the amount and kind of physical activity participated in by young people. This literature usually reports on large-scale quantitative studies using purpose designed surveys (e.g. Booth *et al.*, 1997; Youth Service Survey, cited in Roberts, 1996). The conclusion is generally that young people and particularly certain groups of young people are not as active as they should be and that school and recreational programmes should be designed and funded to enhance their participation (see Roberts, 1996, for a critique of this position). This participation research, through the description of large populations of young people, does provide a context in which to locate an understanding of young people's participation in physical activity. However, by their nature and intent, these studies raise significant questions which cannot be answered by the methodologies so far employed. For instance, they cannot provide information about the place and significance of physical activity in young people's lives as these change for individuals over time (particularly for non-organised sport and recreational activities); they cannot demonstrate how young people deploy the discursive and material resources associated with physical culture to construct their identities in relation to physical activity; and they provide few insights into the place of physical activity in relation to other forms of leisure in young people's lives.

In addition, within the participation literature, girls and young people of cultural minority groups often fare less well in comparisons with the participation of young white males in sport and exercise and thus become identified as 'problems' (Booth *et al.*, 1997; de Knop, 1998). In general, the participation research is not designed to take into account the social, and cultural contexts, local, national and global in which young people participate in physical activity, except as variables with which to compare one group to another. They do not take into account the wide variation within groups nor the circumstances of young people's lives which may allow or prevent their enacting their desires and wants in physical activity. To not participate in this context is to be cast as deficient and delinquent; to fall short of an ideal. This ideal is often framed in relation to healthy lifestyle and performance discourses which privilege middle-class, Anglo, male ways of doing leisure and physical activity (Gilbert & Gilbert, 1998).

This paper reports on the first stages of a qualitative longitudinal study that attempts to address these lacunas. The larger study, while also concerned to enhance the young people's opportunities and experiences of physical activity and physical education, makes an important conceptual shift by recasting and extending the notion of 'participation' to that of young people's 'engagement with physical culture' (Kirk, 1997). Here, physical culture is understood as a range of discourses concerned with the maintenance, representation and regulation of the body through institutionalised forms of physical activity. Focusing on the broader concept of physical culture rather than physical activity is consistent with the call by Crouch (2000) and others in leisure studies to account for the complex interactions of practice, space, subject, knowledge and embodiment in understanding everyday existence. Further, with its implicit relational analysis, it strengthens the research through interdisciplinary study comprising cultural, youth and leisure studies, sociology and education (Deem, 1999).

The larger study will follow three cohorts of young people for three to five years through from primary school to the early years of high school, from the middle years of high school to completion or as school-leavers, and students in their last years of high school on to further study or work. As a first stage of the study, students in three secondary schools were surveyed to identify a range of demographic features and basic patterns of participation which were used to select those students who would be asked to participate in a semi-structured interview. The information collected in the surveys and interviews was then used to identify those students who would be invited to participate in the longitudinal study.

This paper reports on the interpretations of the results of these first semi-structured interviews. As background to these interpretations, the paper will introduce ways of examining physical culture, both empirical and theoretical, before giving further details on the participants and the way we worked with them. Data are presented in terms of how participants recalled physical activity engagement when they were young and their current engagement. It is then discussed through the lens of location, schooling and gender, key factors in a cultural analysis of participation in physical activity.

Physical culture: a relational analysis

In their analysis of the patterns of consumption of young people in former communist countries Roberts and Fagan (1999) point out that leisure is context-dependent—'it is highly sensitive to broader socio-economic conditions and division' (p. 1). Although their premise does not directly address physical activity as leisure, it provides a useful lens through which to interpret the ways in which young people in different geographical and social locations talk about their participation in physical activity. Differences in leisure patterns point to social and cultural divisions within countries as well as between countries. The opportunities to participate in physical activity as leisure, as well as the values attributed to participation, are framed within class and gender relations. For example, in studying the 'tastes' of the French population, Bourdieu (1984) found that the working class was more likely to take up an instrumental relation to their bodies and to pursue sports which demanded 'a high investment of energy, effort or even pain . . . and which sometimes even endanger the body itself' (p. 213). The middle classes and particularly middle-class women, on the other hand, were more likely to be concerned with the cultivation of the healthy body. In those countries which have inherited the colonial legacy of the British public school, organised team sports (including rowing) are imbued with values which are clearly associated with developing the power elite of society. They become central to producing a particular kind of citizen, that is, certain sports are deliberately cultivated to produce a specific *habitus*, a specific embodied relation to the world (Bourdieu, 1984). From the point of view of the individual subject, habitus becomes taken up in the dynamic formation of identit(ies). Habitus in this sense provides one way of understanding identity as formed by and through bodily practices which are themselves socially and culturally located.

All (physical) activity is influenced by and contributes to the making of identity—that is, a person's being in the world and in relation to the world. Young people draw on specific cultural resources to make sense of their participation; their engagement with physical activity and physical culture provides resources with which they make sense of their lives and their interactions with others. The term 'engagement' here is used to signal an interaction with meanings about physical activity which is promoted through direct physical participation in physical activity and sport but also those interactions which may be more reflective: for instance, interactions with mediasport; spectating sport; conversing about sport; rejecting sport. In western societies it is difficult in some way not to construct one's identity in relation to physical activity and/or sport, even it is in rejecting it as part of one's social and cultural life.

There has been considerable writing about the relation between physical activity/exercise and sport in constructing gender identity. Following Connell (2000), masculinity and femininity are understood as 'configurations of practice within gender relations' where gender relations are modelled as a structure that includes 'large-scale institutions and economic relations as well as face-to-face relationships and sexuality' (p. 29). Connell and others (Walker, 1988; Whitson, 1994) have pointed to the central place of sport in shaping gender relations and, in particular, dominant forms of masculinity. I.M. Young (1980) in her classic paper 'Throwing like a girl' has used phenomenology to describe the way femininity can be constructed bodily in opposition to the claims on space and strength which Connell associates with dominant masculinity. Grimshaw (1999) and others (Markula, 1998) challenge this limited analysis of the female body in opposition to the male body pointing to different capacities for movement and the potential for 'empowering' movement offered by aerobics and other none traditional sport activities. Scranton and others (Young, 1997; Scraton et al., 2000) demonstrate the complex ways women negotiate their 'femininity' in the context of traditional male sports and physical activities, on the one hand finding pleasure in the physicality of the sport while on the other concerned to confirm their heterosexuality.

Participation patterns in recreational and organised competitive physical activity continue to be sharply demarcated (ABS, 1997; de Knop, 1998; Mota & Silva, 1999). Recent shifts in patterns of participation again point to permeability of certain gender boundaries and the continued policing of others. Whereas young women are increasingly taking up the various codes of football—soccer, rugby union and rugby league and in Australia, Australian Football—and receiving national and commercial recognition for their achievements, there has been no similar rapid increase in the number of young men in netball, gymnastics and dance. This is despite the promotion of some forms of dance, such as tap dance and rap, as masculine pursuits.

Less has been written about the relationship between physical activity and ethnic identity. In Australia, the importance of soccer to ethnic minority communities groups (Mosley, 1995) and to the identity of young people in those communities has been well documented (Georgakis, 2000), but there has been less written about the importance of other forms of physical activity such as dance, martial arts, tai chi, table tennis and badminton (chosen because they reflect immigration trends in Australia) to the cohesion of specific communities. These forms of physical activity tend to be marginalised (as does soccer in Australia), rarely provided with the recognition accorded traditional mainstream sport, poorly resourced and unlikely to feature in any major way in school curricula despite the interests of students in the school community.

In our attention to structures such as gender, ethnicity and class in the context of examining the specificity of the meanings young people's construct around sport we attempt to follow the injunction of Apple (1999) and others (Layder, 1997; McLaren Farahmandpur, 2000) to avoid focusing solely on the local and the contingent and ignoring structural relations among practices 'as if nothing existed in structured ways' (Apple, 1999, pp. 187–188). We attempt in the following analysis to recognise the ways in which individual choices are constrained by structures of social class, gender and ethnicity but also to attend to the specific place and significance that physical activity has in the lives of the young people interviewed.

The study

The three schools involved in the project were chosen because of their differences from each other and the opportunity to include students from a wide range of social, cultural and geographical locations. They were all located in two of the Australian eastern seaboard States; in one State, students from an elite Protestant boys' school participated in the project, and in the other, students came from a Catholic coeducational parochial second-ary college in a medium-sized city and a secondary coeducational government school in the western suburbs of a major metropolis. Each school and its geographical location provides a different 'space' and 'place', where 'space' is understood as the 'geometric coordinates of interactions that are physical, economic, social and so on' (Massey, cited in Crouch, 2000, p. 66) and 'place' is understood as a human practice 'through which and with which lives are lived and identity and myth made' (Crouch, 2000, p. 64). As Crouch (2000, p. 67) argues, 'specific kinds of cultural practise are achieved in particular places.'

The Catholic coeducation school (Seacliff College) is situated close to the coast and to the surf. It has a very good reputation for pastoral care together with a reasonable academic reputation. This means that it attracts students beyond its immediate parish and many of these students come from middle-class homes. The students who live closer to the school come from a housing estate, as well as from the more affluent homes on the beach front. In other words, its student population is very mixed. The western suburbs govern-ment school (Belleville) tends to draw on students from working-class families or from families with no adult employed in full-time paid work. The proportion of students from cultural minority backgrounds is far greater in this school than in any of the other two.

In marked contrast to both these schools was the well-established, non-government primary and secondary school for boys located in an inner suburb of a large city. Malcos College attracts many students who live on acreage in the outlying suburbs of the city or who are boarders from rural properties and overseas. It is operated by a Protestant Church and most students and staff identity themselves as members of the Church (Courtice, 1999). The students' parents tend to be in managerial/professional occupa-tions and contribute to a strong 'old boy' tradition and network.

The way of working

Consenting students in the first and fourth years of each of the schools were surveyed using a questionnaire adapted from the NSW Fitness and Physical Activity Survey (Booth et al., 1997). Students were chosen from the survey respondents on the basis of their social and cultural location, their orientation to sport and physical activity and their willingness to participate in an interview as indicated on their survey form. In the end, 52 students—28 female and 34 male—participated in 45-minute semi-structured inter-views with common questions across all sites. Interviews were conducted by experienced teachers employed as research assistants or students undertaking doctoral studies associ-ated with the project. The interviews were designed to provide information concerning the perspectives, orientations to physical culture and participation patterns of groups of young people across a range of social, cultural and geographic locations and so students were chosen for their differences from one another. From the results of these interviews a cohort of students was chosen to participate in the longitudinal study.

The interviews were transcribed and data analysis proceeded by entering these tran-scripts into a database supported by the qualitative software package, NUD-IST. The interviews were initially coded for demographic characteristics and then analysed as they answered the questions which structured the interview. The broadest of these were to do with the nature of their physical activity participation at the time of the interview and in the past and the important influences on that participation. Questions were also asked about the young people's engagement with various forms of physical culture such as mediasport, brandname sportswear and, given the timing of the interviews, interest in the Sydney Olympic Games.

This paper will specifically discuss the students' early and current experiences in physical activity and attempt to understand these in the contexts of family, community, school and location. As far as is possible from this first round of interviews some suggestions will also be made as to the possibilities for identity construction which were and were not available from the physical activities described and the contexts in which they took place.

When they were young

Most of the boys interviewed at Malcos College and many of the students at the coast school, Seacliff College, began organised formal physical activities at a very young age. For the boys, this was likely to be competitive sports and for the girls, gymnastics, dance lessons—ballroom and jazz—and swimming training. The range of activities seemed to be wider for the Malcos College students compared to the coast students at Seacliff and for the coast students compared to the city west students at Belleville. For the Belleville students, the range was quite narrow particularly for the boys, with soccer dominating. The following quotes give some sense of this pattern.

> I've been playing soccer since I was about five and I've played that all the way through. And cricket, I started that at about eight . . . And Aussie Rules but I only took that up in grade 8.
>
> (Malcos student)

> I've been doing karate since I was eight—the first few years was Tae Kwon Do and I've done cricket since I was 12 and I've moved on from that.
>
> (Malcos student)

> Since year 4 I've been playing club soccer and then progressively playing rep soccer and State soccer and I still play now. I played cricket at school, soccer at school.
>
> (male Belleville student)

> I started swimming at one, one and a half and I still do that, I did squad training as well as just laps and things and skills like where they perfect your stroke and all that sort of stuff and then I did ballet for a little while and gymnastics, I only quit last year (because of injury) but I still go every now and then.
>
> (female Seacliff student)

The coast and city west students spent much of their primary years participating in a range of backyard and informal activities with friends and family. Most of the coast boys (and some girls) began surfing or joined a surf club at an early age and combined competitive sport with surfing and/or skateboarding. Their early introduction to the surf was usually through their fathers and family picnics were also mentioned frequently by this group. The city west students seemed to spend more of their time alone, watching TV, riding their bikes or listening to music, but also playing in the backyard with friends. The following quote picks up some of the informal forms of activity which were typical of many of the Belleville boys.

> R: Tell me about the sorts of things you used to do after school and on weekends.
> MS: I had a brother and I always used to hang around with him and stuff and toys and go outside and just use my imagination.

And a little later:

> R: What other kinds of things did you do on weekends?
> MS: Oh well, I'd go for a ride with my brother, bike ride around the neighbourhood.
> R: What about with your family?
> MS: Oh when I was really young, they used to take us out to the park, like in to the local park, it was good.

The patterns of participation in 'organised forms of activity' across all students interviewed were relatively predictable and similar to those picked up in the statistical research on participation (ABS, 1997; Booth *et al.*, 1997; Kirk *et al.*, 1997 de Knop, 1998): for instance, the predictably greater participation of the boys in organised team sports and the girls in dance and gymnastics; the greater participation and the greater range of sports for the affluent students as compared to those from poorer families. Thus, Malcos boys' activities frequently required a range of facilities, lessons, and uniforms available either through their school or within the local community, whereas for the Belleville students, the primary school sports afternoon where they competed against other schools was their main form of organised participation.

One obvious explanation for these patterns of participation is that of material disadvantage. This explanation stands in contrast to those health promotion and popular discourses which want to place the responsibility for 'deficiencies' in activity behaviour with the laxity of the individual or the inappropriate attitudes of particular cultural groups (Lupton, 1995; Baum, 1995). Neither structural explanations—economic and cultural— nor those which would blame individual attitudes and behaviours provide an adequate account of how the material and emotional circumstances of young people's intersect with their desires and opportunities to make choices about their leisure activities. This point is exemplified in the following quote from a female Seacliff student. It demonstrates how the particular circumstances of her life provide a very different context for physically active leisure from the rich environment of families and friends who played together and who supported a range of physical activities of her coast peers.

> R: Tell me about the sort of things you used to do when you were younger.
> FS: What kind of things do you mean?
> R: What did you do after school, on weekends?
> FS: I just, not really anything to do on the weekends, 'cause I don't have any brothers and sisters and like the neighbours are all like old ladies. So I just used to play by myself and just go rollerblading in the backyard or something 'cause there's wasn't really much to do.

> R: What about with your parents, did you do anything with them?
> FS: Oh well my Dad died so my mum doesn't really do anything. We just go some places. She doesn't really like to participate in any like sporting activities.

In these early experiences of physical activity the important influence of structures such as place, family configurations and socio-economic resources in framing the potential choices that the young people could make in their lifestyles are already evident.

Play now

As the literature suggests, the patterns of activity manifested in the early years of schooling tended to be indicative of participation in later years (Malina, 1996; Telama *et al.*, 1997), though the level of organisation and competition seemed to increase for those who were serious about their sport.

The Malcos College boys

The Malcos College boys continued to play the activities they had begun in their primary years and added to them. In comparison to the students at the other three schools, the range of activities and the apparent ease with which the Malcos College boys moved in and out of activities was notable. However, where they may have played club sport in primary school this, particularly in the case of football codes and rowing, shifted to school based competition (or both club and school). At the time of the interviews, many of these boys were putting in a considerable number of hours of training before and after school. The following comments are typical of the private school boys' talk about sport.

> I'm playing club cricket this season and then school cricket after Christmas and then AFL—I'll play club earlier in the year and start school later in the year.

> I've been doing basketball recently and I also do water polo . . . I stopped playing cricket because I thought it was too boring, just standing around the field and not much happening. That's the only one I've really stopped . . . oh and soccer 'cause I need to let my anger out a bit more and (you can't) tackle people that hard in soccer.

> I do motor cycle trials . . . more of an obstacle course. And I do rugby **with** club and rowing **with** school. Tae Kwon Do just club. I have done and still do model aircraft flying.

Between club and school sport and homework, the Malcos College students' time was comprehensively accounted for: 'I've got basketball on Monday morning, basketball on Tuesday afternoon, then I've got rowing on Wednesday and I've got tutoring on Thursday and then on Friday I've got rowing'. There were many opportunities to do activities outside the school and participation in these was encouraged by the school through forms of recognition such as a mention in the school newsletter: 'they just have a little bit in the College news that shows that they have got a good place'. However, the students recognised that certain sports were 'preferred' by the school, for instance, rugby union rather than rugby league (played in state schools), thereby making the class differential quite explicit.

As is the case in many if not most elite boys' schools run on a traditional British model (Mangan, 1981; Courtice, 1999), not to do sport was counter both to the culture and the ethos of the school. There were a number of comments that pointed to the subtle pressure from the school and from the boys' peers to do sport. If a boy did not play any sport he might be 'called up to see a teacher' or 'the boys sort of get on your back and rag you about it'; '(w)e practically have to do a sport' in this school and '(w)ithout sport it would be just another normal school . . . sitting in the classroom'. It is also clearly stated in the school policy that participation in sport and other such activities 'while not compulsory is expected'.

At Malcos College there was also a clear investment for the student's family in the sporting life of the school; what could be considered a mutual constitution of identity as children's participation in school sporting events gave parents an *entrée* into the school culture/community (Yang *et al.*, 1996). Families were encouraged to be enthusiastic spectators and to honour sporting success. The confluence of sport with the general aims of the school is evident in a discourse analysis conducted by Courtice (1999) of Malcos's end-of-year Speech Night of 200 prizes, 70 of which were 'sporting'.

While the boys at Malcos have arguably considerably more opportunities and more encouragement to participate in sport, the social practices around sport also serve as powerful disciplinary technologies (Foucault, 1980) whereby particular kinds of citizens, forms of masculinity and ways of interacting with physical activity are shaped. The close monitoring of the students' time, the confluence of the parents' values with those of the school, the investments produced by being successful at sport in many ways suggest a limited and limiting environment for the negotiation of identity.

The coast students

In stark contrast to the Malcos College students, the school was most certainly not the major focus of sport or physical activity participation, nor the source of a culture of participation for the Seacliff students. What was most striking from the Seacliff interviews was the extent to which these students talked about physical activity as a taken-for-granted part of life—particularly, but not only, the boys. You surfed and/or skated and you might also play football; there were no special values attributed to their pursuit of these activities, they were what you did when you weren't at school or, for some of the older students, at work. The following quotes are relatively typical of the mix of activities for the boys amongst this group of students.

> I'm playing cricket at the moment, indoor cricket, and playing rugby league this year and playing a lot with my friend. He lives next door to a facility where you can train so I go down a couple of times a week.
>
> (year 10 student)

R: What's a typical afternoon/weekend for you?

MS: Um . . . sometimes go to work and then um go down to the cricket nets, then go for a surf, that's about it.

And later in the same interview:

R: What takes up most of your time?
MS: Um . . . probably sport and a bit of school.

(year 10 student)

Physical activity and sport was managed quite differently by these boys in comparison to the Malcos students. There was far less a sense of obligation, their time was less pressured and there was a decreased emphasis on formalised team sport and competition.

The young women in the coast group had a more varied range of non-school activities including art and piano. Most, however, were involved in traditionally female activities such as dance, gymnastics, netball or a combination of these. Amongst the younger ones in the first year of high school, there also seemed to be a keen interest in the martial arts (either Tae Kwando or kickboxing).

R: So what sort of things do you do after school and on weekends now?
FS: After school on Tuesdays, I play the piano and I've started kickboxing and that's it.
R: Why did you take up kickboxing?
FS: Uh, because, I don't know. I don't want to like just do nothing and sit at home all day, like I just want to get out and do something.

(female year 7 student)

The coast students were more likely to describe themselves as doing less sport, with their entry into high school and with the increased expectations and obligations such as home-work or paid work that this bought. Most of the students who made these kinds of comments, however, were students who described themselves as having engaged in a considerable amount of formal activity when they were younger. It seemed that they were underestimating current engagement in part because it no longer involved the same degree of formal participation even though they continued by all accounts to be very active. For instance, one of the female students in her fourth year at Seacliff College lamented how her sport had now dropped in priority because of school work and paid work, while at the same time describing how she still exercised regularly with aerobics, weights and on the Air Strider at home, played soccer to get away from competitive running (a State level competitor) and still trained for carnivals now and then. For some of the boys, the demands of organised competitive team sports, such as rugby league and soccer, increased as they got older and most of the coast boys still fitted in surfing and skating into their lives whenever they could.

What came through most strongly at this point in the analysis were the ways in which most of the coast students seemed to epitomise the 'normality' of a particular Australian ideal of physical activity participation. Physical activity participation was taken-for-granted by these students and their families as a way of life. These students described at least one and often both parents as being active and as believers in a 'healthy lifestyle' and as being supportive of their children in their various forms of activity. The fathers often surfed with their sons and less often daughters, and both parents helped coach and/or organise their children's sport.

> R: What about your parents—do they do any particular activities?
> SF: My mum likes to clean the house (laughter) and my dad likes to surf, and rollerblade. And bushwalk.
> R: Do you do any of these things with him?
> FS: Yeah I bushwalk with him and sometimes I go surfing with him and . . .
>
> (female year 7 student)

> R: What about your parents, are they doing activities now?
> MS: Yeah, um sometimes, we go to mini-athletics at B——Park, and my Dad, he has to do this long jump stuff and he has to show the kids and all that and my mum she helps out with the organising it and usually they just have a bit fun in the back garden with us.
> R: What kind of activities do you do on the weekend with the family together?
> MS: Well we go down the beach and we go down the park and play a bit of soccer, play the footy around and throw frisbees.
>
> (male year 7 student)

While the centrality of sport to the lives of the Seacliff students has parallels with the Malcos College story, there were considerable qualitative differences in their relation to sport and the circumstances surrounding their participation. Most of the Malcos and coast students were active in a range of activities, which they had usually begun in childhood and most took their participation in physical activity for granted. Whereas the school was the main source of support and encouragement for the Malcos College boys, for the coast students it was their parents and to a certain extent a physical environment rich with opportunities for individual forms of recreation—surfing, skateboarding, aerobics—as well as competitive team sports. The emphasis on achievement and the social values of competition seems to have little place in the lives of the Seacliff students—perhaps even less so in the lives of the boys as compared to the girls who were more likely to be involved in the competitive environments of athletics, ballroom dancing and swimming.

The coast boys seem to negotiate their identity in relation to a particular kind of masculinity formed in relation to the individual pursuits of skateboarding and surfing, mediated in their case by a close connection to family and location. As Beal (1996) suggests in the context of her study of skateboarders, they combine those aspects of masculinity which are associated with strength and independence with a mild anti-authority and anti-intellectual stance. These positions are still formed in antithesis to notions of femininity and male surfers and skateboarders are generally not welcoming of girls into their activities (Pallotti-Chiarolli, 1998).

The meaning of physical activity for the coast girls was more difficult to interpret. Their lives seemed to be less tied to the beach and their non-school time was as likely to include homework, shopping and work as physical activity. At this stage in the research, physical activity did not seem as central to the girls' identity formation as it was for the boys. However, this ignores the more subtle workings of the place and meaning of physical activity in the girls' lives and the ways they are positioned and position themselves in relation to the discourses of physical activity, in particular those associated with body maintenance and health. The cohort study will allow these aspects to be explored in greater depth.

The western suburbs students

Whereas an interest and desire to participate in physical activity were also part of the stories of the city west students at Belleville, their opportunities seemed to be much more limited. One girl's interview was particularly poignant. Living with her Dad and two younger brothers, having run away from her Mum several years ago, her chances of pursuing those physical activities she enjoys seem to be very much limited by the economic and social circumstances of her life. Not that she necessarily saw it this way:

> FS: I love dancing. I've been dancing since I was in Kindergarten.
> R: What kind of dancing?
> FS: Just normal dancing really.
> R: Like ballet, tap, jazz?
> FS: No, just dance groups like how they dance to songs and stuff.
> R: Is that something you're still doing now?
> FS: I finished last year, that was the last year I done it, I don't know about this year. My dad wants to get me into doing ballet or something like that.
> R: Why did you finish last year, was that because of the change to high school?
> FS: Yeah, and there's no dance groups in year 7.
> R: So it was something that was done through school, so this was the school dance type stuff?
> FS: And going to rock eistedfords. I was always in the rock eistedford and stuff.
> R: We were talking about PE and you said you'd like them to do more dance.
> FS: Yeah, I'd like to do dancing like the year 10s do and stuff but um Miss E, my PE teacher she said that we'd be doing it soon, once we've finished what we're doing, so hopefully soon.

And later again in the same interview:

> R: Are there any sports people that you admire?
> FS: Sports people, I'd love to run like Cathy Freeman, I love running.
> R: Would you like to be able to do it as a competitor?
> FS: Yeah.
> R: Would your dad support you if you said you wanted to do that?
> FS: Yeah, my brother wants to do it too.
> R: Is that something you are going to look at doing this year or next year?
> FS: Yeah, maybe this year, it all depends on what my dad says really and if my brothers are being good.

In contrast to the Malcos and Seacliff students there were more students among those interviewed from Belleville who did not do much organised physical activity at all by their account or were active in ways less readily recognised by participation surveys. For some it was just not an important aspect of their lives and they had not given a great deal of thought to it. For others their physical location restricted what they could do. For the

Belleville students, school physical education and sport were an important site for physical activity/recreation not because of the school ethos but because it was one of the few places where they had access to facilities and equipment. The following quote exemplifies a number of these issues. It helps in reading this to contrast the ease with which a coast student could drop down to the beach for a quick ride after school to the difficulties faced by a student in the western suburbs, where the buses to the beach only run in summer and then only on the weekend.

> R: So you're big on surfing?
> MS: Yeah, oh bodyboarding, I just call it surfing, same thing.
> R: Are you doing competition at all?
> MS: No, I'm not, I'm just doing it for fun.
> R: What sort of things are you doing now after school?
> MS: Um I'm still waiting until it gets a bit warmer, but I'm thinking about starting bodyboarding again.
> R: Do you do much during winter after school?
> MS: No, I just stay inside.

And later when discussing school physical education:

> MS: I like to play football, just touch football, we're doing that now and something to do with football, I like football.
> R: You don't play football after school though?
> MS: No, we play it at lunch time, at recess and before school.
> R: Would you play competition football?
> MS: No.
> R: Why not?
> MS: I just like to do things for fun and I just figure I couldn't be bothered to get up that early on Saturday mornings.

The relationship between family, ethnicity and community, which was a feature of the Belleville interviews, was exemplified by the commitment to baseball by one family from Nicaragua. All the male members of the family play baseball; the family with other members of the local South American community attended as spectators the major baseball events leading up to and including the Sydney Olympics.

> R: What sorts of things do you do as a family on weekends?
> FS: Well, on weekends we get, we're involved with baseball, a baseball commit-
> tee and stuff and my Dad plays baseball and my brother plays baseball and
> usually on, like on Saturdays, we go to school as well, Saturday school languages.
> (female year 10 student)

Baseball as a social practice is as gendered as most team sports. For the female student whom we have quoted above, this commitment was expressed through softball. Her quote again underlines the importance of the school in a location where community support for sport is not always available. It also says something about her relation to the sport and to those who played with her. Her pleasure is in part derived from being 'undefeated' (interesting in that she chose not to use language signifying winning or beating others) and in part from having assisted other girls to play well enough to contribute to this success.

> I used to play softball, last season 'cause this season we couldn't get a team together or a coach to coach us. It was outside of school, and this year, I played for the school for softball as State. We used to have like, sport every Wednesday and a group of my friends, about 10 of us, we'd go play softball and we got through the whole season undefeated, first in the whole, in the whole thing. So we were pretty happy because some of them didn't even know how to play the game and we'd go just do this, I'll tell you what to do.

Whereas the students at Malcos and Seacliff were primarily from Anglo families, there was a far greater diversity of ethnic heritage amongst the students at Belleville and this was reflected in their relation to physical activity. The families from South American were committed to baseball, the young man from the Philippines with the slight American accent played social basketball, and the young man whose family is from Bangladesh played competition cricket after following up a local community advertisement for players.

For many of the young ethnic minority women, the school provided the link between community sporting clubs and young women who wanted to join a sport by communicating requests for players from local clubs and also by advertising clubs requests for players to the students. The school not only provided the information service, but perhaps also a sense of propriety and approval in particular where families may have doubts about the appropriateness of activities for their daughters. This may be perceived as a more important service for young women given the assumptions of the masculine identities of team sport.

More of the students at Belleville also came from poor families where physical activity and sport were not a priority when children had to be fed and clothed and supported at school. There were very few of the less affluent students participating in activities which required equipment, particularly outside of the school programme. In addition, while there was a local commercial gym, this required membership and class fee payment. The local Police Citizen Youth Club (PCYC) did at times conduct gymnastics activities at the high school gymnasium. Again the school was an important location for physical activity for the Belleville students.

Discussion

At this stage in the study, the importance of location has emerged as a key indicator of cultural practice. It is also evident that a qualitative approach provides ways of understanding young people and their relationship with physical activity and physical culture that are rarely talked about in the participation literature. The young people's talk about their involvement in physical activity points to the ways in which they construct their lives and their identities in relation to physical activity and physical culture differently, while at the same time using cultural resources that are similar. How they take up these resources (for instance, mediasport, messages about bodies, physical activity and health) depends very much on the social and economic capital and the salience of particular resources in terms of their cultural, social and geographic location. For instance, whereas 'Adidas' sportswear is a highly valued signifier of identity associated with international soccer players for young men from the western suburbs, it is eschewed by the coast surfers because of its association with 'westies'. As Hendry *et al.* (1993) suggest, young people's tastes and interpretations of cultural texts can be attributed to cultural competencies that are acquired as a consequence of the group's social location. These aspects of culture will be explored further in the longitudinal study.

It is clear that for some of the young people interviewed their choices were highly constrained not only in terms of physical leisure but any notion of leisure as consumption. Poverty, family commitments, including the negotiation of emotionally difficult family relationship all constrained what was possible even to imagine as a 'choice'. In the western suburbs, community facilities and resources were limited and the school looked to as an important site for the provision of opportunities because of this. On the coast, the surf, access to swimming pools, athletic tracks and commercial and community gyms provided an environment in which participation in physical activity was very much a major aspect of leisure, particularly for the boys.

Physical activity was less likely to play a central role in their understanding of who they were and how the world works; the place and significance in their lives was mediated by relations with family, community and school. This is not to say that for some of the young men in the study that playing rugby league, soccer, surfing and skateboarding was not important to how they defined themselves as male. In particular it is likely that surfing and skating provided that time free from the surveillance of adults which seems to be an important aspect of leisure for young people (O'Donnell & Sharp, 2000).

On the other hand affluence and privilege did not always mean that choices were unconstrained, rather the kinds of constraints were cultural rather than economic, but equally class based. While we are concerned not to romanticise the less obvious social and cultural constraints for many of the coast students, the particularities of young people's lives also point to the ways in which disciplinary technologies are differently distributed. On the one hand, the boys from the privileged families at Malcos had a greater range of sports to choose from but in other ways these choices were constrained by the ways in which certain sports were valued as contributing to the ethos of the school and the schools purpose of producing particular kinds of citizens. Their time outside school was comprehensively accounted for by training and competition (and homework) often under the supervision of adults. In addition, the boundaries between leisure and school were blurred—recreational sport was school sport. Participation was for the school (and for the parent, perhaps) as well as for the student.

The well-documented relation between masculinity and sport including the sub-cultural studies of surfing and skateboarding make it an easier task to theorise the significance of physical activity for the male students in the study. It is less easy to do this for the female students. In part this is because their use of leisure is more diverse and they are more likely to be involved in domestic activities, work and/or homework as both evidenced by this study and others (McLennan, 1997). Physical activity does not have the same relation to femininity as it does to masculinity—it is most often written about in terms of exercise and a preoccupation with an ideal body. In this first round of interviews, a preoccupation with exercise and body shape was not obvious, although it does begin to appear in later interviews with the older students. Rather what stood out was the diversity of positions the girls took up in relation to physical activity—some played rugby league, quite a few pursued some form of dance, others played softball—some at close to elite levels and others on a casual and informal basis.

However, young women's introduction to this variety of activities, particularly for team sports whether through high school or community clubs, began later than their male counterparts. The option of primary school team sport does not appear in their histories as for the boys. Early physical activities appear more related to 'traditional' feminised activities, particularly with dance. Yet in high school years, formal dance and gymnastics participation diminishes to almost nil. For the young men, there is more constancy in their options, they played soccer and rugby and cricket at primary school, as well as high school; there was less diversity in their choices and fewer competing options for leisure time as compared to the girls.

At this point in the larger longitudinal study we have been more interested in canvassing the place and meaning of physically activity in the lives of a broad spectrum of young people, across different social, cultural and geographical locations. This approach has already identified the importance of these structural relations in shaping young people's physical activity. The next stage of the study will follow small cohort selected from these young people as they make decisions about physical activity and as they engage in and with contemporary physical culture. Through such an approach we hope to be able to capture in greater depth the specificity of these young people's lives as well as continue to examine the structural relations which shape their leisure choices.

References

Apple, M. (1999) *Power, Meaning and Identity* (New York, Peter Lang).

Australian Bureau of Statistics (ABS) (1997) *Participation in Sport and Physical Activities 1995/96* (Canberra, ABS).

Baum, F. (1998) *The New Public Health: An Australian Perspective* (Melbourne, Oxford University Press).

Beal, B. (1996) Alternative masculinity and its effects on gender relations in the subculture of skateboarding, *Journal of Sport Behaviour*, 19(3), pp. 214–220.

Booth, M. *et al.* (1997) *NSW Schools Fitness and Physical Activity Survey 1997* (Sydney, NSW Department of School Education).

Bourdieu, P. (1984) *Distinction: A Social Critique of the Judgement of Taste* (London, Routledge).

Connell, R. (2000) *The Men and the Boys* (Sydney, Allen & Unwin).

Courtice, R. (1999) All-male schooling: speech night and the construction of masculinities, in C. Symes & D. Meadmore (Eds) *The Extraordinary School* (New York, Peter Lang).

Crouch, D. (2000) Places around us: embodied lay geographies in leisure and tourism, *Leisure Studies*, 19(2), pp. 63–76.

De Knop, P. (1998) Worldwide trends in youth sport, in R. Naul (Ed.) *Physical Activity and Active Lifestyles of Children and Youth* (Paris, ICSSPE).

Deem, R. (1999) How do we get out of the ghetto? Strategies for research on gender and leisure for the twenty-first century, *Leisure Studies*, 18(3), pp. 161–177.

Foucault, M. (1980) *The History of Sexuality: Volume 1. An Introduction*, R. Hurley (Trans.) (New York, Vintage).

Gard, M. & Wright, J. (2001) Managing uncertainty: obesity discourses and physical education in a risk society, *Studies in Philosophy and Education*, 20(6), pp. 535–549.

Georgakis, S. (2000) *Sport and the Australian Greek: An Historical Study of Ethnicity, Gender and Youth* (Rozelle, Standard Publishing House).

Gilbert, P. & Gilbert, R. (1998) *Masculinity Goes to School* (Sydney, Allen & Unwin).

Grimshaw, J. (1999) Working out with Merleau-Ponty, in J. Arthurs & J. Grimshaw (Eds) *Women's Bodies: Discipline and Transgression* (London, Cassell).

Hendry, L., Shucksmith, J., Love, J. & Glendinning, A. (1993) *Young People's Leisure and Lifestyles* (London, Routledge).

Kirk, D. (1997) Schooling bodies for new times: the reform of school physical education in high modernity, in J-M. Fernandez-Balboa (Ed.) *Critical Postmodernism in Human Movement, Physical Education and Sport* (Albany, Suny Press).

Kirk, D. *et al.* (1997) Time commitments in junior sport: social consequences for participants and their families, *European Journal of Physical Education*, 2, pp. 51–73.

Layder, D. (1997) *Modern Social Theory* (London, UCL Press).

Lupton, D. (1995) *The Imperative of Health: Public Health and the Regulated Body* (London, Sage).

Malina, R.M. (1996) Tracking of physical activity and physical fitness across the lifespan, *Research Quarterly for Exercise and Sport*, 67, pp. 48–57.

Mangan, J.A. (1981) *Athleticism in the Victorian and Edwardian Public School* (Cambridge, Cambridge University Press).

Markula, P. (1998) Women's health, physical fitness and ideal body: a problematic relationship, *Journal of Physical Education New Zealand*, 31(1), pp. 9–13.

McLaren, P. & Farahmandpur, R. (2000) Reconsidering Marx in post-Marxist times: a requiem for postmodernism? *Educational Researcher*, April, pp. 25–33.

McLennan, W. (1997) *Youth Australia: A Social Report* (Canberra, Australian Bureau of Statistics).

Mosely, P. (1995) *Ethnic Involvement in Australian Soccer: A History 1950–1990* (Canberra, Australian Sports Commission).

Mota, J. & Silva, S. (1999) Adolescent's physical activity: association with socio-economic status and parental participation among a Portuguese sample, *Sport Education and Society*, 4(2), pp. 193–199.

O'Donnell, M. & Sharp, S. (2000) *Uncertain Masculinities* (London, Routledge).

Pallotta-Chiarolli, M. (1998) *Girls' Talk: Young People Speak their Hearts and Minds* (Sydney, Finch Publishing).

Penney, D. & Evans, J. (1999) *Politics, Policy and Practice* (London, E & FN Spon).

Roberts, K. (1996) Young people, schools, sport and government policies, *Sport Education and Society*, 1(1), pp. 47–58.

Roberts, K. & Fagan, C. (1999) Young people and their leisure in former communist countries: four theses examined, *Leisure Studies*, 18(1), pp. 1–17.

Scraton, S., Fasting, K., Pfister, G. & Bunuel, A. (1999) It's still a man's game? The experiences of top-level European women footballers, *International Review for the Sociology of Sport*, 34(2), pp. 99–111.

Telama, R., Yang, X., Laakso, L. & Viikari, J. (1997) Physical activity in childhood and adolescence as predictor of physical activity in young adulthood, *American Journal of Preventive Medicine*, 13(3), pp. 17–23.

Walker, J.C. (1988) *Louts and Legends: Male Youth Culture in an Inner-city School* (Sydney, Allen & Unwin).

Wearing, B. & Wearing, S. (1990) Leisure for all? Gender and policy, in: D. Rowe & G. Lawrence (Eds) *Sport and Leisure: Trends in Australian Popular Culture* (Sydney, Harcourt Brace Jovanovich).

Whitson, D. (1994) The embodiment of gender: discipline, domination and empowerment, in: S. Birrell & C. Cole (Eds) *Women, Sport and Culture* (Champaign, IL, Human Kinetics).

Yang, X., Telama, R. & Laakso, L. (1996) Parents' physical activity, socio-economic status and education as predictors of physical activity and sport among children and youth: a 12 year follow up study, *International Review for the Sociology of Sport*, 31, pp. 273–289.

Young, I.M. (1980) Throwing like a girl: a phenomenology of feminine body comportment, motility and spatiality, *Human Studies*, 3, pp. 137–156.

Young, K. (1997) Women, sport and physicality, *International Review for the Sociology of Sport*, 32, pp. 297–305.

PART 4

Learners and learning

INTRODUCTION

AS WE NOTED IN THE INTRODUCTION, learning is one component of
pedagogy, along with curriculum and teaching. Until recently, learning was very much
the poor second cousin to teaching in educational research on physical education. This is
why the papers in this section date from the late 1990s even though research in physical
education appeared in earnest in the 1970s. **Rink** in particular makes the case that any
theory of teaching must be based on a sound understanding of how learning happens, and
argues that this point has been overlooked by researchers who in the earlier years of physical education research probably gave too much attention to teaching. Part of the difficulty
here was due to the behaviourist orientation of early educational research on physical
education, which relied on learners' observable actions as proxy measures for learning,
which was seen to be an effect of teaching.

Lee's sustained contribution to research on student cognition marks a clear break
with this behaviourist perspective and frees physical education scholars to consider how
learning may occur even when it is not observed. The paper by **Kirk and Macdonald** builds
on the work of researchers such as Lee and her colleagues to broaden the focus on learning
even further, beyond individuals, to consider how learning is situated within social relationships and settings. The final paper by **Evans** questions assumptions about commonplace
ways of thinking about learning and the emphasis placed in physical education on traditional notions like ability in particular. All four papers mark an important shift in recognition
of the importance of understanding how learning occurs in physical education.

FURTHER READING

Li, W. (2006) Understanding the meaning of effort in learning a motor skill: ability conception. *Journal of Teaching in Physical Education*, 25, 295–306.

Wellard, I., Pickard, A. and Bailey, R.P. (2007) 'A Shock of Electricity Just Sort of Goes Through My Body': physical activity and embodied reflexive practices in young female ballet dancers. *Gender and Education*, 19(1), 79–91.

Tinning, R. and Fitzclarence, L. (1992) Postmodern youth culture and the crisis in Australian secondary school physical education. *Quest*, 44, 287–303.

David Kirk and Doune Macdonald

SITUATED LEARNING IN PHYSICAL EDUCATION

W E WILL ARGUE in this paper that a constructivist approach to learning may offer itself as a useful framework to inform and integrate pedagogical practices in physical education. In the last two decades, theories of learning in physical education have been dominated by the tenets of the mediating variable paradigm. A central notion within this paradigm is that teacher behaviors shape student behaviors. Student behaviors, in turn, are considered to be proximal indicators of learning. Locke (1979) identified instruction and engagement in active performance of learning tasks, or "time on task", as two behaviors which mediate between the teaching and learning of physical activities. As a consequence, research traditions have built up around questions of how best to structure instructional tasks and maximize time on task using ALT:PE instrumentation. While the mediating variable paradigm has continued to dominate ways of thinking about learning in physical education, a number of areas of the school curriculum have benefited recently from the application of constructivist approaches to learning (e.g., Cobb, 1994; Driver et al., 1994). In light of new challenges facing physical education, such as student alienation and a widely discussed crisis in the subject, it may be appropriate to begin to explore constructivism as a means of complementing existing approaches to learning in physical education.

Constructivist approaches emphasize that learning is an active process in which the individual seeks out information in relation to the task at hand and the environmental conditions prevailing at any given time, and tests out her or his own capabilities within the context formed by the task and environment. Relatedly, learning is situated in social and cultural contexts and is influenced by these contexts. Constructivist approaches also stress that learning is developmental, both in the sense that there are identifiable phases in learning physical skills and that the ways people learn change over time due to growth, maturation and experience. A further feature of constructivist approaches is that learning is multi-dimensional in the sense that individuals typically learn more than one thing at a time, often implicitly as in the case of the hidden curriculum. Finally, constructivist approaches attempt to cater for differences in individuals' preferred learning styles.

As Rovegno and Kirk (1995) have shown, physical educators have a long tradition of practices that share some of these features of constructivism, through for example applications of the work of Rudolf Laban to movement education, and in the books of Bilborough and Jones (1963) and Mauldon and Redfern (1969), among others. These authors stressed that learning is an active and creative process involving individuals in interaction with their physical environment and with other learners. While these approaches survive in the practices of some physical educators, it might reasonably be observed that they lack prominence and influence in the 1990s.

A recent *Journal of Teaching in Physical Education* monograph (Rink, 1996) has focused on approaches to learning in sports and games. One approach the monograph highlights is teaching games for understanding. This approach emphasizes game appreciation and tactical awareness as a basis for making game play decisions and meeting skill development needs. In our view, the games sense approach may be consistent with constructivist approaches to learning, particularly due to the emphasis placed on active learning, involving processes of perception, decision making and understanding, and developmental factors involving the modification of games to suit the learner.

Our view is that constructivist influences, sometimes associated with student centered learning, have the potential to contribute to new theoretical perspectives on learning in the physical domain that can regenerate school physical education. Along with Locke (1992) and others we suggest that such regeneration has now, as we approach a new millennium, become a matter of utmost priority for physical educators. Our sense of urgency here derives from widespread concerns about an alleged "crisis" in both primary (Kirk, 1996) and secondary (Siedentop, 1987) school physical education and, in particular, from responses to this crisis that call for "back-to-basics" forms of physical education. These back-to-basics forms conceptualize physical education as the development of non-cognitive and narrowly sport-related "fundamental motor skills" and "physical fitness". We are worried too by widespread reports of physical education's apparent lack of meaningfulness in many children's lives, the allegedly inauthentic ways in which physical education practices relate to other social practices, and by reports of children's alienation from physical activity, from their bodies and from themselves (Graham, 1995).

The apparent neglect of individuals' needs and interests with regard to learning is evident in much curriculum research which has tended to focus more broadly on the social organization of school knowledge. Where individuals have been considered within curriculum research, this has most often been in the context of understanding how people make sense of their experiences as school students or as teachers. Generally, our own individual and collaborative curriculum research programs have paid scant attention to students' learning and we have increasingly come to regard this as a shortcoming that needs to be addressed. We now believe that curriculum development requires an underpinning theory of learning. Any meaningful or useful syllabus, course advice or program of study that presents a selection of sequenced content, teaching strategies, learning experiences and assessment tasks will be embedded, often implicitly, in sets of assumptions about how people learn and what it is important that they learn. In our experience, many well documented "failures" of curriculum development in physical education (see Locke, 1992; National Professional Development Project, 1996; Sparkes, 1990; Tinning & Kirk, 1991) may have owed as much to an underdeveloped concern for learning as to the multifarious other factors so often cited in the curriculum innovation and development literature.

In light of these problems and concerns, our task in this paper is to sketch the beginnings of a theory of learning that can integrate and enrich current pedagogical practices and locate these practices socially and historically. Building on the work of Rovegno and Kirk (1995) and Macdonald et al. (1994), and drawing heavily on Lave and Wenger (1991), we will attempt to demonstrate that a version of situated learning theory could form a basis for integrating other forms of social constructionist research in the pedagogy of physical activity. We begin this paper with a brief comment on some uses of the term "constructivism" in the physical activity pedagogy literature. In a second section, we provide an outline of some of the key tenets of Lave and Wenger's (1991) version of situated learning theory. We then go on to show how this version of situated learning theory can be applied to thinking about the social construction of school physical education using the example of sport education.

Uses of constructivism in physical activity pedagogy

Constructivist theories of learning have had a somewhat limited application to physical education to date. Within the education field generally, there is some controversy surrounding the meaning and use of the term "constructivism" itself. Both Phillips (1995) and Anderson, Reder and Simon (1996) award it the status of a "philosophic position". They see constructivism as a paradigm or set of ideological assumptions, rather than as an operational theory or set of theories supported by extensive empirical research findings. Rovegno and Kirk (1995) note the term's quite different meanings in the fields of motor control and educational learning theory. Besides the papers by Rovegno and Kirk (1995) and Macdonald et al. (1994), where constructivism is used in the same or a similar form to its use in this paper, a number of authors concerned with physical education appear to have been influenced by the theoretical developments that have been located under the umbrella of constructivism. These include Rovegno's work with notions of pedagogical content knowledge in teaching (Rovegno, 1993, 1995) and Ennis's research using the concept of dynamical systems to reconceptualize learning (Ennis, 1992).

Rink, French and Tjeerdsma (1996) suggest that constructivism has gone in and out of fashion over a number of decades, and has been associated primarily with experiential learning, discovery learning, and problem-solving. They suggest research support for constructivist approaches has been lacking as it has been unable to show any clear advantage over other inquiry-oriented approaches. However, they do suggest constructivism, as it has been conceptualized in some programs of study, may produce more positive affective outcomes than other approaches.

Explicit use of the term constructivism as a means of identifying the core theoretical assumptions of their research in physical education has been made by only a handful of authors, including Grehaigne and Godbout (1995), Anderson (1994) and Pissanos and Allison (1993). Taken together these three papers provide a useful illustration of the diversity of interpretations of the term constructivism in the physical activity literature and the uses to which it might be put.

Grehaigne and Godbout (1995) compare and contrast two approaches to learning and performing in team sports such as soccer, hockey and volleyball that they describe as "constructivist" and "cognitivist". Their work is an attempt to move towards the development of a substantive theory of the place of tactical knowledge in team game performance, and in this respect may be viewed as an ecological theory of learning, concerned principally with the relationships between individual, task and environment. Their focus at the level of substantive theory concerned specifically with team games means, however, that their development of a constructivist theory of learning is somewhat restricted in scope at this stage, and may have limited application to learning in other areas of physical activity.

Anderson (1994) attempts a reconciliation between behaviorism and constructivism in the context of physical education teacher education. The thrust of his argument is that it is possible to reconcile both perspectives and integrate some of their key concerns within one learning theory. We think his critique of both "isms" has some value and the synthesis he attempts is laudable. However, rather than explore constructivism's positive contribution to learning theory in its own right, Anderson presents a version of constructivism constrained by the task of correcting what he perceives to be the deficiencies of behaviorism. For example, he claims that constructivism is concerned, in part, with understanding students' perceptions. Once these perceptions are taken into account by the teacher, teaching a skill based on a constructivist approach "would probably appear very much like a behaviorist approach to teaching" (Anderson, 1994, p. 16).

Pissanos and Allison (1993) select one feature of constructivism, "the learner's perspective", and proceed to represent this as a constructivist theory of learning. We agree with their claim that students' perspectives are vitally important to understanding how people learn in physical education. However, we suggest that in addition to incorporating the student's perspective, constructivist approaches need to conceptualize the learner as an active participant, and learning as individualized, developmental and social in character.

While we do not claim this to be an exhaustive survey of the uses of the term "constructivism" in the pedagogy of physical activity literature, we cite these papers to illustrate the diverse ways in which a constructivist theory has been called upon to address instruction and learning in physical education. We cite them also to make the point along with Rovegno and Kirk (1995) that there is no one version of constructivism. However, it appears to us that there is a need for a more theoretically developed view of constructivism if this approach is to be useful in improving our understanding of learners and learning in physical education. We propose that this approach has the potential to integrate thinking about physical education across the pedagogical categories of curriculum, instruction and learning and in relation to individual and societal concerns. The following section outlines Lave and Wenger's situated learning theory as one example of a constructivist approach to learning.

Situated learning as a component of a constructivist approach to physical education

Situated learning theories attempt to broaden attention from the learner as an "isolated" individual to include a focus on the social settings that construct and constitute the individual as a learner (Lave & Wenger, 1991). Situated learning focuses on learning as a social practice in social settings. In its most simplistic uses, the "situatedness" of learning means merely that learning takes place in particular sets of circumstances, in time and space. In addition, it may refer to the fact that learning is social in so far as it may involve interaction between an individual learner and others. Our initial attraction to the work of Lave and Wenger was due to the potential of their approach to assist the development of our understanding of the broad range of social practices of which learning is an integral part. One advantage of such an approach is that it permits the analysis of the learning of physical activities in a whole range of sites (such as community sport and exercise settings), though our particular interest in this paper is specifically in school physical education.

The key concepts in Lave and Wenger's theory of situated learning are the notions of *legitimate peripheral participation* in *communities of practice*. Lave and Wenger suggest that legitimate peripheral participation in communities of practice needs to be understood as a whole concept rather than in terms of its parts, though some consideration of each part in relation to the others can assist our understanding of the whole concept.

Although the term *community of practice* is not clearly defined by Lave and Wenger, it is of central importance to their theory. We understand the notion of community of practice to refer to any collectivity or group who together contribute to shared or public practices in particular spheres of life. Within Lave and Wenger's theory, one example of a community of practice would be an occupational group such as teachers. To build on this example, teachers may also be part of a larger community of practice such as the school where, in addition to teachers as salaried workers, the school includes administrators and other workers and students. The advantage of describing the activities of teachers specifically or the school more generally as "communities of practice" is that this allows us to identify the specific social contexts and activities that shape the learning trajectories of individuals within each community.

Lave and Wenger claim that the activities of a community of practice provide learners with a framework for making sense of this specific sphere of life. In other words, the social and cultural contexts in which a community of practice exists and to which its activities contribute have a significant influence on what is learned and how learning takes place. According to Lave and Wenger (1991, p. 98), the ways in which a community of practice is structured in terms of its social relationships "define possibilities for learning". A key part of this notion of community of practice is a person's identity in relation to other members of a community. This issue relates to affective development and, as Rink et al. (1996) suggest, may be a particular strength of some constructivist approaches to learning.

Lave and Wenger's notion of *legitimate* peripheral participation in a community of practice is intended to convey the sense of authentic or genuine participation, where a person's involvement in the practices of a community are meaningful to them as individuals and also hold significance for other community members. Lave and Wenger suggest that underlying this notion of legitimate peripherality are relations of power in terms of how individuals are positioned and the kinds of access they are able to gain to the resources of particular communities of practice. They note through a series of ethnographic case studies of occupational apprenticeship that it is not uncommon for legitimate peripheral participants to be denied access to crucial human and material resources. Such barriers can adversely affect their learning trajectories towards full participation. In a physical activity context barriers may take the form of limited field time for children in team sports, or personality clashes with a teacher or a coach, or financial, or other material barriers such as lack of equipment.

Lave and Wenger go to some lengths to suggest that legitimate *peripheral* participation is not meant to imply that there is a core or center of a community of practice but rather to suggest that all participation occurs within sets of *relationships* in which people begin as "new-comers" or novitiates and that they may move towards *full* participation involving particular experience and expertise and new sets of relationships. In their words, "peripheral participation is about being located in the social world, *changing* locations and perspectives are part of actors' learning trajectories, developing identities, and forms of membership" (Lave & Wenger, 1991, p. 36, original emphasis). Their notion of legitimate peripheral *participation* signals a concern shared by other constructivist theories of learning for active involvement by persons in the construction of knowledge through meaningful social activity.

Lave and Wenger concede that the place of communities of practice within their theory of situated learning as legitimate peripheral participation requires considerable conceptual sharpening and empirical support. They set this task aside for the future but make the interesting observation that communities of practice may be identified by the cyclical processes through which they reproduce themselves and in which it is possible to discern regularities and patterns of practices. One example of this would be where some of the practices of sport, such as the techniques, tactics and styles of play, and the beliefs and values surrounding sport, may be reproduced in and through lessons in physical education classes.

At the same time, we need to note that the school mediates the reproduction of communities of practice. One explanation of how schools may do this is advanced by Bereiter (1990). Building on the idea of knowledge structures as "contextual modules", Bereiter identifies different modules operating in a variety of learning situations. In schools, he states that the dominant form of learning can be characterized as the "school-work module". Acquisition of the schoolwork module provides children with a means of coping with the hidden as well as the official curriculum of schools, in much the way Jackson (1968) described in his celebrated book *Life in classrooms*. While assisting children to cope with learning in curriculum activities such as physical education, this module simultaneously sets up social relationships and forms of participation that may not necessarily match those in related communities of practice outside the school gates, such as sport, exercise or physical recreation. In short, the form of learning represented by Bereiter's schoolwork module may have little transfer value to related situations outside the school. In Bereiter's terms, the schoolwork module mediates, and in so doing alters, the forms of knowledge produced within the communities of sport, physical recreation and exercise, each of which contributes subject matter to school physical education. This is highly problematic when a typical aim of school physical educators is to prepare children to pursue an active lifestyle in adulthood.

School physical education and communities of practice

In this section we want to show how the concept of legitimate peripheral participation in communities of practice might be applied to understanding situated learning in school physical education. A key point to be considered is *which* communities of practice are being mediated and reproduced in and through physical education classes and, relatedly, what knowledge and other resources for meaning making are provided to young people by these communities of practices?

We suggest that the communities of practice which have strong substantive relation-ships to school physical education are the overlapping fields of sport, exercise and physical recreation. These institutionalized practices form the "physical culture" of most western societies. Sport, exercise and physical recreation provide many of the practices that constitute school physical education, its subject matter, instructional strategies and forms of learning. Teachers, students and their parents, administrators and policy-makers, each draw for the most part differently and unequally on these communities of practice and the discursive resources they provide to make school physical education possible. Using Lave and Wenger's terms, we might argue that school physical education reproduces some aspects of the communities of practice of sport, exercise and recreation through young people's engagement in physical education lessons.

If a typical aspiration of school physical education programs is indeed to prepare young people for an active lifestyle beyond school-age and into adulthood, application of Lave and Wenger's theory of situated learning would suggest that school physical educa-tion may regularly and consistently *fail* to provide young people with opportunities for legitimate peripheral participation in the communities of practice of sport, exercise and physical recreation. The reasons for this failure are many and complex and have been addressed in detail elsewhere (Evans, 1990; Kirk, 1994a; Locke, 1992). We propose that the alleged crisis in school physical education is an outcome of this failure. Part of the reason for this is that physical culture has been undergoing rapid and accelerating change since at least the 1980s and has been taking forms that have been extremely difficult for schools to reproduce, such as media sport, commercialized exercise culture and new physical recreational activities like white water rafting and bungee jumping (Brooker & Macdonald, 1995; Kirk, 1994b).

At the same time, school physical education has not disappeared from the curricula of schools and schools continue to aspire to reproduce some forms of these communities of practice, evident in such ubiquitous aims as "providing the skills to pursue lifelong physical recreational activities" and "enabling children to lead healthy and active lifestyles". We noted earlier Lave and Wenger's claim that the activities of a community of prac-tice provide learners with a framework for making sense (Lave & Wenger, 1991, p. 98). We noted, moreover, that the communities of practice of sport, exercise and physical recreation provide school physical education with its subject matter, its modes of organiza-tion, the forms in which participation might occur and the codes that should inform participants' conduct. Arguably, many aspects of the communities of practice that cur-rently regulate, construct and constitute school physical education no longer exist outside the school setting (Kirk, 1994a). For instance, a "command" style of instruction, derived from a militaristic form of calisthenics, continues to dominate the teaching of school physical education, even though calisthenics and other militarized forms of physical activity such as drilling and marching no longer exist in schools and in the 1990s play a less prominent role in the physical culture of western societies than they did formerly.

It becomes apparent that, in addition to the multifarious other problems that beset school physical education, a crisis exists in school physical education because it is unable in its current forms to reproduce the communities of practice that provide it with meaning and legitimacy among both professional audiences and the lay-public. In circumstances such as these, it is important to note the emergence of new forms of school physical education that are modeled explicitly on currently existing communities of practice. We suggest that there have been several new forms. One is the health-related fitness form of physical education that emerged from the work of Whitehead and Fox (1983) in Britain in the 1980s, which was an attempt to reproduce communities of exercisers by providing students with the knowledge and skills required to engage in health-related exercise. In more general terms, Hellison's (1985) social responsibility model presents another new form of physical education that attempts to reproduce the community of self-regulating citizens by providing young people with opportunities to learn to be accountable for their actions using sport as the medium. Recently in Australia, Alexander and his colleagues have developed a version of sport education that provides an excellent illustration of an attempt to reproduce the contemporary community of practice of sport (Alexander, Taggart & Thorpe, 1996).

The case of sport education

Alexander et al.'s (1996) version of sport education, which owes a considerable debt to Siedentop's work (e.g., Siedentop, 1994), sets up a form of school physical education modeled on community-based sport, though neither Alexander et al. nor Siedentop have theorized sport education as a form of situated learning. However, their descriptions of sport education and their rationale for its development fit this theorization precisely. Sport education operates during regular curriculum time and treats units of work as "seasons" that typically run across ten or twenty sessions. Matched, mixed ability teams compete, often using modified forms of games and sports. Students not only learn to become players in this context, but also have opportunities to become managers and coaches, officials, publicists, and members of the "Sports Board" that has overall responsibility for governing the competition. According to Alexander et al., the teacher may take a directive role early in the season but increasingly becomes a facilitator for the students' achievement of personal and social goals.

Using the language of Lave and Wenger's theory of situated learning, sport education offers young people opportunities to engage in the community of practice of sport as legitimate peripheral participants, in a variety of roles such as player, manager, coach and so on. By providing these opportunities for legitimate or authentic participation, by adopting the format of seasons, in line with community-based sport, and by recasting physical education lessons as matches and training sessions, the school reproduces aspects of the contemporary community of practice as it exists outside the school.

The reasons Alexander et al. give for the development of this form of physical education, again drawing heavily on Siedentop's lead, is the poor educational status of the subject, both in relation to other school subjects and to community and professional sports, and widespread evidence that many young people learn to dislike participation in physical activity through school physical education. On the basis of their research to date, they argue that sport education has achieved considerable success. This success is due, among other things, to its perceived authenticity and relevance by both students and teachers, in other words, to the opportunities for *legitimate* peripheral participation it affords (see also Carlson, 1995).

Alexander et al. state that this version of sport education is only one curriculum model for physical education, and they are careful to note the socially and educationally less desirable aspects of sport as a community of practice. In our view they are correct to do this for two reasons. In the first place, there are, as Tinning (1995) and others have pointed out, aspects of the contemporary practice of sport such as cheating, drug abuse and corruption, that school physical education would clearly not wish to reproduce (see also Curnow & Macdonald, 1995). Since many young people might at best become recreational participants in sport, or more typically spectators of sport, rather than professional athletes, it would seem to us that part of the process of being a legitimate peripheral participant in sport as a community of practice will involve the development of young people's skills of critical consumption of sport as a commodity.

Secondly, there are at least two other substantive communities of practice that can be reproduced through school physical education, exercise and physical recreation, and it appears to us that these have as much claim on curriculum time as does sport. The role of school physical education is to offer young people opportunities to be legitimate peripheral participants in each of these overlapping communities of practice, where "participation" will include one or more of the roles of player or exerciser, volunteer administrator, instructor, coach or helper, consumer, and less likely for the majority, a professional in one of these roles.

Any curriculum model such as sport education will inevitably need to find some means of minimizing the effects of Bereiter's "schoolwork" module in terms of inauthentic participation, while at the same time optimizing the value of this module as a means of institutional survival for students. How sport education does this remains to be seen. Results of studies to date suggest that, at least for some children, this form of sport education that models some of the currently existing practices of community sport is well received and may have some useful carryover beyond the "schoolwork" context criticized by Bereiter.

Discussion and conclusion

We suggest that Siedentop, Alexander et al. and some other advocates for sport education have grasped the need for a form of physical education that offers students opportunities for meaningful, authentic and differentiated participation in a form of physical activity, and that provides imperatives for the ordering of subject matter, for relationships between actors (e.g., player-coach, team mates, opponents), and for forms of identity (e.g., team membership). At the same time, they and others recognize the historically and socially contingent nature of these factors that provide structure and substance to sport education, a matter that can be a subject for study in itself. The community of practice that constitutes sport can therefore be reproduced *and* transformed through the pedagogical form of sport education. It can be reproduced through young people acquiring already existing techniques and knowledge for participating in a range of roles in sport. It can be transformed through young people acquiring the skills of a critical consumer of sport and of the many varied products of the sport industry.

We hope through this paper to have provided some basis for beginning to develop a theory of physical activity pedagogy that has the potential to integrate analyses across curriculum, instruction and learning and in relation to individual and societal concerns. At the same time, much remains to be done. Sport education provides a good example of what might be possible in reforming school physical education, but we need to note a number of issues that require attention before we might claim to have grasped the complete requirements of an integrated theory of physical activity pedagogy.

One issue is the need to recognize that the theory of situated learning discussed here is only one component of a constructivist approach to learning, which in turn can be located in a social constructionist approach more generally. As Rovegno and Kirk (1995) point out, ecological and developmental theories of learning have much to offer such an approach in terms of understanding the interfaces of individual, task and environment in any given pedagogic episode, and how learning develops over time. Along with Rink (1996) and her colleagues, we propose that the teaching games for understanding (Bunker & Thorpe, 1983) model provides one excellent example of an ecological theory of learning that, we claim, would fit well within a constructivist approach generally and the sport education model specifically.

Through the deployment of Lave and Wenger's (1991) notion of situated learning as legitimate peripheral participation in communities of practice, we suggest that it is possible to produce a theory of learning that is historically and socially situated, that has considerable analytical power, and that will be able to guide policy development as well as the development of curriculum and of teacher education programs. A major strength of this theory is that it applies to learning as legitimate peripheral participation in a range of communities of practice in which physical activity is the main medium of learning, such as settings for sports coaching and exercise instruction. Schools and these other communities of practice can then be positioned in relation to one another, a process that demands an integration of theories and their forms of research in order to understand the reproduction and transformation of physical culture.

We suggest that the need for new ways of thinking about old and sometimes perennial problems, such as the relationship of the practices of school physical education to the communities it purports to serve, is increasing at an exponential rate. Reports of crisis in physical education, students' alienation from the subject, and its continuing marginalization in the curricula of many schools, prompt us to explore new possibilities for theorizing learning and in so doing we might better understand the nature of the subject and what it might contribute to the education of young people who face new challenges, risks and opportunities in the new millennium. We are not suggesting that constructivist theories of learning magically provide "the answer" to such compelling questions, but we do argue that such theories provide the potential for more sophisticated and powerful means of thinking about specific issues now confronting physical educators and other workers in the field of physical activity pedagogy.

References

Alexander, K., Taggart, A., & Thorpe, S. (1996). A spring in their steps? Possibilities for professional renewal through Sport Education in Australian schools. *Sport, Education and Society*, *1*, 23–46.

Anderson, A. (1994). How constructivism and behaviorism can complement each other in the preparation of physical education professionals. *CAPHERD Journal*, Fall, 13–18.

Anderson, J. R., Reder, L. M., & Simon, H. A. (1996). Situated learning and education. *Educational Researcher*, *25*, 5–11.

Bereiter, C. (1990). Aspects of an educational learning theory. *Review of Educational Research*, *60*, 603–624.

Bilborough, A., & Jones, P. (1963). *Physical education in the primary school*. London: University of London Press.

Bunker, D., & Thorpe, R. (1983). A model for the teaching of games in secondary schools. *Bulletin of Physical Education, 19*(1), 5–8.

Brooker, R., & Macdonald, D. (1995). Mapping physical education in the reform agenda for Australian education: tensions and contradictions. *European Physical Education Review, 1*(2), 101–110.

Carlson, T. B. (1995). "Now, I think I can". The reaction of eight low-skilled students to sport education. *ACHPER National Journal, 42*(2), 68.

Cobb, P. (1994). Constructivism in mathematics and science education. *Educational Researcher, 23,* 4.

Curnow, J., & Macdonald, D. (1995). Can sport education be gender inclusive? A case study in upper primary. *ACHPER National Journal, 42*(2), 9–11.

Driver, R., Asoko, H., Leach, J., Mortimer, E., & Scott, P. (1994). Constructing scientific knowledge in the classroom. *Educational Researcher, 23,* 5–12.

Ennis, C. D. (1992). Reconceptualizing learning as a dynamical system. *Journal of Curriculum and Supervision, 7,* 115–130.

Evans, J. (1990). Defining a subject: The rise and rise of the new PE. *British Journal of Sociology of Education, 11,* 155–169.

Graham, G. (Ed.) (1995). Physical education through students' eyes and in students' voices [Monograph]. *Journal of Teaching in Physical Education, 14* (4).

Grehaigne, J-F., & Godbout, P. (1995). Tactical knowledge in team sports from a constructivist and cognitivist perspective. *Quest, 47,* 490–505.

Hellison, D. (1985). *Goals and strategies for teaching physical education.* Champaign, Ill.: Human Kinetics.

Jackson, P. W. (1968). *Life in classrooms.* New York: Holt, Rinehart and Winston.

Kirk, D. (1994a). "Making the present strange": Sources of the current crisis in physical education. *Discourse: The Australian Journal of Educational Studies, 15,* 46–63.

Kirk, D. (1994b). Physical education and regimes of the body. *Australian and New Zealand Journal of Sociology, 30,* 165–177.

Kirk, D. (1996). The crisis in school physical education: An argument against the tide. *The ACHPER Healthy Lifestyles Journal, 43,* 25–27.

Lave, J., & Wenger, E. (1991). *Situated learning: legitimate peripheral participation.* New York: Cambridge University Press.

Locke, L. (1979). Teaching and learning processes in physical education: The central problem of sport pedagogy. In H. Haag et al. (Eds.) *Physical education and evaluation.* Proceedings of the I.C.H.P.E.R. World Congress, Schorndorf, Germany.

Locke, L. (1992). Changing secondary school physical education. *Quest, 44,* 361–372.

Macdonald, D., Kirk, D., Rovegno, I., Brooker, R., & Abernethy, B. (1994, November). Cognition and context: revisiting skill learning through a multidisciplinary approach. Paper presented to the Annual Conference of the Australian Association for Research in Education, Newcastle, NSW.

Mauldon, E., & Redfern, H. B. (1969). *Games teaching: A new approach for the primary school.* London: Macdonald and Evans.

National Professional Development Project (1996). *Reviewing curriculum in the health and physical education key learning area.* Canberra: Department of Employment, Education and Training.

Phillips, D. C. (1995). The good, the bad and the ugly: The many faces of constructivism. *Educational Researcher, 24,* 5–12.

Pissanos, B. W. & Allison, P. C. (1993). Students' constructs of elementary school physical education. *Research Quarterly for Exercise and Sport, 64,* 425–435.

Rink, J. (Ed.) (1996). Tactical and skill approaches to teaching sport and games [Monograph]. *Journal of Teaching in Physical Education*, *15*(4).

Rink, J. E., French, K., & Tjeerdsma, B. (1996). Foundations for the learning and instruction of sport and games. *Journal of Teaching in Physical Education*, *15*, 399–417.

Rovegno, I. (1993). Content-knowledge acquisition during undergraduate teacher education: Overcoming cultural templates and learning through practice. *American Educational Research Journal*, *30*(3), 611–642.

Rovegno, I. (1995). Theoretical perspectives on knowledge and learning and a student teacher's pedagogical content knowledge of dividing and sequencing subject matter. *Journal of Teaching in Physical Education*, *14*, 284–304.

Rovegno, I., & Kirk, D. (1995). Articulations and silences in socially critical work on physical education: toward a broader agenda. *Quest*, *47*, 447–474.

Siedentop, D. (1994). *Sport education*. Champaign, Ill: Human Kinetics.

Siedentop, D. (1987). High school physical education: Still an endangered species. *Journal of Teaching in Physical Education*, *8*, 187–270.

Sparkes, A. C. (1990). *Curriculum change and physical education: towards a micropolitical understanding*. Geelong: Deakin University Press.

Tinning, R. (1995). The sport education movement: a phoenix, bandwagon or hearse for physical education. *ACHPER National Journal*, *42*(2), 19–21.

Tinning, R., & Kirk, D. (1991). *Daily physical education: collected papers on health based physical education in Australia*. Geelong: Deakin University Press.

Whitehead, J., & Fox, K. (1983). Student centred physical education. *Bulletin of Physical Education*, *19*(2), 21–30.

Amelia M. Lee

CONTRIBUTIONS OF RESEARCH ON STUDENT THINKING IN PHYSICAL EDUCATION

RECENT EFFORTS TO understand how learning occurs from teaching have included the study of students' thoughts, beliefs, expectations, motivations, attitudes, and feelings about themselves, the content and events in achievement situations. This focus views students as active participants who affect events and interactions in classrooms as much as they are affected by them. The emphasis on the role of student thoughts and feelings as mediators between teaching and learning has resulted in a change in the kinds of questions researchers ask and the methodology used to answer the questions (Knight & Waxman, 1991). The assumed connection between teaching and learning is clarified by including the perspective of the learner. This paper will provide some background information, discuss issues related to self-report measures, and summarize the research designed to contribute to our understanding of the variables that influence students' thinking and the role of student thinking in physical education settings. I draw heavily on my own research and the contributions from classroom settings, but I will try to include other findings that are available in physical education.

Beginnings of research on student thinking

Schunk (1992) suggests that from a historical perspective, an understanding of the current emphases in student thinking can be gained by examining the three editions of the *Handbook of Research on Teaching*. Neither the 1963 edition edited by Gage, nor the 1973 edition edited by Travers contained a chapter on student thinking. In the third edition published in 1986, a chapter written by Merlin Wittrock emphasized how teaching can influence achievement through student thought processes. He highlights the value of studying student thinking by making the following argument:

Perhaps teaching can directly influence achievement, just as learning can sometimes occur without awareness. But research on students' cognitive processes examines and tests the utility of assuming otherwise, that teaching can better be understood and improved, by knowing its effects upon the learners' thoughts that mediate achievement.

(Wittrock, 1996b, p. 297)

Research summarized by Wittrock emphasized the effects of teachers upon the student perceptions, expectations, attentional processes, motivation, attributions, memories, beliefs, attitudes, and learning strategies that mediate achievement. While Wittrock examined how teaching influences what students think, believe, feel, and say, little information was included to help us understand how student thought processes and beliefs affect what goes on in classrooms.

Pedagogical studies of student thinking began to appear when scholars brought attention to the need for researchers to go beyond describing what teachers and students do in classes, stressing that learning is not a passive process. In 1978, Doyle argued for the need to extend the mediating process approach to include the thought processes of students from both cognitive and social perspectives. He stressed the need to analyze how students interpret the content presented by the teacher, and how they go about interacting with the assigned tasks in the social environment of the classroom.

Also in the 1970s, the theoretical basis for cognitive mediators as a central component of motivational behavior appeared in the educational literature. For years it had been suspected that factors other than ability influence whether individuals would exert effort during learning and performance, but the constructs were poorly understood. Once researchers began to emphasize how learners interpret situations, what goals they set for themselves, and how they view their own competence, a consistent body of research was generated.

Nicholls (1984) highlighted the central role of an individual's perceptions of their own competence in motivated behavior. He argued that feelings of accomplishment are maximized by a perception that one has demonstrated ability. Based on the work of Nicholls (1984), Harter (1978), and others (Markus, Cross, & Wurf, 1990) who proposed that feelings of competence, as well as actual competence, affect motivation and performance, the need to focus more on perceived competence captured the attention of researchers. This acceptance of perceived competence as a mediating construct led many to theorize that what children think about their own competence is more important than their actual competence in explaining motivation and learning. While competence in cognitive, social, or physical tasks requires some ability, a sense of what students perceive to be possible for themselves and positive feelings about their own competency are equally essential for effective participation.

Recent literature has offered goal theory as a framework for studying motivation in achievement settings, and this approach has contributed greatly to the present emphasis on student thinking in research. Goal theory integrates many of the constructs appearing in earlier views by describing how goals can influence how students approach and respond to learning situations. The role of student perceptions has long been emphasized in motivation theory and research, but goal theory framework integrates affective and cognitive components as factors representing different ways of approaching and responding to classroom events. Central to this approach and other social cognitive frameworks is the role of achievement-related self perceptions. While a complete description of the constructs defined in goal theory is beyond the scope of this paper, the model assumes relationships between students' goals for achievement, their persistence in learning situations, and their attributional belief patterns. These goals also seem to be related to patterns of cognitive involvement during learning and influence whether students employ effective learning strategies. Two contrasting goal constructs have been defined and contrasted as task/ego by Nicholls (1984), mastery/performance by Ames and Archer (1988), and learning/performance by Dweck (1986). A task, mastery, or learning orientation is more often associated with an intrinsic interest in learning, a focus on learning through effort, and the use of effective learning strategies. Evidence suggests that a task-oriented goal is related to a range of achievement-related variables, including positive affect and persistence in the face of difficulty.

In the 1990s, research on student thinking gained more respect and recognition from constructivist frameworks that stress that learning is a constructive rather than an acquisition process. According to Blumenfeld (1992), learning is social and occurs when learners interact with relevant learning tasks and other students in the class. The approach includes the notion of meaningful experiences gained from work on authentic tasks. Authentic tasks require that students practice self-regulation in the course of active participation with others on activities that are varied and challenging. The constructivism literature views the teacher as one who provides support, but allows students to control their learning. From this perspective, an important challenge for teachers is to design activities that are meaningful to each individual student and planned at an appropriate level of difficulty.

A mediational model of student thinking and behavior

Based upon the available literature, my graduate students and I have developed a model of student thinking and behavior to assist us in visualizing how the different components relate and to see how research on learners' thoughts might mediate achievement (see Figure 1). I can make no claims for the empirical validity of the model, but I offer it as an organizer that might help us make sense of the research I will review. We use the model as a framework to help organize the findings available and to formulate additional research questions.

On the left side of Figure 1 are background variables that serve to shape students' thoughts about what physical education is or should be, what their roles as students should be, how they should approach the content offered, and what their chances of success might be. First, the literature supports the importance of examining students' achievement-related beliefs from a development perspective because children at different ages have different conceptions of ability and different explanations for their successes and failures. Younger children differ from adolescents and adults in how they define the difficulty of a task and estimate their ability to be successful.

The developmental studies have also indicated that children form gender-differentiated perceptions of their abilities and interests in both cognitive and motor tasks even before they enter school. Gender differences in students' perceptions are especially obvious for activities presented or perceived as appropriate for male or female participation.

Perhaps more important to understanding differences in students' entry level perceptions is a need to study the history of participation in physical activity and sport, and the

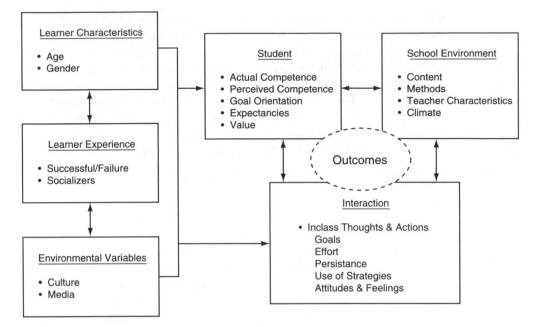

Figure 1 A mediational model of student thinking and behavior.

influence of parents, peers, cultural expectations, and media exposure. Entry level ideas, feelings, and beliefs develop over time and from a variety of sources. There is no doubt that students' initial views about school and their beliefs about themselves and their abilities are shaped by the frequency of opportunities to participate and the feelings associated with successful and nonsuccessful experiences. Children's performance in various activities and their interpretation of success and failure influence their beliefs about their own ability and their choices for future participation.

On the other hand, parents' belief systems and behavior might have an effect on children's self-perceptions. Parents can enhance or diminish their children's competence beliefs by socializing them to expect higher or lower levels of success in various activities. If parents value physical education and want their children to perform well in movement activities, they convey this message by encouraging active participation at home and by reminding them that physical education is an important school subject. The broader social environment, including the cultural context in which students are involved, the role models available in the community, and the exposure to media are also potential influences on student perceptions and attitudes.

Socialization practices of significant others and cultural expectations can also influence children's conceptions of what the content of physical education should be and what their roles as students should be. Students' interpretations of the messages given by parents can shape the students' initial beliefs about what activities are important and how well they can expect to perform. While these background variables may not represent an exhaustive list of early influences, it is clear that entry-level beliefs and attitudes about school and physical education are shaped to some degree by the combined effects of biological factors, experiences, and the culture.

Teaching and learning outcomes

The other components in the model portray teaching and learning as an interaction between students and the environment. Reflecting our belief that both thoughts and initial skill are entry characteristics that combine to influence classroom interactions, both actual and perceived competence are included. Based on the expectancy-value model developed by Eccles et al. (1983), students' interpretations of past experiences and cultural expectations are assumed to determine their expectancies for success and the value they place on various activities. Student engagement during learning is influenced by initial skill and knowledge, operating in combination with a student's subjective perceptions of competency, expectancies, values, and goals. It is proposed that students tend to persist at and exert effort when they expect to do well, value the content, and adopt task-oriented goals.

While these attributes and motivational beliefs help to shape students' initial acceptance of and interactions with the content and processes they face in different instructional situations, teachers can structure classes that might enhance motivational beliefs and the quality of learning for students. For example, the environment can influence student perceptions and motivation by promoting challenge, emphasizing mastery, and offering opportunities to engage in tasks that are meaningful and valued. Teachers shape the environment by the activities offered, the methods they select, the amount of choice afforded students, and the assessment and evaluation techniques implemented. It is important to note that while the environment is influenced directly and indirectly by numerous factors, a description of these is beyond the scope of this paper. The evidence is clear, for example, that teacher knowledge, beliefs, and values influence the kinds of activities they select and the practices they use during instruction (Ennis & Chen, 1995; Ennis, Ross, & Chen, 1992).

The interaction between students and the environment affects the quality of engagement, including the goals students adopt and the quality of their effort, persistence, and use of strategy. In addition, learners' perceptions of the meaningfulness and value of classroom work will shape their attitudes and feelings. If teachers offer tasks, for example, that students do not value, the quality of engagement will most likely be hampered because of a lack of perceived meaningfulness. This perception can influence the achievement-related behavior and affect of students.

In summary, learners' initial skill, knowledge, and thoughts interact with environmental factors to produce learning outcomes. Teachers can design learning tasks and select teaching practices that can promote both positive and negative feelings among students in the class. With careful planning, the environmental features and social climate of the class can enhance ability and value perceptions, promote a commitment to effort and persistence during practice, activate the use of strategies for regulating one's own learning, and foster desirable ways of responding to failure. Finally, these motivational, affective, and cognitive components mediate the effects of teacher behavior on student engagement and learning.

Methods of data collection

The study of student thinking depends heavily on the use of self-reports provided by students in interviews or on questionnaires. Self-report data have been viewed by many as problematic, particularly when obtained from children (Assor & Connell, 1992; Bandura, 1983; Nisbett & Wilson, 1977). Bandura (1983), for example, warns that young children's reports about their own competence are likely to depend on immediate outcomes and, thus, will vary over time. Another concern expressed is the intentional or unintentional distorting of information by respondents.

Over the past 20 years, researchers have tried to improve the validity of self-reports by adhering to certain guidelines (Assor & Connell, 1992). We believe that when carefully collected, self-report data can provide valuable information for researchers and practitioners. Those studying student thoughts have typically used questionnaires, interviews, or stimulated recall to collect students' thoughts about themselves or instruction. We also ask learners to respond to hypothetical situations depicting various classroom situations or teacher practices. Results of recent research indicate that students are aware of their thoughts and are able to report them with sufficient accuracy to yield information that researchers can use to explain how they learn from teaching. The research reviewed here can be categorized into four broad topics: (a) beliefs about ability and competence, (b) beliefs about task values, (c) relationships between student thinking and engagement, and (d) enhancing student motivational thoughts.

Beliefs about ability and competence

The study of perceived ability has a long history and ample support from the empirical literature. The construct has been defined and measured in several different ways, but usually refers to students' judgments about their ability to be successful, their confidence in their skills to perform different tasks, or their estimate of how good they are in different skills. Harter (1982) and others have developed scales to measure children's perceptions of ability in different domains, and these have been used extensively. Another approach is to ask children a question about their beliefs in an activity to which they respond verbally or by using a numerical scale. Assor and Connell (1992) conclude that researchers can collect valid and reliable data with a 4- or 5-point Likert scale from children as young as kindergarten age. Questions for younger children, however, need to be supported with some pictorial information. Our research has shown that reliable estimates can be obtained from students in kindergarten through high school, with higher reliability coefficients for the older age groups. It is recommended that younger children be surveyed individually, but older students prefer the privacy of a group administration (Assor & Connell, 1992).

Research has provided evidence that competency beliefs vary as a function of age, gender, and domain studied. Our research has consistently shown that when compared to older children, younger children have higher, but not necessarily more realistic, expectancies for success (Lee, Hall, & Carter, 1983; Lee, Nelson, & Nelson, 1988). Younger children often set extremely high goals that may not be good predictors of actual performance but that show children in this age group to be optimistic about their own abilities. Many children give themselves the highest possible rating when asked to indicate their confidence in physical education. Using teacher ratings as a measure of actual competence, there is usually no relationship between the children's perceptions of competence and their actual competence before age 7 or 8. The self-ratings of children in third grade and fifth grade began to show significant relationships with more objective measures such as teacher ratings, or achievement scores (Nicholls, 1978; Wigfield & Harold, 1992). Our research is consistent with other studies showing that self evaluation of abilities decreases across age (Lee et al., 1983; Sanguinetti, Lee, & Nelson, 1985).

These age changes can be explained in part by Nicholls and Miller's (1984) explanation of more and less differentiated conception of ability. A less differentiated conception is evident when children under 7 years of age do not recognize the implications of social comparison or the normative conception of ability. This means that young children do not understand that ability is judged on the basis of how one performs relative to others in the class. Evidence suggesting that children in kindergarten and first grade do not consider social comparison information in their beliefs comes from an interview study we conducted recently (Lee, Carter, & Xiang, 1995). When children were asked to explain their competence ratings in physical education, all of the younger children discussed their ability in terms of the movement tasks they could perform. For example, one kindergarten girl explained that she considered herself to be good in physical education because she could catch the ball, jump rope, do gymnastics, and knew how to bowl. In contrast, more of the older children defined their ability by comparing their own performance to that of their peers. A fifth-grade female who gave herself only 3 out of 5 stars, indicating average ability, said, "Well, because sometimes I am not as good as some of the people that play basketball and baseball. I'm just not good at them."

Nicholls suggests that another important development in children's understanding of ability is the distinction between ability and effort. Xiang (1996) found that 68% of the fourth graders she studied had trouble differentiating between effort and ability when asked to respond to a story about two children practicing basketball. One student tried harder than the other student during practice, but they both made the same number of baskets in the end. The younger children believed the students had the same level of ability, but 8th and 12th graders judged the one who tried harder to have less ability. It is important to note that even after children understand the notion of ability as something stable, many will believe that their ability in motor skills and the ability of others can be modified through effort (Lee et al., 1995; Veal & Compagnone, 1995). These findings have powerful implications for teachers. There is evidence (Nicholls & Miller, 1984) to suggest that if the class focuses on task mastery, if activities are challenging, and if evaluation is self-referenced, learners at all ages will employ a less differentiated conception of ability and expect that more effort will lead to greater competence. Our research and the study by Veal and Compagnone (1995) provide some evidence that many older students in physical education believe that if they try hard they will be more competent.

Over the years, researchers have reported gender differences in children's beliefs about their own competence, but these differences vary by task. In general, boys consistently report higher perceptions of their overall competence and are more positive than girls about their ability in most traditional sport activities (Eccles et al., 1989; Harter, 1982; Marsh, Barnes, Cairns, & Tidman, 1984). Based on Lenney's (1977) contention that females do not display a lack of confidence in all situations, our research and that of others (e.g., Clifton & Gill, 1995) have documented that sex-linked movement tasks can mediate gender differences in ability perceptions, with males displaying more confidence on masculine-typed tasks and females displaying more confidence on feminine-typed tasks (Clifton & Gill, 1994; Lirgg, 1991; Sanguinetti et al., 1988).

Results of our research (Lee, Belcher, Fredenburg, & Cleveland, 1996), designed to

examine students' beliefs about the appropriateness of movement activities for participation by males and females, have been consistent with studies using older adolescents
and adults. Students viewed football, basketball, and soccer as more appropriate for
boys, and jump rope, cheerleading, dance, and gymnastics as more appropriate for girls.
Jogging, roller skating, tennis, volleyball, and softball were judged appropriate for both
males and females. In general, boys have higher ability perceptions for activities labeled
more appropriate for male participation, and girls' ability perceptions for the activities
stereotyped as feminine are higher than those of boys.

In an earlier study (Lee et al., 1988), we examined the effects of a manipulated
sex linkage on expectancies obtained prior to engaging in a novel task and found that
the confidence of girls and boys can be influenced by a manipulation, but in different ways.
We selected a novel reaction time task and explained to children that performance was
related to either success in football or dance activities. The success predictions were
similar for girls in a task-appropriate and task-inappropriate activity, but boys indicated
significantly more confidence when the novel task was presented as a measure of abilities
important in football. More important is the finding that although the girls predicted
lower scores than the boys, the girls' performances on the novel task were just as good
and were higher than their predictions. This finding is important since some children can
acquire inaccurate self-perceptions of incompetence, and these erroneous beliefs can lead
to underachievement.

Research findings by Wigfield and Harold (1992) suggest that teachers' beliefs about
children's competence in different domains might reflect society's stereotypes about
appropriate activities for boys and girls and provide evidence that relationships between
teacher beliefs and children's beliefs are quite strong in the sport domain. According
to these researchers, teachers consistently view boys at all ages as being more talented
in sports. Based on Martinek's (1988) research showing that learners in high and low
expectation groups perceive teacher feedback differently, these findings are important.
Although teachers are assumed to be reasonably accurate in judging children's ability in
movement activities, the gender differences some teachers judge for very young students
might not be accurate because few performance differences are evident at these early ages.
The possibility that teachers have stereotypical beliefs about male and female competence
that serve to influence children's beliefs about their own competence is distressing and
needs the attention of researchers.

In a large-scale study (Lee et al., 1996) involving 745 first-, third-, and fifth-grade
children drawn from physical education classes in six different schools throughout the
state of Louisiana, we examined the relationships between teachers' ratings and children's
self-perceptions of ability in physical education. Analyses were performed separately for
males and females at each grade level. Consistent with previous research, significant
relationships between teacher beliefs and student beliefs were found in Grade 5, but the
correlation coefficient was stronger for the boys. The *rs* were .22 and .41 for females and
males, respectively. The findings for first graders are more important. For females there
was no relationship between the beliefs of teachers and students. On the other hand, there
was a positive relationship between the teacher ratings and self-rating for the boys. It
appears that teachers were more likely to agree with the high ratings the young males gave
themselves.

An important question we might ask is, Do teachers adjust their behavior to reflect
their beliefs about abilities of males and females in physical education? Another question of

interest might be, How do students interpret the messages they might receive from teachers with differential beliefs? Findings from a recent study by Solmon and Carter (1995) suggest that some teachers might influence their male and female students' thinking about their performance even when their intentions are to provide a noncompetitive environment where all children can be successful. Ms. Wood, the teacher in Solmon and Carter's (1995) qualitative study, interacted differently with the kindergarten boys and girls, and the children interpreted the differential treatment. Girls referred to good behavior and following directions when asked what the teacher wanted them to learn, but boys' replies focused solely on skill performance. Ms. Wood's actions were inconsistent with her stated philosophy, and she was disappointed when the researchers suggested that the opportunities she had allowed and the reinforcement she had provided were perceived differently by boys and girls. Although Ms. Woods was shocked, she was also reflective, and after thinking about the implications of her actions, she saw reasons to change her approach. These findings suggest that children can interpret the messages teachers send early in elementary school, but more research is needed to determine how these subtle messages might influence student self-beliefs about their competence.

Beliefs about task value

Value-related perceptions (the extent to which various activities fulfill individual needs and provide satisfaction) are thought to be related to achievement behavior (Eccles et al., 1983). Individuals tend to engage in and persist in tasks that they like and see as useful. Luke and Sinclair (1991), in one of the few studies to directly address the dimensions of task value for various movement and sport activities, examined factors that contribute to positive or negative attitudes toward physical education. They found that the curriculum content was the most important determinant of a positive attitude. Students with positive attitudes more often elect physical education, and one can assume that these students also place a higher value on participation and derive more pleasure from involvement in game, gymnastic, and dance activities.

Our research has shown that males and females tend to value activities that they perceive as appropriate for their gender (Lee et al., 1996). Many females, especially those who have personally adopted stereotypical perceptions for themselves, see no value in trying hard and doing well in sports such as basketball. When asked why girls do not try as hard in basketball, a typical response was, "Girls have better things to do; they think it's boring." In contrast, girls are more likely than boys to perceive dance, gymnastics, and other activities with a strong feminine sex link as important for them to learn. In their study of students' constructs of physical education, Pissano and Allison (1993) concluded that gender was more powerful than skill level, academic achievement, participation level, physical size, creativity, timidity, popularity, verbal ability, or impressionability in influencing how students constructed meaning of elementary school physical education. They concluded that teachers must account for gender in curricular practices by acknowledging that males and females might construct different meanings from the same experiences.

Based on our research and studies done by Carlson (1995), Hopple and Graham (1995), and Sanders and Graham (1995), task value might be a critical dimension affecting positive motivational beliefs in physical education. Findings from these studies suggest that feelings of interest, enjoyment, and personal meanings and perceptions of significance, challenge, and usefulness are missing in the physical education experiences of many students. One of Carlson's (1995) participants concluded that she had learned nothing but plenty of games, and that was of no value. Carlson's study also provides evidence of how parents shape students' value perceptions: One student's mother had convinced her that gym was a waste of time and the grade she received was not important. Hopple and Graham (1995) found that students viewed the mile run as a painful, negative experience rather than a meaningful, positive one. Sanders and Graham's study (1995) suggested that even at kindergarten age some activities, especially those not perceived as playlike and challenging, can be a turnoff to children.

Although many students' feelings are obviously a reaction to the types of activities they encounter, we propose that when students enter school, they have already identified activities important and useful to learn. It appears that teachers need to learn more about what activities students place a high value on and then create environments that might enhance the value perceptions in physical education. We need to continue listening to students' voices about what constitutes meaningful, challenging, authentic tasks for them. The *Journal of Teaching in Physical Education* summer monograph edited by George Graham (1995) helps us understand more about the subjective experiences of students in our classes, but now the voices of these students must be used in our decision making.

Dyson (1995), for example, has described an alternative curriculum that enhanced students' perceptions of value and meaningfulness. Additional interviews with students might help us identify what content and types of teacher practices might have the potential to mediate the negative attitudes and value perceptions some students have about physical education. Toward this end, we asked a group of students with rigidly held gender role conceptions to evaluate the effectiveness of various practices that teachers might use to enhance their effort and persistence in activities they perceived to be sex-typed (Lee et al., 1996). Findings indicated that before any teacher practice will be effective, interventions must be planned to reduce the sex typing of activities. More work needs to be done to determine what makes a task interesting, meaningful, and worthy of student effort.

Relationships between student thinking and engagement

According to a cognitive mediational framework students' backgrounds, beliefs, attitudes, and behavioral intentions should be related to their behaviors in physical education classes. Greenockle, Lee, and Lomax (1990) tried to identify entry characteristics that would influence the activity patterns of students in a high school fitness class. Consistent with predictions, findings indicated that for 9th and 10th graders, the effort exerted during a jogging class was influenced by significant others (particularly peers and teachers) and personal attitudes toward jogging. Those students who perceived vigorous exercise to be fun and exciting and who believed in the value of exercise for health and fitness were more likely to participate at a higher intensity level. Students who perceived that teachers and peers expected and approved of fitness activity indicated an intention to take advantage of the class.

The cognitive mediational framework also assumes that students will determine which, if any, learning strategies they will employ during practice of movement activities. Learning strategies are the procedures used by students to enhance the acquisition and retention of information or skills. Locke and Jensen (1974), in an early study using thought sampling, found that individual students differ significantly in their characteristic levels of attention. Students attend to different aspects of the learning environment, and there is some evidence that some students might be so concerned about their inability to perform at an acceptable level that they have trouble implementing strategies to help them learn (Lee, Landin, & Carter, 1992). In a study using stimulated recall, we found that many students reported thoughts relating to their own inadequacy and fear of failure. The fourth graders who experienced a higher level of success during instruction were able to recall specific strategies they used to improve their performance, whereas low-success students were more concerned with their inability to perform the skill than selecting and implementing cognitive strategies.

Previous research in classroom settings (Pintrich & Schrauben, 1992) indicates that students who have positive feelings about their own competence are more likely to be cognitively involved trying to learn the activities assigned by the teacher. In a comprehensive study designed to explore relations between student entry characteristics, in-class activity patterns, and student cognition, Solmon and Lee (1996) hypothesized that children who perceived themselves as competent would pay more attention to instruction, use learning strategies to improve performance, and report higher levels of motivation during practice.

Findings indicated that a combination of skill and perceived competence was related to self-reports of motivation and an ability to make self-correction adjustments during practice. Nevertheless, students who felt more confident about their ability to do well in the activity were less likely to report the use of cognitive learning strategies. On the contrary, it was the students who perceived themselves as lacking the ability to be successful who employed strategies as they tried to learn the skill. From a cognitive mediational perspective, it became apparent that strategies are useful for those who need them, but may not be necessary for everyone, depending on the level of task difficulty. It was possible that the tasks assigned by the teacher were not matched to the students' skill level, and in this case did not create a challenging situation. While the students with high perceived competence were motivated and regulated their own learning by making self-correction, they were able to grasp the basic skill components with minimal levels of cognitive engagement.

Using student goal orientation as an entry characteristic, Solmon and Boone (1993) found that task-involved goals are linked with a range of positive motivational beliefs and play an important role in mediation between teacher behavior and student achievement in a tennis class. Specifically, students exhibiting a task-involved goal perspective selected more challenging tasks, indicated higher levels of interest, and were more likely to use strategies to understand concepts relevant to the task. They reported a willingness to persist in practice and an aptitude to regulate one's own learning. Solmon and Boone concluded that students whose criteria for success or competence is self-referenced and based on the mastery of a skill tend to employ cognitive processes which foster learning.

Enhancing student motivational thoughts

We have evidence that student characteristics and environmental factors influence student thinking and, consequently, the level of student engagement patterns. Since self-perceptions of ability, beliefs about task value, and goal orientation play a significant role in shaping student classroom thoughts and actions, it is important to learn more about what decisions teachers can make to enhance student confidence, convey the value of learning tasks, and create a mastery-oriented learning environment. Given that students' interpretations of past successes and failures affect their entry level perceived competence, teacher practices designed to provide initial success are important. According to Bandura (1986) and others, a student's sense of competence can be enhanced from engagement in activities, allowing individual progression from easy to difficult. Hebert (1995) investigated the role of task progressions on student cognition and found that a gradual increase in task complexity enhanced self-efficacy and motivation, especially for the low-skilled students. From a cognitive mediational perspective, we might advise teachers to focus on designing tasks to raise confidence levels even though increases in performance might not be evident for some time.

Ames (1992) outlined TARGET strategies designed to create task-involved climates that foster effective motivational patterns. These strategies are grouped into six dimensions labeled as task, authority, recognition, grouping, evaluation, and time. Treasure (1993) manipulated the motivational climate in a physical education context, reporting that students in a task-involved climate demonstrated more adaptive patterns of achievement cognition and affective responses that those in an ego-involved climate. Theeboom, DeKnop, and Weiss (1995), in a summer camp program, randomly assigned children to either a task-involved climate or a traditional program for instruction in martial arts. Children in the task-involved condition demonstrated superior skill performance and expressed higher levels of enjoyment compared to children in a traditional sport program.

Solmon (1995) used TARGET strategies to create task-involved climates and a competition ladder to create ego-involved climates for a short instructional period on a juggling task. She and graduate students at Louisiana State University coded practice trials at easy and difficult levels during student practice. Students in the task-involved condition completed a higher number of practice trials at difficult levels when compared to those in the ego condition. This is an important study because it provides the first evidence that students in task-involved climates do not just indicate on self-report measures that they are willing to work hard or that they enjoy activities more than those in ego-involved or traditional programs. In this study, data about what students actually did in classes, as reflected by their persistence during practice at a difficult level, support the contention that task-involved climates can impact student engagement.

Extending this line of research, Jerry Boone (1995) conducted an intervention with real teachers in real classes in real schools. After collecting preintervention data concerning students' perceptions of motivational climates, Boone conducted training sessions designed to encourage teachers to implement strategies in their classes to increase the salience of a task-involved climate. He reported positive changes in students' perceptions of the motivational climate in physical education classes of the teachers participating in the intervention as compared to students in control classes. Students in classes of teachers who implemented TARGET strategies also demonstrated a faster rate of skill improvement than students in control classes.

In summary, the results from this line of research provide strong evidence that we have information teachers can use in their classes to enhance the experiences students have in physical education. First, teachers might need to be more aware of children's entry characteristics and the kind of impact they have on student thoughts and actions during instruction. It is also important that teachers and researchers learn more about the factors shaping students' initial beliefs, attitudes, and values concerning their experiences. Students' perceptions about themselves are influenced by the social and cultural landscape to which they are exposed, by their interpretation of the expectations of others, and by their own successes and failures. For some children, at least, special effort is needed to counteract these early influences. It is clear that children's self perceptions of ability change over the school years; awareness of these changes might encourage teachers to evaluate students on effort and improvement rather than ability. Finally, more knowledge is needed about the types of tasks students find meaningful so that teachers can design activities that will result in positive responses from students.

If we view the world through the eyes of our students and hear the messages embedded in their actions, we will learn things we never knew we did not know. There seem to be some consistent messages from our students—messages about the content of the curriculum, their value perceptions, and the meaningfulness of their experiences.

Acknowledgments

This paper was originally presented as the Special Interest Group: Research on Learning and Instruction in Physical Education Scholar Lecture at the annual meeting of the American Educational Research Association, New York, 1996. I thank Dr. Melinda Solmon, who helped to conceptualize a cognitive mediational framework for studying the teaching-learning process in physical education classes. I also thank Karen Fredenburg, Don Belcher, Ping Xiang, and Jian Luo for their contributions and comments on earlier drafts of this paper.

References

Ames, C., & Archer, J. (1988). Achievement goals in the classroom: Students' learning strategies and motivation processes. *Journal of Educational Psychology*, **80**, 260–267.

Ames, C. (1992). Achievement goals, motivational climate, and motivational processes. In G.C. Roberts (Ed.), *Motivation in sport and exercise* (pp. 161–176). Champaign, IL: Human Kinetics.

Assor, A., & Connell, J.P. (1992). The validity of students' self-reports as measures of performance affecting self appraisals. In D.H. Schunk & J. L. Meece (Eds.), *Student perceptions in the classroom* (pp. 25–47). Hillsdale, NJ: Erlbaum.

Bandura, A. (1983). Self-referent thought: A developmental analysis of self-efficacy. In J. Flavell & L. Ross (Eds.), *Social cognitive development* (pp. 200–239). Cambridge: Cambridge University Press.

Bandura, A. (1986). *Social foundations of thought and action: A cognitive theory.* Englewood Cliffs, NJ: Prentice Hall.

Blumenfeld, P.C. (1992). Classroom learning and motivation: Clarifying and expanding goal theory. *Journal of Educational Psychology*, **84**, 272–281.

Boone, J. (1995). *Achievement goals and motivational climates for physical education.* Unpublished doctoral dissertation, Louisiana State University, Baton Rouge.

Carlson, T.B. (1995). We hate gym: Student alienation from physical education. *Journal of Teaching in Physical Education*, **14**, 467–477.

Clifton, R., & Gill, D. (1994). Gender differences in self-confidence on a feminine-typed task. *Journal of Sport & Exercise Psychology*, **16**, 150–162.

Doyle, W. (1978). Paradigms for research on teacher effectiveness. In L.S. Shulman (Ed.), *Review of research in education* (Vol. 5, pp. 163–198). Itasca, IL: Peacock.

Dweck, C.S. (1986). Motivational processes affecting learning. *American Psychologist*, **41**, 1040–1048.

Dyson, B.P. (1995). Students' voices in two alternative elementary physical education programs. *Journal of Teaching in Physical Education*, **14**, 394–407.

Eccles, J., Adler, T.F., Futterman, R., Goff, S.B., Kaczala, C.M., Meece, J., & Midgley, C. (1983). Expectancies, values, and academic behaviors. In J.T. Spence (Ed.), *Achievement and achievement motives* (pp. 75–146). San Francisco: Freeman.

Eccles, J.S., Wigfield, A., Flanagan, C., Miller, C., Reuman, D., & Yee, D. (1989). Self-concepts, domain values, and self esteem: Relations and changes at early adolescence. *Journal of Personality*, **57**, 283–310.

Ennis, C.D., & Chen, A. (1995). Teachers' value orientation in urban and rural school settings. *Research Quarterly for Exercise and Sport*, **66**, 41–50.

Ennis, C.D., Ross, J., & Chen, A. (1992). The role of value orientation in curricula decision making: A rationale for teachers' goals and expectations. *Research Quarterly for Exercise and Sport*, **63**, 38–47.

Gage, N.L. (1963). *Handbook of research on teaching*. Chicago: Rand McNally.

Graham, G. (Ed.) (1995). Physical education through students' eyes and in students' voices [Monograph]. *Journal of Teaching in Physical Education*, **14**(4).

Greenockle, K.M., Lee, A.M., & Lomax, R. (1990). The relationship between selected student characteristics and activity patterns in a required high school physical education class. *Research Quarterly for Exercise and Sport*, **61**, 59–69.

Harter, S. (1978). Effectance motivation reconsidered: Toward a developmental model. *Human Development*, **21**, 34–64.

Harter, S. (1982). The Perceived Competence Scale for Children. *Child Development*, **53**, 87–97.

Hebert, E. (1995). *Content development strategies in physical education: An exploratory investigation of student practice cognition and achievement*. Unpublished doctoral dissertation, Louisiana State University, Baton Rouge.

Hopple, C., & Graham, G. (1995). What children think, feel, and know about physical fitness testing. *Journal of Teaching in Physical Education*, **14**, 408–417.

Knight, S.L., & Waxman, H.C. (1991). Students' cognitive and classroom interaction. In H.C. Waxman & H.L. Walberg (Eds.). *Effective teaching: Current research* (pp. 239–255). Berkeley, CA: McCutchan.

Lee, A., Belcher, D., Friedenburg, K., & Cleveland, N. (1996). *Gender difference in conceptions of competence*. Unpublished manuscript.

Lee, A., Carter, J.A., & Xiang, P. (1995). Children's conceptions of ability in physical education. *Journal of Teaching in Physical Education*, **14**, 384–393.

Lee, A., Hall, E., & Carter, J. (1983). Age and sex differences in expectancy for success among American children. *The Journal of Psychology*, **113**, 35–39.

Lee, A., Landin, D., & Carter, J. (1992). Student thoughts during tennis instruction. *Journal of Teaching in Physical Education*, **11**, 256–267.

Lee, A., Nelson, K., & Nelson, J. (1988). Success estimations and performance in children as influenced by age, gender, and task. *Sex Roles*, **18**, 719–725.

Lenney, E. (1977). Woman's self-confidence in achievement situations. *Psychological Bulletin*, **84**, 1–13.

Lirgg, C. (1991). Gender differences in self-confidence in physical activity: A meta-analysis of recent studies. *Journal of Sport & Exercise Psychology*, **8**, 294–310.

Locke, L.F., & Jensen, M.K. (1974). Thought sampling: A study of student attention through self-report. *Research Quarterly*, **45**, 263–275.

Luke, M.D., & Sinclair, G.D. (1991). Gender differences in adolescents' attitudes toward school physical education. *Journal of Teaching in Physical Education*, **11**, 31–46.

Markus, H., Cross, S., & Wurf, E. (1990). The role of the self-system in competence. In R.J. Sternburg & J. Kolligan, Jr. (Eds.), *Competence considered* (pp. 205–225). New Haven, CT: Yale University Press.

Marsh, H.W., Barns, J., Cairns, L., & Tidman, M. (1984). Self-description questionnaire: Age and sex effects in the structure and level of self-concept for preadolescent children. *Journal of Educational Psychology*, **76**, 940–956.

Martinek, T.J. (1988). Confirmation of a teacher expectancy model: Student perceptions and causal attributions of teaching behaviors. *Research Quarterly for Exercise and Sport*, **59**, 118–126.

Nichols, J.G. (1978). The development of the concepts of effort and ability, perceptions of academic attainment, and the understanding that difficult tasks require more ability. *Child Development*, **49**, 800–814.

Nicholls, J. (1984). Conceptions of ability and achievement motivation. In R. Ames & C. Ames (Eds.), *Research on motivation in education: Student motivation* (Vol. 1, pp. 39–73). New York: Academic Press.

Nicholls, J., & Miller, A. (1984). Development and its discontents: The differentiation of the concept of ability. In J. Nicholls (Ed.), *Advances in motivation and achievement: The development of achievement motivation* (pp. 185–218). Greenwich, CT: JAI Press.

Nisbett, R.E., & Wilson, T.D. (1977). Telling more than we can know: Verbal reports on mental processes. *Psychological Review*, **84**, 231–259.

Pintrich, P.R., & Schrauben, B. (1992). Students' motivational beliefs and their cognitive engagement in classroom academic tasks. In D.H. Schunk & J.L. Meece (Eds.), *Student perceptions in the classroom* (pp. 149–179). Hillsdale, NJ: Erlbaum.

Pissanos, B.W., & Allison, P.C. (1993). Students' constructs of elementary school physical education. *Research Quarterly for Exercise and Sport*, **64**, 425–435.

Sanders, S., & Graham, G. (1995). Kindergarten children's initial experiences in physical education: The relentless persistence for play clashes with the zone of acceptable responses. *Journal of Teaching in Physical Education*, **14**, 372–383.

Sanguinetti, C., Lee, A., & Nelson, J. (1985). Reliability estimates and age and gender comparisons of expectations of success in sex-typed activities. *Journal of Sport Psychology*, **7**, 379–388.

Schunk, D.H. (1992). Theory and research on student perceptions in the classroom. In D.H. Schunk & J.L. Meece (Eds.), *Student perceptions in the classroom* (pp. 3–23). Hillsdale, NJ: Erlbaum.

Solmon, M. (in press). The impact of motivational climate on students' behaviors and perceptions in a physical education setting. *Journal of Educational Psychology*.

Solmon, M.A., & Boone, J. (1993). The impact of student goal orientation in physical education classes. *Research Quarterly for Exercise and Sport*, **64**, 418–424.

Solmon, M.A., & Carter, J.A. (1995). Kindergarten and first grade students' perceptions of physical education in one teacher's classes. *Elementary School Journal*, **95**, 355–365.

Solmon, M., & Lee, A. (1996). Entry characteristics, practice variables, and cognition: Student mediation of instruction. *Journal of Teaching in Physical Education*, **15**, 136–150.

Theeboom, M., DeKnop, P., & Weiss, M.R. (1995). Motivational climate, psychological responses, and motor skill development in children's sport: A field-based intervention study. *Journal of Sport & Exercise Psychology*, **17**, 294–311.

Travers, R.M.W. (1973). *Second handbook of research on teaching* (2nd ed.). Chicago: Rand McNally.

Treasure, D.C. (1993). *A social-cognitive approach to understanding children's achievement behavior, cognition, and affect in competitive sport*. Unpublished doctoral dissertation, University of Illinois at Urbana-Champaign.

Veal, M.L., & Compagnone, N. (1995). How sixth grades perceive effort and skill. *Journal of Teaching in Physical Education*, **14**, 431–444.

Wigfield, A., & Harold, R. (1992). Children's ability perceptions and values during the elementary school years. In D.H. Schunk & J.L. Meece (Eds.), *Student perceptions in the classroom* (pp. 95–121). Hillsdale, NJ: Erlbaum.

Wittrock, M.C. (1986a). *Handbook of research on teaching* (3rd ed.), New York: Macmillan.

Wittrock, M. (1986b). Students' thought processes. In M. Wittrock (Ed.), *Handbook of research on teaching* (3rd ed., pp. 297–314). New York: Macmillan.

Xiang, P. (1996). *Achievement goals and self-perceptions of ability in physical education: A cross-cultural perspective*. Unpublished doctoral dissertation, Louisiana State University, Baton Rouge.

Judith E. Rink

INVESTIGATING THE ASSUMPTIONS OF PEDAGOGY

RECENT LITERATURE AND RESEARCH in physical education pedagogy has seen a resurgence of the methods "wars." By this I mean that advocates for one type of method of teaching attempt to show that their way of teaching is far better than traditional or other methods of teaching. The most recent conflict in the literature has positioned more traditional, usually meant to imply more direct, styles of teaching against those primarily based on more constructivist and socially based applications of learning theories (Allison & Barrett, 2000; Chandler & Mitchell, 1991; Turner & Martinek, 1995). The most obvious example of this trend is the literature that surrounds the value of a games for understanding approach to teaching sport and sport education and, in a broader context, advocacy for "constructivist teaching" (Almond, 1986; Grehaigne & Godbout, 1995; Hastie, 1996; Metzler, 1999; Siedentop, 1994).

For those of us who were practicing physical educators in the sixties, the methods discussions in the literature are reminiscent of those surrounding movement education and the introduction of Mosston's styles of teaching (Mosston, 1966). During this time period in our history, more cognitive styles of teaching (see Rink, 1998) directly challenged the exclusive use of direct teaching as the "best" and only way to teach physical education. The movement education of this time carried with it a set of assumptions about how students best learn and, more importantly, claims about what students learn if you teach this way (Bilbrough & Jones, 1963; Logsdon, Barrett, Broer, Ammons. & Roberton, 1977; Mauldon & Redfern, 1969). Like our contemporaries in the more general field of education, issues of how to teach were primarily put on an "I believe" basis more appropriately reserved for discussions of philosophy than investigations into how to teach for particular outcomes. The notion of philosophy is used here to imply both issues related to serious discussions of ontology and epistemology related to pedagogical concerns, as well as the less formal and less thought through use of the term meaning a more ideological perspective and disposition toward a particular method. In either case, it is not my intent to pursue a discussion of the philosophical bases of teaching methodologies. For a good discussion of the issues and problems of making teaching methodology philosophy, see the recent ASCD publication *Perceiving, Behaving and Becoming: Revisited* (ASCD, 1999).

Literature on movement education was often accompanied by a recipe for teaching that became commandments for followers. As an undergraduate and beginning teacher I personally became captivated by the notions that I could contribute in such a broad way to student development. I supported the psychology that gave birth to a lot of pedagogy of this time through the works of Carl Rogers (1969), Abraham Maslow (1962), and Arthur Combs (1959), usually referred to as "Third Force Psychology" (Goble, 1970). My early career as a movement education teacher was characterized by an attempt, well founded or not, never to tell a student how to do anything, but to let the student discover for themselves the best way. I was a missionary for the methodology.

The pursuit of a scientific orientation to looking at teaching and teaching methodology would come later (for an historical review of research on teaching for this period, see Shulman, 1986), although red flags were being sent up by several physical educators in the new field of motor learning (Locke, 1969) and in England where movement education was well established (McIntosh, 1972). Early pioneers in motor learning were just beginning to identify the very specific nature of learning, the difficulty of teaching for transfer, and the almost impossible task of doing "methods" studies (Cratty, 1967, Singer, 1980; Wickstrom, 1970). The point of this historical review, in a time when we are faced with similar appeals to wholesale adoption of particular teaching methods, is to suggest that we may learn something from the past.

From my perspective, one of the most important things to understand for those of us involved in pedagogy is that all teaching methodology makes some assumptions about how students learn. A major assumption of "exploration" and "discovery" teaching was that the student would be engaged creatively in a way that would result in better movement responses that were more adaptable (transferable) to more real world use of the responses (Logsdon et. al., 1977; Stanley, 1969). Also inherent in such ideas was the notion that more indirect styles of teaching would have a great advantage over more direct styles of teaching because the "whole" learner would be involved. For the physical education teacher this usually meant more cognitive and affective involvement. What was missing in any discussions about the viability of movement education and problem solving methodologies by advocates was any attention to the fidelity of the assumptions about what children would learn and how they would learn it. What was missing from the practitioner's perspective was any attention to verifying that the intended student processes were in fact taking place.

Oddly enough it was a masters thesis I did in the later part of the sixties (Rink, 1969) that initially caused me to question what was really happening. Four first grade boys were followed over a 6-week period in a class taught using a "movement education approach." Two of the boys were selected by both the classroom teacher and the physical educator because they were "risk takers" and more creative. Two of the boys were more conservative in their interactions and responses. The unit of analysis was the teacher task and the student response(s) to that task. The independent variable was the amount of freedom the student had in each movement task. Task freedom to respond was determined by a word by word analysis of the potential of each task for varied responses, either because of the nature of the task itself (e.g., the difference between the possibilities in a task involving running and a task involving balancing), the number of qualifiers the teacher put on the task (e.g., slowly, three parts the body), or because of the number of responses the teacher asked for (e.g., "how many different ways can you . . .?"). The dependent variables were the number of different responses each student produced to each task and the accuracy of the response relative to what the teacher asked. The results of the study showed that the more creative students did indeed produce more varied responses. The less creative students primarily looked around to see what others were doing and largely "copied" or came up with one or two responses that they stayed with during the time given for the task. The more creative students also produced a much larger number of incorrect responses (i.e., any responses that were not within the framework of what the teacher asked a student to do).

What I learned from this particular investigation was important. I did not learn that movement education didn't work. I learned that as a teacher I cannot assume that particular learning processes are taking place because a particular teaching method has the potential for that process to take place, particularly across all students. The idea of inferring learning (relatively permanent changes in behavior) from observations of behavior has always been problematic. The idea of inferring a particular learning process because a particular methodology is being used is even more difficult and more problematic.

What we see currently in education and in physical education is another reform effort aimed at shifting the focus of educational methodology to the learner, this time based on constructivist learning theory (Prawet, 1995). Cobb (1994, p. 4) in a discussion of constructivism in math and science education commented:

> Pedagogies derived from constructivist [learning theory] frequently involve a collection of questionable claims that sanctify the student at the expense of mathematical and scientific ways of knowing. In such accounts the teacher's role is typically characterized as that of facilitating student's investigations and explorations.
>
> Romantic views of this type arise in part because a maxim about learning, namely that students construct their mathematical and scientific ways of knowing, is interpreted as a direct instructional recommendation.

The same notions of political correctness surround much of the current literature in physical education, which is even more interesting because constructivist methodologies are usually associated with attempts to teach particularly difficult cognitive material (Perkins, 1999). Because all instructional methodologies are rooted in some learning theory, they assume that particular processes are taking place that will lead to particular kinds of learning. If we are to understand the arguments separating any discussion of methods and are to make intelligent choices about what to teach and how to teach what to students and when, then we are going to have to understand the issues that separate learning theories. There are two important issues for pedagogy. One involves the viability of the learning theory: Do students who engage in this process learn what we want them to learn? A second and perhaps more neglected area for pedagogy researchers and teachers is: When teachers teach a particular way, do students engage in a particular process? If we are to do meaningful research we are going to have to begin to investigate whether or not those processes are actually taking place and when and under what conditions they take place. We cannot assume that a particular method or approach to teaching automatically results in a particular process of learning. In order to investigate teaching we are going to have to investigate learning. Investigating learning means that we have to have a better understanding of the learning theories upon which different methods of teaching are based, and the differences between them. Although the discussion of teaching methodologies can take place from many perspectives, the intent of this paper is to explore the issue from the perspective of the assumptions of learning theory.

The learning roots of teaching theories

Most instructional methods or approaches to teaching fall under a continuum of two orientations to instruction: direct to indirect teaching. Direct instruction, and the methodologies attached to it, usually means that teaching is explicit, broken down, step by step, and highly monitored (Rosenshine, 1987). Direct instruction is generally thought to be a more teacher centered approach to teaching methodology and more associated with the term "transmission" (Cobb, 1994). Indirect instruction, and the methodologies attached to it, usually is more implicit, involves larger chunks of content, and is more holistic in its approach to content (Peterson, 1979). Indirect instruction is usually associated with more student centered teaching methodologies. Generally speaking, direct instructional strategies find their roots in more behavioral and information processing theories of learning, and indirect instruction finds its roots in more cognitive strategy orientations that emphasize the role of perception and social learning theories of learning. There are several very important differences that divide these theories that are critical from a pedagogy perspective. These critical differences usually revolve around the following primary issues:

1   What kind of learner engagement and cognitive processing is necessary for learning to occur?
2   How much information does the learner need about the content?
3   What is the appropriate size of the "chunk" of content that the learner should handle at one time?
4   Is learning an independent or socially constructed process?

Learner engagement and cognitive processing

It is important to say from the outset that all approaches to instruction recognize the need for high levels of learner involvement with the content. There is no learning theory that does not recognize the critical nature of the level of student engagement in what they are doing. Even motor skill learning theorists have come to understand the importance of engagement (R. Magill, 1998). Our own pedagogy research on time with the content has documented from an historical perspective the transition from allocated time to motor engaged time to the need for a high level of processing and learner engagement (Ashy, Lee, & Landin, 1988; Metzler, 1989; Silverman, 1990; Silverman, Devillier, & Rammirez, 1991; Solmon & Lee, 1996). Motor skill practice that does not require a high level of student processing may not be the best practice that we can offer, suggesting that rote repetition of responses is not appropriate practice.

The big theoretical issue from a learning perspective is currently an issue regarding the nature of student processing necessary for learning to occur. Although there is consensus on a high level of student engagement with the content, there is less consensus on issues related to the level of cognitive processing essential for learning and whether or not cognitive processing has to be at a conscious or awarness level. Constructivists would advocate a high cognitive level of engagement, sometimes referred to as higher order thinking (Anderson, Reder, & Simon, 1996; Brooks & Brooks, 1993), while the behaviorists are not as concerned with the level of processing as they are with the nature of the response of the learner. The behaviorist is concerned with finding a way to get the learner to produce an appropriate response and then reinforcing that response (Bandura, 1969; Becker, Engleman, & Thomas, 1971). The process the learner uses to produce that response may not be critical.

Level of processing

Constructivist theories of learning are based on the idea that students process information at a higher level in learning experiences designed from a constructivist perspective and therefore learn more and better (Brooks & Brooks, 1993). Learners construct their own ways of knowing (Cobb, 1994). A high level of cognitive processing is facilitated because the learner is encouraged to find their own way through tasks rather than being given explicit detailed information on how the task is to be accomplished. Of course it is not that easy. One of the problems that we have when we look at level of student processing as an indicator of "good practice," or a good indicator of an appropriate learning experience, is that you cannot predict the level of student processing from the methodology a teacher uses. You cannot rule out higher order thinking because a teacher uses a more direct methodology. You cannot predict higher order thinking because a teacher uses a problem solving approach (Styles, 1974). This was made abundantly clear at the recent AISEP conference (1999), in which researchers from France presented their analysis of a teaching episode in which the teacher began asking a class some questions that were designed to elicit some higher order thinking (Amade-Escot, Loquet, & Refuggi, 1999). It became very clear to the researchers that the students were in search of the answer they thought the teacher wanted. Most of us have had the experience of being in a lecture class and struggling to stay awake. Likewise most of us have had the experience of being in a lecture class and hanging on every word of the professor. We have been in group learning environments with similar contrasts in level of engagement.

Just as learners in a motor skill eventually reduce the level of processing needed to perform a motor task to lower and even automatic levels of cognitive response (Fitts & Posner, 1967), learners in cognitive tasks do the same, depending on, among other things, their experience with the task. A process that facilitates a higher level of processing in one student may elicit a lower level in another student for a variety of reasons, including motivation, past experience with the task or similar tasks, the social context of the environment, or perhaps cognitive strategies available to the student. This means that students in a highly structured information processing or more behaviorally oriented pedagogical experience who are highly motivated and involved could be processing at a very high level, and students who are in a problem solving or constructivist oriented learning experience could be processing at a low level. In other words, there is no direct line from a method of teaching to a level of student processing; too many other factors are involved (Styles, 1974). Researchers in pedagogy and, perhaps more importantly, teachers in the field will need strategies to identify the expected nature of processing, if they are to really understand what is happening in particular teaching methodologies. Researchers are going to have to investigate the nature of student processing and engagement and not merely the products of the process in order to understand how to effectively use teaching methodology.

For the researcher and the teacher the idea that learning and process cannot be assumed from method presents many problems. As stated before, just as there is no direct measure of learning and we infer learning from observable products, there is no direct measure of processing. To some extent it is easier to infer processing in motor responses because the process is oftentimes more observable (trials and attempts at a response). On the other hand, direct measures of observable behavior for predicting learning outcomes are mostly inadequate. The current emphasis in psychology on talk-aloud and other self-report kinds of measures holds much promise and has been used in our field by a variety of researchers with some very interesting results (see for instance, Rink, French, & Tjeerdsma, 1996: Solmon & Lee, 1996, 1997).

Conscious level of processing

What we do not know is whether or not there is a difference between the effect of responses produced at a high level of conscious processing and those responses produced perhaps at a high level of processing but not at a conscious level. While constructivists and behaviorists do not address the issue of conscious level of processing, the issue is imbedded in the pedagogy of the constructivist and the behaviorist. The synonym for the terms *direct/explicit* and the synonym for the terms *indirect/implicit* instruction are the terms used by the psychology literature to indicate conscious and unconscious processing, respectively (Biehler & Snowman, 1982).

The dynamical systems literature coming out of motor control and other research on learning clearly alludes to the idea that the learner does not have to process what they are doing at a conscious level in order to make an appropriate motor response to a task (Newell, 1986; Schmidt, Young, Swinnen, & Shapiro, 1989; Singer, Lidor, & Cauraugh, 1993; Starkes & Allard, 1993; Wulf & Weigelt, 1997). In this context the notion of conscious level of processing means to bring an idea to an awareness level. In the dynamical systems literature, the "system" will always choose an appropriate response based on the constraints (Newell, 1986). Constraints in this context means organismic, task, and environmental. D. Magill, in a recent publication (1998), explored the notion that learners can acquire knowledge about how to perform motor skills without being able to verbalize that knowledge. Knowledge, in the context of this work, means environmental critical cues necessary to perform primarily open skills. This work, in its larger context, supports the idea that learners do not have to be given explicit information on how to perform a skill in order to learn the skill, and that brings us to the next issue.

How much information does the learner need about the content?

An exploratory study done by Sweeting and Rink (1999) contrasted the effects of kindergarten and second graders learning a long jump either through direct instruction or through an environmentally designed task approach that elicits the appropriate response from the learner. The direct teaching approach used a whole-part-whole orientation to teaching the task, step by step instruction, learning cues, and student feedback on performance. The environmental design approach put students in a variety of environmentally designed situations where they had to complete the task to accomplish a particular goal like jumping over low hurdles, jumping to achieve marked colored bands on a mat, and so on, using the standing long jump skill. No teacher information on how to do the skill or augmented teacher feedback was given to the students in the environmental group. The environmentally designed task clearly increased initial performance, particularly for younger and less skilled students, but lost its effect with time and increasing skill. An analysis of process characteristics of the jump indicated that students in both groups were strong in different parts of the jump, which means that they learned different things from the two different instructional orientations to teaching the skill. The idea that students may learn different things from different methods was also suggested in the results of a study investigating tactical and skill orientations to teaching badminton (French, Werner, Taylor, Hussey, & Jones, 1996).

A second study that attempted to sort out how much information a learner needs on how to perform was done in the context of volleyball progressions (Rink, French, Werner, Lynn, & Mays, 1992). One group was given helpful information during the practice of a progression on how to best perform and another was not. For most initial tasks in the progression, the success levels during practice were similar. For a later stage of the progression the group that did not receive information from the teacher on how to make an adjustment to a task that had increased in complexity was not successful. Learners in this context were not able to "read" the environmental cues appropriately. This lack of success was maintained through later stages in the progression.

Advocates of a "games for understanding" approach to developing games players suggest that students should not be given information on how to execute motor skills *prior* to needing it in the context of game play. The emphasis of this approach is clearly the attention given to the role of tactics (Almond, 1986; Chandler & Mitchell, 1991). In a sense, games for understanding is another approach that is not supportive of giving a lot of information to learners on how to execute skills, at least not initially in the teaching of games. The results of this research are mixed (Rink, 1996). However, the real issue for all of these orientations is not if but when the learner should receive information on how to execute a motor skill. Does the learner need specific information on how to execute a motor response? Not always but clearly sometimes. Is not giving learners information on how to do a skill non-teaching and trial and error learning, or is the teaching just different? If it is true that beginners do not need, or cannot use, explicit information, are there any principles that guide when and under what conditions learners might need more specific help? Are there any guidelines that help teachers to know how best to construct learning experiences that "lead" the learner without "feeding" the learner? What is at issue here from a theoretical perspective is how much information the learner needs and whether or not the teacher should be communicating anything to learners on how to do a motor skill (Kwak, 1993; Lee, Swinnen, & Serrien, 1995; Rink, 1994; Werner & Rink, 1988). Learning requires processing, regardless of whether information is given by the teacher. Knowing how to get learners processing what they are doing enough to "generate" appropriate motor responses and knowing when to intervene with more specific help and different tasks that elicit more advanced responses may be the art of teaching in physical education and should be a major concern for researchers who would understand teaching. Research on feedback in a physical education setting also seems to suggest that it is an "it depends" issue, which means that teachers should be prepared to understand how and under what conditions learners need particular kinds of information (Lee, Keh, & Magill, 1993; Magill, 1994).

Related to issues involving the amount of information the learner needs are those related to teacher clarity. Part of the justification for the identification of more explicit teaching styles as more effective is related to the notion of teacher clarity (Kennedy, Cruickshank, Bush, & Meyers, 1978). There is no reason to assume that these characteristics of teacher clarity are not still important components of all effective instruction (Werner & Rink, 1988). All of the research indicating the importance of teacher clarity I consider to be part of that group of teaching skills that transcend methodology—those generic teaching skills (Landin, 1995; Magill, 1994). There is a tendency for advocates of, and particularly novices at, indirect teaching styles to confuse being clear and having clear expectations for what students should be doing with telling students exactly what to do. Some of the most effective teachers of movement education use some of the most direct and explicit teaching styles. In a Barrett style of movement education, learner expectations are explicit (Logsdon et al., 1977). Student options for responses are clear within a set of clearly communicated expectations. Using an indirect teaching style does not abdicate a teacher from being clear or having clear expectations for performance.

One of the most important sets of questions for those who would study learning is not necessarily how you help students to produce a response, but the long-term effects of that experience on future learning, the ability of the student to use responses appropriately, and the transfer of learning from one context to another. In terms of future learning, if you can produce the response without a high level of conscious processing, does that have an effect on how you can refine the skill or the more long-term ability of the student to learn other related skills? If the response is not conscious it usually means that the student does not have to have a language label for what they are doing. Is learning motor skills or future motor skills facilitated by a language label? If for instance I have learned to do a drop shot in badminton but do not know it is a drop shot, what effect does that have on future learning? What is clear is that learners can produce appropriate motor responses without processing what to do at a conscious level (Singer, Lido, & Cauraugh, 1993; Wulf & Weigelt, 1997). What is also clear is that there must be some kind of cognitive processing.

One of the assumptions of teaching based on constructivist orientations to learning is that because the learning experience is more appropriately contextually based, which means that the student should be learning the skill in the context in which it is going to be used, the problems of transfer when the context changes are minimized (Brooks & Brooks, 1993). Intuitively this makes sense, but yet to be investigated are assumptions about transfer to different or more complex settings and the difficulties of putting students into environments that may be contextually too complex. Recent work reconceptualizing the transfer issues of learning may support more constructivist orientations to learning, or at least not dismiss them so quickly (Bransford & Schwartz, 1999).

Related to both the type of processing and the level of processing are issues of student motivation, particularly as student motivation relates to levels of student engagement and processing. Recent educational literature has given a lot of attention to notions of student motivation (Lepper, 1988; Pintrich, March, & Boyle, 1993; Wigfield, Eccles, & Rodriguez, 1998) and with good reason. If student engagement is crucial to learning, then how to increase student engagement is critical. Student motivation is certainly a key to engage-ment. Of particular concern are issues related to choosing teaching strategies and creating environmental conditions that facilitate student motivation, which should lead to higher levels of student engagement and therefore higher levels of processing. In school setting both academic and social goals interact to influence learning and are linked to notions of an appropriate learning environment. Although the recent emphasis on more indirect and constructivist methodologies is in part driven by a commitment to make learning more meaningful for individual learners and to the improvement of student motivation, the assumption that students are not and cannot be motivated in non-constructivist and more behavioral orientations to learning cannot be supported. Likewise, using a con-structivist orientation to teaching does in no way guarantee high levels of student motiv-ation, particularly teaching that relies entirely on establishing tasks that motivate learners intrinsically.

Questions related to what kinds of tasks and methods motivate students are beginning to be of interest to pedagogy researchers. This is the level of investigation that should capture the pedagogy researcher interested in issues of motivation. If we are to understand the role of student motivation it is important for us to understand what motivates different kinds of students in teaching (Chen & Darst, 1999). Issues of the nature of the content, the appropriate level of content, design of the task, and lesson and unit pacing are likely to be fruitful avenues of investigation in our attempt to understand how to develop and maintain student interest and motivation for a high level of processing. As the debate of the sixties clarified, waiting for all students to be highly motivated to do a task so that all learning can be intrinsically motivated is a luxury that most educators do not have (Freiberg, 1999).

The size of the chunk of content

The selection of the learning task is perhaps the single most critical decision that the teacher has to face. What constitutes a "meaningful chunk" of content is a critical issue for learning theorists. Current learning theory is concerned that the content the learner is asked to work with has "meaning" in and of itself and is not just a fragmented part of something else (Anderson, Reder, & Simon, 1996; Kirk & McDonald, 1998). The issue is decontextualized learning. Constructivists have advocated that a larger and more meaning-ful "chunk" of content be presented to learners as opposed to breaking down content into less than "wholes" characteristic of more behaviorist orientations to instruction (Anderson et al., 1996; Kirk & MacDonald, 1998). The pedagogy of the behaviorist is concerned with creating small step by step increments of content to create success oriented learn-ing (Mathis & McGagaghie, 1974). So what we have is one group advocating large chunks of content to make sure the content is meaningful and in context and another group advocating smaller chunks of content so that the experience of the learner is successful.

The selection of an appropriate task will largely be based on the teacher's ability to balance the need for student meaning and the need for student success. We need to know more about this process from the learner's perspective. Many behavioral models of step by step instruction may have overemphasized the need for immediate success and become mindless and meaningless exercises for many students. However, learning theories that provide large chunks of content in an attempt to deal with contextualized learning and student meaning for the learner may choose too large a chunk of content for learner success and run the risk of skipping vital stages of development in the learning of some content areas. Designing learning experiences to promote challenge and processing without putting the learning task out of reach of the learner would seem to be the teacher's challenge.

Current thinking regardless of where you are on the continuum of direct to indirect teaching clearly asserts that skills should *ultimately* be practiced in the context in which they are going to be used. Both orientations would support the idea that students are not likely to use in meaningful contexts what they have been taught in fragmented ways and out of context. Ample evidence exists to support the idea that unless safety is an issue, practice of the whole should precede any attempt to temporarily fragment the skill and practice part of a skill. Motor learning theorists have vigorously suggested that it is the whole skill that should be practiced when possible and not the individual parts (R. Magill, 1998).

At first, the idea that the whole is critical would seem to settle the issue of context or chunk of content. However, in the context of physical education content, is a meaningful whole the individual skills of a sport, the game, or something in between? What constitutes a meaningful whole? Does this change with age and experience? At a more micro level the issue for sport skill instruction becomes an issue of whole-part-whole learning: should the teacher break down individual skills? At a more macro level the notion of progressions also involves reducing the complexity of the context in which skills are learned and practiced. No one is suggesting that the learning of motor skills occur in a full game. As a matter of fact research done on skill improvement over time would suggest that players do not improve their individual motor skills by playing the game (French & Thomas, 1987; Parker & O'Sullivan, 1983). Research also supports the idea that reducing skills and learning contexts is essential when students are not successful. In some of the studies done by the author, students who practiced a final skill task in a volleyball study (receiving a pass from one direction and sending it to another direction) were not as ultimately successful as those students who practiced with a progression that initially reduced the complexity and then gradually added it (French, Rink, Rikard, Mays, Lynn, & Werner, 1991; Rink, French, Werner, Lynn, & Mays, 1992). Whether the issue was more related to motivation and meaningful practice or more related to success has yet to be resolved.

Is learning an independent or socially constructed process?

Most learning theories have assumed that learning is a private experience: groups do not learn, individuals do. Social constructivists would say that all learning is social, meaning that learning is socially constructed (Saloman & Perkins, 1998; Vygotsky, 1978). From the perspective of the learner, individual self-perceptions, goals, and the social learning environment all mediate student choices, performance, and effort, and therefore student engagement and learning. Sorting out the specific role created by the learning environment has been most difficult. When translated into practice, the learning environment created by the social learning theorists rest heavily on pedagogy that involves the learner in social ways with others (peer teaching, cooperative learning, creating learning communities, etc.; Johnson, Johnson, & Holubec, 1994).

The issue for research on the learning environment from the perspective of learning theory is related to the kind of learning environment that facilitates learner processing and engagement and how knowledge is constructed (Anderson, Reder, & Simon, 1996; Kirk & McDonald, 1998). The early research on teacher management clearly illustrates the need for a well managed learning environment (Brophy & Good, 1986). What is new about the present discussion of learning environment is the issue of whether learning is a social or an independent process. Much of the research on learning has taken place from the perspective of the individual learner and has been concerned with studying how individuals acquire knowledge and skills that may be facilitated by another or others. Learning from this perspective is primarily construed as an individual process. Additional research has considered the social interaction of students as a critical factor in the ecology of the gym (Hastie & Siedentop, 1999). Research done from a social learning perspective is more concerned with the manner in which learning is actively constructed by a group of learner in particular environments (Salomon & Perkins, 1998; Vygotsky, 1978).

An active construction perspective and an individually acquired perspective on learning can coexist as explanations for different phenomena (Bredo, 1994). Individuals can learn alone. They can acquire skills and knowledge from a facilitator whose role it is to help them acquire particular skills and knowledge (teacher or tutor). They can also learn in group environments devised to encourage interactive processes that help groups construct meaning. Physical education has been studied from the first two situations: individual learning and facilitated learning. Some work on sport education and games for understanding approaches a group learning situation, and this work would indicate that group learning environments are effective in physical education (Hastie, 1996, 1998), particularly in terms of more affective concerns.

Putting students into groups does not insure positive interaction. We know very little about the nonverbal and verbal interaction that takes place in a gymnasium where groups of learners are trying to acquire individual skills but have access to knowledge of the performance of others. We know less about the verbal interaction process between learners that might facilitate the process. Sport education research and research on other processes involving group interaction will need to study the process of group learning to the level of detail that would help us know what is happening and how to facilitate the positive and productive interactions between students so crucial to the assumptions of social learning theory.

Group learning environments are not without their problems and, like most recommendations for pedagogy, should not be considered universally effective for all students in all situations. The research on the effects of group learning environments on students with different characteristics is conflicting (Fradd & Lee, 1999; Lou, Abrami, Spence, Poulsen, Chambers, & d'Apollonioa, 1996). For instance there is some support for the idea that less aggressive students (many girls) and the average student are more likely to not be as involved in the process as males and more highly aggressive students (Mael, 1998). When grouped heterogeneously these students are not likely to be as involved in the interactive process and therefore not likely to learn as much as other students (Salomon & Perkins, 1998). Although most of the research clearly supports the positive effect of heterogeneously grouped groups on low skilled and below average students, like most recommendations for pedagogy the critical issues revolve around for whom and under what conditions a particular pedagogy is appropriate (Driver, Asoko, Leah, Mortimer, & Scott, 1994).

What is significant about the more recent emphasis on constructivism and social learning is the recognition that teaching and learning does not always have to be explicit and is not always an independent experience. While there is sufficient documentation to support explicit teaching and explicit learning, there is now also the beginning of support for teaching and learning that rests heavily on implicit strategies.

Conclusions

So what is the point of this discussion? Put quite simply, there is no single theory of learning that explains learning or the lack of it in all situations, and therefore, there can be no single approach to instruction. Each theory of learning is used to support an approach to instruction. Each has but a piece of a very complex phenomenon we call learning. A lot of the research done on instruction has been framed, not to establish theory or to understand learning, but rather to establish direct links between what a teacher does and what a student learns. Often this research looks at a particular kind of learning, rather than viewing learning more holistically. The advantage of using learning theory to talk about pedagogy is that you get to test the assumptions of the theory—what it is based on. For instance, is it true that constructivist learning environments are more motivating to learners? Is it true that students process more when practice is not rote?

You don't want to know simply that something works—you want to know why it works and how it works in different conditions. Knowing why it works and how it works allows you to develop pedagogy that is consistent with that why. When you build a knowledge base on theory you can test the assumptions of a theory. When you spend all of your effort proving that a particular kind of teaching is better than another kind of teaching, you limit what you can learn about the very complex teaching/learning process. I am not advocating that we do not do methods studies. I am advocating that we ground our work in the theories that are the underlying basis of these methods so that we have a better way to build a knowledge base. This kind of thinking changes the question that we ask from "Which is best?" and "What do I believe?" to "What is happening here, and for what purposes, under what conditions, and in what way should I use this instructional methodology?" There may not be a best way to teach, but there may be a best way to teach particular content to particular learners. Lee (1991) made this point abundantly clear in her review of the research up to this time.

Part of the process of understanding what is happening for both the teacher and the researcher should involve developing an understanding of the assumptions of what is taking place in the learning process and testing those assumptions. Periodically those of us who are involved in studying the teaching and learning process forget that the process involves what students actually do and that the process should result in particular products. We confirm the treatment by looking exclusively at what the teacher does, when in actuality we probably should be focusing more attention on what the student does. This is not a new problem for us. It took the academic learning time research movement to move us out of an era of looking at what the teacher does in our early work. More recent work being done in student cognition and with ideas related to the student as the mediator of instruction are an attempt to refocus our work on the importance of the learner (Lee, 1994). Work being done in Europe on didactics in the instructional process puts a similar emphasis on the process and the critical role of the process of learning from the student perspective (Amade-Escot, Loquet, & Refuggi, 1999). An important difference between the European work on didactics and current work in the United States is the emphasis didactics puts on the role of content. Framing the focus on the student with a learning orientation should organize our quest.

A focus on teaching methodology in professional preparation without attention to the underlying assumptions of that methodology is also problematic. Unless teachers implement methodologies with a knowledge of what processes should be taking place, and unless they are given strategies to confirm that those processes are taking place, we are placing teachers in an untenable position. They too must understand that there is no direct link between what a teacher does and what a student learns.

When newer ideas (or ideas from previous decades) on how to teach and what to teach are introduced into our literature they generate an excitement and an enthusiasm that is good. Teachers get motivated and they try new things, which in and of itself is good. It is not good when any single methodology or approach to teaching becomes more than just a choice from many different teaching methodologies. Pedagogy researchers have an obligation to develop an understanding of approaches to content and methods of teaching that informs the field objectively. Those direct lines that we are looking for between learning theory and student learning and between teaching and learning are mostly not out there.

References

Allison, P., & Barrett, K. (2000). *Constructing children's physical education experiences*. Boston: Allyn and Bacon.

Almond, L. (1986). Reflecting on themes: A games classification. In R. Thorpe, D. Bunker, & L. Almond. *Rethinking games teaching* (pp. 71–82). Loughborough, UK: University of Technology.

Amade-Escot, C., Loquet, M., & Refuggi, R. (1999). *Didactic research in physical education classes: Interest and characteristics of a research programme*. Paper presented at the annual meeting of the International AISEP Congress, April, 8. Besancon, France.

Anderson, J., Reder, L., & Simon, H. (1996). Situated learning and education. *Educational Researcher*, **25**, 5–11.

ASCD (1999). *Perceiving, Behaving and Becoming: Revisited*. Alexandria, VA: Author.

Ashy, M., Lee, A., & Landin, D. (1988). Relationship of practice using correct technique to achievement in a motor skill. *Journal of Teaching in Physical Education*, **7**, 115–120.

Bandura, A. (1969). *Principles of behavior modification*. New York: Holt, Rinehart, and Winston.

Becker, W., Engleman, S., & Thomas, D. (1971). *Teaching: A course in applied psychology*. Chicago: Science Research Associates.

Biehler, R., & Snowman, J. (1982). *Psychology applied to teaching*. Boston: Houghton Mifflin.

Bilbrough A., & Jones, P. (1963). *Physical education in the primary school*. London: University of London Press.

Bransford, J., & Schwartz, D. (1999). Rethinking transfer: A simple proposal with multiple implications. *Review of Research in Education*. Washington, D.C.: American Educational Research Association.

Bredo, E. (1994). Reconstructing educational psychology: Situated cognition and Deweyian pragmatism. *Educational Psychologist*, **29**(1), 23–35.

Brooks, J., & Brooks, M. (1993). *In search of understanding: The case for constructivist classrooms.* Alexandria, VA: ASCD.

Brophy, J., & Good, T. (1986). Teacher behavior and student achievement. In M. Wittrock (Ed.), *Handbook of research on teaching* (3rd ed., pp. 328–375). New York: MacMillan.

Chandler, T., & Mitchell, S. (1991). Reflections on models of games education. *Journal of Teaching in Physical Education, 14*, 467–477.

Chen, A., & Darst, P. (1999). *Situational interest as a function of learning task design: Influence of cognitive and physical engagement in physical activity.* Paper presented at the annual meeting of the American Education Research Association, April. Montreal, Canada.

Cobb, P. (1994). Where is the mind? Constructivist and socio-cultural perspectives on mathematical development. *Educational Researcher, 23*, 7, 13–20.

Combs, A. (1959). Personality theory and its implications for curriculum development. In A. Fraiser (Ed.), *Learning more about learning* (pp. 5–20). Washington, D.C.: ASCD.

Cratty, B. (1967). *Movement behavior and motor learning.* Philadelphia: Lea & Febiger.

Driver, R., Asoko, H., Leah, J., Mortimer, E., & Scott, P. (1994). Constructing scientific knowledge in the classroom. *Educational Researcher, 23*, 5–12.

Fitts, P., & Posner, M. (1967). *Human Performance.* Belmont, CA: Brooks/Cole.

Fradd, S., & Lee, O. (1999). Teacher's role in promoting science inquiry with students from diverse language backgrounds. *Educational Researcher, 28*, 14–20.

Freiberg, J. (Ed.) (1999). *Perceiving behaving becoming: Lessons learned.* Washington, D.C.: ASCD.

French, K., Rink, J., Rikard, L., Mays, A., Lynn, S., & Werner, P. (1991). The effects of practice progressions on learning two volleyball skills. *Journal of Teaching in Physical Education, 10*, 261–274.

French, K., & Thomas, G. (1987). The relation of knowledge development to children's basketball performance. *Journal of Sport Psychology, 9*, 15–32.

French, K., Werner, P., Taylor, K., Hussey, K., & Jones, J. (1996). The effects of a 6-week unit of tactical, skill, or combined tactical and skill instruction on badminton performance of ninth-grade students. *Journal of Teaching in Physical Education, 15*, 439–463.

Goble, F. (1970). *The third force: The psychology of Abraham Maslow.* New York: Grossman.

Grehaigne, J., & Godbout, P. (1995). Tactical knowledge in team sports from a constructivist and cognitivist perspective. *Quest, 47*, 490–505.

Hastie, P. (1996). Student role involvement during a unit of sport education. *Journal of Teaching in Physical Education, 16*, 88–103.

Hastie, P. (1998). The participation and perceptions of girls within a unit of sport education. *Journal of Teaching in Physical Education, 17*, 157–171.

Hastie, P., & Siedentop, D. (1999). An ecological perspective on physical education. *European Physical Education Review, 5*, 9–29.

Johnson, D., Johnson, R., & Holubec, E. (1994). *The new circles of learning: Cooperation in the classroom and the school.* Alexandria, VA: Association for Supervision and Curriculum Development.

Kennedy, J., Cruikshank, D., Bush, A., & Meyers, B. (1978). Additional investigations into the nature of teacher clarity. *Journal of Educational Research, 2*, 3–10.

Kirk, D., & MacDonald, D. (1998). Situated learning in physical education. *Journal of Teaching in Physical Education, 17*, 376–387.

Kwak, E. (1993). *The initial effects of various task presentation conditions on student's performance in the lacrosse throw.* Unpublished doctoral dissertation. The University of South Carolina.

Landin, D. (1995). The role of verbal cues in skill learning. *Quest, 46*, 299–313.

Lawther, J. (1968). *The learning of physical skills*. Englewood Cliffs, NJ: Prentice-Hall.

Lee, A. (1991). Research on teaching in physical education: Questions and comments. *Research Quarterly for Exercise and Sport*, **62**, 374–379.

Lee, A. (1994). How the field evolved. In S. Silverman & C. Ennis, *Student learning in physical education*. Champaign, IL: Human Kinetics.

Lee, A., Keh, A., & Magill, R. (1993). Instructional effects of teacher feedback in physical education [Monograph]. *Journal of Teaching in Physical Education*, **12**, 437–446.

Lee, T., Swinnen, P., & Serrien, D. (1995). Cognitive effort and motor learning. *Quest*, **46**, 328–344.

Lepper, M. (1988). Motivational considerations in the study of instruction. *Cognition and Instruction*, **5**, 289–310.

Locke, L. (1969). Movement education: Description and critique. In R. Brown & B. Cratty (Eds.), *New Perspectives of man in action* (p. 208). New York: Prentice Hall.

Logsdon, B., Barrett, K., Broer, M., Ammons, M., & Roberton, M. (1977). *Physical education for children: A Focus on the teaching process*. Philadelphia: Lea & Febiger.

Lou, Y., Abrami, P., Spence, J., Poulsen, C., Chambers, B., & d'Apollonioa, S. (1996). Within class grouping. *Review of Educational Research*, **66**, 423–458.

Mael, F. (1998). Single-sex and coeducational schooling: Relationships to socioemotional and academic development. *Review of Educational Research*, **68**, 101–129.

Magill, D. (Ed.) (1994). *Communicating information to enhance skill learning* [Monograph]. *Quest*, **46**.

Magill, D. (1998). *Motor learning: Concepts and applications*. Boston: McGraw-Hill.

Magill, R. (1994). The influence of augmented feedback during skill learning depends on characteristics of the skill and the learner. *Quest*, **46**, 314–327.

Magill, R. (1998). Knowledge is more than we can talk about: Implicit learning in motor skill acquisition. *Research Quarterly for Exercise and Sport*, **69**, 104–110.

Maslow, A. (1962). *Toward a psychology of being*. Princeton, New Jersey: Van Nostrand.

Mathis, C., & McGagaghie (1974). From theories of learning to theories of teaching. In L. Styles (Ed.), *Theories for teaching* (pp. 30–50). New York: Dodd, Mead & Co.

Mauldon, E., & Redfern, H.B. (1969). *Games teaching*. London: Macdonald & Evans.

McIntosh, P. (1972). A recent history of physical education in England with particular reference to the development of movement education. In B. Bennett (Ed.), *History of physical education*. Chicago: Athletic Institute.

Metzler, M. (1989). A review of research on time in sport pedagogy. *Journal of Teaching in Physical Education*, **8**, 87–103.

Metzler, M. (1999). *Instructional models for physical education*. Needham Heights, MA: Allyn & Bacon.

Mosston, M. (1966). *Teaching physical education*. Columbus, OH: Charles E. Merrill.

Newell, K. (1986). Constraints on the development of coordination. In H. Wade and H. Whiting (Eds.), *Motor Development Aspects of Coordination and Control*. Dordrect, The Netherlands: Martinus Nijhoff Publishers.

Parker, M., & O'Sullivan, M. (1983). Modifying ALT-PE for game play contexts and other reflections. *Journal of Teaching in Physical Education*, Summer Monograph.

Perkins, D. (1999). The many faces of constructivism. *Educational Leadership*, **57**, 6–11.

Peterson, P. (1979). Direct instruction reconsidered. In P. Peterson & H. Walberg (Eds.), *Research on teaching: Concepts, findings, and implications*. Berkeley, CA: McCutchan.

Pintrich, P., Marx, R., & Boyle, R. (1993). Beyond cold conceptual change: The role of motivational beliefs and classroom contextual factors in the process of conceptual change. *Review of Education Research*, **63**, 167–199.

Prawet, R. (1995). Misreading Dewey: Reform, projects and the language game. *Educational Researcher*, **24**, 7, 13–21.

Rink, J. (1969). *An evaluation of the movement responses of four first grade boys to teacher stated movement problems.* Unpublished master's thesis, University of North Carolina, Greensboro.

Rink, J. (1994). Task presentation in pedagogy. *Quest*, **4**, 270–280.

Rink, J. (Ed.) (1996). Tactical and skill approaches to teaching sport and games [Monograph]. *Journal of Teaching in Physical Education*, **15**(4).

Rink, J. (1998). *Teaching physical education for learning.* Boston: McGraw Hill.

Rink, J., French, K., & Tjeerdsma, B. (1996). Foundations for the learning and instruction of sport and games. *Journal of Teaching Physical Education*, **15**, 397–417.

Rink, J., French, K., Werner, P., Lynn, S., & Mays, A. (1992). The influence of content development on the effectiveness of instruction. *Journal of Teaching Physical Education*, **11**, 139–149.

Rogers, C. (1969). *Freedom to learn.* Columbus, OH: Charles E. Merrill.

Rosenshine, B. (1987). Explicit teaching. In D. Berliner & B. Rosenshine (Eds.), *Talks to teachers.* New York: Random House.

Salomon, G., & Perkins, D. (1998). Individual and social aspects of learning. In P. Pearson & A. Iran-Nejad (Eds.), *Review of research in education* (pp. 1–24). Washington, D.C.: American Educational Research Association.

Schmidt, R., Young D., Swinnen, S., & Shapiro, D. (1989). Support for the guidance hypothesis. *Journal of Experimental Psychology: Learning, Memory and Cognition.* **15**, 352–359.

Shulman, L. (1986). Paradigms and research programs in the study of teaching: A contemporary perspective. In M. Wittrock (Ed.), *Handbook of Research on Teaching* (pp. 3–36). New York: Macmillan.

Siedentop, D. (Ed.) (1994). *Sport education: Quality PE through positive sport experiences.* Champaign, IL: Human Kinetics.

Silverman, S. (1990). Linear and curvilinear relationships between student practice and achievement in physical education. *Teaching and Teacher Education*, **6**, 305–314.

Silverman, S., Devillier, R., & Rammirez, T. (1991). The validity of ALT-PE as a process measure of student achievement. *Research Quarterly for Exercise and Sport*, **66**, 32–40.

Singer, R. (1980). *Motor learning and human performance.* New York: Macmillan.

Singer, R., Lidor, R., & Cauraugh, J. (1993). To be aware or not aware? What to think about when performing a motor skill. *The Sport Psychologist*, **7**, 19–30.

Solmon, M., & Lee, A. (1996). Entry characteristics, practice variables, and cognition: Student mediation of instruction. *Journal of Teaching in Physical Education*, **15**, 135–150.

Solmon, M., & Lee, A. (1997). Development of an instrument to assess cognitive processes in physical education classes. *Research Quarterly for Exercise and Sport*, **68**, 152–160.

Stanley, S. (1969). *Physical education: A movement orientation.* Toronto, ON: McGraw-Hill.

Starkes, J., & Allard, F. (1993). *Cognitive issues in motor expertise.* Amsterdam: Elsevier Science Publishers.

Styles, L. (Ed.) (1974). *Theories for teaching.* New York: Dodd, Mead, & Co.

Sweeting, T., & Rink, J. (1999). Effects of direct instruction and environmentally designed instruction on the process and product characteristics of a fundamental skill. *Journal of Teaching in Physical Education*, **18**, 216–233.

Turner, A., & Martinck, T. (1995). Teaching for understanding: A model for improving decision making during game play. *Quest*, **47**, 44–63.

Vygotsky, L. (1978). *Mind in society.* Cambridge, MA: Harvard University Press.

Werner, P., & Rink, J. (1988). Case studies of teacher effectiveness in second grade physical education. *Journal of Teaching Physical Education*, **4**, 280–297.

Wickstrom, R. (1970). *Fundamental motor patterns*. Philadelphia: Lea and Febiger.

Wigfield, A., Eccles, J., & Rodriguez, D. (1998). The development of children's motivation in school contexts. In P. Peterson and A. Iran-Nejad (Eds.), *Review of research in education* (pp. 73–118). Washington, D.C.: American Educational Research Association.

Wulf, G., & Weigelt, C. (1997). Instructions about physical principles in learning a complex motor skill: To tell or not to tell. . . . *Research Quarterly for Exercise and Sport*, **68**, 362–367.

John Evans

MAKING A DIFFERENCE?
Education and 'ability' in physical education

Introduction

IN THIS DISCUSSION I take up a theme articulated but left rather under-developed in a recent joint venture with Brian Davies and Jan Wright (2004). In that text we were concerned primarily to explore how consciousness is embodied through the practices and rituals of Physical Education and Health (PEH) in schools. However, we were equally eager to emphasize that, if we are interested in improving the lot of more children in schools in the interest of social democratic ideals, then we needed to be as concerned with issues of 'ability' – how it is recognized, conceptualized, socially configured, nurtured and embodied in and through the practices of PE – as with those of sport and health. I begin, then, by asking whether, in the current political culture, we are moving closer or further away from engaging these ideals.

In what has been an extraordinary displacement of professional interest over the last 20 years, physical education (and I use this term inclusively to signify both its subject matter and the people, researchers, teacher educators and teachers who trade in it) has increasingly centred attention on and justified its existence discursively and pedagogically in terms of just about everything other than that which is distinctive and special about itself and its subject matter. Specifically, the discipline's capacity and pedagogical responsibility to work on, effect changes in, develop and enhance 'the body's' intelligent capacities for movement and expression in physical culture,[1] in all its varied forms, has been displaced. PE has become strangely disembodied. It has either ceased to talk about the nature of 'physical education', 'educability', 'educe' (the process of bringing out or developing latent or potential existence) and 'ability' as processes and goals altogether, or reduced it to a dribble of unproblematic assumptions either about motivation and health-related behaviour, or 'fitness' or 'talent' for 'performance' in the interest of health and/or participation in organized sport. Its dominant discourse is a poor substitute for consideration of the nature of PE or the multitude of capacities and desires that find expression in physical culture, though not always within school PE.

This ought to strike us as very odd indeed. We would be hard pressed to find, for example, maths or English teachers justifying their existence principally in terms of what they can do, not for a child's literacy or numeracy, but their mental health, self-esteem or social welfare in and out of school, though both subjects may have better grounds for making such claims than PE. If lack of exercise is bad for your health, long bouts of innumeracy and illiteracy may be worse. Many will be familiar with claims made in the USA, for example, that sport education programmes or 'the application of structured physical fitness programmes' can meet the needs of 'at risk' youth, variously increasing their self-esteem, well-being and acquisition of life skills (like goal setting and planning and values development), while lowering depression and anxiety (Collingwood, 1997). In the UK a raft of policy rhetoric is now emerging from central government and its agencies on the grounds that 'Sport can contribute to neighbourhood renewal by improving communities' performance on four key indicators – health, crime, employment and education' (Policy Action Group 10, Department for Culture, Media and Sport, 1999) and 'Evidence is beginning to show that schools, which have a strong sporting ethos, have fewer truants, fewer exclusions and better academic results' (BBC News, 2003).

Leaving aside the issue of whether such relationships have anything to do with sport or the range of factors (e.g. catchment areas, social class intakes, levels of resourcing, quality of teaching and facilities) rarely mentioned in such reports, we should none the less ask whether PE is for education or wider desires for social control. My point here, however, is not that PE has no part to play in social processes such as these. It is simply that thinking of this kind, especially when adopted by central governments and sanitized of any radical social and economic agenda or intent, while not *determining* the development of PE in the UK and elsewhere, has so *dominated* the discourses of the profession and constrained its agendas that it is now almost impossible to debate the nature of 'ability' and what is educationally worthwhile in the practices of PE.

It is no accident that talk of physically educating 'the body', or of 'educe', has almost disappeared from the discourse of PE in schools and Physical Education Teacher Education (PETE) or Initial Teacher Education Physical Education (ITEPE) as it is called in the UK. In part, we no longer discuss what constitutes 'physical' education or 'educability' because those people whose trade it was to talk of such matters, such as philosophers of education, have largely disappeared from the scene. With 'valued knowledge' increasingly being determined by politicians, governments or their agents, learning for learning's sake, or its discussion have become truly unfashionable ideals. In the UK there is lineage between Kenneth Clarke's (Conservative Secretary of State for Education in the 1980s) ruthless dictum that 'having any ideas about how children learn, or develop, or feel, should be seen as subversive activity' and 'Teacher Educators who have peddled their subversions should be hunted down and hanged from the entrails of every sociologist' (quoted in Stones, 1992: 111) and New Labour's current Secretary of State for Education, Charles Clarke's recent rant about 'useless history' (Times Higher, 2003) taught in university and schools. It has been philosophers who have, more than others, prompted us to think about 'body matters' in relation, for example, to the nature of 'practical knowledge' (Polanyi, 1958), 'physical literacy' (Whitehead, 2001), 'kinaesthetic intelligence' (Arnold, 1979; Best, 1978) or 'puissance', evoked in Brian Pronger's (2002) recent, brilliant evocation of Marxism, phenomenology and Buddhism to reinstate 'desire' and the visceral embodiment of emotion into our pedagogical thinking and ideals. In the brutal culture of individualism and materialism that characterizes contemporary politics, voices such as these, positioned on the margins, inevitably struggle to be heard. And having driven talk of 'education' and 'educability' from the language of PE, it has been all too easy, given the factionalized nature of 'the profession', for powerful commercial forces to successfully privilege the instrumental, self-serving interests of the 'health' and sport industries. Once positioned as having either nothing or little to say about a child's 'physical' development, PE becomes easy pickings for those charged with costing education to suggest that if it isn't 'physical education' that the profession is trading in, then it has no legitimate business being in schools at all. We can note, for example, Stephen Jefferies's (2003) recent lament that in the USA school administrators are increasingly looking to cut costs by removing PE from the school curriculum.

None of this is to suggest that PE in schools should not benefit children and young people socially or in health terms, though there are no convincing arguments or empirical evidence to suggest that PE has any special right or responsibility in these matters. Rather, it is to underscore how PE's relations with sport and health interests may have altered understandings of how 'ability', 'educability' and 'educe' are recognized, conceptualized, cultivated and materialized in the actions of teachers in PE in schools and ITPE. Recent research (see Evans et al., 2004) has illustrated that how PE relates to these interests has a bearing on the way in which 'ability' is recognized and configured in its practice. The powerful discursive forces of health and sport have altered thinking on these matters fundamentally, perhaps irreversibly, in ways that detract from discussion of what educational work on 'the body' in the pursuit of educational ideals should be in PE.

PE cannot compensate for society

As the interests of sport and health pervade and dominate the discourses of PE in Initial Teacher Education and schools in many countries (see Evans et al., 2004) the realities of PE are increasingly being defined as forms of *compensatory education*. Such a perspective implies that something is lacking in the family, culture, class or community and thus, in the child, and that the school has to compensate for that which is missing. Families and children are looked at as deficit systems. The danger in this perspective, of course, is that teachers then develop low expectations of children that many will undoubtedly fulfil and fail to benefit from schools. If children are labelled as 'culturally deprived' (they don't eat the right food, or do 'the right' amounts or type of exercise), 'then it follows that the parents are inadequate; the spontaneous realizations of their culture, its images and symbolic representations, are of reduced value and significance' (Bernstein, 1971: 62). We are already seeing some evidence of this in the teaching of health education within PE in schools (Evans et al., 2004). PE cannot compensate for society's ills, either in its own right, or trading as sport and health. Bernstein (1971) argued that schools cannot compensate for the poverty and deprivation that contribute to working class failure in schools, but they could and should make a difference to their chances by confronting structures of inequality in both society and schools. In his view, however, if the rhetoric of compensatory education became a substitute for schools engaging in a critical analysis of their own practices (their curriculum, pedagogies, forms of assessment and organization) it could compound, rather than help erode, disadvantage, impoverishment and inequality in and outside school. As Bernstein (1971: 60) put it, 'I do not understand how we can talk about offering compensatory education to children who in the first place have not as yet, been offered an education environment.'

He argued that the concept of CE serves to direct attention away from the internal organization and the quality of the educational context of the school and to focus attention instead on the deficits of families and children. It may also have constrained discussion of the quality, form, content and function of PE and its capacity to make a difference to children's 'ability' to relate to and access physical culture and 'health' in and out of schools (see Collins and Kay, 2003; Roberts, 1996; Stroot, 2001).

One expression of compensatory ideology expressed in PE is the notion that teachers can help compensate for the poor health of children by enhancing their interest and enjoyment in and motivation for involvement in physical activity and sport. A whole industry of psychological research has grown up around issues of 'motivation', orientated towards helping practitioners understand how their programmes can better be attuned to the interests and needs of children and young people in schools (e.g. Dweck and Leggett, 1998; Weiner, 1995). In this perspective, neither 'education' nor 'ability' is treated as a problematic concept. 'Ability' tends to be characterized as a one-dimensional, static entity, one among many fixed or incremental 'attributions' (the others being effort, task difficulty, luck). While this has usefully centred attention on the nature of individual decision-making in health and sport, it has little to say about the nature of 'ability' as a dynamic, sociocultural construct *and* process. Education and 'educability' are defined only in relation to the values, ideals and mores that prevail in schools and other social fields, when consideration should be given to the ways in which 'abilities' are configured, recognized, nurtured and rejected within and across the physical cultures of communities, societies and schools.

The reductionism inherent in the literature on attribution and ability lends itself perfectly to those willing converts of recent 'human genome' theory, some of whom may wish to reduce 'ability' to something akin to 'physical intelligence'; a kind of God-given, homogeneous, immutable entity programmed (or not as the case might be) for (top-level) sport. In the UK researchers have recently documented that 'ability' is increasingly understood by policy-makers, politicians and teachers as 'proxy for common sense notions of "intelligence"' (Demaine, 2001: 2). Thinking of this kind now runs through a multiple of grouping and tracking practices that separate out the 'able' and the 'less able' within schools, providing opportunity for teachers and senior managers 'to identify the winners and losers at the earliest possible stages, allowing continual checks to ensure that those predicted success "fulfil" their potential' (Gillborn and Youdell, 2001: 97). In this way schools build on and reproduce, rather than produce, 'ability'; they identify and endorse the individual characteristics that parents invest in, differently, by virtue of their social class (Ball, 2003). The stratification that operates at an institutional level, through ability grouping policies, also has its counterpart at an interpersonal level within classes in terms of the time and attention given to different types of students (Lynch and Lodge, 2002).

The significance of these developments for the social reproduction of achievement, underachievement, educational aspirations, 'ability' and identity in contexts of PE requires detailed exploration. Evidence is beginning to emerge to suggest that stratification and ability grouping, along with the labelling and segregation of the 'gifted and talented' and 'low attainers', are increasingly features of PE departments in some 'specialist' secondary schools in the UK (Penney and Houlihan, 2003). Neither the sciences that feed ITPE nor the discourses of health and sport may do much to interrupt this state of affairs, or help us explore what 'ability' means and how it is configured, performed and displayed in contexts of PE. What do such terms as 'gifted' and 'talented' mean in PE? How are they configured in its practices and with what consequence for the multiple of 'abilities' and desires that children bring to school? What impact will PE have on the differences between the 'abilities' of pupils in contexts such as these? How can we debate such matters and reinstate 'ability' into the discourse and practice of PE in ways that do not view it simply as an attribution or 'entity' or as 'physical intelligence'; a homogenous, immutable, manifestation of a culture free gene?

Towards a sociology of 'ability'

Though not well designed to handle issues of change or intervention, Bourdieu's (1992) development of the concept of 'habitus' offers some steer on how this may be achieved. In Bordieu's view an agent's habitus is an 'active residue or sediment of their past experiences which function within the present, shaping their perception, thought, action and social practice in a regular way' (Crossley, 2001: 93). 'It consists of dispositions, schemas, forms of know-how and competency, all of which function below the threshold of consciousness, shaping it in particular ways' (p. 93). Critically, these dispositions, schemas and competencies are acquired in social contexts structured by social class, gender and ethnicity, whose patterns and underlying principles they incorporate as both an inclination and a modus operandi. It is hardly surprising, says Crossley, that a child brought up in a football-loving household, for example, is far more likely statistically to develop their own love of football and will acquire the 'know how', the dispositions to 'true' appreciation and criticism. In this respect habitus is not just sets of learned dispositions but acquired by children in environments that are classed, 'cultured' and subject to variation. They are not simply cognitive structures but 'dispositions of the body', deep-seated structures of embodied dispositions, many of which become 'doxis', 'unquestioned beliefs embodied in actions and feelings but seldom formulated in words' (Crossley, 2001: 99). They are reflected, for example, in how we eat, walk, 'carry' and communicate with our bodies in everyday interaction. Such competencies carry a cultural value that have an exchange value in certain fields and, as a consequence, can function as 'capital' (Shilling, 1993). Insofar 'as they acquire a value within specific fields, these bodily attributes become desirable to social agents' (Crossley, 2001: 107). In effect they may be perceived as 'abilities', embodied social constructs, meaningful only in their display and are always and inevitably defined relationally with reference to values, attitudes and mores prevailing within a discursive field.[2]

The concept of 'field' is Bourdieu's way of conceptualizing horizontal differentiated social spaces, as they are intersected by vertical differentiation. Figure 1 highlights that social spaces are never constituted independently of the vertical axis of class, gender, 'race', disability and other forms of differentiation (e.g. age, sexuality). 'Horizontal differentiation is diffracted through vertical differentiation and vice versa' (Crossley, 2001: 100). Behaviour displayed in different forms of physical culture horizontally across fields is thus never constituted independently of the vertical axis of gender, class, disability, ethnicity, etc. We cannot 'read' or interpret 'ability', valued aspects of behaviour,

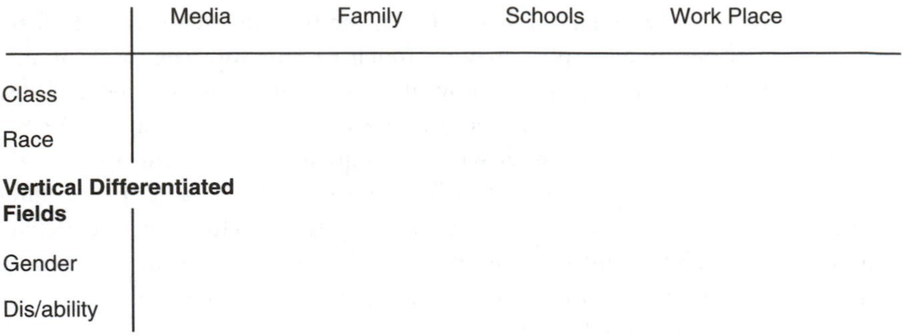

	Media	Family	Schools	Work Place
Class				
Race				
Vertical Differentiated Fields				
Gender				
Dis/ability				

Figure 1 Horizontal/differentiated fields (discrete but overlapping spaces).

without reference to a person's gender, age, ethnicity, 'disability' and the values prevailing within and across particular fields. For example, in contemporary health education class-rooms, the emphasis placed on body improvement and perfection (Evans and Davies, 2004) may configure 'ability' as a willingness to continually work on and engineer the body (through proper diet, more exercise) towards slender ideals. Children, by virtue of their social class or cultural background, may be more or less 'able' and willing to achieve this. Some, perhaps children of the new middle class, may find it relatively easy to achieve. For others, such manifest attention to the body may make little sense at all and have no currency as 'ability' (Salter, 2003; Zaman, 1997). This may be the case, for example, in the homes of Muslim children for whom a body-centred focus may run counter to religious beliefs and may neither be a priority nor a proper concern. Given that individuals are bound to each of these social fields (the school and the family) by a strong, affective grip, introducing new possibilities through education and asking individuals 'to change' will be equally emotionally charged.

Making a difference?

How does this bear on our discussion of education and 'ability' in PE? The emphasis given to sport, health and social goals has been at the expense of talk about the nature of PE. Along with its feeder disciplines' tendencies to endorse a rather limited conception of 'ability', this has displaced meaningful discussion of whether and how PE can make an impact on the 'cognitive embodied differences', 'the abilities' that children bring to school. In remaining relatively silent on these matters PE inevitably remains a conservative force, building on and reproducing rather than challenging and changing the 'ability' deficits and (where appropriate) the differences that children develop outside school. Class, like gender and 'race', is not enacted straightforwardly in schools and classrooms. Middle-class parents no longer claim resources, reward and privilege on the grounds of traditional differences but because of what they have achieved by virtue of their 'ability'. They invest heavily and strategically to ensure that the 'ability' and distinction of their offspring is maintained (Ball, 2003). Men no longer claim superiority over women, for example, in sport because of physical differences, but because they have 'abilities' that women do not. The 'middle classes' and men invest heavily in the cultivation of the physical capital of their offspring from a very early age. And my point here is that 'embodying' means not only inculcating 'the right' attitudes, values, motivations, predispositions, representations but also the right physical capital in terms of skills, techniques and understandings. In the absence of discussion of education and 'ability' we have little idea of how the latter is to be achieved, or how it is variously configured through the practices of the family and the school.

Sociological researchers in PE have been very good at documenting the way in which 'the body' has been inscribed with social value and meaning. As a result, quite properly, pedagogues have set about challenging and changing the attitudes and values that are nurtured discursively across different fields. But a concern to address and alter the discursive elements of habitus and to change people's attitudes towards each other in relation to physical culture may have been at the expense of giving equal attention to the analysis of the physical resources (capital) individuals then require to cross discursive boundaries once reconfigured and changed. In short, we may have become so concerned to make children feel healthy, happy and good about their own and others' bodies that we have overlooked that schools are also there to 'make a difference' by eroding the embodied physical differences that are the product of the class and cultures of the family and the home.

We know that middle-class children have benefited academically much more than working-class counterparts from the expansion of school and university over the past 20 years. In the UK for example, the chance of a boy of high ability from a high-income family becoming a graduate was 76 percent among those born in 1970, up 17 percentage points on 1958. By contrast, 43 percent of high-ability boys born into working-class backgrounds in 1970 gained a degree, an increase of just eight points. The prospects of bright middle-class girls born in 1970 were also much better than those of girls born in 1958, with the proportion who graduated rising 17 points to 77 percent. Over the same period, the proportion of poorer girls who became graduates declined by nine points from 38 to 29 percent (*TES*, 2003: 1). Can we make anything like the same analysis of progress and decline in PE in terms of altering not just the distribution of cultural but physical capital through its processes? We cannot talk authoritatively of having made progress in developing pupils' physical abilities in PE over their 12 years or so of schooling because we have not been overly concerned to identify, nurture and measure such 'ability', let alone make a difference by eroding the disparity between the haves and have-nots. But if we fall back on 'levels of participation' as proxy for discussion of the capacity of PE to develop 'ability', we can contest difference and ensure a more even distribution of physical capital, accepting that some measure of 'progress' is reflected in levels of participation in sport and physical activity in and outside school. In this respect, there is still compelling evidence for the salience of social class in structuring, if not determining, a person's choice, preferences and opportunities in sport in the UK and elsewhere (Collins, 2003; De Knop and Elling, 2001; Kew, 1997; Nagel and Nagel, 2001; Van Der Meulen et al., 2001). As suggested above, these are inequalities compounded by other social characteristics, such as race, ethnicity, dis/ability, age, geography and sexuality that define people's lives. The point here, however, is that class does not just determine choice and preference in sport. It also determines a person's physical capacity, 'their ability' to realize those choices and preferences, let alone extend them.

Conclusion

If we accept the notion of habitus as a set of learned cognitive embodied dispositions then we have, as Nash (2003) maintains, to at least consider 'that durable embodied cognitive schemes, acquired by children in classed and "cultured" (gender and ethnicity) environments, are at least an important, if not the principal cause of observed variation in educational performance', including that expressed in PE. In effect, the 'physical capital' that children acquire outside schools is fundamentally involved in the reproduction of the differences that provide the basis for inequality in education, leisure and health. We have to consider that the primary effects of socialization, what goes on in the family (see Kay, 2000) and the early years of schooling, may be as, if not 'more important than the secondary effects that many sociologists and policy makers have taken as their proper area of concern' (Nash, 2003: 1).

> The framework assumes 'that the economic division of labour generates social classes; that families are located in the class structure; that families in consequence have differential access to resources (financial, educational, and social); that families are engaged in long term actions with the strategic purpose (broadly known to them) of enabling their offspring to maintain their economic, cultural and social position; that schools are involved in this process of 'reproduction' by affording recognition to the skills acquired through a literacy focussed socialisation.

Among other things, this means that we have to be as concerned in policy and pedagogy in PE to address the embodied *physical resources* children acquire in the family and bring to school as we are with their symbolic/discursive cultural resources. Bernstein proposed that 'the schools' curriculum, if it is to be effectively acquired, always requires two sites of acquisition, the school and the home. Curricula cannot be acquired wholly by time spent at school' (Bernstein, 1990: 77). Addressing racism, sexism, motor elitism, or a child's health and social well-being, is not enough. We have to be equally concerned to recognize the differences and deficits in physical capital, constructed outside schools, and address them through culturally relevant pedagogies and curriculum (see Ennis, 1999). Furthermore, if professional understandings of physical 'ability' have become a synonym for an essentialist view of 'physical intelligence', then we need to at least consider whether this discourse supports school practices that generate observed distributions of attainment in PE, or merely 'fails to eliminate variance due to the operations of the cognitive embodied habitus' (Nash, 2003: 6). I share Nash's view that to write and think of embodied cognitive habitus is not 'to encode IQ theory in a radical discourse', an unfriendly act indeed. It is to draw attention, 'in the legitimate tradition of Bernstein, and Vygotsky (1994) to the relationships between classed environments and schemes of language, thought and modes of specialised cognition' (Nash, 2003: 16). It is also to suggest 'that contexts in which embodied cognitive habitus is developed are central to the construction of sound theories of inequality and difference and that the reflex dismissal of all accounts as "deficit theory" is an error' (Nash, 2003: 16). This is not a way of saying that PE should be judged only on its capacity to induct all pupils 'equally' into conventional forms of knowledge, skill and discipline in PE. Parents have a right to know whether their children have been given not just 'equal opportunity' to physical culture in all its varied forms but also the physical capital thereafter to engage with it. Above all else it is to suggest that we redirect attention away from the interests of sport and health towards discussion of what in policy and pedagogical terms needs to be done in PE if an education that enhances children's 'ability' and desire is to be achieved (Light, 2003).

We should ask not only how 'ability' is configured within the practices that define PE but how thinking about 'ability' as teachers and teacher educators is influenced by the knowledge/s that define our fields, how it is encoded by the interests of sport, health and science and how physical capital is reflected, reproduced and perhaps reconfigured and challenged in schools. We should also investigate how physical capital is distributed and allocated in the family, the school and across other fields. What 'abilities' are recognized, valued, nurtured and accepted, while others are rejected by whom, where and why in schools? Can and does PE make a difference to the form, content and distribution of physical capital? Above all else, we need agendas and discussions of physical 'ability', educe, and educability in PE which go beyond those given the profession by the interests of capital, health and sport.[3]

None of this attributes ontological priority to any given 'body', or privileges a particular form of movement, or defines in advance what is to constitute 'ability', 'educability' or 'physical intelligence' in PE. It is intended only to open up the range of thinking on these matters and to at least consider that there are forms of education, 'ability' and educability beyond those that currently prevail.

> I had a dream in which I was a strange dealer: a dealer in looks or appearances. I collected and distributed them. In the dream I had just discovered a secret! I discovered it on my own, without any help or advice.
>
> The secret was to get inside whatever I was looking at – a bucket of water, a cow, a city (like Toledo) seen from above, an oak tree, *(a child)* and once inside, to arrange its appearances for the better. *Better* did not mean making the thing seem more beautiful or more harmonious; nor did it mean making it more typical, so that the oak tree might represent all oak trees; it simply meant making it more itself so that the cow or the city or the bucket of water *(or the child)* became more evidently unique! The doing of this gave me great pleasure and I had the impression that the small changes I made from inside gave pleasure to others.
>
> The secret of how to get inside the object so as to rearrange how it looked was as simple as opening the door of a wardrobe. Perhaps it was merely a question of being there when the door swung open on its own. Yet when I woke up, I couldn't remember how it was done and I no longer knew how to get inside things.
>
> (Berger, 2001: 13–14; my italics)

We would be hard pressed indeed to find a better definition of 'educe' than this, or one further removed from the interests of capital, sport and health. We can only speculate on how we achieve this. Perhaps the real issue is whether we any longer have the opportunity or the desire, given the current political culture, even to debate such things.

Acknowledgements

I am indebted to Professor Brian Davies, Cardiff University and my colleagues David Kirk, Dawn Penney and Kathy Armour for their invaluable advice and support in preparing this paper. The views expressed and their limitations are entirely mine. I am also extremely grateful to the two referees who provided invaluable criticism and helpful advice on the ways in which this paper could be further developed and improved. I have been able to address some but unfortunately not all their concerns in this paper, which remains rather discursive and wide-ranging in its content.

Notes

1   I use the term physical culture to refer to the variety of play, sport, adventure, dance and other leisure physical activities that help define the social fabric of local and national communities.

2   A field is a distinct social space consisting of interrelated and vertically differentiated positions, a 'network, or configuration of objective relations between positions' (Bourdieu and Wacquant 1992: 97, quoted in Crossley, 2001: 100). 'These positions may be occupied by either agents or institutions but what "positions" them, as such, is their concentration or possession of specific "species" of capital and power. They are positions in a specific distribution of capital and power' (Crossley, 2001: 100), signalling, it seems to me, the efficacy, in the last instance, of social class.

3   I am conscious of rather skirting the issue of 'physical ability', what it is and how it is configured as a dynamic of biology and culture. These are matters aired but barely developed in this text and will form the bases for further discussion and development. Shilling (1993) provides an excellent way of accessing these issues.

References

Arnold, P.J. (1979) *Meaning and Movement, Sport and Physical Education*. London: Heinemann.

Ball, S.J. (2003) *The More Things Change: Educational Research, Social Class and 'Interlocking Inequalities'*. Stephenage: Pear Tree Press.

BBC News (2003) 'Sir Alex Demands More School Sport', http://bbc.co.uk/1/hi/education/3033255.stm

Berger, J. (2001) *The Shape of a Pocket*. London: Bloomsbury.

Bernstein, B. (1971) 'Education Cannot Compensate for Society', in B.R. Cosin, I.R. Dale, G.M. Esland and D.F. Swift (eds) *School and Society*, pp. 61–7. Milton Keynes: Open University.

Bernstein, B. (1990) *The Structuring of Pedagogic Discourse*. London: Routledge.

Best, D. (1978) *Philosophy and Human Movement*. London: Unwin.

Bourdieu, P. (1992) *The Logic of Practice*. Cambridge: Polity.

Bourdieu, P. and Wacquant, L. (1992) *An Invitation to Reflexive Sociology*. Cambridge: Polity.

Collins, M.F. (2003) 'Social Exclusion from Sport and Leisure', in B. Houlihan (ed.) *Sport and Society*, pp. 67–89. London: Sage.

Collins, M. and Kay, T. (2003) *Sport and Social Exclusion*. London: Routledge.

Collingwood, T.R. (1997) 'Providing Physical Fitness Programs to At-Risk Youth', *Quest* 49(1): 67–84.

Crossley, N. (2001) *The Social Body*. London: Sage.

De Knop, P. and Elling, A. (2001) *Values and Norms in Sport*. Aachen: Meyer & Meyer Sport.

Demaine, J. (2001) *Sociology of Education Today*. London: Palgrave.

Department for Culture, Media and Sport (1999) *Policy Action Team 10: Report on Social Exclusion*. London: Dept for Culture, Media and Sport, London SW1Y 5DH

Dweck, C.S. and Leggett, E. (1988) 'A Social-Cognitive Approach to Motivation and Personality', *Psychological Review* 95: 256–73.

Ennis, C.D. (1999) 'Creating a Culturally Relevant Curriculum for Disengaged Girls', *Sport, Education and Society* 4(1): 31–49.

Evans, J. and Davies, B. (2004) 'The Embodiment of Consciousness: Bernstein, Health and Schooling', in J. Evans, B. Davies and J. Wright (eds) *Body Knowledge and Control*, pp. 129–148. London: Routledge.

Evans, J., Davies, B. and Wright, J. (2004) *Body Knowledge and Control. Studies in the Sociology of Physical Education and Health*. London: Routledge.

Gillborn, D. and Youdell, D. (2001) 'The New Iqism: Intelligence, "Ability" and the Rationing of Education', in J. Demaine (ed.) *Sociology of Education Today*, pp. 65–97. London: Palgrave.

Jefferies, S. (2003) 'Teaching Cuts in Physical Education NOT Inevitable?' Jefferies@cwu.EDU

Kay, T. (2000) 'Sporting Excellence: A Family Affair', *European Journal of Physical Education* 6(2): 151–71.

Kew, F. (1997) *Sport: Social Problems and Issues*. Oxford: Butterworth, Heinemann.

Light, K. (2003) 'The Joy of Learning: Emotion and Learning in Games through TGFU', *Journal of Physical Education New Zealand* 36(7): 93–109.

Lynch, K. and Lodge, A. (2002) *Equality and Power in Schools*. London: Routledge/Falmer.

Nagel, M. and Nagel, S. (2001) 'Social Background and Top Performance Sport', paper presented to ECSS Congress, 24–8 July, Cologne.

Nash, R. (2003) 'Inequality/Difference in New Zealand Education: Social Reproduction and the Cognitive Habitus', paper presented at the International Sociology of Education Conference, London, 2 Jan.

Penney, D. and Houlihan, B. (2003) *Specialist Colleges National Monitoring and Evaluation Research Project: First National Survey Report*. Loughborough: Institute of Youth Sport, School of Sport and Exercise Sciences, Loughborough University.

Polanyi, M. (1958) *Personal Knowledge: Towards a Post-Critical Philosophy*. London: Routledge & Kegan Paul.

Pronger, B. (2002) *Body Fascism: Salvation in the Technology of Physical Fitness*. Toronto: University of Toronto Press.

Roberts, K. (1996) 'Young People, Schools, Sport and Government Policies', *Sport, Education and Society* 1(1): 23–47.

Salter, G. (2003) 'Maori Culture and Tradition in the Mainstream', *Journal of Physical Education New Zealand* 36(7): 27–42.

Shilling, C. (1993) *The Body and Social Theory*. London: Sage.

Stones, E. (1992) 'Editorial', *Journal of Education for Teaching* 18: 111–13.

Stroot, S.A. (2001) 'Socialisation and Participation in Sport', in A. Laker (ed.) *The Sociology of Sport and Physical Education*, pp. 129–148. London: Routledge/Falmer.

TES (2003) 'Decades of Reform Fail to Close Class Gap' (11 April): 1.

The Times Higher Education Supplement (2003) 'Clarke Lays into Useless History' (9 May): 2–3.

Van Der Meulen, R., Kraylaar, G. and Utlee, W. (2002) 'Lifelong on the Move: An Event Analysis of Attrition in Non-Elite Sport', paper to ECSS Congress, Cologne, 24–8 July.

Vygotsky, L. (1994) *The Vygotsky Reader*, ed. R. Van der Veer and J. Valsiner. Oxford: Blackwell.

Weiner, B. (1995) *Judgements of Responsibility*. New York: Guilford Press.

Whitehead, M. (2001) 'The Concept of Physical Literacy', *European Journal of Physical Education* 6(2): 127–39.

Zaman, H. (1997) 'Islam, Well Being and Physical Activity: Perceptions of Muslim Young Women', in G. Clarke and B. Humberstone (eds) *Researching Women and Sport*, pp. 50–68. London: Macmillan Press.

PART 5

Teachers and teaching

INTRODUCTION

TEACHING HAS PROBABLY been the most visible feature of physical education research. While we maintain that a much greater emphasis needs to be placed on how students learn than has so far been the case, there is little doubt that teacher practices are of great importance in understanding pedagogy. This point is made very clear in **Green's** analysis of the everyday 'philosophies' of teachers. Green is not interested here in the formal theories of philosophers, but rather the implicit, intuitive, often unexamined views about the purposes of physical education. His paper offers an interesting introduction to some influential papers. **Siedentop's** focus is on what he calls 'content knowledge' of physical educators, by which he means the subject content that joins pedagogical expertise as bases of effective teaching. This paper takes in a diverse range of themes, and is worth revisiting, not least for Siedentop's reflections on the repeated tendency for physical education academics to intellectualise the subject, and in doing so downplay the role of physical experience. **Kirk's** paper proposes a critical and potentially radical approach to the professional education of physical education teachers. In discussing the role of an inquiry-orientated approach in helping to articulate the political dimension of schooling, he calls for a teacher education that encourages critical reflection on the act of teaching, itself.

FURTHER READING

Pascual, C. (2006) The initial training of physical education teachers: in search of the lost meaning of professionalism. *Physical Education and Sport Pedagogy*, 11(1), 69–82.

O'Sullivan, M., Siedentop, D. and Locke, L. (1992) Toward collegiality: competing viewpoints among teacher educators. *Quest*, 44, 266–80.

Tinning, R. (2002) Toward a 'modest pedagogy': reflections on the problematics of critical pedagogy. *Quest*, 54, 224–240.

Ken Green

EXPLORING THE EVERYDAY 'PHILOSOPHIES' OF PHYSICAL EDUCATION TEACHERS FROM A SOCIOLOGICAL PERSPECTIVE

Introduction

THIS PAPER PRESENTS the findings from semi-structured interviews with 35 physical education (PE) teachers in secondary schools in the north-west of England. The principal aim of the study was to examine teachers' 'philosophies' of PE from a sociological perspective, in order to identify the existence of philosophical—or, more accurately, ideological—themes therein and to explore the socio-genesis of such 'philosophies'.

Two broad themes have dominated philosophical conceptions of PE since the 1970s: the 'standard' or academic conception of the subject (Reid, 1996a, 1996b) associated with the liberal analytical philosophy of Peters and early Hirst, and one centred on valued cultural (or human) practices (Arnold, 1992; Hirst, 1994a, 1994b) which has, broadly speaking, become associated with the increasingly prominent rhetoric of 'sport education' (Siedentop, 1994).

From the starting point of a figurational sociological perspective on the social 'nature' of knowledge, it was tentatively hypothesized that PE teachers' 'philosophies' would, firstly, bear the hallmark of particular ideologies rather than philosophies, in the abstract academic sense of the term; and, secondly, that the ideological nature of teachers' everyday 'philosophies' would point the way to a more adequate explanation of the socio-genesis of teachers' particular orientations.

Before I say a little more about philosophy and ideology *per se*, I want to add a small caveat to the effect that it is important to bear in mind that of necessity this paper is a synopsis; that is to say, it is inevitably a summary of extensive interviews and, as such, is bound to leave some interesting dimensions of the subject-matter relatively unscrutinized.

Philosophy, ideology and the sociology of knowledge from a figurational perspective

Elias (1978) and Wilterdink (1977) observed 'two main traditions in the study of human knowledge'. On the one hand, there is a *philosophical* tradition, which Elias (1978) referred to as a classical theory of knowledge that centres conceptually upon the notion of 'a solitary individual' who 'thinks, perceives, and performs' in isolation in pursuit of 'definite and certain knowledge' (Elias, 1978, p. 37). On the other hand, there is a *sociological* tradition, wherein 'all knowledge is regarded as culture-bound, socially determined, and therefore *ideological*' (Wilterdink, 1977, p. 110; emphasis added). For Elias, the apparent polarization of views illustrated by the phrases 'philosophical absolutism' and 'sociological relativism' can be seen to represent a false dichotomy, 'in which knowledge can only be true or arbitrary' (Wilterdink, 1977, p. 111).

From the perspective of figurational sociology, it is more accurate as well as more productive to view knowledge as lying along a continuum of greater or lesser adequacy. This is because, for figurational sociologists, one cannot escape the fact that knowledge— or, rather, what people believe to be true—is inherently social and needs to be understood as such. This is a crucial point, for what follows from this is that much philosophical debate remains inadequate whilst it perpetuates the misguided notion that establishing the nature and purposes of social phenomena, such as PE, must begin with an abstract conceptual debate. From a sociological, and specifically figurational perspective, then, it seems more satisfactory to characterize knowledge as a 'structured flux'; that is to say, as a process that tends to be more or less congruent with reality to the extent that people manage to attain the appropriate blend between involvement and detachment corresponding to the topic under investigation. With this characterization of knowledge in mind, it is worth saying a little more about the terms at the centre of this paper: philosophy, ideology and discourse.

The term 'philosophy' has a lexicographic sense which broadly centres upon the rational principles underlying a putative knowledge base, and it will be the academic sense of philosophy that is utilized when referring to educational *philosophy*. When describing the views of PE teachers, however, the term 'philosophy' is placed in parentheses to indicate that this represents a sense which shares more in common with a taken-for-granted, everyday usage as one's view of 'how things should be'; as might be illustrated at a conversational level by a phrase such as 'my philosophy of PE is . . .'. This, as the philosopher Anthony Flew (1984, p. vii) indicates, represents use of the term 'philosophy' 'in a perfectly reputable and *useful* sense' (emphasis added) as:

> . . . a matter of standing back a little from the ephemeral urgencies to take an aphoristic overview that usually embraces both value-commitments and beliefs about the general nature of things.

These differing uses of the term—both with and without parentheses—reflects the concern of the study, at least in part, with the relationship between the philosophies which have been articulated by academic philosophers seeking to define what they consider to be the 'essential' characteristics or nature of PE and, furthermore, ideas about PE held by those at the sharp end, so to speak—the PE teachers themselves. In strictly sociological terms, one might want to term these ideas, 'world-views' or 'habituses'.[1] However, for several reasons, I have preferred to use the term 'philosophies'.[2]

Thus, whilst reference has been, and will be, made in passing to genuine philosophical attempts to make sense of the nature and purposes of PE, the paper will, for the most part, utilize the term 'philosophy' in its more 'everyday' sense to describe the concise and pithy but, nevertheless, frequently intuitive overviews of the nature and purposes of PE held by teachers. These 'philosophies', it will be suggested, are in reality more *ideological* than philosophical.

Through the twentieth century, sociological uses of the term *ideology* have developed away from what have been termed (Mann, 1983) evaluatively *neutral* conceptions— characteristic of lexicographic definitions such as 'a body or system of *ideas*' (Chambers English Dictionary, 1990)—towards definitions that incorporate pejorative and thus evaluatively *negative* connotations, 'implying false or mistaken notions' (Mann, 1983, p. 164). Hence, standard sociological usages of the term have tended to qualify the concept of ideology to incorporate notions of 'falsehood and distortion generated by more or less unconscious motivations' (Flew, 1984, p. 162).

Whilst in the late twentieth century ideologies *per se* may be said to 'have absorbed a good deal of *factual* . . . knowledge' (Elias in Mennell & Goudsblom, 1998, p. 32; emphasis added) they are, nonetheless, best viewed as located along a continuum between involvement and detachment (Mennell & Goudsblom, 1998). From this perspective, Dunning (1992, p. 178) observes that whilst ideologies 'differ in their degrees of reality-congruence . . . they always . . . contain a mythical component', making them what Elias would have termed 'an amalgam of realistic observations and collective fantasies' (Elias in Mennell & Goudsblom, 1998, p. 227).

The crucial distinction between the concept of ideology and a related concept, that of discourse, is also worthy of mention. According to Kirk (1992, p. 23), discourse 'refers to the ways in which people communicate their understanding of their own and others' activities, and of events in the world around them'. In short, discourses in PE are the multiplicity of ways in which those involved with the subject communicate something of what—for their part—PE *means* or *is about*: its nature and its purposes. Discourses are aspects of the processes by which ideologies are not only *articulated* but also *developed*. Sociologically speaking, however, it is important to appreciate that discourse not only reflects thinking, *it is part of thinking itself*. Although, as indicated earlier, several writers view discourse as reflecting *ideology* and as the embodiment of ideological work (Kirk, 1992; Johns *et al.*, 1994), for. figurationalists it is more precise to view discourse as the work of 'doing' ideology. On this view, discourse is best conceptualized as an *aspect* of the ideologies found among particular groups rather than in the reified terms suggested by the claim that discourse embodies ideology. Conceptualizing discourse in this way overcomes any tendency to view discourse and ideology as separate entities.

The task for figurational sociologists is, then, to develop a sociological epistemology and, in so doing, to identify the existence of more or less involved or detached thinking. Thus, in order to make sense of PE teachers' 'philosophies' it becomes necessary to identify and make overt the ideological underpinnings of PE teachers' 'philosophies', prior to making sense of the ways in which teachers' 'knowledge' may be seen as an aspect of the figurations of which they are a part.

Methodology

The study was based upon semi-structured interviews conducted with 35 PE teachers from 17 schools in the north-west of England in late June/early July of the summer 1998 term. The sampling frame for the study was all male and female PE teachers at 25 secondary schools in the State education system in two unitary authorities (formerly one County Council). A purposive sampling method—a non-probability method and one commonly employed in qualitative research (Bowling, 1997)—was utilized. This form of sample selection is used to identify particular people or groups of people—in this case PE teachers—who are broadly known to the researcher and 'with a specific purpose in mind'. That purpose 'reflects the particular qualities of the people . . . chosen and their relevance to the topic of the investigation' (Denscombe, 1998, p. 15). In this vein, the various schools, and PE departments therein, were chosen to represent the city, new town and rural locations typical of the region. In that respect the area was not atypical of non-metropolitan areas in the UK with a variety of urban, suburban and rural communities as well as a broad economic base, albeit with a relatively small ethnic minority population. This purposive sampling frame resulted in a sample that was, in one sense, a convenience sample, in so far as it was constituted of PE teachers at those schools—located variously in a small city, two towns and several villages—that were 'first to hand', as Denscombe (1998, p. 16) puts it. Consequently, the resultant sample consisted of those teachers who responded to the first round of interview requests.

In many ways this configuration of purposive and convenience sampling threw up what—in the absence of available official data—might be plausibly regarded as a suitable cross-section of PE. The resultant sample consisted of 15 male and 20 female teachers from 17 schools of which 15 (eight male/seven female) were heads of department (HoD) and 20 (seven male/13 female) were main-grade teachers of PE. Thirteen of the teachers (of whom three were HoDs) were 30 years of age or younger. Six (two HoDs) were between 31 and 40. Fifteen were between 41 and 50 years (nine HoDs) and one (HoD) was over 50.

The interviews focused upon PE teachers' 'philosophies'; that is to say, their aphoristic or everyday thoughts on the nature and purposes of PE. The broad areas of enquiry which provided the structure for the interviews were: teachers' views regarding what PE should be about; teachers' perceptions of various aspects of PE [e.g. National Curriculum Physical Education (NCPE) and extra-curricular PE]; the relationship between teachers' 'philosophies' and their professed practice; teachers' perceptions of contextual constraints; and teachers' biographies.

Content analysis and categories of meaning

The taped interviews were fully transcribed and subjected to content analysis. Qualitative approaches, such as the one employed in this study, typically involve an attempt to identify the central features of, and patterns within, interviewees' responses via a categorization of content. Texts can be interpreted on a number of levels but an over-riding concern is the attempt to comprehend the perspective of the interviewee. This necessitates an analysis not only of the content of interviews—in terms of the frequency of words, phrases or themes (Keats, 2000, p. 80)—but also an analysis of discourse in the form of an interpretation of such themes. Thus, being 'concerned with the way people understand things' (Denscombe, 1998, p. 207), a qualitative analysis of data generated by semi-structured interviews emphasizes the 'search for meaning' (Arksey & Knight, 1999, p. 150) as well as the frequency of particular words or phrases.

In this vein, the interview data from the study were arranged into what might be termed 'common clusters' or 'categories of meaning' based upon the core themes of the interviews—such as teachers' 'philosophies', their biographies, their views on NCPE and so on. These categories were, in turn, amended to incorporate areas of concern that emerged during the interviews, such as 'enjoyment' and examinations in PE. In this manner, 'the full set of ideas' (Arksey & Knight, 1999, p. 165) to be found in the data were broken down (or collapsed) into units for analysis (Denscombe, 1998; Arksey & Knight, 1999) via the continual and ongoing revisiting of interview transcriptions and field notes in order to refine the categories of meaning subsequently employed as a basis for explaining the data. Grouping teachers' comments together in the above manner—by integrating particular themes that appeared during the research with the aforementioned ideological themes—enabled extraction of the essential features of PE teachers' 'philosophies' from what Evans & Davies (1986, p. 13) have observed might otherwise be an 'overwhelming stream of talk or/and behaviour'. As such, the analysis of content—in the form of categories of meaning—was 'grounded'; that is to say, 'rooted *empirically* in the data and *conceptually* in the research issues' (Arksey & Knight, 1999, p. 164; emphases added).

Findings: the everyday 'philosophies' of PE teachers

This section reports on the data produced by the semi-structured interviews and offers a synopsis of the broad themes identifiable from the teachers' responses. Much of the data that emerged from the 'clusters' or 'categories of meaning' reflected a number of ideological themes identified elsewhere (Kirk, 1992; Green, 1998); in particular, ideologies of sport, health, education for leisure and academic value. Several additional, often related, themes were identifiable and these are incorporated where deemed appropriate. Before dealing with each of the main ideological themes in turn, it is worth referring to one particularly prominent leitmotif of PE teachers' 'philosophies', namely the emphasis placed on 'enjoyment'.

Enjoyment

In almost all responses to the question 'What do you think PE should be about?' the word 'enjoyment' featured prominently and, for the most part, explicitly. Enjoyment was a primary consideration for the teachers, whether male or female, young or old, HoD or main-grade. It tended to be the first thing they mentioned and was something they returned to again and again. Typically, enjoyment formed an initial and immediate response upon which teachers then elaborated. For some teachers, enjoyment was seen as being an end in itself:

> . . . some sort of success and enjoyment. Success might just mean enjoyment
> . . . to me that's as good as being an Olympic champion.

Frequently, however, enjoyment was linked with ideas that resembled justifications based upon a cathartic role for PE. In this sense, PE seemed to be seen not so much as part of the academic content of education, but as a *release from* the academic aspects of school:

> . . . one of the main priorities is that they enjoy themselves . . . it's my job to get them active, release a bit of tension, get some energy out of their systems so they are ready for the rest of the school day.

Thus, whilst for some teachers enjoyment was spoken of as an end in itself, more typically, enjoyment was seen either as a *precondition* and/or a *vehicle* for other outcomes; that is to say, enjoyment was seen as necessary as well as desirable. Some teachers felt the need to veer towards enjoyment in the lesson as a vehicle for *greater control* over the pupils:

> . . . control . . . if somebody is not happy with doing something . . . they're not likely to turn round and say, 'Well, it's good this!' . . . the control will be much better.

Not only was enjoyment a vehicle for achieving practical objectives, for many teachers enjoyment was an *aid to the process of learning* the requisite physical and sporting skills and personal habits that they also took to be a feature of PE:

> If you can get them really involved and enjoying it then they will get more out of it, and they'll take more 'on board' as well.

One HoD illustrated the way in which *enjoyment*, class *control* and *learning* were frequently associated with each other in teachers' minds:

> . . . it's enjoyment . . . Once you have got the fun side and you have got them enjoying the lessons then you can start to educate them in all the other aspects.

As far as teachers in this study were concerned, enjoyment was at the heart of their 'philosophies'. Enjoyment was seen as the key to *control*, to *learning* and, above all, to *participation*.

This emphasis upon enjoyment is worthy of note for several reasons. Firstly, enjoyment is not commonly expressed as a goal of education. In this regard, one might speculate what the Office for Standards in Education (OFSTED) or, for that matter, Her Majesty's Chief Inspector of Schools would have to say about such claims. Secondly, the emphasis on enjoyment suggested that even teachers of PE perceived their subject as somehow 'less serious' than other subjects. The implicit idea appeared to be that PE was a less serious subject and not really 'educational' in the academic sense. Indeed, one could not imagine teachers of other subjects placing quite the same emphasis upon enjoyment. On the contrary, one would expect to find little sympathy amongst educationalists for enjoyment as an educational goal *per se*. Established characterizations of teaching and learning in the academic literature (e.g. Oakeshott, 1972; O'Hear, 1981) incorporate many things but nowhere is mention made of 'fun'—explicitly or implicitly—as a defining feature of either. References to fun were, significantly, also absent from the brief justifications teachers offered for other subjects on the school curriculum. Indeed, teachers appeared to hold quite particular and distinctive views of their own subject.

Sport

The vast majority of teachers in the study identified enjoyment as a central plank of their 'philosophies'. For many it was simply taken-for-granted, implicitly or explicitly, that the *enjoyment* they initially referred to would be of *sport*:

> . . . above all . . . for them (the pupils) to enjoy PE through a medium of participation in sports.

> . . . they (the pupils) have to understand that . . . sport is to be enjoyed . . . sport is enjoyable and something that is good.

Sport tended, then, to be a particularly prominent ideological theme in PE teachers' 'philosophies'. Even where participation was the primary concern of teachers, this tended to be participation in (competitive) *sport* and, frequently, team-games. Indeed, the terms 'physical activity' and 'sport' were regularly used interchangeably and seemingly treated as if synonymous:

> PE should be about getting children involved in physical activity and teaching them about different physical activities . . . (because) *that's what sport's all about isn't it?* (emphasis added)

Various PE teachers (especially male) appeared to assume that competition was an important, if not the *essential*, element of sport and, thus, PE. The importance of achieving competitive sporting success frequently appeared to dominate these teachers' 'philosophies':

> I think it's brilliant having competitive sport in school. It's a real focus and it's a real drive for the children.

Accordingly, an emphasis on performance and skill-acquisition in PE lessons was commonplace; amongst male PE teachers (of all ages and occupational levels) in particular. In this regard, an established male teacher offered the view: 'that's what we need to get back to . . . because the standard in those major team games is slipping'. When I suggested to him that some of the teachers he was criticizing (for allegedly moving away from 'traditional' PE) would also claim that they were trying to encourage 'sport for all' but through a 'recreational' or 'activity choice' approach, he replied: '(S)o, what is the success rate of that attitude of getting pupils to actually *perform* at any *level* whatsoever?' (emphasis added).

In this manner many teachers in the study perceived the acquisition of sporting skills as a central function of PE; particularly in the initial stage of secondary education (at Key Stage 3) ('from Year 7 to Years 8 and 9 . . . they are increasing their repertoire of skills'). Indeed, for some teachers, skill-acquisition remained the role of PE throughout the secondary school life of pupils. Some made no attempt to hide their unequivocal commitment to the acquisition of sports skills in the face of recent developments (such as NCPE):

> Call me old school if you like but it's about *physical* education; it's about the *physical* and . . . (as) the old school say, 'put the physical back into physical education' . . . When I hear 'plan/perform/evaluate', I'd go along with that to a degree, I mean they can plan things like in . . . gymnastics, but I don't think they can plan particularly well the movements for a (rugby) line-out . . . (performance) that's where I'm coming from. (emphasis in the original)

It was interesting to reflect that this male teacher articulated a view implicit in a number of (particularly male) teachers' comments. Yet, at no time did a teacher intimate the contrasting view that might be summarized as 'putting the *education* back into physical education'. The clear impression one formed was that for many PE teachers (and, again, particularly the male teachers) the emphasis in PE *is* and *should remain* on the *physical* rather than the *educational*.

Especially noteworthy was the manner in which such views involved very *particular* and *subjective*, that is to say preferred, conceptions of what PE should be about. In this case, and once again, particularly with males, it was evidently sport and, within sport, team games especially. Needless to say, many (particularly, but by no means exclusively, male PE teachers) were 'happy' with the renewed emphasis upon games in both the revised NCPE of 1995 and the Government's policy statement, *Sport: Raising the Game* (DNH, 1995). Whilst emphasis upon winning and success appeared to conflict with other aspects of teachers' 'philosophies', it did seem to reflect: (a) their own intuitive feelings and values; (b) their views on the traditions of PE; (c) their perceptions of the school's expectations of PE.

Two things became apparent: firstly, that teachers' emphasis upon competitive sport did not sit at all easily alongside their ostensible commitment to 'enjoyment'—not least because, as some teachers recognized, many pupils (perhaps especially girls but also less able as well as disaffected pupils) may be put off by such an emphasis upon achievement and competition. Secondly, it also indicated that they were not given to abstract philosophizing in which emphasis is placed on developing internally consistent and coherent justificatory systems. In other words, and as I will indicate later in this paper, PE teachers' views on the nature and purposes of their subject frequently appeared an amalgam of what sociologists refer to as their particular habituses in figuration with the dominant ideologies within PE, alongside the constraints of day-to-day practice. Teachers' views appeared to reflect an intuitive commitment to a notion of PE as *essentially* sport that had, nonetheless, been more or less penetrated by an amalgam of 'sport for all', education for leisure and health ideological themes. They represented teachers' intuitive responses to their 'gut' feelings interwoven with pragmatic responses to practical circumstances.

It is noteworthy, in this regard, that whilst a number of teachers seemed equivocal about the inclusion of sports coaches in PE they appeared, on the whole, remarkably receptive to their involvement. This is contrary to what one might expect, given that it implies that there is no prior need for a specialist qualification in order to be involved in teaching PE and that this, in turn, might be seen as undermining teachers' claims for specialist status—something which has frequently appeared a preoccupation within the PE subject-community in recent years. Here again, teachers did not tend to respond by outlining a *philosophical* justification, in this case, for the involvement of coaches in the domain of teachers. Indeed, the justification was *no* justification as such. Rather, it was merely an outline of the *practical* benefits to the teacher of the involvement of coaches; that is to say, involving coaches in PE let some teachers 'off the hook'—in terms of saving them work and/or providing 'cover' for areas of inexpertise as well as helping with class motivation and control and, notably, improving the levels of sports performance. Justifications for the inclusion of coaches were similar to justifications for enjoyment as an aim, inasmuch as the primary concerns of teachers appeared to be *pragmatic*.

In relation to the prominence of a sporting ideology within PE teachers' 'philosophies' it was interesting to explore their views regarding extra-curricular PE. It was noticeable that the broad consensus among PE teachers was that extra-curricular PE represented an '*extension* of curricular PE' (emphasis added). Frequently, teachers described extra-curricular PE as an extension of the skills and performance emphasis associated with the sporting ideology:

> Well, it's extensions. (In) curricular PE we start off with the basics (skills) and develop it as we go through.

Despite this consensus, the 'philosophies' of PE teachers with regard to extra-curricular work were quite complex, not to say confused. Typically, their views reflected multiple foci (e.g. sport, health-related exercise and recreation) for extra-curricular work. In this respect, it was noteworthy that teachers claimed a commitment to both 'sport for all' *and* performance sport:

> There are *practices* every break-time, every lunch-time and virtually every night and at weekends. But it's not just for the teams, it's *open*—the whole school can take part. (emphases added)

And yet, despite such professed 'philosophical' commitments to participation as well as performance, the ostensible practice of extra-curricular PE continued to revolve to a greater extent around sport, particularly team sports, and to a lesser extent around team practices or even what will subsequently be referred to as 'sport for all'. It became clear that, notwithstanding professed commitment to involving as many pupils as possible in extra-curricular activity, there was a tension here that had, unsurprisingly, not been thought through, for nothing constrained teachers to reconcile the apparently irreconcilable. Extra-curricular PE provided teachers with a degree of freedom to choose and they chose sport. This predisposition was, in turn, exacerbated by constraints in the form of the expectations and requirements of various groups, prominent amongst which were headteachers and parents. It seems, then, indisputable that—as several commentators (Mason, 1995; Penney & Harris, 1997; Sports Council for Wales (SCW), 1995) have noted—extra-curricular PE is biased towards sport and, within sport, towards team-games. This appears so, not least because many PE teachers like it that way and are more constrained towards such practice than they are constrained away from it.

Nonetheless, closely associated with concern for sports performance in teachers' 'philosophies' of PE as a whole was concern with the value of participation in sport 'for its own sake' as well as the additional benefits participation was alleged to bring. In this regard, a sporting ideology frequently shaded into the related ideologies of education for leisure and 'sport for all'.

Education for leisure

According to Roberts (1996a, 1996b) and Scraton (1992), since the 1970s teachers have been increasingly aware of, and have responded to, wider social trends regarding developments in youth culture. That this has remained the case appeared evident in a number of teachers' comments:

> . . . there's so many other things around now that we have to compete with . . . which are offering . . . adrenaline rushes . . . So, I think we have to try and say, 'Yes, we can achieve a high and an adrenaline from sports, as well as those other things, but on top of that we can offer you extra things and relationships of belonging, of physical well-being'.

Such comments seem to offer support for Roberts' (1996b) claim that one of the reasons that PE has, over the last decade or so, been what he terms 'a success story' in participatory terms, is that PE teachers have been 'in tune' with, and adapted their programmes to take account of, young people's changing leisure lifestyles. Similarly, many teachers' responses suggested that they were also inclined towards encouraging enjoyment and competence in what Roberts & Brodie (1992) have referred to as 'a wide sporting repertoire' on the part of young people:

> . . . so that when they become adults . . . they would have experienced and enjoyed a *cross-section* of sports, so that they are . . . capable (enough) to go on and say, 'Yes, I enjoyed that, I want to keep that going . . . I know where I can go', and they can carry on playing. (emphasis added)

Nevertheless, and once again, it was noticeable that teachers frequently assumed that this continuing participation would be achieved through sport and sports clubs. Indeed, it was also noticeable that some of the older teachers viewed the emergence and development of 'activity choice' as a practical response to the pragmatics of coping with older pupils rather than a 'philosophical', or ideological, response to changes in young people's lifestyles.

'Sport for all'

What might be termed 'sport for all' (after the Sports Council's strategy of recent decades with which it was associated) appeared frequently, often prominently, in the justifications of many PE teachers in this study, both explicitly, as a phrase utilized by teachers to explain their policies, and implicitly, as a theme recognizable in a range of views proffered. There were some unequivocal expressions of commitment to a 'sport for all' 'philosophy':

> I just want to get as many people as involved as possible. I'm not bothered whether they are brilliant teams or whatever, I just want to try and get everybody to like PE.

Interestingly, 'sport for all' was a 'philosophy' particularly common among those teaching in disadvantaged[3] areas ('My job is to try to cater for everybody in my school with various sports'). Teachers in such schools frequently introduced or qualified their statements with references to '*this* school', or this '*type* of area' and even '*these* kids'. Several teachers, working in relatively disadvantaged schools, tendered views similar to those of the following HoD:

> . . . the only opportunity *some* kids get for sport is within school . . . As a PE teacher it's got to be 'sport for all'. (emphasis in the original)

'Sport for all' was a particularly prominent 'philosophy' in relation to (usually female) teachers' views of girls:

> . . . while they're in school I want to teach them these skills and hope that it transfers to later on in life . . . we find that some . . . particularly Year 11 girls, if they don't want to do (PE) they will not. They will sit on the side line, even if they have their PE kit there!

It was noticeable, then, that the comments of a number of PE teachers suggested that their views on PE incorporated degrees of 'localism'. In referring to what they perceived as a need to adapt their aims, expectations and practice to various constraints, these teachers demonstrated a tendency towards degrees of localism that one would not expect to find in other (more academic) National Curriculum subjects. Indeed, the National Curriculum does not cater for such qualifications according to the 'character' or location of the school. Nor, it is worth reminding ourselves, do the philosophies articulated by academic philosophers of PE allow for, let alone expect, degrees of localism in their justifications for the subject.

In so far as teachers' 'philosophies' were often linked with 'activity choice' (as OFSTED (1998) refer to what otherwise has become known as 'option' PE), what the teachers *thought* was usually related to what they had come to believe on the basis of *experience*. Their dispositions towards PE appeared to have altered as their networks encompassed pupils and schools in disadvantaged areas and this, in a variety of ways, had come to constrain their practice of PE—particularly in the case of girls and disaffected pupils.

Offering pupils an element of 'activity choice' was seen as having a positive effect, among other things, upon participation rates ('the participation rate was brilliant . . . our participation rate, our enjoyment rate, the success of the kids'), especially with older pupils and girls—for whom it was perceived as a far more pressing matter. Once again, this was particularly the case in schools located in relatively deprived social areas. Despite the fact that the scope for offering choice has been very much limited by the NCPE, it was nevertheless particularly noticeable that many teachers remained committed to it, for a variety of reasons, and managed to squeeze 'choice' in as, in effect, a continuation of what might be called their 'pre-NCPE' practice.

As committed to 'activity choice' as they appeared, many teachers, nevertheless, still viewed it as following on (chronologically and developmentally) from skill-development. They saw the early years of secondary PE (Years 7, 8 and 9: Key Stage 3) as focusing upon teaching 'the basics'; in other words, the acquisition of 'key' sporting (but also physical) skills that would, in their view, allow a more 'recreational', leisure-oriented emphasis in Key Stage 4 (Years 10 and 11):

> . . . in Key Stage 3 we offer a more narrow curriculum in the more traditional type activities . . . developing their skill . . . Then, perhaps in Key Stage 4, we'd give them a wider choice of activities—things like they could take up when they leave school, things like that.

In light of high-profile concerns of the 1980s regarding the dangers of so-called 'progressive' PE, alluded to by Evans (1990), it is worthy of note that much of what passes as 'activity choice' in the PE curriculum could not adequately be construed as 'revolutionary'; that is to say, it does not involve discarding what might be seen as the 'traditional' (sport and team-game oriented) PE curriculum. Moreover, it seems to bear out Roberts' (1996a, 1996b) observation that the 'options' made available to pupils *supplemented* rather than *replaced* 'traditional' PE:

> We do a little bit (of optional choice) but it's more . . . 'traditional'; you either play hockey, netball, football—very traditional sport. And, again, you are teaching them a specific skill.

This was the case even though many of the teachers in this study were acutely aware that the staple PE 'diet'—of sport and particularly team-games—was not popular with many children ('that . . . can be off-putting to some children if they are made to do something they really don't enjoy').

It appears somewhat ironic, then, that OFSTED, in a recent report, claimed that a 'move away from the "recreational activities" and "activity choice" approach is also raising achievement levels in Key Stage 4' (OFSTED, 1998, p. 1). This is a particularly interesting development for it suggests, quite clearly, that whereas PE teachers' goals are often couched in terms of 'enjoyment', the goals of OFSTED remain phrased in terms of 'achievement levels'. OFSTED emphasizes the *educational* objectives of PE and appears to be trying to move PE towards mainstream educational goals and formally defined criteria which they, and others, can measure in a form that will stand up to public scrutiny.

It is a moot point whether OFSTED are correct in claiming that there has been a move away from 'activity choice' among PE teachers in secondary schools. It is equally debatable whether any movement away is born of necessity rather than teacher choice as such. Also questionable is what is meant by 'raising achievement levels'. Having said this, it is the case that, at the very least, the criteria in terms of which OFSTED measure 'achievement levels' are clear and explicit. PE teachers, by contrast, appeared to have no criteria for assessing the effectiveness of their own preferred versions of PE.

At this point, however, a caveat needs to be added, lest one forms the impression that 'activity choice' is one area in which there *is* a consensus among PE teachers. Not all teachers were converts to 'activity choice'. Whilst 'activity choice' appeared to have been embraced by very many of the teachers in this study, there were those who held out for a more traditional curriculum. These were more likely than not to be established teachers at what one might describe as the more traditional and academically successful schools, with fewer ostensible 'problems' and fewer concerns regarding pupils' participation.

Academic value

The belief, put colloquially, that PE reaches the parts that other subjects cannot, in terms of 'building up the character', as one teacher put it, was quite commonplace. For many this was portrayed as an informal, but nevertheless highly significant, aspect of the PE curriculum:

> . . . it's like a *silent curriculum*, the social side of it . . . we do work at it but it's obviously not in the written curriculum. (emphasis added)

Once more, such a view was expressed particularly forcibly by teachers in the relatively disadvantaged schools in the study:

> In (this area) it's even more of a priority, because a lot of the kids are quite antisocial, so you put them in situations where they depend upon each other for their success.

In addition, a sense of achievement was expected to flow from sporting success and this was particularly prominent amongst teachers faced with the perceived constraints of working in disadvantaged areas:

> . . . giving them (pupils) a sense of achievement . . . for the lower (ability) end . . . teamwork and getting on with each other . . . It's a sense of achievement for them if they are good at sport but not so academically.

It was noticeable, however, that many teachers who claimed personal and social educational (PSE)[4] benefits for PE, when asked if they could identify it in their practice indicated they could not do so. Even those who claimed they could tended to describe it as happening indirectly or subconsciously:

> I don't think you're conscious in saying, 'Yes, I must get moral development'. I think what happens is it (just) comes out of what's happened (in the lesson).

It was striking that the rather vague responses to questions regarding the ability of the teachers to recognize examples of PSE in PE in *practice* suggested that external agencies such as OFSTED would be even less convinced of their efficacy. Academics and philosophers of PE (such as Laker, 1996a, 1996b) might continue to claim its existence in theory but it seems that many would have difficulty—as, indeed, teachers themselves did—finding examples from their professed practice.

Nonetheless, it was noticeable that many teachers perceived a need to put some kind of educational 'gloss' on what might otherwise be viewed, at least in educational terms, as tangential justifications for their subject. In this regard, it was particularly interesting to note the place of examinations in PE (GCSE and A level) in teachers' 'philosophies'. For the most part, their comments on examinable PE did not represent an ideological theme as such. Rather, teachers tended to refer to examinations as a *constraint* rather than something to which they had an ideological commitment. Consequently, numerous teachers described the rapid growth and popularity of examinable PE as a pragmatic response to perceived status problems which left them, as they saw it, with 'Hobson's choice' if they were not to jeopardize the status of their subject, their departments and even their own careers ('they're doing GCSE PE . . . and I must at least have the opportunity for my career and personal development').

Thus, most responses to questions regarding examinations began with references to status concerns on the part of PE teachers. At the same time, however, many teachers were keen to claim more altruistic and educational justifications for the development of examinable PE:

> I think all (PE departments) . . . are looking to broaden . . . their curriculum . . . for the sake of their status . . . generally. I say status, but I don't want to give too much emphasis to that because that's not why we're doing it, that's down the list. We're doing it because we know the kids will enjoy it and respond to it and we as a department are keen.

Amongst those who appeared equivocal about examinable PE, and who were quick to identify the pressures constraining them to accept its introduction to their department, were many teachers who, nevertheless, were keen to identify positive aspects of such a development. These positive aspects were said to be 'opportunities': for those pupils 'keen' on PE ('Well . . . it's about choice and pupils are given a choice and we want to offer them that extra choice'); for those 'gifted' at sport ('we have children with a lot of talent and I think it's important that they should be able to manifest . . . (what) they have talent in'); as well as for those less 'academically able', more 'practically-minded' pupils:

> KG: Why do you do examinable PE?
> Teacher: We've just started it this year, GCSE . . . Basically the Head thought it was a good idea. But I think it gives . . . another window for someone who's interested in PE—who did PE to get some success . . . they can't get elsewhere.

It was noticeable, then, that seemingly altruistic claims regarding examinable PE were often bound up with more pragmatic justifications:

> I knew that there (were) pupils here . . . that (would) excel in it and I knew we were going to get (good) exam results . . . (and the grades) are getting better every year . . . and now we've introduced 'A' level. And all the time it's having a positive effect on the PE department and it's giving pupils something they have not had before.

It was easy, however, to form the impression that the supposed benefits for pupils were frequently a secondary concern for teachers; that is to say, the alleged 'educational' benefits provided, in effect, a convenient justificatory ideology for something that had primarily to do with personal and professional status. In effect, PE teachers appeared to have been engaging in what might be termed a 'cost-benefit' analysis of examinable PE at personal and local levels.

Overall, then, to the extent that an academic ideology was discernible (even tangentially) in PE teachers' comments, it typically took the conventional form (see Blake, 1996; Laker, 1996a, 1996b; Munrow, 1972) of faith among teachers in the utility (taken to be inherent in sport) for the development of the moral and aesthetic dimensions of young-sters' characters. Many of the claims for the alleged moral and character development benefits of PE made by teachers bore the hallmarks of the kind of fantasy-laden thinking that, according to Dunning (1992), characterizes ideology. Occasionally explicitly, but more frequently implicitly, teachers indicated their beliefs that mere involvement in PE —and especially sport and team-games—would be sufficient to bring about PSE benefits. It is worth noting, however, that teachers themselves did not make this connection explicitly or otherwise. This is something one might reasonably have expected them to do had they really believed in the efficacy of PE in PSE terms. Rather, they appeared to turn to PSE more as an afterthought, seemingly utilized to bolster their preferred views with a more overtly educational rationale.

It was also noticeable that views regarding the educational worth of PE were not expressed in a similar manner to other ideological justifications. Indeed, the 'educational' justification frequently appeared as an afterthought; an additional vindication just in case *enjoyment* of *sport* was seen as insufficient. It was almost as if PE teachers were saying 'sport is worthwhile for pleasure's sake' but that they implicitly recognized that many people would not regard this as sufficient justification for the subject and they, therefore, felt constrained to add that PE had a variety of additional 'goods'. Such 'goods' included the 'traditional' and pervasive claim for sport as a vehicle for moral and character development. Alongside, and often in association with such assertions, have been added more recently claims for a role for PE in pupils' intellectual development in the form of examinable PE.

Health

For many teachers in the study, enjoyment was also seen as a vehicle for the development of the kind of *active lifestyles* that would promote health by developing adherence to activity in a manner that would be likely to persist beyond school and into later life:

> I like to think they would go away from my lesson and go and do (physical activity) out of school hours. And if they don't enjoy it in school they are not going to want to do it outside of school.

Indeed, many teachers appeared to view health as *the* issue confronting PE teachers currently:

> . . . the health side of it is more and more important . . . the health and participation part (of PE) . . . and getting them to realise why they're doing it and why it's important . . . with regard to what it's actually doing within your body.

For some, health has even come to overshadow 'traditional' PE—with its emphasis on team-games—as the contemporary *raison d'être* for PE:

> . . . we teach netball, hockey . . . bringing in all your motor skills and that's

important, as is the team aspect, but to me the health-related (aspect) is more important.

Thus, with some teachers health promotion was considered either implicitly or explicitly *the* function of PE:

I think it's our *duty* really that children should be as active as possible. (emphasis in the original)

It is quite revealing and informative that, without having mastered the details or, indeed, the precise implications for their practice, PE teachers have a general idea that PE— frequently in the form of *sport*—'does children good'.

For many PE teachers who subscribed, more or less, to a health ideology, sport was still seen as the main vehicle for health promotion:

. . . my fundamental job is to raise levels of fitness and skill expertise in whatever area I'm working in . . . *we're talking about why we need sport*. (emphasis added)

A permeating theme of this study is recognition of the fact that teachers' 'philosophies' are not especially likely to have been formed by professional, let alone academic, writing on the subject. Yet, with regard to health, some teachers did make reference to develop-ments which they perceived as occurring 'as a result of documents coming out' as well as 'research in a lot of PE articles'. More often, however, the emphasis placed upon health was not perceived by the teachers themselves as having developed in response to the 'call to arms' to be found in the academic press and among academics and teacher-trainers themselves. Rather, PE teachers' views were more likely to refer to the effect of 'news-papers; your own belief . . . (there's) so much more in the news'. It was interesting to note, then, that this was more often on the basis of 'lay' understandings of the relationship between health and exercise than health-related justifications espoused in the NCPE or, for that matter, in the theory underpinning HRE *per se*. It appeared that a common-sense, 'paramedical' role for PE had infused many teachers' 'philosophies'.

Traces of a health ideology were more or less apparent in virtually all teachers' comments in the present study. The health ideology has risen to occupy a prominent place on the ideological high-ground of PE teachers' 'philosophies' and, thus, gradually amidst many teachers' habituses. Nonetheless, one is left with the clear impression that whilst PE teachers are broadly aware of the requirements of NCPE in relation to health and HRE, this remains a rather vague awareness, both of the rationale for HRE and of the manner in which it is required to be implemented according to NCPE.

PE teachers' 'philosophies': an amalgam of ideologies

Analysis of the interview data revealed several prominent ideological themes—sport, health, academic value, education for leisure and 'sport for all'. These themes bore little resemblance to the more academic conceptions of PE to be found in PE theory and documentation. In this vein, teachers' commitment to particular notions, such as enjoyment, begged questions regarding the ostensibly educational element of physical education. It was apparent that many PE teachers' 'philosophies' incorporated several ideas or ideologies. Frequently these 'philosophies' emphasized one dimension, such as sport, among an amalgam featuring several additional aspects, such as health, education for leisure or PSE. Many amalgam 'philosophies', and particularly those of male teachers, placed great emphasis upon sport and the development of sporting skills:

> Well, first and foremost . . . I think enjoyment has got to be one of the key issues; acquisition of skills—obviously—and teamwork/co-operation. Obviously fitness is . . . mixed in with all that as well . . . to play sport, to carry out skills, you've got to have a certain amount of fitness.

Many 'philosophies' incorporated sport, health and education for leisure (with sport implicitly taken to be intimately associated with the promotion of health):

> . . . providing children with positive habits throughout their life, positive sporting habits . . . (The) number one aim as a teacher is to teach pupils various sporting skills and then . . . to enjoy it more, enjoy coming to the lessons . . . then probably the third would be to motivate them to do things.

Other amalgam 'philosophies' emphasized PSE in particular. An example was provided by a teacher who described personal development and health education as her two main aims, but who laid particular stress on PSE:

> I think it's an extremely good way for pupils to develop self-confidence in physical ability, in terms of relationship building, in terms of learning to co-operate with others . . . In terms of keeping themselves healthy for the future, I think it is extremely important.

Yet other amalgam 'philosophies' ostensibly took fitness to be the more substantial aspect of their focus:

> Teaching skills . . . keeping children fit and teaching social skills as well . . . we're all trying to maintain a reasonable fitness—that's part of life. We try to educate them to stay fit in all three areas, really: strength, stamina, suppleness. The social side: they have to work with each other in life, they play games and have to get on with each other . . .

It is clear from the pervasiveness of what I have termed these 'amalgam' philosophies that the comments of many teachers in this study were of a piece with those of the teachers in Mason's (1995) study. Teachers in both studies appeared to hold what might best be described as a mishmash of views on PE: sometimes overlapping, sometimes contradictory, frequently ill thought-through and typically confused.

Discussion

The first point of note from the data provided by the semi-structured interviews, is that PE teachers rarely had anything that could be called philosophies in the sense of inte-grated, coherent sets of ideas. Confusion and contradiction were common features of their views. What PE teachers articulated was typically a kind of check-list of aims and practices frequently centring upon words and phrases like 'enjoyment', 'health', 'skills' and 'character'. If one were to be generous one might describe these as what Reid (1997) referred to as 'value pluralism'—a multiplicity of justifications for PE based on a plurality of values such as health, sports performance and character-development. However, their somewhat vague and unclear statements regarding the purposes of PE indicated that the teachers in this study did not possess the kinds of coherent, reflexive 'philosophies' suggested by Reid and others (e.g. Carr, 1997). Indeed, their 'philosophies' appeared more like justificatory ideologies; that is to say, ideologies that served to vindicate teachers' preferred conceptions of PE.

The distortions characteristic of ideological thinking range, for Mannheim (1960, p. 49; emphasis added), 'all the way from conscious lies to half-conscious and unwitting disguises; from calculated attempts to dupe others to *self-deception*'. Though ideological, the differing views held by PE teachers, did not appear as 'calculated lies'. Rather, and for the most part, they appeared an amalgam or complex of teachers' subconscious predispositions (what, in sociological terms, might be called 'habitus') and the practical situations in which teachers found themselves. In figurational terms, PE teachers' 'philosophies' were on a continuum 'between a simple lie at one pole, and an error, which is the result of a distorted and faulty conceptual apparatus, at the other' (Mannheim, 1960, p. 54). Much of the 'knowledge' incorporated into, and thus constituent of, PE teachers' 'philosophies' appeared, in fact, ideological; that is to say, it was by degrees more or less mythical, more or less false, more or less distorted.

A second, and related feature of PE teachers' 'philosophies' was that they appeared as processes in which intuitions were coupled, frequently, with convenient *ex post-facto* rationalizations or justifications for the things that they did. In this sense, it appeared that teachers' 'philosophies' were more likely to follow practice than precede it in the manner of conventional explanations of the relationship between theory and practice (Reid, 1996b). At the same time, and as processes, teachers' 'philosophies' were likely to develop (even change) over time to the extent that they were constrained to do so.

A third aspect of their 'philosophies' was the manner in which the overt emphasis upon enjoyment, the unusual justification for activity choice, and the emphasis upon sports performance (presumably one of the things which discourages some pupils), amongst other things, suggested that teachers perceived PE as somehow *different* from the rest of the curriculum. Theirs were very special kinds of 'philosophy', characterized by degrees of localism, particularism and subjectivity that stood in marked contrast to what one would expect to find in other areas of the National Curriculum and, indeed, from what OFSTED might demand. One wonders, for example, whether viewing enjoyment as a precondition for the achievement of 'philosophical'—or, more exactly, educational —goals is anything more than a rationalization for the fact that 'fun' would not be seen as a sufficient justification for a school subject. Indeed, in this vein, it often seemed the case that 'philosophical' justifications were presented as after-thoughts—'add-ons' intended to make the intuitive and pragmatic reasons more palatable.

A fourth feature was the existence of widespread continuities alongside (and some-what despite) real change in PE teachers' 'philosophies' and professed practice. According to a number of commentators (e.g. Evans, 1992; Kirk, 1992) this has been a feature of ideological trends in the history of PE in the UK. Nonetheless, real changes are said to have occurred in the ideologies and practices of PE teachers over the course of the 1970s and 1980s. The data in this study support such a claim. HRE has assumed a prominent place in the 'philosophies' and professed practices of PE teachers. At the same time, education for leisure and 'sport for all' (Hendry et al., 1993; Scraton, 1992) and, to some extent, the academic value of PE, have become more central rationales for PE. However, whilst development and change continued to be a feature of the emerging and developing 'philosophies' of teachers in this study, so was the marked persistence of long-standing ideologies. Sport, and especially team-games, continue to be the most prominent activity area in the vast majority of curricula for boys and girls in secondary schools and lie at the heart of many teachers' 'philosophies' of PE; albeit alongside other justificatory ideologies. Based upon their research in the USA, Chen & Ennis (1996, p. 339) claimed that what they term the 'discipline mastery' orientation (a 'focus on developing performance proficiency in sport skills and understanding of performance-related knowledge'), and what here is labelled the sporting ideology, 'was no longer the dominant philosophy in teaching physical education'. 'Teachers' beliefs', they argued, 'varied across the spectrum of the value orientations'. My own study would not support such a claim. PE teachers continuing and strong commitment to sport is a feature of their emergent and processual 'philosophies'. Whilst this may be tempered or even camouflaged by other concerns, such as health and PSE, most of them continue to view sport rather than physical activity as the most suitable and likely vehicle for achieving other 'educational' goals.

Conclusion

Over the last 20 years or so, the literature theorizing education from philosophical and pedagogical perspectives has frequently incorporated an implicit assumption that edu-cational theory can be expected to impact upon, even transform, teachers' thinking with regard to PE and, subsequently, their practice. It also seems to be implicitly assumed that teachers themselves are duty-bound to share such a perspective on educational philosophy. A characteristic of much (analytical) philosophy, McNamee (1998, p. 81) observes, is the tendency to proceed in argumentation 'as if the logic of (the) analysis carries itself forward to a conclusion in the minds of any *reasonable* person' (emphasis added). These 'reasonable' people include, of course, PE teachers, regardless of their prior orientations or dispositions or their practical context (e.g. their newness, the man-agement style of their Heads of Department, or the traditions of the department and the school). And yet, there is very little evidence that teachers reflect upon PE in a manner that bears any resemblance to the kind of abstract reasoning usually associated with philosophical theory itself.

In this paper I have attempted to outline the contours of the everyday 'philosophies' of PE teachers on the basis of data obtained from semi-structured interviews. In attempt-ing to make sense of the relationship between PE teachers' 'philosophies' and the ideolo-gies underpinning these, I have sought to identify and examine what teachers themselves, rather than academics or teacher trainers, think PE is about. Not, it should be noted, in the belief that these 'philosophies' might be taken to be self-evidently 'true' but, rather, in an attempt to construct a more systematic understanding of PE teachers' views of their subject 'in the belief that greater understanding will enhance our capacity to exercise control' (Dunning, 1999, p. 240) over an important aspect of young people's educational experiences.

The impact of philosophy as such on teachers' 'philosophies' was, perhaps unsurprisingly from a figurational perspective, demonstrably very limited. Teachers' 'philosophies' of PE and, for that matter, the practice of PE itself, are best understood as processes rather than states. PE is not something that can be treated as if it has evolved into its final form with the task being to establish the defining features of that final form. PE teachers' 'philosophies' are best understood as a shifting set of practices more or less favoured by PE teachers who, in turn, hold more or less ideological conceptions of PE which are inevitably circumscribed by their habituses and context.

Mannheim (1960, p. 251) might have been describing the relationship between academic philosophy of PE and the 'philosophies' of PE teachers when he referred to the commonplace tendency of 'talking past one another'. In the case of PE philosophy, however, it is not simply a matter of academics and teachers 'talking past one another', not least because in one sense PE teachers are not *talking* (in the sense of philosophizing) about PE much at all. This point is crucial; most teachers simply *do* PE. And their 'doing' appears to interact with their predispositions in influencing their thoughts on the subject.

There is another reason why it would be an over-simplification to talk about PE academics and teachers as 'talking past one another', for educational philosophers *are* dealing with substantive issues. The point is that they are debating the substantive issue of what PE is at an abstract level—PE as a concept—rather than engaging with the reality of PE as practice. It is not so much that they talk past, but that they simply are not talking on the same wavelength, as PE teachers. Thus, it only becomes possible to make sense of PE teachers' 'philosophies' if analysis is not restricted simply to ideas themselves or to the dictat of PE policy-makers as reflected, for example, in the NCPE.

Why, then, do PE teachers hold views that are evidently more or less (and, frequently, more) ideological, more or less mythical? How might one satisfactorily explain or account for their kind of views? In this paper, I have suggested that a figurational sociological approach to making sense of PE teachers' 'philosophies' holds out more promise than a (traditional) philosophical perspective. PE teachers 'philosophies' cannot be reduced to philosophy *per se*; nor, for that matter, to psychology. The knowledge and ideas of PE teachers cannot be explained by studying either the ideas themselves or the teacher (him or herself) in isolation. Knowledge (in terms of people's ideas and beliefs), for figurationalists, needs to be conceptualized as an *aspect* of interdependencies. Thus, PE teachers' thoughts, as well as their teaching behaviours, can only be fully understood when teachers are located in the figurations they form with each other—as inescapably *interdependent* people.

Thus, in a subsequent submission, I will attempt to explain how the 'philosophies' held by PE teachers, and the underlying ideologies therein, are best explained in terms of the networks of social relationships—or figurations—of which they are a part. I will suggest that in order to make sense of teachers' 'philosophies', ideologies and the discourses that manifest them, PE teachers' 'philosophies', need to be viewed in context; that is to say, in the particular figurations which make *particular* interpretations of PE more likely than others. I will suggest that what did impact upon the PE teachers featured in this study was their deeply-rooted attachments and associated convictions (e.g. towards the value of sport) and their practice or, more precisely, the constraints circumscribing their practice. The way teachers thought about PE had been shaped by their past experiences and had become bound up with the job itself. As such, their 'philosophies' tended to be *practical* 'philosophies'; that is to say, 'philosophies' that bore the hallmarks of their prior PE and sporting practice and their contemporaneous practical teaching contexts.

Acknowledgements

I am grateful to Dr Ivan Waddington (Centre for Research into Sport and Society, University of Leicester) and Dr Miranda Thurston (Chester College of H. E.) for their advice on an earlier draft of this paper. I would also like to thank two anonymous reviewers for their helpful comments. I am particularly indebted to the reviewer who, in requiring greater clarity and detail in the methodological section, contributed to what I believe is now a more well-rounded and informative paper.

Notes

1   The concept of habitus refers to 'the durable and generalized disposition that suffuses a person's action throughout an entire domain of life, or in the extreme instance, throughout all of life—in which case the term comes to mean the whole manner, turn, cast, or mold of the personality' (van Krieken, 1998, p. 47).

2   I have chosen to use the term 'philosophy' to describe teachers' views on PE, for the following reasons:

   (i)   in answer to my opening questions regarding their thoughts on what PE should be about, various PE teachers themselves made frequent reference to their 'philosophy' in a manner which bore close resemblance to the aphoristic use of the term that, as I have indicated, has a common currency;

   (ii)   several authors in the broad field of the sociology of PE (e.g. Armour, 1997; Armour & Jones, 1998; Evans, 1992) make use of the term 'philosophy' when referring to teachers' ideas;

   (iii) I am attempting to ascertain the 'surface-level' or, as van Krieken (1998, p. 47) puts it, the 'superficial portion' of their 'consciousness' in the first instance; whilst,

   (iv)   reserving the more sociological concept of 'habitus' for a more specific role in *explaining* PE teachers' 'philosophies'.

3   Measured in terms of the relative percentages of children attending the school entitled to free school meals.

4   I have labelled these alleged social and moral benefits PSE because of the currency of the term in secondary schools as a formal process for bringing about the kinds of objectives PE teachers were claiming for PE.

References

Arksey, H. & Knight, P. (1999) *Interviewing for Social Scientists* (London, Sage Publications).

Armour, K. (1997) Developing a personal philosophy on the nature and purpose of physical education: life history reflections of physical education teachers at Citylimits high school, *European Physical Education Review*, 3(1), pp. 68–82.

Armour, K. & Jones, R. (1998) *Physical Education Teachers' Lives and Careers: PE, Sport and Educational Status* (Basingstoke, The Falmer Press).

Arnold, P.J. (1992) Sport as a valued human practice: a basis for the consideration of some moral issues in sport, *Journal of Philosophy of Education*, 26(1), pp. 237–255.

Blake, B. (1996) Spiritual, moral, social and cultural development in physical education, *Bulletin of Physical Education*, 32(1), pp. 6–16.

Bowling, A. (1997) *Research Methods in Health* (Buckingham, Open University Press).

Carr, D. (1997) Physical education and value diversity: a response to Andrew Reid, *European Physical Education Review*, 3(2), pp. 95–105.

Chambers English Dictionary (1990) *Chambers English Dictionary* (Edinburgh, W. and R. Chambers).

Chen, A. & Ennis, C.D. (1996) Teaching value-laden curricula in physical education, *Journal of Teaching in Physical Education*, 15(3), pp. 338–354.

Denscombe, M. (1998) *The Good Research Guide* (Buckingham, Open University Press).

Department of National Heritage (DNH) (1995) *Sport: Raising the Game* (London, DNH).

Dunning, E. (1992) Figurational sociology and the sociology of sport, in: *Theories of Sport*, Module 2, Unit 3, pp. 147–221 (Leicester, Centre for Research into Sport and Society (CRSS)).

Elias, N. (1978) *What is Sociology?* (London, Hutchinson).

Evans, J. (1990) Defining a subject: the rise and rise of the new PE? *British Journal of Sociology*, 11(2), pp. 115–169.

Evans, J. (1992) A short paper about people, power and educational reform. authority and representation in ethnographic research subjectivity, ideology and educational reform: the case of physical education, in: A. Sparkes (Ed.) *Research in Physical Education and Sport: Exploring Alternative Visions*, pp. 231–247 (London, The Falmer Press).

Evans, J. & Davies, B. (1986) Sociology, schooling and physical education, in J. Evans (Ed.) *Physical Education, Sport and Schooling: Studies in the Sociology of Physical Education*, pp. 11–17 (Basingstoke, The Falmer Press).

Flew, A. (1984) Preface, in: A. Flew (Ed.) *A Dictionary of Philosophy*, 2nd edition, pp. vii–xi (London, Pan Books Ltd).

Green, K. (1998) Philosophies, ideologies and the practice of physical education, *Sport, Education and Society*, 3(2), pp. 125–143.

Hendry, L.B., Shucksmith, J., Love, J.G. & Glendenning, A. (1993) *Young People's Leisure and Lifestyles* (London, Routledge).

Hirst, P. (1994a) Keynote lecture, *National Conference for Physical Education, Sport and Dance*, Loughborough University, July 1994.

Hirst, P. (1994b) Personal communication, *National Conference for Physical Education, Sport and Dance*, Loughborough University, July 1994.

Johns, D.J., Gilbert, K. & Shuttleworth, J. (1994) Justifying terminology and changing discourses: from physical education to human movement studies, unpublished manuscript.

Keats, D.M. (2000) *Interviewing: A Practical Guide for Students and Professionals* (Buckingham, Open University Press).

Kirk, D. (1992) *Defining Physical Education: The Social Construction of a School Subject in Postwar Britain* (London, Falmer Press).

Laker, A. (1996a) The aims of physical education within the revised National Curriculum: lip service to the affective?, *Pedagogy in Practice*, 2(1), pp. 24–30.

Laker, A. (1996b) Learning to teach through the physical as well as of the physical, *The British Journal of Physical Education*, 27(3), pp. 18–22.

Mann, M. (Ed.) (1983) *Macmillan Student Encyclopaedia of Sociology* (London, Macmillan Press).

Mannheim, K. (1960) *Ideology and Utopia. An Introduction to the Sociology of Knowledge* (London, Routledge & Kegan Paul).

Mason, V. (1995) *Young People and Sport* (London, Sports Council).

McNamee, M. (1998) Philosophy and physical education: analysis, epistemology and axiology, *European Physical Education Review*, 4(1), pp. 75–91.

Mennell, S. & Goudsblom, J. (Eds) (1998) *Norbert Elias on Civilization, Power and Knowledge* (Chicago, The University of Chicago Press).

Munrow, A.D. (1972) *Physical Education. A Discussion of Principles* (London, Bell & Hyman Ltd).

Murphy, P., Sheard, K. & Waddington, I. (forthcoming) Figurational sociology and its application to sport.

Oakeshott, M. (1972) Education: the engagement and its frustration, in: R. Dearden, P. Hirst & R. Peters (Eds) *A Critique of Current Educational Aims, Part I of Education and the Development of Reason*, pp. 17–47 (London, Routledge & Kegan Paul).

Office of Standards in Education (OFSTED) (1998) *Secondary Education 1993–97 The Curriculum* (http:www.opengov.gov.uk).

O'Hear, A. (1981) *Education, Society and Human Nature. An Introduction to the Philosophy of Education* (London, Routledge & Kegan Paul).

Penney, D. & Harris, D. (1997) Extra-curricular physical education: more of the same for the more able, *Sport, Education and Society*, 2(1), pp. 41–54.

Reid, A. (1996a) The concept of physical education in current curriculum and assessment policy in Scotland, *European Physical Education Review*, 2(1), pp. 7–18.

Reid, A. (1996b) Knowledge, practice and theory in physical education, *European Physical Education Review*, 2(2), pp. 94–104.

Reid, A. (1997) Value pluralism and physical education, *European Physical Education Review*, 3(1), pp. 6–20.

Roberts, K. (1996a) Young people, schools, sport and government policy, *Sport, Education and Society*, 1(1), pp. 47–57.

Roberts, K. (1996b) Youth cultures and sport: the success of school and Community sports provisions in Britain, *European Physical Education Review*, 2(2), pp. 105–115.

Roberts, K. & Brodie, D. (1992) *Inner-City Sport: Who Plays and What are the Benefits?* (Culemborg, Giordano Bruno).

Scraton, S. (1992) *Shaping Up to Womanhood. Gender and Girls' Physical Education* (Buckingham, Open University Press).

Siedentop, D. (1994) *Sport Education: Quality PE Through Positive Sport Experiences* (Champaign, IL, Human Kinetics).

Sports Council for Wales (SCW) (1995) *The Pattern of Play: Physical Education in Welsh Secondary School: 1990 to 1994* (Cardiff, Sports Council for Wales).

Van Krieken, R. (1998) *Norbert Elias* (London, Routledge).

Wilterdink, N.A. (1977) Norbert Elias's sociology of knowledge and its significance for the study of the sciences, in: P.R. Gleichmann, J. Goudsblom & H. Korte (Eds) *Human Figurations: Essays for Norbert Elias* (Amsterdam, Stichting Amsterdams Sociologisch Tijdschrift).

David Kirk

A CRITICAL PEDAGOGY FOR TEACHER EDUCATION
Toward an inquiry-oriented approach

IN THE LAST DECADE, teacher educators have been influenced by two important developments in the curriculum field: first by the appearance of *Knowledge and Control* (Young, 1971), and more recently by a loosely aligned group of writers labeled by Pinar (1978) as the "reconceptualists." Both "new directions" sociology of education and the reconceptualists have sought to politicize the notions of knowledge and schooling by drawing attention to the roles that schools play in capital accumulation—by sifting and sorting students for the labor market, in legitimation of power relations and social inequality, and in the production of technically utilizable knowledge essential to the maintenance of science-based industrial output (Apple & Weis, 1985; Karier, 1976).

Giroux (1981) has argued that this work is significant for teacher education because schools "exist within a constellation of economic, social, and political institutions which make them a fundamental part of the power structure" (p. 143). Accordingly, teaching can never be a neutral activity, but is always related to "legitimizing the categories and social practices of the dominant society" (p. 149). However, Giroux suggests that teacher education programs have tended to depoliticize the nature of the teaching experience and, in so doing, obscure the relationships between teacher education, schooling, and wider societal interests. Thus, teacher education as it is conventionally approached is caught in a paradox, wherein education is seen on the one hand to provide the means by which "all socio-economic classes [can] learn about and . . . transform the nature of their existence" (p. 143), but on the other, provides a depoliticized teacher education that can only produce teachers who work to reproduce and legitimate social inequality.

In the wake of this reconceptualization of curriculum studies, there has been growing advocacy for a politically aware inquiry-oriented approach (Zeichner & Teitlebaum, 1982) to teacher education (see also Bates, 1981; Pollard, 1984; Smyth, 1984; Woods, 1985).

While Tinning (1985a) has recently argued for such an approach to be applied within physical education teacher education, there are as yet few guidelines for teacher educators that outline in practical terms what an inquiry-oriented approach might involve.[1] This paper attempts to sketch out a framework for such an approach to teacher education that is relevant (though not necessarily exclusive) to physical education.[2]

The inquiry-oriented approach

The inquiry-oriented approach seeks to transcend the perceived inadequacies of other teacher education models (see Zeichner, 1983) and aims to create a critical pedagogy. Zeichner and Teitlebaum (1982) have suggested that teacher education can never be normatively neutral, but instead "the dominant forms of teacher education today largely encourage acquiescence and conformity to the status quo, both in schooling and society" (p. 102).

They claim that teacher education programs lead to students developing utilitarian perspectives[3] on their teaching which "is separated from its ethical, political and moral roots" (see also Apple & Weis, 1985; Giroux, 1981). This, they argue, is largely the result of personalized teacher education programs that focus on survival and craft- or skill-based courses. To counter this rampant pragmatism, Zeichner and Teitlebaum suggest that some conception of social and economic justice is an essential component of every teacher's education.[4] What is called for, they contend, is an inquiry-oriented approach that places less emphasis on the technical and instrumental aspects of teaching and greater emphasis on developing certain critical capacities in students.

> [this critical approach] . . . legitimates a notion of inquiry where education students can begin to identify connections between the level of the classroom (e.g. the form and content of curriculum, classroom social relations), and the wider educational, social, economic and political conditions which impinge upon and shape classroom practice.
>
> (Zeichner & Teitlebaum, 1982, p. 104)

The notion of inquiry-oriented teacher education, and the critical pedagogy it entails, marks a radical departure from other approaches to teacher education by its emphasis on the political dimension of schooling. In the next section of this paper, I wish to explore the notion of a critical pedagogy in more detail by investigating the most recent advocacy of this idea in two important areas of development, one mainly in educational practice and the other in educational theory. This next section will also be a prelude to an attempt to outline what an inquiry-oriented program aimed at developing a critical pedagogy may look like.

Roots of the notion of a critical pedagogy

The roots of an inquiry-oriented approach to teacher education and the notion of a critical pedagogy it encompasses lie in two clearly discernible areas of development in education: action research, and critical social and curriculum theory.

Action research

In the 1960s and early 1970s, much curriculum development in schools was undertaken using large-scale projects (e.g., see Stenhouse, 1980), most building on the rational planning model (Tyler, 1949) of curriculum design. Despite massive private and public funding, however, it was realized that all of this work had brought about little change in the practice of schooling (Doyle & Ponder, 1977–78; Leiberman & Griffin, 1976). For instance, in 1976 MacDonald and Walker, both heavily involved in the curriculum movement themselves, were forced to admit,

> The enduring problem that has plagued the sponsors and planners of curriculum innovation is not the problem of creation, but the problem of impact, the failure to achieve anything like the mass conversion to new aims, new content, and new approaches that they aspire to. The schools have not, it seems, been transformed by all the organised, systematised, specialised efforts of the professional innovators.
>
> (1976, pp. 4–5)

Some commentators have been inclined to blame the teacher as the culpable party in the failure of such programs (e.g., Renshaw's [1976] "unreflective pragmatist"), while others have more reasonably suggested that there are complex factors involved in any attempt to innovate that the teacher can never hope to control fully (Leiberman & Griffin, 1976; Olson, 1983). Whether sympathetic or not, however, the growing acknowledgement of much of this research was that the teacher plays a central role in any effort to initiate innovation in schools. The Humanities Curriculum Project (Elliot & Adelman, 1973) and other follow-up work such as SAFARI (MacDonald & Walker, 1974) represent early attempts to act on this realization by outlining a positive and constructive participatory role for the teacher in curriculum development. Thus, as MacDonald and Walker (1974) seem to confirm, the action-research movement was created, or at least was given an initial push, due to the failures of large-scale curriculum projects.

Stenhouse's (1975) notion of teacher as researcher reflects the mood of this time:

> all well founded curriculum research and development, whether the work of an individual teacher, of a school, of a group working in a teachers' centre or of a group working within the co-ordinating framework of a national project, is based on the study of classrooms. It thus rests on the work of teachers. . . . It is not enough that teachers' work should be studied: they need to study it themselves.
>
> (1975, p. 143)

Through this kind of advocacy, the notions of research-based teaching, teacher as researcher, and action-research have become common in teacher education inservice programs. Action-research in education is being conducted in Britain (see Elliot, 1978, for a characteristic statement of the British view), in continental Europe (see Brock-Ulte, 1980), in the United States (see Tikunoff, Ward, & Griffin, 1979), and in Australia (see Grundy & Kemmis, 1981). Grundy and Kemmis present a definition of action-research in education that reflects something of each of these perspectives.

Educational action research is a term used to describe a family of activities in curriculum development, professional development, school improvement programs, and systems planning and policy development. These activities have in common the identification of strategies of planned action which are *implemented*, and then systematically submitted to *observation, reflection* and change. Participants in the action being considered are integrally involved in all of these activities.

(1981, p. 3)

Action-research, according to this definition, aims to improve educational practice through the involvement, and especially active participation, of educators in dialogue, in the development of understanding, and in strategic action.

The importance of the notion of action-research to a critical pedagogy is its assertion of the teacher as the central figure in any curriculum development effort, as the mediator between educational intentions and eventual outcomes. Furthermore, it thus claims for teachers not only a high level of professional significance but also the need for a degree of autonomy, expertise, and responsibility to control their own educational practice. Clearly, this conceptualization of the teacher's role stands in stark contrast to those attempts to "teacher proof" curriculum packages on some large-scale curriculum projects (Stenhouse, 1975, p. 24). There is evidence to suggest that teachers are becoming involved in action-research through centers like Deakin University in Australia and the University of East Anglia in England, through research projects (e.g., Almond, 1983), and through publication (e.g., Nixon, 1981).

However, in the context of a critical pedagogy, action-research also presents some difficulties (see Hargreaves, 1982a, for some general comments). In particular, there is a problem with confining the teacher's reflective efforts to the classroom and an apparent unwillingness to address some of the wider social and political issues that affect educational action. Much action-research has focused on solving technical or "how to" questions in pedagogy, and has shied away from addressing social, ethical, and political issues (see Bullough, Gitlin, & Goldstein, 1984; Reid, 1978). A critical examination of some of the published products of action-research (e.g., Nixon, 1981) reveals that teachers' efforts are concentrated almost exclusively on questions of how to communicate information and ideas more effectively. This dimension of the teacher's task is clearly important and is not denied here; however, it is precisely the lack of truly *critical* insight into some of the fundamental problems in schooling that much action-research has lacked so far. It is this omission that recent critical social theorists have begun to correct.

Critical social and curriculum theory

Pinar (1978) has suggested that there are at least three main groupings of researchers currently at work in the curriculum field: traditionalists, conceptual-empiricists, and reconceptualists. The latter category is the most recent and its writers have drawn on Marxism and other critical traditions in social theory (see Giddens, 1976, 1982; Mills, 1970) in applying their ideas to curriculum and teacher education.

The "new directions" in sociology of education, and in particular *Knowledge and Control* (Young, 1971), has had a considerable impact in stimulating these developments in curriculum theorizing. Two central ideas presented in *Knowledge and Control* are that (a) the

structure of knowledge in the school curriculum can be seen to reflect and serve particular dominant and self-serving political power and (b) through phenomenological analysis,
the curriculum produced by these structures can be seen to be "an historically specific
social reality expressing particular production relations between men" (Young, 1976).

Hammersley and Hargreaves (1983) have argued that this thesis was significant,
particularly in the context of the "general cultural radicalism" of the late 1960s, because

> it suggested to teachers that since the conception of worthwhile knowledge
> they held and the categories they used to distinguish academic from non-
> academic, bright from dull, able from stupid were . . . not absolutes but
> "socially constructed", then teachers could presumably choose to *redefine* what
> counted as worthwhile knowledge and so avoid labelling working class pupils
> as thick and dull.
>
> (1983, p. 4)

However, as Young (1976) himself subsequently acknowledged, this conception of the
relationship between knowledge and power inappropriately gives the teacher the responsibility of social change through the curriculum, a project that teachers can hardly hope to
fulfill, given the structural constraints embodied in the process of schooling. Bates (1981)
has argued further that while the major thesis of *Knowledge and Control* was to liberate
teachers and pupils from the constraints of absolutist definitions of knowledge, in fact for
many it carried quite a different message.

> many teachers presented with an analysis which saps most of the conventional
> justification of their activities, displays the restrictive conditions of classrooms
> and offers accounts of the incoherence, domination and partiality of teachers
> in their relations with pupils, are likely to either reject the analysis or resign in
> uncomfortable guilt at the damage they are doing to children.
>
> (Bates, 1981, p. 43)

The roots of the contradictory nature of the message to teachers from early "new
directions" sociology of education lay, Bates argues, in a naive and simplistic structural
analysis of schooling, in which "solutions to school problems become attendant upon
changes, but within wider society itself (1981, p. 44).[5]

Thus, as Bates points out,

> The outcome of this juxtaposition of radical structural analysis and a relativ-
> istic phenomenology was a curious contradiction, in that the structural analysis
> offered convincing explanations of the *limits* of change under a system of elite
> control, yet phenomenological analysis asserted that teachers and pupils in
> classrooms constructed *their own* realities.
>
> (1981, p. 45)

More recent critical theorizing in education has sought to wrestle with the ambiguities
of this contradiction that *Knowledge and Control* embodies. Young (1976), for instance, has
suggested that the solution to this problem is the development of a "critical theory of
curriculum" which (a) takes as a starting point the practice of teachers and pupils and their

theorizing on this practice, and (b) addresses fundamental issues of how this practice is structured in and by society. This suggests that liberation and emancipation are issues that are not, and should not be, confined to classrooms. Apple (1976) has similarly argued that a critical analysis of educational practice must begin at the point of rendering problematic the everyday, taken-for-granted world of schools and classrooms. It is only through a process of challenging what he calls "common sense categories of thought" that people will ever be able to "see the actual functionings of institutions in all their positive *and* negative complexity, to illuminate the contradictions of extant regularities, and, finally, to assist others in 'remembering' the possibilities of spontaneity and choice" (Apple, 1976, p. 183).

Both authors, Young and Apple, point to a mediation between the constraining effect of social structures on the possibilities for change through human agency as a key issue in discussions of a critical pedagogy.[6] Indeed, much recent debate in this area has centered on exploring how domination is manifest in and through schooling, and the possibilities of resistance by both teachers and pupils, and the forms that this might take (e.g., Bullough et al., 1984; Bullough & Gitlin, 1985; Giroux, 1981; Walker, 1985). This debate has been critically enjoined by McNeil (1981) and by Hargreaves (1982b). McNeil has argued that much of the theorizing about domination/resistance suffers from incoherence due to faults endemic to the frames of reference (e.g., Marxism) upon which reconceptualist curriculum theorists have drawn.[7] Hargreaves (1982b), in addition to McNeil's criticism, has claimed first that the debate surrounding domination/resistance stands in need of grounding in empirical studies,[8] and second that this debate suffers from a restricted vision of possible alternatives in schooling due to its explicit political stance.

This latter criticism by Hargreaves needs some clarification, however, since it is the "political" nature of educational practice and theorizing that is most commonly misunderstood in discussions of this kind. To argue that all educational action is politically based, in that we cannot avoid the exercise of judgments of value in our daily interactions from classroom through to systems levels (see Reid, 1978, p. 98), is to do no more than describe a state of affairs. Whether or not educational action and interaction *ought* to be political is an interesting abstract question, but ontologically there is little we can do to alter this. Indeed, this existential fact of life in itself carries strong recommendations for a critical awareness of social life because, as Mills (1970) has argued, it is through inaction that forms of power are produced and reproduced and so become pervasive and obdurate.

Thus, to argue (following Giroux, 1981) that a critical pedagogy should involve (a) an understanding that knowledge is socially constructed, and through this see the possibilities for transformative action, (b) an understanding that knowledge is never value-free, (c) an awareness of the importance of concepts such as social justice, and (d) an awareness of the potential *and* limitations of social action, and its possible consequences, does not commit a theorist or teacher to a particular brand of politics (e.g., conservatism, socialism, communism). It may be that the capacity to think critically about social life is more easily achieved through particular political modes, for instance through a democratic rather than totalitarian mode. I would argue that the reconceptualists' politicization of schooling does not imply a particular brand of politics, but more correctly proposes a particular way of looking at the world.

In summary, action-research and critical social and curriculum theory represent two developments that lie at the root of the notion of a critical pedagogy, which is in turn a key concept within an inquiry-oriented model of teacher education. Drawing on interpretative social theory, action-research has emphasized the importance of human understanding and reflection for the improvement of educational practice, and has demonstrated the value of involving teachers in research-based teaching (see Grundy, 1982). While these developments have done teacher education a valuable service, the forging of a methodological basis for research by practitioners has tended to ignore more fundamental questions about schooling and society which penetrate into everyday classroom life. Recent curriculum theorizing, drawing mainly on post-Marxist and other critical social theory, has corrected this onesidedness of action-research by addressing as a central problem the question of how human action and interaction are structured in schools and classrooms. The ongoing debate around the problem of teacher and pupil resistance to domination clearly demonstrates that structure/agency is a complex phenomenon that is manifest in all spheres of social life (see Giddens, 1979).

The challenge facing teacher education is to construct programs that can move teachers beyond the instrumentalism of a "pedagogy of necessity" (Tinning, 1985a) toward a critical pedagogy, wherein ethical, political, and social issues are not accepted as unquestionable but instead are treated as problematic. The major themes or project of any such program can thus be said to be an attempt to engender in students a satisfactory level of technical competence and at the same time an ability to move beyond commonsense categories of thought in order to gain critical insight into the process of schooling.

In the context of teacher education, I would argue that one dimension of structure/agency is the perennial problem of theory *versus* practice. This dichotomy presents a focus for the final part of this paper, as any attempt to outline the components of a program that aims at the development of a critical pedagogy must include an analysis of knowledge that forms the basis of instruction in teacher education.

Toward an inquiry-oriented approach to teacher education in physical education

Knowledge and the problem of theory in teacher education

Theory, it is commonly thought, is only remotely related to the practice of teaching, often to the point of being redundant or even antagonistic, and teachers often consider practical knowledge more valuable than theoretical knowledge (see Ward & Hardman, 1978).

Clearly, the sedimented traditions (Berger & Luckmann, 1971) of teacher education institutions, and of particular school subjects (Goodson & Ball, 1984), will play an important role in shaping the nature of the theory/practice relationship. For example, a program in an institution that has a long and distinguished history in teacher education, and especially if the department, school, or faculty is housed in an older university, will inevitably be shaped to some extent by past practices, often at a deep and unarticulated level. Newer institutions, which don't have the many years of sedimented tradition to structure their actions, may have a relatively greater freedom to develop more innovative approaches to theory and practice.[9]

In the same respect, the nature of the subject that students are being prepared to teach, and particularly its status in the curriculum as perceived by pupils, parents, administrators, and the professional community of teachers, will play an important role in defining the theory/practice relationship in subject pedagogy. For example, physical education has traditionally been seen as a practical subject, and in the early years of teacher training students experienced a broad, practically oriented program closely resembling the activities they were likely to teach in schools (Thomson, 1983). More recently, and particularly through the development of degree courses in the disciplines of human movement studies, considering theoretical topics in the exercise sciences, and sociocultural and philosophical studies, the relationship between what students learn at the pre-service level and what they are expected to teach in schools can be quite disparate (Mangan, 1984).

However, this apparent dysfunction between theory and practice is in itself a product of theoretical discourse.

> Theory and practice are distinct in the sense that they are theoretically distinguishable, just as love and lust or the constituent parts of water are theoretically distinguishable. But it is another matter to try to physically separate love and lust in practice, or to try to physically separate the elements contained in a glass of water.
>
> (Barrow, 1984, p. 12)

Thus, the notion of "theory" versus "practice" as two separate components of the teaching act represents a false dichotomy. Theoretical and practical knowledge, as Entwistle (1969) has shown, are inextricably intertwined in any complex action or series of actions such as teaching. This is not to say, however, that all theoretical knowledge leads to good practice, nor is it to say that good practice necessarily presupposes an awareness of relevant theory. In teacher education, perhaps the problem of theory versus practice has been that for too long the elements of poor theory have been combined with little or no relevant support for the student-teacher's lived experience of teaching, and has in this way reinforced the idea that theory and practice in teaching inevitably are dysfunctional. For instance, Woods has remarked that

> sociology has not served teachers well. Its theoretical abstraction seems remote from the teacher's hard realism, and its terms of debate seem difficult to comprehend. . . . The messages that do get through appear often to be radical and revolutionary, advocating fundamental and long term change. Whatever their desirability, these messages are small comfort to teachers grappling with the myriad mundane, small-scale problems of everyday school life. As they may appear to blame the teacher, either as agents of an evil system or for personal inadequacies, in a way again that offers little advice on how individual teachers might repair their deficiencies.
>
> (Woods, 1985, p. 51)

This problem of the apparent distance of theoretical knowledge from the actual practice of teaching is, I would suggest, fairly widespread in teacher education programs. This is particularly the case in programs that are discipline-based rather than practice-referenced (S.J. Smith, 1985); that is, their starting point in the teacher education process is in the various contributing disciplines to educational theory and this is presented in such a way that theory is contrasted with, rather than referenced to, practice. Stenhouse has commented in this respect that the received doctrine has been that the core of education for teaching lies not in research in education, but in the application to education of research in the "contributory disciplines" of philosophy, psychology and sociology. Most of those teaching these disciplines to teachers have not been able to share a research base with their students, who are clearly quite unlikely to become philosophers, psychologists or sociologists, since they are on professional courses for teachers.

(Stenhouse, 1979, p. 18)

It is possible to see how a dysfunction between theoretical and practical knowledge might occur within discipline-based teacher education. However, as both theoretical and practical knowledge are essential elements in the teaching act, then clearly theory that is irrelevant to practice is bad theory.

Theory, practice, and the teaching act

The kind of theory that should form part of the teacher education process, at least as a starting point, is not discipline-based theory. Rather, the starting point for education for teaching, I believe, following Stenhouse (1975), Young (1976), and Apple (1976), must be in the teaching act itself. In this conception, the teaching act is no longer the endpoint of the process of teacher education but is instead a beginning. It is the point of departure for developing in the student a deeper awareness of the phenomenon of education. It is in this sense that knowledge in teacher education can be practice-referenced; the student's lived experience acts as the "sounding board" of theory, and the relationship between theory and practice is no longer oppositional but is instead dialectical, each sphere of knowledge informing the other.

Woods has suggested in this respect that, "Following from the belief of ethnographers that theory should be grounded in empirical reality, we might argue that teachers' appreciation of educational theory should be grounded in *their* experience, which necessarily has to come first" (1985, p. 57).

Woods' idea is that by involving student-teachers in ethnographic exercises that are action-oriented, focusing on them and their own teaching, we can help student-teachers learn to distance themselves from their own practice and thus create enough analytic space for reflection on this practice. Underlying this proposal is an important acknowledgement that in a critical pedagogy, the teacher needs to take a certain degree of responsibility for his or her own learning. Thus, in reflecting one of the major tenets of the action-research movement, the teacher is seen as an interpretative individual capable of relating knowledge to his or her own lived experience (Elliot, 1978). This idea is echoed in the following comment by Giroux:

Teaching must be viewed, in part, as an intensely personal affair. This suggests that prospective teachers can be given the concepts and methods to delve into their own biographies, to look at the sedimented history they carry around, and to learn how one's own cultural capital represents a dialectical interplay between private experience and history.

(1981, pp. 158–159)

One writer, however, has raised various objections to this notion by pointing out that it is wrong

> to expect teachers to theorize the system rather than their own classrooms, partly because teachers know no-one in power in the system takes their theories about their own classrooms seriously, so they are hardly going to believe them if they begin theorizing about the system; and partly because it needs a particular kind of critical consciousness to theorize context rather than actions; and finally partly because teachers' most immediate concern is with their classroom, so that's where they will begin.
>
> (Tripp, 1984, p. 60)

Tripp is correct to suggest that theorizing about systems is inappropriate for teachers as an exercise in itself; the point is, as he argues, any such thinking must be grounded in the teacher's *own* practice. Zeichner and Teitlebaum (1982) make exactly this point when they suggest that the primary vehicle for achieving critical reflectivity in teachers is through carefully structured courses whereby "macro-contextualized ethnographies" are interposed with teaching in schools. Their idea is to preempt the pragmatic and sometimes cynical utilitarianism that students may develop during the socialization process involving practice teaching in schools.[10] Ethnography here not only creates the analytic space for self-critical reflection, but also for a socially critical consciousness.

However, Tripp's other point, which is that a particular kind of consciousness is implied by this perspective, suggests that the student-teacher himself or herself plays a vital role in the process of seeing the usefulness of knowledge. The student-teacher will attempt to interpret and give structure to this knowledge; thus, lectures, tutorials, teaching experience, and research exercises (e.g., the action-oriented and macro-contextualized ethnographies that Woods as well as Zeichner and Teitlebaum suggest) help to create a dynamic relationship between the student-teacher's own biography and a potentially inert body of ideas and information. As insights are gained, both heuristically and analytically, this knowledge provides the student-teacher with a vocabulary and a framework of concepts to render explicit and coherent his or her own personal experience. This conception of theory, in Woods' terms,

> offers to put a teacher's practice on a reasoned, logical, universal level, rather than an idiosyncratic, chance, hit-or-miss framework many have to work in . . . Theory liberates teachers from myth, fantasy, and ill-founded rumour and permits teachers to construct policy on a realistic basis.
>
> (1985, p. 55)

A program for physical education teacher education

This decision to take the teaching act as the starting point of the process of teacher education suggests in more specific terms two major foci for knowledge. This knowledge is intended to contribute to an individual's development as a teacher, but it should be noted that these foci do not preclude other knowledge components in teacher education programs. Clearly, teachers also need to acquire some knowledge of what it is they are to teach, that is, the substance of their teaching, and this knowledge will be derived from a study of the various subdisciplines of human movement studies (Saunders, 1980). My main concern here is to establish the kind of knowledge that supports the teaching act itself.

The first focus would be on knowledge that feeds directly into the teaching act and aims at the development of competency and a capacity for reflective self-development. This knowledge could be brought together under the rubric "analysis of teaching." This analysis would aim to present studies with general procedures or courses of action for situations arising in the classroom. The knowledge base for this focus lies in the work of researchers such as Smith and Geoffrey (1968), Jackson (1968), and Hamilton (1977) in the qualitative tradition (generally, see Delamont, 1976), and in a prolific number of studies in the quantitative tradition (see Dunkin & Biddle, 1974). The former tradition is closely related to action-research in terms of methods of data collection and frames of reference; in addition, Stenhouse (1978) has outlined in some detail how qualitative materials, like case studies, could be used in teacher education. The latter source of knowledge within the quantitative tradition has produced a broad base of information about teaching which is useful to teacher educators (see Locke, 1982; Siedentop, 1982).

Both traditions provide knowledge that creates the possibility of presenting students with a range of general strategies which can be adapted to suit particular circumstances, so that teachers can choose alternative courses of action as situations demand. For example, many institutions seem to be adopting strategies such as mini and micro teaching (Turney, Clift, Dunkin, & Trail, 1973) as a complementary support for teaching experience, along with the traditional prolonged period of placement in schools. The use of video recordings of student teaching is just one approach within this context that can provide students with invaluable feedback on their teaching performance.

The second focus would be on knowledge that contextualizes the student-teacher's experience of the teaching act, and may be brought together under the title "curriculum studies." By studying the curriculum, student-teachers could begin to broaden their conception of the teacher's role in the classroom, in the school, and in society at large. This broader focus allows them to consider topics such as curriculum design, innovation, and evaluation, and issues such as the nature of knowledge in physical education, how this knowledge can be taught and the possible consequences of different approaches, and how students can and should be assessed. At the same time, student-teachers can begin to examine some of the political, social, and ethical dimensions of these topics and concerns. By focusing on the curriculum, knowledge takes on an action-orientation because these issues are located in the arena within which teachers operate.

It is only by locating the analysis of these issues in this action-frame that teachers can begin to treat commonsense categories of thought as problematic, and see beyond the reified nature of school knowledge. Unless this analysis is empirically grounded, it is less likely that a necessary intersection between analysis and the student-teacher's own biography will be achieved. Similarly, while students must be able to meet the expectations of their prospective employers, and in a less direct way that of the taxpayers, it is only by demonstrating how these expectations are created and then manifested in the practical curriculum context that teachers can avoid repression of their own creativity and individuality to the goals of service (see Bullough et al., 1984; Woods, 1984). The loyal obedience of the teacher as a public servant needs to be supplanted by critical, intelligent praxis, whereby teachers develop insights that help them see beyond the motives of particular groups and so avoid being used for purposes that may conflict with their own deeply felt values.

Thus, through a critical focus on the curriculum and the analysis of abstract concepts and practical issues in this action-frame, the student-teacher may be better equipped with the conceptual tools that allow him or her to move beyond loyal obedience toward creative and intelligent practice.

Indeed, both knowledge components would seek to transcend the arbitrary and dichotomous distinctions between qualitative/quantitative and macro/micro, in an attempt to capture something of the reality of teaching and learning. In other words, both components would seek to ground teacher education in a dialectic that aims at praxis (Small, 1978). Both knowledge components will be validated by different criteria of value within the context of educational praxis. Knowledge aimed at supporting and illuminating the teaching act, for instance, must meet as a basic requirement of its adequacy the criterion of usefulness. That is to say, it should have a general applicability to the kinds of situations teachers are likely to encounter, and so allow the teacher to move beyond crude pragmatism.[11] Knowledge that aims to contextualize the teaching experience, on the other hand, must meet the criterion of meaningfulness; it must make sense when sounded out against the student-teacher's own biography as well as against the intersubjective professional world of monographs, papers, books, and reports.

Conclusion

Knowledge in teacher education can thus be focused to emancipate the teacher from lore and mysticism and to provide, as Woods (1985) has suggested, a vocabulary for the expression of practical experience. It is this process of emancipation that lies at the heart of a critical pedagogy, as it is only by relating the knowledge gained through the teacher education process to his or her own biography that the teacher can begin to operate as an intelligent practitioner, capable of reflective self-development and wise to the complexities of the educational process. It is only when a dialectical relationship exists between knowledge and experience that the teacher can begin to make meaning from his or her professional life and so make a significant contribution to an emancipatory educational process through schooling.

In physical education, the development of an inquiry-oriented approach to teacher education may be assisted by what Hendry (1976) has described as physical education's "marginality" in the school curriculum. While this circumstance may work against the physical education profession in some contexts, it can provide physical educators with a degree of autonomy rarely enjoyed by other school subjects caught up in the straightjacket of syllabuses, examinations, and other accountability procedures. This autonomy can be beneficially employed by teacher educators to encourage an experimental and critical consciousness in their students with less fear of retribution if things don't always work out. It may be that teachers will then see a way of enhancing their status in the school curriculum without being co-opted into the repressive examinations/accountability oriented systems (see Kirk & Smith, in press).

Barriers within physical education will need to be overcome, however, before an inquiry-oriented approach can become a reality in some teacher education institutions. Siedentop (1980) has suggested that, "Physical Education has been a conservative force in a largely conservative educational establishment" (p. 41). This is the problem of sedimented tradition mentioned earlier. There is in addition what S.J. Smith (1982) has referred to as the "hidden curriculum of pedagogical research" in physical education teacher education. He argues that the curriculum of teacher education courses is underwritten by a "science of management," which is in turn reproduced by teachers as a mechanization of human existence through the physical education curriculum. This version of "positivism" (Halfpenny, 1982) is clearly at odds with a critical pedagogy because, as Smith suggests, it denies human beings the fact of consciousness and so the possibility of ever acting in a transformative capacity. This combination of conservatism and positivism represents a major force that may work against the development of a critical pedagogy in physical education teacher education.

In addition, the development of a critical pedagogy cannot be a panacea for all the problems that afflict mass schooling. Clearly, teachers' influence in schools is mediated by many factors in the school environment and in the wider structures of society. This does not mean, however, that teachers have no role to play in the process of educational development and change. Teacher education should be concerned with producing teachers who are critically aware of the complexities of the educational process, of their contribution to this process, and of the potential for change. This need for awareness necessarily involves politicizing the notion of schooling within teacher education courses, not because schooling ought to be subject to political influence but precisely because we need to guard against the use of schooling as an agency of social control and as a representative and perpetrator of vested interests.

Stenhouse (1975) has argued that teachers are the mediators of educational goods, the living link between what society hopes will happen through the process of schooling and the eventual outcome in terms of what pupils learn and of the people they become. Teachers are, then, placed in a special and significant role in the educational process; it must be an important part of the teacher educator's task to ensure, as far as possible, that they are worthy of this responsibility.

Notes

1   See, however, Zeichner (1980, 1981). Writers like Almond (1983) and Tinning (1985b) may wish to argue that their work is inquiry-oriented. However, as I hope to show, it is probably closer to the action-research approach than the model I am advocating here.

2   Although this paper is not a descriptive account of any existent programs, it does represent a rationale for the teacher education program currently being developed in the Department of Human Movement Studies, University of Queensland.

3   Or what Doyle and Ponder (1977–78) have called "the practicality ethic."

4   Siedentop (1982) has made a similar point.

5   Lakomski (1984) makes the same point in relation to "new directions" sociology of education and Bordieu's and Passeron's "theory of symbolic violence."

6   I will have more to say about structure/agency below.

7   Barrow (1984, pp. 259–260) makes the same point, although in both cases this criticism is not substantiated to any satisfactory degree.

8   On this issue, Hargreaves' criticisms *are* well substantiated. See Hammersley (1985), who suggests that not only are conceptual studies in need of empirical grounding but

that many empirical (particularly ethnographic) studies lack theoretical direction and coherence.

9   The 15-year follow-up study by L.M. Smith et al. (1982) of the original study of Kensington (Smith & Keith, 1971) provides an interesting insight into these issues, and also shows how sedimented traditions in society at large penetrated and reshaped in subtle ways the original Kensington ideology of child-centered education.

10   See Woods (1979) for an illustration of this problem.

11   The generalizability of knowledge, if it is to be useful to teachers, is less likely to derive from computations of probability than from contextualized accounts of practice by other teachers that rings true within the reader's own biography of experience. See Stenhouse (1978) for a detailed discussion of this distinction between predictive and retrospective generalization.

References

Apple, M.W. (1976). Commonsense categories and curriculum thought. In R. Dale, G. Esland, & M. MacDonald (Eds.), *Schooling and capitalism* (pp. 174–184). London: Routledge & Kegan Paul.

Apple, M.W., & Weis, L. (1985). Ideology and schooling. *Education and Society*, **3**(1), 45–63.

Almond, L. (1983). *Teaching games for action research*. Paper presented at the AIESEP International Congress for Teaching Team Sports, Rome.

Barrow, R. (1984). *Giving teaching back to teachers: A critical introduction to curriculum theory*. Sussex: Wheatsheaf Books.

Bates, R.J. (1981). What can the new sociology of education do for teachers? *Discourse*, **1**(2), 41–53.

Berger, P., & Luckmann, T. (1971). *The social construction of reality*. London: Penguin Books.

Brock-Ulte, B. (1980). What is educational action research? *Classroom Action Research Network Bulletin*, **4** (Summer).

Bullough, R.V., Gitlin, A.D., & Goldstein, S.L. (1984). Ideology, teacher role, and resistance. *Teachers College Record*, **86**(2), 339–358.

Bullough, R.V., & Gitlin, A.D. (1985). Beyond control: Rethinking teacher resistance. *Education and Society*, **3**(1), 65–73.

Delamont, S. (1976). *Interaction in the classroom*. London: Methuen.

Doyle, W., & Ponder, G.A. (1977–78). The practicality ethic in teacher decision-making. *Interchange*, **8**(3).

Dunkin, M.J., & Biddle, B.J. (1974). *The study of teaching*. New York: Holt, Rinehart & Winston.

Elliot, J. (1978). What is action-research in schools? *Journal of Curriculum Studies*, **10**(4), 355–357.

Elliot, J., & Adelman, C. (1973). Reflecting where the action is: The design of the Ford Teaching Project. *Education for Teaching*, **92**, 8–20.

Entwistle, H. (1969). Theoretical and practical learning. *British Journal of Educational Studies*, **17**, 117–128.

Giddens, A. (1976). *New rules of sociological method*. London: Hutchinson.

Giddens, A. (1979). *Central problems in social theory*. London: MacMillan.

Giddens, A. (1982). *Profiles and critiques*. Berkeley: University of California Press.

Giroux, H. (1981). *Ideology, culture, and the process of schooling*. London: Falmer.

Goodson, I.F., & Ball, S.J. (1984). *Defining the curriculum: Histories & ethnographies*. London: Falmer.

Grundy, S. (1982). Three modes of action research. *Curriculum Perspectives*, **2**(3), 23–34.

Grundy, S., & Kemmis, S. (1981). *Educational action research in Australia: The state of the art*. Paper presented at the Annual Meeting of the AARE, Adelaide.

Halfpenny, P. (1982). *Positivism and sociology*. London: George Allen & Unwin.

Hammersley, H. (1985). From ethnography to theory: A programme and paradigm in the sociology of education. *Sociology*, **19**(2), 244–259.

Hammersley, M., & Hargreaves, A. (Eds.) (1983). *Curriculum practice: Some sociological case studies*. London: Falmer.

Hamilton, D. (1977). In search of structure: A case study of a new Scottish open-plan primary school. *SCRE Publication 68*. London: Hodder & Stoughton.

Hargreaves, A. (1982a). The rhetoric of school-centred innovation. *Journal of Curriculum Studies*, **14**(3).

Hargreaves, A. (1982b). Resistance and relative autonomy theories. Problems of distortion and incoherence in recent Marxist analyses of education. *British Journal of the Sociology of Education*, **3**(2), 107–126.

Hendry, L. (1976). Survival in a marginal role: The professional identity of the P.E. teacher. In W. Whitehead & L. Hendry, *Teaching physical education in England—Description and analysis* (pp. 89–102). London: Lepus.

Jackson, P. (1968). *Life in classrooms*. New York: Holt, Rinehart & Winston.

Karier, C. (1976). Business values and the educational state. In R. Dale, G. Esland, & M. MacDonald (Eds.), *Schooling and capitalism*. London: RKP.

Kirk, D., & Smith, S.J. (in press). How objective are ROSBA objectives? A critique of objectivism in curriculum design. *Curriculum Perspectives*.

Lakomski, G. (1984). On agency and structure: Pierre Bourdieu and Jean-Claude Passeron's theory of symbolic violence. *Curriculum Inquiry*, **14**(2), 151–163.

Leiberman, A., & Griffin, G.A. (1976). Educational change: Inquiry into problems of implementation. *Teachers College Record*, **77**(3), 416–423.

Locke, L.F. (1982). Research on teaching physical activity: A modest celebration. In M.L. Howell & J.E. Saunders (Eds.), *Proceedings of the VII Commonwealth and International Conference on Sport, Physical Education, Recreation and Dance* (Vol. 6, pp. 189–198).

MacDonald, B., & Walker, R. (1974). *SAFARI papers—Innovation, evaluation and research, and the problem of control*. Centre for Applied Research in Education, University of East Anglia, Norwich, England.

MacDonald, B., & Walker, R. (1976). *Changing the curriculum*. London: Open Books.

Mangan, J. (1984). *Physical education: Prejudices, paradoxes, priorities and possibilities*. The "Philip Law Lecture," Philip Institute of Technology, Victoria, Australia.

McNeil, L. (1981). On the possibility of teachers as the source of an emancipatory pedagogy: A response to Henry Giroux. *Curriculum Inquiry*, **11**(3), 205–210.

Mills, C.W. (1970). *The sociological imagination*. Pelican Books. (First published 1959).

Nixon, J. (Ed.) (1981). *A teacher's guide to action research*. London: Grant McIntyre.

Olson, J. (1983). Guide writing as advice giving: Learning the classroom language. *Journal of Curriculum Studies*, **15**(1), 17–25.

Pinar, W.F. (1978). The reconceptualization of curriculum studies. *Journal of Curriculum Studies*, **19**(3), 205–214.

Pollard, A. (1984). Ethnography and social policy for classroom practice. In L. Barton & S. Walker (Eds.), *Social crisis and educational research* (pp. 171–199). London: Croom Helm.

Reid, W.A. (1978). *Thinking about the curriculum*. London: Routledge & Kegan Paul.

Renshaw, P. (1976). Human movement studies and the curriculum. In J. Kane (Ed.), *Curriculum development in physical education* (pp. 46–69). London: Crosby, Lockwood, Staples.

Saunders, J. (1980). Theoretical bases for methods of physical education courses at tertiary level. In L. McGill (Ed.), *Concept of teaching and coaching* (pp. 5–22). Kingswood: ACHPER.

Siedentop, D. (1980). Physical education curriculum: An analysis of the past. *Journal of Physical Education and Recreation*, **51**(8), 40–41, 50.

Siedentop, D. (1982). *Developing teaching skills in physical education* (2nd ed.). Palo Alto: Mayfield.

Small, R. (1978). Educational praxis. *Educational Theory*, **28**(3), 214–222.

Smith, L.M., & Geoffrey, W. (1968). *The complexities of an urban classroom*. New York: Holt, Rinehart & Winston.

Smith, L.M., & Keith, P.M. (1971). *Anatomy of educational innovation: An organizational analysis of an elementary school*. New York: Wiley & Sons.

Smith, L.M., Prunty, J., Dwyer, D., & Kleine, P. (1982). *Kensington revisited: A fifteen year follow-up of an innovative school and its faculty*. Washington DC: NIE.

Smith, S.J. (1982). The hidden curriculum of pedagogical research in physical education. In M.L. Howell & J.E. Saunders (Eds.), *Proceedings of the VII Commonwealth and International Conference on Sport, Physical Education, Recreation and Dance* (Vol. 6, pp. 231–238).

Smith, S.J. (1985). The rhetoric and reality of teacher education: Towards a praxis model. *The Australian Journal of Teacher Education*, **10**(1), 18–33.

Smyth, W.J. (1984). Toward a "critical consciousness" in the instructional supervision of experienced teachers. *Curriculum Inquiry*, **14**(4), 425–436.

Stenhouse, L. (1975). *An introduction to curriculum research and development*. London: Heinemann Educational Books.

Stenhouse, L. (1978). Case study and case records: Towards a contemporary history of education. *British Educational Research Journal*, **4**(2), 21–39.

Stenhouse, L. (1979). *Research as a basis for teaching*. Inaugural Lecture, University of East Anglia, England.

Stenhouse, L. (Ed.) (1980). *Curriculum research and development in action*. London: Heinemann Educational Books.

Thompson, I. (1983). The training and status of physical education teachers in Scotland 1872–1939. *Physical Education Review*, **6**(1), 26–41.

Tikunoff, W.J., Ward, B.A., & Griffin, G.A. (1979). *Interactive research and development on teaching study: Final report*. San Francisco: Far West Laboratory for Educational Research and Development.

Tinning, R. (1985a). *Student teaching and the pedagogy of necessity*. Paper presented at the AIESEP International Conference on Research in Physical Education and Sport, Adelphi University, New York.

Tinning, R. (1985b). *Beyond the development of a utilitarian teaching perspective: An Australian case study of action research in teacher preparation*. Paper presented at the AIESEP International Conference on Research in Physical Education and Sport, Adelphi University, New York.

Tripp, D.H. (1984). Life in a tenured (curriculum) position. *Curriculum Perspectives*, **4**(2), 59–62.

Turney, C., Clift, J.C., Dunkin, M.J., & Trail, R.D. (1973). *Microteaching: Research, theory and practice*. Sydney: University Press.

Tyler, R. (1949). *Basic principles of curriculum and instruction*. Chicago: University Press.

Walker, J.C. (1985). Rebels with our applause? A critique of resistance theory in Paul Willis's ethnography of schooling. *Journal of Education*, **167**(2), 63–83.

Ward, E., & Hardman, K. (1978). The influence of values on the role perception of men physical education teachers. *Physical Education Review*, **1**(1), 59–70.

Woods, P. (1979). *The divided school*. London: Routledge & Kegan Paul.

Woods, P. (1984). Teacher, self and curriculum. In I.F. Goodson & S.J. Ball, *Defining the curriculum: Histories and ethnographies* (pp. 239–261). London: Falmer.

Woods, P. (1985). Sociology, ethnography and teacher practice. *Teaching and Teacher Education*, 1(1), 51–62.

Young, M.F.D. (1971). An approach to the study of curricula as socially organized knowledge. In M.F.D. Young (Ed.), *Knowledge and control* (pp. 19–46). London: Collier-MacMillan.

Young, M.F.D. (1976). Curriculum change: Limits and possibilities. In R. Dale, G. Esland, & M. MacDonald (Eds.), *Schooling and capitalism*. London: RKP.

Zeichner, K. (1980). Myths and realities: Field based experiences in preservice teacher education. *Journal of Teacher Education*, 31(6), 45–55.

Zeichner, K. (1981). Reflective teaching and field-based experiences in teacher education. *Interchange*, 12, 1–12.

Zeichner, K. (1983). Alternative paradigms of teacher education. *Journal of Teacher Education*, 34(3), 3–9.

Zeichner, K., & Teitlebaum, K. (1982). Personalised and inquiry-oriented teacher education: An analysis of two approaches to the development of curriculum for field-based courses. *Journal of Education for Teaching*, 8(2), 95–117.

Kathleen M. Armour and Rebecca Duncombe

TEACHERS' CONTINUING PROFESSIONAL DEVELOPMENT IN PRIMARY PHYSICAL EDUCATION

Lessons from present and past to inform the future

Introduction: CPD in an age of accountability

> Two questions that need to be considered for any accountability system are: (a) What counts? and (b) Who is held accountable?
>
> (Linn, 2003, p. 3)

TEACHER DEVELOPMENT is widely recognised as a key ingredient of successful school improvement strategies (Reynolds & Teddlie, 2000). Thus, the provision of more and better continuing professional development (CPD) is offered as the solution to a range of problems in education (DfEE, 2001; Campbell, 2002). However, in an era defined by an increased emphasis upon accountability (Linn, 2003) there is a growing expectation that the impact of particular CPD programmes and activities will be identifiable (and measurable) in terms of clear and improved learning outcomes for pupils. Moreover, these learning outcomes are often defined narrowly within the political imperatives of current educational policy (Seashore Louis, 2001). Yet, at the same time, it is also widely acknowledged that the process of identifying measurable, causal links between teachers' professional development and impact upon pupils' learning outcomes is fraught with difficulties (Guskey & Sparks, 2002). Moreover, as Guskey (1998) points out, 'more' CPD does not necessarily mean 'better' CPD and, to compound matters, there has been 'relatively little systematic research on the effects of professional development on improvements in teaching or on student outcomes' (Garet et al., 2001, p. 917). It could be argued, therefore, that addressing Linn's (2003) questions about accountability—being clear about what counts and who is to be held accountable—is particularly important in the case of CPD.

Within that broad context, this paper focuses on CPD in physical education (PE-CPD) and, more specifically, CPD for primary school teachers within a new National PE-CPD Programme for Teachers and Others in England. A brief overview of the national programme is provided in section 2. Section 3 comprises of *vignettes* illustrating the PE-CPD experiences of three practising primary school teachers. These accounts highlight the kinds of issues teachers and schools face currently in teaching primary PE and accessing relevant CPD. The stories also raise some questions about the structure and organisation of previous (before the national programme) forms of PE-CPD and so, in section 4, key moments from the history of PE-CPD in England are detailed, focusing particularly on the ways in which earlier attempts to support teachers' learning are reproduced in the new programme. In Section 5, a summary of the international research on teacher learning and effective CPD suggests that new initiatives in PE-CPD may need to be more radical than those proposed in the new national programme if they are to deliver—and be held accountable for—major changes in the standards of teachers' and pupils' learning.

The new PE-CPD context in England

In England, PE is at the forefront of new developments in CPD. In October 2002, the government announced funding of £450 million to transform the quality of physical education, and a key element of the strategy is to fund a National PE and School Sport Professional Development Programme for Teachers (and other adults). In summary, the programme aims to reach all primary and secondary schools. It will assist schools to undertake a baseline evaluation of the quality of the outcomes of their existing PE and school sport provision, select relevant CPD from a menu of modules and resources, implement what has been learned, and then measure improvement against the baseline and in the context of the Programme objectives. It is proposed that the menu of opportunities will be flexible, will meet a diverse range of needs, and will be well supported. The framework is to be managed by a consortium of professional and charitable organisations within PE and School Sport[1] and an independent research project to evaluate the Programme has been commissioned.

The aims and objectives of the new CPD Programme are ambitious. Within the broad aim of improving the quality of teaching, coaching and learning in PE and school sport, the Programme will also seek to support a wide range of other targets to be met through PE including raising educational attainment, contributing to whole school improvement, enhancing health/physical activity links, supporting innovation, and enhancing cross-phase continuity of learning. In order to achieve these outcomes, the programme will consist of nationally developed CPD modules and resources that are locally delivered to agreed national quality assurance standards. The managing consortium will appoint Local Delivery Agencies (i.e. local authorities, universities, or some schools) who can deliver the national programme to agreed standards throughout the country. For primary schools, the CPD provision will comprise:

- a resource-pack explaining the role of CPD and the new opportunities available;
- locally-based workshops for key personnel;
- the development of a CPD action plan for staff in each school;

- access to appropriate modules (courses or resources);
- feedback and dissemination by teachers to other teachers;
- monitoring and evaluation.

Importantly, teachers will be entitled to a certain amount of 'free' CPD funded through the programme, although this will not include any teacher replacement costs incurred by schools.

At one level, therefore, it could be argued that the National PE-CPD Programme, together with the independent evaluation of its impact to ensure accountability, fit well within the broader CPD landscape. Moreover, in involving a range of professional organisations in its management and delivery, and seeking to meet not only PE-specific targets but also wider government aspirations for education, it could be argued that the programme is ideally located in contemporary political and professional agendas, thus maximising opportunities for effectiveness. As such, evaluation of its effectiveness, using the programme's identified success criteria, ought to be a relatively straightforward process. However, in practice, determining impact and effectiveness are likely to be anything but straightforward because of the multi-layered complexities inherent in at least four fundamental aspects of the whole endeavour:

- teachers and their learning (new, current and past);
- pupils and their learning (particularly that which can be attributed to specific teacher learning);
- the nature of individual school contexts;
- the nature of 'effectiveness' in the context of CPD (Craft, 1996; Loughran & Gunstone, 1997; Day, 1999).

Add to this the sheer number of overlapping projects and initiatives currently being directed at schools in England, the difficulties inherent in establishing reliable 'baselines' about teacher or pupil learning, and the problems in collecting relevant evidence that relates to any one initiative alone without 'contamination' from others (Connell *et al.*, 1995) and the picture becomes even more complex. One way into an analysis of this complexity is to examine the PE-CPD issue from the point of view of practising teachers.

Three primary teachers and their PE–CPD

Two of the following vignettes are drawn from ongoing research into primary PE-CPD, and one is an autobiographical account (Sparkes, 2000) of the experiences of one of the authors of this paper (Duncombe) who was, until recently, a primary school teacher responsible for the curriculum leadership of PE. Indeed, it was these experiences that led her to undertake research on this topic. The research took place in two case study primary schools, over the period of one school year (2002–03) and involved interviews, questionnaires, observations and action research with the whole staff in each of the schools (see Duncombe & Armour, *in press*, for further details). Although the vignettes presented here are triangulated from all the data collection methods, interviews were the main source of information. A semi-structured interviewing technique was employed (Gillham, 2000) to find out how these teachers had learnt about teaching PE throughout their careers. The interviewer used a set of predefined questions to guide the interviews but did deviate from the schedule to clarify and probe issues central to the research topic. All interviews were transcribed and then analysed by organising the data into categories and themes (Bogdan & Biklen, 1982; Ritchie & Lewis, 2003). For the purposes of this paper, the relevant data categories were: teachers' experiences of pre-service training in PE, teachers' views on their competence to teach PE, and experiences of PE-CPD and judgements about its value. The resulting vignettes, although brief, suggest that while it appears there may indeed be a need for more and better PE-CPD at the primary school level, a view supported by OFSTED (2001/2002), there are also a series of profound challenges facing the new national programme in England.

(i) *The PE coordinator*

One of the authors (Rebecca Duncombe) is a primary school teacher with two years of teaching experience who is taking time out of the classroom to do research. The first teaching post Rebecca secured required a year four (ages 7/8) class teacher with additional responsibility for coordinating PE throughout the school. To prove her worth as a PE 'specialist', she was required to have neither extra training nor experience in PE. She turned up for the interview with plenty of enthusiasm and a reasonable amount of knowledge and personal experience in netball, hockey, athletics and swimming. In fact, Rebecca had never even taught a PE lesson during teacher training without the support of a mentor teacher. Perhaps more worrying is the fact that she had received only six hours of training in PE, had only ever taught nine lessons of PE (all with support), yet was deemed sufficiently knowledgeable and experienced to lead this curriculum area and guide other staff in their teaching of PE. She couldn't help thinking that she was offered the job just because she was young, enthusiastic and, more importantly, had mentioned a willingness to run some lunchtime clubs and arrange inter-school fixtures.

Once in post, and despite being one of her favourite subjects when she was a pupil, PE was the lesson that Rebecca dreaded most. The children's behaviour seemed worse outside of the classroom, the resources were limited, safety was a nightmare, it was too cold (or too hot!), it rained, the stage was up in the hall, there were tears, there were missing PE kits. Rebecca wouldn't claim to have taught many effective lessons to her own class, yet she was still expected to lead the other staff. Because of her personal sporting experience she was confident that, despite this, she had the ability to teach reasonable games and athletics lessons, but where to start with gymnastics and dance? She felt very insecure in these areas; indeed she often ended up ditching the lesson plan to play dodge ball or going back to the classroom early because the children had 'forgotten' how to listen.

PE-CPD could have been the solution to some of these problems. However, during her time in post, and despite being the school PE coordinator, Rebecca was offered only one course related to PE—a course that focused on assessment rather than more broadly on teaching PE. Despite identifying her needs in NQT (newly qualified teacher) and performance management meetings during those two years, she could find few relevant courses. Moreover, when a course was found, she could not secure funds to attend it. She had, however, attended football, netball and athletics courses during her initial teacher training year, all in her own time and at her own expense. Rebecca regards these as good and helpful courses, and she could recall one or two ideas from them, but the impact of the learning was somewhat reduced because she was not in a teaching post at the time, so there was a long delay between the learning and practice. Reflecting on Rebecca's story, two concerns emerge. Firstly why was this teacher considered to be an acceptable candidate to lead the school in all areas of PE? Secondly, if this teacher was struggling to teach PE, how do other teachers cope, particularly those who have neither her enthusiasm nor the motivation from a personal love of sport? Perhaps the next story provides some illustration.

(ii) *The Newly Qualified Teacher (NQT)*

This is the story of Peter, an inexperienced teacher. After gaining qualified teacher status (QTS) in England, teachers enter their 'probationary' year as newly qualified teachers (NQTs). During this year they are given a mentor teacher to guide them and they are expected to reach set professional standards. They are allocated non-contact time and extra funding for professional development so, for example, they can attend courses and access funds for teacher replacements so they can watch colleagues' lessons and also have their own lessons observed. Peter was a recent appointment (2002) and had two terms' teaching experience at the beginning of the research.

Peter's story is interesting because he is one of those newly qualified teachers who, unlike the teacher in the previous story, would not describe himself as 'sporty'. Indeed, both of the other stories detail teachers who have a keen interest in sport and it is clear that this has supported them in their teaching of PE where more formal training has been lacking. Peter, however, expressed some personal interest in football, but no other areas of PE. His teacher training in PE had been very limited and, at the time of the interview, he had not been offered any additional support by the school and was clearly struggling to cope. The pre-service training received by Peter consisted of 'a couple of afternoon sessions'. He described them as being very good but felt he needed much longer; he suggested 10 or even 20 afternoon sessions. His confidence in his ability to teach PE was very low and he expressed concerns about safety; for example, what it was safe to expect the children to do, especially with the apparatus in gymnastics. In fact, he reported that he had little idea about teaching most areas of the PE national curriculum except, perhaps, football. He also highlighted the 'warm-up' as an area of PE that he knew little about and whilst he accepted that he could seek out resources to explain the principles of an effective warm up, he felt he needed to see them in practice with children. Despite this, no arrangements had been made for Peter to observe PE during his non-contact time, or have his own lessons observed. Peter's lack of knowledge and confidence also meant that he was happy to adopt lesson plans written by another teacher. Unfortunately, Peter explained that sometimes he didn't really understand them or know enough to teach them well. To compound the problem, Peter tended to arrange for his non-contact time to occur when he was scheduled to teach PE so a replacement teacher could take his PE lessons. Whilst this may have been of benefit to the children in his class, it did nothing to enhance his learning in PE and so just displaced the problem.

More positively, Peter felt that he had learned quite a lot about teaching PE through his involvement in this PE-CPD research project. He commented that being able to observe another teacher (the researcher) taking his own class had been particularly beneficial because it made everything 'real' and provided him with ideas for managing his own class. It was clear to him that he needed more activities like this to boost his fragile confidence.

(iii) *The experienced primary school teacher*

Charles is a primary school teacher with 11 years of teaching experience who has taught all Key Stage 2 year groups (ages 7–11). Despite his experience, he identified gaps in his PE teaching knowledge and felt that he lacked confidence when teaching sports where he had little personal experience. This meant, for example, that while he enjoyed teaching gymnastics, he would try to avoid teaching dance. However, unlike other teachers in the research (Duncombe & Armour, *in press*) he did not feel that teaching PE was something to fear, and he drew upon his knowledge of other areas of the curriculum and his own experience to plan and teach his PE lessons.

In terms of his professional development, Charles felt that he learnt something new about teaching PE every time he taught a lesson, and that discussions with colleagues were an important (and under-valued) source of teacher learning. He described his initial teacher training as 'sketchy' and thinks it consisted of approximately two hours every week for three terms. He could not recall the specific content of his pre-service training but did remember that it focused heavily on safety issues. Since qualifying, Charles has attended a limited number of courses; one-day courses in athletics, team games, ball games (rugby, cricket, football) and swimming. Of these, he singled out the athletics course as an example of effective CPD because it had taught him things that he would be able to use in school. Other than these formal courses, he welcomed any opportunities to watch colleagues and felt that he would be more confident to teach dance if he had the opportunity to observe colleagues or specialist teachers, or if he had access to better and more detailed resources. In addition, he recalled some whole school INSET (in-service training) days that had a PE focus but, like most of the PE courses he had attended, these were several years ago.

In discussions about effective CPD, Charles stressed the importance of ensuring that course leaders were interesting and had recent experience in the classroom. He felt that the longer people had been away from the classroom, the more out of touch they were about what was possible in school. However, both finding and funding high quality teacher replacements to enable teachers to attend courses was always problematic, as was the pressure to link professional development to the school's current development plans. In Charles' experience, these two constraints placed severe limits upon what teachers were able to access.

(iv) *Lessons for PE-CPD?*

These stories suggest that a coordinated national PE-CPD programme that is both accessible and relevant would be helpful for these teachers and others like them. However, it is also apparent that such a programme would face a number of challenges. For example: not all primary teachers are enthusiastic about teaching PE and so need to be convinced that time spent on PE-CPD will be interesting and worthwhile; low levels of PE preparation in some initial teacher training courses result in teachers with a very wide range of needs; schools struggle to release teachers from the classroom to attend professional development activities and they face an inherent tension in disrupting pupils' learning in order to improve it; teachers learn in a wide range of ways including both formal and informal contexts; and CPD providers need to be able to tailor their activities to teachers' very specific needs and the exigencies of individual school contexts. Moreover, Charles is not alone in hoping that PE-CPD providers will be realistic and practical in their approach (Armour & Yelling, 2004). What is clear is that the issues raised by these stories are not new; they are the product of the history of previous attempts to support teachers' learning in PE and so whereas a new funded, national, coordinated CPD programme for PE is to be welcomed, it is also essential that it does not simply repeat earlier mistakes. It is suggested, therefore, that an analysis of the history of PE-CPD can provide valuable insights into the potential impact of new programmes and initiatives.

PE-CPD since 1870 or . . . the more things change . . .

This is not intended to be a full account of the history of primary education and physical education in England (detailed accounts can be found in McIntosh, 1952; McIntosh *et al*, 1981, Kirk, 1992). Rather, the focus is specifically upon key moments from the history of primary PE-CPD within the broader history of education and PE. The account begins in 1870 with the Forster Education Act because this act introduced compulsory schooling for children aged 5–13 and although there was no mention of PE, permission was granted for boys to participate in drill and this was extended to girls in 1873. Her Majesty's Inspectors (HMI) then played a part in influencing teachers' practices by identifying the potential health benefits of PE for children and putting forward three recommendations: firstly that physical training should be part of the payment by results scheme;[2] secondly that health should be studied as a subject at school; and thirdly that Physical Training (PT) should become compulsory in teacher training (Kirk, 1992). Interestingly, it was found to be difficult to assess physical education in terms of the 'payment by results' scheme; after all, what were the 'results' to be, so the problem was solved by paying schools the higher grant for 'organisation and discipline'. It is worth noting the enduring nature of the assumed links between PE and pupil discipline and the echoes of these links in the new national CPD programme that will seek to: 'improve the understanding of how high quality PE and school sport can be used as a tool for whole school improvement, particularly in terms of attendance, behaviour management and attainment' (DfES/DCMS, 2003, p. 12). At the same time, it is also interesting to note comments in Rebecca's story (vignette 1) about poor (or perhaps different) pupil behaviour in PE lessons, as compared to the classroom, and the problems this presented.

At the end of the nineteenth century, when PE started to focus less on military drill and more on gymnastics, the Ling system of Swedish gymnastics became popular with teachers and, as a result, the Ling Association was formed in 1899 to support its use in schools: 'Its purpose was to band together teachers trained in the Swedish system to protect and improve their status and to arrange meetings and holiday courses' (McIntosh *et al.*, 1981, p. 207). The Ling Association was, therefore, an important CPD provider during this period. They supported teachers by running courses and providing some demonstration PE lessons to enable teachers to observe 'experts' teaching the system:

> After the first post-war demonstration organised by the Ling Association in the Albert Hall in 1921 they were held frequently up and down the country, and helped to popularise the gymnastic side of education.
>
> (McIntosh, 1952, p. 203)

At this time, it was recognised that the teacher of PE needed more specialist PE knowledge but also needed to be, primarily, an educational expert able to understand children as learners across the curriculum, another tension that can still be recognised today and that has impacted upon teacher learning in PE. It could also be argued that the national CPD programme ought to recognise this tension in its planning and delivery.

The 1919 syllabus and a revision in 1922, changed the face of physical education further by recognising the benefits of dance and games as well as promoting a less rigid style of gymnastics (Kirk, 1992). Particularly important at this time were the links between PE and health that were becoming prominent. Similar to today (although addressing very different health issues) PE was viewed as a form of preventative medicine in order to justify its costs, and dramatic claims were made for the benefits of a healthy body: 'A healthy and vigorous body is essential to a healthy and vigorous mind (Welpton, 1922, p. 92). Even more interesting are Welpton's comments about the essential components of any comprehensive system of physical training: elements of health and strength, skill, thinking/intelligence, challenge and personal/social education. The similarities with the definition of high quality PE that underpins the new CPD programme are remarkable (DfES/DCMS, 2003, pp. 3–4). Other groups besides the Ling Association provided courses and conferences for teachers during this period, for example governing bodies of sport (McIntosh et al., 1981) and local education authorities. Sheffield is one example:

> H.A. Cole was appointed Superintendent of Physical Training in 1913 and he was given wide duties in supervising work in the city's day and evening schools and in training teachers, pupil teachers, and students at the City Training College and at the University. Between Easter 1913, and the end of 1914, 600 teachers in Sheffield attended short courses.
>
> (McIntosh, 1952, p. 158)

There were also summer courses provided by the Board of Education from 1915 to 1919 to support and extend the teaching of Swedish gymnastics. The interesting observation to make here is that the mix of professional development providers for PE evident at that time (professional organisations, sports governing bodies, local authority and central government) closely mirrors that in operation today, including the partnership responsible for delivering the new national CPD programme.

The Hadow Report in 1926 signalled a change in the organisation of education and introduced the notion of different forms of schooling for under and over 11-year old pupils (a system that endures in much of England today). The 1919 PE syllabus was unsuitable for the new format of schooling and so, in 1933, a new syllabus was published (Board of Education, 1933). It was organised into different sections for pupils under and over 11 years of age. Reflecting the continuing links between PE and health, the syllabus recommended daily exercise as a necessity for growing children and it outlined the two essential components of successful practice: 'A practical syllabus and a competent teacher are the first essentials necessary for useful training' (Board of Education, 1933, p. 18). However, as the syllabus also pointed out, teachers need to have a thorough understanding of the effects of PE on the child and although this can be developed through training and experience, it requires teachers to have a 'living interest' in physical education (p. 20). Moreover, the syllabus promotes the notion of a reflective teacher: 'It is incumbent on every teacher to criticise the results of her own teaching' (p. 20). Looking at the contemporary context for primary PE in England, it could be argued that there is, in place, a practical syllabus (the National Curriculum) and now a new national CPD programme that has the potential to help teachers to become competent. Yet, it is unclear how either will create a 'living interest' in PE among generalist primary teachers who are attempting to teach many areas of the curriculum particularly, as in the case of Peter in vignette 2, where they have little personal interest in physical activity or sport.

The 1933 syllabus endured for over twenty years; however, in 1952, dramatic changes took place with the publication of a new type of syllabus. Two books were produced in a new format that more closely adhered to the developing progressive educational theories of the time. The first, 'Moving and Growing', was a short study of physical movement and growing children including information on growth, development, the nature of the child and human movement. The second, 'Planning the Programme', attempted to translate some of the movement concepts into a more concrete form to help teachers to plan lessons. In a much more flexible approach than in the 1933 syllabus, teachers were expected to plan their lessons based on an analysis of their pupils' particular needs. However, this was not universally welcomed, particularly for young and less experienced teachers:

> All the time [in reading the new syllabus] one has the feeling that the writers are automatically assuming that all teachers of PE are (a) full time specialists and (b) burning with enthusiasm for the subject, which of course is far from true.
>
> (Edmundson, 1956, p. 5)

Nor, of course, is it true today, as the earlier teachers' stories remind us. Moreover, this was a development that was supported by more female than male teachers. As Kirk (1992, p. 69) argues 'the stage was set for a debate between male and female physical educators'. However, both generally and in PE, progressive teaching approaches were gaining in popularity culminating, in 1967, in the publication of the Plowden report. For PE, this Report extended what had been suggested in the 1952 syllabus and highlighted the expressive opportunities that dance and 'movement' could offer. It is interesting to note that Charles, the teacher in vignette 3, appears to support such a view, but he feels ill-equipped to provide his pupils with such opportunities.

A milestone in the history of CPD was the 1972 government report on professional development for teachers: The James Report. This was the first official recommendation for in-service training for all teachers:

> The education or training of teachers was seen as falling into three consecutive stages or cycles: the first, personal education, the second, pre-service training and induction, the third, in-service education and training. The Committee gave the last first priority, and recommended that: 'All teachers in schools and full-time staff in further education colleges should be entitled to release with pay for in-service education and training on a scale equivalent to no less than one school term in every seven years of service . . . and as soon as possible the entitlement should be written into a teacher's contract of service'.
>
> (Browne, 1979, p. 213)

The James Report highlighted the necessity of establishing a coordinated, comprehensive and continuous system of high quality professional development. Thus it was anticipated that: 'Throughout a teacher's career the third cycle (concerning in-service training) would provide a wide range of relevant courses and activities' (Evans, 1985, p. 185). However, although the James Report set the wheels in motion for much of the professional development that followed (Bradley, 1991) it has been argued that its full promise has never been realised. Instead, as was vividly illustrated in the teacher vignettes, CPD has remained patchy and uncoordinated, is of variable quality, and suffers from enduring issues of teacher access (Smith, 1999).

The next major event in educational history came in 1988 with the Education Reform Act (ERA). This paved the way for a National Curriculum that, albeit with revisions, is still in place today. For professional development, whole school INSET days were introduced in 1986 where the cascade process was a favoured training strategy in which 'some "super trainers" passed the message to some ordinary trainers who passed it on to someone from each school who passed it on to the rest' (Bradley, 1991, p. 85). This same cascade training approach is a key part of the delivery strategy of the new national PE-CPD programme, however, it is rarely as effective in practice as theory might suggest (Craft, 1996). More recently, Teacher Appraisal (Pluckrose, 1987), Induction Year and, latterly, Performance Management policies have been important on the professional development landscape as schools seek to 'develop' their teachers in the context of national standards and individual school missions. The role of the inspection service (OFSTED—HMI prior to 1992) has also played its part in influencing professional development. Increased emphasis upon school accountability, and public access to OFSTED reports, have ensured that unprecedented levels of preparation precede an inspection, and recommendations following it, of necessity, provide a focus for school development (Porter & Ware, 1997; Tosey & Nicholls, 1999) and are likely to influence the kinds of CPD activities that schools will fund. This may help to explain Charles' comments (in the third teacher vignette) about only being able to access CPD that was linked to a school's current development plan.

Professional development providers for PE in the 1970s and 1980s were still largely drawn from professional associations, sports governing bodies, and local and central government. For example, The Ling Association (which is now known as PEA-UK)

> had long supported the concept of in-service education being well aware that, in a rapidly changing world, teachers could not hope to provide an up-to-date professional service based solely on their initial training. For many years it had actively promoted the idea by the provision of its conferences and courses.
>
> (Bailey & Vamplew, 1999, p. 109)

From 1970 onwards, Local Education Authorities were also very active as they provided INSET for their teachers and developed comprehensive Local Advisory Services to support teachers' learning in many curriculum areas. Thus, it was a well-established career route for PE teachers to become local authority advisors supporting teachers in local schools. Indeed, these advisors became both active and influential, and a number of LEAs (for example, Kent, Durham and Leicestershire) produced detailed curriculum guidelines and resources that were made available nationally. However, as the period progressed, problems with this form of PE-CPD emerged and these were compounded when professional development budgets were transferred from LEAs to individual schools: 'Teachers were finding "increasing difficulty" in obtaining financial support from local education authorities to support their attendance . . .' (Bailey & Vamplew, 1999, p. 109). In addition to this, Evans and Penney (1994) point out that the role of the local authority advisory service switched after the 1988 Education Reform Act from advice to monitoring and inspection, thus heralding a fundamental change in its original supportive philosophy. It is also worth noting that HMI expressed concerns about the quality of primary PE during much of this period (HMI 1978; 1982; 1985); further evidence, perhaps, that the existing systems were not always effective. As a direct result of the changes in funding and philosophy, LEA advisory services shrank, and while some former advisors moved more fully into inspection roles, others became independent CPD providers acting, for example, as private consultants to schools, local authorities and professional organisations. It is interesting to note, therefore, that some of these same consultants are likely to deliver parts of the National PE-CPD programme. It is also intriguing to note that in 1992:

> a successful bid was made to the Sports Council for major funding to work with the standing conference on Physical Education and the British Association of Advisors and Lecturers in Physical Education to develop a national, coordinated framework for the development of resources and in-service training for teachers.
>
> (Bailey & Vamplew, 1999, p. 110)

Members of these groups are also involved in the design and management of the new national PE-CPD programme. Questions might be asked, therefore, about the ways in which the new programme will differ from previous ventures undertaken by similar groups.

As well as providing courses and conferences for teachers, professional associations and commercial groups have also produced publications to keep teachers informed. Examples include the British Journal of Teaching Physical Education that also had a popular 'Primary Focus' supplement (Bailey & Vamplew, 1999) and The Bulletin of PE. There are also several academic publications available that report the findings of national and international research on physical education. However, it is difficult to imagine many primary school teachers accessing such resources. Of more immediate practical significance for teachers, perhaps, is the government body: the Qualifications and Curriculum Authority (QCA) and its publications, particularly the PE & School Sport website (www.qca.org.uk/pess). The QCA is responsible for supporting the delivery of the National Curriculum and so, arguably, offers particularly valuable support to teachers because it links advice on lesson planning and delivery to the official planning, assessment and inspection frameworks.

In 2001, the government produced another general CPD strategy: Learning and Teaching: A Strategy for Professional Development (DfEE). This strategy appeared to echo many of the sentiments of the earlier James Report, including funding for teachers to take sabbaticals and also to undertake research on their practice in the form of Best Practice Research Scholarships. PE teachers have participated in this scheme but, illustrating Smith's (1999) comments about the history of CPD being one of discontinuity, it is interesting to note that the scheme is shortly to be scrapped. However, in what could be viewed as a significant development in enhancing the quality of PE-CPD in England, the government has recently established a Professional Development Board for Physical Education (PDB-PE) as a pilot for other curriculum areas:

> The PDB-PE (England) has been established to assure the quality of Continuing Professional Development of all teachers of physical education for the benefit of young people and to raise standards in physical education . . . The role of the board is to provide a CPD framework embracing the range of career development routes . . . to design and implement a strategy for the quality assurance of professional development provision for teachers of physical education.
>
> (PDB-PE promotional literature, 2003)

The professional bodies represented on this board overlap with those responsible for the new national PE-CPD programme, and yet it is anticipated that the PDB-PE will form part of the quality assurance mechanism for the programme. Another important development since 1997 has been the introduction of Specialist Sports Colleges (SSCs).[3] This has resulted in significant opportunities for primary PE-CPD. All SSCs have a responsibility for the quality of PE in their local schools, including primary schools, and so part of their role is to provide professional development for primary teachers. The Youth Sport Trust, a charity established in 1994, is responsible for SSCs, coordinating training and support for its teachers across a wide range of areas. Interestingly, the Trust also forms part of the consortium responsible for the national PE-CPD programme and it has representation on the PDB-PE. Although none of these links and overlaps necessarily present a problem for quality assurance or accountability, it could be argued that this is an issue for all affected groups to recognise and manage explicitly. Finally, but not exhaustively, it is envisaged that sports coaches will become more closely linked to PE teachers in the future: 'The possibility of coaches taking on activities currently undertaken by teachers has also been explicitly recognised . . .' (DfEE/DCMS, 2003, p. 15). Sports coach UK is a member of the consortium responsible for the national programme thus cementing the links. In theory, therefore, it could be argued that we have moved some way from the historical conflict between physical education and sport (Sage, 1996; Penney & Evans, 1997). However, Kirk (2002, p. 4) points out that 'there is very little evidence to suggest that, since the first appearance of sport-based physical education in universal secondary schooling, programs have been able to achieve their aim of promoting life-long participation', and this may be an important warning for the national CPD programme.

This section has detailed the historical background to the new national PE-CPD programme and, in reflecting upon the events of history, at least three things are immediately striking. The first is that physical education has been somewhere like this before, at least in terms of establishing a national programme and with regard to some of the key partners involved in its management and delivery. A question to be asked, therefore, is what will be different this time? The second issue to emerge is that ambitious aspirations for PE have been held throughout its history, for example, using PE as a form of behaviour management and linking PE to health. At the same time, there is little robust evidence from history to suggest that PE can achieve such outcomes (Kirk, 1992) making accountability a key issue for the future. Thirdly, it is difficult to argue with Smith's (1999) comment that 'the history of the management of the CPD of teachers is . . . fraught with issues of discontinuity and ineffectiveness' (p. 86). In the case of PE and its more recent history, this might be because some CPD initiatives have focused on developing structures to manage access to existing forms of CPD, rather than seeking to devise new structures and learning processes to support teachers' learning more effectively. Indeed, it could be argued that the new national PE-CPD programme is located somewhere between these two positions; some elements of the process are new, but the programme also intends to draw upon existing provision wherever possible. The penultimate area for discussion, therefore, is: what do we know about the nature and structure of effective CPD and in what ways does the national programme reflect that knowledge?

Lessons learned: effective teacher learning, effective PE-CPD

There is a vast body of international research literature on CPD and teacher learning, of which this is only a brief overview. Darling Hammond and McLaughlin (1995, p. 1) suggest that effective professional development 'involves teachers both as learners and as teachers and allows them to struggle with the uncertainties that accompany each role'. Other research has sought to identify 'principles' or characteristics of effective CPD. For example, the National Partnership for Excellence and Accountability in Teaching in the USA (NPEAT, 1998) claims that the most effective professional development:

- Focuses on analyses of student learning, especially the examination of differences between actual student learning outcomes and goals and standards for student learning;
- Involves teachers identifying their own training needs and developing learning experiences to meet those needs;
- Is school based and embedded in teachers' daily work;
- Is organised around collaborative problem solving;
- Is continuous and ongoing with follow up and support for further learning;
- Incorporates evaluation of multiple sources of data detailing student learning and teacher instructional practices;
- Provides opportunities for teachers to link the theory that underlines knowledge and skills they are learning;
- Is connected to a comprehensive change process focused upon improved student learning.

More recently, the National Foundation for Educational Research in the UK (NFER, 2001) found that CPD was most effective when teachers had some autonomy over the direction of their personal development, when CPD activities were delivered with appropriate expertise, and when they contained challenging and up-to-date content that was relevant to classroom practice. It was still found to be difficult, however, to make clear links between CPD and 'impact' upon teachers' practices and pupil earning. Stein *et al.* (1999) point out that if educational standards are to rise dramatically, then improved teacher learning is needed and this will require new forms of CPD. Thus, Garet *et al.* (2001) argue for a move away from traditional forms of CPD and towards 'reform' types that typically take place within the school day, involve collective participation of teachers from the same school or group of schools, and are integrated into practice in the form of study groups, mentoring and coaching. Garet *et al.* argue that these forms of learning are easier to sustain over time and are likely to result in better connections between new learning and existing practice. Similarly, Guskey (2002) argues for an alternative model of professional development. He claims that it is pointless to attempt to change teachers' attitudes and beliefs in the hope that this will lead to changes in practice. Rather, teachers are more likely to change beliefs *after* they have seen the impact of an initiative upon pupils. McLaughlin and Zarrow (2001) follow a similar theme, arguing that many existing models of CPD are 'substantively and strategically incomplete' because they are missing '*data and evidence* about practice and policies at school and classroom levels' (pp. 99–100). There are links here with the work of Newmann *et al.* (1996) in the USA. Their five-year study into the restructuring of schools and the impacts upon teachers' and pupils' learning also resulted in a plea for teachers to focus closely upon their pupils' achievement.

Smith (1999) argues that in England, until recently, the dominant government-sponsored mode of CPD was largely traditional: 'externally designed and delivered off-site courses' but that 'such a model . . . fails to encourage the collaboration, participation and empowerment of teachers . . .' (p. 94). However, there are signs that these views are changing. For example OFSTED (2002, p. 11) has claimed:

> the narrow perceptions that professional development always involves off-site activity, such as attendance at a course hosted by the LEA, is gradually being replaced by a wider and more comprehensive view of CPD.

It is unclear whether this claim has yet been realised in practice. In the case of PE-CPD, there is some evidence that a traditional model has prevailed, and that a sports focus predominates (Armour & Yelling, 2004). However, the three primary teachers in section three of this paper provided fascinating insights into their requirements, echoing the literature on effective CPD; i.e. the need for teacher learning to be closely linked to practice (Rebecca); the need for school-based CPD with own pupils (Peter); and the need for CPD providers to be realistic (Charles). Moreover, they are not unusual teachers as similar comments were made in a recent study by secondary PE teachers (Armour & Yelling, 2004). So, in attempting to map the new PE-CPD programme against the criteria for effective CPD, it could be concluded that the programme has made clear efforts to take a 'reform' approach in Garet *et al.*'s (2001) terms while retaining elements of a traditional approach. Yet, the objectives and success criteria for this CPD programme are ambitious, seeking major changes in the quality of teachers' and pupils' learning. At the same time, historical evidence suggests that while it is apparent that PE-CPD courses have been provided for teachers for many years, robust evidence about major impacts upon practice is difficult to discern. Thus, finally, this discussion turns to where it began: accountability.

Lessons learned? Accountability and shared responsibility

One outcome of the increased government funding for PE in England has been the added emphasis upon accountability. Perhaps more than at any time in its history, the PE profession is being asked not only to clarify its knowledge claims, but also to provide robust evidence of the impact of its programmes upon pupils both within PE and more broadly. If PE programmes are funded but are seen to 'fail', there may be problems securing continued or further funding. In the case of the new PE-CPD programme, it could be argued that the answers to Linn's (2003) question (what counts? and who is to be held accountable?) are clear: the managing consortium has defined its objectives and success criteria and, by identifying targets, holds itself accountable for their delivery. However, as Linn also argues 'accountability must entail broadly shared responsibility . . . to include students, teachers, school administrators, parents, and policymakers . . . researchers also need to share responsibility' (p. 3). This is an important perspective given the scale of the changes proposed by the new PE-CPD programme. It is unlikely that the programme will succeed unless pupils see the point of learning, teachers have enough interest (a 'living interest'?) in PE to learn new practices and improve old ones, schools recognise the value of PE, parents are supportive, and policy-makers realise that large-scale social change takes time to effect (Connell & Kubisch, 1998). Moreover, researchers have identified models of teacher learning that have the potential to be effective, while urging caution in viewing the links between teacher and pupil learning as simple or easily measurable (Guskey & Sparks, 2002). The message for any new CPD initiative is, therefore, quite clear. Dramatic improvements in the standards of teachers' and pupils' learning are likely to require dramatic changes in CPD and strong support from a range of stakeholders. Thus, each of these stakeholders also bears some responsibility for the success or failure of the programme, and so perhaps shares responsibility for accountability. Thus, two questions remain for the new PE-CPD programme in England: is it sufficiently different from previous initiatives to make a real difference; and how can accountability be properly shared? We intend to explore these issues as the programme develops.

Conclusion

This paper has considered the contemporary policy and research context for teachers' professional development and has outlined, as an example, a new national PE-CPD programme to be made available to teachers of PE at all levels of schooling in England. The discussion has focused specifically upon primary PE as this is, arguably, a phase where enhanced professional development for teachers is most needed. Accounts of the PE-CPD experiences of three primary school teachers raised a number of questions about previous and existing CPD structures. An historical analysis of PE-CPD from 1870 provided some answers and it was noted that, as was the case with professional development generally, PE-CPD has been characterised by fragmentation. It also became clear that there are similarities between the new national programme and previous programmes, suggesting that there may be important lessons to be learnt from their study. Finally, an analysis of the contemporary literature on effective CPD has raised the thorny issue of accountability in professional development. The new PE-CPD programme has identified ambitious outcomes for which it will be held accountable. It is argued that such outcomes are inherently complex and multi-faceted and that it may be wise for the programme to seek to share more widely the responsibility for their delivery.

Acknowledgements

The authors would like to express their thanks to the teachers who participated in the case study research, the reviewer who provided valuable feedback on an earlier version of the paper, and the School of Sport & Exercise Sciences for funding the research.

Notes

1   The management of the programme has been awarded by the government Department
     for Education and Skills to consortium comprised of: The Youth Sport Trust, The
     British Association of Advisers and Lecturers in PE, the Physical Education Association
     of the United Kingdom, and sports coach UK.
2   Teachers were paid according to the results they achieved with pupils. This important
     change in policy meant that teachers could be paid for teaching PE.
3   Schools can apply to be granted specialist status in a curriculum area. In 2003, there
     were 228 secondary schools designated as specialist sports colleges, with a target of
     400 to be met by 2005 (Youth Sport Trust, 2003).

References

www.aspeninstitute.org
www.ofsted.gov.uk
www.qca.org.uk/pess
www.youthsporttrust.org
http://www.nsdc.org/library/publications/jsd/guskey194.cfm
www.npeat.org
Armour, K. M. & Yelling, M. R. (2004) Professional 'development' and professional 'learn-
     ing': bridging the gap for experienced physical education teachers, *European Physical
     Education Review*, 10(1), 71–74.
Bailey, S. & Vamplew, W. (1999) *100 years of physical education 1899–1999* (Reading, Physical
     Education Association).
Board of Education (1933) *Syllabus of PT for schools* (London, HMSO).
Bogdan, R. C. & Biklen, S. K. (1982) *Qualitative research for education: an introduction to theory
     and methods* (London, Allyn and Bacon Inc).
Bradley, H. (1991) *Staff development* (London, Falmer Press).
Browne, J. D. (1979) *Teachers of teachers: a history of the Association of Teachers in Colleges and
     Departments of Education* (London, Hodder and Stoughton).
Campbell, A. (2002) Research and professional development, paper presented at the *British
     Education Research Association Annual Conference*, Exeter University, 12th–14th September.
Connell, J. P. & Kubisch, A. C. (1998) *Applying a theory of change approach to the evaluation of
     comprehensive community initiatives: progress, prospects and problems* (Washington, DC, The
     Aspen Institute). Available online at: http://www.aspeninstitute.org (accessed January
     2004)
Connell, J. P., Kubisch, A. C., Schorr, L. B., & Weiss, C. H. (1995) *New approaches to evalu-
     ating community initiatives: concepts, methods and contexts* (Washington, DC, The Aspen
     Institute).
Craft, A. (1996) *Continuing professional development* (Routledge, London).
Darling-Hammond, L. & McLaughlin, M. W. (1995) Policies that support professional devel-
     opment in an era of reform, *Phi delta KAPPAN*, 76(8), 597–604.
Day, C. (1999) *Developing teachers: the challenges of lifelong learning* (Falmer, London).
DFEE (2001) *Learning and teaching: a strategy for professional development* (Nottingham, DfEE
     publications).
DFES/DCMS (2003) Learning through PE and sport: a guide to the PESSCL strategy
     (Nottinghamshire, DfES publications).

Duncombe, R. & Armour, K. M. (2004) Collaborative professional learning: from theory to practice, *Journal of In-service Education*.

Edmundson, J. (1956) *PE teachers' handbook for primary schools* (London, Evans).

Evans, J. & Penney, D. (1994) Whatever happened to good advice? Service and inspection after the Education Reform Act, *British Educational Research Journal*, 20(5), 519–533.

Evans, K. (1985) *The development and structure of the English school system* (London, Hodder and Stoughton).

Garet, S. M., Porter, C. A., Desimone, L., Birman, B. F. & Yoon, K. S. (2001) What makes professional development effective? Results from a national sample of teachers, *American Educational Research Journal*, 38(4), 915–945.

Gillham, B. (2000) *Case study research methods* (London, Continuum).

Guskey, T. R. (1998) The age of our accountability. *Journal of Staff Development*, 19(4). Available online at: http://www.nsdc.org/library/publications/jsd/guskey194.cfm (accessed January 2004).

Guskey, T. R. (2002) Professional development and teacher change, *Teachers and Teaching: Theory and Practice*, 8(3/4), 381–391.

Guskey, T. & Sparkes, D. (2002) Linking professional development to improvements in student learning, paper presented at the annual meeting of *The American Educational Research Association*, New Orleans, April.

HMI (1978) *Primary education in England* (London, HMSO).

HMI (1982) *Education 5–9* (London, HMSO).

HMI (1985) *Education 8–12* (London, HMSO).

Kirk, D. (1992) *Defining Physical Education. The social construction of a school subject in post-war Britain* (London, The Falmer Press).

Kirk, D. (2002) Quality Physical Education: can it be achieved by applying the professional sports model? ISCPES Keynote address, the 12th Commonwealth International Sports Conference, Manchester, July.

Linn, R. L. (2003) Accountability: responsibility and reasonable expectations, *Educational Researcher*, 32(7), 3–13.

Loughran, J. & Gunstone, R. (1997) Professional development in residence: developing reflection on science teaching and learning, *Journal of Education for Teaching*, 23(2), 159–178.

McIntosh, P. C. (1952) *Physical Education in England since 1800* (London, G. Bell & Sons, Ltd).

McIntosh, P. C., Dixon, J. G., Munrow, A. D. & Willetts, R. F. (1981) *Landmarks in the history of Physical Education* (London, Routledge & Kegan Paul).

McLaughlin, M. W. & Zarrow, J. (2001) Teachers engaged in evidence-based reform: trajectories of teachers' inquiry, analysis and action, in: A. Lieberman & L. Miller (Eds) *Teachers caught in the action. Professional development that matters* (New York, Teachers College), 79–101.

NFER (National Foundation for Educational Research) (2001) *Continuing professional development: LEA and school support for teachers* (Slough, NFER).

NPEAT (National Partnership for Excellence and Accountability in Teaching) (1998) *Improving professional development: eight research-based principles*. Available online at: www.npeat.org (accessed September 2003).

Newmann, F. M. & Associates (1996) *Authentic achievement: restructuring schools for intellectual quality* (San Francisco, Jossey-Bass).

OFSTED (2001/02) *Physical Education in primary schools*. Available online at: http://www.ofsted.gov.uk/publications/index.cfm?fuseaction = pubs.summary&id = 3168 (accessed January 2004).

OFSTED (2002) *Continuing professional development for teachers in schools* (London, OFSTED publications, Ref: HMI 410).

Penney, D. & Evans, J. (1997) Naming the game: discourse domination in physical education and sport in England and Wales, *European Physical Education Review*, 3(1), 21–32.

Pluckrose, H. (1987) *What is happening in our primary schools?* (Oxford, Basil Blackwell).

Porter, J. & Ware, J. (1997) Bringing about change after inspection: how can outside consultants help? *Journal of In-service Education*, 23(2), 193–203.

Reynolds, D. & Teddlie, C. (2000) Linking school effectiveness and school improvement, in: C. Teddlie & D. Reynolds (Eds) *The international handbook of school effectiveness research* (London, Falmer Press), 206–231.

Ritchie, J. & Lewis, J. (2003) *Qualitative research practice: a guide for social science students and researchers* (London, Sage Publications).

Sage, G. (1996) Reaction to the role of sport pedagogy, *Quest*, 48(4), 451–452.

Seashore Louis, K. (2001) Teachers' professional development for vital middle schools: what do we know and where should we go? Paper presented at the *Office of Education Conference*, Washington D.C., April 2001. Available online at: http:www//education.umn.edu/carei/Papers/default.html (accessed November 2003).

Smith, P. V. (1999) Managing continuing professional development to support school-based target setting, *Journal of In-service Education*, 25(1), 85–96.

Sparkes, A. C. (2000) Autoethnography and narratives of self: reflections on criteria in action, *Sociology of Sport Journal*, 17, 21–43.

Stein, M. K., Smith, M. S. & Silver, E. A. (1999) The development of professional developers: learning to assist teachers in new settings in new ways, *Harvard Educational Review*, 69(3), 237–269.

Tosey, P. & Nicholls, G. (1999) OFSTED and organisational learning: the incidental value of the dunce's cap as a strategy for school improvement, *Teacher Development*, 3(1), 1–13.

Welpton, W. P. (1922) *Physical Education and hygiene* (London, Clive).

Youth Sport Trust (2003) *Specialist sports colleges*. Available online at: http://www.youthsporttrust.org/yst_schools_sc.html (accessed January 2004).

Daryl Siedentop

CONTENT KNOWLEDGE FOR
PHYSICAL EDUCATION

> The first source of the knowledge base is content knowledge—the knowledge, understanding, skill, and disposition that are to be learned by school children. This knowledge rests on two foundations: the accumulated literature and studies in the content areas, and the historical and philosophical scholarship on the nature of knowledge in those fields of study.
>
> Lee Shulman (1987, pp. 8–9)

MY TASK IS TO DISCUSS issues related to the definition of content knowledge for physical education. While it is clear that current thinking in teacher education favors the view that content knowledge and pedagogy need to be studied together—the domain of the knowledge base that Shulman calls pedagogical content knowledge—it is equally clear that to do so requires that the parameters of the content knowledge domain be identified. In math or English or music or art, the task of defining the content knowledge base would be straightforward. That is because the math, English, music, and art that children learn in school is clearly related to the math, English, music, and art that prospective teachers learn in the university as content knowledge in their teacher preparation programs. To be sure, the university versions of these content fields are more sophisticated, complex, and intellectually rigorous than what is taught in schools, but school curricula in these fields arc obviously a developmental version of the mature subject fields of study in the university.

The content knowledge domain for physical education is not so easily identified. In fact, it continues to be a source of serious controversy in our field. What I will argue this morning is that we, and by "we" I mean particularly the teacher educators in physical education, have largely given up the historic content knowledge of our field, and, in so doing, have virtually eliminated the possibility of developing a serious body of pedagogical content knowledge for teaching physical education. Pedagogical content knowledge is the "main stuff" from which effectiveness and expertise in teaching and coaching derives. But, this much is clear: You can't have pedagogical content knowledge without content knowledge, and all of our advances in pedagogy in physical education can't change that simple truth.

Several of our colleagues have for some time pointed out the degree to which we are emphasizing pedagogy without a corresponding emphasis on content knowledge. Joan Vickers (1987) described this view in Cincinnati at AAHPERD's pre-convention conference on graduate education:

> In this paper it will be argued that the teacher preparation programs today define teaching largely in terms of the methods, processes, and procedures of pedagogy with little attention paid to the subject matter of school physical education.
>
> (p. 179)

Shirl Hoffman (1987), in his perceptive fictional scenario for our future, attributed the demise of school physical education to the fact that physical education teachers were good at organizing and managing, but didn't really know enough about the subjects they were teaching to educate students beyond a very rudimentary level:

> The report went on to point out that it was not difficult to find laypersons whose knowledge and expertise on the activities in physical education ranged far beyond those of teachers themselves. If physical education teachers had any special talent at all, it seemed to be the ability to teach a broad range of skills at an introductory level in environments that promised little hope of success.
>
> (p. 128)

If these criticisms are valid—and I believe they are—we have arrived at a point in our history where we can now prepare teachers who are pedagogically more skillful than ever, but who, in many cases, are so unprepared in the content area that they would be described as "ignorant" if the content area were a purely cognitive knowledge field. To understand this dilemma we need to take a brief trip through our recent history and, particularly, to identify the root problem that best explains the part of that history relevant to the demise of content knowledge in physical education.

The discipline revolution

In 1964 Franklin Henry described the possibility of physical education as an academic discipline—and created a revolution. Henry used chemistry and math as his examples of how a young person whose goal is to teach in high school would study the subject matter to levels far beyond that which would ever be taught in the typical high school curriculum. However, the young person whose goal was to teach physical education, argued Henry, studied only to the level that physical education is taught in the high school, focusing not on higher levels of the subject but instead on how to teach and administer the program.

Henry's solution for this problem was to suggest that the discipline of physical education should be studied as the content knowledge base for physical education.

We all know how completely that revolution has transformed our undergraduate teacher preparation curricula. Most young persons whose goal is to teach and coach now take courses that represent how that discipline has developed in the intervening 25 years—motor learning, motor control, sport psychology, sport history, sport philosophy, exercise physiology, kinesiology, and biomechanics. It is still unclear whether Dr. Henry's proposals were simply misunderstood by those who developed them into the discipline increasingly referred to as kinesiology, or whether Henry himself was unaware of the faulty logic of his chemistry and math analogies. Regardless, the bad logic in the basic argument has been pointed out often (Griffey, 1987b; Hoffman, 1988; Kleinman, 1973; Locke, 1977; Siedentop, 1980). The most compelling analysis of the logic, and its unfortunate consequences, was presented by Larry Locke at the first joint meeting of the NCPEAM and NAPECW in Orlando in 1977:

> Those 30 hours of math are academic, are abstract, and are a difficult test of intellect, but transcripts reveal that the focus is not on study *about* math. Those hours do not consist of the history of math, the sociology of math, or the neurophysiology of math. Most of the 30 hours are spent in doing of math, in the acquisition of progressively higher levels of command over the performance of operations. Mastery of the logic of derivation, facility in calculation, skill in the analysis of problems, and the ability to fit solutions correctly—all demand direct, participatory involvement in the stuff of the subject.
>
> For the physical educator, then, the correct analog for the situation in math would not be to insist our students take more courses about sport and exercise. The correct analog would be to extend and intensify their study of sport and exercise by insisting that they practice sport and exercise—by doing it! We should insist that our students acquire a range of movement skills far more extensive than they would be called upon to teach in the public school.
>
> (p. 38)

In Cincinnati in 1986, David Griffey (1987b) reminded us of the consequences of Henry's argument for professional preparation in our field. Just last December, at the Chicago conference convened to anoint "Kinesiology" as the proper name for our undergraduate pre-professional curricula, Shirl Hoffman (1988) pointed out yet again that the study of what is being proposed as the basic kinesiology curriculum has little to do with the physical education curriculum that is taught in schools. Speaking in the context of 5th-year Holmes type teacher preparation programs, requiring a pre-professional subject matter concentration, Hoffman described the error that by now has become institutionalized, and suggested a more proper focus:

> Physical education professors almost instinctively assume that the logical undergraduate major for physical education students in a five-year model is the "body of knowledge" as manifested in an exercise science major. However, the subject matter taught in school physical education programs is not exercise physiology, biomechanics and sport history, but volleyball, gymnastics, swimming and diving. Thus, strict application of the Holmes recommendation to

physical education should require departments to develop undergraduate degrees that give principal attention to performance of skills, not unlike programs featured in departments of dance or music, where performance is allowed to take center stage, unapologetically.

(pp. 61–62)

While it is clear that the discipline has thrived, a primary consequence of that growth for teacher education programs has been the consistent reduction of sport performance and performance related courses in our curricula. What Locke described as a problem in 1977 has not only grown worse, but now, with the national trend toward post-baccalaureate teacher education, threatens to reach its logical conclusion. In 1977, Locke said:

> Because many of us did not see the correct analogy, some departments have spent a decade trying to divest themselves of those embarrassing skills courses. Graduates with only a narrow, single-sport specialization, or worse, graduates without any particular talent for movement at all, too often have become the norm rather than the exception.

(p. 38)

There are now teacher certification programs in physical education that have no within-program requirements for performance courses, and many more that have seriously reduced the credit hours for such courses, and changed them so that they can be passed off as skill analysis or pedagogy courses, evidently making them more palatable for curriculum review committees.

The root problem in defining pre-professional content

Why has this discipline revolution been so influential in our professional programs? Why have we participated in it? The root problem which has allowed the discipline movement to virtually take over and increasingly define pre-professional curricula in physical education is, from my view, straightforward. There is a general belief that sport performance coursework is not worthy of academic status. or, even more directly, that sport itself is "academically unpalatable" (Kretchmar, 1988) as one of our leading sport philosophers proclaimed at the Chicago anointment.

The problem is not new. It was there at the start of the discipline revolution and, in my judgment, is the largely unexamined assumption that has debilitated professional preparation in physical education. Henry said that "physical education has the doubtful distinction of being a school subject for which colleges prepare teachers but do not recognize as a subject field." That claim was accurate then, and nothing has changed since he made it. The school subject, or course, was then, as it is now, all of the learnings associated with exercise and sport, but mostly the experiential learnings one achieves through direct participation. Henry's proposal was to build the discipline and have *that* become the approved subject field at the university, and his proposal has largely been adopted. Henry mentioned performance only briefly, suggesting that while the development of skill in motor performance was a worthy personal goal, it shouldn't be confused with the academic field of knowledge.

It was G. Lawrence Rarick, one of the influential early disciplinarians, who spoke to the issue directly, as he defined the domain of physical education as a discipline in a 1967 issue of *Quest*:

> The question is sometimes raised: Is one justified in including the execution of a motor skill in and of itself as an integral part of a discipline? The mechanics of the skill can be observed and studied, the physiological responses monitored, the feelings states noted. These are areas of legitimate study and research. On the other hand, do we need to clarify for ourselves the level of cognition that is required in learning and executing semi-automatic motor skills? Can we justify as part of our discipline behavioral responses which are for the most part automatically controlled even through there is conscious direction of certain aspects of the movement and interpretative and affective controls which give to the movement refinement, meaning, and beauty?
>
> (p. 51)

While Rarick didn't follow that question with a declarative "no!" the manner in which the question was framed and the material that followed in his article said "no" as clearly as if he had done so directly.

This, then, is the root problem—the direct study of sport skill and strategy through experiential learning is not considered to be of sufficient academic quality to form the core of an undergraduate degree program. Learning basketball, volleyball, and gymnastics—and all the associated issues of training, technique, performance, and strategy—are not worthy of formal academic credit as the central foci of a pre-professional program. If we cannot confront that core problem, and somehow resolve it, then physical education in schools is doomed.

I am more concerned with being equivocal than redundant, so let me state it from a somewhat different angle. If men and women who aspire to be teachers of physical education study, as the core of their content knowledge, the discipline of kinesiology, and have increasingly fewer academic credit hours devoted to developing direct expertise in sport forms, they will fail as teachers of physical education no matter how well they are eventually prepared in the pedagogical domain. They will fail because they have little command of the content they will need to teach, no ability to take students beyond that introductory unit that seemingly gets taught again and again and again.

Nor should anyone expect them to succeed! As the Pedasport executives who visited university teacher preparation programs in Hoffman's version of the "brave new world" of physical education, any intelligent visitor would come away from many of our current programs wondering how anyone could expect our graduates to be expert instructors in either sport skills or exercise, the programs lacking, sometimes totally, a foundation in the content that teachers are expected to teach.

At the Chicago conference, in open discussion relative to the performance dimensions of the proposed kinesiology major. Karl Newell suggested that perhaps the time was ripe to extend the revolution to school programs—the kinesiology curriculum for the elementary school, for example. The suggestion wasn't received with great enthusiasm, partially, I suspect, because few could sort out immediately what the motor control unit for 2nd-graders or the biomechanics unit for 3rd-graders might look like. Yet, this much is clear: The kinesiology major with a certification in physical education who will be graduating from some of our universities in the near future will be better prepared, from a content point of view, to teach a kinesiology curriculum than he or she will be to teach an exercise and sport curriculum.

The consequences of our retreat from sport performance

The consequence of our retreat from the centrality of sport performance in our pre-professional curricula is several generations of physical education teachers who are ill equipped to teach anything beyond a beginning unit of activity. We have, as David Griffey (1987a) pointed out, denied students the opportunity to master something important. The smattering of content knowledge typically acquired by a physical education major has led to school programs that offer a smattering of activities. As John Taylor and Eleanor Chiogioji (1987) argued, the proliferation of too many activity units into a short time has crippled our ability to achieve important goals. In this case at least, Hoffman's (1987) fictional portrayal of physical education in the year 2020 is firmly rooted in the realities of the present:

> Physical education professionals have been awash in a sea of confusion for years. No two of them can agree on what should be taught. What passes for physical education at any particular school is likely to depend on the whims of the teacher. . . . We can only imagine what might happen were math, science, and English teachers to follow the same destructive course.
>
> (p. 127)

If this continues, physical educators of the future, if there are such persons, will be arrangers, coordinators, and managers of primarily recreational activities. They will undoubtedly be good arrangers and managers, keeping children and youth busy and good, and for the most part even happy, if short-term novelty and recreation can sustain happiness as youth develop. Being primarily arrangers, coordinators, and managers, such persons will look with relish for new, innovative activities for which they can develop yet another introductory unit, thus extending the novelty nature of the subject matter. It has become increasingly clear that "anything goes" in the name of physical education in schools—units in darts and Frisbee having the same substantive value as volleyball and track, with the added appeal of novelty. I will leave it to you to judge the fate of a school subject conceptualized and taught in such a manner.

The nature of knowledge in physical education

If you recall Shulman's definition of content knowledge with which I began the presentation, you will remember that it had two parts: the accumulated studies in the content area *and* the nature of knowledge in that field of study. In distancing ourselves from sport performance as the central core of our content area, we have effectively disavowed our tradition which focuses on and values the physical as experience. Jesse Feiring Williams (1951) articulated that view long ago:

We shall keep the balance even if we remember that the physical experience is physical in its outward manifestation but mental and emotional, social and moral, in its relationships and meanings. Thus, we may help education to abandon the tendency toward an exclusive emphasis upon mind and so change itself into a rational procedure for the education of the whole man.

(p. 465)

As we have moved away from the physical as experience and toward the discipline of kinesiology, we have been reminded along the way of how traitorous our gradual disavowal was becoming. My colleague, Seymour Kleinman, said it most clearly and unequivocally in a 1973 *Quest* article:

For these physical education intellectualists, the value and joy of activity in and for itself was insufficient . . . our attention was subtly directed away from the crux of the matter; from the fundamental grounds upon which this field rests—the activity itself. It suddenly became fashionable not to engage in sport and physical activity but to verbalize about it, explore its implications, utilize it physiologically, psychologically, sociologically, philosophically, anthropologically, historically, and God knows what else.

Now I suppose that all of these, to some degree or other, have some validity, but don't you see what is happening when we pursue these things? They place us farther and farther away from the activity itself.

I'm not telling you anything that, in your guts, you don't already know. If you didn't know it, you wouldn't be in physical education, and if you don't know it by now, you don't belong in physical education.

(p. 93)

Unfortunately, Sy was not right about our ability to see what was happening and to know intuitively how wrong it was. Collectively, we simply took part in the gradual extinction of our historic content in sport and exercise and our historic commitment to the physical as experience.

What to do about it

The odds against us building an appropriate content field for pre-professional curricula in physical education in the current university climate are nearly overwhelming. The trends in many states toward post-baccalaureate teacher preparation, and in other states toward defining "academic" majors for teacher, serve only to exacerbate the problems. The current movement among leaders in our field in research universities, to define the undergraduate major as kinesiology and have it consist mostly of the subdisciplines that have developed in the past quarter century, serves only to lengthen the odds.

Do not mistake me. I am not calling for a return to the way in which skills courses were taught in years past. We know too much about sport performance to simply wish for days gone by. The teacher of physical education and the coach of children and youth sport teams need to have a reasonable mastery of the sport activities they will teach to their students and players—that is their content knowledge.

They should know the technical aspects of the skills involved, the strengths and weaknesses of various strategic approaches to the sport, the training implications for improved performance in the sport, the developmental considerations, the norms, values, and traditions of the sport, the role it does and should occupy in local and national sport cultures, the developing technologies within the sport, the psychosocial considerations associated with individual and group dynamics of players, and the ethical/moral dilemmas posed by competition. And, they should "know" these things intellectually and as performers, each kind of knowledge having its own meaning.

Some courses in the discipline of kinesiology include *some* material that is relevant to that content knowledge, but other courses are largely irrelevant to that content knowledge. The more salient issue, however, is that the discipline of kinesiology is not taught in schools and, therefore, that discipline cannot logically serve as the content knowledge base for pre-professional preparation in physical education.

To clarify this point, and to show how far from thorough content coverage we have come in the preparation of teachers in our field, let me share with you the make-up of the program in dance education at my university (see Table 1). We are a Holmes member, so the program in dance education is a 5- to 6-year program with a BA or BFA in dance followed by an MA in Dance Education. The undergraduate major in dance has two tracks, a performance track and a pre-professional dance education track. The pre-professional track is 88 quarter hours of work. As you can see, the clear emphasis in the program is in technique courses. Those courses are graded into three levels with three parts to each level. There are four courses in composition, suggesting a strong progression within that area. There are two related courses in notation. What is absent, in comparison to a typical physical education major, is the sociology of dance, biomechanics of dance, physiology of dance, etc. There are 8 quarter hours devoted to pre-professional pedagogy experiences.

Students who come from other programs to enter the MA in Dance Education must have at least 40 quarter hours of studio work in order to be certified. The professional program at the graduate level includes two courses in dance for children, I and II, and two 15-quarter-hour student teaching experiences, one at the elementary level and one at the secondary level. There are also the standard education courses in methods, foundations, and developmental psychology. In addition, all certification students are required to take 10 more credit hours in dance technique, at least one course per quarter while they are in the program. Why? The answer is clear when you read the last line of the information sheet that describes the purpose and flavor of the program to prospective students. It says: "At Ohio State, we believe that the best way to become a performer, choreographer, educator, or scholar is – TO DANCE!"

Newly certified students from the dance education tract will have completed more than 40 quarter hours of performance courses, progressively graded to focus on higher levels of technique. Their understanding of and skill in dance is no doubt far greater than they will ever have to teach in a K–12 setting, which is of course exactly what Franklin Henry called for. You will also notice that this dance department has decided on a fairly narrow focus for dance education—there are no required courses in jazz, folk, square, social, or break dancing.

I know of no physical education programs which are analogs to that dance education program. Larry Locke, Charlie Mand, and I (1981) outlined the dimensions and rationale for such a curriculum years ago, but, to borrow a phrase, it remains a model little noted, nor long remembered.

Table 1 Dance education pre-professional requirements in the dance department at OSU

Dance 111	Techniques and Materials of Dance I
111.01	Improvisation
111.02	Dance Fundamentals
111.03	Introduction to Composition
111.04	Modern Technique, Part 1
111.05	Modern Technique, Part 2
111.06	Modern Technique, Part 3
111.05	Ballet Technique, Part 1
111.06	Ballet Technique, Part 2
111.07	Ballet Technique, Part 3
Dance 190	Ethnic Dance Forms
Dance 198	Dance Production Workshop
Dance 214	Dance Techniques II
214.04	Modern Technique, Part 1
214.05	Modern Technique, Part 2
214.08	Modern Technique, Part 3
214.06	Ballet Technique, Part 1
214.07	Ballet Technique, Part 2
214.08	Ballet Technique, Part 3
Dance 257	Overview of Dance
Dance 289	Field Experience in Dance
Dance 489	Dance in Education
Dance 534	Dance Techniques III
534.04	Modern Technique, Part 1
534.05	Modern Technique, Part 2
534.08	Modern Technique, Part 3
534.06	Ballet Technique, Part 1
534.07	Ballet Technique, Part 2
534.08	Ballet Technique, Part 3
Dance 620	Notation 1
Dance 621	Notation 2
Dance 622	Notation *or* Dance 605 Effort *or* Dance 606 Space I
Dance 633	Lighting
Dance 645	Foundations in Dance Composition I
Dance 646	Foundations Dance Composition II
Dance 648	Music & Choreography
Dance 649	Intermediate Dance Composition
Dance 657	History of Dance I
Dance 688	Theory & Practice of Teaching Modern Dance
Dance 689	Directed Teaching in Dance
Dance 650	Advanced Dance Composition

Note: Students who earn the BA or BFA in Dance complete an MA degree program in Dance Education including 2 quarters of student teaching plus additional coursework in Dance and Professional Education.

If I were to develop such a model, I would do so with sport as the root metaphor for the program. Someday, soon I hope, a bachelor's degree in sport will be offered at some university, with a primary emphasis on sport performance. If such a degree were available, it would provide the content knowledge for prospective physical educators. You may be more inclined toward a degree in human movement, or fitness, or activity and exercise, to take Mike Ellis' (1988) recent model. That's fine! Our field would be better off if we all stopped trying to be all things to all people in our notions of school curricula and content knowledge. But, before we continue to criticize school-based physical educators for their short-term multiactivity programs with little progression and few real outcomes, we had best take a hard look at the content knowledge we have provided for them in our teacher education programs. If we do take that hard look, I believe we will see, in our own efforts, the best explanation for why school physical education is as it is today.

References

Ellis, M. (1988). *The business of physical education*. Champaign, IL: Human Kinetics.

Griffey, D. (1987a). Trouble for sure, a crisis perhaps. *Journal of Physical Education, Recreation & Dance*, **58**(2), 20–21.

Griffey. D. (1987b). The future of graduate study in teacher preparation in physical education. *Quest*, **39**, 174–178.

Henry, F. (1964). Physical education: An academic discipline. *Journal of Health, Physical Education and Recreation*, **37**(7), 32–33.

Hoffman, S. (1987). Dreaming the impossible dream: The decline and fall of physical education. In J. Massengale (Ed.), *Trends toward the future in physical education* (pp. 121–135). Champaign, IL: Human Kinetics.

Hoffman, S.L. (1988). The Holmes Group and 5th year licensure. *Big Ten Leadership Conference Report* (pp. 61–63). Champaign, IL: Human Kinetics.

Kleinman, S. (1973). Is sport experience? *Quest*, **19**, 96–100.

Kretchmar, S. (1988). Exercise and sport science. *Big Ten Leadership Conference Report* (pp. 45–58). Champaign, IL: Human Kinetics.

Locke, L.F. (1977). From research and the disciplines to practice and the professions: One more time. *Proceedings NCPEAM*. Orlando, FL.

Locke, L.F., Mand, D., & Siedentop, D. (1981). The preparation of physical education teachers: A subject matter centered model. In *Progress through diversity* (pp. 33–54). Washington, DC: American Alliance for Health, Physical Education, Recreation and Dance.

Rarick, G.L. (1967). The domain of physical education as a discipline. *Quest*, **9**, 50–59.

Shulman, L. (1987). Knowledge and teaching: Foundations of the new reform. *Harvard Educational Review*, **57**(1), 1–22.

Siedentop, D. (1980). *Physical education: Introductory analysis* (3rd ed.). Dubuque, IA: W.C. Brown.

Taylor, J., & Chiogioji, E. (1987). Implications of educational reform on high school programs. *Journal of Physical Education, Recreation & Dance*, **58**(2), 22–23.

Vickers, J. (1987). The role of subject matter in the preparation of teachers in physical education, *Quest*, **39**, 179–184.

Williams, J.F. (1951). The physical as experience. *The Journal of Higher Education*, **22**, 464–469.

PART 6

Curriculum and content

INTRODUCTION

CURRICULUM IS THE THIRD component of pedagogy alongside learning and teaching. When educational research in physical education first appeared in the United States in the late 1960s its main concern was teachers and teaching. Despite the ground-breaking work of curriculum researchers such as Ann Jewett and colleagues and the need to design new curricula for examinable courses and in response to government initiatives, curriculum as a topic remained somewhat neglected by physical education scholars. It is only since models-based practice became prominent from the early to mid 1980s that researchers have in large numbers begun to research the curriculum and content of physical education.

Teaching Games for Understanding (TGfU) and Sport Education are currently two of the most researched forms of models-based practice. The paper by **Kirk and MacPhail** examines the original TGfU model developed by Bunker and Thorpe, and reconceptualises the model in the context of situated learning theory. **Dyson and colleagues** consider the relationships and complimentarity of three forms of models-based practice and advocate the benefits of using all three in conjunction. The paper by **Gard** shifts the focus of the curriculum away from games and sports to the arts and dance, and shows how dance can be a medium for teaching about and combating various forms of social oppression.

FURTHER READING

Azzarito, L. and Ennis, C. (2003) A sense of connection: Toward social constructivist physical education. *Sport, Education and Society*, 8(2), 179–197.

Gorely, T., Holroyd, R. and Kirk, D. (2003) Muscularity, the habitus and the social construction of gender: Towards a gender relevant physical education. *British Journal of Sociology of Education*, 24, 429–448.

Hoffman, S. (1987) Dreaming the impossible dream: The decline and fall of physical education, pp. 121–135, in J. Massengale (ed.), *Trends towards the future of physical education*. Champaign, Ill.: Human Kinetics.

Wright, J. (1999) Changing gendered practices in physical education: working with teachers. *European Physical Education Review*, 5(3), 181–197.

Michael Gard

BEING SOMEONE ELSE
Using dance in anti-oppressive teaching

Introduction

SCHOOLS ARE KEY SITES for the regulation and normalisation of children's bodies and subjectivities (Bourdieu & Passerson, 1977; Connell, 1993; Kirk, 1993, 1998a). This means that only certain ways of moving and thinking are legitimate within schools. But schools are not monolithic. Different schools have their own particular multi-layered geographies in which different ways of moving and thinking are either explicitly or inadvertently produced in different places and at different times. This point is most obviously exemplified by the organisation of school time amongst the various subject areas and it is apparent that different subject areas have their own 'communities of practice' (Kirk, 1998b, 1999). As critical educational researchers working across a range of disciplines have shown, these processes of regulation and normalisation have been and continue to be implicated in the production and reproduction of unjust educational and social outcomes (Apple, 1985; McLaren, 1986; Willis, 1987; Acker, 1994; hooks, 1994).

However, it is only relatively recently that researchers and teacher educators in physical education have begun to incorporate these critiques into their work. For example, while some groundbreaking work has emerged over the last 15 years (for example, Scraton, 1990; Wright, 1996a,b), the insights of feminist scholars have yet to make a significant impact on the practice of physical education teacher education in universities and physical education in schools.

This is perhaps not surprising given physical education's strong and enduring association with males and male power (Flintoff, 1991; Macdonald, 1993; Veri, 1999). This association may also partly explain why it was not until the emergence of so-called 'masculinities' scholarship that interest in analyses of gender in physical education has begun to broaden, particularly amongst male academics.

The emergence of masculinities studies[1] raises some important questions for physical education. For example, might a focus on 'masculinities' simply reinforce boys' and men's privileged location within physical education and, in fact, physical culture more generally? More fundamentally, is it realistic to expect physical education to contribute to justice with respect to gender and other areas of social relations? If it can, what contribution might physical activity itself, as opposed to discussion about physical activity, make? And given that masculinities researchers generally do most of their work in teacher education institutions rather than schools, what is the pedagogical relationship between under-graduate teacher education on the one hand, and primary and secondary school physical education on the other? Is there a relationship at all?

Clearly, these are large and complex questions. However, my purpose in this paper is to address them by considering the potential impact of masculinities studies on school and university physical education. In short, I want to argue that the problematisation of masculinity within masculinities studies has the potential to contribute to anti-oppressive pedagogies in schools and universities and to delineate a particular area of pedagogical attention: the ways in which boys and men deploy their bodies and construct their identities.

A case for 'ad hocery'

In the following three sections I briefly discuss my research into three different social sites in which male bodies and identities are produced and reproduced; theatrical dance, school physical education and university physical education teacher education. In different ways, each area of research explores the relationships between dominant discursive construc-tions of gender and the materialisation of men's bodies. In other words, they focus on the constructedness of embodiment. They show that the ways our bodies 'feel' and the 'natural' capacities which are assigned to them are both intensely political matters. They also suggest that the production of material bodies is not only a matter for the mover and (in the context of this paper) *his* sense of *himself*, but also the viewer/s. That is, embodi-ment is equally a matter of what looks right as well as what feels right.

My use of terms such as 'discourse', 'constructedness', 'materialisation' and 'embodi-ment' indicates that this work is informed by particular theoretical traditions (for example see Rothfield, 1988; Aalten, 1997; Lindemann, 1997; Jackson & Scott, 2001).[2] In general terms, this means an interest in sociologically grounded theories of what has come to be termed 'embodied subjectivity'. By sociological, I gesture towards a discomfort with (although certainly not an out of hand rejection of) more philosophically abstract theories of embodiment (such as Butler, 1990, 1993; Grosz 1994). Instead, I have taken my lead from authors whose focus has been on socially embedded bodies and identities, where structural power relations and everyday interactions produce and re-produce embodied experience (in particular see Burkitt, 1999; Jackson & Scott, 2001; Ramazanoglu, 1995). However, I propose to de-emphasise the theoretical justifications and implications of this research for two reasons.

First, I am most interested in the implications of this research for classroom physical education in schools and universities. It is my hope that, by themselves, the data I present here will suggest some pedagogical responses. It is not my expectation that teachers and student teachers will necessarily be interested in the theoretical conversations which gave rise to this work nor to those to which it might contribute.[3]

Second and following Thomas' (1997) call for more 'ad hocery' in educational research and teaching, I am both ambivalent about the degree to which theory facilitates (as opposed to constrains) innovative thinking,[4] while also acknowledging that if the 'findings' of academic educational research find their way into teaching practice at all, they will often do so in ways which owe little to the complexities of their theoretical geneses. In other words, the work of academics will be taken up in partial, unpredictable, creative and context specific ways.

With this said, let me be clear about my purpose in presenting these data. As will become obvious, this paper is primarily interested in dance, its utterly marginal status within the practice of physical education, and the potential for using dance to address questions of justice in the classroom. More particularly, I am interested in the potential of creative forms of dance to problematise gender, especially masculinity, and sexuality, especially heterosexuality. Although I do offer some points of analysis around these data, these comments are intended to allude to pedagogical possibilities rather than to claim interpretive finality. Elsewhere, I and others (Bond, 1994; Marques, 1998; Gard, 2001b) have attempted to be more theoretically prescriptive about approaches to dance teaching. This is not my intention here. At this moment, physical education needs a reason to start dancing and my argument here is that a focus on masculinity is a good reason to do so.

I begin with some dance history.

I

By 1932, Denishawn, the pioneering American modern dance company founded by Ruth St Denis and Ted Shawn, had given its last performance. The company, which employed both male and female dancers, had been both financially and critically successful. Despite this success, stage dancing of virtually any kind remained in the eyes of many Americans an immoral occupation for women and an absolutely unthinkable one for men. A dancing male body was considered unquestionably 'effeminate' and deviant, and given the prevailing laws against homosexuality, was not far from being a crime.

In the following year, 1933, a new company, Ted Shawn and his Men Dancers, gave its debut performance. Shawn had been toying with the idea of starting an all male company for some time and, with the collapse of Denishawn, it became the focal point of his career. He later wrote:

> Though I, the first American man to make the art of dancing his life-work, had made good, there still was a prevailing prejudice against dancing for men. It was considered to be an effeminate, trivial, and unworthy occupation for the strapping and well-muscled male. I knew this to be utterly false but men were in the minority in every company, including Denishawn, and the public eye had not really been focussed on the problem of men and dancing. I hoped, by touring with a company of men, to make people think about the subject. I was sure that when people saw young American athletes going through masculine dances, prejudice would be overcome and dancing as a career would take its place with other legitimate professions.
>
> (Shawn, 1960, pp. 240–241)

Shawn and the Men Dancers performed across the US for seven years, giving their final performance in Boston in 1940. Throughout its brief life the company battled financial insecurity and hostile audiences while at the same time developing an ultra-macho, ultra-athletic style of choreography which, as the quote from Shawn above suggests, was designed to convince people that dancing was a 'respectable' activity for males. Shawn and his men promoted the 'cause' of the male dancer with extraordinary zeal and obviously considered it a serious matter. In his biography, Barton Mumaw, Shawn's principal dancer in the Men Dancers, even wrote that 'Shawn's fight for the right of men to participate in creative dance in the US was as difficult as the fight of the suffragettes for the right of women to vote, and ultimately as successful' (Sherman & Mumaw, 2000, p. xxiv).

Drawing on something of a mish-mash of Greek philosophy and the ideas of writers such as the 'humanist, sexologist, and dance aficionado' (Foster, 2001, p. 154), Havelock Ellis, Shawn saw dance as the oldest and most significant of all art forms, an ennobling force and the perfect medium through which to celebrate, if only implicitly, what he saw as the highest form of love: that which existed between honourable, intelligent, muscular white men.

On the other hand, Shawn detested 'effeminacy'. He saw 'effeminate' gay men as a 'disgrace' and as traitors to the Hellenic, muscular vision of love between men he extolled in private. Of course, despite and because of the presence of gay men in the company, Shawn regularly and explicitly denounced homosexuality in his speeches and writings, calculating, no doubt accurately, that any suspicion of homosexuality would have brought the entire enterprise to a halt. According to Shawn, dance demanded 'strength, endurance, precision, perfect coordination of mind, body and emotion, clarity of thinking, all distinctly masculine qualities' (quoted in Foulkes, 2001, p. 124). With these as his guiding principles, he created dance which plundered the cultural traditions of what he called 'primitive' societies, as well as images of western and non-western men which he hoped would constitute an unambiguously 'manly' artistic form. The Men Dancers performed pieces called *Negro Spirituals, Workers Songs of Middle Europe* and *Cutting the Sugar Cane*, and others depicting American Indians, factory labourers and athletes. In fact, as Burt (1995) points out, Shawn looked anywhere and everywhere for 'inspiration' except towards his own middle class, educated, suburban background.

He was particularly preoccupied with portraying his Men Dancers as athletes and connecting dance with the heterosexual respectability enjoyed by competitive sports. He deliberately sought to recruit physical education undergraduates into the company and looked favourably on those who had excelled at some form of competitive sport. One of the company's most celebrated pieces, *Olympiad*, depicted fencers, boxers, hurdlers and other stylised sportsmen going about their particular events. On one occasion, the newspaper review for a performance 'appeared smack in the middle of the sports page, a location we heartily approved' (Shawn, 1960, p. 254).

As an object of research, Shawn's life's work is unquestionably rich and complex. It mixes pungently racist, misogynist and homophobic elements with, in my view, a laudable determination to break down a form of prejudice which needed to be broken down. This is certainly not to suggest, as Barton Mumaw implies, that the 'struggle' for the male dancer was a pressing human rights issue. However, it is to try to simultaneously grasp his historical locatedness—particularly the ways in which he was invested in many of the less than progressive attitudes of his time—as well as his peculiarity – the degree to which he was responsible for (relatively) new ways of thinking about and viewing the male body.

The story of his work and the reactions of others to it are also revealing in other ways. They exemplify the ways in which the domains of the social and the sexual, the public and the private, are inextricably linked. Indeed, following Richardson 1996), the virtual prohibition on male dancers at this time shows how the distinctions between social/public and sexual/private are heteronormative constructions. Men were not prevented from dancing because the form of dance they did directly endangered anyone's safety or broke any law, and there were many public spaces in which they could participate in other forms of 'social' dance. They were prevented because this form of dance was associated with a form of sexual ('private') practice. Partner dancing involving a man and a woman could be called 'social', not sexual, because of its association with 'normal', unmarked (hetero)-sex. However, public displays of men participating in 'artistic' dance were seen as unambiguously (homo)sexual, not social, and therefore immoral.

The method Shawn used to try to change attitudes towards male dancers is also telling. Realising that homosexuality was strongly associated (almost to the point of equating with) 'effeminacy', he explicitly chose dancers with muscular bodies, dressed them in clothes which revealed and emphasised these muscles and developed a 'manly' style of choreography.[5] That these methods seem to have been largely successful, particularly his choice of choreographic style, is clear evidence of the ways in which bodies are always sexually inscribed. Shawn wanted his audiences to 'see' heterosexual men on stage or, at the very least, to not 'see' homosexual men. And although we need to be circumspect about claiming to know the minds of others, particularly those alive over 60 years ago, he seems to have convinced many. Although he might not have used precisely these words, he realised that sport was constructed as a thoroughly (hetero)-sexualised practice. As masculinities researchers trying to draw meaning from the past, Shawn reminds us that sport and dance *remain* both discursive as well as material constructions and occupy significant if evolving places within the project of gender identity construction, particularly for boys and men, and the perpetuation of heterosexual male power.

II

In 1999, my colleague Robert Meyenn and I conducted an interview based study with secondary school boys aged between 11 and 14 (see Gard & Meyenn, 2000, for a methodological account of this work). In this study we asked boys to watch video footage of different forms of physical activity, including a range of individual and team sports as well as mime, contemporary dance and ballet.

Although enthusiasm for any form of dance was low amongst most (though not all) of the 23 boys we interviewed, the following short passage struck us as particularly telling. Having asked the two boys in this particular interview if they did any gymnastics or dance in physical education, Trent went into a lengthy description of his limited experiences with gymnastics. When he finished, the other boy, Alex, commented:

Alex: We haven't done dance. Good! I hate it.
Michael: Why do you hate dancing.
Alex: I just don't like it. I don't know why. I just really hate it.
Trent: Dancing with girls is alright, but not just like ballet or nothin . . . Like if

you're on TV doing ballet, lot of people'd call you a girl, say that's a girl's sport . . .

Alex: But you don't sort of think, like if you saw someone dancing you don't go home and think about what you gonna call him. If you just saw him there, and you just thought 'oh!', the first thing that comes into your mind you think 'oh what a girl!'.

There are, of course, a number of ways in which we might interpret this passage and, in particular, Alex's statement about hating dance. Both boys were being interviewed by a man they did not know in a room with a male peer. Were they speaking the 'truth' about what they 'really' felt? Were they simply attempting to establish their position within a heavily gendered social hierarchy in which creative dance movement is associated with homosexuality and where homosexuality is considered abnormal and inferior to hetero-sexuality? Or might these two elements, what they feel and what they say, be closely connected?

My own feeling is that Alex's words were part of a strong emotional response he felt either towards the thought or the video image (or, in fact, both) of a dancing male body. My sense of the interview was that Trent, while not disagreeing with Alex, did not appear to share his depth of feeling. Alex seems to have sensed that he was in something of a 'one-out' position on this matter, but seemed determined to say what he felt. What I am suggesting here is that Alex's words represent more than a discursively constituted per-formance designed to meet the demands of this particular social context. I am suggesting that his words resonated in his body.

In order to explore and develop (although far from 'prove') this assertion, I want to suggest an admittedly speculative but compelling line of analysis. The first point to make is an obvious one. Alex's reaction is not easily explained in rational terms. It seems spon-taneous and visceral. It has the urgency and alarm that we sometimes see in people who have been asked to perform some public act (such as speak in front of an audience) for which they are unprepared and anxious. But Alex was *capable* of dancing; he spoke at length about his involvement in highly vigorous forms of physical activity such as playing rugby football and riding a motorcycle. In my view, the most satisfactory explanation is that the forms of movement Alex associated with dance were not only different from the forms of movement he was most familiar with, but carry with them meaning: meaning which was at odds with the kind of (male) person he saw himself as, or at least desired to be. In other words, I a am going much further than simply suggesting that Alex feared the ridicule that might ensue if he was to admit to liking dance or, indeed, if he actually danced in front of his peers. I am saying that his sense of himself has produced its own realm or, to use a Foucauldian term, 'technology' of bodily pleasures and displeasures. I believe him when he says that he 'really hates' dancing and I can fully imagine the difficulties I would face were I Alex's physical education teacher and was planning a dance module with his class.

There have been a number of important contributions to the physical education literature which have considered dance and the gender politics of the physical education classroom (in particular, see Flintoff, 1991, 1994; Meglin, 1994; Brennan, 1996; Wright, 1996; Talbot, 1997). With varying points of emphasis, each of these authors have high-lighted the ways in which sexism and homophobia amongst male (and some female) students and teachers have contributed to the marginalisation of dance within physical education and disadvantaged those students, predominantly girls and women, who enjoy dancing. However, I would argue that this section of data from my interview with Alex and Trent helps to foreground at least two important areas of discussion which have yet to be explored within the physical education literature.

First, it is notable that Alex not only struggles to find the words to explain his hatred, but that he even feels hatred rather than, say, dislike or disinterest.[6] I would argue that this suggests an opportunity to move beyond simply teaching about (how to do) movement, towards teaching through movement to explore the meanings and emotions generated by moving bodies. Given that many physical education syllabi stipulate the inclusion of creative dance forms, it would seem perfectly reasonable to explore these meanings (including those concerned with gender and sexuality) and emotions (including hatred) with our students. By extension, this also suggests that we could address the connections between the difficulties associated with the verbal elaboration of hatred and the ease of the (violent) physical elaboration of hatred. Here, I am particularly thinking of the connections between homophobic hatred and homophobic violence, but this also relates to male violence more generally.

Second, this analysis helps to problematise any notion of the 'biological' or the 'natural' in terms of the forms of physical activity boys choose to do, a point which has been convincingly made about girls by feminist scholars (in particular Young, 1990). So much of 'common sense' discourse around physical activity and children is concerned with what boys and girls 'naturally' like to do and what boys and girls are 'naturally' good at. Given that physical educators regularly claim to be primarily concerned with expanding the movement choices open to children (Green, 1998, 2000), there seems to be a strong argument in favour of physical education working against, rather than reinforcing, the sexist and homophobic discourses which limit the movement forms children feel safe and comfortable about trying.

Of course, as I have said, Alex's reaction was particularly vehement and readers might legitimately ask why I have singled out his response from all the others. I did so because it is this kind of response, the angry, difficult male student, which, almost to a person, my teacher education undergraduate students raise as their reason for not wanting to teach dance in schools. Despite Alex's apparent atypicality, for many teachers he is a spectre which occupies a disproportionate amount of space within our pedagogical imaginations.

III

Although my teacher education students may not dance with their own students when they start teaching, they dance with and for me. As part of the assessment for the one and only dance module in their degree course, I ask them to form small groups and compose a movement sequence of between three and five minutes duration. For research purposes, I have videotaped the results of their work over the last four years. The results of their work have ranged from the self-conscious to the ecstatic, from music video extravaganzas to literal narratives, and from sombre meditation to humorous self-deprecation.

In one particular performance, five athletically built men walk to the middle of the stage. They are wearing top hats and dinner jackets, pink tutus, black stockings and sports shoes and begin five minutes of well rehearsed movement sequences. They progress deftly from soft-shoe shuffle to oom-pa-pa thigh slapping to slow waltz to heavy metal mosh and more, each section accompanied by its own neatly edited music backing. Towards the end, they strike balletic poses, classical music fills the air and they become prima-ballerinas. Their audience of peers and lecturer, already totally engrossed in the show, scream with laughter. The music stops, the men bow and we roar our approval. We feel good.

In terms of the criteria I had set for this piece of assessment, it was the superior item of its year. I had asked them to explore movement and in five short minutes they had crawled along the floor, flown through the air and almost bounced off the ceiling. However, my reflection on this work and other items like it over the period of this research has brought me closer to the sense that something is missing. The feminist dance educator, Sue Stinson (1998), has discussed the limitations of what we might call 'traditional' approaches to creative dance in which students simply 'explore movement'. She argues that this kind of creative dance can make teachers and students feel happy, but that it produces 'docile' bodies and decontextualised movement. My feeling is that this is an accurate description of much of the dance that has taken place in my own classroom; the students are occupied, they say they had fun, and they usually want a copy of the video tape! But what is it for?

By the same token, Stinson also points to the problematic fantasies of critical pedagogies, not least of which is the idea that we, as academics, can speak about changing the world from the relative safety of the lecture hall, while expecting our students to be change-agents in the very different climates of schools. I agree with Stinson when she argues that there is still a great deal of work to be done in developing critical, feminist and anti-homophobic dance pedagogies.

So what was the dance item that I have just described about and what, if anything, was learned? I do not think the use of humour here is insignificant. As Nayak and Kehily (2001) have argued, the ability to deploy and absorb ridicule is a key feature of heterosexual masculinity in schools and elsewhere, while Brown (1998) and Skelton (1993) have explored the role of sexist and homophobic humour within the macho cultures of undergraduate physical education. So while I would reject glib or singular interpretations of this performance, I would contend that the use of humour by this group (and many of the other all male groups over the period of this research) was one way of managing the discomfort caused by being forced to dance in front of other people. Whereas Shawn used serious, heroic and hyper-athletic themes to convince audiences that his dancers were not gay, these students chose to parody femininity, to perform caricatures of a variety of dance forms and to avoid a more revealing and less ironic 'self display'. Like Alex, I imagine that the thought of dancing, at least in particular ways, made these men anxious. Throughout their performance they rarely looked at the audience, preferring to watch each other, occasionally giggling nervously (apparently) at the situation they found themselves in. There was little sense in which they felt comfortable enough to invite the gaze of the audience and, thereby, announce that this was *them* on stage. The humour and the averted eyes made it clear that it was definitely someone else up there.

But unlike other performances of this kind, this one had been thoroughly rehearsed and they touched and smiled and laughed with excitement when it was all over. They had, I think, derived pleasure from it. The music, the ballet skirts and the context of a performance had given them 'permission' to move in ways they had probably rarely if ever tried. Obviously the performance could legitimately be 'read' as an attempt to use humour as a means of preserving masculine power via the often used image (particularly on Australian television) of 'footballers in women's clothing'. However, I would maintain that the performance also made available new pleasures for both dancers and spectators as well as spaces for moving and 'being' in different ways. These pleasures and spaces are 'new' and 'different' partly because they are so marginal to what physical education is usually understood to be about and partly because this kind of dance is so unlike the kinds of movement experiences (mainly sport) that physical education usually makes available.

One final thought about what other kinds of performances they might have given sticks in my mind. As hard as I try, I cannot visualise the bodies of these five men, well known within their peer group as 'tough', 'cool' footballers, performing an intensely serious, graceful, emotionally charged group dance set to appropriate music. I cannot imagine them doing it and I cannot imagine their audience being able to sit and watch calmly as these bearers of gendered power quietly risked it all.[7] Why is this?

Being someone else

Jackson (1996, pp. 27–28) has written that 'While we are engaging in ever more sophisticated modes of theorising about gender, sexuality and subjectivity, we still have no satisfactory way of approaching the very basic question: How did I get this way?' The lack of certainty that I feel around the problems of theorising gender, sexuality and subjectivity, and my curiosity about the relevance of physical movement to these problems, partly explains my interest in Ted Shawn. From a strictly theoretical point of view, his practices may, at first glance, seem to offer us little. His own discourse both implicitly and explicitly oppressed some groups which were already significantly oppressed. But what was the effect of the moving bodies of his dancers upon those who watched? What pleasures and displeasures did they derive or discover? Even Shawn's most trenchant academic critics do not doubt his influence in legitimating dance as an art form, and, by extension, opening up avenues of artistic expression for many more male and female, gay and lesbian artists than might otherwise have been the case. In my view, and without sanctioning the more egregious aspects of his discourse, Shawn's work suggests that theoretical purity is not the precondition for action. Shawn was, at least in one sense, like all of us, both teachers and academics: anxious to formulate a mode of practice with only fragmentary, incomplete and contradictory knowledge and beliefs to guide.

Fragmentary and incomplete would probably overstate what we presently know about the use of movement to combat oppression. As a teacher and researcher, I have therefore sought to explore the possibility that the relationships between movement and identity are neither unidirectional nor linear. While it is clear that 'who we are' informs how we move and prefer to move, the extent to which movement experiences might make available new ways of thinking and being remains obscure.

However, by making masculinity (as an institution) and masculinities (as identities) the foci of research and classroom practice, it is possible to gain a sense of the extent to which the bodies of boys and men are already disciplined and the difficulties some of us have imagining them moving in other ways. Considering the astonishing gap between what bodies can do and what they 'choose' to do may be one way of foregrounding the disciplining effects of gender and sexuality, and making material the discourses which construct them.

That my interest in dance relates (although is not reduced) to its capacity to make us uncomfortable is a crucial point. There is a tradition within theatrical dance and, by extension, dance education which sees dance as a universal experience, inherently good, essentially pleasurable and capable of changing the world for the better by virtue of its being. This discourse is prominent in the work of Ted Shawn and other 20th century modern dancers. I make no such claim. I am interested in dance's discursive locatedness, its inadvertent political status and its potential at this moment in time to be of use in the classroom.

It should also be clear that although I have mentioned the word 'sexuality' a number of times, my specific concern has been to problematise heterosexuality and to explicate its construction within particular classed, raced and geographical settings. For example, my work on Ted Shawn, far from telling us much about homosexuality, underscores the beliefs and prejudices of some heterosexual people and the ways in which Shawn was able to recognise, co-opt and subvert them. Similarly, by talking to boys about physical activity and watching my undergraduate students dance, I have arrived at the conclusion that movement itself is a potentially powerful pedagogical tool because it articulates the unspoken investments that, in this case, straight identifying boys and men have in particular discourses of gender and sexuality. Through its very materiality, movement highlights the radically constructed nature of the bodies and identities that produce it. And through the emotions it arouses, both for mover and for viewer, we gain a sense of how much is at stake for heterosexual boys and men.

The research I have described above, particularly in sections II and III, suggest that we cannot be sure how students, particularly male students who are accustomed to getting their way in physical education, will react when asked to create and do dance. However, there is one point about which we can be more certain. Dance movement is likely to be (at least initially) an uncomfortable experience for some students and that, whether we acknowledge it or not, much of this discomfort will be related to the gendered identities of these students. While I have heard male students use words like 'weird', 'stupid' and 'dumb' to describe dance movement, my research suggests that the association of dance *per se* and particular forms of dance movement with both feminine and non-heterosexual ways of moving and being remains strong. Indeed, it is this association in the minds of male teachers and students which, more than anything else, keeps dance out of physical education classes. And yet it is this knowledge, the knowledge that bodies carry and construct gendered meanings, which we might address through dance. And while it is true that all forms of movement carry social meanings, creative dance, via its association with non-normative sexualities and its relatively unstructured movement vocabulary (certainly in comparison with the highly codified movement technologies of sport and gymnastics which usually constitute the practice of physical education) is uniquely placed to raise issues such as homophobia, to offer students other ways (besides reading, writing and talking) of 'discussing' this issue, and to allow students the pleasure (and pain) of being someone else.

Notes

1   A number of different terms have been coined to describe the relatively recent literature concerned with the social construction of masculinities. I do not strongly advocate any particular term, but use 'masculinities studies' to refer to work which, to a greater or lesser extent, draws on feminist research into the social construction of gender but which is primarily concerned with male experience.

2   The authors cited here are included to give the reader a general sense of the theoretical traditions that this work draws upon. For a fuller explication of this framework see Gard (2001a).

3   By no means is this comment intended to suggest that teachers and students are incapable of engaging with the theoretical terrain which frames this work. My intention is only to indicate that such an engagement is not a precondition for being able to discuss the substantive issues of justice in schools and universities which I raise.

4   Thomas (1997) is particularly scathing of the use of 'theories' which purport to explain phenomena once and for all. Drawing on the likes of Heidegger, Nietzsche, Feyerabend, Wittgenstein, Foucault and postmodernism more generally, he advocates for an 'anything-goes' 'methodological terrorism', and an explicitly anti-disciplinary approach to educational research. He writes: '. . . perhaps the most serious problem concerning theory is its encouragement to particular kinds of thinking and to the discouragement of . . . diversity of thought' (1997, p. 84).

5   There is not enough space here to go into the details of Shawn's choreography, but as authors such as Burt (1995) and Foulkes (2001) have observed, Shawn's dancers rarely touched except where forceful grips and movements were used, they constantly struck and held tense, muscular poses, they were usually arranged in sharply geometric patterns, they continually stamped their feet and struck imaginary objects against other imaginary objects, and, importantly, never flexed their wrists. Shawn actually seems to have believed that men's wrists were naturally less flexible than women's, and was particularly careful to avoid 'weak wristedness' on stage.

6   I thank Sharon Pickering and Will Letts for helping to clarify these points, as well as for their general feedback on this article.

7   By 'risked it all', I am certainly not suggesting that the material benefits of being young, white, male, middle class and good at football might suddenly evaporate after one dance performance. What I am getting at here is the degree to which the 'unimaginable' dance performance that I am describing is unimaginable because it would juxtapose the men whom the audience 'knows' with a gendered embodiment significantly at odds with this 'knowledge'. What would be 'at risk' in this situation would be our (including the dancers') knowledge of who they are.

References

Aalten, A. (1997) Performing the body, creating culture, in: K. Davis (Ed.) *Embodied Practices: Feminist Perspectives on the Body* (London, Sage).

Acker, S. (1994) *Gendered Education: Sociological Reflections on Women, Teaching, and Feminism* (Buckingham, Open University Press).

Apple, M.W. (1985) *Education and Power* (Boston, Ark Paperbacks).

Bond, K. (1994) How 'wild things' tamed gender distinctions, *Journal of Physical Education, Recreation and Dance*, 65, pp. 28–33.

Bordieu, P. & Passerson, J. (1977) *Reproduction in Education, Society and Culture* (London, Sage).

Brennan, D. (1996) Dance in the Northern Ireland physical education curriculum: a farsighted policy or an unrealistic innovation, *Women's Studies International Forum*, 19, pp. 493–503.

Brown, L. (1998) 'Boys' training': the inner sanctum, in: C. Hickey, L. Fitzclarence & R. Matthews (Eds) *Where the Boys Are: Masculinity, Sport and Education* (Geelong, Deakin Centre for Education and Change).

Burkitt, I. (1999) *Bodies of Thought: Embodiment, Identity and Modernity* (London, Sage).

Burt, R. (1995) *The Male Dancer: Bodies, Spectacle, Sexualities* (London, Routledge).

Butler, J. (1990) *Gender Trouble: Feminism and the Subversion of Identity* (New York, Routledge).

Butler, J. (1993) *Bodies That Matter: On The Discursive Limits of 'Sex'* (New York, Routledge).

Connell, R.W. (1993) *Schools and Social Justice* (Leichardt, NSW, Pluto Press).

Flintoff, A. (1991) Dance, masculinity and teacher education, *The British Journal of Physical Education*, Winter, pp. 31–35.

Flintoff, A. (1994) Sexism and homophobia in physical education: the challenge for teacher educators, *Physical Education Review*, 17, pp. 97–105.

Foster, S.L. (2001) Closets full of dances: modern dance's performance of masculinity and sexuality, in: J.C. Desmond (Ed.) *Dancing Desires: Choreographing Sexualities On and Off the Stage* (Madison, The University of Wisconsin Press).

Foulkes, J.L. (2001) Dance is for American Men: Ted Shawn and the intersection of gender, sexuality, and nationalism in the 1930s, in: J.C. Desmond (Ed.) *Dancing Desires: Choreographing Sexualities On and Off the Stage* (Madison, The University of Wisconsin Press).

Gard, M (2001a) Athletics, aesthetics and art: a study of men who dance. Unpublished PhD thesis (Wollongong, University of Wollongong).

Gard, M. (2001b) Dancing around the 'problem' of boys and dance, *Discourse: Studies in the Cultural Politics of Education*, 22, pp. 213–225.

Gard, M. & Meyenn, R. (2000) Boys, bodies, pleasure and pain: interrogating contact sports in schools, *Sport, Education and Society*, 5, pp. 19–34.

Green, K. (1998) Philosophies, ideologies and the practice of physical education, *Sport, Education and Society*, 3, pp. 125–143.

Green, K. (2000) Exploring the everyday 'philosophies' of physical education teachers from a sociological perspective, *Sport, Education and Society*, 5, pp. 109–129.

Grosz, E. (1994) *Volatile Bodies: Toward a Corporeal Feminism* (Bloomington, Indiana University Press).

hooks, b. (1994) *Teaching to Transgress: Education as the Practice of Freedom* (London, Routledge).

Jackson, S. (1996) Heterosexuality and feminist theory, in: D. Richardson (Ed.) *Theorising Heterosexuality: Telling It Straight* (Buckingham, Open University Press).

Jackson. S. & Scott, S. (2001) Putting the body's feet on the ground: towards a sociological reconceptualisation of gendered and sexual embodiment, in: K. Backett-Milburn & L. McKie (Eds) *Engendering the Body* (Basingstoke, Palgrave).

Kirk, D. (1993) *The Body, Schooling and Culture* (Geelong, Deakin University Press).

Kirk, D. (1998a) *Schooling Bodies: School Practice and Public Discourse 1880–1950* (London, Leicester University Press).

Kirk, D. (1998b) Educational reform, physical culture and the crisis of legitimation in physical education, *Discourse: Studies in the Cultural Politics of Education Education*, 19, pp. 101–112.

Kirk, D. (1999) Physical culture, physical education and relational analysis, *Sport, Education and Society*, 4, pp. 63–73.

Lindemann, G. (1997) The body of gender difference, in: K. Davis (Ed.) *Embodied Practices: Feminist Perspectives on the Body* (London, Sage).

MacDonald, D. (1993) Knowledge, gender and power in physical education teacher education, *Australian Journal of Education*, 37, pp. 259–278.

Marques, I.A. (1998) Dance education in/and the postmodern, in: S.B. Shapiro (Ed) *Dance, Power and Difference: Critical and Feminist Perspectives on Dance Education* (Champaign, IL, Human Kinetics).

McLaren, P. (1986) *Schooling as a Ritual Performance: Towards a Political Economy of Educational Symbols and Gestures* (London, Routledge & Kegan Paul).

Meglin, J.A. (1994) Gender issues in dance education, *Journal of Physical Education, Recreation and Dance*, 65, pp. 26–27.

Nayak, A. & K. Kehily, M.J. (2001) 'Learning to laugh': a study of schoolboy humour in the English secondary school, in: W. Martino & B. Meyenn (Eds) *What About the Boys? Issues of Masculinity in Schools* (Buckingham, Open University Press).

Ramazanoglu, C. (1995) Back to basics: heterosexuality, biology and why men stay on top, in: M. Maynard & J. Purvis (Eds) *(Hetero)sexual Politics* (London, Taylor & Francis).

Richardson, D. (1996) Heterosexuality and social theory, in: D. Richardson (Ed.) *Theorising Heterosexuality: Telling It Straight* (Buckingham, Open University Press).

Rothfield, P. (1988) Habeus corpus: feminism discourse and the body, *Writings on Dance Dance*, 3, pp. 6–12.

Scraton, S. (1990) *Gender and Physical Education* (Geelong, Deakin University).

Shawn, T. (1960) *One Thousand and One Night Stands* (New York, Doubleday).

Sherman, J. & Mumaw, B. (2000) *Barton Mumaw, Dancer: From Denishawn To Jacob's Pillow and Beyond* (Hanover, Wesleyan University Press/University Press of New England).

Skelton, A. (1993) On becoming a male physical education teacher: the informal culture of students and the construction of hegemonic masculinity, *Gender and Education*, 5, pp. 289–303.

Stinson, S.W. (1998) Seeking a feminist pedagogy for children's dance, in: S.B. Shapiro (Ed.) *Dance, Power and Difference: Critical and Feminist Perspectives on Dance Education* (Champaign, IL, Human Kinetics).

Talbot, M. (1997) Physical education and the national curriculum: some political issues, in: G. McFee & A. Tomlinson (Eds) *Sport and Leisure: Connections and Controversies* (Aachen, Meyer & Meyer Verlag).

Thomas, G. (1997) What's the use of theory?, *Harvard Educational Review*, 67, pp. 75–104.

Veri, M.J. (1999) Homophobic discourse surrounding the female athlete, *Quest*, 51, pp. 355–368.

Willis, P.E. (1977) *Learning to Labour: How Working Class Kids Get Working Class Jobs* (Farnborough, Saxon House).

Wright, J. (1996a) The construction of complementary in physical education, *Gender and Education*, 8, pp. 61–79.

Wright, J. (1996b) Mapping the discourses of physical education: articulating a female tradition, *Journal of Curriculum Studies*, 28, pp. 331–351.

Young, I.M. (1990) *Throwing Like a Girl and Other Essays in Feminist Philosophy and Social Theory* (Bloomington, Indiana University Press).

David Kirk and Ann MacPhail

TEACHING GAMES FOR UNDERSTANDING AND SITUATED LEARNING
Rethinking the Bunker-Thorpe model

BUNKER AND THORPE (1982) first proposed Teaching Games for Understanding (TGfU) in 1982 as an alternative to traditional, technique-led approaches to games teaching and learning. Since then, TGfU has attracted widespread attention from teachers, coaches, and researchers (Rink, French, & Tjeerdsma, 1996). While there have been developments of the Bunker-Thorpe approach in the work of researchers such as Griffin, Oslin, and Mitchell (1997), and Gréhaigne and Godbout (1995), there have been no attempts to revise the Bunker-Thorpe model itself.

We believe there have been important advances in educational learning theory since the model first appeared that could be beneficial to the development of TGfU. There has also been a recent resurgence of interest in learning among physical education researchers. Metzler (2000) and Rink (1999) have argued that instructional strategies should be based on learning theory, since without a clear understanding of how learning takes place, teachers cannot expect to achieve intended learning outcomes. As Metzler notes, TGfU is an instructional model focused on developing learners' abilities to play games. As such, a perspective on learning underpins the model. Yet this perspective has not been developed and made explicit, even though there was some early published work on the psychological and philosophical dimensions of TGfU (Kirk, 1983; Piggot, 1982).

We wish to stress at the outset that we do not intend in this paper to provide a model of learning in games, valuable though this may be. We wish to retain, examine, and modify the original TGfU model, with its emphasis on instruction, for a number of reasons. First, the model is well known to researchers and teachers and has been widely used as a developmental tool for teachers and coaches (Australian Sports Commission, 1997a; Butler, 1997; Chandler & Mitchell, 1991; Doolittle, 1995; Griffin et al., 1997). Second, Metzler (2000) provides a sound argument for TGfU to be considered one of a number of instructional models in physical education. Among other things, instructional models provide guidelines to teachers on how to put into practice particular approaches to physical education. Third, as we will argue in this paper, we need to know more from research about how teachers and coaches use the model, as compared to the TGfU approach in general, to structure experiences for learners in games.

Physical education researchers have suggested that approaches to learning to play games such as the TGfU approach may be broadly consistent with cognitive, constructivist, and situated theories of learning (Dodds, Griffin, & Placek, 2001; Griffin, Dodds, Placek, et al., 1999; Kirk & Macdonald, 1998; Rovegno, Nevett, & Babiarz, 2001). These theoretical perspectives emphasize the social, cultural, and physical learning that physical education activities such as games can promote. They also show that learning to play games involves the development of skills such as strategic thinking and problem solving—two important but often understated higher-order cognitive skills that game play can foster (Aspin, 1976). Given traditional resistance in education systems to the idea that physical education can make such a contribution to cognitive development (Kirk & Tinning, 1990), TGfU provides a valuable example of what is possible.

The paper begins with a description of the TGfU approach and overviews recent research on TGfU. A situated learning perspective is then introduced and applied in examining the Bunker-Thorpe TGfU model. The intended outcome of this paper is to produce a revised form of the TGfU model that can inform future directions in the practice of and research on TGfU.

A description of teaching games for understanding

The Teaching Games for Understanding (TGfU) approach developed from the work of Rod Thorpe and David Bunker at Loughborough University during the 1970s and early 1980s (Bunker & Thorpe, 1982; Thorpe & Bunker, 1989). Other terms that describe developments of this approach include the Tactical Games Model (Griffin et al., 1997) and Game Sense (Australian Sports Commission, 1997a). Thorpe and Bunker observed that much games teaching and coaching was dominated by the development of techniques within highly structured lessons. They also observed that in school physical education, the development of techniques took up the majority of lesson time with little time left to actually play the game. Even when game play was included in lessons, teachers and coaches rarely made connections between the technique practices and how and when these techniques should be applied in game play.

A common complaint voiced by teachers and coaches was that the techniques learned laboriously in lessons and training sessions broke down in game play. Bunker and Thorpe's response to this problem was to develop an alternative approach to games teaching and coaching that helped players to learn the tactics and strategies of game play in tandem with technique development. The Bunker-Thorpe TGfU model can be seen in Figure 1.

At the heart of their approach was the use of modified games to suit the developmental level of the learners (Thorpe, 1990). All TGfU teaching and coaching takes place within the framework of game play and the modified game form. Modifications are made to rules, playing area, and equipment. Techniques are developed using drills and other training practices common to the traditional approach. A technique is only introduced when the players reach a level of game play that requires them to learn the technique. As the players' expertise develops, the game form is changed to continue to challenge the

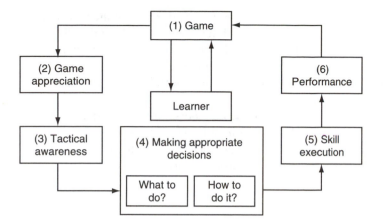

Figure 1 The Teaching Games for Understanding model (from Bunker & Thorpe, 1982).

players in terms of game appreciation, tactical awareness, decision-making, and execution of technique.

In conjunction with the development of the TGfU model, Bunker and Thorpe (1982) argued that some groups of games share key characteristics determined by their rules and tactics. For example, they suggested games such as the following:

1   Soccer, rugby union, and rugby league, as well as basketball, netball, and hockey, can be categorized as invasion games since they share:

   •   the common tactical features of invading territory to make space in attack;
   •   the containment of space in defense;
   •   the use of a goal or similar target for scoring.

2   Net/wall games such as tennis, table tennis, and volleyball share:

   •   the concept of playing the shot so opponents cannot return it;
   •   all players must serve and receive the ball;
   •   the target for scoring is on the playing surface.

3   Striking/fielding games such as cricket, baseball, and rounders share:

   •   the concept of scoring by striking a ball into open spaces;
   •   fielders being placed strategically to prevent runs from being scored.

Bunker and Thorpe suggested that simplified, modified, and generic versions of games could be used to teach the main tactics required by each game in the above categories. An example would be a court-based game with a small number of simple rules for traveling, contact, re-starts, and scoring that serves as a generic lead-up to games such as basketball, korfball, and netball. This is a particularly important consideration for physical education teachers working within severe time constraints in a school setting. This suggestion does raise questions, however, about the extent to which generic game forms can allow players to learn tactics and techniques in tandem, since the techniques of most games are highly specialized.

The terminology of TGfU has had an impact on policy in several countries. In England and Wales, the terminology of invasion, net/wall, and striking/fielding games is enshrined within the statutory National Curriculum for Physical Education (Qualifications Curriculum Authority, 1999). In Australia the same terminology is used to structure the Aussie Sport Program of modified games produced by the Australian Sports Commission (1997b).

While some studies have examined the possibility of transferring tactical understanding among game forms within the same category (Jones & Farrow, 1999; Oslin & Mitchell, 1999), it is the potential of a TGfU approach to facilitate tactical understanding in games that has attracted the most attention from researchers.

Research on TGfU

TGfU began to be scrutinized empirically by researchers around the late 1980s. Much of this research has taken the form of experimental studies that have compared TGfU with the forms of games teaching it is assumed to replace, traditional technique-led approaches (Griffin, Oslin, & Mitchell, 1995; Lawton, 1989; Oslin, Mitchell, & Griffin, 1998; Turner & Martinek, 1992). Rink et al. (1996) noted that research on TGfU has reported positive learning outcomes for students. The most powerful finding across the studies reviewed by Rink et al. was that students who were taught from a TGfU perspective tend to perform better on tests of tactical knowledge than those taught from a technique-led perspective. Some studies (e.g., Griffin et al., 1995; Lawton, 1989) have suggested that a TGfU approach may be perceived by students as more enjoyable than the technique-led approach, thus they may be more highly motivated to participate.

Rink et al. (1996) also noted that, despite some positive findings, the studies reviewed could not provide conclusive support for TGfU over technique-led approaches. They argued that this was due to different research designs, making comparison difficult because studies varied according to the game chosen, the age of participants, the length and nature of the intervention, the variable chosen for investigation, and the ways in which these variables were measured.

Adding to Rink et al.'s point, we propose that the equivocal nature of these findings may also be due to their treatment of TGfU and technique-based approaches as alternative forms of practice. The difficulty here is not that the researchers themselves accept as valid the notion that cognition and physical performance are independent processes, or even that these can be studied as if they were independent. Indeed, most appear to accept Bunker and Thorpe's (1982) insistent claim that teaching for understanding must also include technique development. The difficulty instead may be located in the traditional dualistic divide in physical education between cognition and physical performance, and in the constructs used to theorize this relationship.

Rink et al. (1996) point out that researchers use a range of constructs to describe knowledge and learning in TGfU. The most common constructs are the notions of declarative knowledge, procedural knowledge, strategic knowledge, and technique or movement execution. Before we advance with our examination of the Bunker-Thorpe model, it is important that we clarify our understanding and use of these key constructs.

Constructs for conceptualizing learning in games

In their discussion of expertise in sport, Thomas and Thomas (1994) explain that declarative knowledge is concerned with facts such as game rules, aims, terminology, and etiquette. They define procedural knowledge as knowledge "used to generate action" (p. 299), such as knowing how to get past an opponent in a one-on-one situation in soccer. Thomas and Thomas claim that some measure of declarative knowledge is a precursor to the development of procedural knowledge and that both are present in activities in which it is possible to develop expertise, such as playing chess, programming a computer, or writing an essay.

According to Alexander and Judy (1988), strategic knowledge is a subset of procedural knowledge. Strategies are employed intentionally before, during, and after a performance and are goal-directed. In sport, strategic knowledge is typically dependent on what Alexander and Judy call domain-specific knowledge, which includes declarative and procedural knowledge. The various strategies that may be employed for getting past an opponent in soccer would require some knowledge of the rules and techniques of this game. Dodds et al. (2001) note that although expert/novice studies have investigated aspects of the interaction between domain-specific and strategic knowledge, this is an underdeveloped area of research. They also note that, of the existing studies, few have included children.

The execution of specific movement techniques adds a further dimension to game play that is, according to Thomas and Thomas, a source of error unique to sport. The relationship between each of these elements of knowledgeable performance in games can be summarized as "if-then-do": "declarative knowledge becomes represented as a series of conditions (if statements) linked to action selection (then statements) and then to actions (do statements)" (Thomas & Thomas, 1994, p. 305).

Thomas and Thomas note that the if-then-do relationship is not nearly as straightforward as it sounds. They provide an example of the impact on procedural knowledge of a learner's level of physical and skill development:

> The 5 year old tee-ball player who knows his throwing is not the best and the first baseman's catching is even poorer, often opts to run the ball to first, rather than throwing the runner out. The decision, based on previous experience is to make the safest attempt at the goal. These players apparently know that throwing is what they should do, but based on skill they decide not to throw.
>
> (1994, p. 305)

What this example demonstrates is that the knowledge dimensions of game play are interdependent. In contrast to this point, some of the experimental studies of TGfU seem to have built into their design the notion that TGfU is primarily concerned with developing declarative, procedural, and strategic knowledge, while the traditional, technique-based approaches are primarily concerned with the effectiveness of movement execution.

It appears that such dualistic thinking about cognition and physical performance remains pervasive. A case in point is McMorris' (1998) critique of TGfU from the perspective of motor behavior. McMorris starts with the view that TGfU is a cognition-to-technique approach. Motor behaviorists in contrast recommend a technique-to-cognition approach. On the basis of this view, McMorris claims that criticisms made by proponents of TGfU about traditional technique-based methods of teaching games are criticisms of poor practice rather than of the technique-to-cognition approach itself. He concludes that TGfU research has provided very little new knowledge for motor behaviorists.

Such a conclusion may indeed be warranted on the basis of the evidence produced by experimental studies of TGfU, since their findings demonstrate that cognition and physical performance are both of key importance in learning to play games. However, as we have noted, the design of research studies that have sought to contrast TGfU with technique-led approaches may have inadvertently supported some of McMorris' criticisms.

An ecological version of information processing illustrates the importance of viewing knowledge and technique dimensions of game play as interdependent. According to Abernethy (1996), the information processing approach emphasizes the importance of perception and decision-making as two of the three sequential phases of information processing, with the third being movement execution or acting.

Abernethy argues that during the perceiving phase, an individual is trying to determine what is happening and to identify what information is relevant in a particular set of circumstances. An example is a basketball player who has just received the ball and must identify the position of teammates and opponents, her or his own position on the field or court, distance from the goal, stage of the game and the score, and so on. Abernethy notes that the ability to sift the important information from all the other information available in the environment, and to do this quickly and accurately, is a key characteristic of expert players.

The decision-making phase involves the player deciding the best course of action—in basketball whether to pass, dribble, or shoot, and which is the most appropriate kind of pass or shot. Typically, expert players are much more efficient and faster decision-makers than novices are because they have learned through experience to link their actions to circumstances in the game.

During the movement execution or acting phase, a series of neural impulses recruit muscles to execute the selected movements with appropriate timing, coordination, and force. Movement execution is a vital part of game play. But it is not necessarily the most important part, as the emphasis in traditional technique-led approaches would suggest.

A situated learning perspective

The importance placed by information processing theorists such as Abernethy, Thomas, and Thomas (1993) on the active engagement of the learner with the environment through perception and decision-making is a key assumption that underpins most situated cognition research (Kirshner & Whitson, 1997). A situated perspective assumes that learning involves the active engagement of individuals with their environment (Rovengo, 1999; Rovegno & Kirk, 1995). Rather than merely receiving information transmitted from another source and internalizing that information, as some versions of a cognitive perspective would suggest, individuals actively appropriate information (Kirshner & Whitson, 1998). In so doing, they adapt new knowledge in order to fit it to what they already know (Prawat, 1999).

Dodds et al. (2001) summarize research in science education showing that this prior knowledge varies among individuals and results in learners approaching new learning episodes with alternative conceptions of a topic. For example, Brooker, Kirk, Braiuka, and Bransgrove (2000) reported that for children whose prior knowledge of basketball was formed through their viewing of professional adult sport on television, any modification in school physical education lessons to the "real" media sport was considered as disappointing and unsatisfying. For them, playing basketball was playing the media's version of the game.

Greeno (1997) argues that learning is situated in the sense that it is socially organized. This is particularly the case when learning is constructed and constituted by the institutional requirements of the school. For example, Bereiter (1990) coined the term "schoolwork module" to account for the ways in which individuals respond to the institutional requirements of the school in much the way Jackson (1968) first reported under the rubric of the hidden curriculum. The rules and procedures of the school, and the forms of social interaction they produce, permeate what and how children learn. For example, in the course of learning to play soccer, a child may also be learning about getting along with other children, pleasing the teacher, and her or his own personal abilities and qualities.

Even when a child is working alone, perhaps completing a homework task, learning remains situated because it is socially organized (Greeno, 1997). The student's use of textbooks and computer, access to the Internet, and the study of a task set by the teacher in accordance with school and state curriculum requirements illustrates the layers of social organization of learning, even when it takes place in isolation from others.

Lave and Wenger's (1991) theory of situated learning suggests is necessary to investigate relationships among the various physical, social, and cultural dimensions of the context for learning. This is because the substance of what is learned cannot be disconnected from the communities of practice that generate and sustain knowledge. A key task for schools is to provide young people with opportunities to become what Lave and Wenger describe as legitimate peripheral participants in these communities of practice, whereby they have authentic learning experiences that are valued by themselves and other members of the community of practice. Kirk and Macdonald (1998) suggest that sport education may have the potential to make this connection for young people since it reorganizes most features of competitive sport into an educational form.

A number of key points emerge from this discussion of a situated learning perspective. Learning is an active process of engagement with socially organized forms of subject matter, through perceptual and decision-making processes and the execution of appropriate movement responses. Individuals bring prior knowledge to learning episodes that contain a (sometimes wide) range of alternative conceptions of a topic. The learner's active engagement with subject matter is embedded within and constituted by layers of physical, sociocultural, and institutional contexts. These contexts include the immediate physical environment of the classroom, gym, or playing field, social interaction between class members, the institutional form of the school, and aspects of culture such as media sport.

Rethinking the Bunker-Thorpe model from a situated learning perspective

Next we will examine each component of the Bunker-Thorpe model in light of this situated learning perspective. The revised model is presented in Figure 2.

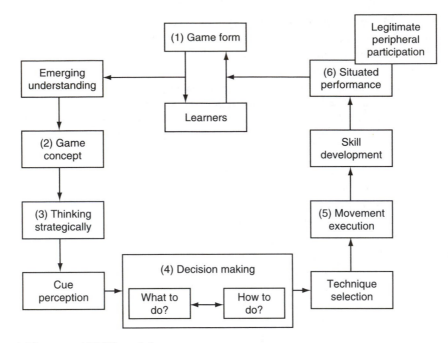

Figure 2 The revised TGfU model.

The game form/learner relationship

The first category in the Bunker-Thorpe model is the game and its relationship to the learner's developmental level. In most situations, consideration of the learner requires the game to be modified, and for this reason Bunker and Thorpe refer to the "game form." For example, modifications to tennis for beginners might involve a "throw-catch" game without racquets, or the use of padder bats and foam balls, lowering the net, and with a corresponding simplification of the rules.

The model requires the teacher or coach to consider the learner and to be knowledgeable about the game form best suited to learner's capabilities. The most obvious consideration is the physical developmental levels of the learners. Consideration of this factor has led to NASPE's advice on developmentally appropriate physical education in the United States (National Association for Sport and Physical Education, 2000), and programs such as Aussie Sport in Australia (Australian Sports Commission, 1997b) and TOPS in Britain (Youth Sport Trust, 2000). These initiatives share the features of modified equipment, resizing of playing surfaces, and simplified game rules. From a situated learning perspective, a number of additional factors need to be considered.

Given the role of prior knowledge and alternative conceptions of domain-specific knowledge in learning, the teacher needs to have some sense of what the learner already understands about the game (Dodds et al., 2001; Rovegno, 1999). This includes, for the learner, direct experience as a participant as well as experience of the game as a spectator. Since the game form is a context in itself, it is also important from a situated learning perspective that the teacher know something about the learner's conceptions of learning in physical education classes (Kirk, Brooker, & Braiuka, 2000).

The tasks set by the teacher that constitute the game form need to make sense to the learner in terms of his or her emerging understanding of the game (Rovegno, 1999). Such connections, between the game form and the learner's understanding of the game, need to be made explicitly in order to overcome the school work module (Bereiter, 1990). The school work form of a task tends to be remote and abstract from the learner's everyday experience outside the school. A good example of this is where children complete a prolonged period of learning isolated parts of a skill before being offered an opportunity to experience how the skills relate to playing the game (Thorpe & Bunker, 1989). In the case of TGfU, this means that the tasks set by the teacher need to be seen as authentic and connected to the game from the learner's point of view.

These requirements of a situated perspective seem demanding enough when considering the relationship between one learner and the game form. The challenge of modifying the game and setting appropriate tasks becomes even more demanding when a group of learners is considered. Taking into account the sense that each member of the group makes of the game form, the relationship of the game form to the game, and learning within the game form context is extremely complex. Practical issues will undoubtedly direct a teacher's actions. However, some form of graded tasks for groups of students, such as manipulating the width of the play area to challenge different ability levels, or loading the attack or defense, may facilitate understanding and game play. Also, explicit contextualization of the game form in relation to what the teacher knows about the learners' perspectives may be necessary, such as using, say, the Olympics to frame a unit of work in track and field.

Game appreciation, tactical awareness, and emerging understanding

In the Bunker-Thorpe model of TGfU, the categories of game appreciation, tactical awareness, and making appropriate decisions align with domain-specific and strategic knowledge. Game appreciation aligns with declarative knowledge, such as knowing rules, player positions, and scoring systems of a game. Making appropriate decisions aligns with procedural knowledge in terms of knowing what to do in response to a game situation, such as how to defend in a one-on-one situation in soccer. Tactical awareness seems to rest somewhere between these two dimensions of knowledge.

Given Bunker and Thorpe's emphasis on players understanding how to play, it seems likely that game appreciation and tactical awareness are intended to go beyond the mere acquisition of rules and other information about a game. The emphasis on understanding suggests that seeing the relationships among pieces of information may be more important to game performance than merely acquiring information (Aspin, 1976).

From a situated learning perspective, game appreciation might be more accurately represented as a player's concept of a game and the ways in which it might be played. Memorizing the rules, positions, and purposes is not the same thing as developing a concept of a game, although these aspects of declarative knowledge are the substance of concept development. The player's concept of the game plays an organizing role in relation to all aspects of game play.

A good way to test an individual's concept of a game is to imagine taking part in an unfamiliar game, say, Australian Rules football. If an individual is a knowledgeable invasion-game player and already knows that Australian Rules football is an invasion game, concept development might be more rapid for this individual than for someone without this prior knowledge. As learning progresses, the concept of Australian Rules football is likely to become increasingly sophisticated. Without some concept of the game, its central purpose, and the relationship of purpose to game form and the player's role, progress in learning to play the game is likely to be slow.

The ways in which the concept of a game may be conveyed to beginners in particular becomes an issue of key importance to teachers and coaches. The insertion in the revised model (in Figure 2) of the notion of emerging understanding between the categories of game form-learner and game concept is intended to provide teachers with a point of focus for helping learners make the connections between the purpose of the game and the game form.

Tactical awareness both feeds and is fed by a player's emerging concept of the game, based on domain-specific declarative and procedural knowledge. Given its central import-ance in TGfU, the term "tactical awareness" may be somewhat imprecise in identifying the assumptions about learning embedded in the model. Players don't need to be simply *aware* of tactics. They need to be able to *deploy* them appropriately (Alexander & Judy, 1988; Aspin, 1976).

The notion of "thinking strategically" may offer a more explicit and focused term for what Bunker and Thorpe intended here. Strategies can of course vary in the level of their generality and specificity. There can be strategies that apply to the whole team or group, and others that are more specific to individual players, strategies for a season, or strategies for specific games. As Alexander and Judy (1988) note, strategies draw on declarative and procedural knowledge. The notion of thinking strategically replaces tactical awareness in the revised model because the notion of strategy conveys a focused, intentional, relational, goal- and action-oriented sense of what the learner does in the process of using declarative and procedural knowledge.

Cue perception and decision-making

The category of making appropriate decisions is common to both information-processing and situated perspectives on learning. Perception can be located here perhaps, between thinking strategically and Bunker and Thorpe's more substantive and instantiated sub-category of decision-making. With perception high-lighted in the model, teachers then have license to facilitate cue recognition. Kirk et al. (2000) argue that even in a TGfU approach, teachers do not teach for cue recognition automatically. An improvement in a player's ability to discern what information is appropriate in any given set of circum-stances, as a wealth of research shows, is a function of experience (Abernethy, 1996). Kirk et al. argue that players must be given opportunities to develop the experience of recog-nizing appropriate cues in a variety of contexts, such as learning that a teammate's outstretched hand is a cue to pass the basketball into his or her path, or when an attacking player is feinting rather than dodging.

Cue perception may be a key factor linking game concept, thinking strategically, and decision-making. Research on TGfU has well established that learners are able to display declarative knowledge of rules and purposes prior to displaying procedural and strategic knowledge (Rink et al., 1996). Kirk et al. (2000) speculate that a failure to display declarative knowledge in game play when it was previously evident in a question-answer session may be explained by a player's inability to recognize the cues that activate particu-lar strategies, especially those relating to positioning and the timing of actions. Teachers

need to make links explicitly between the cues embedded in particular sets of circumstances in a game (such as a defensive formation) and the application of specific strategies
to overcome that formation (such as creating an overlap in offense).

Decision-making, movement execution, and technique selection

If making appropriate decisions involves perceptual activity interfacing with a stock of
declarative knowledge, expressed in the revised model as game concept and thinking
strategically, then decisions about how to act interface with the actual execution of
movement. Bunker and Thorpe's model locates skill execution within a separate category
from decision-making. Thomas and Thomas (1994) claim that decision-making in games is
strongly influenced by knowledge of one's own and others' movement execution capabilities. If this is the case, it may be appropriate to insert a mediating process between
decision-making in terms of how to act and the more specific process of movement
execution. In other words, some elements of procedural knowledge and movement
execution are understood to interface.

A key mediating category to insert here may be technique selection. Technique
selection can be understood to refer to a process of reflection on the appropriate techniques that are actually available to the player and the player's own knowledge of which
technique(s) she or he can execute with confidence. By making this process visible within
the model, teachers can address explicitly "how to do?" as a process of self-reflection and
selection from a range of options.

Skill development and situated performance

The interfaces between skill execution and performance in the original Bunker-Thorpe
model, and between performance and the game form/learner relationship, must be
reconsidered given the developments to the revised model so far. The final category
in Bunker and Thorpe's original model is performance. This category refers to normative criteria, often consisting of an advanced form of a game. This normative category
effectively provides a means of judging the relationship between a learner's progress
through cycles of modified game forms and conventional adult or advanced versions of
a game.

Bunker and Thorpe consistently used the term "skill" to refer to an amalgam of
strategic and technique capabilities in game players. The notion of skill development in the
revised model offers itself as a useful mediating process between movement execution to
performance.

Skill in this context comes close to what Bereiter (1990) describes as a "learning
module." A learning module is a cluster of related, rather than discrete or separate,
capabilities. Skills as modules represent clusters of cue perception capabilities, strategies,
and techniques that are activated together in specific game situations. As players' performances improve, their ability to activate skills as clusters of perception capabilities,
strategies, and techniques becomes smoother and more seamless.

The practice of set drills would seem to provide a good example of an intentional
attempt to cluster or modularize components of game play. For example, soccer players
often practice drills for passing and moving into space in attack. The drill might involve
two or three attackers, opposed or unopposed, with the aim of developing in combination

passing technique, perception of where space is, anticipation of the movement of team-mates, and strategies such as the wall-pass to get around defenders and progress the ball toward the goal.

The second interface to be reconsidered is between performance and the game form/learner relationship. This interface can be understood in terms of a learner's legitimate peripheral participation in a community of practice (Lave & Wenger, 1991). When Bunker and Thorpe were developing their model of TGfU in the late 1970s, the phenomenon of media sport was just beginning to emerge (McKay, 1991). Now more than 20 years later, media sport forms an important community of practice for young people's learning (Kirk, 1999). Young people's everyday experiences are saturated with professional, com-mercial, high-tech, elite adult versions of sports and games. This cultural phenomenon plays a significant part in shaping young people's concept of particular games and their expectations of what it will be like to participate in that game (Brooker et al., 2000). Rovegno (1999) has suggested that more attention needs to be paid to students' cultural conceptions of learning to play games. She claims,

> We must take students' personal and cultural experiences seriously. Students never come to school sport lessons without personal and cultural knowledge, knowledge of how sport and physical activities are portrayed in the mass media, and, with the exception of very young children, without knowledge of how sports are typically taught in schools.
>
> (Rovegno, 1999, p. 11)

The notion of "situated performance" in the revised model might better describe this normative category, reaching out as it does to consider the cultural location of sport and its role in young people's lives as legitimate peripheral participants in this community of practice (Kirk & Macdonald, 1998; Lave & Wenger, 1991). When sport is understood as a complex, multifaceted, and heterogeneous community of practice, it is possible to track players' learning trajectories over time as they begin to understand the broader social, cultural, and institutional practices that constitute games.

This notion of situated performance of TGfU provides one way of understanding the relationship between the game form and the player's prior and alternative conceptions of a game. Without analysis of the popular cultural forms of sport, leisure, exercise, and other related phenomena such as fashion, we may be limiting our understanding of the learner's perspective. We agree with Rovegno (1999) that it is important for young people to grasp the meaning of a game.

Conclusion

By modifying and making additions to the Bunker-Thorpe model, we have been con-cerned with explicating those dimensions of TGfU that seem to be omitted or under-developed. We believe that the interfaces between the elements of the model are worth elaborating upon since they may make crucial links for teachers and coaches. In particular, we suggest that explicit attention to the learner's perspective, game concept, thinking strategically, cue recognition, technique selection, and skill development as the cluster-ing of strategies and techniques, and situated performance as legitimate peripheral participation in games, elaborate upon the already existing but implied learning principles of the Bunker-Thorpe model.

The model has the appearance of a linear process. As Rovegno (1999) notes from her reading of the educational learning theory and motor control literature, learning in a complex medium such as games is not linear. We concur with this point and reiterate that the TGfU instructional model contains embedded assumptions about learning, but it does not seek to represent the learning process. Since this is an instructional model for facilitating understanding, we suggest that the structure needs to be presented in a form that will assist teachers. Here we encounter a key issue. We know relatively little about how teachers use the Bunker-Thorpe model and whether it is in fact useful to them as a model of instruction.

A research program centered on the revised TGfU model or some other form of the model immediately suggests itself. What we believe is required is a systematic examination of the revised model in practice and its further modification and development on the basis of this research program. If the model is to be useful as a means of guiding teaching for understanding in games, it must be able to identify for teachers the key moments in learning to play games that require their attention in terms of designing learning experiences.

When learning to play games is understood as a form of situated learning, we suggest that it becomes possible for teachers to explicitly address aspects of learning that have hitherto at best been understood only intuitively. So, for example, through a situated learning perspective, teachers may be able to address explicitly the authenticity and meaningfulness to children of the experience of learning to play games in school settings by developing better understandings of children's prior knowledge and alternative conceptions (Dodds et al., 2001). Whether the model can assist teachers in this process of reflective teaching is a matter for investigation through research.

Acknowledgement

We wish to thank the teachers at Springfield First School, Worthing, England, for working with us on the model between January and June 2000. We would also like to thank the two anonymous reviewers for their considerable assistance with this paper. Finally, thanks to Rod Thorpe and Len Almond for their valuable feedback on earlier drafts of this paper.

References

Abernethy, B. (1996). Basic concepts of motor control: Psychological perspectives. In B. Abernethy, V. Kippers, L.T. Mackinnon, R.J. Neal, & S. Hanrahan, *Biophysical foundations of human movement* (pp. 295–311). Melbourne: Macmillan.

Abernethy, B., Thomas, K., & Thomas, J. (1993). Strategies for improving understanding of motor expertise (or mistakes we have made and things we have learned!!). In J. Starkes & F. Allard (Eds.), *Cognitive issues in motor expertise* (pp. 317–356). Amsterdam: Elsevier Science.

Alexander, P.A., & Judy, J.E. (1988). The interaction of domain-specific and strategic knowledge in academic performance. *Review of Educational Research*, **58**, 375–404.

Aspin, D. (1976). 'Knowing how' and 'knowing that' and physical education. *Journal of the Philosophy of Sport*, **3**, 97–117.

Australian Sports Commission. (1997a). *Game sense: Developing thinking players*. Belconnen: Author.

Australian Sports Commission. (1997b). *Modified sport: A quality junior sport approach*. Belconnen: Author.

Bereiter, C. (1990). Aspects of an educational learning theory. *Review of Educational Research*, **60**, 603–624.

Brooker, R., Kirk, D., Braiuka, S., & Bransgrove, A. (2000). Implementing a Game Sense approach to teaching Year 8 basketball. *European Physical Education Review*, **6**, 7–26.

Bunker, D., & Thorpe, R. (1982). A model for the teaching of games in the secondary school. *Bulletin of Physical Education*, **10**, 9–16.

Butler, J. (1997). How would Socrates teach games? A constructivist approach. *Journal of Physical Education, Recreation and Dance*, **68**, 42–47.

Chandler, T.J.L., & Mitchell, S.A. (1991). Reflections on 'models of games education.' *Journal of Physical Education, Recreation and Dance*, **61**, 19–21.

Dodds, P., Griffin, L.L., & Placek, J.L. (2001). Chapter 2. A selected review of the literature on development of learners' domain-specific knowledge. *Journal of Teaching in Physical Education* [Monograph], **20**, 301–313.

Doolittle, S. (1995). Teaching net games to skilled students: A teaching for understanding approach. *Journal of Physical Education, Recreation and Dance*, **66**, 18–23.

Greeno, J.G. (1997). On claims that answer the wrong question. *Educational Researcher*, **26**, 5–17.

Gréhaigne, J-F., & Godbout, P. (1995). Tactical knowledge in team sports from a constructivist and cognitivist perspective. *Quest*, **47**, 490–505.

Griffin, L., Dodds, P., Placek, J.H., Carney, M.C., Tremino, F., Lachowetz, T., & Raymond, C. (1999). Middle school students' conceptions of soccer: Their solutions to tactical problems. *Research Quarterly for Exercise and Sport*, **70** (Suppl.), 89.

Griffin, L.L., Oslin, J.L., & Mitchell, S.A. (1995). An analysis of two instructional approaches to teaching net games. *Research Quarterly for Exercise and Sport*, **66** (Suppl.), 65–66.

Griffin, L.L., Oslin, J.L., & Mitchell, S.A. (1997). *Teaching sports concepts and skills: A tactical games approach*. Champaign, IL: Human Kinetics.

Jackson, P.W. (1968). *Life in classrooms*. New York: Holt, Rinehart & Winston.

Jones, C., & Farrow, D. (1999). The transfer of strategic knowledge: A test of the Games Classification Curriculum model. *Bulletin of Physical Education*, **35**, 103–124.

Kirk, D. (1983). Theoretical guidelines for 'Teaching for Understanding.' *Bulletin of Physical Education*, **9**, 41–45.

Kirk, D. (1999). Physical culture, physical education and relational analysis. *Sport, Education and Society*, **4**, 63–73.

Kirk, D., Brooker, R., & Braiuka, S. (2000, April). *Teaching games for understanding: A situated perspective on student learning*. Paper presented at the American Educational Research Association Annual Meeting, New Orleans.

Kirk, D., & Macdonald, D. (1998). Situated learning in physical education. *Journal of Teaching in Physical Education*, **17**, 376–387.

Kirk, D., & Tinning, R. (1990). Introduction: Physical education, curriculum and culture. D. Kirk & R. Tinning (Eds.), *Physical education, curriculum and culture: Critical issues in the contemporary crisis* (pp. 1–21). Lewes: Falmer.

Kirshner, D., & Whitson, J.A. (Eds.) (1997). *Situated cognition: Social, semiotic and psychological perspectives*. Hillsdale, NJ: Erlbaum.

Kirshner, D., & Whitson, J.A. (1998). Obstacles to understanding cognition as situated. *Educational Researcher*, **27**, 22–28.

Lave, J., & Wenger, E. (1991). *Situated learning: Legitimate peripheral participation*. New York: Cambridge University Press.

Lawton, J. (1989). Comparison of two teaching methods in games. *Bulletin of Physical Education*, **25**, 35–38.

McKay, J. (1991). *No pain, no gain: Sport in Australian culture*. Sydney: Prentice Hall.

McMorris, T. (1998). Teaching games for understanding: Its contribution to the knowledge of skill acquisition from a motor learning perspective. *European Journal of Physical Education*, **3**, 65–74.

Metzler, M.W. (2000). *Instructional models for physical education*. Boston: Allyn & Bacon.

National Association for Sport and Physical Education. (2000). Appropriate instructional practice—Developmentally appropriate practice for elementary school physical education. Reston, VA: Author.

Oslin, J.L., & Mitchell, S.A. (1999). An investigation of tactical transfer in net games. *European Journal of Physical Education*, **4**, 162–172.

Oslin, J.L., Mitchell, S.A., & Griffin, L.L. (1998). The Game Performance Assessment Instrument (GPAI): Development and preliminary validation. *Journal of Teaching in Physical Education*, **17**, 231–243.

Piggot, B. (1982). A psychological basis for new trends in games teaching. *Bulletin of Physical Education*, **18**, 17–22.

Prawat, R.S. (1999). Dewey, Pierce and the learning paradox. *American Educational Research Journal*, **36**, 47–76.

Qualifications Curriculum Authority. (1999). *Physical education. The national curriculum for England*. London: Author.

Rink, J.E. (1999, April). *What do students learn in physical activity and how do they learn?* Keynote presentation at the AIESEP Conference, Besancon, France.

Rink, J.E., French, K.E., & Tjeerdsma, B.L. (1996). Foundations for the learning and instruction of sport and games. *Journal of Teaching in Physical Education*, **15**, 399–417.

Rovegno, I. (1999, April). *What is taught and learned in physical activity programs: The role of content*. Keynote presentation at the AIESEP Conference, Besancon, France.

Rovegno, I., & Kirk, D. (1995). Articulations and silences in socially critical work on physical education: Toward a broader agenda. *Quest*, **47**, 447–474.

Rovegno, I., Nevett, M., & Babiarz, M. (2001). Chapter 5. Learning and teaching invasion-game tactics in 4th grade: Introduction and theoretical perspective. *Journal of Teaching in Physical Education* [Monograph], **20**, 341–351.

Thomas, K.T., & Thomas, J.R. (1994). Developing expertise in sport: The relation of knowledge and performance. *International Journal of Sport Psychology*, **25**, 295–312.

Thorpe, R. (1990). New directions in games teaching. In N. Armstrong (Ed.), *New directions in physical education*, Vol. 1 (pp. 79–100). Leeds, UK: Human Kinetics.

Thorpe, R., & Bunker, D. (1989). A changing focus in games education. In L. Almond (Ed.), *The place of physical education in schools* (pp. 42–71). London: Kogan Page.

Turner, A.P., & Martinek, T.J. (1992). A comparative analysis of two models for teaching games: Technique approach and game-centered (tactical focus) approach. *International Journal of Physical Education*, **29**(4), 15–31.

Youth Sport Trust. (2000). *The TOPS programs*. Retrieved Oct. 10, 2000, from the Internet at http://www.youthsport.net

Ben Dyson, Linda L. Griffin and Peter Hastie

SPORT EDUCATION, TACTICAL GAMES AND COOPERATIVE LEARNING
Theoretical and pedagogical considerations

The purpose of this article is to present Sport Education, Tactical Games, and Cooperative Learning as valuable instructional models in physical education. Situated learning is used as a theoretical framework and connection between Sport Education, Tactical Games, and Cooperative Learning. The structures of Sport Education, Tactical Games, and Cooperative Learning allow for participation to occur in a student-centered learning curriculum as opposed to a teacher-centered teaching curriculum. The teacher facilitates learning activities that have the potential to provide students with a holistic education that promotes social, physical, and cognitive learning outcomes. The emphasis is on active learning that involves the processes of decision making, social interaction, and cognitive understanding for students.

MANY EDUCATORS BELIEVE that students rather than the teacher should be at the center of the teaching and learning process. We present three student-centered models to learning: Sport Education (SE), Tactical Games (TG), and Cooperative Learning (CL), which hold specific assumptions about teaching and learning in physical education. The pedagogical implications of using SE, TG, and CL call for the teacher to serve as a facilitator of the learning within a student-centered environment. The teacher purposefully shifts responsibility to the student engaged in authentic, meaningful, and learning tasks.

SE, TG, and CL have the potential to move physical education beyond an activity-driven view of curriculum to a model-based instructional approach to teaching and learning (Metzler, 2000). With concerns regarding physical education as a subject matter in schools, it appears to be time to explore a reconceptualization of K-12 physical education through a models-based instruction (Carlson, 1995; Locke, 1992; O'Sullivan, 1989; Siedentop & O'Sullivan, 1992; Siedentop, Doutis, Tsangaridou, Ward, & Rauschenbach,

1994). In this paper we will argue that SE, TG, and CL have the potential to move physical education beyond a command style multi-activity approach to instruction (Metzler, 2000).

We argue that SE, TG, and CL can provide structures or instructional models for situated learning to occur within a community of practice based on the meaningful, purposeful, and authentic learning activities presented and practiced by students (Lave & Wenger, 1991). Situated learning has emerged as a framework to theorize and analyze pedagogical practices in physical education (Kirk & Macdonald, 1998; Kirk & MacPhail, 2002). Individuals are considered part of a holistic learning enterprise, not acting or participating in isolation. The assumptions and organizing structures of SE, TG, and CL allow for participation to occur in a student-centered "learning curriculum" as opposed to a teacher-centered "teaching curriculum" (Lave & Wenger, 1991, p. 97). This view of a learning centered curriculum moves the teacher off center stage and provides an opportunity for the student (i.e., learner) to help other students learn.

The purpose of this article is to (a) make theoretical connections from situated learning to Sport Education, Tactical Games, and Cooperative Learning; (b) describe Sport Education, Tactical Games, and Cooperative Learning as instructional models; (c) provide pedagogical implications of using these instructional models; and (d) offer challenges to physical educators. SE, TG, and CL each provide a set of structures that allows students to participate in meaningful learning activities.

Theoretical foundations

Situated learning theory will be used as a frame for exploring the potential of SE, TG, and CL as valuable instructional models for physical education. As set forth by Kirk and Macdonald (1998), situated learning theory is conceptualized as one component of a broader constructivist theory of learning in physical education. Lave and Wenger (1991) posit that in this mode of learning, the mastering of knowledge and skills require that novices move toward more advanced participation (full participation) in the socio-cultural practices of the community. In this section, we will begin with a brief overview of constructivism and then discuss situated learning theory as it is applied to SE, TG, and CL.

Perkins (1999) emphasized three tenets of constructivism: the active learner, the social learner, and the creative learner. As active learners, students are not passive recipients of knowledge but are involved in tasks that stimulate decision making, critical thinking, and problem solving. As social learners, students construct knowledge through social interaction with their peers, facilitated by their teachers. As creative learners, students are guided to discover knowledge themselves and to create their own understanding of the subject matter. Individuals draw on prior knowledge and experiences to construct knowledge (Griffin & Placek, 2001).

Situated learning

Situated learning provides an authentic framework in which to position teaching and learning in physical education. Situated learning theory investigates the relationships among the various physical, social, and cultural dimensions of the context of learning

(Lave & Wenger, 1991). Social and cultural contexts contribute to and influence what is learned and how learning takes place. Lave and Wenger (1991) discuss "legitimate peripheral participation within a community of practice" as a key concept for situated learning theory. Lave and Wenger (1991) refer to legitimate peripheral participation as participation that occurs within sets of relationships in which "newcomers" can move toward "full participation" by being involved in particular experiences or practices, and this develops new sets of relationships. Learning is not the reception of factual knowledge or information, but rather the legitimate (genuine), peripheral (complex inter-play of persons, activity, knowledge, and the social world), participation (activity toward a specific task/goal). Lave and Wenger (1991) state that legitimate peripheral participation "obtains its meaning, not in a concise definition of its boundaries, but in its multiple, theoretically generative interconnections with persons, activities, knowing, and world" (p. 121).

Kirk and Macdonald (1998) provide a useful explanation of community of practice. "We understand the notion of community of practice to refer to any collectivity or group who together contribute to shared or public practices in a particular sphere of life" (p. 380). The social and cultural situation of the teaching environment contributes significantly to what is learned and how learning takes place (Kirk & Macdonald, 1998). We argue that SE, TG, and CL can provide structures or instructional models for situated learning to occur within a community of practice based on the meaningful, purposeful, and authentic tasks presented and practiced by students.

SE, TG, and CL develop activities, which provide learners with a structured framework for making sense of learning activities being presented. Legitimate peripheral participation is intended to convey the sense of authentic, meaningful, and purposeful participation by students in an activity. Learning takes place in the interactive social world within social practices or interpersonal relationships that are in the process of production, reproduction, transformation, and change (Lave & Wenger, 1991). Kirk and Macdonald (1998) have argued that "school physical education may regularly and consistently *fail* to provide young people with the opportunity for legitimate peripheral participation in a community of practice of exercise, and physical recreation" (p. 382).

Constructivist and situated learning perspectives have been endorsed as providing a potentially useful reconceptualization of existing approaches to teaching and learning in physical education (Chen & Rovegno, 2000; Dodds, Griffin, & Placek, 2001; Ennis, 2000; Rovegno & Bandhauer, 1997; Kirk & Macdonald, 1998; Rovegno & Kirk, 1995). Consistent with this line of thought, SE, TG, and CL have the potential to represent situated learning within a social constructivist theoretical framework. There are behavioral underpinnings, however, to each of these instructional models, but for this article we have chosen a constructivist perspective. The authors acknowledge that this is our theoretical representation of these models (our ontology) and that there are forms of SE (Alexander et al., 1993; Siedentop, 1994, 2002) and CL that are behavioral (Barrett, 2000; Slavin, 1990, 1996).

SE, TG, and CL have several similar pedagogical principles. First, all of these models advocate a student-centered approach in which learning takes place in a participation framework (Lave & Wenger, 1991). Second, learning activities have the potential to include social, physical, and cognitive learning outcomes. Third, students work in small groups (i.e., communities of practice) and rely on each other to complete the learning activity (positive interdependence). Fourth, the teacher facilitates learning and shifts responsibility to students through learning activities designed to hold students accountable.

SE, TG, and CL emphasize active learning within a social practice and involve the processes of decision making, social interaction, and cognitive understanding of various physical activities. The three models consider developmental factors that involve the modification of activities to meet the developmental needs of the learners in order to optimize the potential for success.

Sport education

Sport education (SE) is an instructional model which links the sport taught in physical education to the wider sporting culture (Siedentop, 1994). Focusing essentially on the notion of authenticity, it is Siedentop's belief that the essential features of sport that lead to its attractiveness are rarely reproduced in physical education. Siedentop lists six key features of the sport experience that make it authentic: (a) sport is done by seasons; (b) players are members of teams and remain in that team for the entire season; (c) seasons are defined by formal competition, which is interspersed with teacher and student directed practice sessions; (d) there is a culminating event to each season; (e) there is extensive record keeping; and (f) there is a festive atmosphere in which the season (and particularly the culminating event) take place. Siedentop (1994) contrasts these features with the typical sports unit within physical education where units rarely last longer than three weeks, team selection is changed daily and is usually ad hoc, and very little (if any) of the particular sport's culture and ritual is transmitted through the experience. The aim of SE is to create competent, literate, and enthusiastic sports players. A system of tasks and learning activities are planned that will result in students not only becoming more skillful, but understanding the histories, traditions, and nuances of the sport, as well as becoming willing participants within the wider sport culture.

SE places students in small-sided teams and takes them through a series of skill practices (planned and carried out by teachers and peer coaches) and through developmentally appropriate games conducted as authentic competition. That is, in contrast to the more common ad hoc game context of physical education where students play in nonconsequented matches, students in sport education become members of teams that stay together for the entire length of a season, and they play in games that are modified in the number of players per team (3-a-side volleyball).

During a SE season, students also take greater responsibility for the organization and management of the sporting experience. A typical SE season involves students not only in skill learning and game play, but also in adopting leadership positions and taking responsibility for the conduct of the unit. Student roles may include coaches, captains, referees, scorers, statisticians and members of the sports organizing board. Thus SE is designed to offer students a more *complete* sport experience than that of simply an isolated player.

As the season progresses, refining and practicing skills take less class time, and the focus shifts to a formal team competition in which the spirit of the competition is to compile points for winning matches, showing good sporting behavior and fair-play, being organized, and completing managerial duties. At the end of the formal competition, a variety of awards are presented such as final standings, referee, fair play, and participation awards.

The essential argument for SE lies in the belief that appropriately conducted sport experiences in community and interscholastic sport capture the enthusiasm of participants and provide experiences that are valued by participants, the significant adults in their lives, and the communities in which they live. Siedentop (1994) writes that skill practice in physical education is frequently decontextualized from how the skills are used in games. Tactical understanding and strategic performance are sometimes stated as goals, but few instructional tasks have this focus (Romar & Siedentop, 1994). Scrimmages, group tasks that simulate game conditions with frequent stop/starts, are fundamental to sport practice but seldom seen in physical education.

SE's conceptual roots were derived from play education, with Siedentop (1980) arguing that the meaning and potential of physical education was best explained in reference to the concept of play. Sport education evolved from play education and is based upon two assumptions. First, that sport, properly understood, is a form of play, and second, that in more mature society, more people are engaged in play and a mature sport culture. "The model is, and always has been, rooted in sport and play" (Siedentop, 2002, p. 415). Siedentop suggests that play can absorb participants in a powerful and complete manner. He argues that play can motivate student engagement and encourage them to be physically active throughout their lives. Emerging from this notion of play education a body of research has emerged to support the implementation of SE in New Zealand (Grant, 1992), Australia (Alexander, Taggart, & Medland, 1993) and the United States (Carlson & Hastie, 1997; Hastie, 1996, 1998; Hastie & Siedentop, 1999).

Kirk and Macdonald (1998) have suggested that by recasting physical education lessons as matches and training sessions, sport education reproduces aspects of the contemporary community of practice, as it exists outside the school. In this aspect of the model, then, SE fits within Lave and Wenger's (1991) theory of situated learning. That is, SE presents students with forms of legitimate peripheral participation in a community of practice. This legitimate participation ". . . is intended to convey the sense of authentic or genuine participation, where a person's involvement in the practices of a community are meaningful to them as individuals and also holds significance for other community members" (Kirk & Macdonald, 1998, p. 380). SE is an example of authentic participation in physical education since it involves participation in some form of "real sporting performance or experience." Wiggins' (1993) notion of bringing a performance to the capability to "execute a task or process and to bring it to completion" (p. 202) is an inherent part of sport education.

Tactical games

Bunker and Thorpe (1982) proposed Teaching Games for Understanding (TGfU) as a shift from a content-based approach with highly structured lessons to a more student-based approach that links tactics and skills in game context. They argued that by reducing the technical demands of the game through appropriate modifications, participants are able to first develop an understanding of the tactical aspects of the game and then build on this understanding with technical or tactical practice to progress toward the advanced game. Tactical Games (TG; Griffin, Mitchell, & Oslin, 1997), which extends TGfU, advocates similar principles and the authors proposed a variety of levels of tactical complexity as well as a more authentic framework for assessing game performance. Griffin et al. (1997) proposed a simplified three-stage model, which focuses on the essential lesson components of the model, namely modified game play, development of tactical awareness and decision making through questioning, and development of skill.

As an instructional model, the goal to be achieved through TG is for students to become improved games players by foregrounding the decision-making process (i.e., tactical awareness). Within games, tactical problems are foregrounded thereby allowing the students multiple opportunities to problem solve and practice the appropriate tactical response (French & McPherson, 2003). In a TG model, students first play a modified game that highlights a particular tactical problem, which becomes the instructional focus. Second, questions are designed to develop tactical awareness (i.e., understanding of what to do to solve a problem). Third, situated practices guide the learner to practice essential skills or movements to solve tactical problems presented by the initial game or game form. Finally, the final game provides students with the opportunity to apply their practice in an authentic setting (Mitchell, Oslin, & Griffin, 2003).

Promoters of the tactical games model (i.e., TGfU, game sense, play practice, and concept-based games) believe that games are highly motivating and thus can be an important part of a physical education curriculum (Thorpe et al., 1984; Griffin et al., 1997). In fact, students in games units usually long to get to game play and in requesting the game they take the position that games, as compared to skills practice, are fun! Games help students develop a sufficient level of skillfulness so that they experience the joy and pleasure of games that will perhaps afford them continued motivation and increased competence to continue to play later in life (Allison, Pissanos, & Turner, 2000; Corbin, 2002; Griffin et al., 1997).

There are three major assumptions about games that underpin TG. First, games can be modified to be representative of the advanced game form and conditioned (i.e., exaggerated by rule changes) to emphasize tactical problems encountered within the game. The use of small-sided games helps to slow down the pace and momentum of the game so there is a better chance for the development of game appreciation, tactical awareness, and decision making. Teachers should view the small-sided games as building blocks to the advanced form, not as ends in themselves. Second, games provide an authentic context for assessment. Assessing students during a game is the most meaningful way for them to receive formative feedback and help the learner's development toward skillfulness and competence as a games player (Corbin, 2002). Third, games have common tactical problems, which form the basis of the games' classification system and serve as the organizing structure for the tactical games model.

The classification system has four major categories: target, fielding/run score, net/wall, and invasion games. Classifying games provides students with a thematic way to view games in which they identify the similarities among games. Advocates of the model argue that many games within each category have similar tactical problems, and understanding these similar tactical problems can assist in transferring performance from one game to another (Bunker & Thorpe, 1982; Griffin et al., 1997). In using TG, teachers may explicitly teach students to transfer knowledge they have about one game to another, simply because they are in the same classification. For example, it needs to be pointed out that pickle ball is a net/wall game, sharing tactical similarities with tennis and badminton.

In the context of TG, questioning is a critical teaching skill the teacher uses to guide students in identifying solutions to the tactical problem presented in the game. As facilitators, teachers will need to know when to use questions and when to provide answers. Literature on tactical games teaching has been consistent in emphasizing the importance of high quality questions (Bunker & Thorpe, 1982; Australian Sports Commission, 1997; Griffin et al., 1997). The quality of questions is critical to problem solving in a tactical games model and should be an integral part of the planning process.

Central to TG are the tactical problems that each classification presents, which must be overcome (solved) in order to score, to prevent scoring, and to restart play. Through games, students identify the various tactical problems a game or game form presents and explore solutions to these problems by making decisions and applying particular movements and skills. Levels of game (i.e., tactical) complexity can help teachers match game complexity with students' game play development. Proponents of a TG model believe that all students can play a game if that game is modified to enable meaningful play to occur (Ellis, 1986; Mitchell, Oslin, & Griffin, 2003; Thorpe, 2001). Games may need to have few skills, few rules, and as few players as possible.

Kirk and MacPhail (2002) have offered a connection between TG and situated learning. They present a modification and extension of the original TG model that draws on a situated learning perspective within a constructivist perspective. Kirk and MacPhail (2002) provide constructs for conceptualizing the teaching and learning of games while rethinking the TG instructional model from a situated learning perspective. Concerning situated learning and the TG model, Kirk and MacPhail (2002) suggest "explicit attention to the learner's perspective, game concept, thinking strategically, cue recognition, technique selection, and skill development as the clustering of strategies and techniques, and situated performance as legitimate peripheral participation in games" (p.189).

Cooperative learning

Cooperative learning (CL) is an instructional model that also shifts the focus of learning to the student. A primary goal in CL is that each student becomes a meaningful participant in learning. Students work together in small, structured, heterogeneous groups to master the content. The students are not only responsible for learning the material, but also for helping their group-mates learn (Antil, Jenkins, Wayne, & Vadasy, 1998; Putnam, 1998).

There is a growing body of research in education that reports the benefits of cooperative learning (Cohen, 1994; Johnson & Johnson, 1989; Kagan, 1990; Slavin, 1990, 1996). Substantial evidence exists to support the idea that students working in small cooperative groups can master material presented by the teacher better than students working on their own (Cohen, 1994; Johnson & Johnson, 1989; Slavin, 1990, 1996). CL also has social outcomes such as positive inter-group relations, the ability to work collaboratively with others, and the development of self-esteem (Cohen, 1994; Johnson & Johnson, 1989; Slavin, 1990, 1996).

There are four major CL approaches: (a) conceptual, (b) structural, (c) curricular, and (d) complex instruction. First, Johnson and Johnson (1989) have developed the conceptual approach, which is based on the premise that teachers can learn the key elements of structuring effective cooperative learning activities. Johnson, Johnson, and Johnson-Holubec (1998) have presented five main elements that they believe are necessary for cooperative learning to be successful. First, positive interdependence refers to each group member learning to depend on the rest of the group while working together to complete the task. Second, individual accountability is defined as practices teachers use to establish and maintain student responsibility for appropriate behavior, engagement, and outcomes. Third, promotive face-to-face interaction is literally head-to-head discussion around the group in close proximity to each other. Fourth, interpersonal skills and small group skills are developed through the tasks and include listening, shared decision making, taking responsibility, learning to give and receive feedback, and learning to encourage each other. Finally, group processing refers to time allocated to discussing how well the group members achieved their goals and maintained effective working relationships.

Second is the structural approach (Kagan, 1992). "The structural approach to cooperative learning is based on the creation, analysis, and systematic application of structures, or content-free ways of organizing social interaction in the classroom" (Kagan, 1990, p. 12). The structural approach to cooperative learning is based on different strategies that Kagan (1990) referred to as structures, such as Jig-saw and Learning Teams. To ensure success when using the structural approach, Kagan (1992) highlighted two main elements, positive interdependence and individual accountability.

Third is the curricular approach, which differs from the content-free structural approach in its grade level-specific and subject-specific curricula (Slavin, 1990). In Slavin's (1996) highly structured approach, he defined group goals as students working together to earn recognition, grades, rewards, and other indicators of group success. The focus is on team rewards, equal opportunity for success (they work on material appropriate to their own grade level), and individual accountability. Individual accountability is assured because students take quizzes and complete assignments that contribute to the team score. Slavin (1996) found that cooperative learning could be an effective means of increasing student achievement, but only if the essential elements of specific group goals and individual accountability are integrated into the cooperative learning methodology.

Finally, Cohen's (1994) complex instruction approach focuses on group work as a strategy for enhancing student social and academic development. Complex instruction is a method of small group learning that features open-ended discovery or a conceptual task that emphasizes higher order thinking skills. Of the four approaches, Cohen's curricula and grade-level nonspecific approach is the least structured in her adherence to a formalized prescription of cooperative learning. Cohen and Lotan (1997) argued that group work is a powerful method for conceptual learning by creating problem-solving situations to facilitate intellectual and social goals and hold students accountable. Group roles such as material manager, harmonizer, and resource person are assigned to students. The teacher's role is to facilitate the group work and emphasize that all skills and abilities are important and relevant for completing the task (positive interdependence).

One of the most appealing attributes of cooperative learning is its dual focus on social and academic outcomes (Antil et al., 1998; Cohen, 1994; Putnam, 1998). Research has shown that CL can have a positive impact on social variables including inter-group relations, ability to work collaboratively with others, and self-esteem (Johnson & Johnson, 1989; Sapon-Shevin, 1994; Slavin, 1996).

Cooperative learning works to place the student at the center of learning. In a cooperative learning lesson, all students contribute to group work, and students rely on each other to complete the task. The teacher acts as a facilitator and works to shift the responsibility to the students while holding them accountable. Putnam (1998) pointed out that educators are not typically aware of the conditions that are essential for cooperative learning to lead to positive outcomes. Putnam (1998) suggested that "simply placing students in groups and asking them to cooperate will not ensure higher achievement or positive interpersonal outcomes" (p. 18). The implementation of cooperative learning is a complex process (Antil et al., 1998; Cohen, 1994; Cohen & Lotan, 1997; Dyson, 2002; Putnam, 1998) and it may take three or more years for a teacher to feel comfortable with this instructional model.

In physical education, CL has enhanced students' goals of the lessons, helped students take responsibility through roles, improved students' motor skills and strategizing, enhanced students' communication skills, improved students' working together, and held students accountable through the use peer assessment and task sheets (Dyson, 2001, 2002). Barrett (2000) found that cooperative structures increased students' trials in sports skills units. In addition, low-skilled male and female students also showed improved performances.

In physical education the structure "Learning Teams" have been used to apply cooperative learning in the gymnasium (Dyson, 2001, 2002). Learning Teams is based on Student Teams-Achievement Divisions (Slavin, 1990) and Learning Together (Johnson & Johnson, 1975). Learning Teams provide students with the opportunity to share leadership and responsibility roles and use collaborative skills to achieve group goals. Learning Teams are useful for teaching any physical education content, although this structure can be readily applied to sports skills and tactics. Student roles and practice tasks are written on a task sheet (Dyson & Rubin, 2003). For example, students could be in groups of four, in roles such as coach, organizer, recorder, and encourager, actively providing feedback to each other. Students could work on the tactical problem "creating space in attack" in soccer using a "give and go" practice task. Students in their groups/teams rely on each other to practice, monitor, and assess their group mates' skills and strategies. At the end of class students discuss their skills and strategies in a group processing session facilitated by their teacher.

In teacher preparation, faculty often use different cooperative learning structures in their programs. For example, in a sport-related games course focused on volleyball, the instructor could set up a CL jigsaw structure to teach the students' skills or tactics. Students could be placed into four even groups and each group could practice a basic skill or tactic: passing a free ball, receiving a serve, setting, or a penetrating setter offense. Each group would then be expected to establish a plan to teach the critical elements of their assigned skill or tactic. Once quality of performance is verified by the instructor, one student from each group (now the expert/coach) would rotate around to each group to teach the other groups the critical elements of the skill or tactic.

Cooperative learning could also be considered an instructional model that represents "legitimate peripheral participation" with student-centered tasks that require student input and experiences that are meaningful, challenging, and authentic for students. The group dynamic in cooperative learning allows for students to take on roles and responsibilities and provides students with the opportunity to achieve tasks while they are socially interacting. Therefore, the situated learning perspective could provide a theoretical construct for conceptualizing cooperative learning.

Pedagogical implications

We argue that SE, TG, and CL can provide structures or instructional models for situated learning to occur within a community of practice based on the meaningful, purposeful, and authentic learning activities presented and practiced by students (Kirk & Macdonald, 1998; Kirk & MacPhail, 2002; Lave & Wenger, 1991). Practitioners need to take into account several pedagogical considerations when implementing any of these three instructional models: (a) the teacher is a facilitator, (b) students are active learners, (c) students work in small groups and modified games, (d) learning activities are authentic and developmentally appropriate, (e) learning activities are interesting and challenging, and (f) students are held accountable.

The teacher is a facilitator

As the facilitator, the teacher sets problems or goals, and students are given an opportunity to seek solutions to these problems. Solutions to the problem are identified through a questioning process and these solutions then become the focus of a situated practice. The teacher also facilitates the practice by either simplifying or challenging based on student abilities. In this way, the teacher is working with the students' prior knowledge to develop new knowledge. The teacher guides the instruction and curriculum as a facilitator of learning.

Students are active learners

In SE, TG, and CL, students have a high rate of engagement. Students take responsibility for organization and management and take on leadership roles. Teachers delegate responsibility so that more students can talk and work together on multiple learning tasks. Therefore, students have positions of responsibility. The teacher is not at the center of instruction and students are active learners, creative learners, and social learners (Perkins, 1999).

Students work in groups or modified games

Grouping is usually heterogeneous in small groups or teams. The behaviors required in cooperative small groups are radically different from the behavior required in traditional classroom settings (Cohen, 1994). Therefore, it is not surprising that developers of CL recommend that prior to implementing cooperative learning, teachers use team-building or social skill-building activities that are designed to develop the appropriate behaviors for cooperation as well as some specific skills for working successfully with others (Antil et al., 1998; Dyson, 2002; Dyson & Rubin, 2003).

Modifying the games allows students to practice their skills and decision-making in "real" game-like situations. Having the teacher emphasize authentic performance puts students in an active learning situation (Darling-Hammond, 1997). For an activity to be considered as authentic in physical education, it must involve some form of observable performance (Wiggins, 1993).

Learning activities are interesting and challenging

When learning activities are either interesting or challenging to students, they are more likely to be satisfying or even enjoyable. The discovery of solutions to various learning activities requires that students contribute to the group or team task. Students will need to rely on each other to complete the learning activity or score the point, which is an example of positive interdependence. Learning activities can also include one or more physical, social, and/or cognitive goals that are aligned with the national standards (NASPE, 1995).

Students are held accountable

Assessment is an ongoing part of instruction, and students are provided with continuous feedback for reflecting on and problem solving about games or physical activity experiences. Assessment should be authentic and therefore aligned with the national standards and specific instructional objectives. Students are held accountable in different ways, which match the basic assumptions of each model. For example, in CL students could be held accountable by having all group members sign task sheets after the learning tasks are completed. In SE, students can be held accountable by both teacher and peer assessments using portfolios (e.g., folders) to keep track of various learning activities students record. Finally in TG, students could be held accountable in game play by using teacher and peer assessments such as the Games Performance Assessment Instrument (Mitchell & Oslin, 1999).

The implementation of any of these instructional models is a complex and labor-intensive enterprise and it may take two or more years for a teacher to be comfortable and effective. Teachers should start by implementing one or two learning activities using their strongest content knowledge. Physical education teachers need guidance and on-going professional development to be successful with any of these instructional models.

The intersection of SE, TG, and CL instructional models

In this paper we have provided situated learning as the theoretical connection between Sport Education, Tactical Games, and Cooperative Learning. Figure 1 provides a representation of the intersection of these pedagogical models. Generally these models are considered as mutually exclusive approaches to teaching. However, if we look at them as examples of situated learning, we can see that each may actually inform practices within the other models.

SE, TG, and CL can intersect in various ways. For example, SE can provide a structure to allow students to organize their own tournament within a TG unit. CL structures can teach students to cooperate in activities and game play so that students can compete more effectively working as a team against another team in a SE unit. TG can foreground the

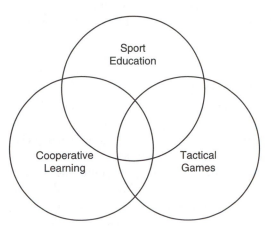

Figure 1 The intersection of Sport Education, Tactical Games, and Cooperative Learning.

decision-making aspect of the games and encourage students to use their problem solving skills in a SE unit. Alternatively, CL or SE could provide the structure for a TG unit by keeping students in small teams for the entire unit and providing clearly defined roles and responsibilities for students. Depending on the teacher's objectives, SE could focus more on competitive games and CL can provide more cooperative games.

We are concerned with the activity-based instruction that predominates our field (Metzler, 2000; Hastie & Siedentop, 1999). It is time to move away from the activity-based instruction that plagues us and develop more sophisticated understandings and practices for our field. It is time to think differently and time to challenge our university programs to develop undergraduates that can be true "change agents" in the field. There are too many innovations that have ended as "innovation without change" (Sparkes, 1991). It is time to challenge teachers to move beyond a "busy, happy, and good" (Placek, 1983) activity-based instruction to provide more educative experiences for their students. It is time for our field to engage in reconstruction of the culture of physical education through models-based instruction that uses pedagogical models, such as Sport Education, Tactical Games, and Cooperative Learning, which can restructure the way teachers do their work. This will not come easily for university faculty or teachers in the field and will require a "conceptual shift" in the way we think about and operationalize our curriculum and instruction. Fullan (1999) has stated that educational change is always messy, chaotic in nature, non-linear, labor intensive, and complicated work. There are no short-term fixes and no one model is a panacea for the complicated myriad of problems that plague physical education in our schools. We believe that Metzler's (2000) models-based instruction is the wave of the future. It is our responsibility as academics to guide this complex and no doubt chaotic process. SE, TG, and CL can be integrated as important components of a teacher preparation program (Oslin, Collier, & Mitchell, 2001; Dyson & Wright, 2003).

Kirk and Macdonald (1998) provided new possibilities for theorizing learning in physical education by presenting situated learning as a theoretical model. They suggested that through exploration of innovative ideas "we might better understand the subject [physical education] and what might contribute to the education of young people who face new challenges, risks, and opportunities in the new millennium" (p. 385). The challenge for our field is to move beyond superficial engagement with these instructional models and for educators to tease out the theoretical constructs, contradictions, and articulations among and between these models to better inform practice (Rink, 2001). This process has the potential to ultimately provide a more comprehensive experience for students in their physical education classes.

SE, TG, and CL represent situated learning in physical education as meaningful, purposeful, and authentic learning activities presented and practiced by students. To gain the full benefits of these instructional models, teachers need to make a conceptual shift and move beyond an activity-driven view of curriculum to model-based instruction (Metzler, 2000). First, the assumptions and organizational structures of SE, TG, and CL provide a student-centered learning curriculum as opposed to a teacher-centered teaching curriculum. A student-center learning curriculum puts students in the role of active learner in which students work together and help each other in the process of learning. Second, the teacher shifts from director (i.e., transmitter) to the facilitator of learning activities. Third, learning activities promote social, physical, and cognitive learning outcomes thus have the potential to provide students with a holistic education. Finally, SE,

TG, and CL emphasize active learning that is socially situated, which involves decision making, social interactions, and cognitive understanding of various physical activities.

We agree with Kirk and Macdonald (1998) concerning the need to explore innovative approaches to the practices of school physical education. Siedentop (1992) stated, "we need to think differently about what we do in the name of physical education" (p. 70). Perhaps it is time that we give Sport Education, Tactical Games, and Cooperative Learning a closer examination.

References

Alexander, K., Taggart, A., & Medland, A. (1993). Sport education in physical education: Try before you buy. *ACHPER National Journal*, **40**(4), 16–23.

Allison, P.C., Pissanos, B.W., & Turner, A.P. (2000). Preservice physical educators' epistemologies of skillfulness. *Journal of Teaching in Physical Education*, **19**, 141–161.

Antil, L.R., Jenkins, J.R., Wayne, S.K. & Vadasy, P.F. (1998). Cooperative Learning: Prevalence, conceptualizations, and the relation between research and practice. *American Educational Research Journal*, **35**, 419–454.

Australian Sports Commission (1997). *Game sense: Developing thinking players*. Belconnen: ASC.

Barrett, T. (2000). *Effects of two cooperative learning strategies on academic learning time, student performance, and social behavior of sixth grade physical education students*. Unpublished doctoral dissertation, University of Nebraska, Lincoln.

Bunker, D. & Thorpe, R. (1982). A model for the teaching of games in the secondary schools. *Bulletin of Physical Education*, **10**, 9–16.

Carlson, T.B. (1995). We hate gym: Student alienation from physical education. *Journal of Teaching in Physical Education*, **14**, 467–477.

Carlson, T. & Hastie, P. (1997). The student social system within sport education. *Journal of Teaching in Physical Education*, **16**, 176–195.

Chen, W. & Rovegno, I. (2000). Examination of expert teachers' constructivist-orientated teaching practices using a movement approach to physical education. *Research Quarterly for Exercise and Sport*, **71**, 357–372.

Cohen, E.G. (1994). Restructuring in the classroom: Conditions for productive small groups. *Review of Educational Research*, **64**, 1–35.

Cohen, E.G., & Lotan, R.A. (1997). *Working for equity in heterogeneous classrooms: Sociological theory in practice*. New York: Teachers College Press.

Corbin, C.B. (2002). Physical activity for everyone: What every physical educator should know about promoting lifelong physical activity. *Journal of Teaching in Physical Education*, **21**, 128–144.

Darling-Hammond, L. (1997). *The right to learn*. San Francisco: Jossey-Bass.

Dodds, P., Griffin, L.L., & Placek, J.H. (2001). A selected review of the literature on the development of learners' domain-specific knowledge. *Journal of Teaching in Physical Education* [Monograph], **20**, 301–313.

Dyson, B. (2001). Cooperative learning in an elementary school physical education program. *Journal of Teaching in Physical Education*, **20**, 264–281.

Dyson, B. (2002). The implementation of cooperative learning in an elementary school physical education program. *Journal of Teaching in Physical Education*, **22**, 69–85.

Dyson, B., & Rubin, A. (2003). How to implement cooperative learning in your elementary education program. *Journal of Physical Education, Recreation, and Dance*, **74**, 48–55.

Dyson, B., & Wright, P. (2003). *Social Responsibility and Cooperative Learning: Comparative and contrasting perspectives*. Paper presented at the Physical Education Special Interest Group, Research on Learning and Instruction in Physical Education at the American Education Research Association, Chicago, IL.

Ellis, M., (1986). Making and shaping games. In R. Thorpe, D. Bunker & L. Almond (Eds.), *Rethinking games teaching* (pp. 61–65). Loughborough, UK: University of Technology, Department of Physical Education and Sports Science.

Ennis, C.D. (2000). Canaries in the coal mine: Responding to disengaged students using theme-based curricula. *Quest*, **52**, 119–130.

French, K.E., & McPherson, S.L. (2003). Development of expertise. In M. Weiss and L. Bunker (Eds.), *Developmental sport and exercise psychology: A lifespan perspective*. Morgantown, WV: Fitness Information.

Fullan, M. (1999). *Change forces: The sequel*. London: Falmer Press.

Grant, B.C. (1992). Integrating sport into the physical education curriculum in New Zealand secondary schools. *Quest*, **44**, 304–316.

Griffin, L.L., & Placek, J.H. (2001). The understanding and development of learners' domain specific knowledge: Introduction. *Journal of Teaching in Physical Education*, **20**, 299–300.

Griffin, L.L., Mitchell, S.A., Oslin, J.L. (1997). *Teaching sport concepts and skills: A tactical games approach*. Champaign, IL: Human Kinetics.

Hastie, P.A. (1996). Student role involvement during a unit of sport education. *Journal of Teaching in Physical Education*, **16**, 88–103.

Hastie, P. (1998). The participation and perceptions of girls within a unit of sport education. *Journal of Teaching in Physical Education*, **17**, 157–171.

Hastie, P.A., & Siedentop, D. (1999). An ecological perspective on physical education. *European Physical Education Review*, **5**, 9–29.

Johnson, D., & Johnson, R. (1975). *Learning together and alone*. Englewood Cliffs, NJ: Prentice Hall.

Johnson, D.W., & Johnson, R.T. (1989). *Cooperation and competition: Theory and research*. Edina, MN: Interaction Book.

Johnson, D.W., Johnson, R.T., & Johnson-Holubec, E. (1998). *Cooperation in the classroom*. (7th ed.). Edina, MN: Interaction Book.

Kagan, S. (1990). The structural approach to cooperative learning. *Educational Leadership*, **47**, 12–16.

Kagan, S. (1992). *Cooperative learning*. (2nd ed.). San Clemente, CA: Kagan Cooperative Learning.

Kirk, D., & Macdonald, D. (1998). Situated learning in physical education. *Journal of Teaching in Physical Education*, **17**, 376–387.

Kirk, D. & MacPhail, A. (2002). Teaching games for understanding and situated learning: Rethinking the Bunker-Thorpe model. *Journal of Teaching in Physical Education*, **21**, 117–192.

Lave, J., & Wenger, E. (1991). *Situated learning: Legitimate peripheral participation*. New York: Cambridge University Press.

Locke, L. (1992). Changing secondary school physical education. *Quest*, **44**, 361–372.

Metzler, M. (2000). *Instructional models for physical education*. Boston: Allyn and Bacon.

Mitchell, S.A., Oslin, J.L., & Griffin, L.L. (2003). *Sport foundations for elementary physical education: A tactical games approach*. Champaign, IL: Human Kinetics.

Mitchell, S.A., & Oslin, J.L. (1999). *Assessment in games teaching. NASPE assessment series*. Reston, VA: National Association of Sport and Physical Education.

National Association of Sport and Physical Education (NASPE). (1995). *Moving into the future: National standards for physical education.* St. Louis, MO: Mosby.

Oslin, J., Collier, C., & Mitchell, S. (2001). Living the curriculum. *Journal of Physical Education, Recreation and Dance, 72*(5), 47–51.

O'Sullivan, M. (1989). Failing gym is like failing lunch and recess: Two beginning teachers' struggle for legitimacy. *Journal of Teaching in Physical Education, 8,* 227–242.

Perkins, D. (1999). The many faces of constructivism. *Educational Researcher, 57,* 6–11.

Placek, J. (1983). Conceptions of success in teaching: Busy, happy, and good? In T. Templin, and J. Olson (Eds.) *Teaching in Physical Education* (pp. 46–56). Champaign, IL: Human Kinetics.

Putnam, J.W. (1998). *Cooperative learning and strategies for inclusion: Celebrating diversity in the classroom.* (2nd ed.). Baltimore, MD: Brookes.

Rink, J. (2001). Investigating the assumptions of pedagogy. *Journal of Teaching in Physical Education, 20,* 112–128.

Romar, J., & Siedentop, D. (1994). *Case studies in teaching physical education.* Paper presented at the World Congress of the Association Internationale d'Ecoles Superieurs d'Education, Physique. Berlin.

Rovegno, I., & Bandhauer, D. (1997). Norms of the school culture that facilitated teacher adoption and learning of a constructivist approach to physical education. *Journal of Teaching in Physical Education, 16,* 401–425.

Rovegno, I., & Kirk, D. (1995). Articulations and silences in social critical work on physical education: Towards a broader agenda. *Quest, 47,* 447–474.

Sapon-Shevin, M.K. (1994). Cooperative learning and middle schools: What would it take to really do it right? *Theory into Practice, 33,* 183–190.

Siedentop, D. (1980). *Physical education: Introductory analysis.* Dubuque, IA: W.C. Brown.

Siedentop, D. (1992). Thinking differently about secondary physical education. *Journal of Physical Education, Recreation, and Dance, 63*(7), 69–72, 77.

Siedentop, D. (1994). *Sport education.* Champaign, IL: Human Kinetics.

Siedentop, D. (2002). Sport education: A retrospective. *Journal of Teaching in Physical Education, 2,* 409–18.

Siedentop, D. & O'Sullivan, M. (1992). (Eds.). Secondary school physical education [Special Issue]. *Quest, 44.*

Siedentop, D., Doutis, P., Tsangaridou, N., Ward, P., & Rauschenbach, J. (1994). Don't sweat gym. An analysis of curriculum and instruction. *Journal of Teaching in Physical Education, 13,* 375–394.

Slavin, R. (1990). *Cooperative learning: Theory, practice, research.* Englewood Cliffs, NJ: Prentice-Hall.

Slavin, R.E. (1996). Research on cooperative learning and achievement: What we know, what we need to know. *Contemporary Educational Psychology, 21,* 43–69.

Sparkes, A.C. (1991). The culture of teaching, critical reflection and change: Possibilities and problems. *Educational Management and Administration, 19,* 4–19.

Thorpe, R. (2001). Rod Thorpe on teaching games for understanding. In L. Kidman (Ed.) *Developing decision makers. An empowerment approach to coaching* (pp. 22–36). Auckland, New Zealand: Innovative Print Communication Ltd.

Thorpe, R.D., Bunker, D.J., & Almond, L. (1984). A change in the focus of teaching games. In M. Pieron & G. Graham (Eds.), *Sport pedagogy: Olympic Scientific Congress proceedings, Vol. 6* (pp. 163–169). Champaign, IL: Human Kinetics.

Wiggins, G. (1993). Assessment: Authenticity, context, and validity, *Phi Delta Kappan, 75,* (3), 200–214.

PART 7

The social construction of bodies

INTRODUCTION

FOR A SCHOOL SUBJECT so specialised in working with and on the body, and with an elaborate vocabulary for talking about the psychology, mechanics and physiology of the body, physical education has for much of its history been blind to the ways in which the body exists in culture as well as in nature. The papers in this section provide examples of the discovery by physical education scholars of the socially constructed body. The social construction of the body refers to a range of what anthropologist Marcel Mauss understood in the 1930s are predominantly educational practices that shape fundamental ways of being embodied, such as walking, running, jumping, climbing, swimming, sleeping, sitting, throwing, using tools and so on. Mauss taught us that these apparently 'natural' bodily movements in fact vary considerably across cultures and that learning to move in some ways rather than others is an expression of the values and preferences of social groups rather than the diktat of nature.

The papers in this section focus on particular examples of this process of socially constructing bodies. **Fitzgerald** uses young disabled people's experiences of physical education and sport as a means of troubling the assumptions and expectations about normality embedded in conventional physical education practices. **Oliver and Lalik** show through sustained conversations with adolescent girls how their bodies are a curriculum, to be shaped, dressed, decorated and cared for in particular ways according to their gendered and ethnic identities and allied perceptions of value and normality. The final paper by **Gard and Wright** shows how the obese body and the certainty with which we talk about its condition, prevalence, treatment and amelioration is a construct of a society in which risk becomes increasingly prominent and difficult to manage. All three papers illustrate the power of the concept of the socially constructed body in better understanding how physical education itself is a site in which the body is constructed in relation to disability, gender and shape and size.

FURTHER READING

Armour, K.M. (1999) The case for a body-focus in education and physical education, *Sport, Education and Society*, 4, 5–16.

Tinning, R. (2004) Ruminations on body knowledge and control and the spaces for hope and happening, in J. Evans, B. Davies and J. Wright (eds) *Body Knowledge and Control: Studies in the Sociology of Physical Education and Health*. London: Routledge.

Wellard, I. (2006) Able bodies and sport participation: social constructions of physical ability for gendered and sexually identified bodies. *Sport, Education and Society*, 11, 105–119.

Hayley Fitzgerald

STILL FEELING LIKE A SPARE PIECE OF LUGGAGE?

Embodied experiences of (dis)ability in physical education and school sport

Introduction

WITHIN CONTEMPORARY SOCIETY public discourse has much to say about inclusion and equity. Indeed, in recent years physical educators have increasingly been concerned with these issues and as a result of this physical education teachers today can draw on a diverse range of resources to assist them with their practice (for example, adapted equipment, guidelines, syllabuses, CD Roms and CPD opportunities). All this, it is anticipated, will provide positive and inclusive experiences for many young people, including those that happen to be disabled. In seeking to explore the nature of young disabled people's physical education and school sport experiences I focus on an important but often overlooked source of information. I centre my concerns on the insights given from young disabled people themselves. As others have argued (Christensen & James, 2000; Christensen & Prout, 2002), I take the position that young people should be listened to and encouraged to participate in research activities. Elsewhere, I have shown how a number of innovative research approaches can effectively be used to engage young disabled people within the research process (Fitzgerald *et al.*, 2003a, 2003b). In this paper, I continue to explore the valuable insights that can be gained from these young people. In doing this, I hope to build upon the limited understandings we currently have of young disabled people's experiences of physical education and school sport (Smith, 2004). Indeed, I believe it is only when these views are listened to that we can begin to better understand the actual nature of physical education and school sport experienced in our schools and the consequences this has on young people's sense of self.

This paper attempts to address the recent call by Aitchison (2003) for researchers within leisure (and I believe these comments are also relevant to physical education and sports researchers) to move beyond the discursive boundaries of the field and engage with wider discourses. In particular, Aitchison (2003) points to the utility of engaging with 'disability studies' in order to develop 'inter-subject field discourses' (p. 956) between leisure and disability. In seeking to contribute to the cross-fertilisation of this discourse I centre my concerns on the embodied experiences of young disabled people within a physical education and school sport context. By positioning my work in this way I believe it will contribute to understandings within physical education and disability studies relating to two key, but interrelated, areas of thinking. First, I will continue the ongoing and growing dialogue found within disability studies that has extended understandings of social model perspectives by exploring the notion of embodied identities of disabled people. By engaging in this discussion I hope to alert writers within physical education and sport to the contested and evolving terrain of social model perspectives and the merits of understanding disability from an embodied position. Second, I also want to develop Evans' (2004) recent discussion focusing on 'ability' and particularly his concern for ability to be conceptualised as a sociocultural and dynamic entity. In this paper then, I will consider data generated from young disabled people in order to explore the ways in which physical education and school sport impact on how their 'abilities are recognised, valued, nurtured and accepted, while others are rejected' (Evans, 2004, p. 104). Although I centre my concerns on the experiences of young disabled people I believe that the arguments developed carry with them important messages that are relevant to the physical education of many young people.

I first of all briefly consider the nature of research that has been undertaken in relation to young disabled people and experiences of physical education and sport. After this, I highlight the literature informing my thinking in this study. In particular, I draw on understandings of disability found within disability studies, conceptions of ability evident in physical education discourses and the notion of embodiment found within the writing of Bourdieu. Following this I identify the methods used to generate the research information. I then discuss the findings emerging from the study relating to four key themes: *activity status, embodying difference through the habitus, legitimate participation and attaining capital* and *the physical education teacher as a nurturer of ability*. Finally, I conclude by reflecting upon the findings in relation to the constitution and practices of physical education in our schools.

Physical education, school sport and experiences of disabled pupils

> The familiar hustle and bustle, murmuring and giggling that follow the instruction 'Get into teams' are always accompanied by the predictable 'Aw Sir, do we have to? Or 'No way are we having him' as the games teachers allocates me to a random team, rather like a spare piece of luggage that no one can be bothered to carry.
>
> (Jackson, 2002, p. 129)

This insightful and frank account given by Luke Jackson provides us with a glimpse of the kinds of experiences he encountered during physical education lessons. More importantly though, from this brief recollection we are able to gain a sense of the way in which Luke perceived himself and the way he believed he was (un)valued by his peers. This account along with other autobiographies of disabled people (Grey-Thompson, 2001) and research relating to broader life experiences (Swain & Cameron, 1999; Viscardi, 2001; Davis & Watson, 2002; Disability Rights Commission, 2002; Shelley, 2002) provide a range of insights into the way in which physical education and sport can impact on the lives of disabled people. Ironically, as I have pointed out elsewhere, physical education and sports researchers seem disinterested in exploring these kinds of insights (Fitzgerald et al., 2003b). Consequently, we currently have to rely on literature from wider sources to extend our understandings in this area. While acknowledging that recent survey work such as that completed by Sport England (2001) is useful, I also recognise this kind of work inevitably falls short of providing in-depth understandings of experiences. The general apathy within physical education and sports research is also coupled with a failure by writers positioning themselves within the sociology of physical education and sport to theorise or sufficiently account for the experiences of disabled people.[1]

The need to explore physical education and sport experiences from the perceptive of disability was highlighted over ten years ago by Barton who suggested:

> Merely adopting a curriculum for able-bodied people without some critical dialogue is unacceptable. The voice of disabled people needs to be heard and seriously examined. This is absolutely essential in the teaching of physical education.
>
> (Barton, 1993, p. 52)

Furthermore, in the context of disability and sport the benefits of exploring participation issues centring on these concepts has also been highlighted by DePauw who argued that:

> The lens of disability allows us to make problematic the socially constructed nature of sport and once we have done so, opens us to alternative constructions, and solutions.
>
> (DePauw, 1997, p. 428)

Since these words were written by Barton and DePauw physical educators have entered into some critical dialogue on issues relating to curriculum and pedagogical aspects of inclusion (Penney & Evans, 1995; LaMaster et al., 1998; Hodge et al., 2003; Smith, 2004). However, the majority of this work has not yet considered Barton's call to listen to the voices of disabled people. This oversight can only be detrimental to the physical education profession, as we will continue to work in ways that are informed by assumptions rather than actual insights from the young people. I believe the implications of this study are wide ranging and although I focus my concerns on the experiences of young disabled people it is worth remembering, as DePauw so eloquently points out, that the kinds of issues I examine and the critique offered will contribute to broader discussions and in particular the growing body of evidence that supports the view that the constitution and practices of physical education in schools are in need of reform (Kirk, 1998; Gorely et al., 2003) if we are to better serve more young people.

Conceptions of disability, ability and embodied abilities

> We all have bodies, but not all bodies are equal, some matter more than
> others: some are, quite frankly, disposable.
>
> (Braidotti, 1996, p. 136, cited in Meekosha, 1999)

Implicit in this statement is the notion that we live in a society that places differing values
on bodies. Indeed, within contemporary society youthful, slim, toned and sensual bodies
are held with the highest regard (Shilling, 1996; Wright, 2000; Oliver, 2001). Bodies
perceived as not achieving this kind of makeup are often seen as undesirable and viewed in
negative ways. In this context, non-conforming disabled bodies are frequently perceived as
'spoilt' (Goffman, 1968) and 'flawed' (Hevey, 1992). In order to understand why it is that
disabled people are often understood in these terms it is useful to briefly review the
concept of disability and ability.

Contemporary understandings of disability are essentially founded on medical or
social model perspectives. The medical model of disability centres concerns on the individual with the impairment and focuses on notions of abnormality and deficiency, as
defined in medical terms (Oliver, 1996; Barnes *et al.*, 1999). Within this perspective
disability is understood as a relatively stable and narrowly defined concept. In contrast, the
social model supports the view that disability is socially constructed and that it is society
that disables people with impairments (Finkelstein, 1980; Oliver, 1996). The social model
has been described as the '. . . . emancipatory force in the lives of disabled people'
(Tregaskis, 2002, p. 457). Indeed, it has been argued that this model '. . . . "speaks" from
the standpoint of disabled people and therefore voices an opinion that has, throughout
modernity, been silenced by the paternalism of a non-disabled culture' (Patterson &
Hughes, 2000, p. 35).

More recently, a number of commentators have argued that the social model has
excluded 'the body' from the experiences of impairment (Morris, 1991; Pinder, 1995;
Hughes & Paterson, 1997, Hughes, 2000; Patterson & Hughes, 2000). Moreover, it has
been suggested that '. . . Within disability studies the term "body" tends to be used
without much sense of bodiliness as if the body were little more than flesh and bones'
(Paterson & Hughes, 1999, p. 600). In this context, Marks (1999, p. 611) believes '. . . .
Individual [medical] and social models of disability represent two sides of the same coin'.
What Marks is suggesting here is that by pathologising the body (the medical model) and
focusing on structural issues (the social model) both models are implicated in failing to
consider the individual beyond these restricted understandings. Although commentators
are increasingly recognising the limitations of the social model it still remains a central,
and persuasive, force for those committed to overcoming the exclusion of disabled people
in social life. Importantly though, as we will see later in this paper, the social model is
not the only way in which the experiences of disabled people can be articulated and
understood.

In many ways, common sense understandings of ability contrast with those frequently
associated with dominant discourses of disability—the prefix of 'dis' provides us with a
constant reminder of the perceived inferior and negative relationship between disability
and ability. According to Gillborn and Youdell (2001), education discourses emphasise
ability as something that is fixed, measurable and can lead to broader generalisations about
potential. Many of these features of ability are also evident in understandings found within

physical education and sport. Indeed, ability is often related to performance and associated with skill and technique (Schmidt, 1991; Xiang *et al.*, 2001). More specifically, it has been argued that physical education and sport supports a normalised understanding of ability that promotes specific bodily ideals. For boys, these ideals are often associated with masculinity and a mesomorphic body type (Tinning, 1990; Light & Kirk, 2000; Tinning & Glasby, 2002). Evans sometime ago warned of the limitations of considering ability through narrowly conceived understandings of performance (Evans, 1990) and recently reaffirmed this view, suggesting that understandings of ability continue to emphasise one-dimensional and static features (Evans, 2004). In representing ability in this narrowly defined manner no account is consequently given of '. . . . the nature of "ability" as a dynamic, sociocultural construct *and* process' (Evans, 2004, p. 99). In seeking to extend discussions concerning the notion of ability within physical education and sport Evans (2004) points to the utility of using the habitus and other associated conceptual tools of offered by Bourdieu (Bourdieu, 1992).

'The Habitus is located within the body and affects every aspect of human embodiment' (Shilling, 1996, p. 129). It is '. . . a bridge-building exercise' (Jenkins, 2002, p. 74) that immerses the relations between structure and agency by incorporating society into the body. According to Crossley (2001) the habitus consists of 'dispositions', 'schemes', 'know-how' and 'competency'. For Bourdieu social life can only be understood by considering the embodiment of individuals within particular fields,[2] such as physical education, through their habitus. According to Bourdieu an individual will be judged on their ability to deploy the relevant habitus within a particular field. Therefore, if an individual's social action is compatible with the style, manner and customs of the field they are likely to be accepted as a member and support the ongoing reproduction of these conditions. Following Bourdieu's thinking, Evans believes that the competencies exhibited as physical education and sports habitus can function as capital and argues that it is these competencies that can and often are considered as abilities.

> In effect they may be perceived as 'abilities', embodied social constructs, meaningful only in their display and are always and inevitably defined relationally with reference to values, attitudes and mores prevailing within a discursive field.
>
> (Evans, 2004, p. 100)

In this paper, I will consider ability as embodied social constructs, and in so doing, attempt to move the thinking offered by Evans forward by exploring how these embodied conceptions of ability are manifest through young disabled people's experiences of physical education and school sport. Moreover, by centring my concerns through the 'lens of disability' (DePauw, 1997) I will also shed new light on questions of ability in the context of disability. As others have illustrated (Edwards & Imrie, 2003) I believe that by using Bourdieu's notions of the habitus and capital and exploring embodied understandings of disability I will bridge the discursive impasse currently evident between medical and social model understandings of disability. Indeed, in this paper I will move beyond these understandings of disability by using an alternative way of recognising and considering the experiences of young disabled people in physical education and school sport.

Methods

The data reported in this paper were generated as part of a larger project involving disabled pupils drawn from thirty-five schools in the Midlands of England. Over four hundred pupils participated in this research project. These young people experience a range of physical and sensory impairments and learning difficulties. The principal methods of data generation used were the completion, by pupils, of physical education question-naires and activity diaries. In addition, a series of 'one off' focus group discussions were undertaken with pupils from six of the thirty-five participating schools. A further set of three focus group discussions were also conducted at two additional schools. The data generated using these collection strategies reflected an approach to data collection enabling deeper understandings to be gained and explored with each strategy used.

This paper will specifically focus on the data generated from one of the schools where three focus group sessions were conducted with five young disabled people.[3] Although it was not my intention to target boys specifically, the five participants were all boys. Essentially, pragmatic reasons relating to timetabling and willingness to participate influenced the selection of participants and the subsequent composition of this focus group.

The paper will draw on data generated in relation to the participants' experiences and understandings of physical education and school sport. Each of the three focus group discussions were recorded on an audiotape and then transcribed. The transcripts were coded into categories, key themes developed and sorted (Glaser & Strauss, 1967). Following the constant comparison method of analysing data (Lincoln & Guba, 1985) I continually reviewed and reworked these categories and themes. Analysis was conducted immediately following each focus group session. In addition to providing an ongoing and evolving insight into the data (Miles & Huberman, 1994) this also enabled preliminary results to be considered and discussed.

Embodied experiences of (dis)ability in physical education and school sport

The status and value attributed to different activities

'It's [an] easy game 'cause I'm playing.'

(Adam)

It is widely recognised that activities undertaken in physical education and sport carry with them value and status. Indeed, according to Bourdieu (1991) participation contrib-utes to the social positioning of those engaging in such activities. The focus group discus-sions revealed a general feeling from all the pupils that a number of activities they undertook in physical education and school sport were not perceived in the same or equal manner as activities undertaken by other pupils. The focus group pupils believed this differential status was sometimes evident from teachers' attitudes towards them. For example, one pupil suggested the physical education teacher lacked any real desire or concern for him to progress in physical education because he did not participate in any 'high status' school teams.

> Well we're not the best and we aren't in the important school teams. If you're in one then . . . You know it's like Mr Evans does the football team and he spends the lesson with the good players and he's not bothered about us.
>
> (Andy)

The continued concern by many writers about the importance and emphasis placed on competition, team games (Talbot, 1997; Penney & Chandler, 2000; Jones & Cheetam, 2001; Penney, 2002) and elite development goals (Siedentop, 2002) are clearly evident from the comment made by this pupil and are reinforced by similar views expressed by other pupils. Interestingly, the pupil mentioned earlier was in the school boccia team and along with other focus group members placed considerable value on being part of this team.

> We had trials. But, and I know there weren't loads of us trying. But it's a school team. You have to go and represent the school. You have to go and play in competitions. It is a proper team. Everyone thinks it's easy to play.
>
> (Steve)

Although the pupils had a positive view of boccia they continually referred to their physical education teachers and the belief that these members of staff did not afford high status to this activity. The pupils did not, however, see all their physical education teachers in this way and believed Mr Jones viewed boccia positively.

> The boccia club is great. Mr Jones coaches us. He thinks we're good, he tells us even if we play bad. It'd be good if some of the other teachers could see us playing. If we had a game then we'd show them, they'd be shocked.
>
> (Dave)

These pupils also believed that some of their peers perceived their membership of the boccia team as having less status than other teams at the school. For this activity it could be argued that the pupils believed the value of their physical and social capital associated with playing boccia was not as great as that given to those pupils participating in other activities or playing in other school teams. Indeed, on occasions the pupils expressed considerable frustration at the lack of recognition afforded to boccia and the indifferent attitudes of their peers and teachers. It seemed that although the focus group pupils wanted their participation in boccia to have an 'exchange value' (Shilling, 1996) this was not the case. Their peers did not recognise boccia as a legitimate activity through which relevant capital could be accumulated or converted.

Throughout the discussions relating to boccia most of the pupils adopted a social model perspective when discussing this perceived low regard for boccia. In this respect, they compared boccia to other activities played at school. They did this rather than focusing on the fact that it was the disabled pupils participating in this activity. One pupil suggested boccia had less credibility and seemed not to be accepted by the wider school population because it was a 'new' school activity.

It's new for everyone. We *are* the first [group] to play [boccia]. When we're in year 11 there'll be more playing. Everyone, like more people, will know about boccia then.

(James)

There seemed to be a belief that over time this activity would become more widely recognised at school. Indeed, the pupils seemed to think that changes to the composition and nature of capital in this field were possible and that this would enhance the value and convertibility of capital associated with playing boccia. However, for the time being boccia did not have the established popularity and value afforded to other school sports.

You don't see it [boccia] played much. Like not everyone here [at the school] plays and not everyone does it in PE. It's just not around like football or basketball or tennis, you know them popular sports.

(Steve)

According to the pupils considerable social capital could be accumulated through involvement in various school activities, including school sports teams. In particular, being 'well known' seemed to be an important quality associated with gaining social capital. In the context of sport James explained how having the role of a team captain could help to make you 'well known'.

Everyone knows who's the football and rugby captain. You get to know . . . But not, most people don't know the boccia captain.

(James)

However, as his comment illustrates being the boccia captain does not necessarily afford you this status. Having said this, within the small group of pupils that play boccia there seemed to be some kudos attached to having the role of boccia captain.

[speculating about the boccia captain for the next academic year]

Dave: Next year, I think I'll be the captain.
Steve: No way, it'll be James. He wins us the games. He can play, he's spot on. He'll be the captain.
Andy: Yeah James *is* captain material.
James: Yeah, I'd like that.

This heated discussion illustrates how some social capital then could be attained. This though did not seem to be recognised within the wider field as a legitimate 'prize' for all to compete for.

It is clear from the comments made by the pupils that their teachers and peers influence their impressions of activities undertaken in physical education and school sport. Although we cannot judge Mr Evans and Mr Clarke on the comments made by the pupils alone, they perhaps provide a powerful indication, from the pupils' perspective, of the influences that these individuals can have on understandings of physical education, the value attributed to activities and an individual's sense of self.

Embodying difference through the habitus

> I'm not going to be as good as the rest of them.
>
> (Steve)

Another key theme to emerge from the focus group discussions was the notion of 'difference'. Indeed, difference manifests itself in a number of ways including through the activities the pupils undertook, the locations of the activities, the exemptions given to pupils and through the pupils' own sense of physicality. For example, the pupils recognised that they sometimes undertook different activities and in different settings during physical education than other members of their class.

> We don't do rugby. We do gym or fitness. The class does rugby, they go on the fields out there.
>
> (James)

When James was asked if he would like to do rugby he suggested:

> Yeh, but it's rough and you get hurt, Mr Jones and mum say I don't have to. So I don't.
>
> (James)

In this instance the differential experiences are legitimised by James using his teacher's and mum's views and although he suggested he would like to participate in rugby he seemed happy to accept that he did not do this activity. This illustrates, as Davis and Watson (2001) found, that young people happily comply and willingly accept the judgements made by others (in this case Mr Jones and mum) if they feel that they will benefit from the situation in some way. On this occasion, not getting hurt and the roughness of the game were deemed by James and, as he indicated, the adults, as sound reasons for him and his peers not to be involved in this activity. Through the informal discursive practices of this mother and physical education teacher James and the other pupils unquestionably accepted as 'fact' that they could not play rugby. In this case it may be that normative values associated with the rules and structures of rugby were rigidly followed by the physical education teachers. In this respect, the teachers were seeking to 'preserve' and 'protect' (Siedentop, 2002) rugby rather than explore any new possibilities that enabled this activity to be more inclusive.

In accepting that they could not play rugby the pupils identified other associated benefits of not participating in this activity. Indeed, it was clear that all the focus group pupils saw this as positive and they even felt that this gave them an additional degree of social capital over other members of their class:

> We all get changed and then go to the gym, gym over there. I know Rob yeh and Simon yeh hate rugby and they've asked to come in but they're not allowed. It's just *us* going up to the gym.
>
> (Steve)

Another pupil suggested it was an advantage not to have to undertake physical education outside in cold weather:

We get to stay in when it's cold. We're not out there, the others have to go out, some of them don't like it, like Simon, Simon says it's unfair.

(Andy)

In relation to playing rugby it is clear that some of the other pupils recognised the focus group pupils were being treated differently than the rest of the class. Simon perceived this situation as 'unfair' and ensured that Andy was aware of his feelings. The 'unfairness' for Simon related to the focus group pupils not having to do rugby or go outside during the cold weather. Interestingly, this was one of the only occasions when the focus group pupils recalled their peers questioning in any way the differential practices in physical education. The issue at stake here for Simon was not about Andy's absence from the 'main' physical education lessons but rather the nature of the perceived preferential treatment given to Andy. In this instance it may be that the discursive practices supporting this segregation serve to normalise the absence of the disabled pupils from the main physical education lessons. Quite simply, it could be that the habitus of participants within this field evokes a disposition that positions the disabled pupils as *not* being treated differently, as it is the norm for the disabled pupils not to always be in the main physical education lesson.

Central to the notion of physical education and sport is physicality. Indeed, it is a certain kind of physicality that is promoted and practised in physical education. For boys this is often associated with aggression, prowess, competition and masculinity (Connell, 1995; Hickey & Fitzclarence, 1999; Light & Kirk, 2000). Importantly, the very nature of these embodied competencies contrast with the ways in which dominant notions of disability are recognised and understood. Indeed, DePauw acknowledges the tensions between sport and disability arguing that '. . . sport, as a place where physicality is admired, has presented a challenge for individuals with disabilities and their active participation in sport appears as somewhat of a contradiction' (DePauw, 1997, p. 423). The tension then arises when 'disabled bodies' are expected to conform to the normalised practices dominating physical education discourse that continue to promote and value a type of physicality that is unobtainable by many disabled people (Barton, 1993). The importance of physicality, and in particular differences in physicality, was also prominent in the focus group discussions. In particular, the pupils often compared themselves with other peers and the consequences this had on their physical education experiences. As James explained:

Most of the boys are bigger than me and I'm not going to get that tall and they're getting bigger and in basketball I haven't got a chance. What it's like, well like I can't get the ball and they don't pass to me and they're bigger and faster and I'll run and try, I'm trying but, that's it, it's hard they're bigger than me.

(James)

Here James clearly highlights the ways in which he perceives his physical capital as not matching up to that of his peers. Barton (1993), DePauw (2000) and Davis and Watson (2002) have argued that disabled people are often measured against idealised notions of normality and it was evident from the responses of the focus group pupils that they too were conscious of the ways in which physical education continues to promote and afford credibility and value to those who match up to the normativity practised in physical education. For Steve, it is clear he believes whatever amount of effort he exerts, he is not going to be able to work towards, or achieve, a level of competence recognised as reflecting a 'good' performance.

> It doesn't matter how much I try I'm not going to be as good as the rest of them. I get mad and I can't do well.
>
> (Steve)

I acknowledge these kinds of understandings are not confined to, or specific to, disabled pupils. Indeed, the recent study by Bramham (2003) illustrates how boys often measure their competencies in physical education against their peers. However, what is important for the pupils in this study is the way normalised values seem to be imposed on all in physical education and the effects that this has on the pupils who fail to match up to these ideas.

Legitimate participation and attaining capital

> They don't want you to be there.
>
> (Steve)

The focus group pupils were aware that various actions of their peers during physical education lessons influenced the extent to which they were considered as legitimate participants within the field. Some of these actions involved peer-led exclusion from physical education activities and serve to illustrate most vividly an absence of 'cooperative' and 'affiliation' dimensions relating to Siedentop's (2002) educative goal to junior sport. Andy recalls a basketball lesson:

> When we were playing basketball last week remember [Andy looks over to James] no one passed us the ball [James acknowledges this with a nod]. What can you do if they won't pass? No one would pass me the ball.
>
> (Andy)

In this instance Andy or James did not directly attribute their disability as being a factor contributing to this situation and they both seemed unsure as to why their peers were not cooperating with them.

> You can shout and shout for it. Shouting loud, you can shout like loud and you still won't. If I get it I'll pass to Andy and we both get a go then, that's what I do. You know I get fed up of shouting and it's just the same. I don't get what it is.
>
> (James)

However, it was clear from a later comment made by Steve that although he perceived this physical capital positively (as he previously had when the discussions focused on boccia) this value seemed not to be recognised by his peers. Indeed, Steve's comment illustrates a sense that his peers do not seem to even accept him within the physical education class.

> I like doing PE but sometimes when we're with the rest [of the group] you can tell some of them, they don't want you to be there. It's not like I'm the worst. They think I am and that's what it's like all the time.
>
> (Steve)

According to Bourdieu an individual will be judged on their ability to deploy the relevant habitus within a given field. Therefore, it may be that Steve's habitus places him at the margins within physical education, what DePauw (1997) describes as 'social' marginality. And even though Steve himself uses a normative comparison (being 'good' at physical education or being 'the worst') and measures himself in what could be considered as a positive light, he believed he was still not accepted or recognised in this normative way by his peers. In part, it may be that the physical absence, referred to earlier, from the main physical education class positions Steve, and the other disabled pupils, temporally as 'part timers' within the field. Consequently, their social practice and ability to become 'endowed with the habitus' (Bourdieu, 1993) of the field seems to be adversely affected and is exhibited through their peers' lack of cooperation and affiliation to the class. Steve then interprets this lack of acceptance within physical education as relating to his peers' discriminatory attitudes and actions.

> 'Cause of me arm and legs I don't fit in. Well, this is what it is, what I mean is they [his peers] don't think that and they go on about it, like it's the biggest thing and its not. 'Cause like my arm doesn't make me the worst.
>
> (Steve)

In addition to peer-led exclusion the focus group pupils highlighted name-calling and other put-downs as actions by their peers that influenced their experiences of physical education. James in particular talked about name-calling:

> Some of them call me. Well I know it's because of my frame and my walking. They're immature, that's what I think and I'm not bothered, they wouldn't like it, it's not nice and if they call you it's not nice.
>
> (James)

Although James indicated that he was not concerned about this name-calling a later comment was perhaps more telling about the way he felt and his reactions to this:

> It doesn't make you feel good about yourself. I get on with things. I ignore them. I sometimes end up shouting and I told Mike his ears stick out [James laughs] and they stick out a lot. Let him see what it feels like to be [name] called.
>
> (James)

Here James illustrates how he uses his agency to respond to the comments made by Mike. Echoing the findings of Davis and Watson (2002) and Priestley (1999) James shows that he can mobilise verbal resistance and challenge the name-calling targeted at him. However, Steve was less vocal in his response to name-calling:

Yeh, I get it and ignore it. Let 'em think you can't hear. Let 'em think you're not bothered.

(Steve)

The name-calling and deliberate exclusion by peers from physical education activities are experiences that other young people also encounter (Groves & Laws, 2000; Brittain, 2004). However, for Steve, Andy and James these kinds of experiences may reinforce dominant discourses of disability that emphasise deficiency, lack, inability and 'otherness' (Barnes *et al.*, 1999). Such actions and reactions by the disabled pupils and their peers perhaps reinforce the centrality of peers in the 'partnership' dimension of Vickerman's (2002) framework for inclusive physical education.

The physical education teacher as the nurturer of ability?

He's not just a PE teacher.

(Andy)

The perceptions young people have of teachers can influence their attitudes and feelings towards a particular school subject, including physical education (Groves & Laws, 2000; Flintoff & Scraton, 2001; Brittain, 2004). Indeed, when discussing their physical education teachers it was notable that the pupils essentially viewed these teachers in terms of their subject specialism. In this context the pupils often referred to specific activities in relation to their teachers. Andy and Adam made the following comments about their physical education teachers:

Mr Evans, he's into football and that's what he does all the time. He's in charge of the team and the coaching and sorting the team out.

(Andy)

Mrs Smith does the netball and hockey with girls. Once we had her for hockey one time. Gemma says she's good at netball.

(Adam)

Mr Evans and Mr Clarke teach the rugby. I've not had them but I've been out and seen it. I heard Mr Clarke, Mr Clarke shouts a lot.

(Adam)

The pupils also made comments about other related tasks that they saw their physical education teachers doing:

[Mr Evans] You see him a lot over the hall doing the team lists.

(Steve)

Other pupils talked about the teachers' attitudes towards them. For example, Adam believed a teacher's low opinion of him generally in physical education and his participation in boccia related directly to his disability:

I know, I think Mr Clarke doesn't see me.

[after being prompted to expand on what this meant]

> Well yeh, yeh and it's like I feel like he's looking down on me and he doesn't
> care and he sees my chair and all things I can't do.
>> Some people see my chair and not me and he's [one of the PE teachers] like
> that. He sees me playing boccia and just thinks it's easy game 'cause I'm playing.
>> (Adam)

In this case, Adam firmly believed this view of him was based on his impairment and essentially founded on a deficit position similar to that evident in the medical model of disability (Barnes *et al.*, 1999).

Another physical education teacher, Mr Jones, was talked about in much broader and positive terms. Mr Jones was acknowledged by all the pupils as being thoughtful and considerate and the pupils reported having very positive relationship with him. The pupils believed Mr Jones paid much attention to their needs when he planned skills and practices in physical education.

> With my [walking] frame it makes PE harder. I don't use it all the time. In one
> lesson I use it. *Not* in all of, *not* all the time and Mr Jones, he'll give me
> goes [skills/practices] for my frame. I'm not saying I use it all the time. When
> I don't [use the frame] then there'll be other gos for me. He doesn't leave
> me out.
>> (James)

James believed these kinds of actions contributed to positive feelings in physical education.

> When I go to PE and see Mr Jones I know I'm okay and have a good time. He
> makes sure I'm doing something and so I like PE with Mr Jones.
>> (James)

Interestingly, Mr Jones was also the Special Educational Needs Coordinator (SENCo) and had considerable contact with these pupils beyond his role in physical education. A number of the pupils identified the additional areas of support given by Mr Jones. One pupil suggested:

> I know he's my PE teacher. He's *not just* a PE teacher. If you get troubles, that
> sort of stuff. Last term there's some trouble with a couple of older lads and Mr
> Jones sorted them out.
>> (Andy)

Another pupil reinforced the positive relationship with this teacher and emphasised the pastoral role he adopted:

> I get on with him well. Yeh, really well and he makes sure I'm okay and I know
> he's there if I need to talk to him, like problems and things happening.
>> (James)

Specific characteristics that the pupil identified about Mr Jones were his fairness and willingness to 'have a laugh'.

> He's fair with everyone, with me and the others. I think he's a good teacher. I like him a lot.
>
> (Adam)

> You can have a laugh with him. I mean I know he's a teacher but he's easy going and you know but not joking around all the time just having a bit of a laugh.
>
> (Steve)

These comments made by Adam, Steve and the other pupils illustrate how a strong relationship can be formed with pupils and how this can be nurtured in a way that contributes to a more positive disposition towards participating in physical education. However, for the other physical education teachers who seem not to have developed such a meaningful relationship it may be that aspects of the subject that exclude pupils are more evident through these teachers' practices. Even though these teachers may advocate and believe that they are working towards inclusive physical education this does not seem to be evident from the pupils' insights. For these teachers it could be that wider issues relating to the structure of the secondary school and the normativity of physical education continue to impinge on their efforts to work towards a more inclusive experience.

Conclusion: reconceptualising (dis)ability through the habitus

This paper has focused on five young people's experiences of physical education and school sport. I believe this work builds on other recent work found within disability studies (Davis & Watson, 2001, 2002; Priestley *et al.*, 1999) and extends these understandings by focusing specifically on experiences of physical education and school sport. Within a physical education and sports context understandings of young disabled people's experiences have typically been expressed through insights from 'others' rather than young people themselves. In this paper, I attempt to address this current imbalance by placing importance on what young disabled people tell us about their experiences. And although I have centred this paper on a small sample I believe this work illustrates the kinds of in-depth insights that can be gained if young people are given opportunities to express their views within a research context.

The data reported in this paper illustrates that a paradigm of normativity prevails in physical education. It would seem the physical education habitus serves to affirm this normative presence and is manifest through conceptions of ability that recognise and value certain characteristics and competences more than others. In particular, the focus group pupils seemed to measure themselves, and perceive that they were measured by others, against a mesomorphic ideal. Earlier in the paper we saw how James was frustrated when playing basketball because his peers were, in his words, 'bigger' and 'faster' than him. In addition, Steve believed he did not 'fit in' because his arms and legs did not work in the same kind of ways as his peers. In both these instances, the pupils were comparing themselves against an ideal that would be impossible for them to attain. However, it is an ideal that contributes significantly to the extent to which their ability is recognised and valued in physical education. Normative conceptions of ability were also manifest through articulations of masculinity that value competitive and aggressive forms of activity. For the focus group pupils not participating in activities that overtly promote these characteristics (such as rugby) and engaging in alterative activities (such as boccia and fitness) did not seem to enable capital to be attained through this conception of ability. Finally, the pupils in this study illustrate how the physical education habitus supports normative conceptions of ability that are manifest through high levels of motoric competence. For example, Andy believed that Mr Evans spent much of his time supporting the 'good' footballers, while Steve recognised he was not going to be 'as good as' many of his peers.

It is perhaps not surprising that motoric competences are valued in physical education contexts that are increasingly driven by agendas seeking to identify 'performances' rather than retaining a focus on educational aspirations. Interestingly, the skills required to play boccia seemed to be universally rejected as constituting a high degree of motoric competence. In part though, this may be explained through the absence of any mesomorphic or masculine characteristics associated with this activity. This study found that to deviate from these kinds of articulation of ability was to be seen as different. This expression of difference was essentially seen in negative terms—to undertake different activities, participate in different places, to be physically different.

Although recent developments relating to adapted programmes would seem to provide the much-needed solutions physical education teachers are looking for to enhance their work with disabled pupils, the contributions and inroads these kinds of programmes can make towards rearticulating conceptions of ability seem minimal. Indeed, it would be a mistake to think these arbitrary and essentially superficial remedies mediate in an any way to disrupt the deep-seated normalised physical education habitus evident in schools. We should perhaps look beyond strategies of adaptation and instead begin to question dominant conceptions of ability embedded through the physical education habitus. By doing this, articulations of ability need to be recast and understood in ways that extend beyond narrowly defined measures of performance and normative conceptions of what is it to have a sporting body. For example, in this study it is clear that, at times, the focus group pupils have very sophisticated understandings of their peers' and teachers' reactions and views. I would argue, in part, that it is this kind of ability that should be recognised and promoted through physical education. What I am proposing here then not only requires the reconceptualisation of the qualities valued in physical education but also a radical rethink about the activities and practices that could best support this work.

Acknowledgements

I would like to thank David Kirk from Loughborough University for his advice and support during the drafting of this paper. I would also like to thank the reviewers for their valuable feedback that has helped to improve this paper.

Notes

1   With the notable exceptions of Borrett *et al.* (1995), DePauw (1997, 2000) and Stone (2001).

2   'A field may be defined as a network, or a configuration, of objective relations bet-ween positions. These positions are objectively defined, in their existence and in the determinations they impose upon their occupants, agents or institutions, by their pres-ent and potential situation (*situs*) in the structure of the distribution of species of power (or capital) whose possession commands access to specific profits that are at stake in the field, as well as by their objective relation to other positions (domination, subordination, homology, etc.)'. (Bourdieu & Wacquant, 2002, p. 97).

3   According to the Pupil Level Annual Schools Census (PLASC) (Department for Educa-tion and Skills, 2003) the following descriptions can be given to the participating pupils. Andy has dyspraxia, a 'Specific Learning Difficulty'. James has cerebral palsy, a 'Physical Disability'. Steve has an arm amputated below the elbow and cerebral palsy, a 'Physical Disability'. Dave has a 'Hearing Impairment'. Adam has a spinal cord injury, a 'Physical Disability'.

References

Aitchison, C. (2003) From leisure and disability to disability leisure: developing data, def-initions and discourses, *Disability and Society*, 18(7), 955–969.

Barnes, C., Mercer, G. & Shakespeare, T. (1999) *Exploring disability: a sociological introduction* (Cambridge, Polity Press).

Barton, L. (1993) Disability, empowerment and physical education, in: J. Evans (Ed.) *Equality, education and physical education* (London, Falmer Press).

Borrett, N., Kew, F. & Stockham, K. (1995) *Disability, young people and school sport*. Paper in Community Studies Number 8 (Ilkley, Bradford and Ilkley Community College).

Bourdieu, P. (1991) Sport and social class, in: C. Mukerji & M. Schudson (Eds) *Rethinking popular culture: contemporary perspectives in cultural studies* (Berkeley, CA, University of California Press).

Bourdieu, P. (1992) *The logic of practice* (Cambridge, Polity).

Bourdieu, P. (1993) *Sociology in question* (London, Sage).

Bourdieu, P. & Wacquant, L. J. D. (2002) *An invitation to reflexive sociology* (Cambridge, Polity).

Bramham, P. (2003) Boys, masculinities and PE, *Sport Education and Society*, 8(1), 57–71.

Brittain, I. (2004) The role of schools in constructing self-perceptions of sport and physical education in relation to people with disabilities, *Sport Education and Society*, 9(1), 75–94.

Christensen, P. & James, A. (2000) Introduction: researching children and childhood: cultures of communication, in: P. Christensen & J. Allison (Eds) *Research with children: perspectives and practices* (London, Falmer Press).

Christensen, P. & Prout, A. (2002) Working with ethical symmetry in social research with children, *Childhood*, 9(4), 477–497.

Connell, R. W. (1995) *Masculinities* (Sydney, Allen & Unwin).

Crossley, N. (2001) *The social body* (London, Sage).

Davis, J. & Watson, N. (2001) Where are the children's experiences? Analysing social and cultural exclusion in 'special' and 'mainstream' schools, *Disability & Society*, 16(5), 671–687.

Davis, J. & Watson, N. (2002) Counting stereotypes of disability: disabled children and resistance, in: M. Corker & T. Shakespeare (Eds) *Embodying disability theory* (London, Continuum).

Department for Education and Skills (2003) *Data collection by type of special educational need* (London, Department for Education and Skills).

DePauw, K. P. (1997) The (In)Visability of DisAbility: cultural contexts and 'sporting bodies', *Quest*, 49(4), 416–430.

DePauw, K. P. (2000) Social-cultural context of disability: implications for scientific inquiry and professional preparation, *Quest*, 52(4), 358–368.

Disability Rights Commission (2002) *Survey of young disabled people aged 16–24* (London, Disability Rights Commission Research and Evaluation Unit).

Edwards, C. & Imrie, R. (2003) Disability and bodies as bearers of value, *Sociology*, 37(2), 239–256.

Evans, J. (1990) Ability, position and privilege in school physical education, in: D. Kirk & R. Tinning (Eds) *Physical education, curriculum and culture: critical issues in the contemporary crisis* (London, Falmer Press).

Evans, J. (2004) Making a difference? Education and 'ability' in physical education, *European Physical Education Review*, 10(1), 95–108.

Finkelstein, V. (1980) *Attitudes and disabled people* (New York, World Rehabilitation Fund).

Fitzgerald, H., Jobling, A. & Kirk, D. (2003a) Listening to the 'voices' of students with severe learning difficulties through a task-based approach to research and learning in physical education, *British Journal of Learning Support*, 18(3), 123–129.

Fitzgerald, H., Jobling, A. & Kirk, D. (2003b) Valuing the voices of young disabled people: exploring experiences of physical education and sport, *European Journal of Physical Education*, 8(2), 175–201.

Flintoff, A. & Scraton, S. (2001) Stepping into active leisure? Young women's perceptions of active lifestyles and their experiences of school physical education, *Sport Education and Society*, 6(1), 5–21.

Gillborn, D. & Youdell, D. (2001) The new IQism: intelligence, 'ability' and the rationing of education, in: J. Demaine (Ed.) *Sociology of education today* (London, Palgrave).

Gorely, T., Holroyd, R. & Kirk, D. (2003) Muscularity, the habitus and the social construction of gender: towards a gender relevant physical education, *British Journal of Sociology of Education*, 24(4), 429–448.

Glaser, B. G. & Strauss, A. L. (1967) *The discovery of grounded theory: strategies for qualitative research* (Chicago, IL, Aldane).

Goffman, E. (1968) *Stigma* (Harmondsworth, Pelican).

Grey-Thompson, T. (2001) *Tannie Grey-Thompson: seize the day* (London, Hodder & Stoughton).

Groves, S. & Laws, C. (2000) Children's experiences of physical education, *European Journal of Physical Education*, 5(1), 19–28.

Hevey, D. (1992) *The creatures that time forgot: photography and disability imagery* (London, Routledge).

Hickey, C. & Fitzclarence, L. (1999) Educating boys in sport and physical education: using narrative methods to develop pedagogies of responsibility, *Sport, Education and Society*, 4(1), 51–62.

Hughes, B. & Paterson, K. (1997) The social model of disability and the disappearing body: towards a sociology of impairment, *Disability & Society*, 12(3), 325–340.

Hughes, B. (2000) Medicine and the aesthetic invalidation of disabled people, *Disability & Society*, 15(4), 555–568.

Hodge, S. R., Tannehill, D. & Kluge, M. A. (2003) Exploring the meaning of practicum experiences for PETE students, *Adapted Physical Activity Quarterly*, 20(4), 381–399.

Jackson, L. (2002) *Freaks, geeks and Asperger Syndrome. A user guide to adolescence* (London, Jessica Kingsley Publishers).

Jenkins, R. (2002) *Pierre Bourdieu* (rev edn) (London, Routledge).

Jones, R. & Cheetham, R. (2001) Physical education in the National Curriculum: its purpose and meaning for final year secondary students, *European Journal of Physical Education*, 6, 81–100.

Kirk, D. (1998) Educational reform, physical culture and the crisis of legitimation in physical education, *Discourse: Studies in the Cultural Politics of Education*, 19(1), 101–112.

LaMaster, K. H., Gall, K., Kinchin, G. & Siedentop, D. (1998) Inclusion practices of effective elementary specialists, *Adapted Physical Activity Quarterly*, 15(1), 64–81.

Light, R. & Kirk, D. (2000) High school rugby, the body and the reproduction of 'hegemonic' masculinity, *Sport, Education and Society*, 5(2), 163–176.

Lincoln, Y. S. & Guba, E. G. (1985) *Naturalistic inquiry* (Beverly Hills, CA, Sage Publications).

Marks, D. (1999) Dimensions of oppression: theorising the embodied subject, *Disability & Society*, 14(5), 611–626.

Meekosha, H. (1999) Body battles: bodies, gender and disability, in: T. Shakespeare (Ed.) *The disability reader* (London, Cassell).

Miles, M. B. & Huberman, M. A. (1994) *Qualitative data analysis: an expanded sourcebook* (Thousand Oaks, CA, Sage Publications).

Morris, J. (1991) *Pride against prejudice* (London, Women's Press).

Oliver, M. (1996) *Understanding disability: from theory to practice* (Basingstoke, Macmillan).

Oliver, K. (2001) Images of the body from popular culture: engaging adolescent girls in critical inquiry, *Sport, Education and Society*, 6(2), 143–164.

Patterson, K. & Hughes, B. (2000) Disabled bodies, in: P. Hancock, B. Hughes, E. Jagger, K. Paterson, R. Russell, E. Tulle-Winton and M. Tyler (Eds) *The body, culture and society* (Buckingham, Open University Press).

Penney, D. (2002) Equality, equity and inclusion in physical education and school sport: in A. Laker (Ed.) *The sociology of sport and physical education: an introductory reader* (London, RoutledgeFalmer).

Penney, D. & Evans, J. (1995) The National Curriculum for physical education: entitlement for all? *British Journal of Physical Education*, Winter, 6–13.

Penney, D. & Chandler, T. (2000) Physical education—what future(s)? *Sport, Education and Society*, 5(1), 71–88.

Pinder, R. (1995) Bringing back the body without the blame?: the experience of ill and disabled people at work, *Sociology of Health and Illness*, 15(5), 605–631.

Priestley, M. (1999) Discourse and identity: disabled children in mainstream high schools, in: M. Corker & S. French (Eds) *Disability discourse* (Buckingham, Open University Press).

Priestley, M., Corker, M. & Watson, N. (1999) Unfinished business: disabled children and disability identities, *Disability Studies Quarterly*, 19(2), 90–98.

Schmidt, R. A. (1991) *Motor learning and performance: from principles to practice* (Champaign, IL, Human Kinetics).

Siedentop, D. (2002) Junior sport and the evaluation of sport cultures, *Journal of Teaching in Physical Education*, 21, 392–401.

Shelley, P. (2002) *Everybody here? Play and leisure for disabled children and young people* (London, Contact a Family).

Shilling, C. (1996) *The body and social theory* (London, Sage Publications).

Smith, A. (2004) The inclusion of pupils with special educational needs in secondary school physical education, *Physical Education and Sport Pedagogy*, 9(1), 37–54.

Sport England (2001) *Disability survey 2000. Young people with a disability and sport, headline findings* (London, Sport England).

Stone, E. (2001) Disability, sport and the body in China, *Sociology of Sport Journal*, 18, 51–68.

Swain, J. & Cameron, C. (1999) Unless otherwise stated: discourses or labelling and identity in coming out, in: M. Corker & S. French (Eds) *Disability discourse* (Buckingham, Open University Press).

Talbot, M. (1997) Physical education and the national curriculum: some political issues in: G. McFee & A. Stevelinson (Eds) *Sport and leisure: connections and controversies* (Aachen, Meyer & Meyer Verlag).

Tinning, R. (1990) *Ideology and physical education* (Geelong, Deakin University Press).

Tinning, R. & Glasby, T. (2002) Pedagogical work and the 'cult of the body': considering the role of HPE in the context of the 'new public health', *Sport Education and Society*, 7(2), 109–119.

Tregaskis, C. (2002) Social Model Theory: the story so far . . ., *Disability & Society*, 17(4), 457–470.

Wright, J. (2000) Bodies, meanings and movement: A comparison of the language of a physical education lesson and a Feldenkrais movement class, *Sport Education and Society*, 5(1), 35–49.

Vickerman, P. (2002) Perspectives on the training of physical education teachers for the inclusion of children with special educational needs—is there an official line view? *The Bulletin of Physical Education*, 38(2), 79–98.

Viscardi, H. (2001) *Me Too! A report by Mencap on play, leisure and childcare for children and young people with a disability in the metropolitan borough of Dudley* (Birmingham, Mencap).

Xiang, P., Lee, A. & Williams, L. (2001) Conceptions of *ability* in physical education: children and adolescents, *Journal of Teaching in Physical Education*, 20(3), 282–298.

Kimberly L. Oliver and Rosary Lalik

THE BODY AS CURRICULUM
Learning with adolescent girls

Some girls don't pay attention to me because I wear a scarf, and I don't like that. Sometimes I just feel like taking my scarf off. When I do, I think everyone will like me, even the boys.

(Khalilah, age 13; journal entry)

THE BODY IS A THEME woven through the literature on adolescent girls' identity development and tangled within the well-documented crisis in girls' lives (Brown and Gilligan 1992, Pipher 1994, Barbieri 1995, Brumberg 1997). Adolescence has been established as the development period during which 'body image' becomes a central concern for many girls (Littrell *et al.* 1990, Rosenbaum 1993, Jaffee and Lutter 1995, Usmiani and Daniluk 1997). Adolescent girls, from Western culture, reportedly spend much time worrying about what their bodies look like to themselves and to others (Brown and Gilligan 1992, Brumberg 1997). Girls' preoccupations with the body are all too frequently interpreted by adults as annoying and foolish narcissism. Such an assessment is common among teachers and others who may daily witness girls frenetically employing combs, brushes and other paraphernalia in attempts to 'improve' their bodies.

In much of the literature documenting girls' concerns, anxieties, and preoccupations with their bodies, including the literature on 'body image', writers have normalized girls' practices (Cash and Pruzinsky 1990, Jaffee and Luther 1995), i.e. they have unreflectively accepted reported beliefs as givens, as just 'how girls are'. This normalizing tendency has accelerated societal acceptance of girls' anxieties about their bodies, as well as the behaviours associated with those anxieties. Currently, such understandings of girls are part of the Western cultural hegemony, the taken-for-granted network of practices and beliefs characteristic of Western society.

With respect to girls' development, one consequence of the normalization process has been that it subverts efforts to help girls resist harmful attitudes and behaviours. Instead, normalizing girls' concerns with their bodies has allowed educators and others to ignore or dismiss destructive behaviours, even as these behaviours may lead to diminished life chances for girls and women. Within the academic literature, school curricula, and everyday practices with adolescents, adults have given insufficient energy to doing what Greene (in Fine 1998: 210) has advocated whenever forms of injustice prevail. That is, adults have ignored opportunities to serve as 'sites of support, comfort, scenes from which to draw strength' (p. 211). Rather than refusing what has been constructed as 'normal' adolescent development, people have all too frequently left girls to fend for themselves within schools and in the larger society.

This abandonment with respect to girls' interests, anxieties, and concerns about their bodies is especially apparent in the USA, where the body is largely ignored as an area for study in school curricula. Indeed, even in middle schools (grades 6–8), where ostensibly school curricula are designed to accommodate the developmental needs of students, little attention is paid to addressing girls' concerns with their bodies.

When the body does appear as the focus of study in school curricula, it is confined primarily to the areas of physical education and health, and presented in a manner that may exacerbate difficulties for adolescents (Tinning and Fitzclarence 1992, Kirk and Tinning 1994). For instance, rather than encouraging students to examine critically issues that influence the ways they are learning to think and feel about their bodies, health and physical educators often objectify the body, constructing it as an object to be controlled and manipulated (Pronger 1995). Furthermore, when guiding study of the body, far too many physical educators present the concept of health as a relationship between fitness and fatness—one in which health is equated with the apparent lack of fat (Tinning 1985).

To complicate matters further, the messages being sent to students about their bodies include the perspective that being fat is not only unhealthy, but it is wrong (Kirk and Colquhoun 1989). Conversely, keeping in shape is all too frequently presented within such curricula as a moral achievement. Moreover, health is generally depicted using images of the body that are unrealistic for many girls. Thus, girls have been observed exerting much time and effort trying to fit into an imagined body structurally inconsistent from their lived forms (Tinning 1985).

Finally, when including the body as a focus of school study, curriculum developers have largely ignored girls' views and experiences of their bodies. In physical education, Kirk and MacDonald (1998: 377) claim 'The apparent neglect of individuals' needs and interests with regard to learning is evident in much curriculum research'. This tendency continues in the face of current knowledge about learning that suggests a viable starting point for study is the knowledge that learners bring with them when they enter classrooms (Ladson-Billings 1994). Instead of drawing on girls' views, educators have persisted in encouraging study of the body that features adults' perspectives. This curricular characteristic is evident in most widely distributed recommendations for knowledge development (National Association of Sports 1995, US Department of Health and Human Services 1996).

For years, feminist theorist have provided insights that should inspire educators to make the body a focal topic in school curriculum and to re-examine the ways that physical educators and others develop curricula of the body (Theberge 1991, Vertinsky 1992, hooks 1995). For example, several writers have described how the seamlessness of human experience operates to damage women's sense of self when the female body is objectified and demeaned in society. Through this theoretical work, feminist have shown that the body plays a crucial role in the reciprocal relationship between women's private and public identities (hooks 1989, 1995, Collins 1990). The social meanings publicly attached to the body can become internalized and exert powerful influences on women's private feelings of self-worth (hooks 1990, Shilling 1993). Women come to understand and experience themselves, in part, through the inequitable social and political systems of their cultures (Sparkes 1997) through which they are all too frequently constructed as 'bodies first, and people second' (Bloom and Munro 1995: 109).

Given the ways in which culture uses women's bodies to perpetuate women's oppression, we are left wondering where in girls' school experiences they are having healthy opportunities to examine their experiences of their bodies. We are also left wondering why adults continue to work from what they have come to consider important body content rather than identifying what girls find important, interesting, problematic, and so on, and starting from there. If educators hope for girls to learn to become healthy women, they need to help them question unexamined claims about the body and girls' development.

One curricular area within which critical examination and human agency are sometimes highlighted is literacy. So, for example, Greene (1995: 186) has written emphatically of the place of the language arts—of reading, writing, speaking and listening—in any curriculum aimed toward societal transformation:

> We are appreciative now of storytelling as a mode of knowing, . . . of the connection between narrative and the growth of identity, of the importance of shaping our own stories and, at the same time, opening ourselves to other stories in all their variety and their different degrees of articulateness.

Greene's views about language arts are consistent with a perspective on literacy described by Freire (1974) and many others who write from the perspective of social reconstructionism (Shannon 1990). Within this tradition, literacy is understood as the ability to read and write the world, i.e. it is understood as the ability to critique the contexts in which people live in terms of equity and justice and to change those circumstances that are unjust, beginning with changing ourselves. In contemporary US society, one of the unjust circumstances confronting all girls is the way the body is controlled and manipulated through dominant cultural narratives and practices.

To be literate, in Freire's sense, one must acquire facility with language, including conventional literacy skills, as well as with a broad array of additional knowledge and skills. Such knowledge would include, for example, bodily knowledge, although this knowledge has been typically ignored or marginalized in the dominant culture. Such literacy also requires moral courage, insofar as those who act in the interests of justice are generally acting against fairly powerful groups who consciously and unconsciously support the structures and processes that encourage inequity.

Freire and others in this tradition (Adams 1975, Weiler 1988, Luke and Gore 1992, Shannon 1992, Shor 1992) have been particularly critical of school literacy education that they claim typically supports the development of complacency in students. They see students at school being taught to go along with the status quo as part of learning how to read and write. Because of their dissatisfaction with conventional schooling practices, social reconstructionists have called for the development of alternative pedagogy (Weiler 1988, Gore 1993). One notable example of such pedagogy is the work of Shor (1992), who has helped university journalism students to examine their worlds and act assertively within them.

More recently, the critical tradition in education has been extended by theorists who address intersections of gender, race, and class in curriculum, schooling and society (Collins 1990, 1998, hooks 1990, 1995, Delpit 1995, Ladson-Billings and Tate 1995). These theorists have been especially articulate in their critique of inequities within existing practices, and have described alternative ways of understanding and acting in the world. Collins (1998: xiv) explains the 'critical' element in these theories:

> Critical social theory encompasses bodies of knowledge and sets of institutional practices that actively grapple with the central questions facing groups of people differently placed in specific, political, social, and historical context characterized by injustice. What makes critical theory 'critical' is its commitment to justice, for one's own group and/or for other groups.

Other theorists in the critical tradition point to the significance of story as a means of addressing issues of injustice. Ladson-Billings and Tate (1995: 57) contend that stories are significant interpretive structures:

> For the critical race theorist, social reality is constructed by the formulation and the exchange of stories about individual situations. These stories serve as interpretive structures by which we impose order on experience and it on us.

We describe herein a curriculum study that grew out of our shared interests in girls' well-being. We developed the project first as collaborators and then as friends. Kim's background is physical education. She is committed to socially just pedagogy and research in physical education. Rosary's background is literacy instruction, and she is particularly interested in critical literacy. Together, we align ourselves with a perspective on curriculum as a relational/structural process. As described by Miller (1990: 2):

> curriculum is created within the relational classroom experiences that individuals share with texts and with one another; at the same time, curriculum also is defined and created by the intersecting forces of existing schooling and social structures.

Thus, curriculum occurs at the intersections of personal and socio-political contexts; the personal and the structural are continually present and interrelating in its expression.

This paper is part of a larger study in which we explored girls' knowledge of their bodies. We examine herein an integrated physical education/language arts curriculum project that Kim developed with Rosary's help. This curriculum project focused on the body as a legitimate area for study and on storytelling, reflection and critical analysis as legitimate learning processes. We believed that in supporting learning and critique, it is essential to start from where girls are. We wanted to develop a curriculum of the body that would begin with girls' experiences, interests and concerns with their bodies, rather than featuring adults' perspectives exclusively. Through this work, we raise issue with the taken-for-granted assertions about the curricular needs of adolescent girls.

We explore three aspects of our work that became central for us. We discuss:

- the curricular processes Kim used as she worked with the girls to help them and us understand how they experienced their bodies in dominant culture;
- the themes of the body that emerged as the girls participated in this curriculum project; and
- the curricular processes and strategies that successfully supported critique.

We saw this work as a social change project, one in which we used activist research, insofar as we gathered knowledge 'in the midst of social change projects' (Fine 1992: 227). We address physical educators' calls for students to become critical consumers of their cultures (Tinning and Fitzclarence 1992, Kirk and Tinning 1994, Brook and MacDonald 1999). We also responded to those literacy educators who construe literacy as societal transformation toward interests of social justice (Freire 1974, 1985). As an example of activist research, 'this work is at once disruptive, transformative, and reflective; about understanding and about action' (Fine 1992: 227).

Ways of working with girls

Selecting collaborators

In 1996, Kim worked with four adolescent girls at Dogwood Middle School, a predominantly African-American magnet school in an inner city in the southeastern USA.[1] In introducing herself and her project, she explained to students in three health and physical education classes that she wanted to learn about the experiences adolescents have of their bodies. To select participants, she asked the students from these classes to do three tasks: to write whatever came to mind on the topic 'someone who is in good shape', to write a story about a 12- or 13-year-old girl or boy who was in good shape, and, finally, to illustrate their story.

She examined the stories for detailed descriptions, comments and illustrations, to determine which students were able and willing to communicate in writing. Given the time constraints on this project it was important that the girls were able to communicate in writing. One limitation to selecting girls who have the ability to articulate in writing is that it further silences those who have not yet developed this ability. Kim selected four girls as participants: Khalilah, Nicole, Alysa and Dauntai.

Khalilah was a 13-year-old African-American/Indian Muslim in the 8th grade. She was from a middle-class family. When asked to describe herself for the purpose of this and other reports of this research, Khalilah wrote, 'I'm 5 feet 2 inches [1.58 m], brown skin, with pretty brown eyes. I wear a scarf on my head for religious purposes. I'm funny sometimes [and] like to have fun all of the time'. Nicole was a 13-year-old 8th-grade African-American from a middle-class family. She described herself as 'light-skinned, nice, intelligent, 5 feet 5 inches [1.66 m], 110 pounds [50 kg], a good entertainer'. Alysa was a 13-year-old 8th-grade Caucasian from a lower-middle-class single-parent family. She described herself in saying, 'I'm nice, funny, caring, 5 feet 2 inches [1.58 m], I wear a

5–6 in jeans . . . I have green eyes and brown hair'. Dauntai was a 14-year-old 8th-grade African-American from a lower-middle-class family. Dauntai described herself as 'I am short, light skin, short hair, hazel eyes. I am a nice fun person to be around. I like doing things with movement'. Because all four girls were students in the International Bound Programme, a high academic track programme, they took all their required classes together. Khalilah, Dauntai and Nicole also spent time together outside school, participating in a teen group devoted to learning a traditional form of choreographed movement called 'stepping'.

Constructing bodily knowledge

Khalilah, Nicole, Alysa, Dauntai and Kim met at Dogwood Middle School every Tuesday and Thursday for 50 minutes during 15 consecutive weeks. During the girls' health and physical education class they met in a private classroom to engage in this alternative curriculum. Khalilah missed one day because of a field trip, and Alysa arrived late on one occasion.

We sought to understand the girls' perspectives. Consequently, it was important to use pedagogical practices that would convey our interest in, and respect for, what they had to say. We worked to support the girls' voices through the questions Kim asked and the tasks she invited the girls to complete. After each small-group conversation, she listened to and transcribed the audio-record made during the session. During our weekly researcher meetings, we reviewed the conversations and planned ways to communicate respectful listening. We also strove to help the girls elaborate their experiences, critique their practices, and imagine alternative and more equitable possibilities for their lives. We agreed with Greene (1995: 23) that:

> Only when the given or the taken-for-granted is subject to questioning, only when we take various, sometimes unfamiliar perspectives on it, does it show itself as what it is—contingent on many interpretations, many vantage points, unified (if at all) by conformity or by unexamined common sense. Once we can see our givens as contingencies, then we may have an opportunity to posit alternative ways of living and valuing and to make choices.

When the girls and Kim first met as a group, Kim asked them to develop personal biographies and personal maps. Our intent was to begin with an unthreatening activity that would inspire a conversation about the girls' experiences of their lives. Hatch and Wisniewski (1995) suggest that understanding individual lives is a central concern in the research process and we thought it might also be appropriate when beginning curricular work. We had structured the personal biography task as a series of questions to which the girls could respond. Thus, each girl wrote about what she liked and disliked, what she enjoyed watching on television, what she liked to read, what she wished adults and her peers understood about her, what physical activity was her favourite, and what made her smile.

To create a personal map, Kim asked each girl to indicate the spaces in which she spent time during the day, from the moment she woke up until the moment she went to bed. Kim asked each girl to label each place on her map, indicating what she did there, how much time she spent there, and who else was there with her. To help the mapping process, she gave each girl six pieces of coloured paper, explaining that the colour of the paper should be changed each time space was changed. The girls were together when they completed their maps. Later, Kim talked individually with each girl about her map and personal biography.

One of the first group activities was a magazine exploration. As multiple forms of representation allow for different meanings to emerge (Eisner 1997, Bustle 1999), we decided to encourage the examination of images. We hoped that magazine images would help the girls reveal meaning about the body that were difficult to express through written or verbal language alone. Secondly, magazines are cultural channels through which meanings of women's bodies are construed and communicated (Berger 1972, Wolf 1990, Pipher 1994). Understanding the girls' interpretations of those images seemed important to understanding how they were constructing the meanings of their bodies.

To complete this task, Kim gave the girls a dozen or so different magazines and asked them to cut out things that were of interest to them and categorize their clippings. Most of the magazines were among those they had indicated they read, including *YM, Ebony, Teen, Glamour*, and *Black Hairstyles*. In addition, we included *Women's Sport and Fitness* and *Shape*, to see if they would select health-related information. When the girl finished working, Kim asked them to explain each category and why each picture was in that particular category (Oliver, 1999).

Throughout her work with the girls, Kim asked them to complete a variety of free-writing responses (Barbieri 1995). The idea behind free writing is that the writer records what comes to mind as quickly as possible, without censoring words or thoughts. The focus is on getting words on paper, not spelling, grammar, being logical or making sense. The hope is to capture what the writer really thinks, to work within a space where energy is unobstructed by social politeness (Barbieri 1995). To encourage free writing, Kim typically used a first sentence as a stimulus and asked the girls to complete the thought using the body as the theme of the writing. For example, using the body as a theme, she asked the girls to develop a series of sentences that began with the words: 'Sometimes I wish . . .', or 'I'm afraid that . . .', or 'I hope . . .'.

The girls also wrote a series of stories and information pieces. The topics they wrote about came from the small-group conversations and the themes that were emerging in the journals. We thought the girls might have an easier time talking if they first had a few moments to reflect through writing. For example, when the girls introduced the term 'fashion out' as an important concept in their experience, Kim asked them to write about what happens to a girl who is labelled 'fashion out'. When the girls mentioned needing the 'right clothes and shoes' to be 'fashion in', she asked them to describe in writing what they meant.

In addition to completing free-writing exercises, written stories, and information pieces, Kim asked the girls to keep journals. We intended that, through journal keeping, the girls would document the times they noticed their bodies. Kim asked them to write in the journals about the times that they noticed their bodies, what they were doing when they noticed their bodies, how they were feeling, and what they were thinking. Since journal writing can serve as a form of self-reflection and self-analysis (Cooper 1991), having the girls begin documenting when they noticed their bodies seemed like a potentially empowering method.

The journals became much more than a place for self-reflection. As Kim responded in writing to the girls' journal entries, the journals became private space for confidential conservations between each girl and Kim. They became spaces within which each girl could express herself without condescension or disapproval from peers.

Since one aspect of this project was to help the girls imagine alternative possibilities for their lives, Kim asked the girls to imagine an alternative society. Rosary had used their technique with student groups at the university, and we thought an adaptation of it might be helpful in this work. To prepare the girls for this task, Kim combined all the major themes from both their journals and group conversations. She presented these themes to the girls and asked them to imagine these things did not exist. For example, imagine a world, she suggested, where everyone was blind, where there were no fashion magazines, no MTV (Music Television), no perms for our hair, no masculine or feminine labels. Imagine a world where girls and boys did not care about what they looked like, they only cared about what people had to say.

The bond that grew between Kim and the girls was palpable for Kim and fuelled conversations about the ethics of the work we had undertaken. As a field researcher, she had become involved in the lives of young people from groups to which neither she nor Rosary belonged. hooks (1989: 43) maintains that such situations are essentially unequal:

> Even if perceived 'authorities' writing about a group to which they do not belong and/or over which they wield power, are progressive, caring, and right-on in every way, as long as their authority is constituted by either the absence of the voices of the individuals whose experiences they seek to address, or the dismissal of those voices as unimportant, the subject-object dichotomy is maintained and dominance is reinforced.

In hopes of framing these girls' experiences of their bodies in the most ethical and authentic way possible, not only do we place the girls' voices at the centre of the curriculum, but we also placed their voices at the centre of the analysis and interpretations (Collins 1990). Nevertheless, our study remains limited by our outsider and potentially oppressive status as adult, middle-class, White, able-bodied, university-based researchers examining the language of four adolescent girls, three of whom identify as people of colour.

Understanding what the girls had to say

We tried to understand what the girls were saying. We supported critical examination of the girls' experiences of their bodies, while respecting the girls' views. In an attempt at critical research, we wished 'to push on the walls of modernity with . . . concerns for autonomy and self-reflection' (Kincheloe and McLaren 1994: 147). We collected several artifacts for this curriculum research project. We acquired transcriptions of the 25 small-group sessions, copies of the four journals, and copies of the materials the girls produced in response to Kim's invitations during the small-group sessions. Our data included articles, stories, life maps, personal biographies, free-writing responses, and magazine collages, as well as Kim's researcher's journal.

We carefully re-read the data many times as we developed a thematic analysis of the girls' linguistic and non-linguistic representations of their experiences of their bodies (Bogdan and Biklen 1998). For each theme, we listed all relevant data from the girls and generated assertions to account for those data. Furthermore, we examined how each girl represented each theme. Through the writing process (Alvermann *et al.* 1996), we refined and limited assertions to represent the data from this study accurately and robustly. We crafted and revised our report of those assertions, selecting examples from the artifacts to bring clarity and verisimilitude to those assertions. Finally, we examined each assertion in our report, questioning its support, and reviewed the data in searching for possible contradictions. We repeated these interpretive processes several times as we organized, elaborated and refined our account.

In spite of our attention to the amount and quality of evidence, we acknowledge that our representation of the girls' perspectives herein is both a partial and perspectival one (Lather 1991). It remains limited, insofar as it is only one of the multiple interpretations possible, given the artifacts and processes of this research project. Furthermore, among the possible multiple interpretations from our evidence, it is limited insofar as it is only one of the several that we two researchers, with our particular histories and social positions in the world, could have developed. Any more grand claim for the knowledge we report here would be 'specious, inauthentic, and misleading' (Lincoln 1996: 10).

In the section that follows, we describe two themes of the body that became salient for Khalilah, Nicole, Alysa and Dauntai as they participated in this curriculum. These were 'being noticed' and 'regulating the body'. Within each theme, we highlight the issue that the girls raised. Because the support of critique is an important intention of this curriculum project, within each theme we noted where and how the girls accepted dominant cultural narratives of the body and where and how they resisted oppressive forms of enculturation.

Themes of the body

Being noticed: experiencing the body through dominant cultural narratives

Khalilah, Nicole, Alysa and Dauntai described their desire for beauty and explained beauty as a means for being noticed by boys and accepted by other girls. Their language revealed the body as a form of collateral they hoped to exchange for being noticed and for developing and maintaining relationships with others. Khalilah's free-writing response to what she 'hopes' in terms of her body points to her desire:

> I hope that I will get prettier and prettier as the years pass on. My mother says that she thinks I'm pretty. I do sometimes and sometimes I don't. I get lots of compliments from older and younger people . . . When mostly boys walk past me, they just glance at me and turn away, but I think if they just look at me for a minute, they will see that I'm very pretty.

Like Khalilah, Dauntai also recognized beauty as a power in attracting boys. She explained in her journal her desire to appear attractive to the 'majority of them', particularly to those boys she finds 'attractive' or 'cute'. Despite this desire, Dauntai was able to carve out for herself spaces within which she did not have to worry about attractiveness or beauty. These social spaces occurred in her home, with family, 'friends that are girls' and friends who are boys and whom Dauntai characterizes as 'brothers'. Dauntai explained why brothers could be treated as exceptions, 'so the way I see it is that if they are my brothers they shouldn't care how I look, and I shouldn't either'.

For Dauntai, making herself attractive was something important not only to herself personally but also to her family. In her journal, she explained that she accepts and appreciates the perspective on beauty she attributes to family members: 'I could understand them wanting me to look nice if we go out somewhere in public, 'cause I would, too'. Dauntai described the press toward beauty in her life as both a personal and familial responsibility.

Although beauty had its social rewards, these young adolescents experienced lack of beauty not as a neutral but as a punitive condition. In a social sense, it was doubly punitive. First, the girls expected a lack of beauty to cause boys to turn away from the 'ugly' girl, leaving her to suffer the lack of their social attention. To make matters worse, they expected other girls to distance themselves from the 'ugly' girl, fearing that their close physical proximity to an 'ugly' girl would cause them, too, to be ignored by boys. Thus, the girl construed as 'ugly' was expected to suffer abandonment from both boys and girls. Khalilah in her journal explained and then personalized this phenomenon among girls:

> Girls do that, too. Some girls don't like to hang around ugly girls because they might make the boys turn away from them. Some girls don't pay attention to me because I wear a scarf, and I don't like that.

At a time in their lives when peer associations are especially prized, lack of beauty was a particularly chilling prospect.

Although desired, beauty did not come without associated costs for these girls. Khalilah considered the conflict between her desire to be noticed for her beauty and her commitment to her familial religious values and practices:

> Sometimes I just feel like taking my scarf off. When I do, I think everyone will like me, even the boys. I think I have a nice figure, but I can't show it. In my religion, the women are only allowed to show their figure to their husband. When I get around 17 or 18, I get to make my decision if I want to be a Muslim or not. I think I am still going to be one, but I'm just not going to wear my scarf. I think I have very pretty hair, and I would like to show it.
>
> (Journal entry, 29-10-96)

Khalilah's words depict the dilemma that she faces as a Muslim adolescent wishing to communicate her beauty in exchange for attention, while recognizing the incongruity between these emerging desires and the beliefs and practices central to her family's religious tradition. From her perspective, she faces a difficult decision.

Nicole also experienced beauty as a double-bind. Although she recognized the need for beauty in attracting social relationships, she explained a drawback of being 'pretty' in her dialogue journal:

> Well, a lot of people say they don't like me because I *think* I'm pretty. Well maybe they don't like me because I really [am] and they aren't. Well I'm tired of silly people who always say I think I'm too good . . . they never have a chance to really get to know me.

For Nicole, the images of beauty carried a price tag of jealousy. Although Nicole understood the importance of beauty in initiating and maintaining relationships, the fallout from being socially labelled as 'pretty' was that she became the envy of other girls. This envy, she suspected, caused other girls to talk about her, or dislike her. For these girls, both beauty and its lack could distance one from other girls.

Kim asked the girls to write about how they experienced their bodies in a variety of settings. Nicole's words reveal how she experienced male dominance in judgements about her beauty:

> When I'm around boys I wonder what they think of me no matter if I like them or not, because I know for a fact that boys look at you. I always wonder, do I look like I'm qualified for what they are looking for?

Nicole sought a standard of appearance and acceptability that she believed boys determined. Although she did not describe the standard explicitly, she believed its attainment was acknowledged in the look or the gaze of the boy. In a very real sense, Nicole, and the other girls Kim worked with, attributed considerable power to male attention.

The girls' explanations of the seductiveness of beauty reminded us of Wolf's (1990: 3) explanation of the disempowering role that beauty plays in much of Western society:

> 'Beauty' is a currency system like the gold standard. Like any economy, it is determined by politics, and in the modern age in the West it is the last, best belief system that keeps male dominance intact. In assigning value to women in a vertical hierarchy according to a culturally imposed physical standard, it is an expression of power relations in which women must unnaturally compete for resources that men have appropriated for themselves.

The language of these girls clearly echoes Wolf's currency metaphor. The girls drew frequently on the construct of currency as they explained how beauty operates within their adolescent lives.

In their pursuits of being noticed, some of the girls negotiated the meanings of their bodies through the lens of white supremacy[2] or the view that White characteristics and patterns of life ought to be the ideal for all human life. hooks (1995: 15) contends that, in using this view, all non-White people—people of various cultures and practices—are viewed as deficient, and all too frequently as deserving of punishment of various sorts:

> If black people have not learned our place as second-class citizens through educational institutions, we learn it by the daily assaults perpetuated by white offenders on our bodies and beings that we feel but rarely publicly protest or name.

For Khalilah, Nicole and Dauntai, the body was a site through which they experienced daily the repercussions of white supremacist values.

Using the white ideal, skin colour becomes a salient human characteristic. When writing about how she experienced her body around girls, Dauntai identified skin colour as a distinguishing feature in appearance, with lighter skin being considered more beautiful than darker skin. Because of her light-coloured skin she 'always wonders how girls look at me'. She worried that she would be considered 'stuck up' because of her lighter skin, as:

> girls like to think or say that light-skin girls are stuck-up . . . think they cute, and think they too good for everybody else and things like that. But I really have no need to worry because I'm not like any of those things, and I think that that comes out of jealousy.

When Kim asked Dauntai to elaborate on her explanation, she accounted for such female jealousy in terms of male attention:

> I think they are jealous of [light-skin girls] because they might think 'we' look better than them or 'you' get a lot of boys that want to talk to you . . . Another reason why dark skin or darker skin girls say things like this is because most boys prefer light-skin girls, and I had people tell me this, and Friday this boy who wanted to talk to me told me he had a thing for light-skin girls.

Dauntai's words revealed how girls become competitive in their quest for male attention. Furthermore, in this quest they often uncritically accepted and internalized a racist image of beauty as a standard for comparison and competition. These girls' experiences are consistent with Fordham's (1996) claim that within the African-American community it is particularly important for women to have light skin.

Resisting oppressive forms of enculturation

Even while the girls spoke eloquently of the significance of beauty in their lives, we noted occasional chords of resistance. Most often we heard those chords in the more private dialogue journal writing with Kim. Occasionally, but not often, they also resonated in the more public small-group conversations. The resistance in the girls' language was similar to the phenomenon of resistance as described by Kanpol (1994: 37):

> Like counter-hegemony, resistance entails acts that counter the oppressive race, class, and gender stereotypes as well as challenges to other dominant structural value . . . As part of resistance, reflecting about one's own subjectivity and multiple identities within the borders of race, class, gender, parent, teacher, husband, lover, and so on is a necessary condition before action can take place to undo oppressive social relations.

We most frequently heard chords of resistance within contradictory explanations about being noticed. The girls would discuss dominant cultural narratives about being noticed for reasons such as physical attractiveness, outer appearance, thinness and paleness when they worked in the group setting. In their journals, they more frequently and elaborately described alternative ways to be noticed.

The resistance we noted varied in intensity, sometimes ringing more clearly and at others occurring in more muted tones. Dauntai's dialogue journal entry is one example of clarity in resistance. It appeared in response to two formal communications. Dauntai had written in her journal about wanting 'cute boys to notice her' for her appearance. Kim wrote in response, 'My question is, do you want "cute boys" or boys you think are "attractive" to be interested in *YOU* as a *whole person* or do you want them to only be interested in "how you look"?'. Dauntai responded in her journal:

> Yes, I do want cute boys or boys that I find attractive to be interested in me as a whole person and not just how I look because my inside is just as pretty as my outside may be. Before anybody judges me by how I look they should get to know me just to see how I really am, then that's when they can judge me. I think that it's OK to be interested in a person how they look, but only before you get to know them because the most important thing is how you are on the inside and that's what people seem to forget. If you just are interested in a person for what they look like, when you get to know them you might not like the person any more and that can hurt their feelings if they really like you a lot. And another problem is that people seem to forget about people who don't look as nice as they want, and that can also hurt a person's feelings because you didn't get to know that person because you judged them by how they look.

For Dauntai, judgements about interest possessed a moral dimension, insofar as she addresses notions of how she thinks we should live together and treat each other (Beyer 1998). For Dauntai, it was important that one acts with caution in one's approach to others, lest one inadvertently causes harm to another.

Dauntai was able to challenge the patriarchal narrative by constructing a counter-narrative even as she conformed at times to the dominant narrative. Although she challenged the institutionalized patriarchal narrative that suggests that women be valued exclusively or primarily for their bodies, she did so only privately through her dialogue journal with Kim. She did not use such resistant language in the more public space of small-group conversation. Her journal responses suggest that during those conversations, Dauntai listened carefully, although she seldom spoke. Dauntai's pattern for voicing resistance is not surprising. The politics of naming and resisting oppression are dangerous for adolescent girls as they struggle to integrate into more adult-like roles, simultaneously wanting to 'fit in' and remain connected with others, while also wishing to distinguish themselves from others (Brown and Gilligan 1992).

Had we limited work with the girls to small-group conversations we may have erroneously concluded that Dauntai had given up her voice to others. Kim's more robust relationship with the girls allowed us to learn that, in spite of a pattern of silencing similar to that frequently observed with other adolescent girls (Gilligan *et al.* 1990, Brown and Gilligan 1992), Dauntai retained a capacity for resistance. Nevertheless, she had taken her voice 'underground', using it only privately within written dialogue. Under such circumstances, it is not surprising that, as Fine and Macpherson (1992: 178) have suggested, feminist scholarship has often overlooked '*how well young women talk as subjects . . . how firmly young women resist—alone and sometimes together*'.

Although, once found, Dauntai's resistance to dominant cultural narratives was more articulate, Alysa's resistance remained more subtle, buried as it was beneath layers of internalized oppression. Alysa's journal explanation, for example, illuminates the cultural narrative that boys are attracted to, or notice, 'skinny girls', 'I think I have to suck in my stomach to look better . . . I think my stomach needs to be flat because guys like skinny girls'.

In this same journal entry, Alysa resists the cultural narrative that suggests girls be noticed only if they are thin, as she writes about *when* she feels noticed:

> I like having company to talk to because unless I'm talking, I'm not happy . . . I like to talk because when I talk I'm noticed and when I don't, I'm not. When I'm talking and giving info to people, or just saying whatever, it just makes me happy. It's hard to explain. When I'm talking people know that I want to be around them.

Alysa's comment suggested her appreciation for alternative means for being noticed. She appeared to be struggling with at least two ways: being noticed for one's ability to talk and give information, and being noticed for one's appearance, particularly for one's thinness. She described her satisfaction with the former. Alysa felt noticed when she was talking. She felt noticed for her voice, for something spoken rather than visual appearance. She felt noticed when she had opportunities to say something to others, about things she knew. For Alysa, talk may be the beginning of agency—that belief that through personal efforts people can influence their world. If so, it would be wise for educators to nurture such emergent power.

Alysa admitted that her experience is 'hard to explain'. Thus, we characterized her resistance as nascent and perhaps more vulnerable than more elaborated forms. Such signs of resistance may be overlooked easily, appearing as they do here amid contradictory assertions, and even then in only grossly articulated forms. In this regard, our data support Grumet's (1988) claim that other 'quieter' stories are more difficult to hear and more dificult to find.

We also heard chords of resistance throughout Nicole's journal, although they are contiguous with oppressive notes. For example, in response to a free-writing exercise on what she hoped with respect to her body she wrote:

> I hope that my body doesn't change; I like my body. I hope that when I put on my bellbottom outfit on Thursday people will like it. I hope that if they don't, I will still be happy. I hope that I can learn to just not care what people think about my body.

For Nicole, the desire to achieve the standard of beauty required for social acceptance was interlaced with the desire to withstand social rejection—to stand her ground so to speak.

This interconnectedness of oppression and resistance may reveal both a possibility and a danger. As a place of contradiction, these expressed hopes may hold potential for nurturing further resistance, particularly through writing. If left unattended, however, this source of contradiction could lead Nicole to develop a consciousness brutalized by the dilemma of wanting to achieve incommensurable goals, i.e. she may hold herself responsible for achieving both the acceptances of dominant perspectives on beauty and their rejection—a no-win situation that could engender a sustained sense of self-disappointment.

Besides addressing the importance of being noticed, the girls also described several ways of regulating the body. In the section that follows, we discuss this theme, showing what it revealed about how the girls experienced their bodies through dominant cultural narratives and where and how they resisted those narratives.

Regulating the body

Experiencing the body through dominant cultural narratives

Dissatisfaction with the body was an experience understood by each of the four girls. Their dissatisfaction manifested itself in their active efforts to monitor, restrict and control their bodies in order to modify their appearance. Alysa admitted privately in her journal just how disappointed she felt with the image of her body, 'I get kind of depressed when I look in the mirror because I always see myself as fat'. In response, Kim wrote in Alysa's journal asking why she thinks she is fat. Alysa wrote in answer, 'I think I'm fat because of my legs'. To understand the standard that Alysa was using, it is important to mention that, at the time of this study, Alysa was 5 feet 2 inches (1.58 m), and weighed 115 pounds (52.28 kg). She wore a size 5–6 in pants. By current health standards, it would be difficult to characterize Alysa as 'fat'.

Alysa was not the only girl to worry about getting fat. Khalilah wrote in her journal:

> Every time I'm about to get in the shower, I always notice my body. I usually think, maybe I need to lose some of this fat on my stomach. I think it looks nasty to have a big stomach . . . Also I think what will people think if they had saw my stomach. It's not really big, I'm just not satisfied with it.

Khalilah's language also depicted her body in a negative light, as an object that somehow exists apart from her and as one that she judged harshly. Her use of the adjective 'nasty' suggests a sense of revulsion with her body. Furthermore, her dissatisfaction with the stomach is particularly disturbing, insofar as the stomach has long been associated in human culture with hunger, desire and appetite—all healthy aspects of being human.

In their attempts to negotiate their dissatisfaction, Khalilah, Alysa, Nicole and Dauntai actively participated in several regulation practices that included monitoring the body as if it were a separate entity from the person. Khalilah's journal entry revealed how pervasive her surveillance of her body had become:

> When I'm around my friends or especially when I'm around girls I don't know, I pay close attention to my body . . . I make sure there are no boogers in my nose. That's one thing I can't stand. When I'm around boys I have to be perfect. I have to make sure everything is right, even my face expression.

The level of conscious attention necessary to conduct such surveillance is considerable and represents an additional cost of beauty.

Khalilah's surveillance was conducted through conscious strategic actions that she incorporated into her daily routines. She explored the effects of certain facial moves by privately trying several out in front of her mirror. Khalilah explained in her journal her efforts to decide which facial expression 'looks best'. 'When I look in the mirror I make faces to see which face looks best and I even model [clothes] to see what I look like'. Besides these private surveillance activities, Khalilah also watched her body while she was in the midst of other activities. She explained that she was particularly attentive during physical activity around others. For example, she wrote:

> I make sure my shirt doesn't come up when my hands are in the air. And also I see if I can see the print of my stomach through my shirt when I put my hands in the air.

While Dauntai was concerned about how she 'looks in a certain shirt or pair of jeans or dress', she was worried about 'bigger things'. Unlike the other girls, she was more concerned about 'hygiene', reporting that she monitored several related matters including 'body odour', 'cleanliness' and 'bad breath'. Dauntai discussed in her journal her reasons for such surveillance:

> I like to make sure that I am clean and don't have body odour because I want to make a good impression on people especially when I meet someone for the first time because of the saying that first impressions always stick.

In addition to controlling how her body smells, Dauntai monitored her face, particularly 'how clean my face is' and what 'bumps that may have appeared or disappeared'.

As part of regulation, these four girls did not simply monitor their bodies, they actively participated in several practices designed to control their bodies in order to conform to standards of beauty as they understood them. In these pursuits, the girls were both active and strategic. They were active insofar as they took matters into their own hands in matters of beauty. They were strategic insofar as the actions taken were intended to address a particular end, in this case the attainment of particular standards of beauty (Oliver 1999).

One standard for beauty that Khalilah, Nicole and Dauntai discussed during the magazine exploration was the need to have 'straight hair'. On several occasions, they mentioned that girls with 'wrinkly' or 'woolly' hair should, treat 'it' with a perm to keep 'it' from 'looking like a doggy'. Images of beauty based on the white ideal are used against all women as a means of creating hierarchical structures of power (Wolf 1990). Therefore, Black girls and other non-White girls may pay particularly very high cultural costs in their pursuit of beauty. They must not only strive for beauty, but they must strive for a beauty that places them in roles as imposters in the social world—people struggling, not so much to claim who they are, but to achieve a standard developed by and for a group from which they have been socially excluded.

Both hooks (1995) and Collins (1990) agree that light skin and long straight hair remain the standards of beauty in the racist imagination. These images of beauty are powerful forms of control that influence Black girls' relationships with Whites, with Black men, and with each other (Collins 1990). hooks (1995: 186) claims that by using the term 'white supremacy', people can begin to see how Black people 'are socialized to embody the values and attitudes of white supremacy', and how these values are used as one means of monitoring other Black people. These girls were using racist images to judge beauty and character in themselves as well as in other girls. The three were learning ways to control their bodies to satisfy the white supremacist images portrayed as socially beautiful.

Although Alysa did not discuss the need to have straight hair (her privilege as a White included straight hair), she practised regulating her body to feel 'skinnier' in an effort to appear more attractive for boys. She revealed through journal writing the extent of her preoccupation with her body, explaining that she 'thinks about her body (looks) all the time'. She also explained why she makes efforts to restrict her body:

> Since I like wearing short shirts, I'm always thinking about sucking in my stomach . . . I think I have to suck in my stomach to look better . . . I think that my stomach needs to be flat because guys like skinny girls.

Alysa not only restricted her stomach around boys, she also did so among girls and with her dad's family:

> When I'm around other girls sometimes we're just sitting around talking, I sit up real straight so my stomach looks skinnier . . . When I'm around my dad's family I try to look as skinny and as pretty as I can because they are all skinny and pretty and my step-brother is kinda cute.

Alysa's desire to appear 'as skinny and pretty' as possible led her to control her body across much of her life.

At home, Alysa developed a concealment strategy to reduce the strain of worry she felt at school about what boys might think of her. As she explained, 'When I'm around boys at school, I wonder if they think I'm fat, but when I'm around guys at home I just wear big shirts to hide my stomach'. When she was not literally constraining her body by pulling in her stomach for fear of appearing fat, she practised modification of the body through concealment. Both were efforts to minimize her body in the world.

Some of the modifications Alysa sought are inconsistent with healthy patterns of human growth and development. For example, she argued, and Khalilah agreed, that it is possible to control pubescent development through the power of will. Alysa's theory of adolescent development crystallized when Kim asked the girl, 'When you look at magazines do you ever look at them and say, "No, these people aren't right; they don't know what they're talking about"?'. Alysa responded, 'Sometimes . . . like those ones that say that when you get this age you like do this or you turn like this or something like that. Sometimes people don't do that or whatever'.

Alysa's response opened a conversational space not only for critiquing magazine content, but also for considering ado adolescent development. Kim asked, 'Let's say, for example, if in one of the magazines it says as you get older your hips are going to get wider'. Alysa answered immediately, 'That's not necessarily true'. Kim asked, 'Is that one of those things that you don't believe?'. 'No', answered Nicole. Immediately Khalilah objected to Kim's comment, 'I wouldn't believe that. I don't believe that'. Kim elicited a prediction, 'What do you think will happen [during pubescent development]?'. Khalilah responded, 'Some people maybe [will develop hips] some people not'. Alysa then presented a theory of development that was somewhat surprising to Kim:

> Whatever you want to happen . . . If you sit there and say OK, this is what's gonna happen and then you sit there and be waiting and waiting for it to happen then it is probably going to happen. But if you say no that's not going to happen and work to make so that it doesn't happen, then it won't.

Disturbingly for us, the rejection of the hips carries with it the rejection, albeit in some unconscious form, of a physiological development that is natural and necessary for the continuance of human life.

In addition to trying to control biological development, Nicole, Alysa and Khalilah practised restricting food intake as a means of regulating their bodies. To regulate her body shape, Khalilah reduced her eating. She explained in her journal one strategy she had used and some of its effects:

> So if my mother makes something for dinner I don't like, I don't eat. A couple of weeks ago I never ate until dinner. When you don't eat for a while, when you do eat you're not hungry. My mother told me I needed to start eating because I was getting tired easy and weak.

Khalilah also expressed an emotional unease with the practice of eating publicly or at least in the public space of the school: 'I don't eat in school because I don't like eating in front of people I don't really know'. These comments suggest that Khalilah was developing several restrictions on her eating practices.

Nicole and Alysa also discussed how they regulated their eating. They were beginning to see how denying oneself food was a perceived means for preventing 'getting fat'.

> *Nicole*: My grandma always pick with me because it was like last year I wasn't this bony, and, um, my grandma told my mom, I think she got ashamed and went on a diet . . . I use to go out to eat every day . . . Then I just, I got tired of eatin'. I said I don't want to eat.
> *Kim*: So you don't eat any more?
> *Nicole*: Yes, I eat, but probably only once a day.
> *Khalilah*: Me, too, 'til dinner.
> *Nicole*: I don't never get hungry because I'm not used to eating any more.
> *Alysa*: Yeah, it's like you get into that way.
> *Khalilah*: I use to eat a lot, I could eat two plates of spaghetti.
> *Alysa*: I think everbody eats a lot when they're kids.
> *Khalilah*: And when I got sick, like last year or year before, then I stopped eatin' a lot.

Taken together, the three girls' explanations reveal a loss of desire for food. Nicole reported how she 'just got tired of eating', and Alysa rang in with hearty agreement. More disturbingly, their conversations foreshadow some of the elements noted in anorexia as described by Bordo (1997: 100):

> Anorexia will erupt, typically, in the course of what begins as a fairly moderate diet regime . . . The young woman discovers what it feels like to crave and want and need, and yet, through the exercise of her own will, to triumph over that need . . . The experience is intoxicating, habit-forming.

Describing this type of self-mastery, Alysa explained how she deals with her hunger, 'Usually if I'm hungry, I find something else to do so I just forget about it'.

Resisting oppressive forms of enculturation

We observed resistance to bodily regulation in the form of criticism, i.e. the girls pointed out some faults of bodily regulation. Although they did not criticize their own eating habits as being detrimental to their health and development, they did critique other girls' eating behaviours. Such form of criticism occurred most often during the small-group discussions. Nicole claimed that anorexia is a means 'other girls' use to prevent developing. She explained having some 'stressed' friends who 'might be anorexic or something because they think, because their body is changing, that they're gonna get fat'. She also claimed that 'other' girls 'think if they eat then they gonna get fatter'. She admitted having heard people say they 'haven't eaten in three weeks'.

Alysa also publicly discussed other girls' habits:

> I know this one girl, she, um, who didn't eat for three days. All she did was drink water and that was it in the morning and at night. That's all she did.

Although Alysa admitted that friends and neighbours were concerned about her eating patterns, she denied their concerns were warranted. 'People think, like everybody in my neighbourhood thinks like I'm anorexic, but I'm not. I eat'. She also showed considerable knowledge on the subject of eating disorders, and easily distinguished anorexia and bulimia:

> Anorexia [is when] you don't eat . . . Bulimia is where you eat but you throw it up . . . It's gross 'cause you stick your finger down your throat and you start throwing up and it will get all over your hands.

Alysa's expertise was not what troubled us, but rather her explanation of the experience of the hands which suggests a personalized knowledge of the bulimic experience. Yet, insofar as Alysa, Nicole, Dauntai and Khalilah were willing to discuss eating habits, even in terms of what other girls do, they may have been offering a form of resistance to their own emerging practices or, as their descriptions suggest, to those of other members of their peer group.

For these girls, regulating their bodies was a common practice in the quest for beauty. Their conversations were consistent with others in which women are described as:

> spending more time on the management and discipline of our bodies than we have in a long, long time. In a decade marked by a reopening of the public arena to women, the intensification of such regimens appears diversionary and subverting.
>
> (Bordo 1997: 91)

In considering the meanings of times when these girls were actively preparing their bodies for attractiveness, holding in the stomachs, straightening their hair, and thinking about what others, particularly males, might think of them, it is important that we, as educators, attend to what is missing from the existential picture. We might, for example, ask what the girls were not doing; what knowledge, talents, skills or other aspects of their human potential were they not developing?

Curricular processes supporting critique

Throughout this project, Kim tried to help Khalilah, Nicole, Alysa and Dauntai name and critique the meanings they were making of their bodies. Critique appeared to us to be a reasonable place to begin in a curriculum project designed to encourage and support agency or active engagement in the world. To create this space for critique, we designed a variety of activities to encourage critical reflection, both within the group setting and the dialogue journals.

Throughout this project, we examined our data to determine what conditions and strategies in our activist research process helped the girls raise questions around taken-for-granted cultural narratives and consider alternative possibilities for their lives. Through analysis, we found that five processes seemed useful:

- tapping girls' interests as a starting place for discussion;
- listening actively and respectfully to what the girls were struggling to say;
- developing strategic questions that supported elaboration or challenged their current views;
- creating safe spaces for expressing alternative views; and
- supporting imagination of alternative worlds.

It is important to note we worked with a small group of girls. Nevertheless, this small-group approach allowed us to look closely at what we were doing and how the girls responded in order to identify aspects of our approach worth adapting for a larger group. In addition, it allowed us to understand some of the complexities of how the girls experienced their bodies, complexities that we would have missed had we worked with large numbers of girls.

Tapping girls' interests

The girls found it compelling to talk with each other about the topics Kim elicited and supported. They pointed to their appreciation for the discussion topics when Kim asked the girls to write in their journals about their experiences in this group. Khalilah explained her interest in the discussion topics:

> I liked talking about all of the things we talked about. I liked this class because we got to talk about things I wouldn't have really talked about w/ [with] my friends . . . I did like working w/ this group. I wouldn't mind working w/ them again.

Like Khalilah, Nicole also found the topics associated with the body interesting, albeit neglected in their school curricula. She wrote: 'I feel that it was a good experience. I got to express a lot of great issues I don't get to talk about all the time'.

Although we were interested in understanding how these girls experienced their bodies, Kim often encouraged the girls to generate topics of interest to them, as she did when she asked the girls to cut out magazine pictures of interest to them. She then used these topics as a springboard for nurturing critique. What we began to realize through this process, was that tapping girls' interests was helpful in understanding their bodily knowledge.

Active, respectful listening

Like tapping girls' interests, we also found that active and respectful listening was of great importance to the girls in this curriculum work. For Kim, active listening meant repeatedly asking herself questions such as, 'What is this girl trying to say?'; 'How can I help her to explain her meaning in greater detail?'; and 'How can I help her better articulate what she means so that all five of us can more fully understand and appreciate her view?' In the small-group discussion, Kim tried to follow the girls' leads even when that meant going in a direction she would not have otherwise gone. Within the girls' journals, she would communicate active listening by writing back to each girl, often asking her to elaborate on something she had previously written.

Active listening was only one part of the listening process that Kim attempted with the girls. We also found that encouraging the girls to talk and listening respectfully as they did so, were very important for supporting critique. Respectful listening often meant putting aside evaluation or judgement of the worthiness of the knowledge that the girls were sharing. At times, this was difficult for Kim when issues of injustice surfaced in the girls' conversations. Nevertheless, careful listening by itself was a type of support, a way to nurture whatever the girls had to say, including their resistance. The girls themselves explained how important active listening was in the context of these conversations:

> *Nicole*: You know, like if [you] come here on Tuesday, on Thursday you come back, and you and you and you, we can tell that you thought about what we said. Because, I mean, you have somethin' to say about it, and then you also go back to . . .
> *Khalilah*: What we said earlier.
> *Nicole*: When we first come in here we might talk about somethin' and then when we leave we might be talkin' about something else. But like when you come in on Thursday we can tell you were listenin' because you still remember, we can tell you thought about it.

The point in our work is that stories must not only be exchanged, they must also be valued. Alysa, Dauntai, Nicole and Khalilah seemed to value Kim's efforts to understand them as well as her willingness to listen to what they thought was important. From their analysis, we learned that they, too, were attentive to Kim. They noticed how she returned to their ideas after each session, and they judged her use of their stories to be evidence that she 'listened'.

Listening and respectfully considering the girls' contributions was a very active process requiring considerable time and energy. It involved Kim focusing on what was happening during the small-group sessions, carefully reading their journal entries, recording many of their conversations, reviewing transcripts of their conversations, and preparing outlines of the points made and issues raised.

Strategic questioning

In addition to active and respectful listening, Kim also encouraged critique and nurtured resistance to bodily oppression by asking small, bridging questions with these ends in mind. The questions she asked were not often the formal critical questions found in the literature on critical literacy, but rather small questions such as 'What do you mean by that?', 'Can you tell me why you feel that way?', and 'Imagine these [oppressive] things did not exist, what would it be like?' Occasionally, her questions challenged the validity of the information or ideas being discussed. So, for example, she asked 'Do you believe all this stuff you read in magazines?' Brooker and MacDonald (1999: 88) claim that 'it is essential that physical educators not only take account of students' shifting understandings of . . . the body, but also adopt teaching approaches that heighten students' critical capacities'.

Kim used such questions to help the girls extend and analyse their language and become more aware of conditions that influence the ways they are learning to think about their bodies. Khalilah described in her journal her experience of the critical processes, 'it was kind of a challenge for me because you wanted us to explain what we had to say, and some of the things were hard to explain'. This finding is consistent with Greene's (1988, 1995) argument that only when people can begin to see their situations as obstacles can they begin to devise plans to overcome these obstacles.

Safe spaces

The spaces that the girls used to voice their resistance were also important. We found that if we wanted to carefully consider adolescents' views, we had to create safe spaces for them to express their views. The two primary spaces Kim used were the dialogue journals and small-group discussions. Although at first the journals were intended as a space where the girls could document the times they noticed their bodies, they soon became a space in which Kim could talk privately, through writing, with each of the four girls.

The content of the girls' journal writing was different in important ways from their small-group conversations. Sometimes they took stances on issues that were different from those they had taken in the small group. Sometimes they expressed views and exchanged information in their journals when they had remained silent in the small group. Sometimes in their journals they elaborated on a point they had made or they introduced a new topic or new piece of information or perspective. Sometimes the girls used the journals to share how they personally experienced many issues raised in the group conversations, and they confided how they felt about some of the small-group conversations. It seemed that the journal had become a space they judged to be safer than the small-group sessions. In their journals, the girls seemed freer to express notions that might have seemed inappropriate or risky during our group conversations. Furthermore, the girls were always eager to see what Kim wrote in response to their entries, and frequently asked at the beginning of each week, 'Did you read my journal?' or 'Did you write anything in my journal?'

The group conversations reflected a more contentious pattern than the journal dialogues. Despite Kim's efforts to sustain a social arrangement in which every voice could be heard and every girl could speak, an unequal conversational pattern developed and persisted. Nicole dominated the conversation, and Khalilah was a close second. Dauntai listened for lengthy periods, but when she spoke all three of the other girls and Kim reflected carefully on what she said. It was as if she spoke in a different tone, one that often forced the group to reconsider an issue or line of analysis. Alysa's role in the group was more worrisome to us. Over time, Alysa became the one whose voice was most often resisted, ignored and otherwise silenced during group conversations. While she spoke during group conversations, the others frequently disagreed with her, or cut her off in the middle of speaking.

A significant difference between the two venues for response lay in the type of comments the girls were likely to make. Small-group conversation and dialogue journal writing served as complementary forms for these girls to reflect on how they experienced their bodies. Within the small-group discussions, the girls described and named oppression, but they seldom expressed outright resistance. However, within the privacy of their journals, the girls expressed nascent forms of resistance to numerous examples of gender, race, class and religious oppression. Through writing, the girls often explored ways of resisting the very stories they told and supported in the more public conversational spaces. Seldom, however, did any girl mention the content from her journal during group conversations. This is a significant finding in our work—one that makes us excited about further developing opportunities for adolescents to use journal writing as a focal activity in efforts to nurture critical reflection.

Several of the girls wrote about why they liked using the dialogue journals. For Alysa, it was a safe place to voice her opinions: 'I like writing in our journal because if I don't want to talk about something I can write it'. For Khalilah, it was a space to say some things that were weighing on her:

> Some of these things I wrote in this journal I can't believe I wrote for someone to see that I didn't really know at first. I usually don't express what I have to say around grown-ups. I don't even tell my mother how I feel. In this journal I have expressed a lot of my feelings and said what I needed to say. I'm glad I said some of these things to get them off my chest. I wish I could do this more often.

For Dauntai, it was an opportunity to confide in an adult:

> I think it has been fun writing in the journals. Some of the things you said or asked me made me think twice or differently about some things. I liked writing about the different subjects, especially about the boys, because I had to tell an older person how younger people feel about boys.

The girls' use of these opportunities supports Collins' (1990: 95) view that 'this realm of relatively safe discourse, however narrow, is a necessary condition for Black women's resistance'. Alysa's use of the journal suggests that journal writing may also be beneficial to White girls.

The girls' response patterns suggest that, although the small-group conversations may have been a reasonable way to initiate discussion of the body, they were not sufficient. Without the more private journal-writing opportunities, the girls may not have resisted the more dominant storylines they developed during group conversations. Clearly more work needs to be done in this area before we can be more definitive. Nevertheless, our work is consistent with the perspective that methods as well as content are important pedagogical agendas. According to Roskelly (1998: 263):

> Some of those methods change patterns of responsibility and authority in ways that promote consciousness of power relationships cross gender, cross race, cross class . . . Journal writing, dialogues, informal responses, and a host of other writing tasks can foster negotiation, challenging received ideas of all kinds, including privilege.

Imagining alternative worlds

Finally, we found that one strategy for helping the girls name forms of enculturation troubling them was to ask them to imagine that things were different and to explain what they hoped for and what they wished things could be like. It was within these spaces that they began to name more accurately how they were constructing the meanings of their bodies within the culture in which they lived, went to school, and in other ways participated. As Greene (1995) has suggested, the girls' responses provided evidence of the importance of imagination in critical activity such as this. According to Greene:

> this passion of seeing things close up and large . . . is the doorway for imagination; here is the possibility of looking at things as if they could be otherwise. This possibility . . . [of] looking at things large is what might move us on to reform.
>
> (p. 16)

Although our initial intent was to have the girls imagine preferred possibilities for their lives through imagining an 'alternative society', we found this to be a particularly difficult task for them. Quite often the girls resisted imagining things as if they could be otherwise. They claimed that they 'couldn't do this', or that 'this is too hard for us'. Through their resistance to this task, however, they began to name more firmly the forms and processes of their own enculturation. When we asked them to imagine something better, they began to articulate more clearly the 'way things were'.

For example, when Kim asked the girls to imagine that there was no such thing as a perm, Nicole responded: 'If we didn't have perms we wouldn't know no better. If we didn't know that they existed we wouldn't want for them'. Kim reminded the girls about the time when Nicole said that African-American people used perms so that their hair would 'be straight like it's supposed to be'. This allowed Kim to ask, 'Who said it's supposed to be straight?' It was not until this point that they began to articulate more clearly the oppression. Nicole stated:

> I mean, some, some races, well when we get perms we try to make, you know better ourselves because some other races already low rate us because of our colour. And being, you know, we just get perms because we don't want our hair to look, you know, despicable.

Conclusion

This curriculum project gives hope to the possibility of transformative physical education and language arts curricula focusing on the body. Through the interplay of opportunities to examine how the body has been represented by various media, with opportunities to write and talk about their experiences of their bodies, the girls were able to express some resistance to culturally dominant perspectives. Kim used an approach that combined course content from physical education and health classes with linguistic processes common in language arts and English classes. This combination of content and process was somewhat useful for the intended purposes, suggesting the wisdom of further study and curriculum development.

For teachers and curriculum workers, these findings suggest the wisdom of exploring the possibilities of thematic study of the body for middle-school students. Such a study might intersect various subjects, not only physical education and language arts/English, while retaining the critical perspective that Kim nurtured through the questions she asked and the tasks she used. Language arts and English can offer the perspective of critical reading that has been identified as an important part of the curriculum in these subjects and defined as:

> Reading a text in such a way as to question assumptions, explore perspectives, and critique underlying social and political values and stances. Critical reading is resistant, active, and focused on both the text and the world. Critical readers bring a range of experiences to texts, and, in turn, use texts to develop critical perspectives on personal and social experience.
>
> (NCTE 1996: 71)

Besides joining these two subjects, we suggest that other curricular areas be included for this effort. Each curricular area can offer specialized knowledge about the body. In this work, however, it will be important to keep the girls' voices and the girls' concerns about their bodies at the forefront. To do otherwise would run the risk, that so many US physical educators have done, of continuing to silence girls by importing issues related to the body that adults find problematic or of interest (Sallis and McKenzie 1991, National Association of Sports 1995, Payne *et al.* 1997, Rimmer and Looney 1997). Brooker and MacDonald (1999: 84) claim:

> While curriculum supposedly exists to serve the interests of learners, their preferences, if sought at all, are marginalized and their voices are mostly silent in curriculum making. This marginalization of student voice is of particular concern in such subjects as physical education . . . in which the essence of the subject is closely linked to the interests and culture of learners.

Indeed, it is notable that the girls seldom discussed the topics of sport or physical activity. In the few instances in which they did so, the topics were typically raised at Kim's prompting, and even then the girls did not sustain conversation on these topics. To keep the girls' voices and concerns central, we suggest the exploration of an inquiry curriculum in which learners are encouraged to ask questions about the body that are important to them and to explore the various curricular areas for evidence to inform their inquiries.

Within the language arts/English/literacy communities, inquiry teaching has been espoused as an empowering curricular process that involves many activities associated with literate behaviours. These include opportunities to interpret texts, say what they mean, relate texts to personal experience, make links across texts, explain and argue with various ideas, make predictions, hypothesize outcomes, compare and evaluate, and talk about doing these things (Heath and Mangiola 1991). This list is remarkably similar to the description of critical reading described in the English/Language Arts National Standards document (NCTE 1996) quoted above, and it is very consistent with our work with our four adolescent collaborators. One suggestion for future efforts at this type of work is to continue beyond the period of a semester. Counter-cultural efforts perhaps require more extended periods of time if they are to have lasting effects.

Although the literacy community talks specifically about how to help students become critically literate, much more work needs to be done in physical education if students are to become critical consumers of popular physical culture (Kirk and Tinning 1990, Tinning and Fitzclarence 1992, Brooker and MacDonald 1999). The academic literature in physical education critically examines forms and processes of enculturation that are often disempowering and destructive to young people (Bain 1990, Theberge 1991, Vertinsky 1992, Kirk and Tinning 1994). This suggests that educators need to make a greater effort at developing ways of working with girls to help them learn these critical processes. Indeed, an important gift educators might give children is to create curriculum through which they can become literate beings whose bodies and minds are experienced as a cherished and inseparable dimension of being.

Acknowledgements

We thank Jerry Rosiek of the University of Alabama, David Kirk of Loughborough University, and the anonymous reviewers for their comments on earlier drafts of this paper.

Notes

1   Pseudonyms are used throughout this paper.
2   The persistence of white supremacy in this part of the USA is evident in how the girls constructed beauty.

References

Adams, F. (1975) *Unearthing Seeds of Fire: The Idea of Highlander* (Winston-Salem, NC: John F. Blair).

Alvermann, D. E., O'Brien, D. G. and Dillon, D. R. (1996) On writing qualitative research. *Reading Research Quarterly*, 31(1), 114–120.

Bain, L. L. (1990) A critical analysis of the hidden curriculum in physical education. In D. Kirk and R. Tinning (eds), *Physical Education, Curriculum and Culture: Critical Issues in the Contemporary Crisis* (London: Falmer), 23–42.

Barbieri, M. (1995) *Sounds from the Heart: Learning to Listen to Girls* (Portsmouth, NH: Heinemann).

Berger, J. (1972) *Ways of Seeing: A Book* (London: British Broadcasting Corporation and Penguin).

Beyer, L. E. (1998) Schooling for democracy: what kind? In L. E. Beyer and M. W. Apple (eds), *The Curriculum: Problems, Politics and Possibilities*, 2nd edn (Albany, NY: SUNY Press), 245–263.

Bloom, L. R. and Munro, P. (1995) Conflicts of selves: nonunitary subjectivity in women administrators' life history narratives. In J. A. Hatch and R. Wisniewski (eds), *Life History and Narrative* (Washington, DC: Falmer), 99–112.

Bogdan, R. C. and Biklen, S. K. (1998) *Qualitative Research for Education: An Introduction to Theory and Methods*, 3rd edn (Boston: Allyn & Bacon).

Bordo, S. (1997) The body and the reproduction of femininity. In K. Conboy, N. Medina and S. Stanbury (eds), *Writing on the Body: Female Embodiment and Feminist Theory* (New York: Columbia University Press), 90–110.

Brooker, R. and MacDonald, D. (1999) Did *we* hear *you*?: issues of student voice in curriculum innovation. *Journal of Curriculum Studies*, 31(1), 83–97.

Brown, L. M. and Gilligan, C. (1992) *Meeting at the Crossroads: Women's Psychology and Girls' Development* (Cambridge, MA: Harvard University Press).

Brumberg, J. J. (1997) *The Body Project: An Intimate History of American Girls* (New York: Random House).

Bustle, L. (1999) Photography as inquiry: image-based research in teacher education. Paper presented at the annual meeting of the American Educational Research Association, Montreal, Canada (Radford, VA: Radford University).

Cash, T. F. and Pruzinsky, T. (eds) (1990) *Body Images: Development, Deviance, and Change* (New York: Guilford).

Collins, P. H. (1990) *Black Feminist Thought: Knowledge, Consciousness, and the Politics of Empowerment*, Perspectives on Gender, Vol. 2 (Boston: Unwin Hyman).

Collins, P. H. (1998) *Fighting Words: Black Women and the Search for Justice* (Minneapolis, MN: University of Minnesota Press).

Cooper, J. E. (1991) Tell our own stories: the reading and writing of journals and diaries. In C. Witherell and N. Noddings (eds), *Stories Lives Tell: Narrative and Dialogue in Education* (New York: Teachers College Press), 91–112.

Delpit, L. (1995) *Other People's Children: Cultural Conflict in the Classroom* (New York: New Press).

Eisner, E. W. (1997) The promise and perils of alternative forms of data representation. *Educational Researcher*, 26(6), 4–10.

Fine, M. (1992) *Disruptive Voices: The Possibilities of Feminist Research* (Ann Arbor, MI: University of Michigan Press).

Fine, M. (1998) Greener pastures. In W. Ayers and J. L. Miller (eds), *A Light in Dark Times: Maxine Greene and the Unfinished Conversation* (New York: Teachers College Press), 209–218.

Fine, M. and MacPherson, P. (1992) Over dinner: feminism and adolescent female bodies. In M. Fine (ed.), *Disruptive Voices: The Possibilities of Feminist Research* (Ann Arbor, MI: University of Michigan Press), 175–203.

Fordham, S. (1996) *Blacked Out: Dilemmas of Race, Identity, and Success at Capital High* (Chicago: University of Chicago Press).

Freire, P. (1974) *Pedagogy of the Oppressed*, trans. M. B. Ramos (New York: Seabury Press).

Freire, P. (1985) *The Politics of Education: Culture, Power, and Liberation* (South Hadley, MA: Bergin & Garvey).

Gilligan, C., Lyons, N. P. and Hanmer, T. J. (eds) (1990) *Making Connections: The Relational Worlds of Adolescent Girls at Emma Willard School* (Cambridge, MA: Harvard University Press).

Gore, J. M. (1993) *The Struggle for Pedagogies: Critical and Feminist Discourses as Regimes of Truth* (New York: Routledge).

Greene, M. (1988) *The Dialectic of Freedom* (New York: Teachers College Press).

Greene, M. (1995) *Releasing the Imagination: Essays on Education, the Arts, and Social Change* (San Francisco: Jossey-Bass).

Grumet, M. R. (1988) *Bitter Milk: Women and Teaching* (Amherst, MA: University of Massachusetts Press).

Hatch, J. A. and Wisniewski, R. (1995) Life history and narrative: questions, issues, and exemplary works. In J. A. Hatch and R. Wisniewski (eds), *Life History and Narrative* (Washington, DC: Falmer), 113–136.

Heath, S. B. and Mangiola, L. (1991) *Children of Promise: Literate Activity in Linguistically and Culturally Diverse Classrooms* (Washington, DC: National Education Association).

hooks, b. (1989) *Talking Back: Thinking Feminist, Thinking Black* (Boston: South End Press).

hooks, b. (1990) *Yearning: Race, Gender, and Cultural Politics* (Boston: South End Press).

hooks, b. (1995) *Killing Rage: Ending Racism* (New York: Henry Holt).

Jaffee, L. and Lutter, J. M. (1995) Adolescent girls: factors influencing low and high body image. *Melpomene*, 14 (2), 14–20.

Kanpol, B. (1994) *Critical Pedagogy: An Introduction* (Westport, CT: Bergin & Garvey).

Kincheloe, J. L. and McLaren, P. L. (1994) Rethinking critical theory and qualitative research. In N. K. Denzin an and Y. S. Lincoln (eds), *Handbook of Qualitative Research* (Thousand Oaks, CA: Sage), 138–157.

Kirk, D. and Colquhoun, D. (1989) Healthism and physical education. *British Journal of Sociology of Education*, 10(4), 417–434.

Kirk, D. and MacDonald, D. (1998) Situated learning in physical education. *Journal of Teaching in Physical Education*, 17(3), 376–387.

Kirk, D. and Tinning, R. (eds) (1990) *Physical Education, Curriculum and Culture: Critical Issues in the Contemporary Crisis* (London: Falmer).

Kirk, D. and Tinning, R. (1994) Embodied self-identity, healthy lifestyles and school physical education. *Sociology of Health and Illness*, 16(5), 600–625.

Ladson-Billings, G. (1994) *The Dreamkeepers: Sucessful Teachers of African American Children* (San Francisco: Jossey-Bass).

Ladson-Billings, G. and Tate, IV, W. F. (1995) Toward a critical race theory of education. *Teachers College Record*, 97(1), 47–68.

Lather, P. (1991) *Getting Smart: Feminist Research and Pedagogy With/in the Postmodern* (New York: Routledge).

Lincoln, Y. S. (1996) Emerging criteria for quality in interpretive research. Paper presented at the National Reading Conference, Charleston, SC.

Littrell, M. A., Damhorst, M. L. and Littrell, J. M. (1990) Clothing interests, body satisfaction, and eating behavior of adolescent females: related or independent dimensions? *Adolescence*, 25 (97), 77–95.

Luke, C. and Gore, J. (eds) (1992) *Feminisms and Critical Pedagogy* (New York: Routledge).

Miller, J. L. (1990) *Creating Spaces and Finding Voices: Teachers Collaborating for Empowerment* (Albany, NY: SUNY Press).

National Association of Sports (1995) *Moving into the Future: National Standards for Physical Education: A Guide to Content and Assessment* (Reston, VA: National Association of Sports and Physical Education, American Alliance for Health, Physical Education, Recreation and Dance; St Louis, MO: Mosby).

National Council of Teachers of English (NCTE) (1996) *Standards for the English Language Arts* (Urbana, IL: NCTE).

Oliver, K. L. (1999) Adolescent girls' body-narratives: learning to desire and create a 'fashionable' image. *Teachers College Record*, 101 (2), 220–246.

Payne, V. G., Morrow, Jr, J. R., Johnson, L. and Dalton, S. N. (1997) Resistance training in children and youth: a meta-analysis. *Research Quarterly for Exercise and Sport*, 68 (1), 80–88.

Pipher, M. (1994) *Reviving Ophelia: Saving the Selvs of Adolescent Girls* (New York: Putnam's).

Pronger, B. (1995) Rendering the body: the implicit lessons of gross anatomy. *Quest*, 47(4), 427–446.

Rimmer, J. H. and Looney, M. A. (1997) Effects on an aerobic activity program on the cholesterol levels of adolescents. *Research Quarterly for Exercise and Sport*, 68(1), 74–79.

Rosenbaum, M.-B. (1993) The changing body image of the adolescent girl. In M. Sugar (ed.), *Female Adolescent Development*, 2nd edn (New York: Brunner/Mazel), 234–252.

Roskelly, H. (1998) We was girls together: race and class and southern women. In J. Z. Schmidt (ed.), *Women/Writing/Teaching* (Albany, NY: SUNY Press), 257–266.

Sallis, J. F. and McKenzie, T. L. (1991) Physical education's role in public health. *Research Quarterly for Exercise and Sport*, 62(2), 124–137.

Shannon, P. (1990) *The Struggle to Continue: Progressive Reading Instruction in the United States* (Portsmouth, NH: Heinemann).

Shannon, P. (1992) *Becoming Political: Readings and Writings in the Politics of Literacy Education* (Portsmouth, NH: Heinemann).

Shilling, C. (1993) *The Body and Social Theory* (London: Sage).

Shor, I. (1992) *Empowering Education: Critical Teaching for Social Change* (Chicago: University of Chicago Press).

Sparkes, A. C. (1997) Reflections on the socially constructed physical self. In K. R. Fox (ed.), *The Physical Self: From Motivation to Well-being* (Champaign, IL: Human Kinetics), 83–110.

Theberge, N. (1991) Reflections on the body in the sociology of sport. *Quest*, 43(2), 123–134.

Tinning, R. (1985) Physical education and the cult of slenderness: a critique. *ACHPER* [Australian Council for Health, Physical Education and Recreation] *National Journal*, 107 (March), 10–13.

Tinning, R. and Fitzclarence, L. (1992) Postmodern youth culture and the crisis in Australian secondary school physical education. *Quest*, 44(3), 287–303.

US Department of Health and Human Services (1996) *Physical Activity and Health*. A Report of the Surgeon General, Centers for Disease Control and Prevention, National Center for Chronic Disease Prevention and Health Promotion, US Department of Health and Human Services, Atlanta, GA, USA.

Usmiani, S. and Daniluk, J. (1997) Mothers and their adolescent daughters: relationship between self-esteem, gender role identity, and body image. *Journal of Youth and Adolescence*, 26(1), 45–62.

Vertinsky, P. A. (1992) Reclaiming space, revisioning the body: the quest for gender-sensitive physical education. *Quest*, 44(3), 373–396.

Weiler, K. (1988) *Women Teaching for Change: Gender, Class and Power* (South Hadley, MA: Bergin & Garvey).

Wolf, N. (1990) *The Beauty Myth* (London: Chatto & Windus).

Michael Gard and Jan Wright

MANAGING UNCERTAINTY
Obesity discourses and physical education in a risk society

Health, healthism and physical education

SINCE ITS INCEPTION as part of the school curriculum in the English speaking world, school physical education has always been associated with the improvement of 'health.' How 'health' has been constituted has varied over time and for different social groups. As Kirk and Spiller (1994) have pointed out, the espoused health goals of physical training/education have played a major role in providing the means to closely monitor and regulate children's bodies in state schools. In the 19th and early 20th centuries this was through postural and other medico-physical assessments. Since the late 1970s the prominence of a health related fitness (HRF) approach has produced new monitoring procedures, such as fitness testing, measurements of weight and other indicators of body size and shape, which have been incorporated into teaching practices in physical education, often with little regard for their effects on individual children (Burns, 1993), or for the messages they suggest about bodies, weight and normality.

In the 1950s research on cardiovascular disease (CVD) which linked heart attacks to a sedentary lifestyle provided physical educators with a source of legitimation which has since been thoroughly mined. As Kirk (1990) has argued, physical education looked to medico-scientific research to enhance the status of the subject and to provide legitimacy in educational contexts where the body/physical was regarded as separate from, and less important than, the mind/intellect. The biomedical research which followed pointed to a range of associations between inactivity and illhealth including the prevention of what were to become known as 'lifestyle diseases', particularly cardiovascular disease. A 'sedentary' lifestyle was established as a 'risk factor.' However, what constitutes a 'sedentary' lifestyle or 'adequate' activity has changed over time and is still far from clear. For example, the duration and intensity of exercise that a person needs to do in order to accrue health benefits remains controversial (Lee and Paffenbarger, 1997; Pate, 1995).

For many physical educators the association between inactivity and illhealth provided the means to argue for an approach to physical education that focused on addressing this problem. Tinning and Kirk (1991) even go so far as to suggest it was in part a response to a perceived threat of irrelevance. This approach, variously known as Health Related Fitness (HRF) or Health Based Physical Education (HBPE) is premised on the assumptions that there is a positive relationship between physical activity and health, that participation in physical activity by children and adults is declining and that this has dire consequences for their health. It also assumed that physical education has a primary responsibility to address this decline by providing opportunities for vigorous activity during lessons and by providing physical skills and positive experiences which are likely to increase students' participation in physical activity now and in the future.

HBPE has many proponents in Europe, UK, USA, Australia and New Zealand (see for instance, Almond, 1983; Corbin and Pangrazi, 1993; Dodd, 1982). There are variations on the assumptions listed above, with some adherents supporting the need for funda-mental movement skills as a basis for participation and others arguing for more fitness based activities and some for both. Its logic is hard to fault, particularly in a context where physical education as a profession and discipline seems to be constantly searching for a definitive purpose (Stroot, 1994). However, it has been criticised by a number of writers (for example, Colquhuon, 1990; Tinning and Kirk, 1991), for the ways in which it uncritically supports the triplex of exercise=fitness=health (where health is determined by body size and shape) and is embedded in a discourse of 'healthism' which constitutes health in terms of a moral imperative of self-control (Crawford, 1980). It is this approach to physical education that relies most heavily on epidemiological and biomedical research to legitimate its research agenda, its presence in the curriculum and its pedagogical practices.

The HBPE approach to physical education received a further impetus in the 1990s with the increase in academic and popular interest in the so-called 'obesity epidemic' (Flegal, 1999). According to Colquhuon (1990), prior to 1960 obesity was rarely men-tioned in the medical literature. However by 1981 concern had grown considerably. Comparative studies in the 1980s pointed to the increasing weight of the 'average' woman and man in populations in the UK, North America and Australia. By the 1990s a pre-occupation with overweight/obesity dominated many governments' health concerns (Jutel, forthcoming 2001). For instance, in the United States, *Healthy People 2000* puts the prevention of obesity at the top of its list of health concerns. In Australia, *Acting on Australia's Weight: A strategic plan of the prevention of overweight and obesity* (NHMRC, 1997) identifies overweight and obesity 'as key risk indicators of preventable morbidity and mortality' (p. 2). It cites the costs to the health system and to individuals as the major reasons for concern.

In this paper we are particularly interested in pointing to the implications of this preoccupation with obesity for physical education. On one hand, we argue that physical education is both implicated in producing and reproducing the obesity discourses and their effects. On the other, we contend that physical education continues to legitimate itself on the basis of claims about obesity and overweight which are not only shaky but ethically irresponsible; that their effects on students and the public are detrimental rather than productive of health; and that it serves our purposes as a profession, to accept these discourses uncritically because of the resources and recognition we accrue.

To achieve our ends we have examined the ways in which obesity discourses become uncritically recontextualised both within and between levels of practice (Bernstein, 1986, 1996). Following a discussion of the theoretical premises deployed in the paper, we examine the ways in which the obesity discourses are constituted by expert practice in the reporting of research in academic journals. Following Beck (1992a, 1992b), our main concern here is the erasure of uncertainty with respect to knowledge about the body, body weight, exercise and health, and the construction of certainty where none seems justified. We examine how this 'expert' knowledge is reconstituted in professional and academic physical education literature. This process should not be imagined as one that is linear. Rather, media coverage of the 'expert' knowledge produced in reports serves to generate a public/popular discourse which speaks to politicians and funding bodies about the levels of community concern generated around the issue and so motivates further discussion – some of which contests the dominant discourse (see Atrens, 2000) but most of which serves to confirm it and spread its effects.

Regimes of truth in risk societies

Beck (1992a, 1992b) has argued that western democracies have become 'risk societies'. Whereas in the past we may have been able to make distinctions between social groupings based on their ability to accumulate wealth or 'goods,' Beck (1992a) argues that new divisions are appearing which cohere around people's ability to avoid risks or 'bads.' It is important to point out that Beck's work has explicitly dealt with global environmental concerns and the spectre of what he calls the environmental 'mega-hazards' of industrialisation. Beck (1992a) argues that all of us, rich and poor, face risks which our societies cannot insure against, such as those associated with nuclear accidents and that more and more of our energy is devoted to avoiding risks.

If risks cannot be adequately insured against, then they must be managed in other ways. In the case of nuclear accidents and global warming, Beck (1992a) has shown how corporations and governments have resorted to relying on 'experts' to allay people's concerns about risks, thus rendering potentially difficult and inconvenient debates about insurance and compensation unnecessary. In a broader sense, these conditions have served to erode public confidence in modernist institutions, such as, governments, industries, corporations and universities, and raise doubts about the very notion of 'progress.'

One of the effects of this has been to alter the conditions under which scientific enterprises proceed. Drawing on this work, Reddy (1996) has suggested that these conditions position the expert as a crucial focus of trust in a modernising process that may seem less and less trustworthy. In effect, the role of the expert in a 'risk society' is to claim knowledge, expertise and an ability to control that which seems to be out of control. The important point is that within a risk society, uncertainty is dangerous because it exposes the degree to which modernist institutions have over-stepped the limits of their own knowledge. Under these conditions uncertainty becomes a scandal and the enemy of the modernising process (Beck, 1992b). By managing uncertainty, the expert becomes central to the construction of a sense of control over the risks we live with.

In public health discourse, the management of uncertainty is accomplished by the quantification of risk through population studies that calculate the likelihood of a phenomenon. Citing Hacking (1990), Lupton (1995, p. 78) describes risk as depending 'on a belief in law-like mathematical regularities in the population, itself dependent upon the collection of data and its tabulation.' Epidemiology and biomedical research become the source of 'expert' knowledge in this context and population studies the only source of valid knowledge about public health. These identify 'risk factors' that effect populations and identify 'populations at risk.' The perceptions of risk are however socially constructed – as Ewald points out (quoted in Lupton, 1995, p. 79) 'nothing is a risk itself until it is judged to be a risk.' This identification or risk is dialectic between expertise and social values and political and economic imperatives.

Fundamental to the notion of risk is that by so naming the risk it can be managed, and uncertainty reduced. By understanding the lines of causality, one can act rationally to avoid it. Lupton (1995) points to the way in which health promotion 'risks' are managed by setting targets for the reduction of mortality or morbidity in particular populations (most at risk from a disease). For instance, in the United States the Surgeon General has set goals of active participation in physical activity for 75% of high school students by 2000 (cited in Savage and Scott, 1998). Once the risk factors identified with morbidity and mortality have been identified the assumption is that targets can be reached 'if only the correct advice is taken' (Lupton, 1995, p. 81). What is not acknowledged is the limited relevance of population predictions to predicting ill health for individuals (Atrens, 2000; Lupton, 1995).

The 'obesity epidemic'

In this paper, we propose that it is possible to employ the notion of 'risk' and 'risk management' to the human body and those who would claim knowledge about it. We argue that the so-called 'obesity epidemic' (Flegal, 1999), which some now claim to be a world wide phenomena, is an example of a field of inquiry in which uncertainty appears untenable and in which a range of experts claim a level of expertise which seems hubristic at best.

Obesity is an interesting condition because it is related to the 'success' of the so-called 'developed' nations and hints at the tensions between human bodies and the project of modernity. That is, despite the ability of 'developed' nations to control and waste a disproportionate percentage of the world's food, their citizens are not free from anxiety about food, albeit anxiety of a very particular kind. Employing Beck's terms, we might say that obesity has been constructed as an undesirable side effect of modern western life and adds to the growing list of risks that this kind of life is charged with generating.

Unlike Beck, our concern in this paper is less with the overtly political deployment of experts by embattled institutions, but with the ways in which certainty about children, obesity, exercise and health is produced in a variety of institutional contexts, and the implications of this process for physical education. Despite an absence of scientific certainty about the causes, incidence, consequences and treatment of over-weight and obesity, the field of physical education continues to operate as if certainty existed. We argue that these unquestioned beliefs have negative effects on the ways in which physical education and exercise are researched and taught, both in schools and universities.

Obesity discourses recontextualised

The work of Bernstein (1986, 1996) on pedagogic discourse is useful in understanding how discourses from outside the field of education become recontextualised to serve educational purposes. According to Bernstein, pedagogic discourse has no particular discourse of its own. Rather, 'it is a principle for appropriating other discourses and for bringing them into a special relation with one another for the purposes of their selective transmission and acquisition' (Bernstein, 1986, p. 210). By this process, pedagogic discourse becomes constituted as a specific and complex discourse (as in physical education) which is concerned with the organisation, and implementation of a particular curriculum area.

The expert knowledge from the primary field of knowledge production, that is biomedical research, is recontextualised to the secondary field as physical education researchers and educationalists appropriate it. It is taken up, refocussed and relocated in ways which make invisible its original complexities and contradictions and exclude contesting positions – an imaginary or mediated discourse removed from its original 'social base, position and power relations' is created (Bernstein, 1996, p. 53). As such, it is more difficult to contest. Obesity as a health problem which is both caused by inadequate amounts of physical activity and which can be treated and prevented by increasing participation in physical activity is reproduced as 'given' knowledge. This 'fact' is then used to argue for the need for physical education in general and for specific kinds of physical education in particular.

Expert knowledge: the biomedical field

An analysis of biomedical research demonstrates that there is a great deal of uncertainty about the levels of obesity/overweight, the relationship between obesity/overweight and health, and the efficacy of physical activity in preventing or treating obesity (see Atrens, 2000; Flegal, 1999; Parsons et al., 1999 for reviews). We have chosen to illustrate these points by focusing on a particular instance of knowledge production, the special November 1999 issue of the American College of Sports Medicine's journal, *Medicine and Science in Sports and Exercise*. This issue presented the findings of the 'Physical Activity and Obesity: American College of Sports Medicine Consensus Conference.' As such, it provides a striking evidence of the way in which uncertainty makes way for certainty, particularly where achieving 'consensus' seems to be the objective (Blair and Bouchard, 1999). In opening the issue, Bouchard and Blair (1999, p. S498) suggest that:

> . . . the body of knowledge on physical activity and relevant obesity outcomes is extremely limited. There are few randomized clinical trials that have lasted 1 year or more, with reasonable statistical power, adequate monitoring of intervention protocols, high levels of compliance, and proper measurement of outcome variables. The net result is a general lack of a solid research database regarding the role of physical activity in the prevention and treatment of overweight and obesity as well as their comorbidities.

These comments are echoed throughout the issue. In her review of research into overweight and obesity levels around the world, Flegal (1999, p. S512), argues that we know 'remarkably little' about the causes of obesity. And despite claims that childhood obesity is increasing (Campbell, 2000; Powell, 2000), Flegal notes that studies of children are rare. In fact, Flegal cites only two examples in which longitudinal comparisons of children are possible. The first of these, a single study from Brazil, shows a small *decrease* in overweight (not obesity) amongst boys aged four years and under (4.7% to 3.8%) and a similarly small increase amongst girls (4.6% to 5.3%). The second involves the authors own work in the United States which suggests more dramatic increases in overweight (again, not obesity) amongst children from ages six through to seventeen.

While demonstrating that far more data regarding adults exist, and that a number of studies around the world show increases for men and women, Flegal notes that these increases are neither universal nor uniform. While some studies show relatively large increases, others show much smaller changes. In a handful of countries, the research reports no change at all. She then argues that despite an increase in obesity "(t)he net health implications of the increases are not completely clear" (p. S511). In a number of countries hypertension, elevated cholesterol, cardiovascular mortality, and average blood pressure have dropped as obesity has gone up. In addition, in the United States, cardio-vascular risk factors remain high amongst the non-obese and non-overweight.

Flegal goes on to comment that '(a)lthough there has been considerable speculation about the reasons for the increases in the United States and in some other countries, solid data are lacking' (p. S511). However, she does note the apparent influence of socio-economics on obesity levels, particularly with respect to gender, race and class. She concludes that 'It is likely that research could benefit from going beyond a narrowly mechanistic focus on eneregy intake and physical activity' and that '(t)he work of economic and social historians, sociologists, and anthropologists may lead to a better understanding of the social forces at work' (p. S512). In effect, Flegal is challenging the standard line of argument, repeated in other contributions to the issue (Bouchard and Blair, 1999; Hill and Melanson, 1999), that since changes in body weight are determined by differences between energy intake and expenditure, people need only manage these two variables in order to manage their weight. Flegal's point, and one that we would support, is that body weight is a complex social issue, and that simply telling people to exercise and eat more carefully is likely to have little impact.

Flegal's representation of the state of knowledge about obesity, exercise and health as partial and contradictory is an exception. Other contributors to the issue are inclined to write in far more straightforward terms. For Bouchard and Blair (1999) the problem is one of changing the 'effortless' (p. S500) lifestyles of western populations. But for whom is life 'effortless'? From whence comes their certainty on this issue? Having admitted in the same article 'the body of knowledge on physical activity and relevant obesity outcomes is extremely limited' (p. S498), they go on to claim that:

> The reduction in energy expenditure associated with physical activity brought about by automation and changing job and professional environmental circum-stances has been nothing but dramatic in the second half of this century.
>
> (p. S499)

This slippage from uncertainty and the lack of valid and reliable data to certainty that there is a problem and that people should change their ways is evident in other contributions. In their review of research into the determinants of overweight and obesity, Hill and Melanson (1999) conclude that:

> Although it is intuitively obvious that improvements in technology over the

past few decades have substantially reduced the energy expenditure required for daily living, this has not been definitively documented. All indications are that work-related physical activity has declined.

(p. S517)

Hill and Melanson do not elaborate on what these 'indications' might be. They are equally speculative when it comes to physical activity and children:

This (decrease in physical activity) is not limited to adults, as it is also likely that significant declines have occurred in the amount of physical activity that children receive in schools. It is not possible to quantify the extent of this decline over the past two to three decades, but the requirement for physical education has declined in most schools as has the number of school children participating in physical education classes.

(p. S517)

A straightforward criticism of these comments is that the authors seem to have assumed that children expend significant amounts of energy in physical education classes. This assumption is at odds with the existing research (Simons-Morton et al., 1993). However, for the purposes of this paper, we are interested in the jump from uncertainty, based on a self-confessed lack of evidence, to certainty. There is perhaps a clue in Hill and Melanson's comment that:

The amount of energy expenditure required for daily living also appears to be declining due to an increase in attractive sedentary activities such as television watching, video games, and computer interactions. Again, we do not have good measures of sedentary activity that would allow us to examine changes over time.

(p. S517)

This comment suggests some interesting value judgements. Why might sedentary activities be more 'attractive' to children than other activities? Two possible explanations for this line of argument present themselves. The first is that authors believe that non-sedentary activities are not pleasurable. The amount of pleasure children derive from physical activity is a complex question, but it is clear that a great deal of organised, adult-led form of physical activity (for example, physical education and competitive sports) are not pleasurable experiences for many children (Portman, 1995). This would appear to be particularly true when the explicit focus of the activity is cardio-vascular fitness and/or weight reduction (Hopple and Graham, 1995). The second possible explanation appears to revolve around a moral suspicion of children and the evils of technology. We would want to ask why the authors believe children of today (as opposed to those of previous generations) find sedentary activities so attractive? A similar moral position seems to run through Bouchard and Blair's (1999) explanations:

The tools available to reverse this unhealthy trend are remarkably simple in appearance as they center on the promotion of eating regular and healthy meals, avoiding high caloric density snacks, drinking water instead of energy-containing beverages, keeping dietary fat at about 30% of calories, cutting down on TV viewing time, walking more, participating more in sports and other energy-consuming leisure activities, and other similar measures. However, it will be a daunting task to change the course of nations that have progressively become quite comfortable with an effortless lifestyle in which individual consumption is almost unlimited.

(p. S500)

Despite the intratextual moves to certainty in the form of moral imperatives to exercise, to reduce time spent watching television and to eat less, at this level of knowledge production there are some spaces for contestation. There is a lack of consensus amongst the experts, the language reporting findings (rather than that making recommendations or suggesting solutions) is tentative and the grounds on which conclusions are reached has to be available for scrutiny by other researchers. While the peer review that occurs is generally based on a narrow set of positivist criteria, it does mean that the methodology is generally described in some detail. In the process of recontextualisation to the educational field of physical education, the means by which the knowledge about obesity is produced becomes hidden and the opportunity for scrutiny radically diminished.

Physical education professional and academic literature

Physical education academics writing in research and professional journals become the recontextualising agents in transforming the knowledge produced by biomedical experts into a set of assumptions which are used in turn to justify physical education practice. The way this happens becomes obvious through an examination of the introductory paragraphs of articles on physical activity and physical education from a range of professional and academic journals. Despite the considerable and increasing debate about the relationships between weight, health, and physical activity, statements are made, with and sometimes without acknowledgment, that uncritically infer the certainty of a detrimental relationship.

The effects of such practices are not only to premise all that follows on somewhat shaky assumptions but also to reproduce a new expert discourse to be drawn on by other academics, teachers and preservice student teachers. The reiteration of the relationship as 'fact' reduces the opportunity for contestation. Moreover, the recontextualisation of obesity discourses in a context where 'healthism' is taken for granted, translates what has been research designed to understand population trends, into an individualist discourse which places the responsibility for health firmly with the individual. Physical education practice thus focuses on individual attitudes and behaviours on the assumption that each individual is at risk of overweight/obesity.

The following examples from the US and the UK are typical articles within the field of physical education which in one way or another argue that there is a problem with current levels of participation in physical activity in and/or out of school contexts and that physical education has a responsibility to increase participation. It follows that they also subscribe implicitly or explicitly to a form of health based physical education.

Fox (1994), writing as an advocate of 'health-related physical activity,' in his article, 'Understanding young people and their decisions about physical activity,' states that:

Inactivity is no now firmly established at the policy-making level as a behaviour that has primary consequences for health. Following the publication of the Allied Dunbar National Fitness Survey (Activity and Health Research, 1992) we now have a Health of the Nation Physical Activity Task Force. Similarly, following a recent rapid increase in the incidence of obesity, nutritionists and physical activity experts have been brought together to seek solutions for the prevention of obesity.

(p. 15)

Several linguistic devices are employed here to recontextualise contested knowledge as 'fact.' For example, the use of the present tense 'is' in the first sentence of the quote, together with the words 'firmly established' leaves few spaces for contestation – grammatically the statement is constructed as 'truth' (Halliday, 1985). In the last sentence, the phrases 'recent rapid increase in obesity' and 'the prevention of obesity' both make invisible the conflicting and complex research that would challenge the assumptions about obesity on which these phrases rely. Activity (inactivity)-obesity-illhealth is linked in an implicit causal relationship which, as is argued above, is not supported by research. In addition, there is some ambiguity over the use of the term 'obesity' – does this conflate with overweight here? Obesity only effects a very small percentage of the population, yet here the moral imperative to be active is directed at all young people.

Savage and Scott (1998) provide another example of the obesity/physical activity discourse. Again the detrimental relationship between obesity and inactivity is (re)produced as uncontestable knowledge. In addition the authors state again without reservations that 'activity and fitness levels of American children and youth have deteriorated significantly over the last 10–20 years' (p. 245). As we have suggested this claim has not been substantiated by research (Goran et al., 1998; Ruxton et al., 1999) and remains in the realms of conjecture. They go on:

A review of relevant literature concerning the health behaviours of children indicate that children tend to be physically inactive (Sallis, 1993) and are not developing activity levels that will endure into adulthood. Physical inactivity is a well-documented risk factor for obesity and other chronic diseases such as cardiovascular disease. Further, activity and fitness levels of American children and youth have deteriorated significantly over the last 10–20 years. This trend may be related to the amount of physical activity available to this population in school physical education classes.

(p. 245)

Consistent with the assumptions with which they begin, this article also assumes a particular kind of physical education as the solution – that is, one where the main purpose of physical education is to contribute to the health/fitness of students. As has been pointed out above, it also makes the dubious assumption that the amount of physical activity in what is generally no more than two, forty or sixty minute lessons physical education a week in secondary schools is likely to make a difference to students' fitness/health.

In the report of another study, which on one level engages socially critical discourses of race, Johnson (2000) also makes an uncritical connection between disease factors, obesity and physical activity. Exploring strategies to promote physical activity among Asian communities, Johnson argues for the need for such strategies on the basis of inequities in health outcomes such as 'circulatory disorders, . . . diabetes and associated renal failure' (p. 51). The link between physical activity and these health outcomes is made through body weight: '(l)ongstanding research has repeatedly found an association with body weight and mass and these conditions, and that raised levels of physical activity can provide a degree of protection from them' (p. 51).

A quick scan of any of the major English language professional and academic physical education journals will soon demonstrate that these examples are not isolated cases. If it were only a matter of a shaky set of assumptions then physical education would not be alone in basing its practices more on 'hope than happening' (Kenway, 1997). However, as we will argue below there are serious and detrimental consequences contingent on assuming the obesity discourses as 'truth' and as legitimate foundations for physical education practice.

An ethical position: why does it matter?

First it is necessary to say that we do not want to deny a relationship between health and physical activity in the context of physical education. Neither are we denying that physical activity should be an integral part of physical education. What we are challenging is the narrow definition of health that has been adopted, that is, the uncritical acceptance of particular narrow health imperatives, notably the 'obesity epidemic' and the effects this has on the research conducted in the name of physical education, on what counts as appropriate physical activity and on physical education practice in schools.

A critique of this issue is not new. Kirk and Tinning (1991) and Colquhuon (1990) have drawn attention to the implications of 'healthism' as the dominant principle underpinning physical education. Tinning (1985) has also drawn attention to physical education's implication (together with the fashion and fitness industries) in the 'cult of slenderness' and the negative consequences of this for young women. With the notion of an 'obesity epidemic' gaining prominence in both academic and popular texts, those espousing health related physical education however have a powerful and seductive rationale for their case. What has not been adequately considered are the merits of the assumptions on which this case rests nor the consequences for school students and the general population of an uncritical acceptance of its premises.

We have argued above that within a 'risk society,' 'experts' have an important role in managing uncertainty through their claim to knowledge. Within the context of health, experts purport to manage the uncertainty of illness and death through the identification of risk factors – that is, factors that are deemed to be largely avoidable through the actions of individuals. The question, then, is why does it matter?

On one level, it matters simply because the successful hegemony of the obesity discourse closes off spaces for other ways of thinking and doing physical education. Other approaches to physical education are available which foreground educational objectives such as critical thinking (Daniel and Bergman-Drewe, 1998), social responsibility (Hellison, 1995) and gender equity (Wright, 1998). But these clearly carry less weight in a context in which healthism, underscored by the moral panic about obesity, holds sway.

On another level, the hegemony of the obesity discourses matters because the knowledges and practices associated with these discourses exert technologies of power which serve to classify individuals (and populations) as normal or abnormal, as 'good' or 'bad' citizens, as at risk and therefore requiring the intervention of the state, in the form of the medico-health system and education. The obesity discourses set up particular modes of regulation. In physical education they allow the measurement and comparison of children and young people with culturally constructed norms which have questionable validity, particularly in relation to determining the present or future health of individuals (Burns, 1993).

These are discourses that allow us to construct those who are overweight as lazy and morally wanting. They give permission on a daily basis for ridicule and harassment and the right to publicly monitor the body shape of others. They stimulate a constant self-surveillance, which if we accept the evidence of surveys suggest that many people do not find themselves as measuring up. They contribute to a process of normalisation that contributes to illnesses such as anorexia and bulimia. The help to produce a lifestyle which Atrens (2000) describes as 'riddled with needless anxiety and conspicuously short of fun' (p. 2).

By accepting the obesity discourses uncritically physical educators are implicated in these processes. It is apparent that body weighing, fitness testing and lifestyle counselling remain standard features of the practice of physical education, despite the highly questionable efficacy and value of these practices. Rather than offering children strategies with which they might critically examine and question body weight norms and the associated moral imperatives to exercise, these approaches to physical education become part of the machinery of surveillance.

We would also argue that the construction of certainty around weight, exercise and health conceals a desire to be certain about the human body; to see it as quantifiable and controllable. However, if the research in this area indicates anything, it is that different bodies respond to exercise and food intake in radically different ways. It may well be that the body is not an object that lends itself at all well to rational quantification. This would certainly seem to be one plausible explanation for the difficulties researchers continue to have in attempting to establish stable 'truths' about weight, exercise and health. It may even tell us something about the motivation for something called a 'consensus conference', such as the one mentioned earlier in this paper. As Beck's analysis of 'experts' in 'risk societies' suggests, it is precisely because stable knowledge in this area has proved so elusive, and will probably remain so, that attempts to find 'consensus' amongst researchers and commentators assume greater and greater importance. The unquantifiable body *is* a scandal, and no doubt, in the future, we will see more concerted efforts to keep the scandal a secret.

With respect to the issues outlined in this paper, we would argue that students of physical education in schools and universities should be allowed and encouraged to conceive of scientific knowledge about the body as contested and unstable. While it is probable that *some* level of physical activity has *some* health benefits for *some* people, there is little else that we can say with any certainty in this area. Therefore, we see a need for physical and health educators to radically expand their definition of what has come to be known as 'informed health decision making.' It has been well documented that anxiety about body weight and fitness has tended to result in 'choosing' to embark on diets or exercise programs. Both of these courses of action have been shown to be of limited value as long term weight control strategies, particularly dieting which appears to result in very little weight reduction (Miller 1999).

Instead, we would like to see people choose to participate in physical activity because they find it pleasurable and to 'know' that their moral and physical integrity does not depend on it. This would require a very different kind of advocacy from the one that currently dominates health and exercise discourse. For physical education, it suggests a more critical engagement with medico-scientific knowledge and a more relaxed and playful approach to physical activity itself. Most of all, we need to be able to see scientific uncertainty about the body, not as a curse, but as confirmation that we are not machines. In the end, Bouchard and Blair's (1999) comment (quoted above) that the 'tools' needed to regulate body weight are 'remarkably simple in appearance' is both untrue and counter-productive. It is untrue because if obesity is the worldwide problem that the experts claim it is (and as we have tried to show, the evidence for this claim is, at best, inconclusive), then it is not simply a matter of energy in/energy out. Clearly, questions of race, gender and class are central to the phenomena, such as it is. And it is counter-productive because it exhorts people to establish relationships with their body based on fear, anxiety and guilt. What does it say about me if weight control is 'simple' and yet I continue to put on weight, no matter how hard I try?

We suspect that it may be better for physical educators to say nothing about obesity, exercise and health, rather than singing the praises of slimness and vigorous exercise and condemning the evils of fat and 'sedentary' life. Failing this, we implore physical educators to look underneath the surface of the discipline's cherished beliefs. While the terror of finding nothing is ever present, we believe that a renewed focus on less instrumental and more child centred approaches to physical activity, and the sheer pleasure of using one's body, may indeed be a liberating experience for all.

References

Almond, L.: 1983, 'A Rationale for Health Related Fitness in Schools', *Bulletin of Physical Education* **19**, 5–11.

Atrens, D.: 2000, *The Power of Pleasure*, Duffy and Snellgrove, Sydney, NSW.

Beck, U.: 1992a, *Risk Society*, Sage, London.

Beck, U.: 1992b, 'From Industrial Society to the Risk Society: Questions of Survival, Social Structure and Ecological Enlightenment', *Theory, Culture and Society* **9**, 97–123.

Bernstein, B: 1986, 'On Pedagogic Discourse', in J.G. Richardson (ed.), *Handbook of Theory and Research for the Sociology of Education*, Greenwood Press, New York.

Bernstein, B.: 1996, *Pedagogy, Symbolic Control and Identity: Theory, Research and Critique*, Taylor & Francis, London.

Blair, S.N. and Bouchard, C.: 1999, 'Roundtable Preface: Physical Activity in the Prevention and Treatment of Obesity and its Comorbidities', *Medicine and Science in Sports and Exercise* **31**, S497.

Bouchard, C. and Blair, S.N.: 1999, 'Introductory Comments for the Consensus on Physical Activity and Obesity', *Medicine and Science in Sports and Exercise* **31**, S498–S501.

Burns, R.: 1993, 'Health, fitness and female subjectivity: What is happening in School Health and Physical Education?', in L. Yeats (ed.), *Feminism and Education*, La Trobe University Press, Melbourne, pp. 78–94.

Campbell, D.: 2000, 'Schools Rear Crop of Couch Potatoes', *The Observer*, Feb 27, p. 6.

Colquhoun, D.: 1990, 'Images of Healthism in Health-Based Physical Education', in D. Kirk and R. Tinning (eds.), *Physical Education, Curriculum and Culture: Critical Issues in the Contemporary Crisis*, Falmer Press, London, pp. 225–251.

Corbin, C.B. and Pangrazi, R.P.: 1992, 'Are American Children and Youth Fit?', *Research Quarterly for Exercise and Sport* **63**, 96–106.

Crawford, R.: 1980, 'Healthism and the Medicalisation of Everyday Life', *International Journal of Health Services* **10**, 365–389.

Daniel, M. and Bergman-Drewe, S.: 1998, 'Higher-order Thinking, Philosophy, and Teacher Education in Physical Education', *Quest* **50**, 33–58.

Dodd, G.: 1982, *The Daily Physical Education Program*, Australian Council for Health Physical Education and Recreation, Adelaide.

Flegal, K.M.: 1999, 'The Obesity Epidemic in Children and Adults: Current Evidence and Research Issues', *Medicine and Science in Sports and Exercise* **31**, S509–S514.

Fox, J.: 1994, 'Understanding Young People and their Decisions about Physical Activity', *British Journal of Physical Education* (Spring), 15–19.

Goran, M.I., Shewchuk, R., Gower, B.A., Nagey, T.R., Carpenter, W.H. and Johnson, R.K.: 1998, 'Longitudinal Changes in Fatness in White Children: No Effect of Childhood Energy Expenditure', *American Journal of Clinical Nutrition* **67**, 309–316.

Halliday, M.: 1985, *An Introduction to Functional Grammar*, Edward Arnold, London.

Hellison, D.: 1995, *Teaching Responsibility Through Physical Activity*, Human Kinetics, Champaign, IL.

Hill, J.O. and Melanson, E.L.: 1999, 'Overview of the Determinants of Overweight and Obesity: Current Evidence and Research Issues', *Medicine and Science in Sports and Exercise* **31**, S515–S521.

Hopple, C. and Graham, G.: 1995, 'What Children Think, Feel, and Know About Physical Fitness Testing', *Journal of Teaching Physical Education* **14**, 408–417.

Johnson, M.R.D.: 2000, 'Perceptions of Barriers to Health Physical Activity Among Asian Communities', *Sport Education and Society* **5**, 51–70.

Jutel, A.: forthcoming 2001, 'Does Size Really Matter?: Weight and Values in Public Health', *Perspectives in Biology and Medicine*.

Kenway, J. and Willis, S.: 1997, *Answering Back: Girls, Boys and Feminism in Schools*, Sydney, Allen and Unwin.

Kirk, D.: 1990, 'Knowledge, Science and the Rise and Rise of Human Movement Studies', *ACHPER National Journal* **127**, 8–11.

Kirk, D. and Spiller, B.: 1994, 'Schooling the Docile Body: Physical Education, Schooling and the Myth of Oppression', *Australian Journal of Education* **38**, 80–97.

Lee, I.M. and Paffenbarger, R.S.: 1997, 'Is Vigorous Physical Activity Necessary to Reduce the Risk of Cardiovascular Disease', in A.S. Leon (ed.), *Physical Activity and Cardiovascular Health*, Human Kinetics, Champaign, IL, pp. 67–75.

Lupton, D.: 1995, *The Imperative of Health: Public Health and the Regulated Body*, Sage, London.

Miller, W.C. 1999: 'How Effective are Traditional Dietary and Exercise Interventions for Weight Loss?', *Medicine and Science in Sports and Exercise* **31**, 1129–1134.

National Health and Medical Research Council: 1997, *Acting on Australia's Weight: A Strategic Plan for the Prevention of Overweight and Obesity*, Australian Government Publishing Service, Canberra, ACT.

Parsons, T.J., Power, C., Logan, S. and Summerbell, C.D.: 1999, 'Childhood Predictors of

Adult Obesity: A Systematic Review', *International Journal of Obesity and Related Metabolic Disorders* **23**(Supplement 8), S1–107.

Pate, R.R.: 1995, 'Physical Activity and Health: Dose-Response Issues', *Research Quarterly for Exercise and Sport* **66**, 313–318.

Portman, P.A.: 1995, 'Who is Having Fun in Physical Education Classes? Experiences of Sixth-Grade Students in Elementary and Middle Schools', *Journal of Teaching in Physical Education* **14**, 445–453.

Powell, S.: 2000, 'One in Four Australian children is Overweight. Slower, Stiffer, Heavier – They are the Cotton-Wool Generation', *The Weekend Australian* (May 27–28), Review 6–8.

Reddy, S.G.: 1996, 'Claims to Expert Knowledge and the Subversion of Democracy: The Triumph of Risk Over Uncertainty', *Economy and Society* **25**, 222–254.

Ruxton, C.H., Reilly, J.J. and Kirk, T.R.: 1999, 'Body Composition of Healthy 7 and 8 Year Old Children and a Comparison with the "Reference Child"', *International Journal of Obesity and Related Metabolic Disorders* **23**, 1276–1281.

Savage, M.P. and Scott, L.B.: 1998, 'Physical Activity and Rural Middle School Adolescents', *Journal of Youth and Adolescence* **27**, 245(9).

Simons-Morton, B.G., Taylor, W.G., Snider, S.A. and Huang, I.W.: 1993, 'The Physical Activity of Fifth-Grade Students during Physical Education', *American Journal of Public Health* **83**, 262–264.

Stroot, S.A.: 1994, 'A Contemporary Crisis or Emerging Reform? A Review of Secondary School Physical Education', *Journal of Teaching in Physical Education* **13**, 333–341.

Tinning, R.: 1985, 'Physical Education and the Cult of Slenderness', *ACHPER National Journal* **107**, 10–13.

Tinning, T. and Kirk, D.: 1991, *Daily Physical Education: Collected papers on Health Based Physical Education in Australia*, Deakin University Press, Geelong, Australia.

U.S. Department of Health and Human Services: 1996, *Physical Activity and Health: A Report of the Surgeon General*, Dept of Health and Human Services, Centres for Disease Control and Prevention, Atlanta, GA.

Wright, J.: 1998, 'Reconstructing Gender in Sport and Physical Education', in C. Hickey, L. Fitzclarence and R. Matthews (eds.), *Where The Boys Are: Masculinity, Sport and Education*, Deakin Centre for Education and Change, Geelong, pp. 13–26.

PART 8

Researching physical education

INTRODUCTION

PHYSICAL EDUCATION RESEARCH may well encompass the widest range disciplines and traditions of any educational field; certainly, it is the only sub-ject area informed by research from both the natural and social sciences. Such diversity has resulted in an unusually rich body of research, but has also often meant that different research communities can work in isolation from each other, and from practitioners too, and that can seriously undermine the applicability and value of their work. **Macdonald** and her colleagues provide a valuable review of some of the main theoretical perspectives of pedagogy research. They also offer a caution to physical education researchers: while theory is essential to high quality research, it should not obscure the need to ask good questions, and seek ways of knowing and communicating. **Hastie and Siedentop** take a complimentary approach, drawing attention to the content and methods of researching physical education teaching. They review what they call the 'classroom ecology paradigm', which involves examining the interactions between teachers and students, and conclude that rather than viewing teaching in terms of performance and outcomes, there is a need to turn towards the contextual, day-to-day activity in physical education lessons.

FURTHER READING

Bailey, R.P. (2001) 'Overcoming veriphobia – learning to love truth again'. *British Journal of Educational Studies*, 49(2), 159–172.

Clarke, G. and Humberstone, B. (1997) *Researching Women and Sport*. London: Macmillan.

Ennis, C. (1999) A theoretical framework: the central piece of a research plan. *Journal of Teaching in Physical Education*, 18, 129–140.

Macdonald, D. (2006) Introduction to Section 1 – theoretical perspectives in physical education research. In D. Kirk, D. Macdonald and M. O'Sullivan (eds) *Handbook of Physical Education*, London: Sage.

Sparkes, A. (1992) *Research in Physical Education and Sport: Exploring Alternatives Visions*. London: Falmer Press.

Doune Macdonald, David Kirk, Michael Metzler, Lynda M. Nilges, Paul Schempp and Jan Wright

IT'S ALL VERY WELL, IN THEORY

Theoretical perspectives and their applications in contemporary pedagogical research

T HE INCREASING INTERNATIONALIZATION of journal publications, research projects, postgraduate study, and employment opportunities in universities raises questions about how effectively researchers in physical education pedagogy can communicate across national, cultural, and paradigmatic boundaries. Central to this communication is what and how theory shapes their work. As revealed in 1999 and 2000 editions of *Educational Researcher*, current debates about educational theory are concerned with the relationship between knowledge and power and thereby issues such as who possesses a "truth" and how have they arrived at it, what questions are important to ask, and how should they best be answered (e.g., Anderson & Herr, 1999; McLaren & Farahmandpur, 2000; H. Wright, 2000). As such, these debates revolve around questions of preferred, appropriate, and useful theories.

A theory may be understood to refer to a unified, systemic explanation of a diverse range of phenomena and thereby aid prediction. Alternatively, depending upon the intentions and purposes of the research process, theory constitutes an attempt to interpret or make sense out of what we know concerning phenomena (Glesne & Peshkin, 1992; LeCompte & Preissle, 1993). Although theory may be defined in different ways, it generally provides a framework for conducting research (Ennis, 1999; Wiersma, 1995). Mouly (1978) says that if nothing else, a theory is a convenience—a necessity—organizing a whole slew of unassorted facts, laws, concepts, constructs, and principles into a meaningful and manageable form through its assistance in guiding research design, analysis, and interpretation and revealing gaps, inconsistencies, and future directions. "Good" theory may be viewed as that which is grounded empirically, allows for deductions arising to be investigated, has a strong explanatory/interpretive power, and is stated simply (Mouly, 1978).

Individual researchers do not act in a vacuum but within a community of scholars who share similar conceptions of proper questions, methods, techniques, forms of explanation, and, perhaps, theories. Such research affiliations and the conceptions of the problem, methods, and theories they share are referred to as paradigms or frameworks that function as maps or guides for designing and carrying out inquiry (McKenzie, Powell, & Usher, 1997). Sparkes (1992) argues that a paradigm, as a world view and a general set of beliefs, permeates every act even tangentially associated with inquiry, such that any consideration even remotely attached to inquiry processes demands rethinking to bring decisions into line with the world view embodied in the paradigm itself. Therefore, a discussion of theory cannot be divorced from a discussion about paradigms in terms of the ontological (nature of existence) and epistemological (nature of knowledge, the rules of knowing) theories which inform them (Crotty, 1998).

Paradigmatic allegiances can determine the theories, perspectives, or operationally, the theoretical frameworks that shape the research process. While there is a good deal of slippage in the literature between the definitions and interpretations of paradigm, theoretical framework, and theoretical perspective, we will use the term theoretical perspective to orient our discussion. There is widespread agreement that a theoretical perspective connotes a philosophical stance, a view of the human world, that broadly informs the research process through making assumptions explicit (e.g., Crotty, 1998; LeCompte & Preissle, 1993).

The following discussion introduces various theoretical perspectives that inform physical education research and which are framed by modernist through to postmodernist/ poststructuralist positions. Modernity is, or was, an historical period that began in Western Europe in the seventeenth century with profound social, structural, and intellectual formations as a precursor to industrial society. Modernity is "associated with order, certainty, harmony, humanity, pure art, absolute truth" and sustained by "design, manipulation, management and engineering" (Sarup, 1996, p. 50). Thus, modem social theory is shaped by the person as object and truth lying in finding systems within time and space. Postmodern/poststructuralist theories represent a shift from concerns with time to questions of space and difference and how social spaces are constructed and subjectivities made. While the following theoretical perspectives are introduced in a sequence of positivist, interpretivist, critical, poststructuralist, and feminist, they should not be seen as a continuum nor mutually exclusive. Each section considers how the perspective informs the questions we ask, shapes the conduct of research, and determines what is contested with respect to the perspective and by whom. The paper concludes with some "cautions" about allegiances to and use of theories in line with concerns for the applicability of educational research to pressing social issues.

Before we proceed, a cautionary note. We believe it presumptuous for a group of individuals to authoritatively and definitively claim to identify any theoretical or research perspective. If research is the process by which scholars come to know, and theory is embedded in human thought, then we concede that all research endeavors, including this paper, are ideologically/paradigmatically positioned and therefore biased. We also acknowledge that many of the points contained within this essay are largely based upon our collective experience with the tenets and procedures of traditions that dominate physical education research across the four continents with which we are most familiar. Nevertheless, we offer this review with a view to alleviating possible "theory anxiety" (LeCompte & Preissle, 1993, p. 117), giving a snapshot of contemporary theoretical perspectives in our field and providing a platform for ongoing communication about theory in physical education research.

The positivist perspective

Of all the perspectives represented in this discussion, only positivism is based in the natural sciences. Its purpose is to use objective measurement to establish predictable relationships (and sometimes causal ones) between two or more sets of variables. At its roots, it is much more closely aligned with the scientific traditions of biology and neurology than those of sociology (Johnston & Pennypacker, 1980). The positivistic epistemology and research tradition has been applied in many fields, some of them quite disparate: medicine, agriculture, psychology, economics, statistics, and education. Those traditions and practices in educational research are more often identified with psychology, in particular operant psychology or behaviorism. This is not to suggest that behaviorism represents the entire range of positivistic thought, only that its central tenet, that scientific laws can be uncovered through the objective measurement and systematic manipulation of relevant variables, applies in this discussion most often to the behavior of teachers and learners in school settings. Certainly, other applications of positivistic thought, in particular, methods that employ statistical correlations, have made valuable contributions to educational research as well. The eventual goal of any positivistic research is the prediction and control of human behavior in ways that can lead to quicker, more efficient, and longer-lasting socially-acceptable changes (one of which is learning) in targeted client groups, such as children in schools—regardless of the specific positivistic tradition used.

Positivism has steered thought and conduct in many areas, including the science of human behavior developed most prominently by B.F. Skinner. This branch of positivism is mentioned here because it most directly led to the research tradition that shaped early research on teaching in physical education. Some or all of the four strategies of a science of behavior were present in research on teaching and learning in physical education as that research area emerged (a) an emphasis on objective description, (b) the use of absolute unit-based measurement, (c) experimental analysis, and (d) a search for and statement of functional relations between variables (Johnston & Pennypacker, 1980). Even though several lines of sport pedagogy research have incorporated all four strategies, most of the initial inquiry was limited to simple description of teacher and learner behaviors in the gym (Anderson, 1980).

Early classroom research on teaching focused on presage variables, positive personal characteristics of teachers that were hypothesized to relate to student achievement. That line of research uncovered few salient relationships between what kind of person a teacher was and his/her students' learning in the classroom. In the mid-1970s, Dunkin and Biddle (1974) proposed a powerful model for the study of teaching that included a process-product paradigm, in which teacher and student behaviors would be measured in situ, and then correlated with objective measures of student achievement, essentially ignoring the personal characteristics of the teacher (Shulman, 1986).

Because process-product research attempted to make direct links between what teachers and students did in class with student achievement, there was a need to develop valid and reliable instruments for the process stage in this paradigm. This methodological strategy had long been one of the hallmarks of a science of behavior, allowing existing technologies to be adapted easily by those wishing to observe and measure behavior in the classroom. The lack of validated and relevant achievement measures in physical education was a limiting factor on the product side of this paradigm, but a number of studies were able to demonstrate some generally accepted results in physical education (see Rink, 1996). For the first time, researchers were able to make some empirically defensible statements about teachers' and children's behaviors in physical education classes and how those contributed to what children learned.

Experimental studies using systematic observations of behavior followed by planned interventions have long been a part of the positivist tradition in physical education pedagogy (e.g., McKenzie, Alcaraz, Sallis, & Faucette, 1998; Turner & Martinek, 1992). From this line of experimental research, we have been able to devise better ways for teachers to manage classes, develop more efficient engagement patterns for learners, improve teachers' verbal and nonverbal interactions, increase academic learning time, improve the conduct of student teacher supervision, and promote the development of effective teaching skills in preservice teacher education programs (see Rink, 1996). Attributable to the interventionist values inherent in a science of behavior as it has been applied in sport pedagogy (Siedentop, 1982), one could make a case that no other research tradition in physical education has contributed more to the conduct of in-service practice and preservice preparation to this point in our history.

Several of the authors' early personal research agendas were based in the positivist tradition, most notable descriptive research on teachers, student teachers, and physical education students and experimental research that attempted to alter process variables that could lead to increased student achievement. There are several advantages to conducting research in this tradition:

1   It maintains a strong focus on teacher and student behavior (independently and interactively) during instruction. It addresses what we think is a central purpose of what teaching, and our research of it, should be about—trying to develop and maintain demonstrable learning outcomes in physical education.
2   It places a high value on observing teacher and/or student behavior as it happens in the most ecologically valid settings possible (e.g., gymnasiums, playing fields), although the contextual subtleties of these settings are not addressed.
3   It eschews "snapshot" description in favor of time series analyses of behavior, conducted over extended periods of time and lessons.
4   It does not stop at simple descriptions of behavior. The inherent values in the tradition ultimately compel researchers to develop ways to improve practice, increase learning, and search for generalizable interventions that can be effective across many settings, people, and content.

Even though positivistic thought and its research traditions have contributed much in the first 25 years of physical education pedagogy, it must be recognized that the theory and practice of a science of behavior are being staunchly challenged in education, teacher education, and physical education. In fact, newly-ascending perspectives, some of which follow in this paper, have replaced positivism as the dominant discourse in journals, conferences, and teacher education. There has been an unmistakable shift from research rooted in the traditions of behavioral psychology to those based in the cognitive and social sciences. We have simply started to ask different questions in pedagogy research, many of which have taken us away from what some might argue is the core activity of our profession—instruction—in K-12 classrooms and teacher education programs (Metzler, 1992).

Positivistic thought in physical education pedagogy is not in descendency because its underlying theory was shown to be in error, its methodologies flawed, or its applications ineffective. It is being contested these days, not from within its own enclave of researchers, but rather more by the larger physical education teacher education community that has branched out into the social sciences, leaving aside many unanswered questions that might be addressed within this tradition.

Meetings for the Association for Behavior Analysis annually featured a semiscripted, sometimes humorous, often insightful dialogue between B.F. Skinner and his colleague Fred Keller. Once, in the early 1980s, as psychologists and educational researchers had begun the move to the cognitive and social sciences, Keller "set up" Skinner with a question that went something like, "Why so few of us?" looking over a small audience at a modestly attended conference. Skinner thought for a moment and said, "The question should not be 'Why so few of us?' Rather, it should be 'Why so many of them?' " This is an interesting question in physical education pedagogy research today, as well, as we desperately need to find ways to instruct children, prepare teachers, and assess physical education programs in schools, while many in the pedagogy research community pursue quite different interests.

The interpretive perspective

The work of Wilhelm Dilthey (1961) is generally recognized as the seminal influence in interpretive scholarship. Dilthey argued that the human sciences should be steeped in hermeneutics (interpretation) for the purpose of recognizing the meaning-perspectives of the people studied. More contemporary influences in interpretive research can be traced to the work of scholars such as Merleau-Ponty (1962), Rorty (1979), and others. In his discussion of phenomenology, Merleau-Ponty made the case for the significance of meaning in the interpretation of lived experiences, while Rorty suggested that collective acts and conversations represent meaning constructions unique to the time, place, and individuals, rather than a set of standards transferable to other groups. In educational research, the works of such noted scholars as Denzin (1997), Eisner (1991), Lincoln (1995), and Wolcott (1994) have provided perspectives on the epistemology and practice of interpretive research that have advanced interpretive scholarship.

There are a number of epistemologies (e.g., constructionist, subjectivist), methodologies (e.g., ethnography, life history, action research), and other theoretical perspectives (e.g., feminist, critical) that interpretive researchers have used to guide study design, inform data collection, and provide structure for data analysis. However, scholarship in the interpretive tradition shares some fundamental epistemological and methodological characteristics. Among these characteristics is the premise that social organizations are constructed based on purposeful actions of individuals as they negotiate their social roles and define status within the collective social group. People make use of learned meaning acquired and constructed through the symbol systems of a culture (e.g., language, politics, ethnic beliefs, negotiations of gender roles, distribution of power within a group). Another premise of the interpretive perspective is that meaning making is both an individual and collective action. Put another way, a person is viewed as both a unique individual and a part of a larger social organization.

The key questions asked in interpretative research are "What is happening here?" and "What do these events mean to the people engaged in them?" (Erickson, 1986,

p. 124). Thus, this perspective is useful when attempting to identify the specific sequence and significance of a particular social phenomenon. In other words, what is happening in this particular place at this particular time and why? Questions appropriate to interpretive inquiry allow researchers to link participants' meanings and actions in a time and place of interest in ways that may offer insightful explanations of events. In doing so, a range of alternative actions not visible from other research perspectives may come to light. Interpretative research, however, goes beyond simply telling the story of what a selected set of events means to a certain group of people. For example, Sparkes (1994a, p. 179) persuasively argues that research focused on the life history of individuals "has the potential to help individuals view themselves and the occupation of teaching in new and emancipatory ways."

The data collection methods and analytic techniques commonly found in interpretive research have their roots in anthropological and selected sociological research traditions. These methods place a primacy on participants telling their story. Developing a full and accurate narrative is dependent upon the researcher establishing an open and trusting relationship with the research participants. Virtually any method that will allow the participants to speak is an authentic and detailed fashion about what they do or do not do and why is acceptable data gathering. Interviews, journals, informal conversations, and fieldwork where the researcher listens and documents the participants' discourse are common techniques. With respect to phenomenological research, Kerry and Armour (2000, p. 9) make the point that "the purpose of writing is to bring the essences of the lived experiences into being."

An interpretive research perspective began to find its way into the sport and physical education literature in the 1980s (e.g., Evans, 1986; Griffin, 1985; Placek, 1983). By the 1990s it had become an accepted research perspective and is now commonly found in scholarly papers and publications. As might be anticipated with any research tradition, the interpretive perspective grew in methodological sophistication and theoretical strength as it gained currency and acceptance in the physical education community. Researchers incorporated new and richer methods in the process of gathering data and increasingly relied on theories drawn from a variety of disciplines to shape the research design, guide data analysis, and interpret findings.

The interpretive perspective has made it possible to investigate a range of questions. For example, Macdonald and Tinning (1995) mapped the experiences and values of a PETE cohort to reveal the hegemony of biophysical, masculine, and technically oriented knowledge in their program. Schempp, Sparkes and Templin (1993) investigated the meanings and actions of physical education teachers during their induction year of public school teaching, while Armour and Jones (1998) offer additional insight on teacher socialization from an interpretivist perspective. A constructivist perspective and extensive field work was employed by Rovegno and Bandhauer (1997) in attempting to understand how environmental constraints influenced the experiences and interpretations of a public school physical educator. Research by Sparkes (1994b) revealed how being a lesbian physical educator harbored a unique set of meanings and subsequently called into play a set of actions that both preserved the individual's safety and passively resisted oppressive cultural norms. Interpretivist perspectives have also shaped physical education curriculum inquiry in attempts to understand how teachers' work and school cultures shape change processes (e.g., Doutis & Ward, 1999; Kirk & Macdonald, 2001). While these examples represent only a few of the interpretive studies conducted in physical education, they demonstrate the variety of questions that can be addressed from this perspective that take the focus of research beyond instructional concerns.

However, we acknowledge that no research perspective can adequately service all questions or gaps in a body of knowledge. It is not surprising that some scholars take issue with an interpretive perspective for its failure to adequately address many of the issues in physical education pedagogy, such as questions of power, opportunity, and social change. Unlike claims of the positivist tradition, an interpretive perspective neither predicts nor generalizes behavior, events, or actions. Thus, the findings from one study are difficult to compare with the findings of another study. Time, place, and participants all differ and, therefore, so will the findings of an interpretive study. Those looking to generalize a set of behaviors from which effective teaching or efficient student learning can be established will find little satisfaction in an interpretive perspective.

Due to the subjective nature of meanings people assign to their actions, an interpretive researcher is often charged with attempting to confirm their own perceptions and beliefs rather than seeking the meanings of the participants. There are questions of how interpretive research can "give voice" to participants and expand the limited impact it often has on the lives of participants and/or wider societal structures (e.g., Carr & Kemmis, 1986). Recent interpretive work in Australia that also draws on feminist post-structuralist perspectives has, accordingly, included participants in the framing of research questions, regularly informed them of the progress of data analysis, and presented their voices with minimal commentary from the researchers (e.g., Webb & Macdonald, 2000).

Finally, an interpretive perspective possesses an epistemological problem for individuals schooled in traditional research perspectives with respect to the constitution of truth. Traditional positivist researchers are frequently working to find a single, testable truth. Interpretive researchers, however, support the notion of multiple truths. That is, truth is seen as a social construction and inextricably linked to the meanings of the study's participants. If the participants, time, and/or location is changed, "truth" is likely to change as well. The notion of multiple truths has proven problematic for many scholars.

Interpretive research has made a significant contribution to the physical education pedagogy body of knowledge as it has led to insights into meanings participants give to their sport and physical education experiences. Topical areas of socialization, teacher education, curriculum change, and student learning have all benefited from this perspective. As new methods are incorporated and additional theories relied upon for guidance, the interpretive perspective will continue as a valuable aid in assembling a body of knowledge in physical education pedagogy.

The socially critical perspective

Similar to an interpretivist perspective, a socially critical perspective accepts that all knowledge is theory dependent or, in other terms, value laden. As such, researchers working within this perspective attempt to make explicit the assumptions about, and purposes for, physical education that they believe influence their research. The assumptions and purposes that underpin and guide a socially critical perspective include a commitment to social justice, equity, inclusivity, and social change (Carr & Kemmis, 1986; Leistyna & Woodrum, 1996; Macdonald, 2002; Wink, 2000). While other perspectives also work toward realizing such commitments (e.g., Hellison's, 1989 interpretivist work), researchers who adopt a socially critical perspective frame their research around these assumptions and purposes.

Typically, socially critical researchers ask questions about other people's assumptions and purposes as well as their own. Some underlying premises of socially critical research include (a) some groups in society are powerful while others are powerless, (b) powerful groups have a vested interest in maintaining power, (c) the purpose of inquiry is to challenge status quo and impart social change, and (d) social reconstruction is brought about by first changing individual and group consciousness (Sparkes, 1992). For example, in *Knowledge and Control* (1971), Michael Young and his colleagues addressed the social conditions of knowledge production and the influence of these conditions on educational institutions, teachers, and learners. This work has been extended by a range of socially critical scholars (e.g., Apple, 1979; Giroux, 1981; Whitty, 1985) who have a vested interest in power and ideology and its relationship to educational policy and practice. Others such as Goodson (1988) use curriculum history to put names and faces to the individuals and groups of people responsible for constructing school knowledge.

Throughout the late 1980s and 1990s, work within socially critical perspectives has addressed a variety of issues, across a breadth of sites, using a range of generally qualitative methods. For example. Tinning (1991) investigated the imbalance between discourses of performance and discourses of participation in physical education teacher education and explored the unjust consequences for school physical education. What remains distinctive about the research is that it continues to pursue explicitly commitments to educational reform and social change based on the values of social justice, equity and inclusivity in schools, and other physical activity settings. The process of making values explicit and using them to frame research requires reflexivity on the part of the researcher (Hammersley & Atkinson, 1981). Reflexivity entails an awareness of oneself as a knowledge producer who "generates" rather than "collects" data and so as far as possible must write themselves into their studies.

Recent work within the critical perspective has focused on such issues as continuing inequity for girls in physical education (e.g., Williams & Bedward, 1999), the alienation of ethnic minorities from sport (e.g., Vescio, Taylor, & Toohey, 1999), exclusionary practices in physical education teacher education (e.g., Skelton, 1993), and teacher involvement in curriculum development initiatives (e.g., Macdonald & Glover, 1997). Still others have investigated how sedimented and taken-for-granted practices in contemporary physical education programs carry forward, albeit in altered form, the forces and concerns operating at various crucial times in history (e.g., Kirk, 1998). Such research has identified inequitable values underlying school structure, teaching and administrative practices, approaches to learning, and particular conceptions of subject matter, and foregrounded social and political issues, not so much in terms of party politics (though some have done this), but more in terms of the operations of power in society.

The exploration of instantiations of broader structuring properties of society (such as geographic location, race, or class) in physical education practice is as yet a relatively under-elaborated aspect of socially critical work, though this criticism can be made of most social theory more generally (Giddens, 1984). Further, we would argue that socially critical researchers are still in the process of refining their theories, their methods, and their strategies for making their research practice-referenced. Some of this work has already produced attempts to integrate theoretical constructs and research methodologies. For example, in physical education, work with situated learning is an attempt to integrate social, historical, and psychological theories around the problem of learning (Kirk & Macdonald, 1998). Nevertheless, more work needs to be done by researchers to move out of disciplinary and paradigmatic boxes in order to develop more powerful theories and methodologies for developing and renewing practice.

Some socially critical researchers in our field have been criticized for seeing their role as critical intellectuals and occupants of the moral high ground (O'Sullivan, Siedentop, & Locke, 1992). Yet, social critique, asking awkward questions about assumptions and taken-for-granted purposes, is absolutely necessary although this must be done constructively, not destructively (Rovegno & Kirk, 1995). The gentle arts of persuasion, drawing on anthropological insight, employing scholarship but also reflexivity, and, indeed, genuine partnerships between the researcher and the researched should occur in action research (e.g., Kemmis & McTaggart, 1982); these need to be the tools of the socially critical researcher's trade if they are to more fully engage the profession and the public.

Critical perspectives invited the field of physical education to reflect upon what purpose physical education serves and what circuits of power maintain its practices—new and confronting questions. In doing so, the research has at times been long on critique but short on strategies and action aimed at promoting inclusivity (e.g., Hickey, 2001; Macdonald, 2002). Nevertheless, those researchers and teachers who have embraced this perspective have provided ways of understanding why physical education is often reproductive and also provided ways of doing physical education differently.

The poststructuralist perspective

The terms *postmodernism* and *poststructuralism* are often used interchangeably and in the following section on feminist perspectives, we have chosen to do so. According to Scheurich (1997), North American educational and social science researchers have little familiarity with the latter term, it being used primarily in Europe and by those drawing more directly on European poststructuralist theory. However, this section focuses on poststructuralist research because (a) it more accurately identifies the debt to Michel Foucault and (b) feminist poststructuralist research has made a considerable contribution to understanding how social practices affect gender relations in physical activity settings (Connell, 1995; Kenway & Willis, 1997; Wright 1995).

Before proceeding, it is important to explain the differences and commonalities between the two terms. The proviso is that, in keeping with both positions, the terms are constantly shifting and will be taken up and interpreted differently in different contexts. A good starting point is Scheurich's (1997, p. 2) suggestion that

> postmodernism is Western civilization's best attempt to date to critique its own most fundamental assumptions, particularly those assumptions that constitute reality, subjectivity, research, and knowledge.

Critiquing well-established practices and theories is not always an easy or popular task as was suggested in the previous section. However, a reflexive approach to the assumptions that underpin physical education practice and research seems important if we are to avoid a position that continues to endorse, unquestioningly, deep seated biases based on the centrality of certain kinds of thinking—for instance, western, scientific, patriarchal views of the world.

While there are a number of writers in physical education who take up this challenge, there are fewer examples of those who translate postmodernism into a research agenda. And indeed this may almost be a contradiction in terms. Postmodernism does not easily fit with any one way of working with data. This is one of the reasons we might look to poststructuralism for its potential as a theory to inform empirical research projects. Like interpretivist, critical, and postmodern perspectives, poststructuralism rejects notions of a reality that is fixed and a humanist/modernist view of the rational autonomous meaning making individual.

Poststructuralist research goes beyond the rejection of positivist assumptions to investigate how selves and social relations are constituted in particular relations of power-knowledge. Rather than being fixed or constituted in specific embodied individuals, selves are taken to be constructs. The terms *subject* and *subjectivity*(ies) are used to denote the ways in which selves are formed in and through language and other systems of meaning. In recent poststructuralist work on the body, the term *embodied subjectivities* has come to be used in an attempt to demonstrate that subjectivities are not simply mental constructs but that bodies are inscribed with meanings which are produced in specific relations of power (Bordo, 1990; Foucault, 1979; Wright, 2000a, 2000b).

The relationship between meaning and power is captured in the term *discourse*(s), a term defined and redefined in poststructuralist writing but generally taken to mean systems of beliefs and values that produce particular social practices and social relations. According to Ball (1990, p. 2), "(d)iscourses are about what can be said and thought, but also who can speak, when and with what authority." Foucault (1972, p. 49) describes discourse as "practices that systematically form the objects of which they speak . . . Discourses are not about objects; they constitute them and in the practice of doing so conceal their own intervention." It is through discourse that meanings, subjects, and subjectivities are formed. While discourse in this sense is differentiated from language, choices in language as social practices provide indicators to those discourses being drawn upon by writers and speakers and to the ways in which they position themselves and others. Questions can therefore be asked about how language works to position speakers (and listeners) in relation to what discourses and with what effects? Further, poststructuralism does by its very nature raise questions about how selves are constituted, how power-knowledge relations change across times, places, and in the context of different social, political, and cultural contexts.

As a theoretical perspective, poststructuralism does not immediately suggest a methodological practice (except perhaps in the case of historical work), so different researchers have taken up the perspective in different ways. However most of the data-based or empirical poststructuralist research in education draws on qualitative methodologies, although it is not unimaginable that numbers might be involved. Researchers tend to use interviews, observations, collect documentation, and take field notes. If specifically interested in the way language or visual images work to constitute meanings and subjectivities, they may record teacher-student interactions or collect media texts.

What differentiates poststructuralist research from interpretivist and/or socially critical research are the kinds of questions which drive the planning of the research, the collection and interpretation of the data, and the conclusions derived from the data. For instance, a poststructuralist researcher is generally not primarily interested in data as constructing a particular reality (e.g. boys' experiences of dance in physical education), as would be the case with interpretivist research. Rather the researcher would be interested in the discursive resources (e.g., notions of masculinity in the family, family's and friends' cultural practices, media) the interviewee (and perhaps the interviewer) draw on to constitute themselves as subjects and the consequences of this in terms of power and their social and cultural positioning and responses. In recent physical education literature, we have some examples of this kind of work in the collection of essays in Fernandez-Balboa's *Critical Postmodernism in Human Movement, Physical Education and Sport* (1997), Gard and Wright's (2001) interrogation of obesity discourses, and Nilges' (2000) study of gender as a nonverbal discourse and the textualization of qualitative data (2001). More specifically, one of the key questions underpinning a recently funded study of the place and meaning of physical activity in young people's lives (Wright, Macdonald, & Wyn, 2001, p. 3) reads as follows:

> How do young people from different cultural and social locations shape their identities and social relations in the context of the cultural and institutional discourses around physical activity, bodies and health which currently have prominence in Australia society and in school physical and health education programs?

In this study, interviews are being used to collect the data to answer this question. The interpretation of the interviews will rely on collateral data collected from the media, the literature on bodies, and the commodification of youth and physical culture to understand how and what cultural resources are deployed by young people in talking about themselves and their lives.

Using a slightly different approach. Gore's (1995) work on feminist pedagogies used observations to code the ways in which social practices across a number of pedagogical sites served to position the participants. Gore's interest is in how these practices worked as technologies of power to produce "normalizing," "regulating," "classifying," and "surveillance" effects. Wright (2000b) draws on this work to analyze the ways in which language, as a social practice, comes to constitute particular embodied subjectivities and social relations in a physical education lesson. An important question is raised in all of this: What are the consequences of such social practices on subjectivities, social relations, and the constitution of power-knowledge in physical education?

In understanding the work of the discourses, it is important to interrogate the operation of power in constructing knowledge, that is, how particular truths are systematically constituted. Foucault uses the term *genealogy* to differentiate between the more traditional "narrative" histories and investigations of historically situated social practices in specific political, social, and economic contexts. In physical education. Kirk (1997), Kirk, Macdonald, and Tinning (1997), Wright (1996), and Burrows (1997) have taken up the challenge of interrogating the discursive construction of physical education from this perspective. In her analysis of developmental discourses in physical education, Burrows (1997) asks these questions: What is the nature of developmental discourses in physical education? What are the conditions that have enabled them to prevail? What are their effects on educational practices and how do they create particular notions of the "normal" child? Further examples of poststructuralist feminist work will be provided in the section to follow.

Fundamental to poststructuralist and postmodernist perspectives is an acknowledgment of a particular epistemological and ontological position that requires a great deal of reflexivity about how the research is conducted and what interpretations can be made. This has generated criticism that poststructuralism/postmodernism is "hyperindividualistic" with an overemphasis on identity politics, consumerism, pluralism, and choice and has lost sight of reproductive power and structural constraints such as class and gender (McLaren & Farahmandpur, 2000). Quite contrary to some of these criticisms, the centrality of power to the perspective enables an interrogation of the effects of discourses and social practices on groups as can be seen in questions of what physical education means to the lives of particular young people. Moreover, people and practices are never seen in isolation but in the context of complex webs of social relations and institutions. Poststructuralist research makes visible what has been invisible; it provides new ways of seeing, and therefore acting, and thereby makes a difference.

The feminist perspectives

Feminism has never been a unified body of thought (Bryson, 1999). Over the past 40 years, different perspectives have surfaced within feminist theory in an attempt to more fully explain woman's oppression and offer solutions for its elimination (Scraton & Flintoff, 1992; Stanley, 1990; Tong, 1998; Weedon, 1999). The sometimes-contradictory positions that comprise feminist thought reflect the broader conceptual shift over the later years of the 20th century toward a socially constructed understanding of human action. As such, interpretive, socially critical, postmodern/poststructuralist, and feminist researchers often share theoretical space when the topic of study directly relates to gender.

Although different points of departure exist within each feminist perspective, feminists are united in their attempt to unpack taken-for-granted assumptions about gender and empower women by improving their social standing and/or circumstance (Stanley, 1990). Collectively, feminist theory offers a unique research perspective that (a) situates "women" and "gender" as necessary and valid categories of inquiry and (b) is overtly political in its commitment to changing women's lives (Hall, 1996; Tanesini, 1999).

As a site where women have historically been cast as separate, different, and unequal, physical education and sport offers a rich but underutilized context for feminist scholarship (Hall, 1996; Nilges, 1998; Scraton & Flintoff, 1992). This section focuses on liberal, radical, and postmodern/poststructural feminist perspectives and the application of these to the growing complexity of options for feminist scholarship in physical education and sport. Each approach has developed in response to particular issues identified in feminist thinking and writing and in relation to other theoretical perspectives more broadly. Although liberal and radical feminism predate postmodern/poststructural approaches, all perspectives continue to inform feminist research.

Stanley (1990, p. 14) contends that "Feminism is not merely a 'perspective,' a way of seeing; nor even this plus an epistemology, a way of knowing; it is also an ontology, a way of being in the world." Liberal, radical, and postmodern/poststructural feminists share a similar ontological position that supports the belief that "reality" exists and it is constructed in ways that oppress women. Therefore, "real" women share a common experience in oppression, although these experiences may differ greatly and extend from different circumstances. For researchers in physical education and sport, this belief opens the door for questioning (a) whose knowledge is reflected in daily practices in physical education and sport and (b) how this knowledge has, intentionally or unintentionally, limited, misrepresented, or denied women access and social power in the arena of physical education and sport.

For liberal feminists, the "oppressor" of women in sport and physical education is lack of opportunity on the basis of biological sex and the concomitant gendered patterns of socialization (Harding, 1986). The goal of liberal feminists, therefore, is to correct this condition by exposing inequities and granting women the rights, privileges, and space that have historically been held by men in the arena of physical education and sport. This may include increased access to a broader range of activities, facilities, and/ or funding.

Liberal feminist research in physical education has been referred to as "distributive" in that it attempts to quantify and explain gender difference in terms of biological sex (Hall, 1996). Methodologically, such research tends to rely on empirical evidence that is analyzed using quantitative methods as opposed to concerning itself with the construction of meaning. For instance, researchers in physical education and sport have empirically documented gender differences in children's attitudes toward physical activity (Luke & Sinclair, 1991), physical education doctoral candidates (Crase & Hamrick, 1994), the scholarly productivity of university professors in HPERD (Shuiteman & Knoppers, 1987), and the preferred teaching strategies of physical educators (Vertinsky, 1984). Liberal feminist research provides a useful starting point for exposing andocentric (i.e., male) bias in physical education and sport resources and opportunities for the purpose of initiating changes to legislation, policies, and practices.

Radical feminists fault liberal feminist thinking for failing to capture gender as a socially constructed, human practice with an historical and cultural dimension. They contend that masculinity, femininity, and gender relations have historically been constructed within the social regulating discourse of patriarchy. Therefore, the fundamental cause of oppression is not merely biological sex but a complex and relationally defined sex/gender system of meaning where masculinity is constructed as "more powerful" than femininity in ways that legitimate the subordination of women in a variety of social spaces (e.g., work, school, family, leisure/sport). Thus, radical feminists' questions shift from concerns with, for example, how more girls/women can be included in sport to questions of why it is that men dominate the sporting media, playing fields, and gymnasia (Macdonald, 1997). Unlike the biological determinism that is endorsed by liberal feminism, a radical standpoint assumes that patriarchy, enmeshed in our histories and practices as a form of social control, has an inevitable effect on how power comes to be granted to men over women.

The connections between physical activity, sexuality, physicality, gender, and power are central to a radical feminist perspective (Scraton, 1987). This leads to research that investigates how gender relations of male dominance and female subordination are constructed and played out in a variety of social contexts, including sport and physical education (Clarke & Humberstone, 1997). Because gender is viewed as a constructed rather than predetermined category, research from a radical feminist perspective tends to use qualitative methods that allow context, meaning, and discussions of social power to be captured and considered (e.g., Chepyator-Thompson & Ennis, 1997; Nilges, 1998). In addition, the ways medical-physiological reasoning and patriarchal views of female physicality have historically combined to disempower girls and women in sport has been considered (Lenskyj, 1986).

In the later years of the 20th century, as many feminists began to fault the "essentialist" nature of feminist perspectives that left little room to investigate differences within "woman" and/or "man" as categories of analysis, they too drew on postmodernist/poststructuralist perspectives. A postmodernist or poststructuralist feminist perspective challenges the universal and oppressive nature of biological and patriarchal truths and suggests that these truths do not have a universal structure and effect on all women. Gender is understood from a multifaceted and complex position where a variety of identity categories (e.g., race, class, physical ability, sexual orientation) intersect with context in the construction of gender identity. Therefore, one overarching explanation or solution to the oppression of women is resisted and local and individual circumstance is highlighted (Tong, 1998). As such postmodernist/poststructuralist feminists (a) believe there are more differences than similarities in the gender reality of women, (b) seek to expose and challenge the local and contextual perspective of diverse women, and (c) recognize that gender identity may vary for any given individual across different social contexts (Brooks, 1997) and thus recognize plurality and difference.

Methodologically, postmodernist/poststructuralist feminists identify individual and small groups of women as an appropriate unit of analysis and focus upon the construction of discourses. Data collection is generally qualitative in nature in order to capture the complexities of diverse women's lives. In physical education and sport, Clarke (1997) has studied how lesbian physical education teachers reflexively manage their subjectivities across their worlds of home and school, while Webb and Macdonald (2000) considered the gendered discourses associated with school structures, the body, family, and physical activity that limited women's promotional opportunities. Working with girls and boys, Hunter (in press) has used photographs, journals, observations, and interviews to examine the gendered, embodied discourses that shape and constrain individuals' learning in physical education. There have also been studies on masculinity discourses and their impact upon boys and physical activity, much of which draws on feminist postmodernist/poststructuralist theory as a resource (e.g., Hickey, Fitzclarence, & Matthews, 1998).

As with other theoretical perspectives, feminist perspectives have not been readily conceded to or uncritically accepted. Hall (1996) suggests there are several reasons why feminism often remains marginalized in physical education and sport. First, much of the existing gender research in physical education and sport is "feminist friendly" (i.e., it seeks to better and/or make visible the position of women in physical education and sport) but fails to be fully grounded in the goals of various feminist perspectives. As such, this research lacks praxis, or a committed political position, that positively impacts those who are studied to the same extent as the person(s) conducting the study (a criticism shared with the socially critical perspective).

Second, feminist research has experienced an uneasy relationship with some in physical education and sport for methodological reasons related to bias. As previously suggested, this second criticism has been made of all those perspectives that use predominantly qualitative methods. However, for the intent and credibility of feminist research to be maintained, it must recognize not only the subjectivity of participants but also the inherent intersubjectivity between the researcher and the researched. Stanley (1990) suggests that credible research grounded in feminist theory must be "unalientated" in that (a) the researchers' thinking, views, and conduct are grounded in the study and

(b) the act of coming "to know" is treated as critically as "what is known." Therefore, the investigation process that has traditionally been viewed as bias might be more accurately equated with good feminist research.

Finally, feminist perspectives have been criticized for recreating binary patterns of thinking about gender in the process of studying it and indeed generally studying the experiences of women only. In physical education and sport, Hall (1996) suggests binary thinking is particularly dangerous in the realm of the feminine because the profession has traditionally been defined by male standards. As long as gender is dichotomized for study, differences between genders are likely to be seen as more interesting than similarities in ways that potentially hinder the cause of equity in physical education and sport. Recent work in the study of masculinity (e.g. Connell, 2000) goes some way toward addressing this criticism by highlighting the shared powerlessness and marginalization of some girls and boys.

There is no straightforward means of applying feminist perspectives to research in physical education and sport. While readers may find one more convincing than another, each provides a frame that can be used to inform the study of gender in physical education and sport. These theories should not be viewed as the only possible feminist approaches, nor negatively because they are fragmented and splintered, but rather as an opportunity to give voice and visibility to women in physical education and sport.

Cautions and conclusion

Individually, and as a global research community, it is imperative that we can communicate in terms of theoretical perspectives that generate and shape our work. Smyth and Shacklock (1998) argue that researchers need to be able to locate their study in the context of the "big thinkers" that lie behind the research tradition/s upon which they are drawn. Further, Ennis (1999) explains how important theoretical frameworks are to guiding a robust research process. Yet, the use of, and allegiance to, particular theoretical perspectives increasingly comes with some warnings. Listed below are five such warnings that relate to research questions and practices regardless of the theoretical perspectives employed.

1. *Connect theory to important political, economic, and cultural issues.* While Apple suggests that theoretical interventions and the interrogation of theory are important to the growth of the academy, he questions whether theorizing allows us to experience the world of social research vicariously without getting our hands dirty:

> I am not interested in theory as a subject in and of itself. . . . The production of endlessly refined accounts of supposedly new perspectives has created a situation in which theory has become an academic pursuit of its own. Theory needs to be connected to the important political, economic and cultural issues of our time.
>
> (Apple, 1999, p. 14)

At a practical level, Anderson and Herr (1999) also discuss the importance of getting our hands dirty through forming alliances with practitioners in the process of conducting inquiry regardless of the perspective being used. If we are to "find more effective and equitable ways to educate children" (Anderson & Herr, 1999, p. 20), then theory should improve the conditions in which and through which teaching and learning occur and provide new ways of understanding and looking at contemporary issues in education.

2. *Connect theory to observations and data collection.* Distinctions between theory and observations/data have been strongly criticized regardless of the theoretical perspective, and it is generally accepted that there is a dynamic interplay between theory and data. The debate in a 1999 *Educational Researcher* with respect to curriculum theory is an interesting case in point. Wraga (1999, p. 4) argues what he sees as a theory-practice split as "detrimental to the academic field of curriculum and the prospect for improving curriculum practice in schools."

> As theory is exalted in reconceptualised curriculum studies, improved practice is an afterthought, typically an incidental, indirect by-product rather than an intentional effect. This bifurcation of theory and practice sanctions a convenient relationship of curriculum theorists to our system of education, which conceives of the theorist as critic and contemplate with little responsibility to seek solutions to problems that affect the lives of millions of students, teachers, and administrators, nor to submit their theories to the test of practice.
>
> (Wraga, 1999, p. 4)

Selecting and using one or more of the theoretical perspectives discussed here to design and conduct inquiry represents a conscious choice by a researcher interested in a given topic. It is only by taking theory off the table and into the field that attention can be drawn to the needs of people and children in schools in ways that are socially responsive. At the same time, theory itself can only be refined and advanced when tested and tried out in the field. In this way, the relationship between theory and practice is necessarily a reflexive one.

3. *Avoid theory becoming instrumental in academic self-promotion.* The relationship between theory and practice can be viewed as instrumental. An instrumental view presupposes that those with knowledge are in a position of power to alter social conditions and to control social and psychological processes (e.g., Anderson & Herr, 1999). Within the academy, those who wave theory from the balcony are more likely to be rewarded through academic advancement. In particular, Apple (1999, p. 17) criticizes instances where "post" theories have been captured by the new middle class academic "intent on engaging in status and mobility politics within the academy" and Scott and Usher (1999) argue, they perpetuate "knowers" of theory and a theory-practice binary.

Kirk also recognizes the potential of theory to alienate the people that educational research is bound to assist:

> Theory has a bad name with teachers. Often they complain that it is hopelessly remote from the everyday pressures and problems of work in schools and classrooms, redundant when it comes to informing their judgements and practices, and guilty of making the simple seem complex, and the concrete, abstract. On top of this, theory's alleged irrelevance is made worse by the

theorist's claim to superior knowledge and insight, and the expectation of respect and deference from the practitioner.

(Kirk, 1989, p. 123)

If researchers are to work with teachers, then they need to forge theoretical perspectives that allow them to consider both the inner workings of the everyday life-world and the structuring and interpenetration of this world and of human consciousness by wider social forces.

4. *Avoid theoretical fads*. Researchers are often tempted by theoretical perspectives that are popular today but need to be wary of theoretical fads. For example, Schempp (1990, p. 82) observes:

> Research paradigms, like most educational movements, are often susceptible to fads. . . . While it is often enjoyable to bask in the warmth and light of such nova, it is usually short lived and soon passed over in favour of the next latest and greatest idea. . . . In ushering in a new paradigm, we must also be cautious. Preservation and celebration of present research traditions are important conditions for continuing the expansion of our body of knowledge.

Apple reinforces the need to be cautious of theoretical fads suggesting, "There are gains and losses in new theories and in new approaches to understanding the complex power relations involved in education" (1999, p. 16). He goes on to warn consumers of research about the "trendy arcane overtheorization" in much current work (Apple, 1999, p. 19). Like Apple, McLaren and Farandmandpur (2000, p. 28) are also contemptuous of "theoretical-chic."

5. *Retain and develop our collective memory*. Linked to a wariness of fads is a concern that we recognize that gains that have been made through the deployment of various theoretical perspectives and that "a little trespassing may be a good thing here" (Apple, 1999, p. 188). To do so, Sparkes (1992) argues for polyvocality in the research community in order to enhance our theoretical vitality. If one voice or perspective dominates, there is a danger they may end up speaking to themselves. More specifically, Apple (1999) warns against the uncritical acceptance of some "post" theories despite their giving space to an increased number of voices and introducing a welcome return to the concrete analysis of particular ideological or discursive formations. Yet these theories can suffer from the same silences as earlier theories and important questions about the state and social formations are simply overlooked "as if nothing existed in structured ways" (Apple, 1999, pp. 187–188). Researchers should not have to choose between a politics of recognition (cultural studies) and a politics of redistribution (modernist, structuralist positions) but rather incorporate structural and poststructural perspectives in their work as appropriate.

In discussing, debating, or even aligning ourselves to particular theoretical perspectives, we should not lose sight of the significance of beginning the research process by asking important questions. Take, for example, the little researched area of students' perspectives on physical education and, in particular, students' positioning in class interactions. A positivist approach in addressing this issue might employ the theory and methods of interactional analysis to quantify student talk and seek correlations between student talk, teacher talk, content, teaching strategies, and the like. That descriptive work may or may not lead to an intervention when undesirable rates and/or patterns of interaction are observed. An interpretivist inquiry could focus upon the students' experiences in the class and, through interviews, ascertain how and why students contribute in class. Taking a more proactive position, one that would aim to make the classroom a more democratic environment, critical theorists would work with the school, teachers, and students, possibly using an action research model, to find ways to give the students a stronger voice in the teaching/learning process. Postmodern/poststructural perspectives might begin with the question of how the learning environment came to be as it is and how different students have different experiences within the one class. Again through predominantly qualitative techniques, they would seek to map the discourses that facilitate, shape, and constrain students' voices. Feminists would be particularly concerned with the impact of classroom interactions on girls and explore if and how patterns were gendered and what was the impact of these on girls' engagement with physical education.

In providing these contrasting theoretical perspectives in relation to a common question, we are reminded of the richness that multiple theoretical perspectives can bring to the same question and the possibilities that open up for rigorous and far-reaching improvements in physical education when this occurs. Yet, we also reiterate our concern that while theory is indispensable to quality research, it should not obscure the need to ask good questions, seek well-considered ways of coming to know, and communicate in ways that are inclusive if the field is to progress as strong and cohesive.

References

Anderson, G., & Herr, K. (1999). The new paradigm wars: Is there room for rigorous practitioner knowledge in schools and universities? *Educational Researcher*, **28**(5), 12–21, 40.

Anderson, W.G. (1980). *Analysis of teaching in physical education*. St. Louis: Mosby.

Apple, M. (1979). *Ideology and curriculum*. New York: Routledge.

Apple, M. (1999). *Power, meaning and identity*. New York: Peter Lang.

Armour, K. & Jones, R. (1998). *Physical education teachers' lives and careers*. London: Falmer Press.

Ball, S.J. (Ed.). (1990). *Foucault and education: Disciplines and knowledge*. London: Routledge.

Bordo, S.R. (1990). The body and reproduction of femininity: A feminist appropriation of Foucault. In A. Jaggar & S. Bordo (Eds.), *Gender/body/knowledge* (pp. 13–33). New Brunswick: Rutgers University Press.

Brooks, A. (1997). *Postfeminisms: Feminism, cultural theory and cultural forms*. New York: Routledge.

Bryson, V. (1999). *Feminist debates: Issues of theory and political practice*. Washington Square, NY: New York University Press.

Burrows, L. (1997). Analysing developmental discourses in physical education. In J. Wright (Ed.), *Researching in physical and health education* (pp. 127–148). Wollongong, NSW: University of Wollongong.

Carr, W., & Kemmis, S. (1986). *Becoming critical: Education, knowledge and action research*. Geelong, Victoria: Deakin University Press.

Chepyator-Thomson, J., & Ennis, C. (1997). Reproduction and resistance to the culture of femininity and masculinity in secondary school physical education. *Research Quarterly for Exercise and Sport*, **68**, 89–99.

Clarke, G. (1997). Playing a part: The lives of lesbian physical education teachers. In. G. Clarke & B. Humberstone (Eds.), *Researching women and sport* (pp. 36–49). London: Macmillan.

Clarke, G. & Humberstone, B. (1997). *Researching women and sport*. London: Macmillan.

Connell, R. (1995). *Masculinities*. Sydney: Allen & Unwin.

Connell, R. (2000). *The men and the boys*. Sydney: Allen & Unwin.

Crase, D., & Hamrick, M. (1994). Gender and race differentials among physical education doctorates. *Physical Educator*, **5**(3), 162–168.

Crotty, M. (1998). *The foundations of social research*. Sydney: Allen & Unwin.

Denzin, N.K. (1997). *Interpretive ethnography*. Thousand Oaks, CA: Sage.

Dilthey, W. (1961). *Meaning in history*. London: Allen and Unwin.

Doutis, P., & Ward, P. (1999). Teachers' and administrators' perceptions of the saber-tooth project reform and of their changing workplace conditions. *Journal of Teaching in Physical Education*, **18**, 417–427.

Dunkin, M.J., & Biddle, B.J. (1974). *The study of teaching*. New York: Holt, Rinehart, and Winston.

Eisner, E. (1991). *The enlightened eye: Qualitative inquiry and the enhancement of educational practice*. New York: Macmillian.

Ennis, C. (1999). A theoretical framework: The central piece of a research plan. *Journal of Teaching in Physical Education*, **18**, 129–140.

Erickson, F. (1986). Qualitative methods in research on teaching. In M.C. Wittrock (Ed.), *Handbook of research on teaching* (3rd ed.; pp. 119–161). New York: Macmillan.

Evans, J. (Ed.). (1986). *Physical education, sport and schooling: Studies in the sociology of physical education*. London: Falmer Press.

Fernandez-Balboa, J-M. (Ed.). (1997). *Critical aspects in human movement: Rethinking the profession in the postmodern era*. Albany, NY: SUNY Press.

Foucault, M. (1972). *The archeology of knowledge* (A. Sheridan, Trans.). London: Tavistock. (Original work published 1972).

Foucault, M. (1979). *Discipline and punish: The birth of the prison* (A. Sheridan, Trans.). Harmondsworth, UK: Penguin. (Original work published 1977).

Gard, M., & Wright, J. (2001). Managing uncertainty: Obesity discourses and physical education in a risk society. *Studies in Philosophy and Education*, **20**(6), 535–549.

Giddens, A. (1984). *The constitution of society*. Cambridge, UK: Polity Press.

Giroux, H.A. (1981). *Ideology, culture and the process of schooling*. London: Falmer Press.

Glesne, C., & Peshkin, A. (1992). *Becoming qualitative researchers: An introduction*. New York: Longman.

Goodson, l.F. (1988). *The making of curriculum: Collected essays*. London: Falmer Press.

Gore, J. (1995). Foucault's poststructuralism and observational research: A study of power relations. In R. Smith & P. Wexler (Eds.), *After postmodernism: Education, politics and identity* (pp. 98–111). London: Falmer Press.

Griffin, P.S. (1985). Teachers' perceptions of and responses to sex equity problems in a middle school physical education program. *Research Quarterly for Exercise and Sport*, **56**, 103–110.

Hall, A. (1996). *Feminism and sporting bodies: Essays on theory and practice*. Champaign, IL: Human Kinetics.

Harding, S. (1986). *The science question in feminism*. Milton Keynes, UK: Open University Press.

Hellison, D. (1989). Our constructed reality: Some contributions of an alternative perspective to physical education pedagogy. *Quest*, **40**, 84–90.

Hickey, C. (2001). "I feel enlightened now, but . . .": The limits to the translation of critical social discourses in physical education. *Journal of Teaching in Physical Education*, **20**, 227–246.

Hickey, C., Fitzclarence, L., & Matthews, R. (1998). *Where the boys are: Masculinity, sport and education*. Geelong, Victoria: Deakin University Press.

Johnston, J.M., & Pennypacker, H. (1980). *Strategies and tactics of human behavioral research*. Hillsdale, NJ: Lawrence Earlbaum Associates.

Kemmis, S., & McTaggart, R. (1982). *The action research planner*. Geelong, Victoria: Deakin University Press.

Kenway, J., & Willis, S. (1997). *Answering back: Girls, boys and feminism in schools*. Sydney. Allen & Unwin.

Kerry, D.S., & Armour, K.M. (2000). Sport science and the promise of phenomenology: Philosophy, method, and insight. *Quest*, **52**, 1–17.

Kirk, D. (1989). The orthodoxy in RT-PE and the research/practice gap: A critique and an alternative view. *Journal of Teaching in Physical Education*, **8**, 123–130.

Kirk, D. (1997). Schooling bodies for new times: The reform of school physical education in high modernity. In J.-M. Fernandez-Balboa (Ed.), *Critical aspects in human movement: Rethinking the profession in the postmodern era* (pp. 39–64). Albany: SUNY Press.

Kirk, D. (1998). *Schooling bodies*. London: Leicester University Press.

Kirk, D., & Macdonald, D. (1998) Situated learning in physical education. *Journal of Teaching in Physical Education*, **17**, 376–387.

Kirk, D., & Macdonald, D. (2001). Teacher voice and ownership of curriculum change. *Journal of Curriculum Studies*, **33**, 551–567.

Kirk, D., Macdonald, D., & Tinning, R. (1997). The social construction of pedagogic discourse in physical education teacher education. *The Curriculum Journal*, **8**(2), 271–298.

LeCompte, M., & Preissle, J. (1993). *Ethnography and qualitative design in educational research*. San Diego: Academic Press.

Leistyna, P., & Woodrum, A. (1996). Context and culture: What is critical pedagogy? In P. Leistyna, A. Woodrum, & S. Sherblom (Eds.), *Breaking free: The transformative power of critical pedagogy* (pp. 1–7). Cambridge: Harvard Education Review.

Lenskyj, H. (1986). *Out of bounds: Women, sport and sexuality*. Toronto: Women's Press.

Lincoln, Y. (1995). Emerging criteria for quality in qualitative and interpretive inquiry. *Qualitative Inquiry*, **1**, 275–289.

Luke, M., & Sinclair, C. (1991). Gender differences in adolescents' attitudes toward school physical education. *Journal of Teaching in Physical Education*, **11**, 31–46.

Macdonald, D. (1997). The feminisms of gender equity in physical education. *CAPHERD Journal*, **63**(1), 4–8.

Macdonald, D. (2002). Critical pedagogy: What might it look like and why does it matter? In A. Laker (Ed.), *The sociology of physical education and sport: An introductory reader* (pp. 167–189). London: Taylor & Francis.

Macdonald, D., & Glover, S. (1997). Subject matter boundaries and curriculum change in the health and physical education learning area. *Curriculum Perspectives*, **17**(1), 23–30.

Macdonald, D. & Tinning, R. (1995). PETE and the trend to proletarianization: A case study. *Journal of Teaching in Physical Education*, **15**, 98–118.

McKenzie, G., Powell, J., & Usher, R. (1997). *Understanding social research*. London: Falmer Press.

McKenzie, T., Alcaraz, J., Sallis, J., & Faucette, N. (1998). Effects of a physical education program on children's manipulative skills. *Journal of Teaching in Physical Education*, **17**, 327–341.

McLaren, P., & Farahmandpur, R. (2000). Reconsidering Marx in post-Marxist times: A requiem for postmodernism. *Educational Researcher*, **29**(3), 25–33.

Merleau-Ponty, M. (1962). *The phenomenology of perception*. New York: Humanities Press.

Metzler, M.W. (1992). Bringing the teaching act back into sport pedagogy. *Journal of Teaching in Physical Education*, **11**, 150–160.

Mouly, G. (1978). *Educational research: The art and science of investigation*. Boston: Allyn & Bacon.

Nilges, L. (1998). I thought only fairy tales had supernatural power: A radical feminist analysis of Title IX in physical education. *Journal of Teaching in Physical Education*, **17**, 172–194.

Nilges, L. (2000). A nonverbal discourse analysis of gender in undergraduate educational gymnastics sequences using Laban effort analysis. *Journal of Teaching in Physical Education*, **19**, 287–310.

Nilges, L. (2001). The twice-told tale of Alice's physical life in Wonderland: Writing qualitative research in the 21st century. *Quest*, **53**, 231–259.

O'Sullivan, M., Siedentop, D., & Locke, L. (1992). Toward collegiality: Competing viewpoints among teacher educators. *Quest*, **44**, 266–280.

Placek, J. (1983). Conceptions of success in teaching: Busy, happy, and good? In T. Templin & J. Olson (Eds.), *Teaching in physical education* (pp. 46–56). Champaign, IL: Human Kinetics.

Rink, J.E. (1996). Effective instruction in physical education. In S.J. Silverman & C.E. Ennis (Eds.), *Student learning in physical education: Applying research to enhance instruction* (pp. 171–198). Champaign, IL: Human Kinetics.

Rorty, R. (1979). *Philosophy and the mirror of nature*. Princeton, NJ.: Princeton University Press.

Rovegno, I., & Bandhauer, D. (1997). Norms of school culture that facilitated teacher adoption and learning of a constructivist approach to physical education. *Journal of Teaching in Physical Education*, **16**, 401–425.

Rovegno, I., & Kirk, D. (1995). Articulations and silences in socially critical work on physical education: Toward a broader agenda. *Quest*, **47**, 447–474.

Sarup, M. (1996). *Identity, culture and the postmodern world*. Edinburgh: Edinburgh University Press.

Schempp. P. (1990). Culture, change and teaching in PE. In R. Telema et al. (Eds.), *Physical education and lifelong physical activity: Proceedings of the AIESEP World Convention* (pp. 73–84). University of Jyvaskyla, Finland.

Schempp, P., Sparkes, A., & Templin, T. (1993). The micropolitics of teacher induction. *American Educational Research Journal*, **30**, 447–472.

Scheurich, J. (1997). *Research method in the postmodern*. London: Falmer Press.

Scott, D., & Usher, R. (1999). *Researching education*. London: Cassell.

Scraton, S. (1987). Images of femininity and the teaching of girls' physical education. In J. Evans (Ed.), *Physical education, sport, and schooling: Studies in the sociology of physical education* (pp. 71–94). London: Falmer Press.

Scraton, S., & Flintoff, A. (1992). Feminist research and physical education. In A. Sparkes (Ed.), *Research in physical education and sport: Exploring alternative visions* (pp. 167–187). London: Falmer Press.

Shuiteman, J., & Knoppers, A. (1987). An examination of gender differences in scholarly productivity among physical educators. *Research Quarterly for Exercise and Sport*, **60**, 159–165.

Shulman, L.S. (1986). Paradigms and research programs in the study of teaching: A contemporary perspective. In M.C. Wittrock (Ed.), *Handbook of research on teaching* (3rd ed.; pp. 3–36). New York: Macmillan.

Siedentop, D. (1982). Teaching research: The interventionist view. *Journal of Teaching in Physical Education*, **1**, 46–50.

Skelton, A. (1993). On becoming a male physical education teacher: The informal culture of students and the construction of hegemonic masculinity. *Gender and Education*, **5**, 289–303.

Smyth, J., & Shacklock, G. (1998). Behind the cleansing of socially critical research accounts. In G. Shacklock & J. Smyth (Eds.), *Being reflexive in critical educational and social research* (pp. 1–12). London: Falmer Press.

Sparkes, A. (1992). *Research in physical education and sport: Exploring alternative visions*. London: Falmer Press.

Sparkes, A.C. (1994a). Life histories and the issue of voice: Reflections on an emerging relationship. *Qualitative Studies in Education*, **7**, 165–183.

Sparkes, A.C. (1994b). Self, silence and invisibility as a beginning teacher: A life history of a lesbian experience. *British Journal of Sociology of Education*, **15**, 93–118.

Stanley, L. (1990). *Feminist praxis: Research, theory and epistemology in feminist sociology*. New York: Routledge.

Tanesini, A. (1999). *An introduction to feminist epistemologies*. Malden, MA: Blackwell Publishers Limited.

Tinning, R. (1991). Teacher education pedagogy, dominant discourses and the process of problem setting. *Journal of Teaching in Physical Education*, **11**, 1–20.

Tong, R. (1998). *Feminist thought* (2nd ed.). Boulder, CO: Westview Press.

Turner, A., & Martinek, T. (1992). A comparative analysis of two models for teaching games. *International Journal of Physical Education*, **24**(4), 15–31.

Vertinsky, P. (1984). In search of a gender dimension: An empirical investigation of teacher preferences for teaching strategies in physical education. *Journal of Curriculum Studies*, **16**(4), 425–430.

Vescio, J., Taylor, T., & Toohey, K. (1999). An exploration of sports participation by girls from non English speaking backgrounds. *Australian Council for Health, Physical Education and Recreation Healthy Lifestyles Journal*, **46**(2/3), 14–19.

Webb, L., & Macdonald, D. (2000). Beyond dualisms: Leadership in health and physical education. *International Review of Women and Leadership*, **6**(2), 33–47.

Weedon, C. (1999). *Feminism, theory and the politics of difference*. Malden, MA: Blackwell Publishers Limited.

Whitty, G. (1985). *Sociology and school knowledge*. London: Methuen.

Wiersma, W. (1995). *Research methods in education*. Needham Hts., MA: Allyn & Bacon.

Williams, A., & Bedward, J. (1999). *Games for the girls: The impact of recent policy in the provision of physical education and sporting opportunities for female adolescents*. Summary report of a study funded by the Nuffield Foundation. Winchester, UK: Winchester King Alfred's College.

Wink, J. (2000). *Critical pedagogy: Notes from the real world*. New York: Addison, Wesley, Longman.

Wolcott, H. (1994). *Transforming qualitative data: Description, analysis and interpretation*. Thousand Oaks, CA: Sage.

Wraga, W. (1999). 'Extracting sunbeams out of cucumbers': The retreat from practice in reconceptualized curriculum studies. *Educational Researcher*, **28**(1), 4–13.

Wright, H. (2000). Nailing jell-o to the wall. *Educational Researcher*, **29**(5), 4–13.

Wright, J. (1995). A feminist post-structuralist methodology for the study of gender construction in physical education: Description of a case study. *Journal of Teaching in Physical Education*, **15**, 1–24.

Wright, J. (1996). Mapping the discourses in physical education. *Journal of Curriculum Studies*, **28**, 331–351.

Wright, J. (2000a). Bodies, meanings and movement: A comparison of the language of a physical education lesson and a Feldenkrais movement class. *Sport Education and Society*, **5**, 35–49.

Wright, J. (2000b). Disciplining the body: Power, knowledge and subjectivity in a physical education lesson. In A. Lee & C. Poynton (Eds.), *Culture and text* (pp. 152–169). Sydney: Allen & Unwin.

Wright, J., Macdonald, D., & Wyn, J. (2001–2003). *Physical activity in the lives of young people.* Funded project through the Australian Research Council, Canberra.

Young, M.F.D. (Ed.). (1971). *Knowledge and control: New directions for the sociology of education.* London: Collier-Macmillan.

Peter Hastie and Daryl Siedentop

AN ECOLOGICAL PERSPECTIVE ON PHYSICAL EDUCATION

RESEARCH ON TEACHING physical education has been mostly descriptive (Silverman, 1991), carried on within the dominant paradigm of quantitative research underwritten by standard assumptions that students are in school to learn subjects and develop as individuals, and the main role of teachers is to teach them those subjects and aid that development in an efficient manner (Tinning, 1991). One of the research streams cited by Silverman (1991) was the classroom ecology stream, which he identified solely with ethnographic and interpretive methods. Griffey (1991), in his reaction to the Silverman review, cited the potential efficacy of the 'task structure' model for understanding the complex dynamics of instructional physical education, but noted that 'Siedentop's call for research on task structures in physical education has gone unanswered' (Griffey, 1991: 383).

The 'call' referred to has not in fact gone unanswered; indeed, there is sufficient physical education research using the ecological model to warrant the review which follows. Nevertheless, like all emerging areas of research, many questions remain unanswered. The purpose of this paper is first to review the major findings of physical education research using the ecological model and, following the guidelines for reviews proposed by Cooper (1989), to extend this summary to include what data are missing. An agenda for future research will then be proposed.

The task structure model cited by Griffey developed from the work of Walter Doyle, who first suggested the saliency of viewing classrooms as interrelated systems, in which change in one system might dramatically influence action in other systems. Doyle called this model the 'classroom ecology paradigm' (Doyle, 1977: 183) and although it developed in classroom research using qualitative methods, its applications in physical education have used a variety of methods.

Scope of the paper

Papers for this review were selected through an examination of four sources; the *Dissertations Abstracts* database, the journals of *Research Quarterly for Exercise and Sport* and the *Journal of Teaching in Physical Education*, and through an ERIC search using the terms accountability, ecology, and physical education as the main identifiers.

Tousignant and Siedentop (1983) published the first in a series of studies at Ohio State University that began to explore the salience of the ecological model for physical education. This was followed by Tinning and Siedentop's (1985) application to student teaching, Alexander's (1983) examination of a secondary golf unit, Marks's (1988) development of a systematic observational protocol, and Jones's (1992) use of a modified version of that protocol to study a veteran and novice elementary specialist. By the mid-1980s the results of these studies had confirmed, with some minor variations, that the basic findings from classroom ecology research tended to replicate in physical education classes.

The Ohio State programme in the USA, accompanied by the development of more sophisticated research protocols, then embarked upon a series of 10 related studies that attempted to analyse why some physical education classes seemed so remarkably alive with learning potential and why others seem so devoid of that very characteristic. These studies included Graham's (1987) ecological analysis of middle school volleyball instruction, Son's (1989) study of Korean secondary physical education with emphasis on task congruence and student work, Fink and Siedentop's (1989) study of the development of the managerial task systems by effective elementary specialists, Lund's (1992) descriptive analysis of accountability in secondary school volleyball units, Rauschenbach's (1993) study of how curricular values related to the ecology of student work in elementary gymnastics units, Romar and Siedentop's (1995) case analysis of goals related to student work, Romar's (1995) study of espoused and enacted theories of action, Fortin and Siedentop's (1995) study of the learning ecology of expert dance teachers and how that related to their unique curricular backgrounds, and Kutame's (1997) study of how teacher knowledge related to the instructional ecology and student work in elementary gymnastics.

This programme of studies at Ohio State has been complemented by Hastie and Saunders's (1990) study of monitoring in secondary school physical education, their study of accountability systems in secondary classes (Hastie and Saunders, 1991), Hastie's (1994a) study of teacher behaviours and student task performance, his study of active supervision (Hastie, 1994b), as well as Hastie and Pickwell's (1996) examination of the student social system. More recently, Hastie (1997) has provided the first intervention study, which directly manipulated the ecology of a physical education class. Silverman and his students at the University of Illinois have also used the concepts of task structures and accountability in studying the key process variables affecting student learning in physical education (Silverman et al., 1995; Silverman et al., 1998).

In an application to studying curriculum, Carlson and Hastie (1997) examined the student social system within the sport education curriculum model. In addition, applications have begun to be made to sport settings. Griffin (1991) used the model to study a high school girls' volleyball setting, while Hastie and Saunders (1989, 1992) studied elite junior rugby and volleyball settings. Hastie (1993) has also found that athletes in sport settings seemed more task oriented than reliant on external sanctions.

The classroom ecology paradigm

An ecological model portrays the behavioural dynamics of classrooms in a way that helps teachers interpret, predict and respond to those dynamics (Siedentop, 1988). In contrast to those models which seek to explain pupil achievement, a primarily distal concern, research in the ecological paradigm focuses on the work students do in their classrooms. It examines the proximal issues of how the organization and programme of action of a class affect student work. The ecological model is a study of classroom life as it naturally unfolds, and, in that sense, represents an anthropological view which can only be accomplished through regular and long-term observation of that life.

The model represents class life as a set of three interrelated systems (managerial, instructional, and student social), in which changes in one system are likely to influence changes in another. Clearly, order and academic work are the two key issues in the ecological model, and the two are intimately linked (Doyle, 1986). For example, changes in student behaviour (either positively or negatively) have clear implications for the amount of academic work that can be achieved. If students begin to misbehave, it is more likely that the teacher will act to restore order, thereby temporarily suspending the instructional focus of that lesson. Likewise, if teachers maintain rigorous standards for performance in the managerial system, opportunities for student socializing may be diminished. Indeed, findings from the earliest studies in physical education using this model confirmed that the compelling agenda for physical education teachers is the establishment and maintenance of order through a managerial system that typically focuses on cooperation rather than compliance. However, it has also been noted that many teachers gain and maintain such cooperation in the managerial system by reducing the demands in the instructional system.

For the purposes of describing the completed work in this paradigm, the concept of the programme of action (Doyle, 1986) needs to be foregrounded. The term is used to identify that place where the issues of subject-matter content and management come together in ways that are not easily separated. The programme of action, then, encompasses the positioning and sequencing of content and management within lessons. Having a specific direction, momentum and energy, the programme of action determines appropriate behaviours for students during different instructional contexts.

Merritt (1982) suggests that classroom activities contain 'vectors' that, once entered into, pull events and participants along their course. The term vector is used purposefully, suggesting that the programme of action draws events and participants along its course. Primary vectors are manifested in those agendas that the teacher has for the lesson, and define both action and the order necessary for the action to move forward smoothly. Secondary vectors are typically student initiated, and serve to test the robustness of the primary vector with its teacher-controlled or content-embedded accountability. Students initiate secondary vectors for a variety of purposes: to reduce the demands of a task, to lessen the chances of being held accountable, to seek a more 'interesting' task, to engage socially with peers, or even out of boredom. Teachers often react to these secondary vectors, and how and when they do will 'define the boundaries and strength of the primary direction vector and shape its direction' (Doyle, 1986: 420).

The programme of action is presented through a series of tasks which focus attention on three aspects of student's work: (i) the products students are to formulate, (ii) the operations used to generate these products, and (iii) the resources available for these products. Whatever the task, there will be some response by the students, ranging from full engagement to passive or active non-engagement, and this will be followed by some teacher response. Thus, the programme of action is not a fixed commodity set in place and left undisturbed, but rather a dynamic vector, the direction and momentum of which is determined by how teachers monitor and respond to the potential or presence of student-initiated secondary vectors. It should be noted that secondary vectors initiated by students might have the potential to improve or strengthen the programme of action, although most research reveals that the more frequent effort is to weaken the primary vector.

Doyle (1980, 1983) has made a number of important statements relating to accountability. First, accountability drives a task system, be it managerial or instructional. Without accountability there is no task, and students will only do as much as they are motivated to by their own interests. In addition, the student response a teacher accepts and rewards defines the real tasks in classes, and the strictness of the criteria a teacher used to judge the acceptability of these responses has consequences for task accomplishment. Thus it is only the tasks for which students are held accountable that they tend to treat seriously: 'If no answers are required or any answer is accepted, then few students will actually attend to the content' (Doyle, 1983: 186).

The level of accountability will determine the difference between the 'stated task' (that is, the instructions given to the student by the teacher) and the 'real task' (that is, what the students are allowed to produce and what is accepted by the teacher). Teacher consequences determine the nature of tasks more than teacher instruction, and students often learn more about the tasks required from a teacher's reactions to performance than they did from the teacher's original instructions. Alexander (1983) refers to this as a contingency-developed instructional task system.

To understand a programme of action, however, it is critical to note that a class ecology is a dynamic, interdependent process. It should not be construed as being uni-directional. Indeed, Doyle was particularly concerned with research that focused only on teacher variables. He argued that an assumption of unidirectionality, that the teachers were directly causing student outcomes, was an oversimplification of how work gets produced in classrooms. According to Doyle (1977), several studies demonstrated the reverse, that is, that teacher behaviour is often influenced by student behaviour. It is only for the purposes of outlining the research using this model that its segments are presented sequentially.

Task and task presentation

Fundamental to the study of a class ecology is the notion of tasks and task systems. Doyle (1980) was the first to produce an examination of classroom tasks. With reference to instruction, Doyle (1983) invoked a concept of 'academic work', and stated that the curriculum can be seen as a collection of 'academic tasks' or subject-matter tasks. The task designates the situational structure that organizes and directs student thought and action (Doyle and Carter, 1984).

Tousignant and Siedentop (1983) first identified three dimensions that define task systems in physical education: managerial, transitional and instructional. Managerial tasks are those which relate to attendance, behaviour, and in some subject areas, appropriate dress. Transitional tasks are defined as 'the operations that the students were expected to do to accomplish the instructional tasks' (Tousignant, 1982: 99). Instructional tasks are those related to the achievement of subject-matter goals. Within the physical education context, there are several options for categorizing these tasks. One way is to focus on whether the task represents practice, scrimmage or game situations. Rink (1993) has proposed that instructional tasks can be categorized by the instructional purpose related to skill development: *informing tasks*, those which provide information to students about the upcoming task, particularly an explanation of task requirements, *refining tasks*, those concerned with improving the quality of the performances by the students, *applying tasks*, those which provide students with opportunities to apply their skills in game or scrimmage situations, and *extending tasks*, which are progressions of previous tasks which challenge students to perform in more difficult situations.

Following the category development of Tousignant and Siedentop (1983), Graham (1987) provided the first account within physical education of how the nature of the task influences the pattern of motor skill responses for students. Graham (1987) expressed concern with research in physical education that had examined end-of-instruction performance scores, claiming a need to focus on the subject-matter work of students in physical education. Using Rink's categories of instructional tasks, and examining student engagement and success rates during instruction, Graham demonstrated that teachers frequently differentiated movement tasks for high and low skilled students to allow for similar response rates. Jones (1992) followed Graham's study on teacher and student performance through the analysis of the task systems operating in elementary physical education. Jones showed that students produced minimal task modification in the managerial task system, and produced high levels of compliance in instructional tasks. However, while students were consistently on task, they were not very successful (between 18 and 35 percent). Several studies have shown that the most typical task development pattern is informing followed by applying tasks, with less attention paid to extending tasks and very little to refining tasks, which, arguably, are the building blocks of successful skill development.

Descriptions of academic tasks have also been presented in a number of settings outside the physical education class. For example, Tinning and Siedentop (1985) examined the characteristics of the task systems that operate in student teaching. In this study, it was shown that the student teacher must balance the demands of those tasks systems that have consequence for pupils, but also those tasks relevant to the cooperating teacher and the university supervisor. In other words, the student teacher is both master and servant, putting in place tasks for pupils and responding to their outcomes, while at the same time, attempting to fulfil tasks set by the higher authority. The work of Tinning and Siedentop (1985) has been adapted for use in training cooperating teachers and university supervisors by Ocansey (1989).

Hastie and Saunders (1992) and Griffin (1991) have examined the task systems operating in a sports team. Similarities between teaching and coaching were identified in that managerial, transitional and instructional tasks systems were operational in both settings. However, an additional task system emerged in the coaching setting, the match play task system, while a subset of instructional tasks, 'role specific instructional tasks', was also identified. These were tasks designed for specified players, and were not practised by all team members, examples being the specialist setter on a volleyball team or the quarterback on an American football team.

The ecological paradigm provides an analysis of collective life in classes, both in its social and academic dimensions, and how those dimensions interact. Life in classes across time with children and adolescents is highly social. Allen (1986) first foregrounded the importance of a student social system by suggesting that students had two major goals, those of socializing and of passing the course. Siedentop (1988) argued that the student social agenda could be interpreted as a task system, one that has strong potential to interact with the managerial and instructional tasks systems in ways that influence the ecology of class life.

The student social system in physical education has received considerably less attention than the managerial and instructional task systems. While some research has mentioned the influence of student's social agenda in affecting classroom processes (e.g. Jones, 1992; Son, 1989), only the studies of Hastie and Pickwell (1996) and Carlson and Hastie (1997) have focused on this system. Nevertheless, this research on the student social system shows it to be a no less critical component in determining the nature and extent of subject-matter work within physical education.

In a systematic study of a dance unit within an eleventh grade physical education class, Hastie and Pickwell (1996) identified a number of strategies that the boys used to get out of instructional tasks they deemed uninviting or unimportant. These strategies allowed them to attend to their social agenda. Indeed, inventing and testing strategies to reduce their involvement in dance tasks actually became part of this social agenda. Furthermore, since the number of boys exceeded the number of girls in this class the teacher informally accepted much of this behaviour provided it did not interrupt the smooth running of the lesson. As Hastie and Pickwell (1996: 183) comment with reference to Placek's (1983) 'busy, happy, good' findings; 'by being busy, happy, and good, the students can give the teacher what he or she wants [that is] the absence of critical events that lead to misdemeanors and deviant student behavior'. The student social system then, was confirmed as a strong influence in the ecology of this class.

The student social system has been determined as a powerful driving force in other activity based settings. In particular, the student social system has been seen as a key impulse in the accomplishment of managerial and instructional tasks during units of sport education (Carlson and Hastie, 1997), and off-campus in adventure education settings (Hastie, 1995). In both these studies, the social nature of the settings tended to promote involvement in the instructional and managerial tasks. In both sport and adventure education, working with one's friends to achieve instructional objectives was an attractive part of the setting. Students enjoyed the significant peer interaction that was available either at the climbing wall or ropes course in the adventure setting, or in developing team strategies and skill during peer coach led practices in sport education. Further studies in sport education (e.g. Hastie, 1996, 1998) have confirmed the key role that student leadership and responsibility plays in maintaining – and even strengthening – the primary vector for subject-matter work.

From these findings, it is reasonable to suggest that some curriculum models may have features embedded within them that produce a programme of action that has considerable strength; for example, sport education (Siedentop, 1994) or adventure education. These models seem to have explicit goals that students see as authentic, and reasonably clear paths to attaining these goals, which no doubt helps sustain the primary vector of the programme of action. These models also display what one might describe as 'content-embedded accountability'; that is, there is accountability intrinsic to the manner in which the activities develop and the goals are to be achieved. These models also tend not only to accommodate, but also indeed to explicitly depend upon, the student social system as a positive attribute of the learning ecology. They help define the social system in ways that contribute to rather than detract from the work agenda.

Students' responses to tasks

Irrespective of the type of task system, tasks vary with the amount of information that they detail. This in turn sets the boundaries within which students can provide acceptable responses. Instructional tasks, and the subsequent student work related to them, depend mostly on the programme of action. If that programme of action is strong and there is strong accountability (either intrinsic to the curriculum or extrinsically developed by the teacher), then students will tend to demand that tasks be explicit. Explicit tasks are those where operational and outcome criteria are clear.

A further component of a task which affects potential student involvement is the ambiguity and risk associated with that task. Ambiguity refers to the extent to which a precise answer can be defined in advance or a precise formula for generating an answer is available. Risk refers to the stringency of the evaluative criteria a teacher uses and the likelihood that these criteria can be met on a given occasion (Doyle, 1983).

Other tasks may be implicit or general. Implicit tasks are those students have previously practised and in which they know how to play the role of a participant. Some researchers have labelled these as routine tasks. When tasks are presented so that the skill, tactic, or knowledge to be acquired is described in general, researchers typically categorize them as general rather than specific. These tasks are often high in ambiguity, but just as often low in risk, and students can be free to modify them without risking corrective reactions from the teacher. Instructional tasks are frequently less explicit than managerial tasks, and often carry less risk for accountability. This is particularly true for those managerial tasks that are introduced early in the term and counted on to become routine (Fink and Siedentop, 1989).

Despite the explicitness of a task, students can choose between a number of behavioural responses, and Marks (1988) has outlined a list of possible responses. In deriving the first instrument for the systematic observation of classes using the ecological model, Marks (1988) developed categories which included off-task (including deviant or non-participant), task modification (where a student alters the stated task to make it either more difficult or easy) and on-task.

Son (1989) introduced the concept of 'task congruence', in order to determine the extent to which the initial response of students corresponded to teachers' stated tasks. Son's analysis was made on two levels: responses to antecedent task statements, and subsequent consequences. The results of this investigation demonstrated that congruent student responses to stated tasks were more likely to be influenced by informal contingencies and/or other important variables, such as the nature of sport activities or student interest, than by antecedent task statements such as a task specification or the formal accountability system. Son (1989) showed that in the Korean context, one of the most important of those informal contingencies was aversive control, where teachers would threaten and physically punish inappropriate behaviour.

Doyle (1986) notes that order can often exist in a class without full and continuous engagement by all students. He adds that 'passive nonengagement is not necessarily problematic in establishing and sustaining order even though it may be unsatisfactory for learning' (Doyle, 1986: 396). In physical education, there is also the possibility of 'fake engagement'. Tousignant and Siedentop (1983) have described the 'competent by-stander', those students who are extraordinarily skilled at staying well within the boundaries of the managerial system but cleverly avoid participation in the instructional system. Son (1989) also showed how some skilled students participate in a practice task appropriately and successfully for a few repetitions, then reduce the task demands subtly and continue participation but also engage in social conversation with their partner(s). When such activities persist or become too widespread, and become noticed by the teacher, the managerial cohesion of the class becomes threatened, even though there is not overt misbehaviour, often influencing the teacher to reduce the instructional demands or change the task.

Doyle (1986) notes that students' responses to work create pressures on the management system of a class. Where these threats are problematic, teachers often simplify task demands and lower the risk for mistakes. Where tasks are relatively simple and routine, classes tend to proceed smoothly with little hesitation or resistance.

In the development of tasks, then, a considerable degree of negotiation can occur. First identified by Woods (1978), negotiation is defined as any attempt by students to change tasks, to change the conditions under which tasks are performed, or to change the performance standards task completion is judged by. Students negotiate in various ways. While in classrooms negotiations are typically verbal interchanges, in physical education they are more often accomplished through student modification of learning tasks. Students modify tasks to make them more or less challenging, to increase their chances of success, or to hide their social interactions. Students may also try to avoid participating in tasks and try to hide their non-participation from the teacher.

If there is accountability for task performance, students will typically seek to increase the explicitness of the task demands (e.g. reduce ambiguity) and will also seek to reduce demands, typically by seeking to perform an easier version of the tasks. Students learn about tasks in various ways other than listening to teacher explanations. They can ask peers about tasks during transitions from explanations to participation, or they 'hang back' and watch the eager performers make their first practice trials.

This understanding of how students attempt to influence the subject-matter demands of the class is seen clearly in Alexander's (1983) initial evidence of a contingency-developed tasks system. The extent to which a task initially explained by a teacher becomes the 'actual' task practised by students and accepted by the teacher depends upon the teacher's supervision and accountability practices. A programme of action that has a strong work orientation, especially when students work toward some authentic curricular goal, typically results in high congruence between tasks as stated and those practised by students. Without the content-embedded accountability, however, a strong work orientation typically requires active supervision and strong teacher imposed accountability.

Negotiation is also less likely to take place where the stated task involves little risk. Where the teacher has not specified the conditions or criteria for successful completion, then almost any answer becomes acceptable, and hence students do not need to reduce the task demand. That is what Doyle (1986) meant when he said that without accountability the instructional task system is suspended. A teacher's skill and will to anticipate and then deal with negotiations typically reveals the likelihood of a strong or weak programme of action.

Trading-off is that situation where teachers negotiate with students to produce the necessary cooperation in the managerial system by reducing the demands of the instructional system. They also might allow for certain kinds of student social interaction to gain the necessary cooperation (as found by Jones, 1992, in the elementary setting, and Hastie and Pickwell, 1996, in the secondary school setting). At times, teachers might even suspend the instructional task system and allow students to engage in non-disruptive socializing tasks, provided they complete the managerial tasks, as was found to be the case with one teacher in the study of Hastie and Saunders (1990).

The degree to which teachers trade-off depends upon the difficulty of the context in which the teaching is taking place, as well as the intention and expectations of the teacher for learning and achievement. Sanders and Graham (1995) found that teachers have a 'zone of acceptable responses' for the tasks they present to children. In their study, on some occasions, teachers allowed significant adaptation when children made attempts to change a particular task, but then allowed no freedom for other tasks.

A further factor affecting teacher negotiation is the degree to which the teacher possesses effective teaching skills. Doyle (1986) notes that effective teachers in difficult situations tend to push students through the curriculum as a way of achieving and sustaining order. This notion of teaching skills was wholly supported in the study of effective elementary physical education specialists (O'Sullivan et al., 1989). For these teachers, one could contend that the overall programme of action had the capacity to engage students and keep them engaged enthusiastically. However, where teachers encounter difficulty in gaining the cooperation of students in the intended tasks, they often retreat to a 'curricular zone of safety' (Rovegno, 1994). Here teachers often restrict their content to application tasks (nearly always game play) and reduce the level of accountability to simply one of compliance in the managerial system.

Research on ambiguity, risk, negotiation and trading-off within physical education is scarce. This is perhaps because, particularly within the secondary school setting, tasks usually appear to contain little risk. This teaching/learning environment has been described as 'no sweat' (Siedentop et al., 1994), by which these authors referred to classes characterized by modest task demands, little student disruption, and a strong social orientation.

The intervention study of Hastie (1997) outlines the key factors involved in the process of moving students from this position of no sweat to a level of quality performance. Through an action research methodology, Hastie (1997) identified three factors that seemed crucial for such a change. These included recognizing how students see that particular subject in the perspective of schooling, the provision of instructional tasks which contain variety, uncertainty and challenge, and creating a class climate in which students want to be engaged.

Teacher response and accountability

When students are (or are not) performing classroom tasks, the teacher makes a number of decisions about their performance. Should the students' responses to the task be satisfactory, the decision most likely is to continue with the task. At the other extreme, where students are not responding to a satisfactory degree, the teacher may stop the task and present a new task. A less drastic measure would be to modify the task without abandoning it altogether. Doyle (1986) comments that when order becomes unstable, a more sensible option is this one of repair, since he claims that even in the best circumstances, transitions to new work are difficult to manage.

Nevertheless, regardless of the nature of the original task, and how explicit the original task might be, it is the subsequent supervision and accountability that determines the work students accomplish. Teachers communicate evaluations to students during practice periods by commenting on the appropriateness of behaviour, effort, or performance, and by offering general or specific information relative to those. Doyle (1983) states that this evaluative climate connects tasks to a reward structure, which defines the accountability system operating in the class. Becker et al. (1968) originally referred to student accountability in this context as existing where there was an exchange of rewards or grades for performance. It is important to note, however, that grades are not solely the marks on a report card. It is more relevant to think of grades as one form of reward structure. This reward structure may be formal, where the performance counts towards a final grade, such as an examination, a skills test, or a squash tournament. More common in physical education, however, is informal accountability, where the performance does not directly contribute towards a grade. Indeed, in Jones's (1992) study of elementary school classes, no instances of formal accountability were identified. Examples of informal accountability in physical education include a practice exam, active monitoring and commentary, sitting out, public recognition, and teacher feedback (Lund, 1991).

When teachers in physical education hold students accountable only for managerial tasks (i.e. dressing and attendance), the instructional tasks system is suspended. Students then are able to do only as much of the instructional task as they wish, a situation Lund (1992: 353) defines as 'pseudoaccountability'. Siedentop (1988) has commented that it would appear that good teachers have a knack of stating tasks in ways that allow for minimal modification to match abilities and interests, but move quickly to redirect modifications that wander too far from the stated task. This reinforces the critical link between curriculum and ecology. Where a programme of action is weak (from a motivational perspective), supervision and accountability become paramount, since when students do modify tasks they tend to do this rather quickly, adjusting for a variety of reasons, many of which promote secondary vectors which diminish the momentum of the primary vector. Teachers who do not supervise carefully inevitably suspend the informal accountability system, with the result that boundaries for acceptable responses become distanced from the stated task (Hastie, 1994a; Lund, 1992). On the other hand, where the programme of action is based on a strong, authentic curricular model, much of the accountability is embedded in tasks leading to the unit goals, requiring less teacher supervision. Indeed, sport education and adventure education programmes typically use peer accountability mechanisms to motivate student work toward unit goals. Interestingly, both of these curricular models also shape the student social system so that it strongly supports the programme of action, rather than being a potential distraction to it.

Research on accountability within physical education was initially descriptive. For example, Tousignant (1982) outlined a continuum of accountability within the instructional task system of physical education. She stated that students might be held accountable at four levels. At the lowest level, students can be held accountable for 'minimal participation', no matter how good or average the performance. In this case, the students are expected to present themselves at class ready to participate. At the next level, students are held accountable for their 'effort', so that the student is at least engaged in the task. At the next stage on the continuum, some 'performance' level is expected. At this level, the teacher is likely to either chastize students for sloppy work, or alternately praise students for a 'great move' or 'good extension'. 'Evaluation' of how the performance was achieved is the fourth stage of the accountability continuum described by Tousignant.

In accountability research dealing with the managerial task system, Fink and Siedentop (1989) found that good class managers had clear, consistent, and fairly rigid boundaries for managerial tasks and gave students sufficient practice and support that the tasks became routinized. A positive effect of formalizing teacher expectations for performance has also been demonstrated (Hastie, 1994a). In this study, the teacher who achieved the highest degree of task compliance and student involvement was that teacher who most often stopped the class to reinforce his behavioural and performance standards.

More recent research on student accountability has linked teacher and student behaviours. These studies have focused more on the accountability systems that were teacher-focused rather than content-embedded. In these cases, Lund (1992) found that monitoring is the precursor of accountability and, as the instructional task system becomes more demanding, the complexity of this monitoring increases. The act of supervising student work was also found to be a strong factor in the accountability system operating in the classes investigated by Hastie and Saunders (1990). However, an intricate interrelationship between supervision, student involvement, and the opportunity to respond was identified. In terms of accountability, students were least likely to be off-task when the teacher was working directly with the students, and most likely to be off-task when the teacher could not see the student. Non-supervised students tended to become deviant where the opportunity to respond was high (such as when a large number of students can be actively involved at the one time), but tended to avoid involvement where the opportunity to respond was low (such as when required to wait for a turn to participate).

While active supervision has been shown to be the basis of most accountability, higher response rates and greater percentages of correctness and success have been achieved with accountability systems that had more than just this (Lund, 1992). In studies of secondary physical education (Hastie, 1994a; Hastie and Saunders, 1991), active supervision was demonstrated to be a powerful determinant of students' task involvement. Active supervision, which occurs when teachers constantly and verbally reinforce task demands and the desired standards of performance, has been determined as a common component of the teaching behaviours of more effective teachers. Lessons with the greatest levels of appropriate student involvement contained large components of active supervision, coupled with little time spent in passive observation.

In one study of five high school teachers in volleyball units (Lund, 1991), the most effective teacher had the lowest amount of practice time, but within that time student responses occurred at a higher rate, and a higher proportion of those responses were appropriate and successful, for more and for less skilled students. This was accomplished through a pedagogical strategy where each instructional task had an individual or group challenge as part of the task demands, and the teacher took time after each short practice bout to assess performance through public reporting and recognition.

The essential message from all the studies that focus on accountability seems to be that the work that eventually gets done in classes depends upon the strength of the programme of action. That is, where the primary vector contains sufficient strength (one, which contains achievable yet challenging tasks) and durability (in which there is some authentic outcome which can accommodate students' social agendas), it is capable of pulling events and participants along a course toward quality performance.

While active teaching behaviours have been associated with higher levels of student intensity in physical education, the relationship between teacher and students behaviours is also mediated by the context of the lesson. For example, Hastie (in press) has shown that students produce variable levels of congruent motor behaviour, modifying and off-task behaviours depending on whether they are engaged in skill practices, scrimmages, or game play. Students produce more significantly off-task behaviour and modifying responses when in skill practice contexts, in contrast with their performance in scrimmage and game play. This seems to occur even when teacher behaviours remain constant across these contexts. Nevertheless, higher frequencies of teacher accountability and other active behaviours are a good predictor of congruent student performance.

Doyle (1986) suggests a delicate balance exists between attending to the primary vector and attention to inappropriate behaviour. To date, little or no research exists within physical education as to how teachers achieve this balance. While it is known that many classes lack intensity, and require little effort from students, research is warranted into those settings characterized by strong programmes of action. How teachers achieve this is only speculative. Siedentop (1988: 121) has suggested that it might be through 'a certain kind of technical virtuosity', where instruction takes place so as to accommodate the student social system within the instructional task setting. This might enhance productivity and reduce the potential outbreak of secondary vectors. Studies that have examined curricula with content-embedded accountability, that is, those which accommodate students' social agendas, would support this idea. Siedentop (1998) has recently argued that researchers have not paid sufficient attention to how the curriculum model contributes to or detracts from the establishment and maintenance of the programme of action. The idea here seems to be that technically sound teaching is not sufficient, in and of itself, to sustain a programme of action, especially in situations where an ordinary multi-activity curricular format is in place. Teachers certainly can create strong accountability systems that keep a less-than-exciting instructional programme going forward (Siedentop, 1988), verification of which was presented in Hastie's (1997) study, but the question is whether it can be sustained over long periods of time and at what cost to the teacher.

Benefits of taking an ecological perspective within physical education

The main benefit of research using the ecological model is that it presents a realistic description of 'life in the gym'. It highlights that considerable negotiation takes place within many classes, where teachers trade-off a reduction in the demands of the instructional system and any rigorous accountability for cooperation in the management system. The student social system is generally allowed to flourish, as teachers are more concerned with creating and maintaining a classroom environment where they and their students can live peacefully throughout the year. As noted, many teachers gain and maintain student cooperation in the managerial system by reducing demands in the instructional system, with these trade-offs or 'treaties' (Tomlinson, 1992) more evident in middle and secondary physical education than in elementary physical education.

A second key benefit of the applying research using this paradigm is that it forces us to examine not only teacher actions, but also those of students through the analysis of tasks.

One particularly rich example of this comes from Romar's (1995) study of middle school teachers. In this work, one teacher described her purpose of a basketball unit as helping children to play a 'well played game', a most praiseworthy goal. Nevertheless, in an analysis of the instructional tasks of this teacher, it was revealed that (a) there were no tactical tasks, and (b) even the skill tasks were not game-contextualized. As a result, the games played toward the end of the unit saw poor levels of play, and the teacher was disappointed. Notably, the teacher, like all the teachers in this study saw herself as a good teacher because she performed many of what we know are appropriate teaching skills. All the teachers in this study had good demonstrations, clear explanations and they gave quality feedback. These self-perceptions were, for the most part, accurate. Many teachers *do* use skills appropriately and their students *do* typically enjoy classes. The point here is that these self-evaluations are based on perceptions of their own teaching behaviour rather than on estimates of student performance gains. However, there was little concern with the tasks the students were being asked to perform. This focus on tasks has shown that teachers in physical education generally do not ask students to complete difficult work. Accountability is primarily to keep students within the managerial boundaries of lessons, rather than to drive any significant production of motor skill performance. This under-scores one of the most important lessons we have learned; to whit, if you want to understand the effectiveness of a teacher, don't watch the teacher, watch the students.

What's missing within research on physical education?

Doyle has written in considerable depth about the importance of establishing and main-taining order in classes. Studies in physical education have shown consistently that the instructional task system is frequently 'low-risk'. There is some evidence that this can be partially attributed to the marginalization of the subject-matter in the school ecology (O'Sullivan et al., 1994). We have little evidence about how some teachers manage to break out of this marginalization and build and sustain strong programmes of action, although our speculation at present is that the nature of the curriculum model may be a promising answer. Curricula that present authentic activities with real outcomes tend to motivate students and sustain them in participation without high levels of teacher supervision. Certainly, in the sport education literature there is evidence that teachers shifted their roles from traffic directors and policing to being content and strategy resource persons (Grant, 1992). Further, these teachers felt tested in this new role because of the demands students placed on them for content-related information and support, which leads us to believe that in such situations students have taken over the sustaining of the momentum of the primary vector.

As described, much of the research on teaching in physical education has been descriptive, with little taking an interventionist approach. Furthermore, much of the research has been completed on cohorts of teachers best described as 'solid' or 'main-stream'. Where studies have used the best available teachers, these teachers have been chosen based upon teaching skills rather than the nature of their programme. More attention needs to be given to those teachers who produce high levels of student work, not just high levels of behavioural cooperation. Of particular interest would be to examine how these good teachers develop and sustain a primary vector devoted to learning and skill performance. Valuable questions include: what is the nature of the curricular model, how do teachers 'sell' it to students, how do teachers establish and maintain cooperation towards the model's goals, and how do students become important factors in sustaining the momentum of the programme of action related to the model?

The essential goal of the classroom ecology paradigm is to investigate how teachers and students operate together to get work done. To understand life in physical education classes, one has to observe and analyse the ecology over extended periods of time. Teachers and their students live together for long periods of time and that collective life has to be reasonably peaceful. Peace is achieved through orderliness, predictability and a balance of subject-matter demands that is negotiated between students and teacher.

Those studies that have examined either teacher behaviours or student performance without examining the classroom behaviours of the other face the risk of making claims that are trivial, or altogether misleading. Moreover, of critical consequence is the examination of the tasks being set for students. Since performance in the subject-matter is the salient criterion for judging teaching effectiveness, to neglect this aspect of the programme of action, and failure to use response-based protocols to examine student work, is both unfair and conceptually counterproductive.

To understand teaching, one has to understand it as work. While there are clear performance aspects to teaching, and there are skills to be learned and perfected, it is a mistake to view teaching primarily from a performance aspect, as, for example, one might judge a musical recital. It is rather the class-to-class, day-to-day, week-to-week work of teachers that needs to be foregrounded, and it is their perseverance in that context that needs to be analysed.

References

Alexander, K. (1983) 'Behavior Analysis of Tasks and Accountability in Physical Education', doctoral dissertation, The Ohio State University, 1982, *Dissertations Abstracts International* 43: 3257A.

Allen, J.D. (1986) 'Classroom Management: Student's Perspective, Goals, and Strategies', *American Education Research Journal* 23: 437–59.

Becker, H.S., Geer, B. and Hughes, E. (1968) *Making the Grade: The Academic Side of College Life*. New York: Wiley.

Carlson, T.B. and Hastie, P.A. (1997) 'The Student-Social System within Sport Education', *Journal of Teaching in Physical Education* 16: 176–95.

Cooper, H.M. (1989) *Integrating Research: A Guide for Literature Reviews*. Newbury Park, CA: Sage Publications.

Doyle, W. (1977) 'Paradigms for Research on Teacher Effectiveness', in L.S. Shulman (ed.) *Review of Research in Education*, pp. 163–98. Itasca, IL: F.E. Peacock.

Doyle, W. (1980) 'Student Mediating Responses in Teacher Effectiveness: Final Report', unpublished paper, North Texas State University. (ERIC Document Reproduction Service No. ED 187 698).

Doyle, W. (1983) 'Academic Work', *Review of Educational Research* 53: 159–99.

Doyle, W. (1986) 'Classroom Organization and Management', in M.C. Wittrock (ed.) *Handbook of Research on Teaching*, 3rd edn., pp. 392–431. New York: Macmillan.

Doyle, W. and Carter, K. (1984) 'Academic Tasks in Classroom', *Curriculum Inquiry* 14: 129–49.

Fink, J. and Siedentop, D. (1989) 'The Development of Routines, Rules, and Expectations at the Start of the School Year', *Journal of Teaching in Physical Education* 8: 198–212.

Fortin, S. and Siedentop, D. (1995) 'The Interplay of Knowledge and Practice in Dance Teaching: What We Can Learn from an Atypical Dance Teacher', *Dance Research Journal* 27(2): 3–15.

Graham, K.C. (1987) 'A Description of Academic Work and Student Performance During a Middle School Volleyball Unit', *Journal of Teaching in Physical Education* 7: 22–37.

Grant, B.C. (1992) 'Integrating Sport into the Physical Education Curriculum in New Zealand Secondary Schools', *Quest* 44: 304–316.

Griffey, D. (1991) 'The Value and Future Agenda of Research on Teaching Physical Education', *Research Quarterly for Exercise and Sport* 62: 380–3.

Griffin, L.L. (1991) 'Analysis of the Instructional Task System in an Interscholastic Volleyball Setting', doctoral dissertation, The Ohio State University, *Dissertations Abstracts International* 52: 2580A.

Hastie, P.A. (1993) 'Players' Perceptions of Accountability in School Sports Settings', *Research Quarterly for Exercise and Sport* 64: 158–66.

Hastie, P.A. (1994a) 'Selected Teacher Behaviors and Student ALT-PE in Secondary School Physical Education Classes', *Journal of Teaching in Physical Education* 13: 342–59.

Hastie, P.A. (1994b) 'Improving Monitoring Skills in Physical Education: A Case Study in Student Teaching', *Journal of Classroom Interaction* 13(2): 11–20.

Hastie, P.A. (1995) 'An Ecology of a Secondary School Outdoor Adventure Camp', *Journal of Teaching in Physical Education* 15: 79–97.

Hastie, P.A. (1996) 'Student Role Involvement during a Unit of Sport Education', *Journal of Teaching in Physical Education* 16: 88–103.

Hastie, P.A. (1997) 'Factors Affecting the Creation of a New Ecology in a Boys-Only Physical Education Class at a Military School', *Research Quarterly for Exercise and Sport* 68: 62–73.

Hastie, P.A. (1998) 'The Participation and Perceptions of Girls during a Unit of Sport Education', *Journal of Teaching in Physical Education* 18: 157–71.

Hastie, P.A. (in press) 'Effect of Instructional Context on Teacher and Student Behaviours in Physical Education', *Journal of Classroom Interaction*.

Hastie, P.A. and Pickwell, A. (1996) 'A Description of a Student Social System in a Secondary School Dance Class', *Journal of Teaching in Physical Education* 15: 171–87.

Hastie, P.A. and Saunders, J.E. (1989) 'Coaching Behaviours and Training Involvement in Elite Junior Rugby Teams', *Journal of Physical Education and Sports Science* 1(1): 21–32.

Hastie, P.A. and Saunders, J.E. (1990) 'A Study of Monitoring in Secondary School Physical Education', *Journal of Classroom Interaction* 25(1–2): 47–54.

Hastie, P.A. and Saunders, J.E. (1991) 'Accountability in Secondary School Physical Education', *Teaching and Teacher Education* 7: 373–82.

Hastie, P.A. and Saunders, J.E. (1992) 'A Study of Tasks and Accountability in Elite Junior Sports Settings', *Journal of Teaching in Physical Education* 11: 376–88.

Jones, D.L. (1992) 'Analysis of Task Systems in Elementary Physical Education Classes', *Journal of Teaching in Physical Education* 11: 411–25.

Kutame, M.A. (1997) 'Teacher Knowledge and its Relationship to Student Success in Learning a Gymnastics Skill', doctoral dissertation, The Ohio State University, 1997, *Dissertations Abstracts International* 58: 1637A.

Lund, J.L. (1991) 'Student Performance and Accountability Conditions in Physical Education', doctoral dissertation, The Ohio State University, 1990, *Dissertations Abstracts International* 51: 3358A.

Lund, J. (1992) 'Assessment and Accountability in Secondary Physical Education', *Quest* 44: 352–60.

Marks, M.C. (1988) 'Development of a System for the Observation of Task Structures in Physical Education', doctoral dissertation, The Ohio State University, 1990, *Dissertations Abstracts International* 51: 3358A.

Merritt, M. (1982) 'Distributing and Directing Attention in Primary Classrooms', in L.C. Wilkinson (ed.) *Communicating in the Classroom*, pp. 223–44. New York: Academic Press.

Ocansey, R. (1989) 'A Systematic Approach to Organizing Data Generated during Monitoring Sessions in Student Teaching', *Journal of Teaching in Physical Education* 8: 312–17.

O'Sullivan, M., Siedentop, D. and Tannehill, D. (1994) 'Breaking Out: Codependency of High School Physical Education', *Journal of Teaching in Physical Education* 13: 421–8.

O'Sullivan, M., Stroot, S.A. and Tannehill, D. (1989) 'Elementary Physical Education Specialists: A Commitment to Student Learning', *Journal of Teaching in Physical Education* 8: 261–5.

Placek, J. (1983) 'Conceptions of Success in Teaching: Busy, Happy and Good?' in T. Templin and J. Olson (eds) *Teaching in Physical Education*, pp. 46–56. Champaign, IL: Human Kinetics.

Rauschenbach, J.W. (1993) 'Case Studies of Effective Physical Education Specialists: Relationships among Curricular Values, Teaching Strategies, and Student Involvement', doctoral dissertation, Ohio State University, 1992, *Dissertations Abstracts International* 53: 3842A.

Rink, J. (1993) *Teaching Physical Education for Learning*. St Louis: Mosby.

Romar, J.-E. (1995) *Case Studies of Finnish Physical Education Teachers: Espoused and Enacted Theories of Action*. Abo, Finland: Abo Akademi University Press.

Romar, J.-E. and Siedentop, D. (1995) 'Cooperation and Body Control as Goals in Physical Education: A Case Study of a Basketball Unit', in C. Pare (ed.) *The Training of Teachers in Reflective Practice of Physical Education: Better Teaching in Physical Education? Think about it!*, pp. 205–22. Proceedings of the AIESEP International Seminar, Trois-Rivieres, Canada.

Rovegno, I. (1994) 'Teaching within a Curricular Zone of Safety: School Culture and the Situated Nature of Student Teachers' Pedagogical Content Knowledge', *Research Quarterly for Exercise and Sport* 65: 269–80.

Sanders, S. and Graham, G. (1995) 'Kindergarten Children's Initial Experiences in Physical Education: The Relentless Persistence for Play Clashes with the Zone of Acceptable Responses', *Journal of Teaching in Physical Education* 14: 372–83.

Siedentop, D. (1988) 'An Ecological Model for Understanding Teaching/Learning in Physical Education', in *New Horizons of Human Movements: Proceedings of the 1988 Seoul Olympic Scientific Congress*. Seoul: SOSCOC.

Siedentop, D. (1994) *Sport Education: Quality PE through Positive Sport Experiences*. Champaign, IL: Human Kinetics.

Siedentop, D. (1998) 'In Search of Effective Teaching: What we have Learned from Teachers and Students', paper presented at the National Convention of the American Alliance for Health, Physical Education, Recreation and Dance, Reno, NV, 5–9 April.

Siedentop, D., Doutis, P., Tsangaridou, N., Ward, P. and Rauschenbach, J. (1994) 'Don't Sweat Gym: An Analysis of Curriculum and Instruction', *Journal of Teaching in Physical Education* 13: 375–94.

Silverman, S. (1991) 'Research on Teaching in Physical Education', *Research Quarterly for Exercise and Sport* 62: 352–64.

Silverman, S., Kulinna, P.H. and Crull, G. (1995) 'Skill-Related Task Structures, Explicitness, and Accountability: Relationships with Student Achievement', *Research Quarterly for Exercise and Sport* 66: 32–40.

Silverman, S., Subramaniam, P.R. and Woods, A.M. (1998) 'Task Structures, Student Practice, and Student Skill Level in Physical Education', *Journal of Educational Research* 91: 298–306.

Son, C.T. (1989) 'Descriptive Analysis of Task Congruence in Korean Middle School Physical Education Classes', doctoral dissertation, Ohio State University, completed 1988, *Dissertations Abstracts International* 50: 2379A.

Tinning, R. (1991) 'Teacher Education Pedagogy: Dominant Discourses and the Process of Problem Setting', *Journal of Teaching in Physical Education* 11: 1–20.

Tinning, R.I. and Siedentop, D. (1985) 'The Characteristics of Tasks and Accountability in Student Teaching', *Journal of Teaching in Physical Education* 4: 286–99.

Tomlinson, T.M. (1992) 'Hard Work and High Expectations: Motivating Students to Learn', Washington, DC: US Dept. of Education.

Tousignant, M. (1982) 'Analysis of the Task Structures in Secondary Physical Education Classes', doctoral dissertation, Ohio State University, *Dissertations Abstracts International* 43: 1470A.

Tousignant, M. and Siedentop, D. (1983) 'A Qualitative Analysis of Tasks Structures in Required Secondary Physical Education Classes', *Journal of Teaching in Physical Education* 3: 47–57.

Woods, P. (1978) 'Negotiating the Demands of School Work', *Journal of Curriculum Studies* 10: 309–27.

Index

Please note that references to Notes will have the letter 'n' following the note